ROUTLEDGE LIBRARY EDITIONS:
THE AMERICAN NOVEL

Volume 14

MARK TWAIN'S HUMOR

MARK TWAIN'S HUMOR
Critical Essays

Edited by
DAVID E. E. SLOANE

Taylor & Francis Group

LONDON AND NEW YORK

First published in 1993 by Garland Publishing, Inc.

This edition first published in 2018
by Routledge
2 Park Square, Milton Park, Abingdon, Oxon OX14 4RN

and by Routledge
711 Third Avenue, New York, NY 10017

Routledge is an imprint of the Taylor & Francis Group, an informa business

© 1993 David E. E. Sloane

All rights reserved. No part of this book may be reprinted or reproduced or utilised in any form or by any electronic, mechanical, or other means, now known or hereafter invented, including photocopying and recording, or in any information storage or retrieval system, without permission in writing from the publishers.

Trademark notice: Product or corporate names may be trademarks or registered trademarks, and are used only for identification and explanation without intent to infringe.

British Library Cataloguing in Publication Data
A catalogue record for this book is available from the British Library

ISBN: 978-1-138-09946-3 (Set)
ISBN: 978-1-351-25544-8 (Set) (ebk)
ISBN: 978-1-138-30067-5 (Volume 14) (hbk)
ISBN: 978-1-138-30069-9 (Volume 14) (pbk)
ISBN: 978-0-203-73321-9 (Volume 14) (ebk)

Publisher's Note
The publisher has gone to great lengths to ensure the quality of this reprint but points out that some imperfections in the original copies may be apparent.

Disclaimer
The publisher has made every effort to trace copyright holders and would welcome correspondence from those they have been unable to trace.

Mark Twain's Humor
Critical Essays

David E.E. Sloane

Garland Publishing, Inc. • New York and London

1993

© 1993 David E.E. Sloane
All rights reserved

Library of Congress Cataloging-in-Publication Data

Mark Twain's humor : critical essays / [edited by] David E.E. Sloane.
    p. cm. — (Garland studies in humor ; vol. 3) (Garland
reference library of the humanities ; vol. 1502)
  Includes bibliographical references
  ISBN 0-8153-0620-2
  1. Twain, Mark, 1835–1910—Humor. 2. Humorous stories,
American—History and criticism. I. Sloane, David E.E., 1943– . II.
Series. III. Series: Garland reference library of the humanties ; vol.
1502.
PS1342.H62M37 1993
818'.409—dc20   92-14927
                                                                         CIP

Printed on acid-free, 250-year-life paper
Manufactured in the United States of America

CONTENTS

General Editor's Note	vii
Acknowledgments	ix
Chronology	xi
Introduction	xiii
David E. E. Sloane	

The Early Writings of Mark Twain: The Growth of the Comedian

Edgar M. Branch. "'My Voice Is Still for Setchell': A Background Study of 'Jim Smiley and His Jumping Frog.'"	3
Franklin R. Rogers. "Burlesque Travel Literature and Mark Twain's *Roughing It*."	31
Pascal Covici, Jr. "From the Old Southwest."	51
Louis J. Budd. "A Curious Republican."	85
David E.E. Sloane. "Toward the Novel."	109

The Middle Career of Mark Twain from *Tom Sawyer* to *Pudd'nhead Wilson*: The Comedian as Major Author

"Novels of the Week: *The Adventures of Tom Sawyer*." *Athenaeum*.	135
Walter Blair. "On the Structure of *Tom Sawyer*."	137
William Dean Howells. "Mark Twain."	155
Rufus A. Coleman. "Trowbridge and Clemens."	165
Blackwood's Magazine. "Musings without Method."	177
George Ade. "Mark Twain and the Old Time Subscription Book."	189
Will M. Clemens. "Mark Twain on the Lecture Platform."	193
Durant Da Ponte. "*Life* Reviews *Huckleberry Finn*."	213
Leslie A. Fiedler. "*Huckleberry Finn*: The Book We Love to Hate."	217
Henry Nash Smith. "A Sound Heart and a Deformed Conscience."	235

Contents

Edward F. Foster. "*A Connecticut Yankee* Anticipated: Max Adeler's *Fortunate Island*."	265
James M. Cox. "Yankee Slang."	271
Alan Gribben. "'I Kind of Love Small Game': Mark Twain's Library of Literary Hogwash."	295
Clyde Grimm. "*The American Claimant*: Reclamation of a Farce."	313
Henry Watterson. "Mark Twain—An Intimate Memory."	337
"The Book Hunter." [Review of *Pudd'nhead Wilson*]. *The Idler*.	349
Martha McCulloch Williams. "In Re 'Pudd'nhead Wilson.'"	351
Shelley Fisher Fishkin. "'The Tales He Couldn't Tell': Mark Twain, Race and Culture at the Century's End: A Social Context for *Pudd'nhead Wilson*."	359

The Later Career of Mark Twain: The Comedian as a Cultural Representative

William Dean Howells. "Mark Twain: An Inquiry."	391
Archibald Henderson. "The International Fame of Mark Twain."	409
Edith Wyatt. "An Inspired Critic."	423
The Ladies' Home Journal. "The Anecdotal Side of Mark Twain."	439
A. C. Ward. "3.—Mark Twain"	455
Review of *Tom Sawyer Abroad*. *The Academy*.	465
Susan K. Harris. "'Hadleyburg'": Mark Twain's Dual Attack on Banal Theology and Banal Literature."	467
John Kendrick Bangs and Mark Twain. "Is the Philippine Policy of the Administration Just?"	487
Susanne Weil. "Reconstructing the 'Imagination Mill': The Mystery of Mark Twain's Late Works."	503
Michael J. Kiskis. "Coming Back to Humor: The Comic Voice in Mark Twain's Autobiography."	539
Laura E. Skandera-Trombley. "'The Mysterious Stranger': Absence of the Female in Mark Twain Biography."	569
Selected Bibliography	591
Index	617

GENERAL EDITOR'S NOTE

David E.E. Sloane's *Mark Twain's Humor: Critical Essays* is the third volume in Garland's "Studies in Humor" series. Each volume in the series is devoted to an assessment of the work of an individual major humorist or group of authors within a specified category and consists of collections of both previously published and original articles on subjects such as S.J. Perelman, Black Humor, Geoffrey Chaucer, Classical Greek and Roman Humorists, Woody Allen, and American Women Humorists, among others.

The intent behind this series is to supply in a single volume a representative sample of the best critical reactions by the humorist's contemporaries and from subsequent scholarly assessments. Typically, the contents of each volume will include: a chronology of the author's life and writing; the volume editor's introduction to the writer's canon; reviews (book, play, and/or film); interviews; essays focusing on specific works (this section may contain both journal articles and parts of books); general essays treating particular aspects of the humorist's canon; a selected, annotated bibliography; and an index. This structure provides access to essential scholarship (some of which may no longer be easily obtainable) on the most important and best examples of the humorist's work as well as demonstrating popular reactions to that work and allowing for comparisons to be made in critical and popular reactions over the course of the writer's career.

Mark Twain is generally considered America's preeminent literary humorist. The nature of his humor and his purpose in creating it, though, have been the subject of a critical debate that began early in his career and continues still. In this

General Editor's Note

collection Sloane has displayed the elements of this critical discourse by focusing on Twain (both as a person and a persona) and his work in three chronological periods: the early writings, in which the essays included detail the growth of the comedian; the middle career from *Tom Sawyer* to *Pudd'nhead Wilson*, in which the comedian as major author is considered; and the later career, in which the comedian is discussed as a cultural representative. There are thirty-four selections included, written by preeminent scholars of the early and the late Twain. In addition, Sloane has furnished an introduction, a selected, annotated bibliography, and an index.

What Twain says at different times as his career evolves and how what he says relates to his experiences and perceptions of life and his hopes and fears for humanity are brought together in a way that makes the works clearer and more accessible as well as bringing readers a better understanding of the man who created the canon. It is especially valuable to be able to see how critical opinions and emphases have shifted over the years, as is evident when the reviews written by Twain's contemporaries are compared with the three original essays written in 1992 that are included in the collection.

David E.E. Sloane is Professor of English at the University of New Haven. The author of *Mark Twain as a Literary Comedian*, *Adventures of Huckleberry Finn: American Comic Vision*, *The Literary Humor of the Urban Northeast, 1830–1890*, *American Humor Magazines and Comic Periodicals*, and several articles on Twain, he was the first Henry Nash Smith Fellow at the Center for Mark Twain Studies at Quarry Farm. He has also been a USIA lecturer on American humor in Brazil and a frequent speaker on Twain, and he is presently president of the Mark Twain Circle and Executive Director and Past President of the American Humor Studies Association.

Steven H. Gale
Kentucky State University

ACKNOWLEDGMENTS

Grateful thanks is extended to the following for permission to reprint articles or portions of chapters to which they hold copyrights.

Walter Blair, *Modern Philology*, the University of Chicago Press for permission to reprint "On the Structure of *Tom Sawyer.*"

Edgar Branch, "'My Voice Is Still for Setchell': A Background Study of 'Jim Smiley and His Jumping Frog'," is reprinted by permission of the Modern Language Association of America from *PMLA*.

Louis Budd.

"Yankee Slang" from James M. Cox, *Mark Twain: The Fate of Humor*. Copyright © 1966 by Princeton U.P. Reprinted by permission.

Pascal Covici, Jr., Department of English, S.M.U.

American Quarterly, 19 (Spring 1967), pp. 86–103. Reprinted by permission of the author and Johns Hopkins U.P.

Leslie Fiedler, "*Huckleberry Finn*: The Book We Love to Hate" originally appeared in the Fall 1984 issue of *Proteus, A Journal of Ideas*, and is reprinted here by permission.

Allan Gribben, "'I Kind of Love Small Game': Mark Twain's Library of Literary Hogwash" reprinted with permission of the editors of *American Literary Realism*.

Shelley Fisher Fishkin, U of Texas, Austin.

"*A Connecticut Yankee* Anticipated: Max Adeler's *Fortunate Island*" © *Ball State University Forum*.

Susan K. Harris and *American Literary Realism*.

Michael Kiskis.

Acknowledgments

Life Reviews *Huckleberry Finn* by Durant Da Ponte. *American Literature* Vol. 31 (1959) published by Duke University Press, Durham. Reprinted with permission of the publisher.

Franklin R. Rogers, "The Road to Reality: Burlesque Travel Literature and Mark Twain's *Roughing It*" © 1963. The New York Public Library, Astor, Lenox, and Tilden Foundations, Reprinted by permission.

Laura Skandera-Trombley.

"A Sound Heart and a Deformed Conscience" reprinted by permission of the publishers from *Mark Twain: The Development of a Writer* by Henry Nash Smith, Cambridge, Mass.: The Belknap Press of Harvard University Press, copyright © 1961 by the President and Fellows of Harvard College.

Susanne Weil.

CHRONOLOGY

1835	Samuel Langhorne Clemens born on 30 November to Jane Lampton and John Marshall Clemens in Florida, Missouri.
1839	Clemens family moves to Hannibal, Missouri.
1847	John Clemens dies; Sam Clemens begins working as a printer's apprentice.
1852	The Boston *Carpet-Bag* publishes "The Dandy Frightening the Squatter" in company with sketches by the young Charles F. Browne and Charles H. Derby.
1857	Becomes an apprentice pilot on the Mississippi River.
1861	Leaves the East to accompany brother Orion to Nevada.
1862–4	Reports for the Virginia City, Nevada *Territorial Enterprise*, taking on the pen name "Mark Twain" in 1863.
1865	"The Celebrated Jumping Frog of Calaveras County" appears in November to instant national success.
1869	*Innocents Abroad* published.
1870	Marries Olivia Langdon. Lectures actively during this period.
1871	Moves to Nook Farm, Hartford, CT.
1872	*Roughing It* published. Son Langdon dies in infancy.
1873	*The Gilded Age* published.
1874	"A True Story" brings Twain to the pages of the respected *Atlantic Monthly*.

Chronology

1876	*Adventures of Tom Sawyer* published.
1880	*A Tramp Abroad* published.
1882	*The Prince and the Pauper* published.
1883	*Life on the Mississippi* published.
1885	*Adventures of Huckleberry Finn* published.
1888	Yale awards Twain an A. M. degree.
1889	*A Connecticut Yankee* published.
1892	*American Claimant* published.
1894	*Pudd'nhead Wilson* published. Twain enters bankruptcy due to the failure of the Paige Typesetter.
1895	Twain begins around-the-world lecture tour to pay off debts.
1896	*Joan of Arc* published. Daughter Susie dies.
1897	*Following the Equator* published.
1901	"To the Person Sitting in Darkness" published as lead article in *North American Review*.
1904	Wife Livy dies.
1906	*What Is Man?* published.
1906	Oxford University awards Twain Litt. D. degree.
1909	Daughter Jean dies.
1910	Mark Twain dies on 21 April.

INTRODUCTION

David E. E. Sloane

Mark Twain was a comedian. His art and his thought both came from a humorous response to a world which *claimed* to be good and kind and humane but *acted* badly and sometimes evilly, cruelly, and inhumanely. Beyond using detailed description to protest the atrocity of individual and corporate actions—seen in whippings, beatings, and lynchings in the novels, seen in the reversal of animal traits with human traits, or through self-deluded behavior in the short stories—Twain had relatively little of a positive political program for reforming the world. He did, however, have a compelling humanity, based not on the letter of biblical or constitutional law but on its spirit, a contentious quasi-religious humanism which he advanced from his earliest writing about the Holy Land through his last final reversals of the satanic and the human in an attempt to wrestle with the meaning of grief and death. The selections reprinted in this volume are intended to provide the case history of a literary life built on these premises. The literary life is both that of the persona Mark Twain—revered as an American icon—and of his canon—that body of literature associated with him and rising to its highest visionary level in *Adventures of Huckleberry Finn*, but shadowed everywhere in even his seemingly most trivial productions.

Much of my own scholarly career has been based on an attempt to understand Twain's humor as central to his vision and also as a representative artifact of American culture. Twain's humor, irony, sarcasm, and even comic allusions advance his uncompromising pragmatism about the centrality of freedom from self-interested authority as the basis of human well-being. Critical responses to my discussion of Twain have often complained that this sort of material wasn't funny. Even more so, this has been argued in relating Twain to the secondary northeastern humorists on whose tradition, as much as that of the Southwest, he leaned for precedents in language, metaphor, and minor characterization. Those responses were, in truth, more accurate than the critics intended. American humor as a literary and as an economic production is often not very funny; it is a record of obvious and avoidable social failures, and as a result it is angry. American humor is the humor of non-acceptance of "reality," and the "real," either literally in fact or idealistically as a literary model. In Europe the absurd is existential; in America, the absurd is a counter-irritant to the observed and a protest and demand for change. In many cases, the burlesque and grotesque exaggerations of American humor—and exaggeration has been the hallmark of European descriptions of American humor for two centuries—are restatements of the triumph of imagination over harsh surroundings, as is suggested in such anthologies as Roger Welsch's collection of Great Plains folk humor *Shingling the Fog* or Walter Blair's *Horse Sense in American Humor*, or even in collections of old-time New England humor such as those by B. A. Botkin.

Twain's humor is purposive. He intended his comic protests to change hearts and minds, to clarify vision, and to improve mankind. His despair is not a product of eastern deracination any more than is Voltaire's or Swift's. Claims that it is based on a profound superficiality of viewpoint characteristic of literary critics turned psychobiographers. Serious students of the canon find it to be consistent—and pessimistic underneath its idealism—throughout. The reason for this is simple. The optimistic idealism of the comedy is based on political premises of equality. Surrounded by the love of his wife Livy (see Laura Skandera-Trombley's article here), the pragmatic Christianity of Joe Twichell (see Leah Strong's book cited in the Bibliography but not easily

Introduction

excerpted), the nurturing realism of William Dean Howells (see Howells's two assessments of Clemens here), the applause—and cash receipts—of the crowd (see the hunger for Twain anecdotes in *The Ladies Home Journal* and George Ade on the subscription book), this idealism could be dominant. More important, it was the external product which writer gave reader, speaker provided audience. Underneath, the despair of a man who saw death, selfishness, and a universe out of control was not a reasonable vision to put forth. First, it was not something likely to improve mankind for the better—this is the importance of Nook Farm (and Quarry Farm as well, by the way)—on Twain: they were places populated by meliorists, and with them he was one, too. Second, his philosophical mechanism was compelling to him, but as a world-view it was half-baked, not a finished product which he shared as much because it was inartistic as because it was warmed up in hell—he published plenty of hellish satire in his later years, including "To the Person Sitting in Darkness" which John Kendrick Bangs tried so unsuccessfully to dispute in *Harper's Weekly*. Thus, a book like *What Is Man?* sneaked into print; it was unfunny, but it was also an enlarged expression of the comedian's anger which had to be vented. Partly it might have hurt his economic standing, he guessed, but also he knew it to be the product of his grief and anger, broadened by his personal losses, but something that he had always carried in him, not necessarily as the stuff of great literature. He didn't publish much of his pessimistic outpouring because it was self-indulgent. The real problem with these later manuscripts is that the scholarly community and a hungry public accept their standing in his canon as higher than it should be. There were many pieces Twain chose not to reprint from his writings. Why? Because they crossed the border between serious humor and mediocre humor. We should recognize the difference; the three essays by younger Twain scholars—Skandera-Trombley, Michael Kiskis, and Susanne Weil—are helpful in analyzing the later Twain in a modern way which leads us to this recognition and do much to extend Susan Harris's study of "Hadleyburg" to the end of Twain's career.

These statements should help focus the selections offered here, divided into groups of essays indicating the nature of Twain's early background as a technician and comic social philosopher, his middle career as a writer to be differentiated from other comedians but still abrasive to many readers, and, lastly, as a world figure whose writings, even when less visionary than the major novels, represented important cultural documents to detached observers. All the analytic critics are consistent in finding in Twain's writing a comic methodology that derives from his time and his culture and eventuates in an outcome that attempts to be socially visionary. That product is intrinsically wrapped around a humane and idealistic meaning. It would have been Christian had Twain been able to reconcile himself with the institutional church, but he could not do that except in the person of Joe Twichell, neither generally nor in the overwhelming evidence of authoritarian Catholicism; Twain was always a good American Know-Nothing. Nor could he come to terms with a true God—which God seemed determined *not* to send him a clear and unequivocal sign no matter how hard he prayed on his knees beside Twichell for belief. So, Twain created work after work out of the comic materials surrounding him, which he found abundant in the failure of the world to live up to its own image of itself. His unrest with other writers—as suggested in Alan Gribben's article on literary small game and in Walter Blair's discussion of *Tom Sawyer* — reflects this impatience with goals which were too limited, accounting, I think, as well, for the oddly distant relationship between Twain and Trowbridge so admirably captured by Rufus Coleman. He semi-fictionalized himself to create the character in the travel books and in part his major heroes, as essays by Franklin Rogers, David Sloane, Henry Watterson, and Edgar Branch suggest. He borrowed the spread-eagle rhetoric and biblical hypocrisies that were the common currency of his day just as he would borrow the

Introduction

pseudo-economic business and world-politick jargon of ours were he alive in the 1990s. In everything he did, however, he tapped into our cultural mainstream—A. C. Ward's trenchant point as an outside observer of American culture, but consistent with discussions of Twain by *Blackwood's* a generation earlier and by Mme. Th. Bentson two generations before that as reflected in Archibald Henderson's discussion of Twain's "international fame." The continuity of his popularity and its growth is testimony to the completeness with which his comedy incorporated the underlying forces of our culture, made clear even in the essay on farce and *The American Claimant* by Clyde Grimm. It may be that American culture as a culture shares his antagonism to reality—seen benignly in the Colonel Sellers observed by Watterson or the seemingly haphazard but actually methodical lecturer Twain seen by Will Clemens—and the pragmatic humor which overcomes it, a form of whimsy far different from other humor. Twain would have missed the humor of other cultures such as the native American cultures, which he despised for the savagery which he held in a contempt that would only have been rivalled by his contempt for the street violence of today's culture. In studying the works, then, we are studying a cultural exercise as well as a literary one. The selections here were chosen because their authors seem aware of the background of culture but maintain a focus on the mechanics of the comedian. As readers move through this book, they should find an array of minute observations which suggest a mechanic at work, but a mechanic with a cultural position. Yet, none of these essays is ideologically didactic, nor do they need to be, although I hope my own assertions in this introduction give a context which raises issues beyond belletristic ones.

The order of essays here is roughly according to the subjects that the essays deal with. Thus, an essay from *Blackwood's Magazine* published in 1907 but focused on writings from the 1880s—revolving around *Life on the Mississippi*, and one by Edith Wyatt in the 1920s—which has salient observations about *Joan of Arc*—come after scholarly criticism of Twain's early work by writers of the post-1950s era—Edgar Branch on the "Jumping Frog," Louis Budd on *The Gilded Age*, and Franklin Rogers on *Roughing It*, but before other scholars treating Twain's last decade. Practically speaking, this arrangement retains the shape of Twain's overall career as well as reprinting some worthwhile treatments of Twain's humor which have never appeared together in one volume. Three works by five younger Twain scholars appear in this volume for the first time in print and are grouped at the end of the volume. Partly this reflects an increased interest in explaining Twain's later work by writers of the late-1980s and 1990s in response to the biographical and textual mix coming out of the popular thirst for "new" Twain materials and the production schedule of the Iowa-California edition (which seemed early on to favor later unpublished, more pessimistic works) and to the several debunking biographies which take strong positions on Clemens's later life. The findings of these recent essays in many ways confirm insights into Twain's work which were current in his own day, and they are thus both "fresh" and conservative—a valuable reminder that awareness of cultural context enhances critical perception.

The purpose of this volume is to lay out documents which give an estimate of Mark Twain as a humorist in both historical scope and in the analysis of modern scholars. A number of excellent essays on various Twain topics and *Adventures of Huckleberry Finn* are omitted because (1) they are easily available in other anthologies, and (2) they tend to lead away from humor to deal with the themes of *Huck Finn*. This is not a bad thing in itself, but not necessarily the only way into the vast array of Twain's humor spread over his more than fifty years as a writer—Lionel Trilling on *Huckleberry Finn* is one obvious example. The emphasis in this collection is on how Twain developed from a contemporary humorist among many others of his generation into a major comic writer and American spokesman and, in several recent essays by younger Twain scholars, the outcomes of that development

Introduction

late in his career. The thrust of these inquiries lies in determining how the humor takes on meaning and importance and how the humor works in a number of ways in the literary canon and even in the persona of Mark Twain.

In some but not all cases, this volume offers materials that have been difficult to locate. Such is the case with the debate over the Philippine war teaming Twain's "To a Person Sitting in Darkness" with a response by popular 1890s humorist John Kendrick Bangs in *Harper's Weekly* of 1901—a "popular" controversy showing Twain's humor as contributing to a national argument over a universal democratic premise. Such a document gives us another way of considering Twain through an interchange that is otherwise lost to us; it shows the humorist taking political responsibility in a controversial area. It is also fascinating to see Bangs, one of the most popular humorists of the 1890–1910 period, trying to stake out a pro-imperialism position, ineptly defending the "Charity Organization Society" against Twain's fiery sarcasm at the "Blessings of Civilization Trust." Even the *ad hominem* shift fails Bangs as he cites Twainian arguments (such as Twain's acrid "Taels, I win, Heads you lose" comment for John C. Ament's insistence on indemnity and the Catholic demand for 680 heads—executions—to accompany the payment of thousands of dollars in Chinese Taels as compensation for deaths in the Boxer Rebellion) which don't even appear in the shortened version of the piece published in the facing pages of the *Harper's* production. Martha McCulloch Williams's erroneous attack on the "shoot my half" story from *Pudd'nhead Wilson* is likewise important not because of her failure to recognize the story as a Yankee story derived from P. T. Barnum's *Life* but rather because it shows a Southerner's anger at Twain's intellectual position, as further drawn out in its racial consequences in Shelley Fisher Fishkin's essay on the same work.

An item from the *Ladies Home Journal* for 1898 reports a variety of anecdotes about Twain. Since the *Journal* at that time was one of the most widely read magazines in the United

States, the short pieces suggest how much Twain was a personality as well as an author. They are offered here because they put Twain in the human context in which his readers read his works. In fact, it would be fair to say that more than any other writer of modern times, Twain is read as if he were in a dialogue with the reader through the pages of his books, rather than as if he were absent and the text stood alone. Consequently, the persona of Mark Twain is of more than passing interest and more integral to his canon than is the case with other figures of his era. Aside from that, the anecdotes give family history that has some merit as part of his record. No extreme critical insight should be claimed for them, and none is. Yet taken together with the article by George Ade, and the analysis by Durant Da Ponte and Leslie Fiedler of the reception of *Huckleberry Finn*, and Edith Wyatt on *Joan of Arc*, such materials give us a broadened picture of an author whose works were bound up in a culture in ways unparalleled in twentieth-century literature.

Several of the analytic pieces in this volume provide extraordinary technical insights into the construction and background of pieces by Twain. Walter Blair on *Tom Sawyer*, Edgar Branch on "The Notorious Jumping Frog," Henry Nash Smith on *Huck Finn*, Louis Budd on the humorist's writings in the late 1860s and early 1870s, Susan Harris on "Hadleyburg," Michael Kiskis on *Mark Twain's Autobiography*, and Susanne Weil on the "Mysterious Stranger" fall into this category, as do significant parts of other essays.

Pascal Covici's study of Mark Twain's humor is particularly valuable in showing how much the southwestern and northeastern blend in Twain's canon, especially since the "Is he dead?" joke in *Innocents Abroad* discussed at the end of the selection, is from easterner Artemus Ward. "From the Old Southwest," however, is particularly useful in giving us specific citations and sources of a less theoretical nature than those in Kenneth Lynn's *Mark Twain and Southwestern Humor*. Covici is helpful in making a trenchant distinction between the real subject matter of the Southwest and Twain as

Introduction

a realistic comedian. James M. Cox on *A Connecticut Yankee* is correspondingly illuminating on that book specifically.

Louis J. Budd helps us understand how innately conservative Twain's comic radicalism actually is. Indeed, Twain held fast to the basic American concepts of democracy in ways that by no means accepted the ugly side of mass culture. Like John Hay and others of his class and time, Twain came to terms with mass labor movements with some difficulty, and his approval of mass action often presumes, as is presumed in the early works discussed by Budd, that humankind will have to be educated up to revolution grade before being emancipated. This is a rather covertly gloomy vision, but it is consistent with concepts expressed in Henry Nash Smith's discussion of *Huck Finn* in "A Sound Heart and a Deformed Conscience" which takes as its premise the idea that social dictates vary from innate human decency—a premise of all of Twain's work, and a necessary assumption for any reforming egalitarian. Although this essay is generally available, it fills an appropriate place between Leslie Fiedler's historical overview and the fulminations of Robert Bridges reflected in *Life*'s 1885 review of *Huck*, and so it completes a rounded view of *Huck Finn* which is a microcosm of the larger collection.

Edward F. Foster, in showing what Max Adeler did with the same materials as found in Twain's *Connecticut Yankee*, draws back from an outright charge of plagiarism against Twain because the real value of his article is in showing the intersection of interests in chivalry versus modernity in literary comedians generally. After all, Max Adeler's "The Fortunate Island" was not the only chivalric-modern satire predating Twain; one could also cite Edgar Fawcett's dreadful verse satire, *The New King Arthur* (1885) among others, including a piece by Twain published in 1871 in *Galaxy* magazine and readily available (See *Mark Twain as Literary Comedian* for further references on this subject).

George Ade shows the context into which Twain's actual printed volumes were plunged. He suggests that while his writings were in opposition to staid works of morality, they were also placed among them. All of Twain's concerns with his writing and public seem to confirm that he, like Ade, was aware of his special, privileged place in the popular libraries of middle America. Therefore, he used their language and their context directly. Oddly enough, Theodore Dreiser also used popular terminology in *Sister Carrie* (1900) but with a stunningly different effect and outcome. The comic reversals of Twain are different from the ironic reversals of Dreiser, though critics could find plenty to dislike in both writers. An astute reader could see interesting comparisons in the use of diction and metaphor by applying Arun Mukherjee's *The Gospel of Wealth in the American Novel* (Totowa, NJ: Barnes & Noble, 1987) backwards from Dreiser's novels to Twain's *A Connecticut Yankee in King Arthur's Court*. Even the late, brief dismissal of *Tom Sawyer Abroad* by the London *Academy* in 1894, ending with a line well-known to be from Artemus Ward, Twain's chief precursor in the English concept of American humor, identifies Twain's works as being regarded within the context of his writing as a humorist, irrespective of the dismal quality of that particular novel.

Blackwood's Magazine in 1907 paid tribute to *Life on the Mississippi* and in passing to Huck and Tom, but this is after the debacle in British eyes of the irreverent *A Connecticut Yankee*. *Blackwood's* has not forgotten that novel, and thus moves freely through a spectrum of life in Britain and finds even in it traces of similar exaggerated cheapening and debasement. In a memorable phrase, they pillory Twain the specialist in travesty as "a bull in the china-shop of ideas," and the argument is worthy of consideration, whether right or wrong, for it highlights the fact that writers such as Twain were radical precursors of modern dissent. *Blackwood's* final objection to Twain is consistent with the position staked out by them half a century before (in "Revelations of a Showman" in volume 47: 187–201 for February 1855) in lambasting P. T. Barnum for his chicanery. Actually, the essay is testimony to sheer consistency of vision for both the Barnum-Twain-

Introduction

Artemus Ward sort of American exaggerated figure and for the English cultural milieu opposed to such Americanism as a social phenomenon. Hating his "imbecile lack of taste," *Blackwood's* reminds us again of the importance of Brander Matthews's comment on Twain in "The Penalty of Humor" (not reprinted here since only a page of its several pages deals with Twain in general terms) that he had suffered more for the reputation of a humorist because he was more of a humorist than any other living writer. Controversy lies at the heart of the acceptance of Twain by disputants like Brander Matthews, H. L. Mencken, James T. Farrell, and others who admired his craft for its social content put forth in the very way that increased the offence to more pretentiously classically oriented critics, along with his rejection at the hands of Edgar Lee Masters in *Mark Twain, A Portrait*. Space precludes including these essays, but they will be found in several lists in the anthologies of Twain criticism at the back of the book. The truth is that Twain appealed through humor to a subversively unorthodox element within genteel America at the same time that his directedness toward "the belly and its members" offended the more officiously mannered of that ilk.

Edith Wyatt's "An Inspired Critic" represents the cultivated appreciation of Twain that came to dominate intelligent readers' view of him through the 1900–1920 period. *Life on the Mississippi* is effectively appraised by her, but she goes on to make a strong statement for the social truth of Twain's humor to "Chicago" and the United States generally—the real places as well as the fictional settings. Her praise of *Joan of Arc* for its "pragmatic validity" is worth noting, and her concluding paragraph is a powerful statement of Twain's popularity as a democratic idealist. Clyde Grimm's study of *The American Claimant* shows that novel to contain some rather sophisticated thinking about the nature of democracy as a sham and as a reality in response to the sham of aristocracy. Since it follows so closely on the heels of *A Connecticut Yankee*, the proximity and shared subject matter of English nobility versus American democracy make *The American*

Claimant more interesting than is allowed by those who over-hastily dismiss it as a rambling farce.

The two chapters from William Dean Howells's *My Mark Twain* are arresting because they show him trying to run counter to prevailing estimates of both periods, emphasizing Twain's seriousness in the early 1880s and his regionalism in the latter period when Twain was coming to his full stature as a world writer. Thus, we see Howells emphasizing "The Recent Carnival of Crime in Connecticut" and noting the success of the play from *The Gilded Age* with a Col. Sellers who is actually drawn from real life. In 1902, he throws his net wider, finding Twain's socio-economic basis and even some nascent feminism, a theme playing through the items offered here by Henry Watterson at the turn of the century and Laura Skandera-Trombley as a recent critic. In fact, as a humorist, Twain was a rule-breaking writer, and it is to focus on this characteristic of his comic indignation and to stress its literary side as well as its social side that Alan Gribben's article "'I Kind of Love Small Game': Mark Twain's Library of Literary Hogwash" is valuable and insightful reading. Twain responded emotionally to form as well as function, and his hatred of the staged and false in literature and in life represents both an aesthetic and a philosophical underpinning of his humanity as irony, sarcasm, exaggeration, burlesque, and satire express it.

Of particular interest is a group of essays by Twain scholars which have not before seen print: those by Kiskis, Skandera-Trombley, and Weil place the literary artifact and an accurate reading of historical detail ahead of ideology in their interpretations. Kiskis's on Twain's *Autobiography* shows how the writer's humor came full circle, in his phrase, depending on narrative patterns that he had used from the very first. Weil makes the point, responding to provocative work by Hamlin Hill and William Gibson, that even supposedly unsatisfactory later works have an identifiable place in Twain's ever-changing comedy. Her discussion of the later works helps place them properly in perspective as part of his comic canon,

The Lyceum Committeeman's Dream—Some Popular Lecturers in Character

making her contribution an important one. Skandera-Trombley, in taking up the place of women in Twain's constellation of psychological traits, brings us back to insights first broached by Henry Watterson, but too long forgotten in the face of Van Wyck Brooks, that there was a strong "feminine" consciousness in Twain, an intrinsic component of his life and art and welcome in his life, not a trivializing eastern consciousness or censorship.

Finally, the selected bibliography has been developed to help readers find essays and books which deal with Mark Twain's humor as such. For this reason, the full contents of several anthologies of criticism should be a helpful finding tool not otherwise available. A special word of thanks must be extended here to Thomas Tenney's extraordinary compilation of critical abstracts in *Mark Twain: A Reference Guide*; this exhaustive collection of materials on Twain provides thousands of insights into specific publications on Twain. Tenney's work materially advanced the work here. The bibliography offers two sections. The first provides tables of contents for several valuable and easily obtainable anthologies of secondary criticism on Mark Twain, and especially on *Adventures of Huckleberry Finn*. The second offers those articles and books, listed alphabetically by author, that deal most directly with aspects of Mark Twain's humor. This section is focussed as tightly as seems possible, and it does not include many "standard" works on Twain because of their more general and comprehensive nature. For further aid in developing sources, the supplements to Tenney's work in the *Mark Twain Journal* and the annual analytic bibliographies in *American Literary Scholarship: An Annual* year by year are unfailingly informative, and were useful also in making this compilation. Bibliographies in Walter Blair's *Native American Humor* and David E. E. Sloane's *Mark Twain as a Literary Comedian* might also be consulted for further references, and a wide array of bibliographies of Twain criticism can be found in the books cited above and elsewhere. The bibliography extends through 1989.

The Early Writings of Mark Twain:
The Growth of the Comedian

"My Voice Is Still for Setchell": A Background Study of "Jim Smiley and His Jumping Frog"

Edgar M. Branch

I

For the past fifteen years scholars have examined many facets of Mark Twain's "Jumping Frog": its narrative techniques and some of its textual history, its relation to folklore, American humor, and Clemens' theory of humorous gravity, and its political, regional, and cultural bearings.[1] This article, by focussing on the personal background to the tale, tries to cast light on the imagination that created the famous yarn. It first relates some of the tale's narrative elements—episodes, characters, names—to Clemens' prior experience, especially to some activities reflected in newly discovered examples of his San Francisco journalism of 1864 and 1865. Then it relates the tale to strong emotional currents in his life during the fall of 1865. Finally the article proposes a date of composition for the "Jumping Frog" and a reading of the tale that emphasizes the level of personal meaning.

Clemens left Nevada for San Francisco 29 May 1864, almost eighteen months before the first printing of the "Jumping Frog" on 19 November 1865, and for fifteen of those months he lived in the city. Soon after arriving he became the local reporter of the San Francisco *Call*. Probably he worked for the paper from 6 June to 10 October or possibly until a week later. During these four months he published hundreds of unsigned news items as well as feature articles and sketches in the *Call*. Growing dissatisfied with his job, he took an assistant in September and began working fewer hours for lower pay. Also he began to publish more ambitiously conceived sketches in C. H. Webb's *Californian,* nine in all between 1 October and 3 December. On 4 December he went to Jim Gillis' cabin at Jackass Hill. He remained there and at nearby Angel's Camp (from 22 January to 20 February) until his return to San Francisco 26 February 1865. From 18 March Through October Clemens published twelve additional sketches in the Californian and placed a few elsewhere. At least by 20 June he had begun his correspondence for Joseph T. Goodman's Virginia City *Territorial Enterprise*—a working relationship he continued into 1866—although he may not have started his daily letter to that paper until the fall. The third major professional connection he made during 1865 was with the San Francisco *Dramatic Chronicle.* He appears to have worked as a *Chronicle* staff writer for about two months, beginning 16 October. He contributed a few sketches and some squibs, and at least part of the time he compiled the column "Amusements," which included the theater notices.

II

Clemens' experience of Angel's Camp was of course basic to the "Jumping Frog." The remote, primitive community, soggy with rain for days on end, gave him the setting for the frame and for the internal narrative, and it supplied the perfect environment to motivate nonstop indoor yarning like Simon Wheeler's. Ben Coon, whom Clemens met there, is usually regarded as the pattern for Wheeler, and Coon's yarn of Coleman and his frog is well recognized as the immediate source for the contest in which Jim Smiley's trained frog is frustrated in his specialty by "a double-handful of shot." Clemens' synopsis put down the main facts: "Coleman with his jumping frog—bet stranger $50—stranger had no frog, & C got him one—in the meantime stranger filled C's frog full of shot & he couldn't jump—the stranger's frog won."[2] Very likely Coon's deadpan manner and vernacular language made a strong impression on Clemens and helped him establish Wheeler's point of view. The frame narrator of the tale, the character Mark Twain, finds Wheeler's speech "monotonous" and "interminable" yet "exquisitely absurd" in its earnest, gravely serene progression: a mixture of feelings that may approximate Clemens' original reaction to Ben Coon.[3] But this characterization of Wheeler's narration may have been suggested to Clemens by other mining camp acquaintances as well. Before he recorded his meeting with Coon and before he summarized Coon's yarn, he wrote: "Mountaineers in habit telling same old experiences over & over again in these little back settlements. Like Dan's old Ram, while [sic] he always drivels about when drunk. And like J's [Jim Gillis'?] account of the finding of the Cardinal... & other great pocket, & the sums they produced in a few days or weeks (50 to 100 lbs gold a day)."[4] At least one other notebook observation made at Angel's Camp seems to reflect experience that supplied a narrative detail. Clemens developed Jim Smiley as a resourceful, dedicated gambler. Simon Wheeler says of him that "if he even see a straddle-bug start to go any wheres, he would bet you how long it would take him to get wherever he was going to, and if you took him up he would foller that straddle-bug to Mexico but what he would find out where he was bound for." That passage may be compared to this notebook entry: "Louse betting by <sold> discharged soldiers coming through from Mexico to Cal in early days. The man whose louse got whipped had to get supper. Or place them on the bottom of a frying pan—draw chalk circle round them, heat the pan & the last louse over the line had to get supper."[5]

The appeal of the mining camp raconteur to Clemens' imagination is evident in "An Unbiased Criticism," his first published sketch after his return to the city. Gladys C. Bellamy (*Mark Twain as a Literary Artist*, Norman, Okla., 1950, p. 146) has correctly recognized in this sketch a rehearsal for the "Jumping Frog." Its major figure, simply called Coon, almost immediately takes over from the Mark Twain persona, as though by force of character. Coon lacks some of Simon Wheeler's "winning gentleness" and ungrudging admiration of others, and his use of the comic *non sequitur*, a device Artemus Ward liked, perhaps adds an artificial touch. But essentially his vision and speech are Simon Wheeler's. Coon, who seems to know everything about everybody for miles around, discourses on his "mighty responsible old Webster-Unabridged, what there is left of it." The miners

> started her sloshing around, and sloshing around, and sloshing around. . . , and I don't expect I'll ever see that book again; but what makes me mad, is that for all they're so handy about keeping her sashshaying around from shanty to shanty and from camp to camp, none of 'em's ever got a good word for her. Now Coddington had her a week, and she was too many for *him*—he couldn't spell the words; he tackled some of them regular busters, tow'rd the middle, you know, and they throwed him; next, Dyer, *he* tried her a jolt, but he couldn't *pronounce* worth a d—n; . . . and so, finally, Dick Stoker harnessed her, up there at his cabin, and sweated over her, and cussed over her, and rastled with her for as much as three weeks, night and day, till he got as far as R, and then passed her over to 'Lige Pickerell, and said she was the all-firedest dryest reading that ever *he* struck."[6]

Although Coon's voice is silenced before he can spin a tale, he speaks with Simon Wheeler's rambling omniscience and rhythms. His imagination like Simon's swarms with lively grotesques whom he observes with discriminating eyes. His dictionary takes on human outline too: something like an old hand-me-down prostitute who still is more than a match for her baffled and inadequate clients. The worthy book has some of the betrayed integrity of the dog Andrew Jackson, it goes through paces as frantic as those of Smiley's fifteen-minute nag, and it is "as likely a book as any in the State," just as

Dan'l Webster "can out-jump any frog in Calaveras county." Both tale and sketch project a feeling of time hanging heavy. Their people are eccentrics preoccupied with oddities and committed to trivia. To a degree the two writings share an identical vocabulary to describe analogous details: a mouth (or door) "prized" open, a dog (or dictionary) "harnessed," a frog (or man) turning a double "summerset." Coon's monologue in "An Unbiased Criticism" permitted Clemens to test the mentality through which he later dramatized the statement: "Why, it never made no difference to *him*—he would bet on *anything*—the dangdest feller." It signals Clemens' discovery of the appropriate style to express Wheeler's consciousness in the tale.

III

The available evidence indicates that Ben Coon's narrative was restricted to the episode of the shot-laden frog and that it played up the idea of human trickery and not animal idiosyncrasy.[7] Also by 1865 Clemens was adept at creating humanized animals. Almost certainly, then, he alone—with no dependence on any mining camp raconteur—conceived the full range of Smiley's love for betting and his paternalistic exploitation of talented animals. Significantly Clemens kept the memory of Coon's yarn alive in his imagination by joking about it with Jim Gillis and Dick Stoker as all three panned for gold, and before writing the published version he may have sketched the tale in a letter to Artemus Ward and may have told it to Bret Harte and other San Franciscans.[8] The imaginative enlargement of Coon's anecdote that occurred in the long gestation is in fact partly traceable. In particular, when he composed the episodes of the fifteen-minute nag and the dog Andrew Jackson, it now appears that Clemens drew upon experience he gained as a San Francisco reporter.

Among the hundreds of local news items appearing in the *Call* during the time Clemens worked on the paper are several on the horse races held in the new and lavishly equipped Bay View Park, located on the bay shore west of Hunter's Point. Two of these turf reports are reprinted below. Although they are unsigned, in my opinion they are by Clemens and form part of the background out of which Jim Smiley's mare comes "cavorting" down the track.[9]

> The Hurdle-Race Yesterday.—The grand feature at the Bay View Park yesterday, was the hurdle race. There were three competitors, and the winner was Wilson's circus horse, "Sam." Sam has lain quiet through all the pacings and trottings and runnings, and consented to be counted out, but this hurdle business was just his strong suit, and he stepped forward promptly when it was proposed. There was a much faster horse (Conflict) in the list, but what is natural talent to cultivation? Sam was educated in a circus, and understood his business; Conflict would pass him under way, trip and turn a double summerset over the next hurdle, and while he was picking himself up, the accomplished Sam would sail gracefully over the hurdle and slabber past his adversary with the easy indifference of conscious superiority. Conflict made the fastest time, but he fooled away too many summersets on the hurdles. The proverb saith that he that jumpeth fences with ye circus horse will aye come to grief.[10]

Six days later the *Call* published the lengthy "Race for the Occidental Hotel Premium." The first half of this report factually describes four heats in the trotting contest subsidized by the Occidental Hotel, where Clemens boarded. The horse Kentucky Hunter ran first in each race. The reporter then continues:

> Previous to the Occidental contest, a tandem race came off for a purse of one hundred and twenty-five dollars, mile heats, best 3 in 5. "Spot" and "Latham," driven by Mr. Covey, and "Rainbow" and "Sorrel Charley," driven by Mr Ferguson, ran. Before the first half mile post was reached, Ferguson's team ran away, and Covey's trotted around leisurely and won the purse. The runaways flew around the race-track three or four times, at break neck speed, and fears were entertained that some of this break-neck would finally fall to Ferguson's share, as his strength soon ebbed away,

and he no longer attempted to hold his fiery untamed Menkens, but only did what he could to make them stay on the track, and keep them from climbing the fence. Every time they dashed by the excited crowd at the stand, a few frantic attempts would be made to grab them, but with indifferent success; it is no use to snatch at a cannon ball—a man must stand before it if he wants to stop it. One man seized the lead horse, and was whisked under the wheels in an instant. His head was split open a little, but Dr. Woodward stitched the wound together, and the sufferer was able to report for duty in half an hour. Mr. Ferguson's horses should be taught to economize their speed; they wasted enough of it in that one dash, yesterday, to win every race this season, if judiciously distributed among them. The only Christian way to go out to Bay View, is to travel in one of the Occidental coaches, behind four Flora Temples, and with their master-spirit, Porter, on the box, and a crowd inside and out, consisting of moral young men and cocktails. Mr. Leland should be along, to keep the portable hotel.[11]

In the "Jumping Frog" Clemens writes of the mare whom the boys called

the fifteen-minute nag, but that was only in fun, you know, because, of course, she was faster than that—and he used to win money on that horse, for all she was so slow and always had the asthma, or the distemper, or the consumption, or something of that kind. They used to give her two or three hundred yards' start, and then pass her under way; but always at the fag-end of the race she'd get excited and desperate-like, and come cavorting and spraddling up, and scattering her legs around limber, sometimes in the air, and sometimes out to one side amongst the fences, and kicking up m-o-r-e dust, and raising m-o-r-e racket with her coughing and sneezing and blowing her nose—and always fetch up at the stand just about a neck ahead, as near as you could cipher it down.

Like Kentucky Hunter, Smiley's mare is a consistent winner, capable of rousing herself and coming from behind to score. But clearly Sam's claim to be her sire is superior to Kentucky Hunter's. Competitors of both Sam and the mare "pass" each horse "under way," thus momentarily confirming to all observers the expected role of each underdog horse as an also-run and adding that much more excitement to the eventual upset victories. Although Sam takes the hurdles gracefully, his slabbering form as a runner suggests the spraddling mare scattering her legs around, and suggests, too, that when the chips were really down, the easygoing Sam, like Smiley's nag, possibly would show up as a lathering slob. To be sure, Sam is as educated as Smiley's frog, and no doubt this training explains his casual confidence and his feeling of superiority, so different from the mare's female excitability and air of desperation. Sam's victory over the speedy Conflict, in fact, is a monument to "cultivation" in contrast to what must surely be an impressive "talent"—no less than that of the dog Andrew Jackson's—in the badly handicapped, snuffling nag. Yet these very differences help us to see that both the "Jumping Frog" and the *Call* report of the hurdle race humorously utilize, with varying emphases, the twin ideas of natural endowment and acquired training (facets of Clemens' more general speculations of necessity and freedom), ideas often linked in his thinking and writing.[12] The two unorthodox race horses are close kin in Clemens' large family of exceptional, strong-minded animals.[13]

IV

Smiley's mare was a consistent winner and so was the bull-pup Andrew Jackson until he "got shucked out bad" by the dog "that didn't have no hind legs, because they'd been sawed off in a circular saw." The disfigured hero who retired Andrew Jackson for good is a significant minor character. So far as we know, he was Jim Smiley's only nemesis before the tricky stranger walked into camp. His surprise triumph over Andrew Jackson resulted from a circumstance much less usual than the duplicity shown by the stranger. Presumably his victory might have suggested to Smiley more forcibly than it did that a sure thing, even a scrupulously educated and gifted frog, can never be taken for granted. It appears that the original of this unsung conqueror of Andrew Jackson claimed Clemens' attention during the third week of October 1865.

In a revealing letter dated 19 October 1865 and addressed to Orion and Mollie Clemens, but meant primarily for Orion, Clemens wrote: "I am also in debt. But I have gone to work in dead earnest to get out. Joe Goodman pays me $100 a month for a daily letter, and the Dramatic Chronicle pays me or rather *will* begin to pay me, next week—$40 a month for dramatic criticisms. Same wages I got on the Call, & more agreeable & less laborious work."[14] It seems clear that when Clemens wrote this letter he had begun his duties of the *Dramatic Chronicle* as a recently recruited staff member and was not, as an old hand, taking on a new assignment at an increase in pay.[15] Two days before, he had published his first sketch in the *Dramatic Chronicle*, "Earthquake Almanac," which customarily noticed the daily offerings at the theaters, museums, and resorts, included the following account of James White's Museum of freaks:

White's Museum

Meigg's wharf is the favorite resort of the little ones on Sunday. No one who goes to this part of the city should leave without paying a visit to White's Museum, where a most wonderful collection of curiosities, fully equal to anything which Barnum has, are on view. The three-quartered dog, a fine handsome fellow, and as intelligent and good-natured an animal as we have ever had the pleasure of being introduced to, is a most wonderful freak of nature. Poor fellow! Richard III was—

"Cheated of feature by dissembling nature,
Deformed, unfinished,"

but this dog is actually cheated of a quarter by dissembling nature, who sent him into the world only three parts finished. However, he does not seem to mind it a bit; he is as strong and lively as any four-legged dog, and more intelligent than many two-legged puppies.[16]

This strong dog who accepts his defect is a fit model for the conqueror of a champion. Neither he nor Andrew Jackson's opponent is as vitally handicapped as Andrew Jackson, whose rigid habitual responses and tender-minded conviction that Smiley owed him a set-up prove to be a fatal combination. But Andrew Jackson is a more important character than his conqueror and in conceiving him Clemens dug more deeply into his past. Simon Wheeler says that "to look at him you'd think he warn't worth a cent, but to set around and look ornery, and lay for a chance to steal something." Here Clemens may be remembering the orneriness and thievery of Curney and Tom, two dogs he wrote up in his Keokuk *Gate City* later of 6 March 1862. But to describe Andrew Jackson's pugnacity when the "money was up on him" he reverted to sterner imagery from his piloting days: "his under-jaw'd begin to stick out like the for'castle [sic] of a steamboat, and his teeth would uncover, and shine savage like the furnaces." Andrew Jackson with his steam up was as lethal as the riverboat with its "long row of wide-open furnace doors shining like red-hot teeth" (*Writings*, XIII, 131) that smashed Huck's and Jim's raft.

Any San Franciscan writing of dogs at this time would almost automatically recall the famous friends Bummer and Lazarus, two dogs constantly publicized during the early 1860's in the San Francisco press. Clemens was aware of them and published an account of Bummer's death.[17] Andrew Jackson was not a vagrant like Bummer, but like Andrew Jackson, the valorous Bummer was a respected fighter. Clemens commented on his dignity, a quality similar to Andrew Jackson's pride that helped to undermine his will to live after "he saw in a minute how he'd been imposed on." Disillusioned, wounded to the heart, and mildly reproachful, Andrew Jackson "limped off a piece" to die alone, a defeated romantic. This comic sentimentality may be compared to the last moments of the more sociable Bummer, who "died with friends around him to smooth his pillow and wipe the death-damps from his brow, and receive his last words of love and resignation; because he died full of years, and honor, and disease, and fleas."

V

Clemens' experience as a San Francisco journalist may have influenced—consciously or not—his choice of names for some characters in the "Jumping Frog," if only by making those names available for selection because of his recent awareness of them. His 1864 editorial "It Is the Daniel Webster" praises the Daniel Webster Mining Company for daring to make its records public at a time when most companies were not disclosing how they spent assessments. As a stockholder, Clemens suffered from the drain of assessments and had fretted about their misappropriation by secretaries and managers of mining companies.[18] The Daniel Webster Mining Company he now saw as a symbol of probity, "worthy of the name of Daniel Webster." Its policy eventually would force other companies to "adopt the system of published periodical statement." On the day, he exulted, stockholders would hear from Virginia City corporations that sport "costly and beautiful green chicken-cocks on the roof, which are able to tell how the wind blows, yet are savagely ignorant concerning dividends. So will other Companies come out and say what it cost to build their duck ponds; . . . another that we have in our eye will show what they did with an expensive lot of timbers, when they haven't got enough in their mine to shingle a chicken-coop with. . . and why they levy a forty-thousand-dollar assessment every six weeks to run a drift with. Secretaries, Superintendents, and Boards of Trustees, that don't like the prospect, had better resign."[19]

During the 1860's the name Daniel Webster still had considerable currency, and Clemens had used it sparingly for many years. The physical resemblance of any frog to the famous politician is enough to have recalled the name once again to an imagination that often visualized animals as people, although Clemens' naming of Smiley's frog no doubt drew upon many interwoven associations, including the one deriving from his attack on the mining companies.

Through much of 1864 and 1865 in the *Call*, the *Dramatic Chronicle*, and the *Territorial Enterprise* Clemens repeatedly sniped at Albert S. Evans, the city editor of the San Francisco *Alta California* who was commonly known by his pen names Fitz Smythe and Amigo. Writing in the *Alta California* in mid-1864, Evans invented a stooge whom he named Armand Leonidas Stiggers, surely one of the dreariest comic characters of all time. Clemens ridiculed the labored jokes Evans constructed around Stiggers. His fondness for the name Leonidas is evident during late 1865 and 1866 in his continuing bouts with Evans, whom he rechristened Armand Leonidas Fitz Smythe Amigo Stiggers. Leonidas, an improbable name at best, in one sense suits the mythical friend who was not there, "the Rev. Leonidas W. Smiley" of the tale, whom Artemus Ward asked Mark Twain to look up. Yet to make a minister of God lion-like is almost as incongruous as the comic ennobling of Smiley's frog and bullpup by naming them after great human leaders.

The name Smiley that supplanted Ben Coon's "Coleman" was Clemens' most brilliant choice. Paired with "Leonidas" it aptly describes the mocking phantom who lives only within the realm of Ward's practical joke on Mark Twain. Joined with "Jim" it admirably fits the wily gambler, adept and enduring in a man's world. Its source may be the case of the *United States vs. Thomas J. L. Smiley* publicized in the San Francisco papers during the summer of 1864 when Clemens was local reporter on the *Call*. In 1862 the ship *Golden Gate* out of San Francisco with almost $1,500,000 in treasure had sunk off the coast of Mexico near Manzanillo. The adventurer Smiley was indicted in the United States Circuit Court for salvaging and appropriating some of the treasure. But on 29 August 1864 Judge Ogden Hoffman ordered a *nolle prosequi*, and the *Call* reported that Smiley had compromised a second suit brought against him. The settlement left him "in the quiet possession of a large amount of the treasure-trove." The *Call* reporter, whether Clemens or another, gratuitously insinuated in a vein not foreign to Clemens' manner on occasion, that "Mr. Smiley, during his arrest, has moved about at his pleasure, attended by a Deputy of the Marshal, which courtesy will doubtless meet its due reward at the hands of the fortunate wrecker."[20]

Clemens characterized the appropriately named Simon Wheeler as a simple, earnest soul, gentle in character but an unswerving steamroller in his storytelling. The surname may have suggested itself to Clemens as a consequence of his acquaintance with Reverend Osgood Church Wheeler. Wheeler lectured widely for the California Branch of the United States Sanitary Commission and served as its secretary. During September Clemens reported the Mechanic's Institute Industrial Fair in San Francisco. Various Fair exhibits collected money for the Sanitary Fund to aid the Civil War wounded, a cause Clemens helped to promote. In one of the Fair writeups the *Call* reporter credits Wheeler with supplying him statistics on public contributions to the Fund. But exactly one week earlier in the *Call* the local reporter had complained of a brush-off at Wheeler's office. He concluded: "We would like, in order to benefit the commission, to give publicity to the names of contributors to the Fund; but on applying for the list, recently, were all but peremptorily refused. The individual who attends to the business of receiving and recording the subscriptions is either too lazy or too disobliging for the position. He prefers his own case to the interest of the Commission."[21] Whether the offending individual was Wheeler or a clerk is not known, but by his complaint the reporter brought his man to account—following precisely the technique Clemens used more violently in "A Small Piece of Spite" (*Call*, 6 Sept. 1864, p. 1) three days later to flatten the Coroner's clerk in Atkins Massey's funeral establishment who had denied him information.

VI

Clemens' original version of his tale begins: "Mr. A. Ward, Dear Sir:—" A minor character not present in person, Ward serves to motivate the meeting between the frame narrator Mark Twain and the internal narrator Simon Wheeler. The reference to him was Clemens' indirect acknowledgment of Ward's invitation to contribute a sketch to this forthcoming book, *Artemus Ward: His Travels,* a request Clemens recorded in his 1865 note book: "26th—Home again—home again at the Occidental Hotel, San Francisco—find letters from 'Artemus Ward' asking me to write a sketch for his new book of Nevada Territory travels which is soon to come out. Too late—ought to have got the letters 3 months ago. They are dated early in November."[22] Those letters of Ward's marked his second eruption in Clemens' life, the first having come in late December 1863 when Clemens heard his "Babes in the Woods" lecture in Virginia City and became personally acquainted with him. On both occasions Ward precipitated publications that helped Clemens' career. The opportunity that Clemens on 26 February believed he had missed opened up in succeeding months as Ward continued to press for a contribution.[23] Surely Ward, the generous friend, was alive in Clemens' thoughts during the incubation of the "Jumping Frog."

The less surprising, then, that Ward, the lecturer and writer, was alive in Clemens' literary imagination when he finally wrote the tale. One notes the letter form that begins the "Jumping Frog," suggesting the way Ward began some of his sketches. Ward's "Babes in the Woods" was a series of digressions: anecdotes and pronouncements given coherence by Ward's platform presence. Similarly the main substance of Clemens' tale, the history of "thish-yer Smiley," is a kind of self-perpetuating digression that unerringly expresses Simon Wheeler's personality. In both the lecture and the tale, as Clemens in effect demonstrates in "How to Tell a Story," the humor is founded on character that is displayed in the manner of telling. What counts is the wandering, bubbling, spun-out discourse, punctuated by studied pauses and afterthoughts, that is spoken by a narrator who is simple, innocent, earnestly sincere, unselfconscious—either naturally like Ben Coon or Simon Wheeler, or by calculated pretense like the platform artists Ward, Twain, Dan Setchell, or James Whitecomb Riley. The genius of the "Jumping Frog" dwarfs Ward's talent; in style, subtlety of organization, character creation, intellectual content, and imaginative power Clemens' tale transcends Ward's influence. Yet Ward must be counted a pioneer of the broad literary approach Clemens followed in writing the tale that made such imaginative use of a personal experience including originals like Coon and Ward himself.

Beyond strictly literary influence, however, Ward probably played a crucial role in Clemens' psychology when the "Jumping Frog" was written. Years later Clemens affirmed that "Babes in the Woods" was the funniest thing he had ever listened to, and after hearing Ward lecture in 1863 he wrote: "There are perhaps fifty subjects treated in it, and there is a passable point in every one of them, and a hearty laugh also for any of God's creatures who have committed no crime, the ghastly memory of which debars him from smiling again while he lives. The man who is capable of listening to the Babes In The Woods from beginning to end without laughing, either inwardly or outwardly, must have done murder, or at least meditated it, at some time during his life."[24] Here Clemens contrasts the worthy result of Ward's humor—a life-giving laughter common to most of "God's creatures"—with murder, an act of violence and final separation. In his letter of 19 October he confides to Orion: "I *have* had a 'call' to literature, of a low order—*i.e.* humorous. It is nothing to be proud of, but it is my strongest suit" (*MDB*, p. 6). He then makes an important commitment. He asserts he will "strive for a fame— unworthy & evanescent though it must of necessity be" by turning his attention "to seriously scribbling to excite the *laughter* of God's creatures" (*MDB*, pp. 8,6). The similar phrasing in letter and review inevitably suggests an imaginative identification of his commitment with Ward's accomplishment, the writing of humorous literature, and it reveals his concept of their identical purpose, the creation of beneficial laughter.

In "How to Tell a Story" Clemens associated Ward and the popular comedian Dan Setchell, Ward's good friend, as masters of humorous technique. His early piece from the mid-1860's, "A Voice for Setchell," further defines the value he finds in laughter. There he wrote that in "a long season of sensational, snuffling dramatic bosh, and tragedy bosh, and electioneering bosh" the people were "learning to wear the habit of unhappiness like a garment" until Setchell appeared as Captain Cuttle in John Brougham's extremely popular adaptation of *Dombey and Son* "and broke the deadly charm with a wave of his enchanted hook and the spell of his talismanic words, '*Awahst! awahst! awahst!*' And since that night all the powers of dreariness combined have not been able to expel the spirit of cheerfulness he invoked. Therefore, my voice is still for Setchell. I have experienced more real pleasure, and more physical benefit, from laughing naturally and unconfinedly at his funny personations and extempore speeches than I have from all the operas and tragedies I have endured, and all the blue mass pills I have swallowed in six months."[25] Murder, Clemens seems to say, excludes laughter, but laughter buoys up the spirit and expels dreariness. As an antidote to misery, it ultimately offers escape from self-murder. His letter of 19 October closes: "I am utterly miserable... If I do not get out of debt in 3 months,—pistols or poison for one—exit *me*. There's a text for a sermon on Self-M[urder,]—proceed" (*MDB*, p. 9).

In 1865, then, Clemens undoubtedly valued laughter and consequently humorous writing for at least one important reason. Later he would appreciate more fully the social value of laughter and humor. On the other hand, in 1865 his implied reluctance to pursue literature "of a low order" that was "nothing to be proud of" is an early expression of later recurrent doubts about the fitness of a career in humor for a serious writer. In view of this conflict it may be supposed that the commitment expressed in his letter resulted less from a sudden dedication to literary values—after all, he had been writing and publishing since 1852—than from his need to get our of debt and keep that way, especially at a time when his mining stocks were proving worthless. In addition to its intrinsic but "low order" value, humorous writing that was more seriously pursued presumably offered him at least a chance for success—to make a name for himself if the stuff was in him.

Clemens' commitment also was supported by Orion's faith in him and, more significantly, by a favorable press in the East. Clemens continued in his letter: "*You* see in me a talent for humorous writing, & urge me to cultivate it. But I always regarded it as brotherly partiality on your part & attached no value to it. It is only now, when editors of standard literary papers in the distant east give me high praise, & who do not know me & cannot of course be blinded by the glamour of partiality, that I really begin to believe there must be something in it" (*MDB*, pp. 7–8). He was alluding to a recently published article on American humor in the New York *Round Table* ("American Humor and Humorists," 9 Sept. 1865, p. 2). The anonymous author, possibly one of the editors, H. E. Sweetser or C. H. Sweetser, broadly characterized American humor and surveyed native humorists. He placed Mark Twain "foremost among the merry gentlemen of the California press"; Twain's writing gave promise that "he may one day take rank among the brightest of our wits." On 18 October, the day before Clemens wrote to "My Dear Bro," the *Dramatic Chronicle*, whose staff he had just joined, reprinted ("Recognized," p. 3)[sic] the part of the article that praised him.

Three days later came Clemens' newspaper writeup of the three-quartered dog. If, as I believe, that dog was the model for Andrew Jackson's conqueror, thereby evoking him in Clemens' awareness of the museum freak at this precise time is a key piece fitting superbly into the puzzle of the date the "Jumping

Frog" was composed. It seems probable that Clemens wrote "Jim Smiley and His Jumping Frog" during the week of 16–23 October. He had a new job in which he covered the city's amusements and plays. He was making every effort to clear away debt. A favorable press was waiting to be used. A clear-sighted self-examination arising from his unhappiness had called forth a commitment to write laughter-provoking humor, another name for "literature of a low order"—"a villainous backwoods sketch" (*Letters,* I, 101) was what he called his laughter-provoking tale three months later. Nor is it likely that he undertook his commitment lightly. A proud man who four years earlier had come West with dreams of wealth, he still was in a subordinate position. He believed in his talent for humor, but still it was "nothing to be proud of." He had come to know already that success of any kind came hard and that a writer's life meant a continuing risk. Finally, if he made his commitment as the best immediate way to become and remain solvent, he must have seen it partly in terms of a life-risk: success or "exit *me.*"

The suggested time of writing is late, for it comes midway in the two-month period spanning the date Ward's book is said to have been published and the appearance of the tale.[26] Yet some evidence suggests that Clemens delayed excessively in writing the tale and that it arrived late in the East.[27] Also it should be observed that given Clemens' interest in freaks, he might have visited White's Museum in the summer or early fall, a supposition that supports an earlier dating of the Andrew Jackson episode assuming one grants the causal relationship between the two handicapped dogs suggested above. Yet, an earlier visit is purely speculative. So far as we know there was no specific motive for it and, if it was made, no visible consequence of it leading into the tale, other than possibly the Andrew Jackson episode itself. On the other hand, the requirement of covering the city's amusements for the *Dramatic Chronicle* was a strong motive for an October visit to White's Museum even if he had been there earlier. The newspaper writeup with its fresh impressions working actively in his imagination—the merging images of the deformed dog and Richard III—suggests both a recent visit and an available bridge to the tale.

VII

The "Jumping Frog" itself supports the date of composition proposed for it in this paper. When Clemens wrote his letter to "My Dear Bro" the uncertainties of his present and future were so troubling that he felt compelled to reexamine his past: "I never had but two *powerful* ambitions in my life. One was to be a pilot, & the other a preacher of the gospel. I accomplished the one & failed in the other, *because* I could not supply myself with the necessary stock in trade —*i.e* religion. I have given it up forever. I never had a 'call' in that direction, anyhow, & my aspirations were the very ecstasy of presumption" (*MDB*, p. 6). The ministry, for Clemens a chimera of his distant boyhood, was for Orion, he believed, a real possibility founded on a "talent" for preaching. "You are honest, pious, virtuous," he wrote; "—what would you have more? *Go forth & preach"* (*MDB*, p. 7). Orion should become "a minister of the gospel," not a "mud-cat of a *lawyer*" (*MDB*, pp. 8, 7). The general principle was simply "that to do the right you *must* multiply the one or the two or the three talents which the Almighty entrusts to your keeping" (*MDB*, p. 6). As a climax to his own sermon, he offered to strike a bargain with Orion: each would agree to develop his natural talent, "to do what his Creator intended him to do" (*MDB*, p. 7). This proposal, which links his own performance to Orion's, further qualifies the seriousness of Clemens' commitment to humorous literature. Moreover his letter was a perfect opportunity to over-dramatize his troubles before a sympathetic audience, and it is doubtful that any resolution, however seriously intended, could keep the pluralistic Clemens in a single path for very long. Yet after all allowances are made, we cannot miss the real unhappiness in the letter, or the latent bitterness: "I have a religion. . . It is that there is a God for the rich man but none for the poor" (*MDB*, p. 9). Nor can we miss the sense of loss as he touches on the old problem of natural endowment versus training ("the Almighty did His part by me—for the talent is a mighty engine when supplied with the steam of *education*— which I have not got" [*MDB*, p. 7]), the genuine uncertainty about his future, and his keen awareness of the element of risk that lay ahead in his life. The fact that these feelings were pressing for expression at that precise time—and perhaps were not so dominant a few days before or after—strengthens the probability that the tale was composed the week of 16–23 October. For those feelings fit the tale in a deeply personal way and help us to understand it in a new and intimate dimension.

Whatever else "Jim Smiley and His Jumping Frog" may be, it also is an unwittingly articulated parable of Clemens' complex state of mind, the pass he had come to, about the time he wrote his letter to Orion. The constructive imagination that built the tale seized on the conflicts and concepts, the forebodings and ambitions, that were at work within. In the tale the character Mark Twain (in life, the relatively unknown but promising humorist) is directed by the character Artemus Ward (in life, the nationally acclaimed maker of laughs) to find "a cherished companion" of Ward's boyhood, "Rev. Leonidas W. Smiley—a young minister of the gospel." The minister turns out to be a chimera, a shade, and for the character Mark Twain to have sought him was indeed a good joke, the "very ecstasy of presumption." Yet by this means Ward brings the seeker Mark Twain (who, in life, seeks to "multiply" his talent for humor) face to face with Simon Wheeler, and Mark Twain wakens the dozing humorist. With utmost seriousness, Wheeler awake seems to give over his entire being to his humorous narration. To his visitor's question about the minister Wheeler responds as though his long irrelevant answer were perfectly proper, as though, in fact, it were really relevant to another, unexpressed question in his listener's mind. His visitor sees that Wheeler accepts his own tale as "a really important matter," and Wheeler speaks with no condescension or irony or hint of trickery. As a storyteller Wheeler is a natural. Evidently of slight education, he performs, to God's own fulness, "what his Creator intended him to do," and he does it with an impressive objectivity. It is deeply appropriate that the character Mark Twain should sit silent before this man (as one might absorb a natural wonder), letting him "go on in his own way" without interrupting him once.

By means of his narrative Wheeler introduces Mark Twain, not to a pious, virtuous minister who knows the language of exhortation like Parson Walker of the tale, or like Orion, but to Jim Smiley, a resourceful adventurer who will slop around in the mud to get what he wants, a man who has done very well in a chancy world. Smiley works his talent for betting for all it is worth. He is enterprising and makes his own opportunities. He counts on the hopes of others and on the strengths of those he bets on. Although "he would bet on *anything*," "he was lucky—uncommon lucky"; and his luck is evidence that usually he knows what he is about. He knows the importance of persistent effort born of desperation (in the mare), of talent (in Andrew Jackson), and of talent combined with training (in Dan'l Webster). Knowing these things, he is equipped to win what victories he can by calculated means. From Andrew Jackson he presumably learns about the weakness of the sensitive romantic who expects too much from the world. From Dan'l's honest belch he learns once again that the unexpected can explode in his overconfident face, but when it does he responds vigorously. He has the courage to bet even when the outcome is totally unpredictable—which bird will fly first from a fence?—and he makes risk the condition of his existence. As Mrs. Wendy Stallard Flory has said, "he embraces chance itself as a way of life."[28] Jim Smiley is the hero of a fabulous world as "exquisitely absurd" as Wheeler's manner, but that world is very real too in the limitations and possibilities it holds for men.

Clemens made Wheeler and Smiley extreme individualists, as though already he were obscurely probing the implications of seriously making humor the business of his life. For Wheeler is the complete humorist. No mere trickster, he is absorbed like a true creator in the world he fashions through his patiently vivid imagination and his serene, rhythmic style. And Smiley, the mundane hero of that world, is the shrewd and determined man of action. He believes in rational effort but knows very well the full range of risk in life. His conduct implies courage and tough-minded hope. "Mr. A. Ward," Simon Wheeler and—through the lens of Wheeler's vision—Jim Smiley, his animals, and the fateful stranger are all meaningful configurations in Clemens' consciousness at a time of uncertainty and resolve, when he wanted to give a new but risky direction to his life.

Although the "Jumping Frog" was not soon equalled by Clemens, it was an important breakthrough in the long process of his development. Years of journalism still lay ahead, but by October 1865 he must have known that San Francisco journalism held little more for him. By 7 March of the next year he was more than ready to sail for the Sandwich Islands, an assignment that would offer fresh experience and the opportunity to cast off "the habit of unhappiness like a garment." But he was not yet ready to recognize fully the heights of humor he had reached in the "Jumping Frog" or to build upon them. His creation was more complex and profound than he knew. The tale is, in fact, a number of things: a blown-up frontier anecdote, a teasing fable that suggests various social and political meanings—although these, I believe, were negligible in the creative impulse behind the tale—and, as Paul Baender has convincingly shown, a thoroughgoing illustration of Clemens' theory of humorous gravity. The voice that had spoken up for Setchell spoke for itself in the "Jumping Frog," which above all else is a first-rate yarn taking extraordinary delight in humorous expression and character. As such, the tale appears to be also an intimately personal creation rising in shapely form from depths previously unsounded by Clemens, a consideration that helps to explain its compelling appeal and its poetic unity. For if the argument of this paper is correct, in writing "Jim Smiley and His Jumping Frog" Clemens utilized, consciously or not, two main areas of his personal background: past events experienced in San Francisco as well as in the mining camps, and certain tension-laden problems, closely connected with his need to find himself, that were pressing for immediate resolution.

Notes

1. See Paul Baender, "The 'Jumping Frog' as a Comedian's First Virtue," *Modern Philology*, LX (1963), 192–200; Walter Blair, "Introduction," *Selected Shorter Writings of Mark Twain* (Boston, 1962), pp. xxi–xxiv; Hennig Cohen, "Twain's Jumping Frog: Folktale to Literature to Folktale," *Western Folklore*, xxii (1963), 17–18; Rufus A. Coleman, "Mark Twain's Jumping Frog: Another Version of the Famed Story," *Montana Magazine of History*, III (Summer 1953), 29–30; Pascal Covici, Jr., *Mark Twain's Humor* (Dallas, Tex., 1962), pp. 48–52; James M. Cox, *Mark Twain: The Fate of Humor* (Princeton, N.J., 1966), pp. 24–33; Roger Penn Cuff, "Mark Twain's Use of the Comic Pose," PMLA, LXXVII (1962), 297–304; Sydney J. Krause, "The Art and Satire of Twain's 'Jumping Frog' Story," *American Quarterly*, XVI (1964), 562–576; Kenneth S. Lynn, *Mark Twain and Southwestern Humor* (Boston, 1959), pp. 145–147; Paul Schmidt, "The Deadpan on Simon Wheeler," *Southwest Review*, XLI (1956), 270–277; Henry Nash Smith, *Mark Twain: The Development of a Writer* (Cambridge, Mass., 1962), p. 11; J. Golden Taylor, introductory remarks to "The Celebrated Jumping Frog of Calaveras County," *American West*, II (Fall 1965), 73–76.

References to the "Jumping Frog" in this article are to the first printing, "Jim Smiley and His Jumping Frog," New York *Saturday Press*, 18 Nov. 1865, pp. 248–249.

2. TS of Notebook 3, p. 8, Mark Twain Papers, Berkeley, Calif.—hereafter cited as MTP; reprinted with changes in *Mark Twain's Notebook*, ed. Albert Bigelow Paine (New York, 1935), p. 7.

3. In his "Private History of the 'Jumping Frog' Story," *North American Review*, CLVIII (1894), 447, Clemens wrote of Coon and his audience of miners: "in his mouth this episode was . . . the gravest

sort of history. . . ; he was entirely serious, for he was dealing with what to him were austere facts, and . . . he saw no humor in his tale . . . none of the party was aware . . . that it was brimful of a quality whose presence they never suspected—humor."

4. TS of Notebook 3, p. 5, MTP. Copyright @ 196- by The Mark Twain Company.

5. TS of Notebook 3, p. 8, MTP. Copyright @ 196- by The Mark Twain Company.

6. *Californian*, 18 Mar. 1865, p. 8; reprinted with some changes in *Sketches of the Sixties*, ed. John Howell (San Francisco, 1927), pp. 158–165.

7. See Clemens' emended version of "Private History. . .," *How to Tell a Story and Other Essays* (Hartford, Conn., 1900), pp. 121–122; *Mark Twain's Letters* (New York, 1917), I, 170.

8. *How to Tell a Story*, p. 126; T. Edgar Pemberton, *The Life of Bret Harte* (London, 1903), pp. 73–75; "'The Jumping Frog of Calaveras' by Mark Twain With an Introductory and Explanatory Note by J. G. H.," *Overland Monthly*, XL (Sept. 1902), 20–21; *Letters*, I, 170.

9. As recently as Oct. 1863 Clemens had written up the races at the first annual fair of the Washoe Agricultural, Mining and Mechanical Society held in Carson City. See *Mark Twain of the Enterprise*, ed. Henry Nash Smith with the assistance of Frederick Anderson (Berkeley and Los Angeles, 1957), pp. 80–86. My article "Mark Twain Reports the Races in Sacramento," to appear in *Huntington Library Quarterly*, shows that Clemens undertook a week's racetrack assignment at the 1866 California State Fair for James Anthony of the Sacramento *Union*.

10. *Call*, 4 Sept. 1864, p. 1. Reports in other city papers name the winner as Strideover, nicknamed Sam. John Wilson was the proprietor of the circus at the Jackson Street Pavilion. Sam's "easy indifference of conscious superiority" is a phrase carrying almost the force of a signature. It marks the horse as one of Clemens' large class of self-assured characters who enjoy lording it over others because of superior skill or style or experience. For examples of Clemens' use of the phrase and its variants see: "San Francisco Correspondence," Napa County *Reporter*, 11 Nov. 1865, p. 2; *The Writings of Mark Twain*, Definitive Edition (New York, 1922), XII, 46, and XIV, 317. Hereafter this edition will be cited as *Writings*.

11. *Call*, 10 Sept. 1864, p. 1. I have omitted the four concluding sentences that notice races to come. George N. Ferguson and Harris R. Covey were racetrack drivers. Wadsworth Porter owned a livery stable. Dr. George F. Woodward was the surgeon and physician of the United States Pension Bureau. Clemens' friend Lewis Leland was the

proprietor of the Occidental Hotel and Clemens often joked about him in print.

Clemens' comic use of "Christian" was routine, and he echoes his earlier review of "Mazeppa" in the phrase "fiery untamed Menkens" (Smith, *Enterprise*, pp. 78–80). Typical of his comic vision is the merging of discrete modes of being and the resulting implicit puns. Quality becomes commodity, as in the use of "break neck" and "break-neck." A burst of speed necessarily indivisible in time is coolly partitioned and distributed among several races (economizing speed for economic gain). Moral young men and cocktails combine (in two ways) to constitute a crowd (animate and animated). The bold, offhand formula for stopping a cannonball and the casually aloof phrasing of "His head was split open a little" familiarly echo the magisterial dispenser of advice and remedies and the Washoe reporter of gory prize fights.

12. It is interesting that Conflict's awkward "double summerset" is a sign of a serious limitation by virtue of his lack of training in hurdle racing, whereas Dan'l Webster's graceful "one summerset, or maybe a couple," is a sign of his free mastery of conditions through training. The fated dog Curney in Clemens' letter in the Keokuk *Gate City*, 6 Mar. 1862, turns "somersets" as he races over the desert. In *Roughing It* "the rawest dog," probably modeled on the alkalied Curney, "threw double somersaults" in his frenzy (*Writings*, III, 260).

13. For examples of Clemens' later use of turf imagery and terms relating to the *Call* pieces and to the "Jumping Frog" see: *Writings*, I, 32; IV, 99, 287; XII, 372; XIII, 206; XIV, 119; XXVII, 176; Walter F. Frear, *Mark Twain and Hawaii* (Chicago, 1947), p. 294.

14. *My Dear Bro,* ed. Frederick Anderson (Berkeley, 1961), p. 8— hereafter cited as *MDB* and documented in text.

15. See "Dictation of M. H. DeYoung," Bancroft Library, Berkeley. DeYoung helped establish the *Dramatic Chronicle* in 1865. His memory of Clemens' connection with the paper is faulty in some details.

16. "Amusements," *Dramatic Chronicle*, 21 Oct. 1865, p. 3. The comparison with Richard III (whom Huck, the Duke, and the Dauphin knew all about), the punning, the easy slide from the factual into the fanciful, and above all the familiar delight in humanizing an animal suggest Clemens' comic imagination at this time.

17. Extant as "Exit 'Bummer'," *Californian*, 11 Nov. 1865, p. 12, from the Virginia City *Territorial Enterprise*, 8 Nov. 1865. In "The Art and Satire..." (see n. 1) Sydney J. Krause argues that the bull-pup is Clemens' satirical portrait of the historical Andrew Jackson. He feels, e.g., that the pup's appearance of not being "worth a cent but to set around and look ornery and lay for a chance to steal something" is

"an analogue of the legendary flashes of temper with which Jackson is known to have frightened opponents into submission" (p. 570). Referring to Mark Twain's sentence quoted in the text and comparing the pup's under-jaw to a steamboat's fo'castle, Krause writes: "In addition to its suggesting the fearful union of savagery with avarice, the idea that Smiley's pup has caught the gambling fever also carries a lurking reference to the stories of Jackson's fabulous exploits in gaming" (pp. 570–571). I feel that this view is overstated.

18. See, e.g., "The Evidence in the Case of Smith vs. Jones," *Golden Era*, 26 June 1864, p. 4, collected in *The Washoe Giant in San Francisco*, ed. Franklin Walker (San Francisco, 1938), p. 82.

19. *Call*, 21 Aug. 1864, p. 2. A clipping of the item is in Moffett Scrapbook 5, p. 58, MTP. In "The Art and Satire...," p. 573, Krause argues that the portrait of Dan'l the frog is Clemens' political satire of Daniel Webster, showing "how completely Twain had *done* Webster in almost every characterizing detail." It should be noted that Webster died in 1852 and that Clemens' few references to him prior to 1865 are not politically hostile. See *Mark Twain's Letters in the Muscatine Journal*, ed. Edgar M. Branch (Chicago, 1942), p. 20; Franklin R. Rogers, *The Pattern for Mark Twain's Roughing It* (Berkeley and Los Angeles, 1961), p. 35. I feel that Krause is unduly hard on Dan'l's integrity and accomplishment because he reads into him unflattering characteristics attributed to Daniel Webster the politician.

20. "A Wrecking Party in Luck," *Call*, 3 Sept. 1864, p. 2.

21. "California Branch of the U.S. Sanitary Commission," *Call*, 3 Sept. 1864, p. 1. The later *Call* item is "A Philanthropic Nation," 10 Sept. 1864, p. 1.

22. TS of Notebook 3, p. 10, MTP.

23. *Mark Twain: A Biography*, ed. A. B. Paine (New York, 1912), I, 277. Paine's chronology here is vague, but his account suggests that considerable time passed before Ward renewed his invitation and that even then Clemens delayed his composition of the tale.

24. "An Inapt Illustration," Virginia Evening *Bulletin*, 28 Dec. 1863, as preserved in Notebook 4, Carton 3, Grant H. Smith Papers, Bancroft Library, Berkeley. Courtesy of the Bancroft Library.

25. "A Voice for Setchell," *Californian*, 27 May 1865, p. 9. The article is signed "X" but is unmistakably by Clemens. The editor of the *Californian* hints broadly at the authorship, and a clipping of the piece is in Clemens' *Scrapbook of Newspaper Clippings...*, Beinecke Library, Yale Univ. Reviewers of Setchell's acting often compared his manner and humor to Ward's. In June 1865 Setchell played the part of Ward in *Artemus Ward, Showman*, a three-act play written for him by Fred. G. Maeder and Thomas B. Macdonough.

26. Jacob Blanck, *Bibliography of American Literature* (New Haven, Conn., 1955), I, 314, No. 1527. Blanck notes that ten years after Ward's book appeared his publisher gave 23 Sept. as the publication date. The listing of Ward's book as received in the 14 Oct. issue of the New York *Saturday Press* may indicate a later publication date. West Coast periodicals noticed the book in late Nov. and early Dec. James M. Cox (*Mark Twain: The Fate of Humor*, p. 32) believes, as I do, that Clemens wrote the "Jumping Frog" and his letter of 19 Oct. 1865 about the same time. My article was accepted for publication in its present form several months before I read Cox's excellent book.

27. See n. 23. Clemens usually claimed that the tale reached George W. Carleton too late for inclusion in *Artemus Ward: His Travels*, although he contradicts this in *Mark Twain in Eruption*, ed. Bernard DeVoto (New York, 1940), p. 144. See *Letters*, I, 102; Yale *Scrap Book*, opposite clippings of the "Jumping Frog"; *Notebook*, p. 7. Henry Clapp's admiring editorial preface to the "Jumping Frog" in the *Saturday Press* of 18 Nov. barely hints that the tale was inserted at the last moment.

28. From "A Defense of 'Jim Smiley and His Jumping Frog'...," an unpublished seminar paper. In my comments on Smiley I am indebted to Mrs. Flory.

Burlesque Travel Literature and Mark Twain's *Roughing It*

Franklin R. Rogers

In July 1870, Elisha Bliss of the American Publishing Company completed a contract with Samuel L. Clemens, the latest arrival among the ranks of the American comic writers, which called for the delivery by January 1, 1871 of sufficient manuscript to make a 600-page book. Bliss, of course, expected the author to furnish something which would repeat the success of *The Innocents Abroad*, which had been published the previous year, and Clemens proposed to outdo himself, if possible, this time with a tale based upon his trip across the Plains in 1861 and his six years' sojourn in Nevada and California. The six months allotted by the contract proved entirely too short for the completion of the projected book. The protracted illness and finally the death of Clemens's father-in-law, Jervis Langdon, and the illness and death of a house-guest, Emma Nye, consumed much of the author's time, and progress on the manuscript was further retarded by a dissatisfaction with the product of his labors which led to extensive revisions. Even an additional six months did not free him from the sense of pressure. As a result, the book which he finally produced exhibits at least two major flaws. One is the awkward break in tone, structure, and point of view evident in the last eighteen chapters, the consequence of his

Reprinted from the *Bulletin of the New York Public Library* 67 (March 1963): 155–68.

hasty incorporation at the last moment of the series of letters written from Hawaii for the *Sacramento Union* in 1866. The other is the padding of the text with statistics and quotations, principally from his newspaper clippings, which characterized a number of the earlier chapters. But despite its imperfections the book proved quite acceptable to Bliss, and its subsequent success apparently stilled any misgivings Twain himself may have had on the score of his patchwork. Interested as he no doubt was in securing another comic bestseller, Bliss ignored its faults; he probably also failed to appreciate the essential importance of the manuscript which Clemens sent him in batches during the first months of 1871. For while *Roughing It* marks the culmination of a seventy-year-old tradition in burlesque travel literature, it also represents the successful transformation of burlesque travel literature conventions into the means for significant literary expression.

The tradition to which *Roughing It* owes a substantial debt begins with William Combe's *The Tour of Dr. Syntax in Search of the Picturesque* which first appeared serially in the *Poetical Magazine*, 1809–1811. Written in a pseudo-Hudibrastic verse which "may wel be rym dogerel," the tour proved a popular success. Combe exploited its popularity with an edition in book form in 1812 and two sequels, *The Second Tour of Dr. Syntax in Search of Consolation* (1820) and *The Third Tour of Dr. Syntax in Search of a Wife* (1821); during the next half-century several British publishers managed to keep the three tours before the reading public.[1] As the title of the first poem suggests, it is a burlesque of the popular late eighteenth-century literature of picturesque travel to which Wordsworth's *An Evening Walk* and *Descriptive Sketches* are closely related. In its general conception Combe's poem reflects the work of such writers of picturesque travel poetry as Anthony Champion, Thomas Maude, and George Cumberland; the central figure, Dr. Syntax, is a caricature of William Gilpin, Rector of Boldre, who has been fittingly called "the high priest of the picturesque."[2] George Crabbe reacted to this literature with a grim realism which a hundred years later won Edwin Arlington Robinson's admiration; Combe reacted with a satire conveyed primarily through his character, Dr. Syntax, whose excessive fastidiousness and sublimity of taste cause him to reject and suppress the disturbing truths which Crabbe fastened upon. Dr. Syntax is the very quintessence of the artist in search of the picturesque, the artist who, in order to achieve the picturesque, must take liberties with the actuality before him, blinding himself to that which offends his taste and freely substituting from his imagination that which will heighten his gratification, thus forcing the observed reality into a preconceived ideal pattern of the picturesque. "What man of taste," Dr Syntax asks,

> my right will doubt,
> To put things in, or leave them out?
> 'Tis more than right, it is a duty,
> If we consider landscape beauty:
> He ne'er will as an artist shine,
> Who copies Nature line by line.[3]

According to Combe, this character stems from the mock-heroic tradition; in Canto XII of the first tour, he wrote:

You'll see, at once, in this Divine,
Quixote and Parson Adams shine:
An hero well combin'd you'll view
FOR FIELDING and CERVANTES too. (p. 41)

Certainly in structure, the Dr. Syntax poems are a derivative of the knight errant tradition on which *Don Quixote* is built, but, despite the doctor's encounter with highwaymen which is in the same vein as the battle with the huntsman's hounds in *Joseph Andrews*, very little of the mock-heroic actually appears in the series. An important difference between Don Quixote and Dr. Syntax is that Cervantes' character is deranged, totally dissociated from the actuality through which he moves; the doctor perceives the actuality, but for reasons of taste ignores some aspects of it and, ignorant of worldly matters, fails to understand others. Instead, in his extreme sentimentality and his frequent soliloquies upon picturesque or melancholy scenes, he is much closer to Mr. Yorick of Sterne's *Sentimental Journey.*

The popularity of Dr. Syntax and his adventures is demonstrated not only by the frequent editions and reprints but also by the extent to which subsequent humorists resorted to them for guidance in shaping their own burlesques of travel literature. Apparently it was not so much the doctor's pretense to refined taste and sentiment which attracted the later humorists as it was the comic possibilities inherent in the coupling of this attitude with his artistic and scientific aspirations. Armed with sketchbook and notebook, the doctor traveled about England ever ready to preserve the picturesque scene which fluttered his pulse or the "curious" information which excited his mind. As a result of this combination, a third dimension, as it were, could be added to the burlesque. Not only is the reader moved to laughter by the contrast between the traveler's expectations and the actuality encountered; he is also moved to laughter by the traveler's subsequent interpretations in the form of wretched poetry, crude drawings, or fantastic scientific theories. A host of similar travelers each equipped with sketchbook or notebook or both and eager to present the results of his travels to the reading public, crowd the pages of the British comic magazines down through the first twenty years of *Punch*, that is, from the 1840s to the 1860s, and appear in such less well-known humor magazines as *Fun, Judy,* and *Punch and Judy.* But only two of Dr. Syntax's progeny, Thackeray's Michael Angelo Titmarsh and Dickens' Mr Samuel Pickwick, P.C., have won a permanent place in literature.[4]

Imitative of the British periodicals, the American humor magazines also afford several examples of the type. Generally, the American humorists appear to have modelled their work after the current British burlesques, without any direct reference to the original tours of Dr. Syntax, but in at least one instance the American by-passed the contemporary British examples and returned directly to Combe's work. In the first issue of his *Illustrated California Magazine* (1856), J. M. Hutchings began a burlesque entitled "Dr. Dotitdown in Search of the Picturesque, Arabesque, Grotesque, and Burlesque." The title contains, of course, references to Combe's *Tour of Dr. Syntax in Search of the Picturesque* and to Poe's *Tales of the Grotesque and Arabesque.*

By the 1860s Combe's conception had undergone several mutations. One was the very early abandonment of his doggerel verse in favor of prose; another was the addition of a traveling companion who bears a distant relationship to Sancho Panza, a more immediate one to Sam Weller. A vernacular character, this companion, usually a servant or a young relative or family friend, serves a function slightly different from Sancho Panza's. As far as the reader is concerned, one of Sancho's major services is to report the actuality which the Knight, because of his delusions, cannot see. The companion of the nineteenth-century burlesque constantly reminds the reader and the traveler himself of those unpicturesque elements of the actuality which the traveler has chosen to ignore and contributes a knowledge, sometimes surprisingly full for one of his years, in those fields where the traveler in his innocence, is totally uninitiated: the properties of a wide variety of strong beverages, the wiles of worldly women, the art of gambling, and the devices of a wide variety of tricksters, swindlers, and other petty criminals. With predilections for such activities as those indicated by his knowledge, the companion is the major source of conflict for the traveler. With the emergence of the companion, this type of burlesque, some fifty years after Dr. Syntax first set out on his sway-backed mare, had become fairly conventional: the traveler is a refined and sophisticated gentleman bent upon studying art, discovering sources for other ponds of Hampstead, or devising further theories of tittlebats; his companion is his antithesis in taste, sentiments, and interests; their itinerary takes the pair to scientific wonders, monuments of antiquity, or paintings of the Masters; and a series of arguments and mishaps, precipitated by the companion, disappoint or deflate the gentleman's expectations.

The conventional character of these burlesques is suggested not only by the frequent reappearance of the same elements but also by the failure of the British magazines to keep pace with developments in travel literature. Long after the focus of interest in travel books had shifted from the haunts of the Romantics in Italy, France, and Germany, to scenes of intrepid adventure in the Near East, the Orient, Africa, and the western United States, the travelers in the burlesques still studied their art in the Louvre and the Capitol and sought the picturesque in the Lake District, the Rhine Valley, the Black Forest, and the Harz Mountains. The result, in the British magazines of the 1860s, was a dissociation of the burlesques from the literature upon which they should have fed, with a consequent loss of vitality which is reflected in the mutation of the central character, who is reduced from a caricature of the sentimental traveler to a simple straightman. No longer mad, not even north-north-west, he has become to a great degree merely the center from which we measure the antics of his ebullient companion and others. The mutation is quite visible in one of the longest of such burlesques, "Our Roving Correspondent," which began in the first issue of *Punch* for 1860. In the July 27, 1861 issue, the refined traveler, Jack Easel, comments upon young female tourists at the Italian art galleries:

> The ease and rapidity with which these charming critics form acquaintance with and discuss the merits of the Old Masters is truly astonishing. I once heard a young lady... remark, that she had "done" the Capitol between the hours of breakfast and lunch, adding that she would be able to give me a full description of the Borghese Collection by the time we met at dinner. "*Per Bacco!* Ma'am," I exclaimed—you know we were in Italy, and I always ejaculate, if possible in the language of the country where I am residing—"*per Bacco!* What a muff is your humble servant. Here have I

been spending months in the study of a single gallery and am half inclined to throw up my profession in despair, at my ignorance."

Although the comment about ejaculations suggests the exaggerated sophistication of earlier travelers who did things "by the book," the passage in general demands that the reader regard Jack Easel as the standard against which the charming critics are measured and found wanting.

In the United States the type retained a great deal of its vitality simply because, while British readers were exploring the mysteries of the Middle East in such books as Warburton's *The Crescent and the Cross*, Curzon's *Monasteries of the Levant*, and Burton's *A Pilgrimage to Al-Medinah and Meccah*, the Americans were re-discovering a picturesque Europe in such books as Sara Jane Lippincott's *Haps and Mishaps of a Tour in Europe*, Harriet Beecher Stowe's *Sunny Memories of Foreign Lands*, and Bayard Taylor's *Views A-Foot*. As Professor Willard Thorp has noted in his study of such American travel books:

> The less imaginative of the professional writers soon evolved a sort of standard pattern for the travel book. The author must begin with the excitements of the ocean voyage itself and devote at least a portion of a chapter to the thrill, so long anticipated, of setting foot on foreign soil. From this point on he should mix architecture and scenery. . . , skillfully work in a little history. . . , taking care to add a touch of sentiment or eloquence when the occasion permitted. If the essay or book required a little padding, it was always possible to retell an old legend or slip in an account of dangers surmounted in crossing the Alps.[5]

That is, the travel books which American writers were producing lent themselves well to the sort of burlesque treatment we have been considering; it is not surprising to find them getting such treatment from Artemus Ward, Petroleum V. Nasby, J. Ross Browne, and, of course, Mark Twain.

In *The Innocents Abroad*, the most famous burlesque product of this spate of American travel books, we find Mark

Twain building upon the pattern which Thorp has noted. The first paragraph contains a passage which is, with its alliterations, rhythms, hyperboles, and clichés, at once a revelation of the delusions of the passengers and a parody of the effusive statements of anticipatory thrills in the books upon which it is modelled:

> [The passengers] were to sail for months over the breezy Atlantic and the sunny Mediterranean; they were to scamper about the decks by day, filling the ship with shouts and laughter—or read novels and poetry in the shade of the smoke-stacks, or watch for the jelly-fish and the nautilus, over the side, and the shark, the whale, and other strange monsters of the deep; and at night they were to dance in the open air, on the upper deck, in the midst of a ballroom that stretched from horizon to horizon, and was domed by the bending heavens and lighted by no meaner lamps than the stars and the magnificent moon—dance, and promenade, and smoke, and sing, and make love, and search the skies for constellations that never associate with the "Big Dipper" they were so tired of: and they were to see the ships of twenty navies—the customs and costumes of twenty curious peoples—the great cities of half a world—they were to hobnob with nobility and hold friendly converse with kings and princes, Grand Moguls, and the anointed lords of mighty empires!

But although *The Innocents Abroad* is a burlesque of travel literature, the controlling fiction of the conventional Dr. Syntax type of burlesque, the conflict between a sentimental traveler and his irrepressible companion, is missing, or rather is subordinated to such an extent that it appears only in occasional episodes.

The Innocents Abroad is actually an intermediate stage in a series of experiments through which Twain gradually shaped the burlesque conventions to his own artistic purposes. The first stage in the sequence dates from 1866, when Twain built the controlling fiction of his Sandwich Islands letters directly upon the conventional traveler-companion conflict. Adopting for these letters the pose of Mr.

Twain, a traveler with all the sensibilities and most of the aspirations of Dr. Syntax, and creating a companion, Mr. Brown, as bitter an enemy to sentiment as any of his predecessors, Twain tried to fulfill the two major conditions of his contract with the *Sacramento Union*, that he write a humorous travel sketch and that he furnish factual information about the Hawaiian Islands for the *Union* readers. The attempt to fulfill these two conditions involved Twain directly in a problem inherent in this type of burlesque from its beginnings: how to convey to the reader a clear concept of the actuality which moves the sophisticated traveler to sentimental tears or his companion to snorts of derision. As long as the burlesque is written in the third person, there is no problem. The author, on his own authority, presents the actuality and then permits the two characters to give their interpretations of it. But when, as in the greater portion of the burlesques of this type, the author chooses the first person form of narration, the problem becomes central. Whether he adopts for himself the pose of the traveler or the companion, he must accept as the price a blindness to and ignorance of certain elements in the actuality before him. Of course, he may very easily work in the reactions and interpretations of his associate as, from his point of view, shocking examples of blindness or ignorance, but the reader must discern the actuality for himself somewhere between the two extremes resulting from the traveler's exaggerated sentimentality and the companion's exaggerated skepticism and unregeneracy.

Here we can perceive what may well have been the reason for the failure of the British burlesques to keep pace with the mid-century developments in travel literature. As long as the books being burlesqued dealt with countries which the anticipated audience knew with a fair degree of intimacy, the humorist could depend upon the reader's knowledge to supply the information which his chosen pose prevented him from presenting in the burlesque. But when British travelers pushed on into new and relatively unknown regions, the humorist could not follow unless he forged new tools for his art. Mark Twain faced exactly the same problem, but one cannot say he solved it; he merely ignored the demands of consistency, slipping easily out of his pose to the role of reporter as frequently as he wished, apparently without even asking himself whether such a course indicated Emersonian greatness or artistic weakness.

The letters written for the *Alta Californian* describing Twain's journey from San Francisco to New York by way of the Isthmus in 1866–67 and the *Quaker City* excursion retain the same controlling fiction and exhibit the same disregard for consistency, but in the reworking of these letters for *The Innocents Abroad* Twain took the first major step toward the achievement of *Roughing It* when he attempted to fuse the characteristics of the traveler and his companion in one narrator. The fusion involved him in further difficulties, for this new narrator must exhibit on the one hand the sophistication and sentimentality of the traveler, on the other the uncouthness and insensitivity of the companion, and as necessary the judiciousness of the reporter. Once again he ignored the demands of consistency and let the contradictions stand. For example, his narrator is disdainful of sentimental tears after weeping over the graves of Abelard and Heloise and then learning their history, but he weeps as copiously as either Dr. Syntax or Mr. Yorick when he views Adam's tomb. Then, in order to justify his denunciation of William C. Prime's sentimental tears on the shores of Galilee, Twain must cast his narrator in the role of a clear-eyed and judicious reporter of the observed reality.

In that portion of *Roughing It* which concludes with the departure for the Sandwich Islands, Twain devised a method of reconciling the opposed points of view. *Roughing It* opens with a passage which is both similar to and subtly and significantly different from the statement of anticipatory thrills in the first pages of *The Innocents Abroad*:

> I was young and ignorant, and I envied my brother. I coveted his distinction and his financial splendor, but particularly and especially the long, strange journey he was going to make, and the curious new world he was going to explore. He was going to travel! I never had been away from home, and that word "travel" had a seductive charm for me. Pretty soon he would be hundreds and hundreds of miles away on the great plains and deserts, and among the mountains of the Far West, and would see buffaloes and Indians, and prairie dogs, and antelopes, and have all kinds of adventures, and maybe get hanged or scalped, and have ever such a fine time, and write home and tell us all about it, and be a hero. And he would see the gold mines and the silver mines, and maybe go about of an afternoon when his work was done, and pick up two or three pailfuls of shining slugs, and nuggets of gold and silver on the hillside. And by and by he would become very rich, and return home by sea, and be able to talk as calmly about San Francisco and the ocean, and "the isthmus" as if it was nothing of any consequence to have seen those marvels face to face.

The significant difference is in the pronoun used in each instance. The pronoun *they* in the earlier passage directs the ridicule toward the other *Quaker City* passengers and to travelers who write travel books. It implicitly exempts the narrator himself. The shift in point of view to the first person in the *Roughing It* passage focuses the ridicule upon the narrator himself and tends to remove travelers as a class to the background, if not out of the picture.

A change of plan during the composition of *Roughing It* reveals Twain's struggle with the problem of the point of view. On March 4, 1871 he wrote to his brother, Orion, that "right in the first chapter I have got to alter the whole style of one of my characters and re-write him clear through to where I am now."[6] Since the narrator himself is the only character who appears with sufficient frequency to require the sort of extensive revision suggested by this comment, the letter reflects some important discovery Twain had made relative to the point of view to be used, and his determination to act upon it.[7] The discovery was made as Twain pored over several letters he had written to the Keokuk *Gate City* in 1861 and '62 describing his adventures in Nevada, and therefore was apparently connected with them.[8] In these letters, Twain had adopted the pose of an unsophisticated, unregenerate "bitter enemy to sentiment" whose letters home were designed primarily to shatter the illusions of a pious, genteel, and excessively sentimental mother. That is, the relationship between the fictive mother and son in these letters prefigures the Mr. Twain-Mr. Brown relationship of the Sandwich Islands letters.

No evidence exists to indicate clearly the details of Twain's first draft of *Roughing It*, but a logical deduction from the available evidence is that, after the difficulties encountered with the point of view in *The Innocents Abroad*, he had returned to the Mr. Twain-Mr. Brown conflict of the Sandwich Islands and *Alta Californian* letters, patterning his narrator after Mr. Twain and his companion, renamed Bemis, after Mr. Brown. In the finished text, the narrator's gullibility, revealed in his prevision of the journey, and his sentimentality, his predisposition to view things through the "mellow moonshine of romance," are indications of his kinship with Mr. Twain and ultimately with Dr. Syntax.[9] And certainly Bemis exhibits in his infrequent appearances most of the characteristics of Mr. Brown not only when he climaxes the "noble sport" of buffalo hunting ignobly treed by the bull but also when he launches out on his own in Salt Lake City and experiments with a local concoction known as "valley tan" with predictable results. Such traces of the burlesque conventions in the finished text strongly suggest a more fully developed traveler-companion relationship in the first draft, that is, before the revision which Twain described to his brother.

Apparently, then, the *Gate City* letters taught Twain how he could dispense with such a character as Bemis and how he could link the contradictory points of view of a Mr. Twain and a Mr. Brown in the one character. As Professor Henry Nash Smith has demonstrated (p. 212), in the prevision of the journey and in much of the subsequent text "the pronoun 'I' links two quite different personae: the tenderfoot setting out across the Plains, and the old-timer, the veteran, who has seen the elephant and now looks back upon his own callow days of inexperience." Sophisticated and sentimental at the outset, the narrator's romantic expectations are shattered by the experiences of his journey and residence in the mining districts of Nevada. Envisioned at first as a character analogous to Mr. Twain, the narrator is transformed by his experiences into a character analogous to Mr. Brown.

Such a manipulation of the point of view, in itself a relatively simple affair, has enormous consequences for the art of that fiction which strives to build the illusion of objective reality. Stendahl's contribution to the development of literary realism, according to Erich Auerbach, is the technique of placing fictive characters in an externally real historical and social continuum: "Insofar as the serious realism of modern times," he declares, "cannot represent man otherwise than as embedded in a total reality, political, social, and economic, which is concrete and constantly evolving... Stendahl is its founder."[10] To the sort of time-perspective exploited by Stendahl, Twain added an internal time-perspective gained by the evolution of his narrator from tenderfoot to old-timer, an evolution which is implicit in the point of view from the very beginning of the narrative when, in introducing the tenderfoot's prevision of the journey, the old-timer comments, "I was young and ignorant." A great deal of the verisimilitude in the subsequent narrative derives from this manipulation of the point of view. By presenting the tenderfoot's prevision in a burlesque tone and coupling with it the old-timer's explicit disdain of his youthful folly, Twain predisposes the reader to a willing suspension of disbelief when the reader encounters the fictive reality which has transformed the tenderfoot into old-timer and upon which the old-timer bases his judgment. As far as the reader is concerned, the technique contributes materially to the obscuring of the distinctions between the fictive world in which the narrator moves and the external reality of travel across the Plains and life in the silver-mining regions of Nevada in the early 1860s.

The internal time-perspective, the movement from youthful delusion to mature skepticism, is not the only important consequence of the change in point of view. The movement is one in space as well as in time, almost literally a journey along a road to reality, and the wisdom of the old-timer results not so much from the time elapsed since he started out on his journey as it does from his removal from one geographical region to another and his consequent initiation, as Professor Smith has noted, into a new society, the society of the mining regions (p. 214–219). The shift in the point of view has produced a shift in the nature of the conflict which now becomes an internal one based on the differences between the mores of the East and those of the West. Bearing with him on his journey not only the heritage of his youth in the eastern United States but also highly erroneous concepts gleaned from his readings about the West, the tenderfoot must learn to adjust to the mores of the new society before he can become the old-timer. The insecurity, the humiliation, and occasionally the danger attendant upon actions performed and attitudes revealed while one is ignorant of the basic rules of the "curious new world" in which he finds himself are at the heart of the first thirty-three chapters, that is, to the point where the introduction of a new tenderfoot, General Buncombe, signals the narrator's own emergence into the community of old-timers. One humorous illustration of this inner conflict is the narrator's encounter with the desperado Slade:

> The coffee ran out. At last it was reduced to one tincupful, and Slade was about to take it when he saw that my cup was empty. He politely offered to fill it, but although I wanted it, I politely declined. I was afraid he had not killed anybody that morning, and might be needing diversion. But still with firm politeness he insisted on filling my cup, and said I had traveled all night and better deserved it than he—and while he talked he placidly poured the fluid, to the last drop. I thanked him and drank it, but it gave me no comfort, for I

could not feel sure that he would not be sorry, presently,
that he had given it away, and proceed to kill me to distract
his thoughts from the loss.

As a further consequence of the shift in point of view, Twain transformed burlesque into a remarkable effective fictive representation of the experience of those sensitive Americans whose adult lives spanned the Civil War years. With basic convictions, often excessively optimistic, formed in the pre-Civil War era, such Americans suffered a most intense disillusionment in the post-war era while at the same time they gained the sobered maturity of, say, the Walt Whitman of "Out of the Cradle Endlessly Rocking." Vernon L. Parrington was correct when, in opening his discussion of Mark Twain in the third volume of his *Main Currents*, he identified the narrator of *Roughing It* as the image of the post-Civil War American. Certainly Twain's old-timer is as powerful an image for this period as Cooper's Natty Bumppo is for the former. But Parrington was quite wrong when he chose the tenderfoot's brief spree in stock speculation to epitomize the American of the Gilded Age. The American whom Twain epitomized with the narrator of *Roughing It* is one who, nurtured in one culture, suddenly finds himself faced with the necessity of adjusting to another, or succumbing. One indication of the accuracy of Twain's image appears in the parallel between the narrator of *Roughing It* and the Henry Adams of *The Education*. What Twain achieved with the two personae merged in the pronoun "I," Adams achieved by writing his autobiography in the third person: the detachment and distance of the educated Adams from the Henry Adams who was undergoing the painful and seemingly fruitless education. Like Twain's old-timer, the Henry Adams of the twentieth century looks back with disdain upon what it pleased him to call his deluded "eighteenth-century youth," chronicles the events which produced the maturity, and reveals what is implicit in Twain's narrative, the loss as well as the gain of education. Although we can perceive it in the book, Twain did not make much of the point that the gaining of maturity necessarily involves a loss of that freedom from reality upon which the romantic imagination is based. The point is, nevertheless, implicit in the *Weekly Occidental* episode which occupies a rather prominent place toward the end of the adventures in Nevada. In this episode, the narrator and several fellow old-timers attempt to write a "sensation" novel in installments for their literary weekly. But the narrator and his fellow novelists are totally unable to produce such flights of the imagination as those upon which the tenderfoot's preconception of the Far West had been based. Later, in *Old Times on the Mississippi*, Twain was more explicit. Commenting upon the results of the cub's education as a river pilot, he wrote,

> Now when I had mastered the language of this water and had come to know every trifling feature that bordered the great river as familiarly as I knew the letters of the alphabet, I had made a valuable acquisition. But I had lost something, too. I had lost something which could never be restored to me while I lived. All the grace, the beauty, the poetry, had gone out of the majestic river!

The hero which Twain thus developed differs somewhat from the Young Man from the Provinces, whom Professor Lionel Trilling discerned as the defining hero in "a great line of novels" running "through the nineteenth-century as . . . the very backbone of its fiction." Professor Trilling describes the Young Man as one who "need not come from the provinces in literal fact, his social class may constitute his province. But a provincial birth and rearing suggest the simplicity and the high hopes he begins with—he starts with a great demand upon life and a great wonder about its complexity and promise. He may be of good family but he must be poor. He is intelligent, or at least aware, but not at all shrewd in worldly matters. He must have acquired a certain amount of education, should have learned something about life from books, although not the truth."[11] Twain's hero differs primarily in the assurance which is his as a result of his illusions. Confident of his superiority, or at least of his equality, in ability, social station, and sophistication, he eagerly embarks upon a penetration into a strange society, only to be exposed by his very illusions in a series of experiences to the painful truth that he has been deluded, that he must discard his previous self-conception. The successful learning of this lesson, although it involves the loss of youthful ebullience, brings mature self-knowledge.

All this is to say that the conflict which Twain developed from the mutation of the burlesque conventions anticipates that of the international novel later developed by Henry James, which Professor Oscar Cargill had defined as a novel "in which a character, usually guided in his actions by the mores of one environment, is set down in another, where his learned reflexes are of no use to him, where he must employ all his individual resources to meet successive situations, and where he must intelligently accommodate himself to the new mores, or, in one way or another, be destroyed."[12] The anticipation suggests a relatively close bond between Twain and James. But the closeness is obscured by Professor Cargill's failure to stress in his definition two essential elements: the initial illusory self-conception which precipitates a course of action leading toward an anticipated conquest in the new society, and the self-discovery resulting from the disappointment of his hopes.

Twain took the comic view; James, the tragic, first in *The American*. In doing so James created a character, Christopher Newman, whose attitudes, background, and even physical appearance are close enough to those of Twain or his fictive counterparts in *The Innocents Abroad* and *Roughing It* to cause the reader to suspect a direct indebtedness. James, of course, gave to the theme perhaps its most embracing significance when almost as if he were retelling the story of Hawthorne's Miriam, he took another American innocent, Isabel Archer, along the road that led to Rome. "Rome was actual," Henry Adams discovered on the eve of the Civil War: to him Rome meant the first painful realization of the enchainment, the confinement of the romantic imagination, the anchoring of a soaring idealism to the hard and heavy facts of actuality. To Isabel, Rome finally signifies substantially the same thing. Envisioning happiness, at the outset of her European adventures, as dashing over a strange road in a coach and four on a dark night, so self-confident and assured of a special destiny that she refuses Lord Warburton with but little trepidation, she discovers herself in Rome married to Gilbert Osmond, confined to a "dark narrow alley with a blind wall at the end." Rome is indeed the actual for her when she turns away from Caspar Goodwood's impassioned embrace to follow the "very straight path" back to Osmond.

When we recall the differences between the two writers, the fact that James was impelled to express in his fiction a theme almost identical with Twain's attests to the accuracy and, one might almost say, the universality of the image of the American evoked by the mutation of the burlesque conventions in Twain's *Roughing It*.

Notes

1. At least ten English editions and reprints appeared between 1821 and 1868.
2. Christopher Hussey, *The Picturesque* (London and New York, 1927), 111.
3. *Doctor Syntax's Tree Tours* (London, 1868), 7.
4. Franklin R. Rogers, *Mark Twain's Burlesque Patterns* (Dallas, 1960) 30–35. Further information, especially on Combe's influence on *The Pickwick Papers*, appears in Wilhelm Dibelius, "Zu den Pickwick Papers," *Angliz* XXXV (1912), 101–110.
5. "Pilgrim's Return," *Literary History of the United States*, ed. Robert E. Spiller, et al. (New York, 1953), 831.
6. *Mark Twain's Letters*, ed. A.B. Paine (New York and London, 1917), I 186.
7. On this question see also Henry Nash Smith, "Mark Twain as an Interpreter of the Far West: The Structure of *Roughing It*," *The Frontier in Perspective*, ed. Walker D. Wyman and Clifton B. Kroeber (Madison, 1958), 210, and Martin B. Fried, "The Sources, Composition, and Popularity of Mark Twain's *Roughing It*," unpublished Ph.D. dissertation (Chicago, 1951), 16.

8. Franklin R. Rogers, *The Pattern for Mark Twain's Roughing It: Letters from Nevada by Samuel and Orion Clemens, 1861–1862* (Berkeley, 1961), 19–21.

9. Rogers, *Mark Twain's Burlesque Patterns*, 61–66.

10. *Mimesis: The Representation of Reality in Western Literature* (New York, 1957), 408.

11. Lionel Trilling, "The Princess Casamassima," *The Liberal Imagination* (New York, 1950), 61.

12. Oscar Cargill, "The First International Novel." *PMLA* LXXII (Sept., 1958), 419.

From the Old Southwest

Pascal Covici, Jr.

I

Mark Twain's relationship to the humor of his region is probably less direct than it is usually thought to be. That the humor of the old Southwest is indeed part of his heritage can be, and has been, demonstrated; the proposition is by now axiomatic. Mark Twain transcends this tradition. Faced with the literary problem of presenting many of the themes and moods that in various ways attracted such diverse minds as Poe, Hawthorne, Melville, Henry James, and Henry Adams, Twain, to be sure, found solutions different from theirs. But this difference is not to be measured solely by the scale of Twain's adherence to the models of his southwestern predecessors.

Nevertheless, to understand Mark Twain's use of humor is, at least partly, to put oneself in tune with the early frontier and western humor of America. Many scholars, among them Franklin Meine, Mody C. Boatright, Bernard DeVoto, and, most recently, Kenneth S. Lynn, have shown in a multitude of ways how oral humor became more than mere pastime for hunters and keelboatmen confronting violence and loneliness and for any raw westerner confronting the snickering East. Such personal uses of humor only gradually became literary,

Reprinted from *Mark Twain's Humor: The Image of a World* (Dallas: Southern Methodist U. P., 1962), pp. 3–36, 257–8.

however, for the literate tellers of tales in the pre-Civil War Southwest almost without exception were newcomers to the regions in which their stories were set. As a result, they were moved by compulsions different from those of the "natives." Lawyers, judges, and doctors, educated on the Atlantic seaboard and suddenly thrust into the continent, they looked with wonder at the "manners, customs, amusements, wit, dialect" so different from what they had left behind.

The stories that flowed from this wonderment were largely organized around two impulses: a need to belittle and a desire to report. The gentlemen from the East looked upon their presence in the West—Alabama, Georgia, Mississippi—as a blessing to the barbarous natives from whom the Gentleman must always be careful to distinguish himself, at least in print. The lawyer might slap backs all he chose, but his duty was to make sure that the barbarian knew his place, that the political and economic fortunes of the new country were safeguarded by his own kind from public ravishment. An illuminating and just emphasis is Kenneth Lynn's on the political bias revealed through the framework of countless yarns in which a "Self-controlled Gentleman"[1] presents the actions of an uncouth lout. Lout and gentleman are separated by dialect as well as by action; there is no chance that a reader might confuse the two.

This need of gentlemanly authors to establish a moral and cultural distance between themselves and the places where they earned their living was at one with, and perhaps even helped to develop, the second impulse behind the humorous tales of the Southwest, that of realistic description. A writer who views his environment from a distance is less likely to take that environment for granted than is one wrapped up in the mores of the people he is observing. The living habits of the folk—how they talk, the pranks they play, what interests them—will seem worth reporting in proportion to their variation from the "normal" life left behind. One can see now that the striving for objectivity implicit in the aim of setting down the oddities of a new sort of civilization—or lack of one—clashed with the feeling of superiority so meticulously cultivated by the writers. Brutality and coarseness were blown up out of all proportion in order to solidify the position of the detached witness; most of the events narrated could never have been enacted by mere human beings: the half-horse, half-alligator men of the Mississippi, in fact, a whole menagerie of frontier titans, were used to accommodate the Gentleman's need for low behavior from which to disassociate himself.

But beneath the violence and exaggeration of mid-nineteenth-century southwestern humor there lies an impulse toward realism, toward a faithful presentation of the life of the region. Repeatedly, the stories about Simon Suggs, Sut Lovingood, Major Jones, and their picaresque brethren are introduced as offering intimate knowledge of a particular locality and its particular citizens. William Tappan Thompson, as he says in his preface to *Major Jones's Chronicles of Pineville* (1843), "endeavored, in a small way, to catch [the Georgia "cracker's"] 'manners living as they rise'. . . I claim no higher character for my stories" than that they present "a glance at characters not often found in books, or anywhere else, indeed, except in just such places as '*Pineville*,' Georgia." The vividness with which the frontier and the backwoods live for Americans today is at least partial testimony to the realistic bent of Thompson and his fellows. Although they dealt in exaggeration, tall tales, impossible violence, satire, and other distortions of reality, their intention to be faithful to the felt quality of life in their region cannot be mistaken.

The realism in the stories of George Washington Harris, W.T. Thompson, Augustus Longstreet, Johnson J. Hooper, et al. implies more than close observation and a nice ear for the spoken word. The expressed intention "to supply. . . the manners, customs, amusement, wit, dialect, as they appear in all grades of society to an ear and eye witness of them"[2] yielded time and again to the more subtle, less often articulated, pressure to crack the local yokels, or the damn-yankees, on their presumptuous and ill-bred snouts. The content of these satiric thrusts was apt to be anything but realism, narrowly considered, yet the distance, or disengagement, from local life that provided the perspective for satire also fostered the careful reporting of minute detail. But no sense of a transcendental oversoul, infusing both squatter and sophisticate, pervades the realism of the Southwest. Although the writers described the commonplace, they did not, with Emerson, embrace it. The effect of their stories upon a reader is to insulate him from any emotional involvement or identification with events, characters, or region.

These pre-Howells realists present the externals of action and dialogue. Had they explored through their fiction interior states of being or even acknowledged through analysis the existence of human feeling in their characters, we could not laugh at the predicaments set before us. A concern limited to the realistic surface of behavior is made almost obligatory in the case of the southwestern humorists by the nature of the humor which the "school" employed. If a reader is asked to respond to victimized protagonists, or to protagonists' victims, as though they were of the same flesh and spirit as himself, he is not going to laugh as he watches their cruel and exaggerated suffering. When Sut Lovingood leaves half of his skin stuck to his shirt by some newfangled, gluelike starch, one can laugh only if Sut is nothing more than the "nat'ral born durn'fool" he represents himself to be. The quality of Sut's humanity is so removed from ours that the distance between the two is never bridged, nor was it meant to be. On the other hand, were Huck Finn to be comparably flayed, the reader would wince, not smile; no one laughs when Nigger Jim is bitten by a snake, or when Huck hides out from the Shepherdsons by climbing a tree.

The realism of the southwestern humorists consists, then, of content—a report on what life looks like in the sticks—and of an aesthetic distance, or psychological detachment, from the object of scrutiny. The juxtaposition of educated gentry and boorish locale goes far toward accounting for the content and the attitude that shaped so much of the writing which poured out of the region. But the seeds of this village realism in a still more important way came from outside, just as did the writers themselves. Behind the attitude of objective disdain lies an assumption right out of the rationalistic eighteenth century: that a man of common sense can distinguish truth from falsehood, reality from appearance, can know what is right, can see with clarity and dispassion the world around him. The unambiguous treatment of material reinforces the epistemology of realism: direct sense-impressions are to be trusted; what seems to be, is.

For the reader who aligns himself with the rational author, the world is no mystery. Sut Lovingood shatters the slumber of an unwelcome intruder by tying a nine-foot length of intestines to the man's shirttail: the terrified "snake-bit Irishman" lights out for home, convinced that "'a big copper-headed black rattil-snake is crawlin up [his] britches,'"[3] but the reader never for a moment needs to doubt the reliability of his own senses. The boorish victims, on the other hand, repeatedly suffer from an inability to distinguish between the real and the pretended, for the discrepancy between what seems to be and what actually exists forms the crux of numerous pranks perpetrated by southwestern scalawags. It is not only Simon Suggs among them whose "whole ethical system lies snugly in his favorite aphorism—'IT IS GOOD TO BE SHIFTY IN A NEW COUNTRY.'"[4] Repeatedly, characters are victimized because they fail to recognize that "reality" has been altered for their special benefit. William Tappan Thompson's "How to Kill Two Birds with One Stone"[5] ironically applauds young lawyer Jenkins' wisdom in persuading two men that each has stolen from the other when the lawyer himself has hidden Si Perkins' wagon in Absalom Harley's cellar, in turn loading Si's wagon with Harley's bacon and other articles, in order to foment a double lawsuit and pocket double fees. The ruse works perfectly, and the reader appreciates with a Whig's awareness the "democratic" acuteness of Thomas Jefferson Jenkins while condemning with a laugh the litigious pretensions of his victims. The characters are fooled; the reader is not.

The refined reader is encouraged to trust his sense of ethics as well as his sense of what is real. The behavior of the fictional characters is held up against an implicit standard accessible to all men of reason. Again, simply the surface of what happens, the mere action, speech, and setting as they impinge upon the senses of the realist, is adequate to the purpose of the writers. What really counts is "manners"; the way in which the characters act is of more import than what they do or why they do it. When Sut Lovingood works himself into that fancily-starched shirt which subsequently rips the hide off him, he isn't being unethical, but, rather, pretentious. His pretensions to city grandeur do not mesh with his backwoods ignorance, and one laughs because Sut is ridiculous.

If there is any one pattern basic to the humor of the Southwest it is precisely this: a character is pushed by the author into a situation in which he either exposes the pretensions of others or himself emerges as ridiculous because of his pretentious behavior. The eighteenth-century concept of decorum comes to mind in this connection; what is being criticized more often than not is a failure to adhere to the standards of a cultivated civilization, a failure—so annoyingly common in raw, frontier democracy—to recognize and to accept one's inferior position in society. By considering himself to be as good as the next man, the country democrat becomes pretentious, at least in the eyes of the transplanted easterners whose aloof standards shaped the Southwest humor of the nineteenth century.

The satire embedded in this humor is a satire of the ridiculous, which means that when we talk about the humor of the American Southwest we are really talking about the kind of humor described by Henry Fielding in his preface to *Joseph Andrews*, the humor of eighteenth-century England. The tales so often and so delightfully anthologized that Americans think of as so particularly their own are American in content but English in theory and in organization. Through affectation, "the only source of the true ridiculous," according to Fielding, characters are made into figures of fun. Sometimes the affectation is motivated by vanity, "which puts us on affecting false characters, in order to purchase applause," sometimes by hypocrisy, which "sets us on an endeavor to avoid censure by concealing our vices under an appearance of their opposite virtues." Hypocrisy and vanity—under which headings outsiders could lump almost all attempts to transcend the unmannerly boorishness of a frontier community—lead to affected behavior, and "from the discovery of this affectation arises the Ridiculous—which always strikes the reader with surprise and pleasure." Fielding had no need to add that the reader's pleasure depends on his identifying with the objective viewer rather than with the vain or hypocritical character, for the very attribution of vanity or hypocrisy automatically establishes the proper aesthetic distance between author and reader on the one hand, ridiculous character on the other.

A careful reading of southwestern "American" humor will give substance to the suggestion that this particularly American tradition is in fact derived explicitly from English theory and practice of the eighteenth century. Hooper, Harris, Thompson, and others show a keen sense of the ridiculous as Fielding defines it. Repeatedly, their humor embodies Fielding's contention that "from affectation only, the misfortunes and calamities of life, or the imperfections of nature, may become the objects of ridicule." The victims of Simon Suggs's camp meeting, for example, endure considerable misfortune and calamity when the worthy Captain rides off with the dollars they have donated toward his pretended efforts to establish a church. One might expect to find a reader's sympathies aroused for the swindled congregation, but, instead, one finds oneself chuckling along with wicked old Simon as he canters off at the end of the story. Simon's victims are ridiculous, not because of what they are, necessarily, but rather because the reader has been made to observe them from the point of view of a refined and rational being.

As Hooper leads his reader into the camp meeting, he first describes realistically and objectively the various kinds of religious hysteria manifested by the throng. Then he kills off any incipient identification with the masses that may have sprung up in the reader's open mind: "The great object of all seemed to be, to see who could make the greatest noise—

> 'And each—for madness ruled the hour—
> Would try his own expressive power.'"[6]

One of the ministers, under the guise of religious zeal, is "lavishing caresses" upon the prettier among the young women. The Negro woman who is most profoundly moved by religious emotion is "huge" and "greasy," adjectives which cast doubt on the delicacy of her spiritual awakening. The minister to whom Simon attributes his spectacular—though bogus—conversion is a presumptuous ass; the whole crew get what's coming to them.

> "I-I-I can bring' em!" cried the preacher. . . in a tone of exultation—"Lord thou knows ef thy servant can't stir'em, nobody else needn't try—but the glory aint mine! I'm a poor worrum of the dust," he added, with ill-managed affectation.[7]

Affectation renders the people ridiculous and permits one to laugh at them. At the very moment when Simon is cajoling them into contributing money so that he can found a church "in his own neighborhood" and "make himself useful as soon as he could prepare himself for the ministry," his smooth talk is aimed not at their religious enthusiasm but at their desire to appear wealthy and generous before their neighbors: "Simon had excited the pride of purse of the congregation, and a very handsome sum was collected in a very short time."[8]

Nineteenth-century Americans not only ridiculed the affectations of louts, but also went still farther into eighteenth-century English practice when aiming at more specific targets.

By pretending that the object of attack was simply affecting the qualities that made him dangerous—courage, intelligence, power, or whatever—Jonathan Swift, and many others, could cut their enemies down to size, denying in the process that the enemy was worth taking seriously in the first place. George Washington Harris, for one, borrows a page from Swift when he recounts Sut Lovingood's travels with "Old Abe Linkhorn"[9] in a way that "diminishes" Lincoln to the disappearing point. The leader of the antislavery faction so inimical to Harris is too stupid to be dangerous, too cowardly to be feared. Moreover, his ugliness is inhuman enough to suggest that he can be disposed of as easily as any other harmless amphibious reptile:

> I ketched a ole bullfrog once [says Sut] and drove a nail through his lips into a post, tied two rocks to his hind toes and stuck a darnin needle into his tail to let out the moisture, and left him there to dry. I seen him two weeks after'ards: and, when I seen old Abe, I thought it were an awful retribution come onto me, and that it were the same frog—. . . same shape same color same feel (cold as ice), and I'm damned if it ain't the same smell.[10]

This technique of belittling the object of attack is by no means limited to eighteenth-century England but belongs to a tradition of literary satire familiar to any classically educated American of the nineteenth century. Since *meiosis*,* whether

---

*The "technique of rendering devils flabby is a common literary device which was discussed in rhetorical handbooks under the Greek title *meiosis*, meaning, literally, 'belittling' or 'diminuation.' Diminuation may be described briefly as the use of any 'ugly or homely images' which are intended to diminish the dignity of an object. . . diminuation is any kind of speech which tends, either by the force of low or vulgar imagery, or by other suggestion, to depress an object below its usually accepted status." (John M. Bullitt, *Jonathan Swift and the Anatomy of Satire: A Study of Satiric Technique* [Cambridge: Harvard University Press, 1953], p. 45.)

applied to northern Presidents or backwoods boobs, was so frequently and deliberately and even characteristically employed, it is fair to say that no matter how firmly anchored to American experience their lives and writings might be, the pre-Civil War humorists of the Southwest had at least one eye on foreign literary sources.

II

The characteristics of southwestern humor, then, are those of realism in content and in epistemology. Even the satirical intentions behind the humor call upon the reader to agree to the existence of clearly defined standards, identically visible to all thinking men. Instead of the moral hesitancies to be found on a frontier where old codes are daily called in question by the exigencies of a new life, this humor reflects the bland assurance of eighteenth-century men of reason that the cultivated mind can measure all things.

But to Mark Twain there was little, if any, validity in the realistic assumptions behind the humor of the frontier. When, in *Mark Twain at Work*,[11] Bernard DeVoto asserts that Twain's aim in writing *Huckleberry Finn* was to record life by the banks of the Mississippi, his comment is less applicable to the complex and ambiguous novel Twain wrote than to the literary tradition from which most of Twain's work emerges. Twain uses the materials of realism—the events and objects of the daily life of the region—but in a way that Americanizes American humor and puts it more closely in touch with the metaphysical facts of life in a new land and in our modern world: his effects do not, ultimately, depend on a detached objectivity that permits the reader to look upon scoundrels and boors as nonhuman beasts of no importance, or on a sense of the ridiculous as it arises from affectation, but, instead, on a knowledge—paid for by experience—that human reason is cruelly limited, too often unable to discriminate between what is and what seems; that the shibboleths of one generation are the jests of another; and that the powers of irrationality, rather than the deliberate exercise of will, make people appear to be other than what they are.

This is, to be sure, taking humor seriously. Yet even in the simplest episodes of Twain's narrative humor lies the basis for such a contrast between what Twain does and what his predecessors did with similar raw material. In Chapter XX of *Huckleberry Finn* (1885), the king attends a camp meeting at Pokerville much like the one to which Johnson J. Hooper had sent Simon Suggs forty years earlier. Both meetings are minutely described, and both congregations are subtly robbed. The essential difference is between the frailties that in each case lead the people to allow themselves to be cheated. Simon Suggs defrauds those who are guilty of affectation: the laity are purse-proud, and the clergy are concerned either with taking up the collection or with hugging the prettiest girls. Simon's benefactors give money to create the impression of wealth; their show of pious charity is transparently hypocritical and vain, and they are made to seem ridiculous because of affectation. Mark Twain's king exploits a very different sort of meeting: his victims, not "ridiculous through affectation," neither hypocritical nor vain, are victimized because they share humanity's penchant for romantic excitement. The king, improbably representing himself as a pirate, succeeds completely in taking in the communicants because they want to believe that an Indian Ocean pirate could brush against their own dull lives. In exchange for this fatuous belief they are willing to pay their money: "The king said. . . it warn't no use talking, heathens don't amount to shucks alongside of pirates to work a camp-meeting with" (XIII,184–85).[12] This has nothing to do with vanity or hypocrisy—and, therefore, has no connection with affectation, either. The gulled ones are just as charitable and religious as their actions suggest, but they are motivated less by charity and zeal than by their desire to share in a sensation. This, however, they do not know about themselves. In contrast to the earlier tradition, the people of

Pokerville are not trying to appear to be what they are not. Rather, they are by their very nature other than they seem.

Mark Twain's fictional world is different from that of his immediate regional predecessors because it is organized around a real, and not a contrived, discrepancy between reality and appearance. The orderly and comprehensible universe presided over by the Self-controlled Gentleman is one in which author and readers can all relax together, assured that only those who stand outside their circle can be deceived by the contrived accidents that befall frontier clowns. Sut Lovingood gladly swallows Sicily Burns's "love-potion," with terrific results, but the civilized reader knew all along that it was soda. Such assurance is foreign to the nineteenth-century American fiction most cherished today. Nathaniel Hawthorne's explorations of the effects of sin on the human heart force one to reorganize one's sense of what sin itself is, and Melville's presentation of the Mount of Titans in *Pierre*, and of Moby-Dick himself, compels one to question the seeming beneficence of smiling nature. More to our immediate purpose, Mark Twain, using the materials and surroundings of his southwestern literary progenitors, throws into doubt—as they never do—a reader's complacent evaluation of common sense as applied first to daily human behavior, and finally to man's role in the universe.

Twain's preoccupation with revealing a discrepancy between seeming and reality is central, not peripheral, to his work. A striking example, built from bits of Twain's frontier heritage, is Huck's trip to the circus to counterpoint through humor one of the most somber episodes in *The Adventures of Huckleberry Finn*. In Chapter XXI, Old Boggs, a harmless drunk, is shot down in cold blood by the ruthless but gentlemanly Colonel Sherburn. Huck Finn is the one sympathetic witness of the slaying. An orphan himself, Huck is especially touched by the pathos of Boggs's daughter as she weeps over the dying man. "She was about sixteen, and very sweet and gentle looking, but awful pale and scared." The other witnesses are totally detached. In fact, "the whole town" watches callously as Boggs breathes his last in a drugstore window, a weighty Bible laid upon his chest to ease his departing soul and increase his agony. They might be watching a show, to hear the people farther back from the window talk to those hogging the front row: "'Say, now, you've looked enough, you fellows; 'tain't right and 'tain't fair for you to stay thar all the time, and never give nobody a chance; other folks has their rights as well as you'" (199; all page numbers are to *The Writings of Mark Twain*, "Definitive Ed." NY: Harper, 1922–25).

Huck subsequently (Chapter XXII) watches another drunk at a local circus whose life is endangered not by pistol-fire but by his insistence that he be permitted to attempt equestrian acrobatics. Finally the patient ringmaster acquiesces; amid howls of laughter and derision, the drunk mounts a horse, "his heels flying in the air every jump, and the whole crowd of people standing up shouting and laughing till tears rolled down." The horse breaks loose from the roustabouts, and the drunk seems headed for certain death, to the vast delight of the audience. "It warn't funny to me, though," says Huck; "I was all of a tremble to see his danger" (206). The seeming "drunk" turns out to be a seasoned performer, a member of the circus-troupe who rides like an angel, and the laugh is on naïve Huck Finn, so easily taken in by a circus act. Huck has been sentimental, the reader may feel, in separating himself from the crowd that first jeers, then laughs at the performer. His delicacy of feeling is worthless, for the crowd's callous merriment has injured no feelings. The laughers, indeed, have added to the effect of the circus routine. As for the heartlessness of their instinctive response, well, their sympathies were as unsought as they were unstirred.

But when the reader remembers the similar excitement of this same toughened crowd when it witnessed the murder of Boggs and the drama of his death, he sees that though Huck is naïve, his simple compassion is preferable to the "smart" sensation-seeking of the empty-headed mob. Not only had the people clustered around the store window in which Boggs lay dying, but they also had had the cold-blooded detachment to enjoy a re-enactment of the slaying after the event, even offering their flasks to the "long, lanky man" who "done it perfect . . . just exactly the way it all happened" (200). In each case, Huck's reaction differs from the crowd's. Moreover, Huck's sympathy for Boggs arises from the same qualities of spirit that make Huck a gull at the circus, just as the same shallow craving for excitement motivates the crowd in both instances. Thus, although Huck's attitude at the circus appears to stem from a foolish and valueless naïveté, its true source is his fineness of soul. The reader, therefore, is compelled to reinterpret the "reality" that has been set before him. What has seemed to be and what is are inexorably opposed.

We know that Twain's murder of Boggs is in itself "realistic," for it is "almost without a hairsbreadth of variation" a duplication of Judge John Clemens' account of the shooting of "Uncle Sam" Smarr by William Owsley in Hannibal, when Sam Clemens was just over nine years old.[13] Moreover, the circus incident itself was borrowed from an earlier southwestern writer. What is at issue here, though, is something more than a question of how photographic the writer's memory happens to be. The murder and the circus not only are events in themselves; they also reveal hidden duplicities in the world. The analogue of Twain's circus scene, however, concerns itself with no such opposition between what seems and what is; it never challenges the reader to revise his first impressions. William Tappan Thompson's circus in "The Great Attraction! or The Doctor Most Oudaciously Tuck In"[14] anticipates by some forty years the one Huck attends: in each case, a conventional equestrian act precedes the pseudo-drunken "head-liner"; a witty clown cracks jokes of surpassing cleverness; and then comes the rider who turns out to be sober after all and astonishes his beholders by rising to his feet on the horse's back, then stripping off assorted suits of clothes, "twenty or more" for Thompson's hero, a mere seventeen for Twain's.

From the Old Southwest

The effect of Thompson's circus is considerably simpler than that of Twain's. It appears to be, and it is, a short satire on pretension. Doctor Jones, the unhappy protagonist of the piece, is insufferably impressed with his own sophistication. Denizen of Pineville though he be, he has once visited Augusta, "that Philadelphia of the South," and feels that he is "—to use one of his own polished expressions—'bully of the tan-yard.'"[15] Everything about Augusta is immeasurably superior to whatever Pineville has to offer, and Jones, because of his exposure to the metropolis, includes himself among its wonders. He has seen everything, done everything; and he knows everything, too. When he guides the untutored young ladies of Pineville to their first circus, he assures them that what they are seeing is "nothing to what he had seen in Augusta."

Thompson's attitude toward Jones is one of ironic scorn, as any reader quickly perceives. The Doctor is pretentious. Vanity leads him to affect a sophistication, a *savoir-faire*, that he doesn't really possess, and the circus proves to be his undoing. When the "drunk" tries to ride, thus interrupting the performance, Doctor Jones rushes to the ring, intent on being the hero of the hour. Despite explicit warning by two of the townsfolk that "that chap belongs to the show," he tries valiantly to prevent the ride, only to be rudely rebuked by the clown and finally jostled into the colored section. The Doctor has failed to understand the niceties of circus shenanigans, and so is made a laughingstock, "oudaciously tuck in." Needless to say, the citizens of Pineville rejoice in his downfall. "'Is that the way they does in Augusta?'. . . and a hundred other such jeers" bring both the story and the Doctor's local glory to a close.

Thompson's story is excellently organized and accomplishes the effect that one can assume Thompson meant it to have. Because his aim was not Twain's is no reason to criticize Thompson, whose consciousness of theme is embodied even in his language. Doctor Jones's refinement is called into question by a report of his own coarse epithet for himself—"bully of the tan-yard"—a bit of backwoods lingo echoed in the description of big Bill Sweeney as the rough and tough "bully of the county." Mr. Sweeney, whose place in the story is quite subordinate, shares with Jones the fault of pretentiousness. His pretensions are not to sophistication, however, but to gentility. When he refuses to remove his hat so that others can see the show, the ensuing fracas reveals that he has no right to sit among gentlefolk, just as the main action of the story annuls the Doctor's claims to intellectual supremacy. Both men, each in his different way, have striven to "purchase applause," in Fielding's words, by "affecting false characters." There are no hidden subtleties in the story, no extraneous reverberations. Its satiric impact is obvious and direct. The motives of the characters appear clearly at the start, and one never needs to revise his estimate. This is not true of the king's camp meeting victims or of Huck Finn at his circus.

The two examples of the circus and the camp meeting suggest that although Mark Twain's writing draws upon the traditions and materials utilized by earlier southwestern humorists, its humor goes beyond an exposure of deliberate affectation. In psychological awareness, Twain is closely akin to Melville and Henry James, for he presents human beings as more disposed to misunderstand themselves, as do Pierre and the first-person protagonists of *The Turn of the Screw* and *The Sacred Fount*, than to mislead others deliberately. Consequently, his technique, his literary organization of material, is more concerned with laying bare the human heart than with presenting the rogue's world as it was at a given time and place. Anyone who reads carefully the introduction to the king's camp meeting cannot help but be impressed by the meticulous acuteness of the description, even down to benches "made out of outside slabs of logs, with holes bored in the round side to drive sticks into for legs" (XIII, 181). To say that Twain is not concerned at all with the surface appearance of the life surrounding his characters is clearly to overstate the point. It is his particular use of appearances that sets him off from his humorous predecessors.

III

The most direct way to suggest the unique quality in Twain's use of surface, or reportorial, realism is to turn from specific analogues to a technique as general as the use of spoken language. That Twain cared about reproducing the exact inflections of dialect, and that he was proud of his abilities in this direction, the author's "Explanatory" to *Huckleberry Finn* makes clear. Seven distinct varieties of speech are mentioned, and, we are reminded, "The shadings have not been done in a haphazard fashion. . . but painstakingly, and with the trustworthy guidance and support of personal familiarity with these several forms of speech" (XIII, xxi). Repeatedly he tries to make his people talk as their environment and training might make them talk in real life, adopting the vocabulary and imagery that will most precisely evoke the varieties of backwoods experience.

His westerners, for example, repeatedly speak the language of the poker table, and in this respect they are not alone in nineteenth-century fiction. Poker talk was a common device of local-color characterization in the writings of the transplanted lawyers and judges who found rural Tennessee, Georgia, Alabama, and Mississippi strikingly different from the metropolitan East they had left behind. There were many stories about gamblers in the new country, and the vocabulary of gambling provided a quick metaphorical index to the habits and origins of the speaker. "No matter what sort of a hand you've got. . . take stock!'" exhorts Simon Suggs. "'Here am *I*, the wickedest and blindest of sinners—has spent my whole life in the sarvice of the devil—has now come in on *narry pair* and won a *pile!*'"[16] That Simon presents his recent "conversion" in poker language serves to place him as a backwoods con man; also, one notes the dramatic irony of his words, for Simon's sinful life prior to the camp meeting, his newly-won "pile" as a joyful allusion to God's free grace which Simon appears to be experiencing, whereas the reader is aware that Simon is planning to win a "pile" of money on the strength of his pretended conversion, his bluff "hand" with "narry pair" in it. When he urges unrepentant sinners to join him on the mourners' bench, he reassures them that "'The bluff game aint played here! No runnin' of a body off! Every body holds four aces, and when you bet, you win!'"[17] Summing up his achievement at the end of the story, Simon concludes that "'Ef them fellers aint done to a cracklin, . . . I'll never bet on two pair again!'"[18] The principal effect of this terminology is to present Simon as a cardsharper, willing to gamble on the gullibility of the average man. But this the reader knew from the opening pages of the story. The poker talk has revealed nothing new about the Captain; it is simply part of the author's impulse toward realism, toward presenting the audible surface of the time and place.

In a bit of Mark Twain's earlier writing the same limited effect appears: poker vocabulary denotes the westerner but tells nothing specific about him as a man. Describing a rising river in 1859, Sergeant Fathom "would suggest to the planters, as we say in an innocent little parlor game, commonly called 'draw,' that if they can only 'stand the raise' this time, they may enjoy the comfortable assurance that the old river's banks will never hold a 'full' again during their natural lives."[19] This is an amateur's imitation of a technique: the effort to westernize the speaker is unsupported by dialect, and the humor is heavy-handed. Fathom is a stick figure who never comes to life. But Twain was to discover the possibilities latent in simple speech: the preparations for Buck Fanshaw's funeral in *Roughing It* not only amuse one but present a fully-drawn character as well. Scotty Briggs and the minister converse for seven pages of western slang and eastern elegance where a single page of less characteristic talk might have sufficed, but one finds that Scotty emerges in the round because of the way he talks.

The first stage of the interview presents Scotty's effort to tell the minister that Buck is dead and that the "boys" would appreciate a few comforting words at the funeral."

"'Are you the duck that runs the gospel-mill next door?'" (IV,45) asks Scotty. After the minister counters that he is, rather, "'the spiritual adviser of the little company of believers whose sanctuary adjoins these premises,'" Scotty "scratched his head, reflected a moment, and then said: 'you ruther hold over me, pard. I reckon I can't call that hand. Ante and pass the buck.'"

Scotty's perplexities increase. The minister asks for simpler language, but the request is too complexly worded. "'I'll have to pass, I judge.'" "'How?'" "'You've raised me out, pard'" (46).

Eventually the two understand each other. But the minister wonders about Buck Fanshaw's religious affiliations in language that leads Scotty to complain, "'Why, you're most too many for me, you know... Every time you draw, you fill; but I don't seem to have any luck. Let's have a new deal.'" "'How? Begin again?'" "'That's it.'" "'Very well. Was he a good man, and—'" "'There—I see that; don't put up another chip till I look at my hand'" (50).

Apart from giving the western flavor that Twain explicitly means to impart (42–43), poker terminology here accomplishes two ends. First, the metaphoric equation of chips and cards with words ties the episode together by providing a secondary story line. The inability of Scotty and the minister to communicate becomes as much the subject of the brief scene as is the arranging of Buck Fanshaw's funeral. The two confuse each other with their language, and a reader wonders how long their differences of terminology will keep each from "seeing" the other's point. The minister, slick though sickly easterner that he is, keeps on talking, and Scotty is "raised" out of several conversational "pots" by his flow of words. Finally, however, Scotty can "call"—"'I see that'"—and the episode comes to a close with mutual comprehension.

Secondly, Scotty's poker vocabulary displays his character. Never does he try to bluff. He admits the minister's ability to "draw and fill"; he quickly acknowledges the inadequacy of his own "hand"—his comprehension of language—and forthrightly "passes," having been "raised out." When he understands the minister's words—the "bet"—he will "see that," but he wants to "look at [his] hand" before any more chips—words—fall. Scotty's discourse is scrupulously honest and manly; his terms never suggest that he thinks the minister's ignorance is presentation of him as a sympathetic Sunday-school teacher whose rendition in slang of Bible stories "was listened to by his little learners with a consuming interest" (53). The contrast between East and West is clearly presented, but the story differs from most western stories of the time in that the contest and victory are moral and are presented through language, not through violent action: the rough westerner, in the terms of his own rough game, shows himself to be a more honest man than the educated easterner. The language of poker ties Scotty's character and story together into a simple, kindly unit.

Scotty's simplicity of 1871 contrasts with the simple-minded duplicity of Saladin Foster in "The $30,000 Bequest" (1904). The anecdote of Scotty and the minister is more or less a "set piece," an exhibition of language for its own sake. The story of the Fosters, on the other hand, has a definite plot organized around a specific theme; its concern is not to demonstrate speech but to use it to reveal character. Saladin's use of poker metaphor establishes him as an unpretentious, rather commonplace man—which is important for the total effect of the story, since the reader is supposed to feel that what happens to Saladin might happen to anyone—and simultaneously reveals his understanding of himself. The effect of the device is double: it both vivifies him and foreshadows his actions.

Saladin exhibits more self-awareness than Scotty. When his wife expresses joy at the news that his rich uncle—from whom they expect to inherit $30,000—is still living, Saladin derides her for being "'immorally pious'" (XXIV, 12). Electra is tartly certain that "'there is no such thing as immoral piety,'" and Saladin is soon overwhelmed because he doesn't know when to stop talking. He multiplies his excuses, only to entangle himself still further. "Then, musingly, he apologized to himself. 'I certainly held threes—I *know* it—but I drew and didn't fill. That's where I'm so often weak in the game. If I had stood pat—but I didn't. I never do. I don't know enough'" (13).

Saladin, one sees, laments two things. Superficially, he bemoans his unavoidable failure to "fill"—and superficially the story is built upon the Fosters' expectations (doomed to disappointment) that the uncle will make the bequest that he promised. No one can control the run of the cards at poker; likewise, Saladin is not responsible for his uncle's malicious deceit. But Saladin does have a weakness and sees it clearly: he knows that he cannot bluff successfully, whether before or after the draw. Later, as the Fosters come to live more and more in their imaginations, daydreaming about their lives as millionaires once the bequest shall have been invested a few dozen times, Saladin sinks to degrading debaucheries. He gambles; he drinks; he fornicates. His transgressions are purely mental, but Electra detects the glazed eyes and the slack face as he sits lost in fantasy. He is unable to "bluff" her; he cannot deny what in imagination he has been up to, and the happiness of their marriage is blighted. The misery that results from his failure to "stand pat" is a direct outgrowth of the character revealed through the poker-talk monologue.

Finally, to choose an example near the chronological middle of Twain's career, when Hank Morgan presents himself in Arthur's dining hall near the beginning of *A Connecticut Yankee in King Arthur's Court* (1889), one finds an intensive use of American frontier, or "Yankee," poker talk not only to characterize the protagonist but also to anticipate theme and prepare for the satiric irony behind the story. Faced with the dismal fact that he is either in the sixth century or in a lunatic asylum, with no way to determine which until an eclipse occurs or fails to occur, Hank decides to dismiss the problem from his mind: "One thing at a time, is my motto—and just play that thing for all it is worth, even if it's only two pair and a jack" (XIV, 16). Ironically, Hank Morgan's career as "The Boss" will be an attempt to inculcate the masses of Great Britain with the habits of rationality and the attributes of reflective intelligence; his whole program will be one of education in the "Man-factory." But here, he shows that he is a man who will play a bluff with the best, and foreshadows his successful eclipse-bluff, his repeated "miracles," and his final saturnalia of destruction when his "bluff" is called. The conflict between reason and irrationality, between, one may say, the doctrines of the perfectibility of man and of innate human depravity, is played off against the background of Hank's poker-faced opportunism. In the great tournament between the "magic of fol-de-rol" and the "magic of science" (396), the magic of science triumphs, but "it was a 'bluff' you know. At such a time it is sound judgment to put on a bold face and play your hand for a hundred times what it is worth; forty-nine times out of fifty nobody dares to 'call,' and you rake in the chips" (395).

Such a passage is of the frontier tradition; it is the realistic speech of an uneducated man who, by speaking the way he does, convinces a reader of the existence of his environment. Yet it accomplishes a good deal more. Hank Morgan's use of poker terminology is more significant than that of Captain Simon Suggs at his camp meeting. Suggs's poker metaphors come at the end of his story, when the reader already knows all about the Captain, but Hank's "two pair and a jack" serves to introduce both his character and the essential conflicts to be presented in his story. Hooper's satire, moreover, has nothing to do with the characterization of Simon Suggs through poker talk. Simon is no outsider whose entrance into a previously stable society disrupts the status quo. He is immediately recognized as "the very 'chief of sinners' in all that region,"[20] his physiognomy as familiar as his reputation. His vocabulary adds little to the meaning of the story, because Simon's function—to victimize the affected—does not depend on his origin as signaled by his talk. Hank Morgan, however, is an unknown quantity. His very clothing seems miraculous, and his vocabulary repeatedly sets him off from his captors. His mere presence in Arthur's court will serve to contrast Yankee ingenuity and energy with Arthurian romance and sloth; the contrast between his American language and sixth-century, knightly habits of thought will be essential to the development of the book's theme.

IV

Even when Hank Morgan is roaming the streets of Old England, his Americanism is guaranteed by his poker talk. Of even broader usefulness in suggesting nationality is the poker face, more a way of saying something, or nothing, than a vocabulary. Because it embodies an attitude rather than a regional heritage, the frontiersman's poker face was more widely appropriated than his slang by writers presenting an American to the outside world; and from the very beginning, the outside world was inescapably present in the American consciousness. Distant though he was, the frontier settler was fair game for the polished easterner, the easterner himself open to wisecracks from abroad. The conflict embodied in such antitheses as country and city, West and East, became a theme common to writers as far removed from the conventional eighteenth- and nineteenth-century nature-civilization dichotomy as Twain, Henry James, and Sinclair Lewis. In many cases, what began as western humor was quickly pressed into service on behalf of the national honor.

One may think of the tall tale as a traditionally western way of cutting the pompous outsider down to size. The heaping up of exaggerations by a narrator who never cracks a smile, or in any other way indicates that he is joking, stretches to the breaking point the stranger's predisposition to assume the worst about the new region. The Texan who disdainfully put a braggart in his place by saying, "'Only after my fourth killing, gentlemen, did I consider myself worthy of becoming a citizen of Texas,'"[21] is satirizing an unthinking acceptance of malicious anti-Texas gossip; the previous speaker, with but one corpse to his credit, plays the role of straight man.

This is folk humor hot off the range, but the technique antedates the frontier. As a defense against slander, the tall tale and the poker face enabled no less a man than Benjamin Franklin to counteract falsehoods about America that were circulating in London in 1765. Rather than attack detractors in passionate rage, Franklin quietly admitted in a letter to a London newspaper that no story, however extravagant it seemed, could give a false picture of America, which was itself so grandiose. He went on to speak of the cod and whale fishing on the Great Lakes, concluding that

> Ignorant People may object that the upper Lakes are fresh, and that Cod and Whale are Salt Water Fish: But let them know, Sir, that Cod, like other Fish when attack'd by their Enemies, fly into any Water where they can be safest; that Whales, when they have a mind to eat Cod, pursue them wherever they fly; and that the grand Leap of the Whale in the Chase up the Fall of Niagara is esteemed, by all who have seen it, as one of the finest Spectacles in Nature.[22]

In fiction, however, the development of a poker-faced manner was a sophisticated refinement that occurred only after more violent techniques of presenting western antipathy toward eastern elegance had been fully explored. The rough squatter of Hannibal, in Sam Clemens' "The Dandy Frightening the Squatter" (1852), wastes no words, forthrightly punching the overarmed but unmanned Dandy into "the turbid waters of the Mississippi."[23] Sut Lovingood frightens his intrusive Irishman right back across the ocean, to the land where there are no snakes. Thompson's Doctor Jones is led to the circus for the single purpose of being "oudaciously tuck in," for Augusta, "the Philadelphia of the South," has rendered him objectionable to his fellows at Pineville. Even in real life, the young men of Hannibal, incensed at the citified airs of one of their number who had returned from Yale in all the appurtenances of eastern fashion, turned to action, not talk: they "dressed up the warped negro bell ringer in a travesty of him—which made him descend to village fashions."[24]

The country resents the city, the West resents the East, and the theme of this hostility toward what is different—and therefore threatening—is expressed in countless stories, first by those who were intent on capturing the feelings of the folk around them, regardless of where their own sympathies lay, and, later, by men who identified themselves at least partially with their adopted, or even natal, home on the frontier. This same opposition found its way into serious fiction as a contrast between America and Europe, although as early as Revolutionary times Royall Tyler's comedy—titled, of course, *The Contrast*—was elevating the manly American above the effete Englishman. By the last third of the nineteenth century, though, the contrast had become considerably more complex. For many writers, to place an American in a European context was to provide the *donnée* for infinitely suggestive adventures. This confrontation carries with it a minor, but interesting, literary problem: how shall the author establish implicitly the particular qualities of his characters' nationality without writing an essay? Mark Twain, in *The Innocents Abroad* (1869), points the way to one sort of solution through characters whose use of a poker face stamps them as Americans from a frontier rawer than a genteel reader will approve yet worthy of respect for its clear-sighted resistance to humbug.

The immediate impulse of Twain's traveling Yankee is to disguise emotion, whether fear of Europe as it threatens an American's self-image or awe of Europe as it suggests unexplored possibilities of experience. Accomplished poker-players that they are, they deceive for gain on the byways of the Continent as expertly as they might at the card table. When Twain-the-character and his friends in *The Innocents* plague a series of guides, all rechristened "Ferguson," the iron-visaged idiocy displayed leads to one very specific gain: "The guide was bewildered—nonplussed. He walked his legs off, nearly, hunting up extraordinary things, and exhausted all his ingenuity on us, but it was a failure; we never showed any interest in anything" (I, 306). By criticizing "Christopher Colombo's" poor penmanship, by asking if an Egyptian mummy is dead, the Doctor—who "asks the questions, generally, because he can keep his countenance, and look more like an inspired idiot, and throw more imbecility into the tone of his voice than any man that lives" (303)—forces the guide of the moment on to ever greater exertions.

Like any clever poker-player, the Doctor is versatile. When a guide persists in taking Twain, Dan, and the Doctor to silk stores rather than to the Louvre, the masquerade of boredom changes to one of simulated enthusiasm. As "Ferguson" foolishly persists in his commercial scheming, the Doctor's mounting anger expresses itself as aesthetic pleasure: "'Ah, the palace of the Louvre; beautiful, beautiful edifice! Does the Emperor Napoleon live here now, Ferguson?'" (115) And at the third silk store: "'At last! How imposing the Louvre is, and yet how small! how exquisitely fashioned! how charmingly situated! Venerable, venerable pile—'" (116). This reaction is, strictly speaking, irony, but, as an attitude adopted by the Doctor for slicing through a foreigner's deceit, it also belongs to the species "poker face."

When the Doctor stonily asks, "'Is, ah—is he dead?'" before every statue, he is clearly deceiving for gain. The guide, intent on drawing a conventional show of enthusiasm from the passive Doctor, works much harder than he is paid to do in the hopes of shattering his employer's calm. But there is another side to the coin. The Innocents are impressed by what they see, for if they were not, they would find no practical advantage in pretending to be bored. "We came very near expressing interest, sometimes—even admiration—it was very hard to keep from it" (306). But the pretense means more than just a desire to gain additional sights, as one sees when the group visits the vault beneath the Capuchin Convent. The walls are decorated by the dismembered skeletons of dead monks. The guide—in this case one of the monks who will some day add his mite to the communal fresco—has shown them everything, and now they stop to examine in particular one skeleton, robed and intact, whose skull has preserved "a weird laugh a full century old!" "It was the jolliest laugh, but yet the most dreadful, that one can imagine" (II,5). Terror and humor coalesce: "At this moment I saw that the old instinct was strong upon the boys, and I said we had better hurry to St. Peter's. They were trying to keep from asking, 'Is—is he dead?'" (5)

In this instance, the poker face gains a very real but immaterial advantage for its user: it allows him to inject humor into a situation that frightens him. Certainly this is a common technique all through *The Innocents Abroad*. When Twain, the American narrator, is overwhelmed by Europe, he can find relief by laughing at it, or simply by laughing, a response similar to that of Melville's Ishmael who emerges from his first violent brush with a whale to conclude that life's vicissitudes, from "small difficulties" to "extreme tribulation" and "peril of life and limb," must be taken "for a vast practical joke" if sanity is to be retained.[25] That Twain's American laughs does not mean, always, that he is happily at ease in his world.

Twain's awareness of the impact of Europe on Americans abroad is hardly the central theme of his fiction. Still, he helped to develop the terms through which American writers were to confront the Old World with representatives of the New. The fears and insecurities that Twain revealed through humor became the clichés of the future tourist class, whether from Lewis' Zenith or from James's New York City. The materials of the humorist became touchstones of allegiance for the novelists.

Like other Americans in Europe, the Innocent Abroad is troubled; the "dreadful" laugh that is "a full century old"— older than the town of Samuel Clemens' birth, or of most nineteenth-century Americans' birth—is different from anything Mark Twain has ever known. The very existence of the skeleton suggests a way of looking at life that is foreign, for the fashions of American interior decoration have never emulated the Capuchin vaults. Twain's fascination with that ancient, that noticeably "un-American," laugh suggests Lewis' Sam Dodsworth, who is at first intrigued by and attracted to the laughter of the Count von Obensdorf, his wife's future lover: "'Kind of like an American, this fellow—this count,' said Sam. 'got a sense of humor. . . .'" But Sam is wrong.

> "Oh no, it's a very different thing," Fran [Sam's wife] insisted. "He's completely European. Americans are humorous to cover up their worry about things. They think that what they do is immediately important and the world is waiting for it. The real European has a sense of a thousand years. . . behind him."[26]

Dodsworth does "worry about things." He cannot keep from himself "a deep and sturdy recognition of his own ignorance,"[27] and on many occasions we are told, more or less directly, that "he suddenly felt insecure."[28] When he successfully orders French station-attendants around, "he admitted that he was possibly being the brash Yankee of Mark Twain."[29] But Sam Dodsworth eventually chooses a European way of life, and Lewis pointedly foreshadows Sam's un-Americanism by contrasting his unexpected appreciation of art with "the Mark Twain tradition," in which "the American wife still marches her husband to galleries from which he tries to sneak away."[30] His appreciation is unexpected because Sam Dodsworth is first presented as being very much in the tradition: "He liked whiskey and poker,"[31] and his fondness for poker is referred to often enough and in the proper contexts to make it a metaphor of his desire to be with and like Americans.[32]

Now the American poker-player's approach to European art is established for all time by Mark Twain, and the establishment sanctioned by no less a pontiff than Henry James. Twain's Innocent tells us that he "could not help noticing how superior the copies were to the original. . . . Wherever you find a Raphael, a Rubens, a Michael Angelo, a

Caracci, or a Da Vinci (and we see them every day) you find artists copying them, and the copies are always the handsomest" (I, 190). Henry James gives us, in his *The American* (1877), the transitional step between the completely westernized narrator of *The Innocents Abroad* and the potential renegade of *Dodsworth*. Christopher Newman is a synthesis of American types. He looks back upon the isolated spirit of Natty Bumppo as "he laughed the laugh in which he indulged when he was most amused—a noiseless laugh, with his lips closed."[33] He shows a more sociable sort of frontier experience, too, for—like Twain—"Newman had set with Western humorists in knots, round cast-iron stoves, and seen 'tall' stories grow taller without toppling over, and his own imagination had learned the trick of piling up consistent wonders."[34] Finally, he is mythologized as an American titan in the "*légende*" of western wealth and power that the stout Duchess, Madame d'Outreville, invents for him,[35] a myth that will be echoed by Lewis in Dodsworth's determination, at the start of his travels,[36] to return to America and create such a city as is attributed to Newman.

In our first view of him, Newman is presented most simply as the "specimen of an American," as "the American type," and although his visit to the Louvre fills him, "for the first time in his life, with a vague self-mistrust,"[37] his habitual front possesses "that typical vagueness which is not vacuity, that blankness which is not simplicity."[38] He is aware of his fears, but, good American that he is, he is poker-faced. Like Sam Dodsworth, he has gambled quite literally, in business and in sport, "glad enough to play poker in St. Louis."[39] Unlike Twain's *persona*, he has come to Europe—as so many of James's people do—to learn; but his European education does not begin until after his first stroll through the Louvre, when he is most pointedly still the American: Newman looks "not only at all the pictures, but at all the copies that were going forward around them, . . . and if the truth must be told, he had often admired the copy much more than the original."

Newman's poker-faced admiration of Mlle. Nioche's copies soon gives way to an acknowledged emotional involvement with Claire de Cintré, and to Newman's efforts to register directly on his feelings a sense of Europe. Mark Twain, playing the game of the American in Europe, retains the poker face that Newman struggles to put off, that is torn from Dodsworth by fate. (Dodsworth is not trying to educate himself into an involvement with Europe; events conspire to educate and to involve him despite himself.) For Lewis and James as well as for Twain, the American approaching Europe is poker-faced, and his reactions to European culture and customs are similar, initially, for all three writers. As James's and Lewis' protagonists succumb in their respective ways to the lure of the Continent, they lose their poker-faced detachment that has served as a defense against involvement, but their point of departure is defined by Twain's Innocent.

The three authors are concerned with tracing three variations of their common theme. For James, the impact of Europe as a civilizing force on the visiting American—Christopher Newman, Isabelle Archer, Lambert Strether, et al.—is the central concern, whether the force initiates a progression that culminates in grandeur or in futility. Lewis' *Dodsworth*, as one of the many novels in which Lewis presents America as seen through the eyes of H.L. Mencken, stresses the tawdry quality of American society, touching on the world of George F. Babbitt and focusing on the insubstantial character of Fran Dodsworth's worship of all things European. The actual impact of Europe on Sam Dodsworth is great—he chooses to leave America and live in Italy—but the weight of Europe itself is felt less throughout the book than is the density of the America from which Sam turns. The behavior of Mark Twain's Innocent merely suggests the rejection of America, and even the suggestion is only occasional. Most of the time, he appears brashly complacent in his Americanism. Indeed, his fear of Europe drives him happily back to his native shores, although he captures undertones that will become more significant in Twain's later work.

Twain's protagonist is really the most subversive of the three. Happy though the traveler returned may be, his first official act is to summarize the pilgrimage for the New York *Herald*, as Twain in fact did do, and his summary is not flattering to his fellow-Americans. His sarcastic irony—"We always took care to make it understood that we were Americans—Americans!" (II, 401)—evokes such samples of nationalism as the expedition's criminal archeological activities among the pyramids and their bad manners among the French. Boorishness and ignorance are the two most conspicuous qualities of these wandering representatives of God's latter-day Chosen People, as their spokesman's newsletter paints them. There clearly is more to Twain's treatment of America than simpleminded adulation. His ambivalence is as real as James's and Lewis', although one must see it in a more finished work to appreciate it.

Twain's use of the theme—Europe and America, East and West—and the central image for embodying this theme (the poker face) both arise from his immediate background in the humor of the southwest, of the frontier. The same theme and the same image became equally part of the equipment of writers totally removed from both the frontier and the Southwest. Twain's use of this material differs from that of James and Lewis; the gap between Twain and his own tradition is equally significant. To be clear on this point one has only to remember Hank Morgan in Arthur's Court and Simon Suggs at his camp meeting: they are both slang-slinging adventurers, out for what they can get, but Hank's use of poker talk achieves effects that Simon's does not even suggest. Mark Twain's adaptation of the standard elements of frontier humor enlarged their usefulness for literary art. How radical some of his departures were we have yet to see.

Notes

1. See *Mark Twain and Southwestern Humor* (Boston: Atlantic-Little, Brown, 1959), pp. 6ff.
2. Quoted from Augustus B. Longstreet by Donald Day, "The Humorous Works of George W. Harris," *American Literature*, XIV (January, 1943), 393.
3. George Washington Harris, *Sut Lovingood: Yarns Spun by a 'Nat'ral Born Durn'd Fool'* (New York, 1867), p. 111.
4. Johnson J. Hooper, *Simon Suggs' Adventures* (1845, reprinted Philadelphia, 1881), p. 26.
5. *Major Jones's Chronicles of Pineville* (Philadelphia, 1843), pp. 99–135.
6. Hooper, *op.cit.*, p. 132.
7. *Ibid.*, p. 138.
8. *Ibid.*, pp. 142, 143–44.
9. Reprinted from the Nashville *Union and American*, February 28, March 2, and March 5, 1861, in *Sut Lovingood*, ed. Brom Weber (New York: Grove Press, 1954), pp. 219–37.
10. *Ibid.*, pp. 221–22.
11. *Mark Twain at Work* (Cambridge: Harvard University Press, 1942), p. 69.
12. All volume and page references, unless otherwise indicated, are to *The Writings of Mark Twain*, "Definitive Edition" (37 vols, New York: Harper & Bros., 1922–25).
13. Dixon Wecter, *Sam Clemens of Hannibal* (Boston: Houghton Mifflin, 1952), pp. 107–8.
14. In *Major Jones's Chronicles of Pineville*. Twain, says DeVoto, "was thoroughly familiar with Thompson's work" (*Mark Twain at Work*, p. 68n).
15. *Major Jones's Chronicles of Pineville*, p. 18.
16. Hooper, *op.cit.*, p. 141.
17. *Ibid.*, pp. 141–42.
18. *Ibid.*, 144–45.
19. In Edgar M. Branch, *The Literary Apprenticeship of Mark Twain* (Urbana: University of Illinois Press, 1950), p. 227.
20. Hooper, *op.cit.*, p. 136.
21. In Mody C. Boatright, *Folk Laughter on the American Frontier* (New York: Macmillan, 1949), p. 22.
22. Quoted in F. O. Matthiessen, *American Renaissance* (New York: Oxford University Press, 1941), p. 639.
23. Reprinted in Branch, *op.cit.*, p. 218.

24. Quoted from Mark Twain Papers by Henry Nash Smith in "Mark Twain's Images of Hannibal," *Texas Studies in English*, XXXVII (1958), 3.
25. *Moby-Dick*, chap. xlix, "The Hyena."
26. *Dodsworth* (New York: Modern Library ed., 1929), p. 231.
27. *Ibid.*, p. 121.
28. *Ibid.*, p. 76.
29. *Ibid.*, p. 112.
30. *Ibid.*, p. 119.
31. *Ibid.*, p. 11.
32. *Ibid.*, pp. 139, 140, 188, 190.
33. *The American* (Rinehart ed.; New York: Rinehart, 1949), p. 332. See Cooper's *The Prairie* for Natty's silent laugh (Rinehart ed.; New York: Rinehart, 1950), pp. 437 and *passim*.
34. *The American*, p. 98.
35. *Ibid.*, p. 212.
36. *Dodsworth*, p. 23.
37. *The American*, p. 2.
38. *Ibid.*, p. 3.
39. *Ibid.*, p. 21.

"A Curious Republican"

Louis J. Budd

I am a candidate for the legislature. I desire to tamper with the jury law. I wish to so alter it as to put a premium on intelligence and character.—Roughing It

By moving to Buffalo, in mid-August of 1869, Twain put himself well within the orbit of the Langdon family and what he described to his future father-in-law as a "high eastern civilization." There is no sign he was reluctant to raise his social level, however apologetic he may have felt about his rough edges. Though he did not court Olivia Langdon for her money, it impressed him almost as much as her breeding and posed another challenge. Instead of gloating like a prospector who had made a lucky haul, he took the proper Victorian attitude that he had to justify her father's faith in him by working harder than ever.

The respect with which he met Jervis Langdon can be seen indirectly through his "Open Letter to Commodore Vanderbilt," attacking a notorious Wall Street pirate for his personal crudities and "lawless violations of commercial honor."[1] When this drew a defense of Vanderbilt for creating more wealth and new jobs, Twain accepted it as "able bosh"—bosh because it nicked him as well as claiming too much for a ruthless profiteer but able because it persuasively stated the case for capitalists in general. His taunts had not meant to criticize solid businessmen, who in fact resented the

Chapter Three reprinted from *Mark Twain: Social Philosopher* (Bloomington: Indiana University Press, 1962), pp. 40-63, 221–223.

disruptive forays by the robber barons as much as anybody, and he felt no impulse to bait Langdon or ridicule him behind his back. Soon after pushing into the family circle Twain gladly tried to help him collect a half-million dollars from the city of Memphis for wooden pavement.[2] There must have been backslapping around the fireside when Twain's influence produced a scolding editorial in the New York *Tribune* that did some good.

Langdon's main energy went into a network of mines and retail outlets for coal. When some voices around Buffalo accused the big companies of price-fixing, Twain answered them firmly in his own newspaper with "The 'Monopoly' Speaks," which complained that the public was listening too naively to the consumers' side and argued that legitimate market pressures were driving up the price of coal as winter came on.[3] Though Langdon put up the $25,000 with which he bought into the *Express*, Twain would not have gone so far and so openly if he agreed with the other side or cared little about the economic principles involved. Even where his loyalties were not aroused, he took up serious issues as soon as he got oriented in his new job, vaguely hoping to lift the *Express* into the class of often quoted newspapers like the Springfield *Republican* or the Toledo *Blade*. This meant he could not ignore politics. Property holders, large or small, had their stake in the state and expected to be kept informed about it. Furthermore, while they looked down on the city boss and ward-heeler, most educated or well-to-do northerners already felt a proprietary concern in the future of the Republican party.

Having finally committed himself, Twain harried the Democrats with original material in the *Express*. A typical piece, "Inspired Humor," professed to see comedy in their latest call for an honest legislature in New York and derided them as hypocrites "whose religion is to war against all moral and material progress, and who never were known to divert to the erection of a school house moneys that would suffice to build a distillery."[4] His frontal attacks were reinforced by a then standard maneuver of pointing up news items the way he did with "A pig with a human head is astonishing South Carolina. Are they rare, there?" but it so happened in the fall of 1869 that baiting the Democrats was easier than praising the Republicans, at least in New York where the spoilsmen had taken over both sides and even worked together across party lines. Letting other hands keep the *Express* filled with partisan cheers, Twain used his positive moods on more basic Republican planks like the need to recall the greenbacks issued during the war—the point of his "Adventures in Hayti," another sketch that looks weightless today as it clowns about ridiculously high prices for everyday items.

After his furious debut as an editor Twain made the lecture rounds again and then put all his thoughts into getting married. When he got back to writing for the *Express* he was more impartial and relaxed but not aimless. Unfortunately, to know that "A Curious Dream"—about corpses that move their coffins to a better neighborhood—was lampooning the rundown state of a Buffalo cemetery does not make this grisly sketch any funnier. However, such insight builds alertness to worthwhile content behind the slapstick of pieces like "A Mysterious Visit," an account of his dealings with a tax assessor which finally criticized the wealthy sharpers who falsify their returns. This restless dislike of hypocrisy soon killed his dream of being an editor. After openly complaining that "Cain is branded a murderer so heartily and unanimously in America, only because he was neither a Democrat or Republican," he acted out his disgust in "Running for Governor," a parody on a state election in New York that saw two corrupt machines splatter each other with muck. Ominously, this parody attacked the press of both parties without favor.

For the rest of his life after leaving the *Express* Twain thought of most newspaper editors as noisy puppets, and in 1871 he willingly took a big loss to set himself free. Even before then be branched out in monthly "Memoranda" for the *Galaxy* but not as an escape from writing about current affairs.

Along with frothier humor he kept turning out items like "The Coming Man," a superbly witty warning against making some ward-heeler our new minister to England. Put together while the "Memoranda" were appearing, *Mark Twain's (Burlesque) Autobiography and First Romance* had about the same mixture of ingredients. It extended his campaign to project a colorful front and gave further sign of his literary instincts, but its third facet, a sequence of cartoons on the Erie Railroad scandal, showed he had not deserted from guarding the public conscience.

Though Cornelius Vanderbilt was the best-known villain in the Erie scandal it also established Jay Gould's lurid fame, and much later Twain would pick Gould as the prime corrupter of our "commercial morals." Even in 1870 there was widespread comment in this vein—especially by conservatives like brahmin Charles Francis Adams, Jr., who also protested at length that such doings sapped the health of sound business. Keyed by apt variations on the nursery jingle about the house that Jack built, the cartoons in the *Burlesque Autobiography* proved that Twain had gathered every whisper about Jim Fisk's sex life and the payoffs to judges and editors.[5] In fact he capitalized on popular reaction instead of saying anything new; cartoons like those in his book were common and the parody on the nursery rime belonged to current folksay. But he was revolted rather than amused by the Erie tragi-comedy, which attuned him to the looming furor about Tweed's burglaries and other scandals that lead to *The Gilded Age*.

In the meantime, this mounting disgust was allowed to have only a side-effect on *Roughing It* (1872). His appetite was whetted by a steady sale for *The Innocents Abroad*, and he worked hard at spinning another best-seller. More fiction than history wherever the change might please the reader, *Roughing It* is his sunniest book. If it offended Senator Stewart, he was being too touchy. If its passing sarcasms really belittled the old territorial legislature, Twain's experiences could have inspired a much more trenchant critique. Indeed, when he refreshed his mind in 1871 by going over some

"A Curious Republican"

clippings of his feisty columns for the *Territorial Enterprise* he scribbled a comment about the resemblance between Carson City graft and the national scandals that were building up. A few years later he made promising notes for a book about a Senator Bonanza, who routinely bought off state legislatures. Much later he jotted down ideas for a social history from 1850 that would include the effects of the "California sudden-riches disease."[6] Still, though it gave edge to *The Gilded Age*, little of this insight showed up in *Roughing It*, least of all in the now ignored Appendix C—which jeered at an alkali populist who was resisting the push of the mining companies for cozier tax laws.

Roughing It also gave darker signs of misdirected bias from Twain's western years, especially when the Indians slouched across its pages. From the time he crossed the plains he felt only contempt for the red men, and loudly and often said so. In *The Innocents Abroad*, his celebrated ear failing him, he orated against Tahoe as a primitive name not good enough for the famous lake—where he had carelessly burned a stand of trees while toying with the notion of staking out a rich timber claim. In the *Galaxy* he derided the Indian with a white settler's passion as a "filthy, naked scurvy vagabond" whose extinction by the army should continue in spite of the "wail of humanitarian sympathy" from the older sections of the country.[7] There is no good reason why he reacted so violently. Dan De Quille, his crony in Nevada, took a much kinder, more relaxed attitude, and Bret Harte could burlesque James Fenimore Cooper's stagy figures without winking at mistreatment of their flesh and blood counterparts. The ugly truth is that Twain as yet had little respect for any peoples who were outside the pattern of an industrial society. Though he managed to see more humor in tropical languor than in the Digger Indians' struggle to subsist, he also came down harder on the Hawaiian natives than he had in the letters he revised to swell his book to subscription size.

The circle of his sympathy was still actually too small to include even all classes of white Americans. In spite of his eloquent if incidental tribute to the forty-niners as "stalwart, muscular, dauntless young braves," he grimaced at the heavy "scum" on the western surge and, damning politicians as their "dust-licking pimps and slaves," fumed about the absurdity of letting this scum serve on juries. With a steadier eye on his intentions than usual, he gave an exotic picture of the mining frontier; but his colors were occasionally somber or clashing. The continual references in *Roughing It* to the "flush times" suggest that he had a secondary motif in mind and, like another old Whig, meant to highlight the ludicrous yet deplorable crumbling of order before the speculative flood. Somewhat lamely he rang the same note as Joseph G. Baldwin's *The Flush Times of Alabama and Mississippi* in his final "moral": "If you are of any account, stay home and make you way by sober diligence."

Roughing It was western and democratic in the finest sense of these terms only when Twain described himself as a tenderfoot who fraternized with seedy prospectors and shared their sourdough dreams, when readers were asked to take Scotty Briggs as a man of sterling character under his roughness and profanity or were assured that though Dick Baker was "slenderly educated, slouchily dressed and clay-soiled" his heart was "finer metal than any gold his shovel ever brought to light." Scotty's slang and Dick's muscular idiom belong to the supreme achievement of Twain's personal democracy—the sinewy vernacular that controls the choicest passages of *Roughing It*. To adapt a figure he once exploited, he was better at the tune than the words in 1871—his political attitudes needed reshaping but he rose to magnificent cadences when he chanted the virtues of his motley friends. Later, in *Huckleberry Finn* and *A Connecticut Yankee*, the vernacular style would support themes greater than robust camaraderie, and the result would be even more satisfying.

Appropriately, Twain dedicated *Roughing It* to Calvin Higbie, another "Genial Comrade" of his Washoe days. But he had first planned instead on honoring Cain as a consolation for "his misfortune to live in a dark age that knew not the beneficent Insanity Plea" to excuse his murder of Abel. This uninspired idea at least proves that Twain was not lost in a haze of Washoe memories. When a trial in 1870 set the precedent for pleading mental illness as a defense, he had reacted quickly with two protests in the Buffalo *Express* and another in the *Galaxy*, opposing what he took to be merely a legal dodge that interfered with the state's main job—the punishment of thieves and murderers.[8] It is only fair to realize that he was staggered by the first impact of questions that are still troublesome to modern minds when the defense rushes to plead temporary insanity, and that many of his contemporaries were just as afraid of encouraging crime through softness. Before he started coming around to a more humane stand, he also got excited abut juries that helped to pamper the sinners against property rights and personal safety. *Roughing It* erupted with criticism for our jury system as the "most ingenious and infallible agency for *defeating* justice that human wisdom could contrive"; and, just as *The Gilded Age* was being finished, he raged openly at the stalling and softsoaping of the defense in a highly publicized case of wanton murder.

The friends Twain was finding in New England had no reason to mistrust him as a brash westerner who undervalued law and order, even if he wore a sealskin overcoat or was likely to veer suddenly into clowning. Indeed it soon became evident that the clowning could be harnessed to their solemn purposes, as when he dashed off a long and madly punning "ballotd" in 1871 about how the Democrats had tried to steal the last election for governor of Connecticut. Somebody, perhaps in the Hartford *Courant* office, saw fit to print it as a broadside.[9] As always making himself at home had included mixing in local politics; in old age he recalled guiltily that once he even gave twenty-five dollars to buy votes after being assured the Democrats had started playing dirty first.[10] Such close partisanship demanded of course that he do his special bit in national elections too. On the day the 1872 campaign formally began he sent the Hartford *Courant* an unsigned skit titled "The Secret of Dr. Livingstone's Continued Voluntary Exile," which claimed that the missionary, recently contacted in the heart of Africa, had decided to unpack his trunks and "unlearn" his "civilization" because of disgust at the news of Horace Greeley's accepting the Democrats' support for the presidency.[11] Committed at least as much to the Republican party as to its general, Twain hailed the results of the election as a "prodigious victory for Grant—I mean, rather, for civilization and progress."

In spite of deserting his post on the Buffalo *Express*, he had obviously remained an active citizen who studied his daily newspaper, and not just any newspaper either. Around 1870 he toyed with "Interviewing the Interviewer," which would have scolded the New York *Sun* for aiming to "achieve the applause of the bone and sinew of the backstreets and the cellars."[12] He had especially come to admire the New York *Tribune*; and, when there was a fight in 1872 over its future, he showed inside knowledge of the men and issues involved.[13] After Whitelaw Reid came out on top against the odds, Twain congratulated him, "I grieved to see the old Tribune wavering & ready to tumble into the common slough of journalism & God knows I am truly glad you saved it." At this time Reid was prominent for imploring the better classes to counteract the tyrannical, gullible majority as well as the party boss.

Less than a week after he took over the top *Tribune* slot, Reid asked Twain for "something, no matter what" and soon arranged for two long letters on Hawaii, which was again in the headlines because American planters there were again pushing for a closer link with the United States. In these letters Twain deployed his humor with a politician's touch, genially approving the royal claims of the planters' choice but echoing the *Tribune*'s distaste for the expansionist clique here and making the Kanakas look undesirable as fellow Americans.[14] Feeling secure as a valuable sport player on the new *Tribune* team, he also sent in several unsolicited letters, which were published promptly, and a telegram (signed

"Public Virtue") protesting against the raise in salary that Congress had given itself. With obvious self-satisfaction he chortled to Reid: "God knows I was intended for a statesman. I can solve any political problem that ever was invented."[15] He saw no difficulty either in expecting the *Tribune* to help the advance buildup for *The Gilded Age*. Before he suddenly decided that Reid was a "contemptible cur" and the *Tribune* must not get a review copy, there was even an editorial on the forthcoming feast of humor and wisdom. Seemingly the break came because Twain expected still more and flashier free advertising. In any event, though he added broader reasons for hating Reid as time went by, the split was personal rather than political at first. Unfortunately, it ended the flow of his squibs and letters for the *Tribune*. Reacting with his usual vehemence, he stopped buying it, much less writing for it; the dignified New York *Evening Post* became his supplement to the Republican fare of the local *Courant*. However, he had read the *Tribune* carefully between 1871 and 1873, and skimming any week's run from that period will supply at least one clue to the reference in some passage of *The Gilded Age*.

Of course *The Gilded Age* also had deeper roots drawing on Twain's basic attitudes and past experience. His Nevada days had left a suspicious contempt for men like James W. Nye, tagged by several reviewers as the senator who mails seven crates of personal odds and ends as official matter; and serving as a private secretary and a reporter in Washington had broadened his insight. Without really needing it he got a quick review by going back in July, 1870 to lobby for a bill favored by "our Tennesseans."[16] This bill probably involved the famous Clemens tract of land though the tie-up was fittingly so devious that nobody had figured it out. Exploiting old friendships he bustled around the capital for several days and, whether for business or curiosity's sake, had lunch with venal Senator Samuel C. Pomeroy. More out of disgust than prophecy, he grimly wrote to his wife: "Oh, I have gathered material enough for a whole book! This is a perfect gold mine." When the chance to collaborate on a novel with Charles Dudley Warner did come along, he was fully primed.

The fact that Warner co-authored *The Gilded Age* (1874) poses no serious problem. Twain wrote almost all the political chapters, though Warner's daily routine as editor of the Hartford *Courant* led him into the latest tunnels under public affairs. Whatever the reason for this sharing of the work, they agreed easily on the line to follow; if any minor snarls did develop, Twain was mostly the one pulling to the right. In an essay published the same year as their novel, Warner darkly preached against "loose commercial and political morality," but he also showed himself stoutly hopeful about the democratic way and nettled rather than dismayed by the growing sores of corruption.[17] Anybody who sees Hartford life as a reactionary pressure on Twain should compare Warner's ideas with his: seldom will Warner be found the more conservative, even in the 1880's.

Above all, Twain and Warner could work together smoothly because neither wanted to change anything more basic than manners and public morals. Accepting the framework of their society, they flayed minor evils like steamboat racing, religious journals that took dishonest advertising, or the rudeness of clerks and railroad conductors. In spirit, this last, recurring note harmonized with the heavy satire on parvenus who ape the ways of their betters and with the key epithet of "gilded," which appeals to owners of the real thing. Righteous gentility also guided the approach to a more serious matter, the health of our system for punishing criminals. Besides raising angry eyebrows at allowing temporary insanity as a defense, the handling of Laura's trial—spotted in New York City for the purpose—sneered at the fiasco of Boss Tweed's first trip to court. Braham, Laura's crafty lawyer, openly parodied the John Graham who protected Tweed with foxy calm but broke into sobs over his own pleadings for mercy to his client.[18] Furthermore, *The Gilded Age* stressed the Irish background of the jury and judge so heavily that anybody who had heard of Tammany Hall got the point.

The references to affairs in Washington were just as obvious for the informed. Laura's career there fitted in with a buzzing about woman lobbyists of uncertain virtue; more specifically, in the description of Lincoln's statue, alert readers found a direct criticism of a sculptress who had lately inveigled a commission through her youthful charm rather than proved ability.[19] Yet in good Victorian fashion the Lauras turned out much less blamable than men, and especially congressmen, whose trading of legislative favors for everything from railroad passes to stock in shady corporations was typified in *The Gilded Age* by giving one busy lawmaker the name of Trollop. There were also plenty of damning allusions to specific solons; and Dilworthy matched his real life model, Senator Pomeroy, with daring closeness both in mannerisms and the brazenly venal dealings that an ignominious Senate committee refused to censure. For once Twain was not exaggerating: the truth about "Old Subsidy" Pomeroy or his henchmen was extreme enough and too obvious; and when even Colonel Sellers took insult at the idea of becoming a congressman, he merely capped a standard joke of the day.

Nobody had trouble seeing also that Twain and Warner's immediate lesson was, as one magazine put it, "PURIFY THE SUFFRAGE." Yet *The Gilded Age* said little to prevent future Dilworthys from refining platitudes into bullion when it called for a return to the "old-style" congressman—the founding fathers can easily be used for a smokescreen too. It was more sensible when it scolded "good and worthy" citizens for continuing to "sit comfortably at home and leave the true source of our political power (the 'primaries') in the hands of saloon-keepers, dog-fanciers and hod-carriers," though this slur on the hod-carriers, added to numerous other slurs on voters who had a brogue or whose mouths were shaped for living on potatoes, put far too much blame on Irish immigrants. In its economics *The Gilded Age* was just as clearly genteel, preaching against the hunger "to get on in the world by the omission of some of the regular processes which have been appointed from of old." This has Warner's ring and like other, often stuffier passages in the Gilded Age is a happy reminder that Twain was at least not given to buttering the gospel of hard work with Christianity. But his basic attitude was just as narrow. In 1867, deploring the postwar boom, he had predicted a crash and growled like a bondholder that "the sooner it comes in its might and restores the old, sure, plodding prosperity, the better."

The Gilded Age carried over this suspicion of the boom but did not ask if the profit motive was dangerous in other ways. In fact Twain's preface for the British edition hedged strongly about "speculativeness":

> It is a characteristic which is both bad and good for both the individual and the nation. Good, because it allows neither to stand still, but drives both forever on, toward some point or another which is ahead, not behind nor at one side. Bad, because the chosen point is often badly chosen.

He went on to tip the balance cleanly, "Still, it is a trait which it is of course better for a people to have and sometimes suffer from than to be without." To forestall charges of hypocrisy from critics in the 1920's, he should also have added that he still drew a sharp line between the piratical raids by Gould or the will of the wisp chases by a Sellers and the healthy, shrewd business gambles almost always backed some invention—from the adjustable vest-strap to the typesetter—that was supposed to increase human comfort or productivity.

The closing chapters of The Gilded Age solemnly totted up the rewards for the different kinds of enterprise. Named for his true mettle, Philip Sterling made good after toiling hard and long and enduring a penance of discouragement for his passing interest in wildcat ventures. His success was a practical reprimand to Harry Brierly and Mr. Bolton, among others, for drifting into the clutch of promoters who angled for favors from legislatures. Digging on his own, he found a coal mine while the lobbyists went bankrupt or, like Colonel

Sellers, retreated from Washington nursing a worthless old trunk. To pull off this contrast it was necessary to glide over the Union Pacific clique and play up tinhorn operators, brokers of mudflat real-estate, and the idle apprentice who sank toward the fleshpot of federal subsidies—small fry who could not have got past Gould's secretary.

Modern critics of the robber barons have found ammunition in *The Gilded Age*, and some Wall Street entrepreneurs of 1874 must have hoped it would flop. Yet Twain and Warner were only asking for a chaste retreat. As they were getting their book into shape, E. L. Godkin, who rallied the middle class with his new weekly *Nation*, argued that corruption mainly came from the power of Congress to make grants, and he concluded: "The remedy is simple. The Government must get out of the 'protective' business and the 'subsidy' business and the 'improvement' and 'development' business. It must let trade, and commerce, and manufactures, and steamboats, and railroads, and telegraphs alone." *The Gilded Age* fully backed up this demand for pure laissez faire instead of legislative planning, and its main case of boodle hit the reformer as hard as the fixer. With no harm to what was a thin part of the plot anyway, it might have used the Tennessee land for satirizing the prodigal right-of-way grants to railroads or the windfalls from the protective tariff rather than the relatively minor larceny in a bill to found a university open to any race, creed, or sex. In fact *The Gilded Age* showed no sympathy for the common man economically or otherwise. Angrily, it implied that he deserved none since he let jackals like Tweed or Pomeroy into the public larder and was too ready to share the spoils, and one British reviewer actually took it as a terrifying picture of mob rule. Though this was too strong it did sneer at the coarser varieties in the democratic garden, saying of the jury at the Hawkins trial: "Low foreheads and heavy faces they all had; some had a look of animal cunning, while the most were only stupid. The entire panel formed that boasted heritage commonly described as the 'bulwark of our liberties.'" *The Gilded Age* was the first serious outbreak of Twain's lifelong suspicion that the mass of mankind is venal, doltish, feckless, and tyrannical, that the damn fools make up a majority anywhere.

Distinctly less penetrating than John W. De Forest's *Honest John Vane* (1875), which covered similar ground, the scolding of speculators and grafters in *The Gilded Age* only pleaded for a middle-class code of doing business. Its readers had not bought a Trojan horse in a book that fleshed out the longing of its preface for a happy hunting ground "where there is no fever of speculation, no inflamed desire for sudden wealth, where the poor are all simple-minded and contented, and the rich are all honest and generous, where society is in a condition of primitive purity and politics is the occupation of only the capable and the patriotic." There was a limit to how much of this line Twain himself could swallow, and "Life As I Find It," dashed off around the same time, parodied the homily about the boy who got his big break because his elders saw him thriftily picking up stray pins. Still *The Gilded Age* did not even side with the discontented farmers in the current debate, unheretical as their "granges" were. If the conservative side can be defined as putting fear of "paternalism" above corrective federal or state action and elitism above majority rule, then Twain's alignment was clear beneath the American habit of mixing ideas loosely.

Elsewhere he expanded on two matters handled too loosely in *The Gilded Age* for firm sense. His diatribe on "The License of the Press" indicates he had meant the novel to attack the standards of American journalism—and with just cause, seeing the way most newspapers served political and corporate masters. Yet, at least partly out of character, he merely charged that the press too often made fun of religion as well as purveying cheap sensation that further confused the "stupid" majority. Ironically, this hauteur had one happy influence. As late as 1871 he had planned to amuse the lyceums with "An Appeal in Behalf of Extended Suffrage to Boys"—a satire on the "general tendency of the times," meaning especially the rise of the suffragettes—[20] but in 1873 his essay on "The Temperance Crusade and Woman's Rights" argued that it was unreasonable to keep educated ladies from voting "while every ignorant whisky-drinking foreign-born savage in the land may hold office, help to make the laws, degrade the dignity of the former and break the latter at his own sweet will"—a position still short of Nook Farm's ideas on the subject.

These two essays, it should be noted, were done for the sake of progress. For his next bread and butter work after *The Gilded Age* Twain planned a book about England and negotiated with Thomas Nast to illustrate it. They had tried to lay out a joint project several times before, as when Nast proposed to do cartoons for a pamphlet of items that would include "The Great Beef Contract." When Twain approached him in 1873, "Nasty" Nast—as his enemies called him—was the leading political cartoonist of a hard-hitting period: this was exactly his chief lure for Twain, who assured his publisher that his text would fit Nast's genius at caricature. Their dealings fell through again, but Twain's offer is a good sign of the mixed purposes that kept his book from ever getting written.

Though he could straddle as nimbly as a circus rider, in 1872-73 his feeling about England galloped off in directions too varied even for him. Like most working journalists he had now and then twisted the lion's tail since the Civil War. Yet, though he was interested in British history and literature and swayed by the Yankee intellectuals who were eager to close the widened breach, his preface for a British edition of *The Innocents Abroad* played on the "mother-country" theme with a fervor beyond the call of politeness or profit. One enduring side of Twain paid homage to tradition, the more bejewelled and escutcheoned the better. When he trod British soil in 1872 for his first visit, he lingered awestruck in famous abbeys or castles to exclaim eventually, "God knows I wish we had some of England's reverence for the old & great."[21] His awe flowed over into admiring the Victorian present and confiding to his wife that he "would rather live in England than America—

which is treason." British audiences made the affection mutual when he started to lecture.

But he was weighing more than the nobby guards at Buckingham Palace or the crowds at his lectures. A few years afterward he claimed that he had not written a breezy book on England because he had been able to think only about "deep problems of government, taxes, free trade, finance" during his visit.[22] If this was tomfoolery it even took in the Hartford *Courant*, the newspaper least likely to misunderstand Twain. If he had typically overstated, his next comments made sober sense: England was perhaps the "most real republic" in the world, with shortcomings no worse than ours and a civil service less infested by party leeches. Over-reacting against the miasma of Grantism, he admired the British blend of elitism and democracy much more than he expected to when he asked Nast to become his illustrator.

This does not mean he had been undiscriminating as he affably raked in his lecture fees and looked after his copyrights. Anyway, he could not ignore party lines if he wanted to: the Tory-Conservative element was hostile to Yankees and quick to say so. After allowing for casual socializing it becomes clear that, like most American visitors, he gravitated toward Liberal circles, especially in his contacts with newspaper men. He was taken to Parliament by a political editor who wanted him to write for a Liberal weekly; and Frank D. Finlay, owner of the Belfast *Northern Whig* (which stuck to the Gladstone banner in hostile territory), soon rated as "one of the closest friends I have."[23] The effect of such friendships probably underlay both the six hostile pages about Prince Albert in his notebook and his cautious sympathy toward the Tichborne claimant, supposedly a prime example of the freaks that fascinated him.[24] Though he had several reasons for compiling a special scrapbook about this fight over a titled inheritance, it had become a favorite subject for Radical orators, who charged that Tory prejudice and Catholic influence were swaying the courts and denied that the claimant's sloppy manners proved he could not be blue-blooded. Twain's general scrapbook for 1872 also saved other anti-Conservative clippings about a rally to oppose the state church, a non-Anglican who refused on principle to pay tithes, and the wastefully archaic game laws that the nobility kept in force.

Unknowingly, he had stored up ammunition for *A Connecticut Yankee*, but he did a little sniping even before he finally left England in 1873. The O'Shah letters chuckled over the knighting of nonentities who had well-placed friends; a speech before a London social club joked cuttingly about the new ruling that kept plebeians out of Hyde Park. No matter how humbly he looked up to the self-made prince of industry, he held on to a Yankee Doodle hostility toward social class that was based on birth, as he showed again in his parting shot. Nettled because the nobility failed to grace his lecture audiences, he had apologized—in a letter to a stiffly Tory paper—for not arranging the "attendance of some great members of the Government to give distinction to my entertainment," and then swung into a mock alibi about having hired dressy wax figures that got ruined in transit. This was reprinted in Finlay's *Northern Whig* with the comment that "Mark Twain has been audaciously poking fun at the snobbish tendencies of the great British public."[25]

For the present this letter was his most forceful statement on England though he had time and energy to spare for the book he had counted on as his next bestseller. Disgusted by Grantism he liked what he saw there but vacillated between reverence for stability under Queen Victoria and enthusiasm for middle-class reform under Gladstone. Perhaps he was also baffled by problems more complex in many ways than those at home and posed along unfamiliar lines; while attracted to the Liberals mostly, he switched erratically to Conservative or Radical ideas. To complicate matters further, if he happened to think in terms of the Old World against the New he suddenly changed his tone, as when his preface for the British edition of *The Gilded Age* ended with a hopeful forecast on American politics. The fumbling in the O'Shah letters indicates clearly that his confusions would have sapped the fiber of any book he completed.

No major indecisions silenced or lowered his voice as he turned again to the latest affairs at home, picking up where *The Gilded Age* had left off. When a Hartford crowd met a hometown businessman after he was forced out of the cabinet by the sharks around President Grant, Twain chimed in with an appropriate bit of comedy.[26] The letter he sent to a supper for the local Knights of Saint Patrick was much less genial; imploring their patron saint to drive out reptiles like a secretary of war who saved $12,000 annually from a salary of $8,000, it witheringly scolded the President and the swarming grafters of both parties. Restlessly searching for the source of the widespread "ulcers" he settled more heavily than before on universal suffrage, elaborating his diagnosis with a paper for the Monday Evening Club and summarizing it with epigrams such as one sent to a Tammany satrap, "We know there is Unrestricted Suffrage, we *think* there is a Hell; but the question is, which do we *prefer*?"[27] His family and friends must have heard Twain's own answer many times. A house guest from Boston, who kept a diary, recorded about her host:

> He has lost all faith in our government. This wicked ungodly suffrage, he said, where the vote of a man who knew nothing was as good as the vote of a man of education and industry; this endeavor to equalize what God had made unequal was a wrong and a shame. He only hoped to live long enough to see such a wrong and such a government overthrown.

After a visit filled with lively talk she concluded that this "growing man of forty" was in "dead earnest" about life.

As Howells always claimed, it seems that to know Twain well was to take him seriously. Yet his reputation in 1875 was far short of this discovery, and he had the *Atlantic Monthly* for October publish "The Curious Republic of Gondour" without his name, not to hide from rebuttals but to get a respectful hearing. This outburst charged that the "bottom layer of society"—the "ignorant and non-taxpaying classes"—had seized control through the ballot-box, raising the problem of how to reinstate the power of "money, virtue, and intelligence." Bowing to the demagogic realities Twain merely proposed a system of extra votes but allowed these votes so generously for more property or higher education that the "hod-carriers" and their cohorts from the "ginmills" and jails would become a minority on election day at least. It is cheering to note at least that women voted in his utopian Gondour and held office, that free education ran up through the colleges, that the educated served as a "wholesome check" on the rich and as "vigilant and efficient protectors of the great lower rank," and that a top quota of votes was a higher status symbol than money. Though he never said so again, some scholars gratefully emphasize the fact that Twain also suggested more votes for education than property and implied he would mostly go in for college degrees under such a system.

The best perspective, however, is to see how closely "The Curious Republic of Gondour" was connected with other warnings that natural-rights democracy had run aground. During the stock-taking for the centennial of glorious 1776, many disciples of Manchester Liberalism openly doubted that the mob could police itself or else refrain from a feckless tyranny of its own; since monarchy belonged to the outmoded past, they called for a new patrician leadership based on brains and wealth. In the context of this debate, which raged almost as hotly here as in England, Twain's scheme of plural votes was not eccentric—though simpler proposals for giving a vote only to property-owners got heavier support. The skeptics about pure democracy also found in Gondour related features that they had been talking up like permanent judgeships and a civil service system staffed by a career elite who ran the government impartially and stopped the extorting of bribes. Such reforms, it was fondly hoped, would protect business from pickpockets like Tweed and control pirates like Vanderbilt who hired politicians to sanction their raids and would clear the road for the grand march of technology.

By now Twain had an ungilded, twenty-four-carat right to class himself among the propertied and almost as much right to consider himself well informed, with more than enough leisure to think, talk, read—the house guest from Boston said "study"—and write about what interested him. To help support this leisure he could still drop back into empty vaudeville; though Howells' review found a "growing seriousness of meaning in the apparently unmoralized drolling" the items Twain chose for *Sketches, New and Old* (1875) were more often nonsense than meaningful satire. Designed to ride a rising market for stories about boys, *The Adventures of Tom Sawyer* (1876) was another offering with a shrewd eye on his expenses though it showed more concern for ideas by quietly refracting his characters through his deepening moral skepticism. Also adult in effect, but conventionally so, was its close variation on the popular success story with the climactic boon of a fortune rightly earned. All except his best novels would assuringly end with a big cash award to somebody deserving: the emphasis on the treasure in *Tom Sawyer* as against Jim's freedom in *Huckleberry Finn* typifies the gap between the two books.

The explicit touches of social doctrine in *Tom Sawyer* were not always so reassuring. While Injun Joe fitted the local color, his cold cruelty was meant to spread the alarm about misguided softness toward criminals. In February 1876 one of Twain's strangely assorted friends sent him a general petition already endorsed by Longfellow, Whittier, and men of matching stature. He jotted on the envelope, "From that inextinguishable dead beat who has infested legislatures for 20 years trying to put an end to capital punishment. No answer."[28] For Injun Joe's case a petition was signed freely, and many "tearful and eloquent" meetings produced a committee of "sappy" women to "wail around the governor, and implore him to be a merciful ass and trample his duty under foot." Such acidities kept *Tom Sawyer* from turning saccharine as they steadily played over the townspeople drifting behind its plot. When shiftless Muff Potter was framed, the town discovered he was a murderous-looking rascal and talked about a lynching; when he was cleared, the "fickle, unreasoning world took Muff Potter to its bosom and fondled him as lavishly as it had abused him before."

Intermittently, suspicions about mass man had assailed Twain almost from the start, long before he climbed up in the world—though his first fictional use of Hannibal obviously did not record memories from the bottom layer in that village. As for his broodings about the democratic process, they would have come no matter where he was living in 1875. Reasonable cause was available to anybody who read the magazines and newspapers, and Twain was making a dogged effort to think for himself. In religion he had already moved beyond the relaxed dogma of Nook Farm, and his later feeling that he had long hidden the boldest edge of his mind referred partly to these furtive probings. But he mainly used political examples to carry the point of his dark conclusion in 1905 that "free speech is the privilege of the dead."[29] If this included his ideas on government during his first years in the Hartford house, it is because he was aware of standing often to the right of his friends as a curious Republican—hot to pry into current events but badly tempted to doubt that democracy was worth saving.

At least what he said in public made good sense to some people. The Chicago *Times* for January 27, 1876, reported:

> Mark Twain was proposed as an independent candidate for the mayor of Hartford, Conn. . . Mr. Twain, himself a considerable property-owner, would, it is intimated, accept the nomination. . . . The Hartford people believe that he would give them a decent police force, and would not be the tool of any caucus or set of politicians.

But snatches of his "Punch, brothers, punch," jingle were run in between these sentences. The country liked Twain as a funnyman and, considering his frightful monthly bills, he could not afford as yet to wish otherwise.

Notes

1. *Packard's Monthly*, I (March, 1869), 89–91; Dixon Wecter, ed., *Mark Twain to Mrs. Fairbanks* (San Marino, CA, 1949), 86–7.
2. Mark Twain Papers (hereafter, MTP), autobiog. dict. of Feb. 16, 1906; Albert Bigelow Paine, *Mark Twain: An Autobiography* (NY, 1924) II: 135; New York *Tribune,* June 15, 1869, p. 4; MTP, copies of letters from Twain to Whitelaw Reid, dated [June] 15 and June 26, 1869.
3. Dixon Wecter, ed., *The Love Letters of Mark Twain* (NY, 1949), 68–69, 108–09; Buffalo *Express*, Aug. 20, 1869. There is a core of *Express* items that can be assigned clearly to Twain; I use those assembled in MTP (HNS).
4. "People and Things," Aug. 18, 31, Sept. 1, 1869; "Inspired Humor," Aug. 19; "Which?", Aug. 24; "The Democratic Varieties," Aug. 31; "The Legend of the Sharks," Sept. 11; Franklin R. Rogers, *Mark Twain's Burlesque Patterns* (Dallas, 1960), 114–16.
5. In MTP, a letter dated Dec. 31, 1870, from Isaac E. Sheldon, publisher of the *Burlesque Autobiography*, shows Twain was a moving spirit behind the cartoons.
6. Samuel C. Webster, *Mark Twain, Business Man* (Boston, 1946), 115; Henry Nash Smith, *Mark Twain of the "Enterprise"* (Berkeley, 1957), 100; MTP, DV 791—notes for Senator Bonanza story; Kenneth R. Andrews, *Nook Farm: Mark Twain's Hartford Circle* (Cambridge, Mass., 1950), 238.
7. "The Noble Red Man," X (Sept., 1870), 427–28.
8. Albert Bigelow Paine, ed., *Mark Twain's Letters* (NY, 1917), 188; "The New Crime" and "Our Precious Lunatic," *Express*, April 16, May 14, 1870; "Unburlesquable Things," Galaxy, X (July, 1870), 137–38.
9. "A Ballotd. Owed phor the Tymz; Not the Knusepaper" (copy in Yale Univ. Lib.); it was signed "Twark Main." Blanck, *Bibliography of American Literature,* II, item 3596, doubts Twain's authorship but offers no evidence. Andrews, III, notes how closely Nook Farm followed this election.
10. MTP, Nbk 36 (1903), 8.
11. July 20, 1872, p. 2, the *Courant* announced for Grant of course. As a *Tribune* contributor Twain had good reason not to sign this attack, but his authorship is established by a letter from C.D. Warner, dated July 19,1872 (MTP), as well as by obvious similarities with Twain's speech before the Whitefriars Club-reported in New York *Sun*, Aug. 7, 1872.
12. MTP, DV 306—apparently unpublished.

13. Arthur L. Vogelback has written three excellent articles that are relevant: "Mark Twain: Newspaper Contributor," *American Literature*, XX (May, 1948), 111–28; "Mark Twain and the Tammany Ring," *PMLA*, LXX (March, 1955), 69–77; "Mark Twain and the Fight for Control of the *Tribune*," *American Literature*, XXVI (Nov., 1954), 374–83.

14. Vogelback, "Twain: Newspaper Contributor," 119–24, shrewdly analyzes his position, which is confirmed in a letter to Reid on Jan. 3, 1873. Philip S. Foner, *Mark Twain: Social Critic* (NY, 1958), 242, goes too far in stating the anti-annexation tendency of Twain's *Tribune* letters.

15. Letter on March 7, 1873, copy in MTP. The "Public Virtue" original, dated March 8, is in the New York Pub. Lib. Reid wrote on it, "Letter Editor/must."

16. *Love Letters of Mark Twain*, 153–54. This volume omits Twain's earlier and more revealing letter from Washington on July, 6, 1870 (MTP).

17. "Thoughts Suggested by Mr. Froude's 'Progress,'" *The Complete Writings of Charles Dudley Warner* (Hartford, 1904), XV.

18. Invaluable for reading *The Gilded Age* is a broadside reprint of newspaper reviews—seen in MTP.

19. Twain's comments on sculptress Vinnie Ream are reprinted in Johnson, 182–83, and *Mark Twain Quarterly*, V (Sum., 1942), 10–11. Twain's scrapbook for 1872 (MTP) included a clipping on abuses in commissioning statues of Civil War heroes.

20. *Twainian*, N.S. II (May, 1943), 6; *American Publisher*, July, 1871, p. 4; MTP, letter to Frank Bliss, dated June [1871].

21. *Mark Twain to Mrs. Fairbanks*, 175; William Dean Howells, *My Mark Twain* (NY, 1910), 12, 77; *Love Letters of Mark Twain*, 177; Howard G. Baetzhold, "Mark Twain: England's Advocate," *American Literature*, XXVIII (Nov., 1956), 334–35.

22. Hartford *Courant*, May 14, 1879, p. I.

23. *Mark Twain: An Autobiography*, II, 231–32; Stephen Gwynn, *Life of Sir Charles Dilke* (London, 1918), I, 160; Lillian Whiting, *Kate Field* (Boston, 1899), 289; *Love Letters of Mark Twain*, 188; MTP, Olivia Clemens' letters to her mother, Aug. 10–11 and Aug. 31, 1873, and Twain to one Fitzgibbon in 1873–74.

24. MTP, DV 69 and Tichborne scrapbook; in *Following the Equator* Twain referred in detail to attending one of the claimant's "showy evenings." Twain kept a copy of *The Anti-Game Law Circular* for Oct. 12, 1872.

25. H.R. Fox Bourne, *English Newspapers* (London, 1887), II, 286, 308, describes as uncompromisingly Tory the London *Morning Post*,

to which Twain's letter was addressed. The letter was reprinted in the *Northern Whig* of Dec. 13, 1873.

26. Hartford *Courant*, July 25, 1876.

27. Undated AMS in Webster letters, MTP; *Mark Twain: A Biography* (NY, 1912), 541–42; M. A. D. Howe, *Memories of a Hostess* (Boston, 1922), 251–56.

28. MTP, letter from Marvin L. Bovee, dated Feb. 10.

29. MTP, Paine 249 (dated Sept. 18, 1905).

Toward the Novel

David E.E. Sloane

Twain's voice—the persona—focuses the literary comedy. The 1860s was a time for experimentation with this voice in a variety of subjects—burlesques, travel narratives, semiserious reporting—and he never really stopped developing, as his travel narratives show. Twain advanced literary comedy significantly by using the flexibility of his voice to blend plot and author, playing humor against the dramatization of events. The literary comedian thus came to occupy a place inside the novel by virtue of his characteristic attitude toward social and political events. The recording of Pap's "call this a gov'ment" speech in Huck's voice is a natural out-growth of this management of tone, the technique which originates in the burlesques of the 1860 period. Twain's letters to the *Alta California* and a series of letters for the *Missouri Democrat* in 1866 and 1867 give particularly clear revelations of Twain's experiments in such forms. The resolution which he achieved shapes his novels.

The literary interests of the San Francisco bohemians probably encouraged Twain to attempt an increasingly elevated tone in his writing, and [Artemus] Ward had attempted to refine his voice similarly in the course of his development. Twain's writing, aside from the jumping frog story which he sent east to Ward, included reviews, city news, burlesques of plays as well as of the local government, miscellaneous items on the spiritualists, fashions, and local

Reprinted from *Mark Twain as a Literary Comedian* (Baton Rouge: L.S.U.P., 1979), pp. 84–103.

amusements, and, of course, travel letters. Edgar Branch notes the entrance into the San Francisco writing of a sense of Twain's own past, enriching descriptions with a more broadly implicative consciousness, as in the case of a mural at a local establishment which is described with mock piety as being as gorgeous "as a Presbyterian picture of hell." His letters from Hawaii are in Twainian voice, but with a perspective that reverses later views; in order that San Francisco get more whaling business, he suggests that the city "cripple your facilities for 'pulling' sea captains on every pretense that sailors can trump."[1] His later egalitarian ethics solidified on his trip from San Francisco to New York.

Where Ward's national popularity was based on contemporary events, religious sects, and local events like the visit of Albert Edward, Twain's reputation was based on more literary-seeming material, the frog story and travel letters which were identified for their representation of the narrator's American egalitarian viewpoint. His pose was not burdened with any visual limitation such as the cacography that Ward, and following him Josh Billings, labored under. The transition from reportorial commentator to lyceum lecturer was consequently more natural and corresponded comfortably to the establishment of the lyceum agency, which brought such lectures to predetermined audiences. As Twain's audience became sophisticated culturally, politically, and economically, his stance as a comedian was flexible enough to permit him to speak to them. Where Ward was aware of contemporary literature and employed the burlesque freely, Twain was not only literary but also religious in his exact biblical references and cosmopolitan in his mixture of colloquial and sublime diction and attitudes to build comic statements into longer narrative formats.

Experimenting in humorous modes, Twain recast columns of reportorial comedy into dramatic pieces. His burlesques began to capture the political and moral overtones of the democracy. A series of paralleling newspaper items exist from the 1860s which show Twain presenting material in reportorial format and then reworking the same material into dramatic pieces. He touched on marriage and morality, Barnum's candidacy for Congress, and the woman's suffrage question, exploring the possibilities of comic writing in the dual formats. A vulgar persona like Barnum or Captain Ned Wakeman could sometimes demonstrate a point through burlesque; at other times Twain the semiserious reporter could speak. The moralist of the main was finding a dramatic voice.

Twain's treatment of Barnum's American Museum in conjunction with his bid for Congress is well beyond Ward's showman even though both are burlesques of the same figure as an American type. Dated March 2, 1867, Twain's report on Barnum's museum to the *Alta California* was published on April 9, 1867, under the title "How Are the Mighty Fallen!"; "Barnum's First Speech in Congress," a variant of this article, appeared in the New York *Evening Express* on March 5, 1867.[2] In "How Are the Mighty Fallen!" Mark Twain the reporter visits Barnum's museum in New York because Barnum's running for Congress imbues everything connected to him with a new interest. He notices the stairs running from floor to floor, the crowds, and the general seediness of the museum. The eight-foot-high woman merely sits, for "there was no one to stir her up and make her show her points," a phrase reminiscent of the frog story. The giant, too, merely sits, making Twain declare that if he was impresario of the "menagerie," he would "make that couple prance around some, or dock their rations." Two dwarfs, a speckled Negro, and a Circassian girl "complete the list of human curiosities." Otherwise, Twain comments that Barnum's museum is "one vast peanut stand now."

The reporter is commenting on the same things that would preoccupy him in Europe. Experiences held out to be elevating turn out to be vulgar or fraudulent; this is more obviously the case with Barnum and such exhibits as the "Happy Family." The lions and other beasts that make up the show sleep all the time, and Twain notes the spiritless bear, mangy puppies, and meek tomcats—all "bossed and bullied" by a monkey who

111

cuffs the rabbits and raccoons and chases all the other animals away from the feed tub. Twain remarks that "the world is full of families as happy as that," but the monkey who lost his tail to the boss monkey will have to find his solace in philosophy. The reporter Twain also describes the dust-covered Venus and the leering drunken waxwork representing Queen Victoria. These displays and the moral drama called the "Christian Martyr" compose the attraction of Barnum's show, and Twain concludes that "if he has no better show to get to Congress, he ought to draw out of the canvass." This is acerbic Twain, both expository and narrative with the description of the "Happy Family" approaching burlesque.

The parallel item to "How Are the Mighty Fallen!" is a dramatized speech to Congress by Barnum, delivered to Twain out of the future by "spiritual telegraph." The introduction which frames Barnum's speech is a considerable advance over the formal style of Twain's youthful writing, for it is cast in the relatively modern reportorial style of the 1860s rather than in the formal diction of Longstreet. Twain observes that it would be a "genuine pity" if Barnum could not find a way of dovetailing business and patriotism "to the mutual benefit of himself and the Great Republic." Barnum's burlesque speech begins crassly: "Mr Speaker—What do we do with a diseased curiosity? Sell him!" This mood is developed as Barnum takes the opportunity of the speech to praise his animals, Jenny Lind, his low admission price—reminiscent of Artemus Ward's claims for his show—and the numerous peanut stands, "two peanut stands to each natural curiosity," recapturing an idea stressed in the narrative article. Stating that his numerous curiosities are no excuse for him to become complacent, Barnum describes his spotted Negro, camels, "Sacred Cattle from the sacred hills of New Jersey," and "two plaster of Paris Venuses and a varnished mud-turtle." The last line doubles the number of Venuses from Twain's account—exaggeration—and adds the mud turtle to undercut the speech through anticlimax. The narrative account is consequently expanded through comic devices when it is placed in the voice of a character. This is a chief reason why the narrators of Twain's novels embody many of his important social ironies in their own deadpan comic presentations, and it is a controlling factor in the texture of Twain's major works.

As Barnum's speech continues, the same exhibits that Twain the reporter noticed appear as part of the boast of the burlesque congressman. Twain's line that he would dock the rations of the giant is transformed into a consistent strain of materialism in Barnum. The objective irony becomes part of the dramatization of the character. Artemus Ward's only such creation, besides the showman himself, was Jim Griggins. Barnum, however, like the congressmen in *The Gilded Age*, is a self-burlesquing dramatic entity: "Shall I bask in mine own bliss and be mute in the season of my people's peril? No! Because I possess the smallest dwarfs in the world, and the Nova Scotian giantess, who weighs a ton and eats her weight every forty-eight hours; and Herr Phelim O'Flannigan the Norwegian Giant, who feeds on the dwarfs and ruins business; and the lovely Circassian girl; and the celebrated Happy Family." Ward's style of comic rhetoric is almost reversed in this passage. Instead of using moral and political sentiments as a means of describing his show, Barnum in Twain's hands is made to employ the mentality of a showman to decide the course of the nation. In similar cases, Ward's sentiments were expressed as an incongruously idealistic projection of his professional experience, not as a part of the fabric of his commercial enterprise. By connecting the showman with this sort of submerged venality, Twain is attacking a double corruption, first of Congress, and second of the real role of businessmen. Significantly, Twain's dramatization carries an implied rejection of the likelihood of a moral truth coming from a "vulgar" person.

As Barnum continues speaking, more of the facets of his museum are drawn into the texture of his supposed world view, even including the arrangement of stairs to direct attention of displays. His mind, in fact, begins to run his show and the Congress together, as he appeals to "every true heart in this august menagerie" to save the nation from demagogues who beard the starry-robed woman in her citadel while "to you the bearded woman looks for succor." The conflict between the executive and the legislative branches of government over the Fourteenth Amendment is breaking up the happy family of the Union. Barnum further complains that the poor Negro is only white in spots like his Leopard Boy and has gained universal suffering rather than universal suffrage. By the close of the speech, Twain has completely submerged Barnum's radical Republicanism in the museum curiosities dominating the burlesque rhetoric. Irony has become literary characterization as the materialistic mind is discredited through its incapacity to sever its selfishness from the concerns of government:

> The country is fallen! The boss monkey sits in the feed-tub, and the tom-cats, the raccoons and the gentle rabbits of the once happy family stand helpless and afar off, and behold him gobble the provender in the pride of his strength! Woe is me!
> Ah, gentlemen, our beloved Columbia, with these corroding distresses upon her, must soon succumb! The high spirit will depart from her eye, the bloom from her cheek, the majesty from her step, and she will stand before us gaunt and worn, like my beautiful giantess when my dwarfs and Circassians prey upon her rations! Soon we shall see the glory of the realm pass away as did the grandeur of the Museum amid the consuming fires, and the wonders the world admires shall give place to trivialities, even as in the proud Museum the wonders that once amazed have given place to cheap stuffed reptiles and peanut stands! Woe is me!
> O, spirit of Washington! forgotten in these evil times, thou art banished to the dusty corridors of memory, a staring effigy of wax, and none could recognize thee but for the label pinned upon thy legs! ... Woe is me!
> Rouse ye, my people, rouse ye! rouse ye! rouse ye! Shake off the fatal stupor that is upon ye, and hurl the usurping tyrant from his Throne! Impeach! impeach! impeach!—Down with the dread boss monkey! O, snake the

> seditious miscreant out of the national feed-tub and reconstruct the Happy Family!
>
> Such is the speech imparted to me in advance from the spirit land. Mark Twain.

The happy family, the inactive giantess, the museum fire of 1865, and the wax figures that annoyed the reporter Twain all become parts of Barnum's mental apparatus. The speaker's attack on Andrew Johnson, made obvious by the references to the Fourteenth Amendment and Negro suffrage, as well as to the "Executive," is discredited by the ridiculous boss-monkey metaphor; Barnum's rhetorical "woe is me!" suggests a repetitious posturing that also casts doubt on his argument. Twain's restraint in the final sentence, which frames the story without any comment, is an ironic contrast.[3]

"Barnum's First Speech in Congress," like Twain's other experiments in this political idiom in 1867 and 1868, is a partial reflection of the influence of Ward's success in the old showman persona. Twain rejected the mind of Barnum as he understood it at that time but employed the comic representation of legislators and legislative jargon, much as Ward used the showman figure and contemporary social events. Another piece of social commentary handled similarly was based around Captain Wakeman's marriage of two runaway lovers on the trip from San Francisco to the Isthmus, recorded in *Mark Twain's Travels with Mr. Brown.*[4] Conventional morality is thrown into colloquial dialect as Wakeman advises the lovers to "splice and make the most of it," an ironic proposal since the couple placed no value on marriage, according to Twain. The dominant feeling imparted by Twain is genteel skepticism, and the bride's father is given an imaginary line—"You miserable, heartless dog, you have stolen away my child!"—which melodramatizes the incident; reporting is approaching fiction increasingly in such a piece.

Twain's newspaper burlesques on the woman's suffrage question show an even wider range of techniques in imaginative fiction than the other items from the 1867 period. They burlesqued the newspaper letter, reportorial prose, and legislative debates. "Cannibalism in the Cars," which represents a finished application of political burlesque to fiction writing, belongs to the final stage of this development. Taken together, the materials indicate a unity in Twain's newspaper writing in the late 1860s and foreshadow the political sections of *The Gilded Age.*

The suffrage items are as clearly transitional as anything Twain had previously done. In the first item, Twain creates a list of pseudo-government positions, such as "State Crinoline Directress" at $10,000 salary per year, to be filled by greedy female officeseekers. Lists of offices, as in *The Gilded Age,* are mixed with echoes of the coal oil lamp era of political canvassing seen in Ward's Baldinsville. "Mr. Twain" concludes, as a "family" man, which he was not, that his wife will leave him to such chores as wet nursing. He was following Billings in this irony; Billings said he would rather a woman beat him at nursing a baby than at a stump speech or a lecture on veterinary practice. Twain's second item uses the letter convention to present burlesque attacks on him as an opponent of female suffrage. The first two letters are closely parallel diatribes by Mrs. Mark Twain and Mrs. Zeb Leavenworth.[5] Both spend a paragraph berating Twain and threatening him with violence; they conclude with pious hopes that their arguments may have benefited the cause, enabling the two to die "happy and content." The fullness of the repetition projects the suffragists as uniformly bloody-minded harridans. More importantly, Twain's characteristic diction and exaggeration flow into his characterizations; the way was being paved toward fiction.

Twain's third letter on the suffrage issue was written in response to a real letter to the *Democrat* and was written in yet another reportorial voice. In stating his serious premises before turning to burlesque, he reveals that he, like Ward, was genteel and idealistic: "I never want to see women voting, gabbling about politics, and electioneering. There is something revolting in the thought. It would shock me inexpressibly for an angel to come down from above and ask me to take a drink with him (although I should doubtless consent); but it would shock me still more to see one of our blessed earthly angels peddling election tickets among a mob of shabby scoundrels she never saw before." The reactionary sentiment—like Ward, showing a dislike for the ignorant and loathsome with the vote[6]—is blended with the parenthetical pose of the loose-moraled reporter—an almost all-inclusive pose.

Twain describes suffragette women as interested in abolishing tobacco, alcohol, late evenings out for men, and little else. He complains that women will even want to go to war. The piece is drifting, however, toward a better stance as the irony broadens: "We will let you teach school as much as you want to, and we will pay you half wages for it, too, but beware! We don't want you to crowd us too much!" Humorous devices—the comic aside, the termagant type, legislative burlesque—are being turned to the uses of social criticism. As Louis Budd points out, the mixture of attitudes is unsatisfying in its failure to coalesce into a single unified statement.[7] Yet Ward, without the variable persona, had struggled with similar topics in similar ways. The flexibility of Twain's newspaper voice is an advance that brings him near to the first-person narratives of the travel books and novels. He is ready to offer multiple viewpoints, and his sense of ethics, and justice is beginning to form his material and infuse his voice.

The next suffrage piece, "Petticoat Government," is a dramatic burlesque along the lines of Barnum's burlesque speech to Congress.[8] The women betray their personal preoccupations—with gored dresses and waterfall hair styles—to the exclusion of any legislative business other than antidrinking and antitobacco laws. The speeches and asides are recorded as formal oratory, while interspersed among the digressions on fashion are a few harried male attempts to invoke parliamentary rules; the men's chief concern—and here Twain's consciousness is again clearly at work—is the granting of five million dollars for the relief of the Great Pacific Railroad. Beginning the report he had remarked that if women entered government "there would occur almost as disgraceful scenes as have lately blurred the record of Congressional proceedings," and he continues to make a broad application of the burlesque through the overly rhetorical complaint of Mr. Slawson, of St. Genevieve, that the tirade on fashions was "a matter trivial enough at any time, God knows, but utterly insignificant in the presence of so grave a matter as the behests of the Great Pacific Railroad." Add plot continuity and setting to this sort of humor, and the texture of *The Gilded Age* or some portions of *Roughing It* is present in mature form. In *The Gilded Age*, the antirailroad populism was converted into the symbolic encounter between Philip Sterling and Conductor Slum; the rhetoric went to Senator Dilworthy and his cohorts.

The legislative burlesque, which gave Twain scope for ironic exaggerations in diction, was a seductive medium for literary comedians, and Twain was no exception. He already knew that satire could succeed as travesty, as in "The Petrified Man" and the "Bloody Massacre" story, if the travesty did not overwhelm the satire.[9] In "Cannibalism in the Cars," Twain's ability in this area reached its most sophisticated level of expression.

"Cannibalism in the Cars," published in England somewhat later than the other burlesques in this series, is based on an inversion of social and political formality. Here, Twain used political hypocrisy in a more generalized manner than local issues such as Barnum and suffrage allowed. The representatives themselves are the subjects for discussion as various candidates for a cannibal stew. "I liked Harris," or "I have conceived an affection for you. I could like you as well as I liked Harris himself, sir," become dubious compliments.[10] When the narrator of the cannibalism story remarks to his auditor, "This decision created considerable dissatisfaction among the friends of Mr. Ferguson, the defeated candidate," the ironic reversal shows how political terms mask distorted purposes—and also shows how vanity can be contradicted by reality.

The sketch is actually more generalized than earlier related pieces through its comic diction. The frame is unobtrusive, and the story begins in a sublime suspense, in which such phrases as "eternal night" and "in the shadow of death" mark the early going. As the parliamentary rhetoric increases, however, the disjunctions between language and events become more grotesque. Even nature is personified, dragging in a sort of antipastoral element: "Nature had been taxed to the limit [by hunger]—she must yield. RICHARD H. GASTON of Minnesota, tall, cadaverous, and pale, rose up. . . . Only a calm thoughtful seriousness appeared in the eyes that were lately so wild."[11] The formal "yielding" of nature is between high comedy and pun. When the narrator comments, following the nomination of prospective dinners, that "some little caucussing followed," the diction holds the deadpan pose essential to a burlesque of democratic formuli. Human nature is actually at issue, for it is the catastrophic event and the passengers' response which is the action of the story. Cannibalism establishes the importance of the events to the nominees in exaggerated form.

Twain's diction, which seems the source of his humor, is actually subordinated to plot development as Ward's was not. The frame sequence, as with the jumping frog story, has removed the anecdote from the author's own mouth. The "member of Congress" who tells the story deserves a place beside Simon Wheeler, however, for he too is using digression and the deadpan as a means of stating his "experience." Even more significant is Twain's combination of the storyteller with a burlesque based on contemporary American materials; appropriate to the milieu of the literary comedians, the story takes place in a railroad car rather than in the backwoods. Hank Morgan, Huck Finn, and a number of lesser characters grow out of similar combinations. Because the experience is a narrated story, it has only a nominal reality; as fantasy, the social irony of self versus manners underlies the humor. The story is no more a characterization of its teller, really, than is the frog story of Simon Wheeler. Corporate ethics are at issue just as vanity is at issue in the "Jumping Frog." Many episodes in Twain's longer works depend on this effect; they are applicable as philosophical experience even though the reader knows they are unreal.

Twain is creating literature out of the material of the 1860s in "Cannibalism in the Cars." Egalitarian notions of government offer a comic mode for treating situations, and Twain is able to use such notions outside the Civil War context of Kerr and Nasby. Yet Twain's irony is inescapable. When "on the sixth [ballot], Mr. Harris was elected, all voting for him but himself," the point is again made that no amount of parliamentary rhetoric obscures the practical consideration of an individual's well-being; and so it was when Artemus Ward stepped forward and offered the vicarious sacrifice of his brother-in-law and uncle if need be to win the Civil War. The frame sequence that ends the story allows this "slurred nub" to remain an abstraction, clearly untrue but still horrifying to the auditor in the car. The texture of Twain's fiction, created by his diction and irony—his persona—appears in finished form in this short story. To understand how comparable materials condition a reader's understanding of Twain's viewpoint, it is necessary to examine the open framework for humor which Twain's travel fiction provided, and which became part of his machinery for creating the novel.

The Travel Narrative

The Innocents Abroad and the material related to it provide particularly clear relationships between literary tradition, Twainian pose, and ethical intention. In these relationships, the extension of the narrative into a rudimentary story foreshadows the novels' picaresque structure, as the material just studied foreshadows their texture. Twain's intention as a writer of literary comedy was set when he undertook the *Quaker City* voyage, and the writer's problem was thus to fit actual experience into a preconceived pose—a thoroughly literary exercise. Allusions to the Ward-Barnum tradition helped establish his viewpoint, and the interplay between the persona and the foreign milieu establish the tension between Old Europe and the new American viewpoint for which the book became famous. The book's events also coalesced around this viewpoint, however, and developed an increasingly serious demonstration of humanitarian qualities.

The book *The Innocents Abroad* was preceded by travel letters that were varied in quality but maintained the flexibility of persona and voice distinguishing his other work. Phoenix had written travel burlesques, as had Ward. Mortimer Thomson, whom Twain corresponded with about the *Quaker City* voyage, had published comic and burlesque travel adventures as early as 1855 in *Doesticks, What He Says*. Twain's own intention is shown most clearly in his letter describing Bierstadt's picture of Yosemite, which was on display in New York when he was there: "It is more the atmosphere of Kingdom-come than of California. As a picture, the work must please, but as a portrait I do not think it will answer. Portraits should be accurate. We do not want feeling and intelligence smuggled into the pictured face of an idiot, and we do not want this glorified atmosphere smuggled into a portrait of the Yosemite where it surely does not belong. I may be wrong, but still I believe that this atmosphere of Mr. Bierstadt's is altogether too gorgeous."[12]

Twain's sense of the Old Masters, as shown in "The Second Advent," applied the same realistic test to sentimentalized religion. Twain's notebooks show this skepticism toward the Holy Land even before he had been there, as Dewey Ganzel has pointed out, and he had already bracketed passages in guidebooks for special treatment. The literary comedian expresses his vision by describing, in Mr. Ganzel's words, "Missouri in Venice, the commonplace surroundings of the exotic, a pattern he was to use again and again in *IA*."[13] The vulgarian's commonplace, almost the viewpoint of the low thief, would control the responses of the

American vandal abroad and reveal the psychology of "Mark Twain."

The beginning complaint of Twain's letters is almost an unnecessary vehicle for expressing his American vision through comedy. He complained that the travel books had shamefully deceived him, in a passage that was dropped from the Turkish Bath sequence before it went into *The Innocents Abroad*: "What is a Turkish bath in Constantinople to a Russian one in New York? What are the dancing dervishes to the negro minstrels?—and Heaven help us, what is Oriental splendor to the Black Crook?" To flesh out this view with humor, Twain borrowed freely from the tradition of literary comedy. Ward complained that all the jugs in the British Museum were of uncertain age—which did not affect him until he discovered that his chicken at lunch was also "of a uncertain age." Twain captured the same experience in a "Turkish Lunch" (II, 86–87) and expanded upon it with "euchre" terms from the American frontier. "Bishop Southgate's Matinee," in the *Alta* letters, copied Ward's burlesque panorama, which featured a drunken projectionist, from his 1866 tour. Both writers drew comic relationships between religious quackery and the Constitution. P. T. Barnum, earlier, and Twain, later, tested guides for truthfulness in the same way, and both found they lied.[14] Other jokes follow the same tradition.

The circus motif, which Barnum and Ward had developed as an American literary tradition, influences Twain's pose significantly, particularly in the crucial area of religion. In the opening sequence of the book, he masquerades as a minister with claims to the "missionary business" looking for a "show," a sort of Simon Suggs-Artemus Ward compound. Perhaps due to the presence of a Barnum agent on the *Quaker City*, many of Twain's reports reflected the circus. The cathedral at Milan was "bossed" by a "gorgeous old brick" who was mummified and displayed: "It's not part of the regular circus, you know, and so you have to pay extra." Other priests run little sideshows and perform as if they were performing outside a menagerie. Recapturing his Barnum items from St. Louis, Twain said that an Italian dwarf wouldn't stand any "show" in Constantinople: "A beggar has to have exceedingly good points to make a living" there.[15] The diction serves a distinct function in such passages, reflecting the outraged humanity of the narrator. Such brief encounters, exaggerated through ironic diction, also pile up a series of episodes that establish tension between European civilization and the angry, show-conscious traveler. The traveler finally becomes an antagonist, and his travels take on some of the aspects of a plot in which corporate Europe is the enemy.

Twain's treatment of Constantinople offers another point that indicates his method of converting the materials of the comic tradition to fit his own persona. After labeling gilt script inside the dome of St. Sophia "as glaring as a circus bill," he turns his attention from the shoddy atmosphere to the "old-master worshippers from the wilds of New Jersey," combining in a phrase the ideas of art, religion, false reverence, and provincialism. Ward, treating such persons and their entertainers in "The Show Business and Popular Lectures," complained that nine out of ten people "don't have no moore idee of what the lecturer sed than my kangaroo has of the sevunth speer of hevun." Twain complains that his set of traveling American farmers "don't know any more about pictures than a kangaroo does about astronomy."[16] Ward's showman idiom has been altered in tone and generalized to express a yankee cosmopolitanism.

Not only in single lines but also in set pieces and comic vignettes does the tradition contribute to "Twain's" experience. Barnum in Liverpool was assaulted by beggars whom he took for nobility in his innocence; and after him Artemus Ward in London said, "I don't remember a instance since my 'rival in London of my gettin into a cab without a Briton comin and purlitely shuttin the door for me, and then extendin his open hand to'ards me, in the most frenly manner possible. Does he not, by this simple yit tuchin gesture, welcum me to England?" Twain, sharing the American background of Barnum and Ward, shows the same surprise at European beggars but extends his dramatization in an *Alta* letter: "A crowd of bare-footed and ragged and dirty vagabonds, of both sexes, received us on the wharf, and with one hospitable impulse held out their hands. With one grateful impulse we seized the hands and shook them. And then we saw that their hospitality was a vain delusion—they only extended their hands to beg."[17] The earlier travelers had stopped their narrative after showing their own naïveté; Twain continues to define the community—"eminently Portuguese—that is to say, it is slow, poor, shiftless, sleepy and lazy." Continuing, Twain even locates a villain: "The good Catholic Portughee crossed himself and prayed to God to shield him from all blasphemous desire to know more than his father did before him."[18] Burlesque travel narratives take on through such identifications a tension between the narrator—Twain the American—and the milieu—dominated by static religiosity, the corporate church.

Before finishing the discussion of this nascent plot structure in the travel narrative, one or two other crucial borrowings from the tradition need to be developed as sources of the "American" persona, "Mark Twain." In Ward's London letters, the stealing of spoons, as Ward's "Uncle Wilyim" does, burlesques types who try to place themselves in an elevated social context, and newspaper items in Twain's era treat the subject of spoon stealing as comedy rather than with the life-and-death seriousness of *Moll Flanders*. Ward's letters and the Jim Griggins item use the joke as a representation of the venality of the small crook and to indicate his relative harmlessness—a sort of innocence. Twain used the "spoon stealing" joke three times in *The Innocents Abroad*, making it into a *motif* underlying the meeting between the *Quaker City* pilgrims and the Russian Czar. Twain had called into question the good sense and Christian charity of his fellow travelers early (I, 130), and here turns to satire, including through his special flexibility of voice even himself in the group. In the first reference, Twain states that he wants to steal the emperor's coat, claiming, "When I meet a man like that, I want something to remember him by (II, 110)." Then he described the tour by the *Quaker City* party: "We spent half an hour idling through the palace, admiring the cozy apartments and the rich but eminently homelike appointments of the palace, and then the imperial family bade our party a kind good-by, and proceeded to count the spoons" (II, 110). The implication of the passage is that such travelers as the pious voyagers were "low" and vulgar, sharing the traits that Jim Griggins blamed on his lack of education. Twain's borrowing from Ward thus strikes at the essence of the trip, a social pretension by upwardly mobile post-Civil War Americans. And Twain thus develops a theme. Visiting the Russian grand duke, "We bade our distinguished hosts good-by, and they retired happy and contented to their apartments to count *their* spoons" (II, 114). The ship's sailors are even supposed to expand the burlesque of the Russian reception when the third cook—Twain would make it the *third* cook—of the *Quaker City* plays the Czar, damns the formal speech of the visitors and tells his first groom to "proceed to count the portable articles of value belonging to the premises" (II, 121). There is little likelihood that such events occurred as narrated, particularly since there is a literary tradition behind Twain's line. The "low" characterization is no longer attached to a low figure—it has become almost philosophical in its ironic implications about social vanity, and Twain thus reasserts the values of the American comedians even while traveling in a cosmopolitan guise and speaking in a normal colloquial voice.

A second borrowing from Artemus Ward is equally illuminating. Artemus Ward's "Is he dead?" joke shows a British landlord's skepticism about spiritualism in "The Green Lion and Oliver Cromwell." The landlord didn't want to speak to the spirit of the historical figure, he only wanted the spiritualist's room rent. This sort of aggressive practicality, intolerant of historical humbug, is the fund upon which Twain was drawing when in *The Innocents Abroad* he shows his "boys" confronting the guides with the same question. As the guides make a sideshow out of Columbus and an Egyptian mummy, Twain's characters play credulous naifs: "Christopher Columbo—pleasant name—is—is he dead?" (I, 305). The one-line joke is elaborated into a scene and into a motif, as with the spoon-stealing joke. It appears twice in the last chapter of Book I and again in the opening chapter of Book II (I,305, 307; II,5). The transference of the joke from the municipal palace of Genoa (and before that from Ward's London surroundings) through the Vatican Museum at Rome and finally to the catacombs under the Capuchin Convent gradually extends Twain's irony about historical showmanship into the area of European Catholicism. The elaboration of the joke is more sophisticated than Ward's digressions, and the turning of the joke from European fraud to the church's view of man is appropriate to Twain's moral and humanitarian concerns in his fiction. Rather than signifying merely a verbal relation cloaking disparate and antagonistic intentions, as Bernard DeVoto has written, such open borrowings of jokes like the "Is he dead?" formula reflect the unity of viewpoint underlying the various American humorists generally.[19] Twain's elaboration and expansion of such jokes in language and format is his development of the tradition into a vision beyond the level of contemporary newspaper humor.

Finally, Twain's social reflections and religious commentary are pulled together in the Holy Land in burlesque scenes such as the Tomb of Adam sequence and in genteel statements such as those on Godfrey of Bouillon. The rhetorical high point, however, comes during the race into the Holy Land before the Sabbath. Twain's outrage at this point proves the value of his flexible voice, for his statement is intended to be taken seriously and is not burdened with a comic pose or inflection. He had made sarcastic comments about the Plymouth Collection of Hymns dominating ship life and remarked that Balaam's ass was "The patron saint of all pilgrims like us" (II,173). He is beyond this sarcasm and outside of his fictional character in attacking formulaic

Christianity as he saw its immediate consequences in the Holy Land:

> They *must* press on [the "pilgrims" trying to reach a holy point before Sunday]. Men might die, horses might die, but they must enter upon holy soil next week, with no sabbath-breaking stain upon them. Thus they were willing to commit a sin against the spirit of religious law, in order that they might preserve the letter of it. It was not worth while to tell them "the letter kills." I am talking now about personal friends; men whom I like; men who are good citizens; who are honorable, upright, conscientious: but whose idea of the Savior's religion seems to me distorted.
>
> (II, 172).

Josh Billings had commented in *His Sayings* in 1865 that "Heathen are alwus kind tew hosses, it iz only among Christian people, that a hoss hez tew trot 3 mile heats, in a hot da, for $2500 kounterfit munny," and other analogues to the attitude, notably in Dickens' *Hard Times*, predated Twain.[20] Yet so directly is the ethical position stated that problems of pose and persona become largely irrelevant. Twain has shifted from the literary comedian to the "real" (equally literary, of course) persona without apology and caused the hidden plot-action to appear in a single episode. His flexibility of voice allows for the expression of his own ethical background, fixed in his childhood and in the West as well as inherited from the comic tradition of egalitarianism. Burlesque donkey-riding sequences in Fayal at the opening of the book come to have a foreshadowing thematic relationship to the rest of the travels, and the ethics which underlie the narrator's viewpoint—the viewpoint which rejects corrupt corporations and governmental bodies in the novels and dissents from a host of social and religious vanities—protest the treatment of animals in a brief moment in the travel narrative.

There are a number of comparisons between the works of Artemus Ward and Mark Twain, but the most significant comparisons are those that show Twain's growth as an independent process. He was developing a sustained vision of society and an ethical stance out of the materials and techniques available in American literary comedy. Twain's innocent faces a more sophisticated environment than Ward's showman, and Twain's techniques are more mature and more flexible. His experiments with burlesque dramatization, as in "Barnum's First Speech in Congress," show him developing fictional characterizations to express the broad social and aesthetic criticism that distinguishes the literary comedians from the Yankee correspondents and Twain from the literary comedians in turn. The continuing presence of Ward's humor in Twain's mind through the writing of *The Innocents Abroad* is an indication of how much the tradition offered Twain in the expression of his own ethics. As he developed into a writer of books, he began to sustain and elaborate these themes from the comic tradition in his own way, deepening the form of the cosmopolitan travel burlesque as we have seen. He became capable of expressing a variety of sentiments in a variety of comic and serious modes. His writings of the 1860s are thus clearly the products of the school of literary comedy in America and just as clearly foreshadow the voice of the novelist.

Notes

1. Branch, *Literary Apprenticeship of Mark Twain*, 130; Day (ed.), *Mark Twain's Letters from Hawaii*, 94–95.

2. "How Are the Mighty Fallen!" is reprinted in Franklin Walker and G. Ezra Dane (eds.), *Mark Twain's Travels with Mr. Brown* (New York: Alfred A. Knopf, 1940), 116–19, as part of Letter XI. "Barnum's First Speech in Congress" has been made available to me by Professor Louis Budd. This selection from the New York *Express* matches a portion of the letter reprinted in Brown, 286, as being from the New York *Telegram* and subsequently the *Alta*.

3. There is a paradigm for Twain's depiction of Barnum in "Artemus Ward in Washington" in which the showman employs the terminology of national politics in conjunction with his private interests: "I'm reconstructing my show. I've Bo't a collection of life-size wax figgers of our prominent Revolutionary forefathers. I bo't'em

at auction, and got'em cheap. They stand me about two dollars and fifty cents (2 dols. 50 cents) per Revolutionary forefather. Ever as always yours, A. Ward."

4. Walker and Dane (eds.), *Travels with Mr. Brown*, 13–15, 18–19, 23–25.

5. Mark Twain, "Female Suffrage/Views of Mark Twain," St. Louis *Missouri Democrat*, March 12, 13, 1866; "Female Eddikashun," *Josh Billings: His Sayings* (New York: Carleton, 1866), 26–27. As a tangential point, the use of "Mrs. Zeb Leavenworth," offers evidence of the continuity of Twain's mind in holding comic formulations. In 1864, three years earlier, he signed the name "Zeb Leavenworth," a pilot friend from his Mississippi days, to a burlesque letter in "Those Blasted Children" which also uses strong language treating Twain as an advice-giver, while mentioning loss of hair. Here, Mrs. Leavenworth threatens to "snatch hair out of his head till he is as bald as a phrenological bust." The phrase and joke were retained together with their context and later recast to suit current needs. This ability bears on the relation between Twain and previous literary comedians.

6. Mark Twain, "Female Suffrage/The Iniquitous Crusade." St. Louis *Missouri Democrat*, March 15, 1867; Ward, *Works*, 417.

7. As Ward's Betsy Jane threatened to do in "A War Meeting," Ward, *Works*, 251. Louis Budd, *Mark Twain, Social Philosopher* (Bloomington: University of Indiana Press, 1962), 23–24.

8. Mark Twain, "Female Suffrage/Petticoat Government," New York *Sunday Mercury*, April 7, 1867, p. 3.

9. "Memoranda," *Galaxy*, IX (June, 1870), 858, reprinted in *Contributions to "The Galaxy"*, 47.

10. Mark Twain, "Cannibalism in the Cars," reprinted in *Sketches, New and Old*, 339–51. It originally appeared in *Broadway*, November, 1868, a house organ for the publishing firm of Routledge, Twain's British publisher at this time. An analogue for this story, which Artemus Ward created in London in 1866, appears in "Artemus Ward and Mark Twain," by Aaron Watson, *The Savage Club* (London: T. Fisher Unwin, 1907), 120–22, and anticipates the story in many details. Twain reduced the story to a one-line joke in "Riley— Newspaper Correspondent," *Contributions to "The Galaxy"*, 90: "had a grand human barbecue in honor of [the cannibal flag], in which it was noticed that the better a man liked a friend the better he enjoyed him."

11. Twain uses names of friends Dan Slote and Charles Langdon. Ward's "The Fair Inez" supplies a precedent for this coterie device in using names of his Cleveland friends, and the practice was probably a common one.

12. "Letter 24," *Alta California* (dated New York, June 2, 1867), in Scrapbook Seven, Mark Twain Papers, University of California, Berkeley.

13. John S. Tuckey (ed.), *Mark Twain's Fables of Man* (Berkeley: University of California Press, 1972), 50–68; Dewey Ganzel, *Mark Twain Abroad* (Chicago: University of Chicago Press, 1968), 146, 221.

14. Daniel Morley McKeithan (ed.), *Traveling with the Innocents Abroad* (Norman: University of Oklahoma Press, 1958), 132; Ward, *Works*, 444; *Travels with Mr. Brown*, 95–97. Compare Ward, *Works*, 44 on the Shakers, "said world continners to revolve round on her own axletree onct in every 24 hours, subjeck to the Constitution of the United States," with Twain's more refined addition to his letter in *The Innocents Abroad*, I, 68–69; "Antiquarians . . . agree that [Hercules] was an enterprizing and energetic man, but decline to believe him a good, bona fide god, because that would be unconstitutional." Barnum, *Life*, 268.

15. Ganzel, *Mark Twain Abroad*, 54; McKeithan (ed.), *Traveling with the Innocents Abroad*, 50–51, 115–16.

16. Ward, *Works*, 83; McKeithan (ed.), *Traveling with the Innocents Abroad*, 117.

17. Barnum, *Life*, 250–51; Ward, *Works*, 437; McKeithan (ed.), *Traveling with the Innocents Abroad*, 4.

18. McKeithan (ed.), *Traveling with the Innocents Abroad*, 16, 17.

19. DeVoto, *Mark Twain's America*, 220–21. More recently, Edwin H. Cady, *The Light of Common Day* (Bloomington: Indiana University Press, 1971), 80, has said that this "seems to me one of the classic instances of American humor, especially as it peaks in Chapter XXVII of *The Innocents Abroad*." Twain later took this same "Is he dead?" formula one step further in fabricating a story to define his attitude toward John Altgeld, who was running for the Illinois governorship on the platform that he would enforce all the laws of the state fully. Twain pretended that his anecdote was an actual experience from a circus in Little Rock, Arkansas, which was displaying an Egyptian Mummy:

> As the guide was giving (his talk) to the party of ten-cents-apiece customers, pointing out the various features of interest, a solemn-looking fellow, Bert Wheeler, interrupted him.
> "Is this man dead?" he asked.
> "Oh, yes, of course. He—"
> "How did he die?" persisted Bert.
> "Don't know," returned the attendant. "He—"
> "Ever been an inquest held over him in this country?" broke in Bert.

"No, you see, he's been dead for a long time," said the attendant. "Maybe four thousand years. So you see—"

"Makes no difference," snapped Bert, "I'm the coroner of this county, and if you haven't already a certificate on this man's death, he's got to have an inquest. That's the law. Boys, bring the deceased along. The laws of this county must be upheld."

Opie Read, *Mark Twain and I* (Chicago: Reilley & Lee, 1940), 119. This story was presented as a "real" experience, even though the "Is he dead?" element identifies it as an extension of the traditional skepticism of the literary naif. So completely does Twain come to believe in the literary expression that it finally becomes a new anecdote from the "old" Southwest to express his political views. One must not underestimate the value of this insight into Twain's use of local and vernacular-seeming materials.

20. Cited in Jesse Bier, *The Rise and Fall of American Humor* (New York: Holt, Rinehart, and Winston, 1968), 84. Sleery, the showman in Dickens' novel on factory life in England, expresses his humanity in his treatment of horses, so this idea can be seen as a cosmopolitan metaphor rather than a strictly western American one. Sleery delivers the following speech while offering to apprentice the orphaned Sissy Jupe, thus providing her with a permanent home and security: "But what I thay, Thquire, ith, that good tempered or bad tempered, I never did a horthe a injury yet, no more than thwearing at him went, and that I don't expect I thall begin otherwithe at my time of life, with a rider. I never wath much of a Cackler, Thquire, and I have thed my thay." Charles Dickens, *Hard Times* (New York: Holt, Rinehart and Winston, 1963), 35. To find an analogue for Twain's statement in a "vulgar" character such as Sleery reinforces the difference between "genteel" religion and the blunter humanism of the Twain persona as expressed in *The Innocents Abroad*.

The Middle Career of Mark Twain from *Tom Sawyer* to *Pudd'nhead Wilson*: The Comedian as Major Author

Novels of the Week:
The Adventures of Tom Sawyer

The name of Mark Twain is known throughout the length and breadth of England. Wherever there is a railway-station with a bookstall his jokes are household words. Those whose usual range in literature does not extend beyond the sporting newspapers, the *Racing Calendar*, and the 'Diseases of Dogs,' have allowed him a place with Artemus Ward alongside of the handful of books which forms their library. For ourselves, we cannot dissociate him from the railway-station, and his jokes always rise in our mind with a background of Brown & Polson's Corn Flour and Taylor's system of removing furniture. We have read 'The Adventures of Tom Sawyer' with different surroundings, and still have been made to laugh; and that ought to be taken as high praise. Indeed, the earlier part of the book is, to our thinking, the most amusing thing Mark Twain has written. The humour is not always uproarious, but it is always genuine and sometimes almost pathetic, and it is only now and then that the heartiness of a laugh is spoilt by one of those pieces of self-consciousness which are such common blots on Mark Twain's other books. 'The Adventures of Tom Sawyer' is an attempt in a new direction. It is consecutive, and much longer than the former books, and as it is not put forward as a mere collection of "Screamers," we laugh more easily, and find some relief in being able to relax the conventional grin expected from the reader of the little

Reprinted from *The Athenaeum* No. 2539 (24 June 1876): 851.

volumes of railway humour. The present book is not, and does not pretend to be a novel, in the ordinary sense of the word; it is not even a story, for that presupposes a climax and a finish; nor is it a mere boys' book of adventures. In the Preface the author says, "Although my book is intended mainly for the entertainment of boys and girls, I hope it will not be shunned by men and women on that account, for part of my plan has been to try pleasantly to remind adults of what they once were themselves, and of how they felt and thought and talked, and what queer enterprises they sometimes engaged in." Questions of intention are always difficult to decide. The book will amuse grown-up people in the way that humorous books written for children have amused before, but (perhaps fortunately) it does not seem to us calculated to carry out the intention here expressed. With regard to the style, of course there are plenty of slang words and racy expressions, which are quite in place in the conversations, but it is just a question of whether it would not have been as well if the remainder of the book had not been written more uniformly in English.

On the Structure of *Tom Sawyer*

Walter Blair

I

Since, as several critics have suggested, *The Adventures of Tom Sawyer* (1876) attacked earlier juvenile literature in something roughly like the way *Joseph Andrews* attacked *Pamela*,[1] a note on the structure of the novel may well start (though it should not, I think, terminate) with a consideration of Clemens' book in its literary contexts. Such a consideration, by indicating the nature of the writings attacked and the way Mark Twain and other American humorists assaulted them, may emphasize certain architectural peculiarities in the volume and suggest more clearly than critics have done,[2] a unifying narrative thread.

Notable in earlier juvenile fictional works had been their characters, their preachments, and their plots. The children portrayed had been, for the most part, characterized with extraordinary simplicity: they had been good or bad, and that had been an end of it.[3] Horatio Alger's street boy heroes in the sixties, to be sure, had been more inclined towards naughtiness than flawless Little Eva or even beautifully trained Little Rollo had been.[4] But Alger's Ragged Dick, though he used profanity, patronized the Old Bowery Theatre, smoked, and played jokes on country folk, was "above doing anything mean or dishonorable.... or imposing upon younger boys.... His nature was noble and had saved

Reprinted from *Modern Philology* 37 (August 1939): 75–88.

him from all mean faults."⁵ And as a rule, as a critic of the Alger books has recently remarked:

> Our hero was. . . . a good boy, honest, abstemious (in fact sometimes unduly disposed to preach to drinkers and smokers), prudent, well-mannered (except perhaps for preaching), and frugal. . . . Nor did any subtleties of character-drawing prevent one from determining who were the good characters and who were the bad ones. They were labeled plainly.⁶

The bad children—as lacking in complexity as the good— had been distinguished, perhaps, more by their proclivities toward sin than by their accomplishments. Their crimes had ranged all the way from simply being lazy or playing truant to the most horrible outrages within their infantile powers— lying, stealing, battering the helpless and the weak, swearing, smoking, and even drinking. In short, with few exceptions, a bad child had been as totally depraved (in intention) as the non-elect of Calvinistic theology.⁷

The authors of juvenile tales, employing these angelic or villainous children, had provided sermon-like commentaries and had fashioned lesson-teaching plots. Constantly these writers had "extolled the precocious child, deprecated wholesome pleasure, and delighted in didactic sentimentality,"⁸ patting good children on the back, and scolding bad children sternly. Even when he had skipped the sermons, the reader of a typical story had been able to get its point by noticing that the author's dénouement observed the strictest poetic justice. In stories following what seemingly was the earliest pattern—the best known instance of which is the tale of Little Eva—the pallid virtuous child had died at the age proverbially prescribed for the Good, but had promptly gone to Heaven. The Alger boys, somewhat better adapted to the Gilded Age, had survived childhood to become successful business men. But the bad boy who had played truant "and was not really sorry for what he had done . . . went from one bad thing to another, and grew up to be a very wicked man, and at last committed a murder"; while naughty Thomas, who loafed all day or played with his kite, had a depressing adulthood:

> Without a shilling in his purse,
> Or cot to call his own,
> Poor Thomas went from bad to worse,
> And hardened as a stone.[9]

During the years before *Tom Sawyer* appeared, such good-bad-child tales, with their preachments and predetermined conclusions, had suggested incongruities between fiction and life useful to many American humorists. Beginning in the forties comic writers had sporadically beguiled readers with amoral portraits of unregenerate boys. Johnson J. Hooper's Simon Suggs had cheated his father at cards in 1845,[10] and in the fifties adolescent Sut Lovengood and young Ike Partington had perpetrated sundry deviltries. Ike, perhaps the most notorious of these juvenile delinquents, in the first volume in which he had appeared, had told lies, scratched letters on a newly japanned tray, broken countless windows, stolen oranges and cakes and doughnuts, hanged a cat, and imitated the hero of *The black avenger, or the pirates of the Spanish Main*.[11] In the seventies Max Adeler's Cooley boy was creating commotions in church, and kindred spirits in the writings of other humorists were behaving, in sketches, as Tom was to behave in a book. Doubtless the incongruity between these youths and those in contemporary books not only augmented their comic appeal but also molded the form of stories about them.

At least as early as the sixties, various authors had begun an even more direct onslaught upon juvenile fictional characters. Henry Ward Beecher, for example, had said in an essay written for a New York paper:

> The real lives of boys are yet to be written. The lives of pious and good boys, which enrich the catalogues of great publishing societies, resemble a real boy's life about as much as a chicken picked and larded, upon a spit, and ready for

delicious eating, resembles a free fowl in the fields. With some honorable exceptions, they are impossible boys, with incredible goodness. Their piety is monstrous. A man's experience stuffed into a little boy is simply monstrous. . . . Boys have a period of mischief as much as they have measles or chicken-pox.[12]

In 1869, Thomas Bailey Aldrich had launched his somewhat mild full-length portrait of Tom Bailey with a defiant passage calling attention to the difference between the Model Boy and the human youngster:

I call my story the story of a bad boy, partly to distinguish myself from those faultless young gentlemen who generally figure in narratives of this kind, and partly because I really was *not* a cherub. I may truthfully say I was an amiable, impulsive lad, blessed with fine digestive powers, and no hypocrite. I didn't want to be an angel. . . . and I didn't send my little pocketmoney to the natives of the Feejee Islands, but spent it royally on peppermint drops and tiffy candy. In short, I was a real human boy, such as you may meet anywhere in New England, and no more like an impossible boy in a story-book than a sound orange is like one that has been sucked dry.[13]

The story carrying this foreword could swell the circulation of *Our young folks* in 1869, and, in book form, could quickly run through eleven editions.[14]

By the middle of the seventies, the Moral Boy had become a dependable butt for humorists. During the year 1873, when *Tom Sawyer* was incubating, James M. Bailey was surmising that the nine-year-old Concord boy whose ability to repeat the multiplication table backwards had been recorded in a news item was the same hateful paragon who had lived next door to Bailey in his childhood—a youth who "always went to bed at eight o'clock. . . . brushed his hair back of his ears, and carried a store handkerchief. . . . He was the model boy, the boy our parents used to point to, and speak of. . . . while unfitting us for sitting on anything harder than a poultice."[15] The year before *Tom Sawyer* was issued, a Detroit humorist published sketches, "The good boy" and "The bad boy," satirizing some of the excesses of Sunday school fiction.[16] In the year Clemens' novel appeared, Robert Burdette humorously referred to "well-known 'good boys' who wash their faces every morning, keep their clothes clean, wear white collars, and don't say bad words."[17]

None of these attacks, it is probable, can be thought of as a direct inspiration of Mark Twain's book about boys. They are useful only to show a common conception of the humor of childhood and the nature of children of which he could take advantage. As a matter of fact, Twain himself had been rather early in the field with "The story of the good little boy who did not prosper" (1867) and "The story of the bad little boy who didn't come to grief" (1870)—both burlesques.[18] Jim, the hero of the former sketch, stole jam without the usual consequences: "all at once a terrible feeling didn't come over him. . . . He ate that jam and said it was bully." He stole apples and survived, purloined the teacher's penknife and shifted the blame to "the moral boy, the good little boy of the village, who always obeyed his mother, and never told an untruth, and was fond of his lessons, and infatuated with Sunday-school." Jim was delighted when the paragon was whipped, because he "hated moral boys. Jim said he was 'down on them milksops.'" Thus "everything turned out differently with him from the way it does to the bad Jameses in the books." In manhood, Jim "got wealthy by all manner of cheating and rascality; and now he is the infernalest wickedest scoundrel in his native village, and is universally respected, and belongs to the legislature."

Jacob Blivens in the 1870 sketch behaved so abnormally—refusing to play hookey, to lie, and to play on Sunday—that other children decided he was "afflicted," though the real trouble was simply that he "read all the Sunday-school books. . . . This was the secret of it." Again there was an attack upon the endings of stories about children. In them, the models "always had a good time, and the bad boys had the broken legs; in his case there was a screw loose somewhere, and it all happened the other way."

II

One who turns to *Tom Sawyer* with the conventional literature and the humorous attacks on that literature by various writers including Twain in mind may see some important achievements of Clemens' novel. These were suggested by a contemporary critic who said:

> This literary wag has performed some services which entitle him to the gratitude of his generation. He has run the traditional Sunday-school boy through his literary mangle and turned him out washed and ironed into a proper state of collapse. That whining, canting, early-dying, anaemic creature was held up to mischievous lads as worthy of imitation. He poured his religious hypocrisy over every honest pleasure a boy had. He whined his lachrymous warnings on every playground. He vexed their lives. So when Mark grew old enough, he went gunning for him, and lo, wherever his soul may be, the skin of the strumous young pietist is now neatly tacked up to view on the Sunday-school door of to-day as a warning.[19]

That the attack thus suggested may have been responsible in part for the organization of the narrative becomes clear if the story is restated in the way it would have been handled in the literature attacked. The opening chapter of Clemens' novel reveals a character who, in terms of moralizing juvenile literature, has the indubitable earmarks of a Bad Boy. As the story opens, Tom is stealing. Caught in the act, he avoids punishment by deceiving his aunt. He departs to play hookey, returns to stand slothfully by while a slave boy does his chores for him, then enters the house to deceive his aunt again. His trickery exposed by his half-brother Sid, he dashes out of the door shouting threats of revenge. A few minutes later, he is exchanging vainglorious boasts with a stranger whom he hates simply because the stranger is cleanly and neatly dressed. The action of the chapter concludes with Tom pounding the strange boy into submission (for no righteous reason), then chasing him home. "At last," says the author, "the enemy's mother appeared, and called Tom a bad, vicious vulgar child. . . ." If earlier moral writers had had a chance at Tom, they would have been much more eloquent, for within a few pages he has committed many of the enormities against which they had battled for years.

But as the story continues, Bad Boy Tom continues to sin (as these authors would have put it) in a fashion almost unprecedented in the fiction of the time. Up to the last page of chapter x, he piles up enough horrible deeds to spur the average Sunday school author to write pages of admonitions. His actions are of a sort to show that he is—in the language of such an author—thievish, guileful, untruthful, vengeful, vainglorious, selfish, frivolous, self-pitying, dirty, lazy, irreverent, superstitious and cowardly.

What a chance for sermonizing! But Clemens makes nothing of his opportunity: he indicates not the least concern about his hero's mendacity. In fact, his preaching (such as it is) is of a perverse sort. Instead of clucking to show his horror, he writes of Tom's sins with a gusto which earlier authors had reserved for the deeds of Good Boys, and on occasion (as when he tells about the whitewashing trick), he actually commends the youth for his chicanery. A ragged ruffian named Huckleberry Finn who smokes and swears is set up as an ideal figure because:

> . . . he did not have to go to school or to church, or call any being master or obey anybody; he could go fishing or swimming when and where he chose, and stay as long as it suited him; nobody forbade him to fight; he could sit up as late as he pleased; . . . he never had to wash, nor put on clean clothes; he could swear wonderfully. In a word, everything that goes to make life precious, that boy had. So thought every harassed, hampered, respectable boy in St. Petersburg [chap. vi].

On the other hand, the sort of spiteful disdain which had been used to chasten Bad Boys in other books is actually employed here to introduce an indubitable Good Boy. To church on Sunday, says Clemens,

> .... last of all came the Model Boy, Willie Mufferson, taking as heedful care of his mother as if she were cut glass. He always brought his mother to church, and was the pride of all the matrons. The boys hated him, he was so good. And besides, he had been "thrown up to them" so much. His white handkerchief was hanging out of his pocket behind, as usual on Sundays—accidentally. Tom had no handkerchief, and he looked upon boys who had, as snobs.[20]

The ending of the book departs as determinedly from the patterns of juvenile fiction. It staggers the imagination to guess the sort of punishment which would have been deigned fitting for such a monster as Tom by fictionists who had felt hanging in adulthood was an appropriate result of youthful truancy. From their standpoint, the author of *Tom Sawyer* must have outraged poetic justice to the point of being hideously immoral. Here were Tom and his companions, who had run away, played truant, and smoked to boot, actually lionized because they returned from Jackson's Island. Here was Tom cheered to the echo because he saved an unjustly accused man, compared with George Washington by Judge Thatcher because he took Becky's punishment, lionized because he saved the girl from the cave.[21] More shocking, here was even the unregenerate Huck dramatically saving the life of the Widow Douglas. And to top it all, these boys were allowed at the end to accumulate a fortune of the size exclusively awarded to only the best of the Alger heroes.

Thus the characterization, the perverse preaching, the unconventional ending of the book, which gave the volume in its day a comic appeal now all but irrecoverable, also, it is possible, did much to mold the form of the narrative. The simplest explanation of the arrangement of happenings in Clemens' book is that it represented a fictional working-out of the author's antipathy to the conventional plot so broadly developed in "The story of a bad little boy who didn't come to grief"—a more serious handling of a reversed moralizing narrative.

III

One effect of this method of telling a story was, of course, to give youthful readers exactly the sort of a series of happenings likely to please them.[22] Here was the story of a character who, in their opinion, was a real boy, a character who, furthermore, time after time, when he was idolized for his achievements, fulfilled the sort of daydreams which had been their own.[23]

A second effect was perhaps even more important. In attacking in other than a burlesque fashion fictional representations of boys who were unreal, Clemens was faced with the problem of depicting, through characterization and plot, boys who were real.[24] What a real boy was was suggested by the very terms of the attack: he was not simply good or bad but a mixture of virtue and mischievousness. And he could play pranks at the same time he was developing qualities which would make him a moral adult.

This concept allowed elements of incongruity which an author might develop humorously. In this view, youngsters of Tom's age were diverting combinations of ignorance and wisdom, deviltry and morality, childhood and adulthood. These incongruities, of course, were useful to Clemens again and again.[25] But the incongruities of boy nature not only had humorous possibilities; they also had potentialities—far beyond those in good-bad-boy books—for plot structures closely linked with developing characters. As a "real" boy grew up, the common sense theory implied, unlike the consistent actions of the static character in goody-goody books, the nature of his actions would change. Not only would they change from year to year but also from month to month. Less and less, he would behave like an irresponsible and ignorant savage; more and more he would act like a responsible and intelligent adult.

If *Tom Sawyer* is regarded as a working out in fictional form of this notion of a boy's maturing, the book will reveal, I believe, a structure on the whole quite well adapted to its purpose. My suggestion, in other words, is that Clemens' divergence from the older patterns of juvenile fiction and his concept of the normal history of boyhood led him to a way of characterizing and a patterning of action which showed a boy developing toward manhood.

That this was the unifying theme of the story will be indicated, perhaps, by a consideration of the units of narrative, the lines of action, in the novel. There are four of these—the story of Tom and Becky, the story of Tom and Muff Potter, the Jackson's Island episode, and the series of happenings (which might be called the Injun Joe story) leading to the discovery of the treasure. Each one of these is initiated by a characteristic and typically boyish action. The love story begins with Tom's childishly fickle desertion of his fiancée, Amy Lawrence; the Potter narrative with the superstitious trip to the graveyard; the Jackson's Island episode with the adolescent revolt of the boy against Aunt Polly, and Tom's youthful ambition to be a pirate; the Injun Joe story with the juvenile search for buried treasure. Three of these narrative strands, however, are climaxed by a characteristic and mature sort of action, a sort of action, moreover, directly opposed to the initial action. Tom chivalrously takes Becky's punishment and faithfully helps her in the cave; he defies boyish superstition and courageously testifies for Muff Potter; he forgets a childish antipathy and shows mature concern for his aunt's uneasiness about him. The Injun Joe story, though it is the least useful of the four so far as showing Tom's maturing is concerned, by showing Huck conquering fear to rescue the widow, has value as a repetition—with variations—of the motif of the book.

That these actions are regarded by the older folk of St. Petersburg as evidences of mature virtue is suggested in each instance by their reactions. Every subplot in the book eventuates in an expression of adult approval. Sometimes this is private, like Aunt Polly's discovery that Tom has come from the island to tell her of his safety, or like Judge Thatcher's enthusiastic comments upon Tom's chivalry at school. Sometimes it is public, like the adulation lavished on the hero after the trial and after the rescue of Becky, or like the widow's party honoring Huck Finn.

The book contains various episodes extraneous to these lines of action—episodes whose only value in the scheme is variation in the display of the incongruities of boy nature from which the actions arise, but it is notable how much of the novel is concerned with these four threads. Only four of the thirty-five chapters are not in some way concerned with the development of at least one of them.[26] Hence a large share of the book is concerned with actions which show the kind of development suggested.

More important is the fact that, if the novel is regarded as one narrative including the alternately treated lines of action and the episodes as well, as the story progresses, wholly boylike actions become more infrequent while adult actions increase. No such simple and melodramatic a device as a complete reformation is employed: late in the book, Tom is still capable of treasure hunts and fantasies about robber gangs. (Clemens remarked that he "didn't take the chap beyond boyhood.")[27] But actions which are credible late in the story—actions such as Tom's taking Becky's punishment (chap. xx) or testifying for Potter (chap. xxiii)—would, I think, seem improbable early in the book.[28] One of a few slips Clemens makes strengthens this point: in chapter xxiv, Tom tells Huck that when he is rich he is "going to buy a new drum, and sure 'nough sword, and a red necktie and bull pup, and get married." Mr. Edgar Lee Masters finds this jarring. "Can any boy of that age," he asks, "be imagined talking in this way. . . . ?"[29] It is jarring in chapter xxiv, to be sure, but at any point in the first five chapters of the book, say, it would be highly appropriate.[30]

There is perhaps, then, reason for believing that the theme, the main action, and the character portrayal in the novel are one—the developing of Tom's character in a series of crucial situations. Studying the progress of the novel with this in mind, the reader will see, I believe, that though the earlier chapters emphasize Tom's mischievousness, and though a

Sunday school fictionist would therefore call him a Bad Boy, there are potentialities in these chapters for his later behavior.[31] To put the matter negatively, his motives are never vicious; to put it positively, he has a good heart. In his aunt's words, he

> .... warn't *bad*, so to say—only misch*ee*vous. Only just giddy, and harum-scarum, you know. He warn't any more responsible than a colt. *He* never meant any harm, and he was the best-hearted boy that ever was. ... [chap. xv].

An appeal to his sympathy, he himself indicates in chapter ii, is more efficacious than physical punishment or scolding. "She talks awful," he says to Aunt Polly, "but talk don't hurt—anyways it don't if she don't cry." Inevitably then, when at the end of chapter x, his aunt weeps over him, "this was worse than a thousand whippings." And a chapter later, tender-hearted Tom is ministering to poor Muff Potter as he languishes in jail.

Significant, too, is Tom's acceptance, in times of stress in the early chapters, of the adult code of the particularly godly folk of idyllic St. Petersburg.[32] His feeling that it would be pleasant to die disappears when he remembers that he does not have "a clean Sunday-school record" (chap. viii), and the howling dog's prophecy of his death brings regret that he has been "playing hookey and doing everything a feller's told *not* to do." "But if I ever get off this time," he promises, "I lay I'll just *waller* in Sunday-schools!" (chap. x). Surrounded by night on Jackson's Island, he inwardly says his prayers, and a little later, his conscience gnaws as he recalls his sins (chap. xiii). He wants to be a soldier, or a plainsman, or a pirate chiefly in order that he may stroll into the drowsy little St. Petersburg church some Sunday morning and bask in the respect of the village (chap. viii). And his impelling desire for a place of honor in the community is a key to his initiating three of the four lines of action,[33] hence the plot strands are closely linked with his character.

Beginning with the final pages of chapter x, these potentialities for something more mature than inconsiderate childhood begin to develop. Tom is touched by his aunt's appeal to his sympathy; his conscience hurts because of his silence about Potter's innocence; he suffers pangs because he realized he has sinned in running away; he worries about his aunt's concern for his safety, and so on. And well in the second half of the book, in a series of chapters—xx, xxiii, xxix, xxxii—come those crucial situations in which he acts more like a grownup than like an irresponsible boy.

IV

There are some indications that Clemens was aware of the pattern I have suggested. He was aware, undoubtedly, of the divergence from the older fictional models patently burlesqued in his "Bad boy" and "Good boy" travesties. Did he perceive, however, that deliberate divergence from older patterns had led him to create a new structure of his own, nearer to the history of boyhood as he and others conceived it? It is impossible to be sure, but some facts may have a bearing on the problem.

In Clemens' "Conclusion" to *Tom Sawyer* (the italics are his) he wrote: "So endeth this chronicle. It being strictly a history of a *boy*, it must stop here; the story could not go much further without becoming the history of a *man*." When in 1875 he wrote Howells asking him to read the manuscript, Mark Twain asked him particularly to "see if you don't really decide that I am right in closing with him as a boy."[34] And writing to Howells, shortly after the critic had read the manuscript, the humorist said he had decided to discard or not to write what would have been chapter xxxvi, and to add nothing in its place. "Something told me," he said, "that the book was done when I got to that point"—presumably, from the context, the present concluding chapter (xxxv) of the book.[35]

The concluding passage in this chapter tells how Huck Finn, tired of civilization, sneaked away from the widow and started to live again a life free from adult restraints. In chapter vi, it may be recalled, this sort of life had been, in Tom's opinion, most enviable: "everything that goes to make life precious, that boy had." So Tom had thought when all adult curbs had been hateful to him, when grown folk had seemed to be natural enemies, and their ways unnatural ways. But now Tom, bent on dragging Huck back to that civilization, tells the runaway that everybody lives cleanly and according to schedule, "And besides," he urges, "if you'll try this sort of thing just awhile longer you'll come to like it." Craftily, when Huck's chance remark helps Tom "see his opportunity," Tom dangles the bait of the robber gang. But though in chapter xiii Huck in rags was eligible for piratehood and even as late as chapter xxxiii his savagery has not been mentioned as a bar to his joining the robbers, now, to lure the boy back to the Widow's, Tom insists that Huck the Red-handed will have to live with the good woman and be "respectable" if he is to be allowed to join the gang. Something has happened to Tom. He is talking more like an adult than like an unsocial child. He has, it appears, gone over to the side of the enemy.

Notes

1. Critics who have noted the departure of the novel from conventional literature about children include Carl Van Doren, *The American Novel* (New York, 1921), p. 168; Stuart P. Sherman, "Mark Twain," in *The Cambridge History of American Literature* (New York, 1921), III, 15; and Percy H. Boynton, in his "Introduction" to the Harper's Modern Classics ed., pp. xx–xxii.

2. A typical comment is that of F.L. Pattee who, in his *American Literature since 1870* (New York, 1915), pp. 59–60, says of Twain's writings (including *Tom Sawyer*): "They are not artistic books. The author had little skill in construction. He excelled in brilliant dashes, not in long continued effort." Compare Carl Van Doren, p. 169, speaking of *Tom Sawyer:* "To a delicate taste, indeed, the book seems occasionally overloaded with matters brought in at moments

when no necessity in the narrative calls for them. . . . Nor can the murder about which the story is built up be said to dominate it very thoroughly. The story moves forward in something the same manner as did the plays of the seventies, with entrances and exits not always motivated." More recently A. H. Quinn, in *American Fiction, an Historical and Critical Survey* (New York, 1936), p. 256, has asserted that Clemens' "definition of the humorous story as one that 'may be spun out at great length and wander about as much as it pleases, and arrive nowhere in particular' is illuminating in its explanation of his strength and weakness as a writer of fiction. Like Bret Harte he is best in his episodes, and it is through them that he built up the characters. . . . by which he will be remembered," including Tom Sawyer.

3. Exceptions, in some ways, to these generalizations, had been some characters in novels by Louisa M. Alcott, Elijah J. Kellogg, and J. T. Trowbridge. The exceptions, however, do not, I think invalidate the generalizations.

4. Little Rollo, created by Jacob Abbott in 1834 to survive at least twenty-four volumes of boyhood, was surrounded by wise instructors who quickly reasoned him out of impulses toward sin. The same careful nurture kept upright his brothers and sisters in four series of books. Goodrich's Peter Parley narratives, in much the same tradition, were roughly contemporaneous.

5. *Ragged Dick* (Philadelphia, [n.d]), pp.15–18. During the course of the book, however, Dick reformed, and his evil habits were replaced with good ones. It is notable that Alger indicated his departure from the tradition of the completely virtuous hero when he said, "I have mentioned Dick's faults and defects because I want it understood, to begin with, that I don't consider him a model boy."

6. Frederick Lewis Allen, "Horatio Alger, Jr.," *Saturday Review of Literature*, XVIII (September 17, 1938), 4.

7. Some exceptions included, in addition to some Alger boys, the heroes of Oliver Optic's *In School and Out* (1863) and of Francis Forrester's *Dick Duncan* (1864), who, after sinning divertingly for several chapters, were allowed to reform. See Richard Allen Foster, *The School in American Literature* (Baltimore, 1930), pp. 134–35.

8. K. K. Maxfield, "'Goody-goody' Literature and Mrs. Stowe," *American Speech*, V (February, 1920), 201.

9. The story of the truant, which appeared in a reader, and the poem about the idle boy, from *Youth's Casket* (1857), are reprinted in E. Douglas Branch, *The Sentimental Years 1836–1860* (New York, 1934), pp. 312–13. For details concerning the preachments in the McGuffey readers, see Mark Sullivan, *Our Times* (New York, 1927), II, 23–45.

10. He had so far observed the amenities as to grow up to be a rascal, but since his creator obviously delighted in his rascality, Hooper was considered a most immoral person by contemporaries.

11. B. P. Shillaber, *Life and Sayings of Mrs. Partington* (New York, 1854). Ike, for all his resemblance to the later Tom Sawyer, was a rather sketchy character because, as a rule, he committed his crimes in the final lines of a narrative chiefly devoted to his aunt.

12. *Eyes and Ears* (Boston, 1862), pp. 73–74.

13. *The Story of a Bad Boy* (Boston, 1869), pp. 8–9.

14. Feris Greenslet, *The Life of Thomas Bailey Aldrich* (Boston, 1908), p. 92.

15. *Life in Danbury* (Boston, 1873), pp. 72–73. A section on pp. 275–83 called "The Danbury youth" burlesques the old rewards-and-punishment fiction by remarking that "boys who put stones in snow balls grow up to be bad men, and finally die a miserable death in a New York custom house" and foreshadows passages in *Tom Sawyer* by recounting how a boy "whose imagination had become diseased by too much close devotion to dime novels started off yesterday to seek fame as a slayer of bears and Indians. He. . . . was gone nearly two hours."

16. M. Quad [C.B. Lewis], *Quad's Odds* (Detroit, 1875), pp.379–87. The Bad Boy, like Tom Sawyer after him, had "an ambition which nothing could check. He wanted to be a bold pirate and sail on the raging main. . . ." "Jeems," on pp. 354–55 of the same volume, tolerantly told of the difficulty a mother had getting her son started to Sunday school.

17. *The Rise and Fall of the Mustache and Other Hawk-Eyetems* (Burlington, 1877), p. 165.

18. The former first appeared in *The Celebrated Jumping Frog of Calevaras County and Other Sketches* (New York, 1867), the latter in *The Galaxy* for May, 1870. Both were frequently reprinted before their inclusion in *Sketches New and Old* (Hartford, 1875). Both therefore appeared early enough to merit consideration as germinal for Clemens' famous story of boyhood.

19. Quoted in Will M. Clemens, *Mark Twain: His Life and Work* (Chicago, 1894), p. 126. The writer is identified as "a well-known literary critic," and the passage is drawn from a review. I have been unable, however, to find the original review.

20. Chap. v. See also chap. i, in which the author says, approvingly, of Tom: "He was not the Model Boy of the village. He knew the model boy very well though—and loathed him."

21. A female critic so strongly conditioned by preachy literature that she managed to find a moral, of all places, in *Huckleberry Finn*, in 1887 called attention to outstanding examples of Tom's nobility.

"Only a noble and tender heart," she said admiringly, "could have taken the blame upon itself when Becky accidentally tore the teacher's book, and received 'without an outcry the most merciless flogging that even Mr. Dobbins had ever administered'; and 'when he stepped forward to go to his punishment the surprise, the gratitude, the adoration that shone upon him out of poor Becky's eyes seemed pay enough for a hundred floggings.' The scene in the cave, of the rough boy folding in his arms the lost and weeping little girl, is a beautiful one"—Sarah K. Bolton, *Famous American authors* (New York, 1887), p. 369.

22. "My story," said the author in his preface, "is intended mainly for boys and girls." He made changes in his manuscript with his childish audience in view. (See *Mark Twain's letters* (New York, 1917), I, 272, 273.) However, he was not always sure that the book was not for adults.

23. Booth Tarkington's shrewd suggestion is that Clemens gave his youthful character "adventures that all boys, in their longing dreams, make believe they have. He made extravagant, dramatic things happen to them; they were pitted against murderers, won their ladyloves, and discovered hidden gold. He made them so real that their very reality is the stimulus of the adult reader's laughter, but he embedded this reality in the romance of a plot as true to the conventional mid-nineteenth century romantic novel-writing as it was to the day-dreams the boy Mark Twain himself had been"—Introduction to Cyril Clemens, *My Cousin Mark Twain* (Emmaus, Pa., 1939).

24. Clemens at least wanted to do this. "Part of my plan," he said in his preface, "has been to try to pleasantly remind adults of how they thought and talked, and what queer enterprises they sometimes engaged in."

25. The famous whitewashing scene, to cite one example, played upon some of these discrepancies: Tom, vainly trying to escape his chore, was the mischievous and ignorant boy. When, later, he got other boys, less canny than he, to do the job for him, he displayed the sort of wisdom—perhaps even of morality—becoming to an adult. "He," said his approving historian, "had discovered a great law of human action, without knowing it namely, that in order to make a man or boy covet a thing, it is only necessary to make the thing difficult to attain."

26. Chaps. i (which is expository), v, viii, and xxi. Chap. xxii, however, contains only one sentence concerning the Becky Thatcher story. This narrative occurs in twelve chapters, the Injun Joe story twelve, the Jackson's Island episode seven, and the Muff Potter subplot five. Eight chapters contain elements of two lines of action.

27. *Letters*, I, 258.

28. Two kinds of probability are, I believe, theoretically involved here—one that which represents the intelligent person's general conception of the way a boy matures, the other that which derives from a study of the character of Tom as it is displayed in the book. In this instance, I think, the two kinds of probability coincide.

29. *Mark Twain: a Portrait* (New York, 1938), p. 125. Tom's age is not specified in the book, except by his actions. The fact that the action of the book requires only a few months seems irrelevant, since fictional rather than actual time is involved.

30. It is not incongruous, for example, with the list of Tom's treasures in chap. ii.

31. If Clemens' book was to be on a level above that of travesty, such potentialities had to be indicated. A rule of literary art which Twain himself formulated in "Fenimore Cooper's Literary Offenses," in *Literary Essays* (New York, 1899), p. 81, was "that the characters in a tale shall be so clearly defined that the reader can tell beforehand what each will do in a given emergency." Thus his very divergence from the simple motivation of earlier fictional works necessitated more complex characterization than they contained.

32. Kind-hearted Muff Potter, the grave-robbing Dr. Robinson, and the Temperance Tavern keeper who bootlegs are the nearest approach to native sin. Injun Joe and his vague companion from somewhere "up the river" are not of the community. The chief hints of vice Tom picks up anywhere are in the novels he reads.

33. The Becky Thatcher story, the exception, is, as has been suggested, also a natural expression of Tom's character.

34. *Letters*, I, 259.

35. Clemens wrote: "As to that last chapter, I think of just leaving it off and adding nothing in its place. Something told me the book was done when I got to that point—and so the temptation to put Huck's life into detail, instead of generalizing it in a paragraph was resisted" (*ibid.*, I, 267).

Mark Twain

William Dean Howells

In one form or other, Mr. Samuel L. Clemens has told the story of his life in his books, and in sketching his career I shall have to recur to the leading facts rather than to offer fresh information. He was remotely of Virginian origin and more remotely of good English stock; the name was well known before his time in the South, where a senator, a congressman, and other dignitaries had worn it; but his branch of the family fled from the destitution of those vast landed possessions in Tennessee, celebrated in *The Gilded Age*, and went very poor to Missouri. Mr. Clemens was born on November 30, 1835, at Florida in the latter State, but his father removed shortly afterward to Hannibal, a small town on the Mississippi, where most of the humorist's boyhood was spent. Hannibal as a name is hopelessly confused and ineffective; but if we can know nothing of Mr. Clemens from Hannibal, we can know much of Hannibal from Mr. Clemens, who, in fact, has studied a loafing, out-at-elbows, down-at-the-heels, slaveholding Mississippi River town of thirty years ago, with such strong reality in his boy's romance of *Tom Sawyer*, that we need inquire nothing further concerning the type. The original perhaps no longer exists anywhere; certainly not in Hannibal, which has grown into a flourishing little city since Mr. Clemens sketched it. In his time the two embattled forces of civilization and barbarism were encamped at Hannibal,

Section VII reprinted from *My Mark Twain* (NY: Harper & Bros., 1910, pp. 113–123) originally published in *Century Magazine* XXIV (September 1882), 780–83.

as they are at all times and everywhere; the morality of the place was the morality of a slaveholding community: fierce, arrogant, one-sided—this virtue for white, and that for black folks; and the religion was Calvinism in various phases, with its predestinate aristocracy of saints and its rabble of hopeless sinners. Doubtless, young Clemens escaped neither of the opposing influences wholly. His people like the rest were slaveholders; but his father, like so many other slaveholders abhorred slavery—silently, as he must in such a time and place. If the boy's sense of justice suffered anything of that perversion which so curiously and pitiably maimed the reason of the whole South, it does not appear in his books, where there is not an ungenerous line, but always, on the contrary, a burning resentment of all manner of cruelty and wrong.

The father, an austere and singularly upright man, died bankrupt when Clemens was twelve years old, and the boy had thereafter to make what scramble he could for an education. He got very little learning in school, and like so many other Americans in whom the literary impulse is native, he turned to the local printing-office for some of the advantages from which he was otherwise cut off. Certain records of the three years spent in the Hannibal *Courier* office are to be found in Mark Twain's book of sketches; but I believe there is yet no history anywhere of the *wanderjahre*, in which he followed the life of a jour-printer, from town to town, and from city to city, penetrating even so far into the vague and fabled East as Philadelphia and New York.

He returned to his own town—his *patria*—sated, if not satisfied, with travel, and at seventeen he resolved to "learn the river" from St. Louis to New Orleans as a steamboat pilot. Of this period of his life he has given a full account in the delightful series of papers, *Piloting on the Mississippi*, which he printed seven years ago in the *Atlantic Monthly*. The growth of the railroads and the outbreak of the Civil War put an end to profitable piloting, and at twenty-four he was again open to a vocation. He listened for a moment to the loudly calling drum of that time, and he was actually in camp for three weeks on the rebel side; but the unorganized force to which he belonged was disbanded, and he finally did not "go with his section" either in sentiment or in fact. His brother having been appointed Lieutenant-Governor of Nevada Territory, Mr. Clemens went out with him as his private secretary; but he soon resigned his office and withdrew to the mines. He failed as a miner, in the ordinary sense; but the life of the mining-camp yielded him the wealth that the pockets of the mountain denied; he had the Midas touch without knowing it, and all these grotesque experiences have since turned into gold under his hand. After his failure as a miner had become evident even to himself, he was glad to take the place of local editor on the Virginia City *Enterprise*, a newspaper for which he had amused himself in writing from time to time. He had written for the newspapers before this; few Americans escape that fate; and as an apprentice in the Hannibal *Courier* office his humor had embroiled some of the leading citizens, and impaired the fortunes of that journal by the alienation of several delinquent subscribers.

But it was in the *Enterprise* that he first used his pseudonym of "Mark Twain," which he borrowed from the vernacular of the river, where the man heaving the lead calls out "Mark twain!" instead of "Mark two!" In 1864, he accepted, on the San Francisco *Morning Call*, the same sort of place which he had held on the *Enterprise*, and he soon made his *nom de guerre* familiar "on that coast"; he not only wrote "local items" in the *Call*, but he printed humorous sketches in various periodicals, and, two years later, he was sent to the Sandwich Islands as correspondent of a Sacramento paper.

When he came back he "entered the lecture-field," as it used to be phrased. Of these facts there is, as all English-speaking readers know, full record in *Roughing It*, though I think Mr. Clemens has not mentioned there his association with that extraordinary group of wits and poets, of whom Mr. Bret Harte, Mr. Charles Warren Stoddard, Mr. Charles H. Webb, and Mr. Prentice Mulford, were, with himself, the most conspicuous. These ingenious young men, with the fatuity of gifted people, had established a literary newspaper in San Francisco, and they brilliantly co-operated to its early extinction.

In 1867, Mr. Clemens made in the *Quaker City* the excursion to Europe and the East which he has commemorated in *The Innocents Abroad*. Shortly after his return he married, and placed himself at Buffalo, where he bought an interest in one of the city newspapers; later he came to Hartford, where he has since remained, except for the two years spent in a second visit to Europe. The incidents of this visit he has characteristically used in *A Tramp Abroad*; and, in fact, I believe the only book of Mr. Clemens's which is not largely autobiographical is *The Prince and the Pauper*: the scene being laid in England, in the early part of the sixteenth century, the difficulties presented to a nineteenth-century autobiographer were insurmountable.

The habit of putting his own life, not merely in its results but in its processes, into his books, is only one phase of the frankness of Mr. Clemens's humorous attitude. The transparent disguise of the pseudonym once granted him, he asks the reader to grant him nothing else. In this he differs wholly from most other American humorists, who have all found some sort of dramatization of their personality desirable if not necessary. Charles F. Browne, "delicious" as he was when he dealt with us directly, preferred the disguise of "Artemus Ward" the showman; Mr. Locke likes to figure as "Petroleum V. Nasby," the cross-roads politician; Mr. Shaw chooses to masquerade as the saturnine philosopher "Josh Billings"; and each of these humorists appeals to the grotesqueness of misspelling to help out his fun. It was for Mr. Clemens to reconcile the public to humor which contented itself with the established absurdities of English orthography; and I am inclined to attribute to the example of his immense success, the humane spirit which characterizes our recent popular humor. There is still sufficient flippancy and brutality in it; but there is no longer the stupid and monkeyish cruelty of motive and intention which once disgraced and insulted us.

Except the political humorists, like Mr. Lowell—if there were any like him—the American humorists formerly chose the wrong in public matters; they were on the side of slavery, of drunkenness, and of irreligion; the friends of civilization were their prey; their spirit was thoroughly vulgar and base. Before "John Phoenix," there was scarcely any American humorist—not of the distinctly literary sort—with whom one could smile and keep one's self-respect. The great Artemus himself was not guiltless; but the most popular humorist who ever lived has not to accuse himself, so far as I can remember, of having written anything to make one morally ashamed of liking him. One can readily make one's strictures; there is often more than a suggestion of forcing in his humor; sometimes it tends to horse-play; sometimes the extravagance over-leaps itself, and falls flat on the other side; but I cannot remember that in Mr. Clemens's books I have ever been asked to join him in laughing at any good or really fine thing. But I do not mean to leave him with this negative praise; I mean to say of him that as Shakespeare, according to Mr. Lowell's saying, was the first to make poetry all poetical, Mark Twain was the first to make humor all humorous. He has not only added more in bulk to the sum of harmless pleasures than any other humorist; but more in the spirit that is easily and wholly enjoyable. There is nothing lost in literary attitude, in labored dictionary funning, in affected quaintness, in dreary dramatization, in artificial "dialect"; Mark Twain's humor is as simple in form and as direct as the statesmanship of Lincoln or the generalship of Grant.

When I think how purely and wholly American it is, I am a little puzzled at its universal acceptance. We are doubtless the most thoroughly homogeneous people that ever existed as a great nation. There is such a parity in the experiences of Americans that Mark Twain or Artemus Ward appeals as unerringly to the consciousness of our fifty millions as Goldoni appealed to that of his hundred thousand Venetians. In our phrase, we have somehow all "been there"; in fact, generally, and in sympathy almost certainly, we have been there. In another generation or two, perhaps, it will be wholly different; but as yet the average American is the man who has risen; he has known poverty, and privation, and low conditions; he has very often known squalor; and now, in his prosperity, he regards the past with a sort of large, pitying amusement; he is not the least ashamed of it; he does not feel that it characterizes him any more than the future does. Our humor springs from this multiform American experience of life, and securely addresses itself—in reminiscence, in phrase, in its whole material—to the intelligence bred of like experience. It is not of a class for a class; it does not employ itself with the absurdities of a tailor as a tailor; its conventions, if it has any, are all new, and of American make. When it mentions hash we smile because we have each somehow known the cheap boarding-house or restaurant; when it alludes to putting up stoves in the fall, each of us feels the grime and rust of the pipes on his hands; the introduction of the lightning-rod man, or the book-agent, establishes our brotherhood with the humorist at once. But how is it with the vast English-speaking world outside of these States, to which hash, and stovepipes, and lightning-rod men and book-agents are as strange as lords and ladies, dungeon-keeps and battlements are to us? Why, in fine, should an English chief-justice keep Mark Twain's books always at hand? Why should Darwin have gone to them for rest and refreshment at midnight when spent with scientific research?

I suppose that Mark Twain transcends all other American humorists in the universal qualities. He deals very little with the pathetic, which he nevertheless knows very well how to manage, as he has shown, notably in the true story of the old slave-mother; but there is a poetic lift in his work, even when he permits you to recognize it only as something satirized. There is always the touch of nature, the presence of a sincere and frank manliness in what he says, the companionship of a spirit which is at once delightfully open and deliciously shrewd. Elsewhere I have tried to persuade the reader that his humor is at its best the foamy break of the strong tide of earnestness in him. But it would be limiting him unjustly to describe him as a satirist; and it is hardly practicable to establish him in people's minds as a moralist; he has made them laugh too long; they will not believe him serious; they think some joke is always intended. This is the penalty, as Doctor Holmes has pointed out, of making one's first success as a humorist. There was a paper of Mark Twain's printed in the *Atlantic Monthly* some years ago and called "The Facts Concerning the Late Carnival of Crime in Connecticut," which ought to have won popular recognition of the ethical intelligence underlying his humor. It was, of course, funny; but under the fun it was an impassioned study of the human conscience. Hawthorne or Bunyan might have been proud to imagine that powerful allegory, which had a grotesque force far beyond either of them. It had been read before a literary club in Hartford; a reverend gentleman had offered the author his pulpit for the next Sunday if he would give it as a homily there. Yet it quite failed of the response I had hoped for it, and I shall not insist here upon Mark Twain as a moralist; though I warn the reader that if he leaves out of the account an indignant sense of right and wrong, a scorn of all affectation and pretence, an ardent hate of meanness and injustice, he will come indefinitely short of knowing Mark Twain.

His powers as a story-teller were evident in hundreds of brief sketches before he proved them in *Tom Sawyer* and *The Prince and the Pauper*. Both of these books, aside from their strength of characterization, are fascinating as mere narratives, and I can think of no writer living who has in higher degree the art of interesting his reader from the first word. This is a far rarer gift than we imagine, and I shall not call it a subordinate charm in Mark Twain's books, rich as they otherwise are. I have already had my say about *Tom Sawyer*, whose only fault is an excess of reality in portraying the character and conditions of Southwestern boyhood as it was forty years ago, and which is full of that poetic sympathy with nature and human nature which I always find in Mark Twain. *The Prince and the Pauper* has particularly interested me for the same qualities which, in a study of the past, we call romantic, but which alone can realize the past for us. Occasionally the archaic diction gives way and lets us down hard upon the American parlance of the nineteenth century; but mainly the illusion is admirably sustained, and the tale is to be valued not only in itself but as an earnest of what Mr. Clemens might do in fiction when he has fairly done with autobiography in its various forms. His invention is of the good old sort, like De Foe's more than that of any other English writer, and like that of the Spanish picaresque novelists, Mendoza and the rest; it flows easily from incident to incident, and does not deepen into situation. In the romance it operates as lightly and unfatiguingly as his memory in the realistic story.

His books abound in passages of dramatic characterization, and he is, as the reader knows, the author of the most successful American play. I believe Mr. Clemens has never claimed the reconstruction of Colonel Sellers for the stage; but he nevertheless made the play, for whatever is good in it came bodily from his share of the novel of *The Gilded Age*. It is a play which succeeds by virtue of the main personage, and this personage, from first to last, is quite outside of the dramatic action, which sometimes serves and sometimes does not serve the purpose of presenting Colonel Sellers. Where the drama fails, Sellers rises superior and takes the floor; and we forget the rest. Mr. Raymond conceived the character wonderfully well, and he plays it with an art that ranks him to that extent with the great actors; but he has in nowise "created" it. If any one "created" Colonel Sellers, it was Mark Twain, as the curious reader may see on turning again to the novel; but I suspect that Colonel Sellers was never created, except as other men are; that he was found somewhere and transferred, living, to the book.

I prefer to speak of Mr. Clemens's artistic qualities because it is to these that his humor will owe its perpetuity. All fashions change, and nothing more wholly and quickly than the fashion of fun; as any one may see by turning back to what amused people in the last generation; that stuff is terrible. As Europe becomes more and more the playground of Americans, and every scene and association becomes insipidly familiar, the jokes about the old masters and the legends will no longer be droll to us. Neither shall we care for the huge Californian mirth, when the surprise of the picturesquely mixed civilization and barbarism of the Pacific Coast has quite died away; and Mark Twain would pass with the conditions that have made him intelligible, if he were not an artist of uncommon power as well as a humorist. He portrays and interprets real types, not only with exquisite appreciation and sympathy, but with a force and truth of drawing that makes them permanent. Artemus Ward was very funny, that can never be denied; but it must be owned that the figure of the literary showman is as wholly factitious as his spelling; the conception is one that has to be constantly humored by the reader. But the innumerable characters sketched by Mark Twain are actualities, however caricatured—and, usually, they are not so very much caricatured. He has brought back the expression of Western humor to sympathy with the sane orthography in John Phoenix; but Mark Twain is vastly more original in form. Derby was weighed upon by literary tradition; he was "academic" at times, but Mr. Clemens is never "academic." There is no drawing from casts; in his work evidently the life has everywhere been studied: and it is his apparent unconsciousness of any other way of saying a thing except the natural way that makes his books so restful and refreshing. Our little nervous literary sensibilities may suffer from his extravagance, or from other traits of his manner, but we have not to beat our breasts at the dread apparition of Dickens's or Thackeray's hand in his page. He is far too honest and sincere a soul for that; and where he is obliged to force a piece of humor to its climax—as sometimes happens—he does not call in his neighbors to help; he does it himself, and is probably sorry that he had to do it.

 I suppose that even in so slight and informal a study as this, something like an "analysis" of our author's humor is expected. But I much prefer not to make it. I have observed that analyses of humor are apt to leave one rather serious, and to result in an entire volatilization of the humor. If the prevailing spirit of Mark Twain's humor is not a sort of good-natured self-satire, in which the reader may see his own absurdities reflected, I scarcely should be able to define it.

Trowbridge and Clemens

Rufus A. Coleman

Even among those reading widely in American literature, John Townsend Trowbridge today is little more than a name to be remembered chiefly for some verses about a boy named Darius, who, with his home-made contraption buckled to his back, made an early attempt to fly by jumping from a barn loft.[1] And yet in the seventies and eighties, Trowbridge was almost as popular a poet as Longfellow (he was a favorite with the elocutionists) and was, in addition, as editor of *Our Young Folks* and a leading contributor to the *Youth's Companion* and *St. Nicholas*, exceedingly popular with the younger generation. One critic went so far as to write that with Trowbridge a new era in juvenile literature began in America.[2] In his *Autobiography*, Theodore Roosevelt bore witness to his own allegiance, in these words:

> As a small boy I had *Our Young Folks*, which I then firmly believed to be the very best magazine in the world—a belief, I may add, which I have kept to this day unchanged, for I seriously doubt if any magazine for old or young has ever surpassed it. Both my wife and I have bound volumes of *Our Young Folks* which we preserved from our youth. I have tried to read again the Mayne Reid books which I so dearly loved as a boy, only to find, alas! that it was impossible. But I really believe I enjoy going over *Our Young Folks* now nearly as much as ever.[3]

Trowbridge (1827–1916) lived through nearly all of the nineteenth century as well as the first years of the twentieth, a

Reprinted from *Modern Language Quarterly* 9 (June 1948): 216–223.

large share of this time being spent at his Arlington home, a few miles, by trolley, from Cambridge and Boston. A man of many contacts, he met writers as widely dispersed chronologically as Mordecai Noah and Booth Tarkington. He knew many of the New England group intimately, for years being a member of the Boston Authors Club. He was a lifelong friend of Walt Whitman, a "judicious" friend, however, not an out-and-out disciple of the Bucke, Traubel, and Harned variety.

In view of such rich associations, it may seem surprising that Trowbridge did not number Samuel L. Clemens[4] among his intimates, especially since Clemens was a close friend of W. D. Howells who, for a few years, also lived at Arlington not far distant from Trowbridge. But despite common literary interests, the two met infrequently and then chiefly on public or semipublic occasions. Then, too, Trowbridge was critical of Clemens both as a speaker and as a writer, considering him diverting but prolix, episodic, and at times tiresome. Trowbridge was a stickler for form, and it was the lack of this quality and the presence of repetitiousness that prompted his critical disapproval of Whitman. Whitman's ideas on oratory especially disturbed him, as they had likewise done his friend Lewis B. Monroe,[5] for many years dean of the School of Oratory of Boston University, and editor of a series of popular school readers. An enthusiastic disciple of Delsarte, Monroe had even given Trowbridge an occasional lesson in public speaking, which accounts for the latter's frequent comments upon the poor stage presence of such men as Hale or Higginson, whose voices trailed off to a whisper so that only those in the front rows could hear them.

Trowbridge's relationship to Clemens, then, though friendly, was casual, similar in nature to his acquaintanceship with Howells, except, of course, that with the latter there was in addition a business association through the medium of the *Atlantic Monthly*.[6] Yet if the conjectures of scholars are correct, Clemens in his teens wrote his first sketch for Shillaber's *Carpet-Bag*[7] at the same time that Trowbridge, masquerading as "Paul Creyton," was one of its leading contributors.[8]

Both, however, were present at the famous Whittier dinner of 1877. Indeed, Clemens was very much in evidence. Initiated by H.O. Houghton, the enterprising publisher, this dinner was intended not only to honor the poet, but also to celebrate the twentieth anniversary of the *Atlantic Monthly*. The Boston *Daily Advertiser*[9] declared that Houghton and Company had "invited the contributors of the magazine both present and past, to meet in a never before attempted meeting," and that "the company was without doubt the most notable that has ever been seen in this country within four walls." When one casts his eye over the elaborate seating chart handed to each of the guests, one is inclined to agree with this assertion.[10]

Since Whittier disliked any kind of public display, it was considered a great piece of luck when the publishers were able to announce that the guest of honor would be there in person. After the dinner at 10:15 p.m., Whittier's brief and hesitant remarks were supplemented with the reading of some of his verses by Longfellow.[11]

The most striking episode in the whole occasion, however, was "that hideous mistake of poor Clemens,"[12] a phrase coined by Howells who, as toastmaster, was really put on the spot. To understand the extent of the offense, one should keep in mind the extreme veneration with which Holmes, Whittier, Longfellow, and Emerson were looked upon sixty or more years ago, an attitude somewhat like the Englishman's regard for his king. In this instance, however, the respect was intensified threefold. The newspaper reporter (one from the *Daily Advertiser*) reflected but the common esteem[13] when he wrote, "The three, Whittier, Emerson, and Longfellow gave a reverend, almost holy, air to the place, and their gray hairs and expressive faces, formed a beautiful group." Then what did the irrepressible Clemens do but spin a yarn about three disreputable miners masquerading as three of these mighty four, a choice part of which ran as follows:

> Mr. Emerson was a seedy little bit of a chap, red-headed. Mr. Holmes was as fat as a balloon, he weighed as much as three hundred, and has double chains all the way down to his stomach. Mr. Longfellow was built like a prize fighter. His head was cropped and bristly, like as if he had a wig made of hair brushes. His nose lay straight down his face, like a finger with the end-joint tilted up. They had been drinking—I could see that.

To make matters worse, the jokester did not reveal until the very close of his speech that these reprehensibles were imposters. Carefully planned and executed as it was, his hoax failed utterly to go over. There followed a dead silence which poor Howells had to bridge over as best he could. Neither he nor Clemens got over their chagrin for months.[14] In a letter to Norton written only two days later Howells likened his friend's conduct to "demoniacal possession." Clemens spent much of the next few days writing apologetic letters. The whole affair seemed to have affected the principals more devastatingly than it did the other guests, for Trowbridge, who sat across the table from Clemens, made no reference to the incident either in notebook, letter, or autobiography. But the diplomacy of the press seldom appeared to better advantage. The reader of next morning's paper, on coming across this choice piece of mendacity, could never have guessed what had happened: "The humorist of the evening was next introduced and the amusement was intense, while the subjects of his wit, Longfellow, Emerson, and Holmes enjoyed it as much as any."

When the speaking was about half over, Whittier unobtrusively slipped away, and shortly after Trowbridge also left, despite the fact that he was on the program. His contribution, a poem entitled "The Story of a Barefoot Boy," published in the *Youth's Companion*,[15] described an episode in Whittier's life, the details of which had been furnished by Matthew Franklin Whittier, the poet's younger brother.[16] Having found that they could lift each other, the two youngsters evolved the bright idea that perhaps they might raise themselves to the ceiling, and, if they went outdoors, perhaps even higher. To be safe, however, they experimented first in their bedroom, standing on their bed. Trowbridge added his own philosophy in the following stanza:

> 'Twas a shrewd notion, none the less
> And still, in spite of ill success,
> It somehow has succeeded.
> Kind nature smiled on the wise child,
> Nor could her love deny him
> The large fulfillment of his plan,
> Since he who lifts his fellow man
> In turn is lifted by him.

That Whittier appreciated the poem is shown by the following hitherto unpublished letter:[17]

>   Oak Knoll
>   Danvers
>   1 Mo.[Jan.] 6, 1878
>
> Dear Friend Trowbridge:
>   Thanks for thy letter, & paper; and the bright & pleasant account of F's and my experiments in levitation. I wish it had been read at the dinner, it was just suited for such an occasion.
>   Cordially thy friend
>   John G. Whittier
> Remember me to Mrs. N.[18] and thy wife.

The two celebrities met again many years later at a session of the Boston Authors Club,[19] where Clemens was the principal attraction. At the turn of the century his fame was at its peak, and in consequence a large crowd filled the three rooms open for visitors. Mrs. Julia Ward Howe read an introductory poem in his honor "by the light of a candle on a table by a wall, near a doorway, where Mark was seated"— lines of which ran:

> Mark Twain, welcome guest,
> Master of heroic jest;
> He who cheers man's dull abodes
> With the laughter of the gods;

> To the joyless ones of earth
> Sounds the reveille of mirth.
> Well we meet, to part with pain
> But ne'er he and we be Twain.[20]

Clemens was placed in a central position so that his voice could reach the adjoining rooms. When Mrs. Howe had finished, he mounted a chair. Trowbridge's notebook impressions read:

> The talk was about his two-weeks experience in Mo., the point of which was that Grant, then a Col., was personally afraid of the still more frightened squad of 23 men of whom Twain was one; then various things, chiefly his undertaking to teach the art of off-hand speaking in one lesson, his example, on the chance chose subject of portrait painting, being enlivened by ludicrously irrelevant anecdotes 'sarsparilla,' & 'more chalk' stories and others. He must have rambled on nearly an hour being diffuse and almost wearisome at times, getting in good things occasionally with a drollery that convulsed his audience. He told a good story of the 'moral' effect of stealing a green watermellon in his boyhood, & to my surprise retold the anecdote of the whistling cure for stammering which Raymond as Col. Sellers, told on the stage much better, years ago. . . .[21]

Trowbridge was a perspiring spectator at the Aldrich Memorial Services (June 30, 1908) at Portsmouth, New Hampshire, on one of the hottest days of an unusually hot month. Mrs. Aldrich had arranged for two special cars to take her guests from Boston to Portsmouth. Many, who naturally thought their tickets had been paid for, were sharply disillusioned when the conductor came around to collect fares. Despite heat, cinders, and other inconveniences, Trowbridge was not too cast down to make a pun. To a group on the train discussing the question as to whether or not Clemens' popularity was holding its own, he replied that he personally hadn't noticed any "Mark (T)wain in book sales."[22]

An excellent contemporary newspaper account of the proceeding was written for the Boston *Globe*[23] by Caroline Ticknor, who, first comparing these services with the similar memorial to Longfellow in the Old Boston Museum in 1867, went on to inform her readers that:

> At the celebration today, however, were literary people—famous—some of them scarcely heard of 21 years ago, and many of whom have won their Laurels within a decade. All the so-called 'schools' of American literature were represented. There was Colonel Thomas Wentworth Higginson, 85 years old, of that school which has become classic in America—the school of Emerson, Whittier, Bryant, and Lowell. There was John Townsend Trowbridge, 81 years, and there was Mark Twain, William Dean Howells, and Richard Watson Gilder who may be said to typify the second era; then came Hamilton Wright Mabie, Thomas Nelson Page, Prof. Barrett Wendell, Prof. Arlo Bates, Miss Sarah O. Jewett, Frank Dempster Sherman, John Kendrick Bangs, Mrs. Deland, Nathan Haskell Dole, Prof. Edward S. Morse, Peter Finley Dunne, T. Russell Sullivan, Robert Bridges, Nixon Waterman, Charles Warren, Edward W. Bok, Charles Gibson, and several hundred other men and women writers, and altogether about 1000 admirers, who traveled from far and near to pay their tribute of respect to the memory of one of the most genial characters in American literature—Thomas Bailey Aldrich.

Here briefly was the order of the speakers. The first literary man was Mabie, who discussed Aldrich's place in literature. Higginson came next with remarks concerning Aldrich's relation to the older school of writers. Gilder related Aldrich to the younger school, ending with his poem, "The Singing River,"[24] written especially for the occasion. Page represented the Southern group. Howells spoke of personal relations with Aldrich on the *Atlantic Monthly* staff. Then followed Clemens, who saw that to offset this monotonous and deadly eulogy something radical must be done. So lugubrious was the flow that three days later he had not recovered, writing in his notebook an excoriating account of the whole ceremonial, which, deleted from his *Autobiography*, did not appear until 1940 under the careful editorship of Bernard DeVoto.[25] Always a hater of pretension, Clemens was capable of writing of his hostess; "A strange and vanity-devoured, detestable woman! I do not believe I could ever learn to like her except on a raft at sea with no other provisions in sight."

Miss Ticknor's less jaundiced report is worth extended quoting:

> Mayor Hackett in introducing Mark Twain told of the man who took an hour to introduce Mark at one time and this left Mark only half an hour to tell all he knew. This gave Mark a cue to say a few words about long introductions, which embarrass the person who is being introduced and make the audience feel uncomfortable.
>
> He said one of the briefest introductions he ever had was out west in the mining country one time at a place called Red Dog. He had been announced to lecture and the little hall was filled with rough miners, but there was nobody to introduce him. One of the miners, appreciating the situation, stepped on the platform and said, "I don't know what to say about this fellow. I only know two things about him; one is that he has never been in jail; and the other is that I don't know why."
>
> Mr. Clemens then said that his folks had warned him in the morning to be dignified and serious, "and they insisted that I must wear black clothes. So here I am in these dark clothes all day. They seemed to think this was a funeral I was coming to, when, in point of fact, it is a resurrection and an occasion of joy. I have come here dressed in black, which I hate, and it is hot here; but while I have been sitting here I have made 150 speeches waiting for the riff raff to get through.
>
> "Aldrich's life was cheerful and happy I knew him 40 years. He was one of the brightest men it has been my fortune to meet. Some 29 years ago I met him one day at a certain place in a hotel and he looked pained; looked as if somebody had died and it wasn't the right person. I asked him why he looked so troubled, and he said, 'It is all on your account! You used to be the most popular author in this country, but that popularity has all gone.' 'How do you know?' I said. 'Come with me.' He took me around the corner to a book store, and he stepped up to the man in the place and said, 'Have you any of T.B. Aldrich's works?' and the man said 'No!' Then he said: 'Have you any of Mark Twain's works?' 'Yes,' said the man, 'I've got a whole shelf

full of them there.' 'Got any more than that?' asked Aldrich. 'Yes, the cellar's full of them,' was the reply. Then Aldrich took me out and said, 'You see your popularity has all gone. I'm popular now. He's sold out all my books.'"[26]

Outside, when the speeches were over, Trowbridge greeted Clemens with outstretched hands and mutual jokes. Clemens began it with, "Trowbridge, are you still alive? You must be a thousand years old. Why I listened to your stories while I was rocked in the cradle." Not to be outdone, Trowbridge flashed back, "Mark, there's some mistake. My earliest infant smile was wakened with one of your jokes." Albert Bigelow Paine from whom I take the above anecdote went on to say that the two were photographed in the blazing sun, their backs to a fence.[27] In one of his notebook entries Trowbridge presented more confidential impressions, referring to being photographed with Clemens and ending his notation rather caustically:

> Services in the Music Hall (which was crowded) were altogether & most excessively eulogistic, and so monotonous & tiresome (11-1) enlivened by Twain's rambling drolleries & stories (the best of them about Aldrich taking him into a bookstore). Howells undertook to speak some memorized remarks, broke down, then started to read again, got mixed up & broke down again, but finally got through. . . The lunch was served to them who had "breakfast tickets"—standing—and not well dispensed. Fortunately three or four young men and women volunteered to help me and I got a poor and tasteless sandwich, a spoonfull of salad (not bad), a glass of tepid "Iced tea," and best of all, ice cream. I was thirsty.[28]

In all likelihood this was the last time Clemens and Trowbridge saw each other, as Clemens died two years later. At any rate, Trowbridge's notebooks and several hundred of his letters make no reference to a later meeting.

Notes

1. "Darius Green and His Flying Machine" first appeared in *Our Young Folks*, March, 1867.
2. *Cambridge History of American Literature*, II, 402.
3. Theodore Roosevelt, *An Autobiography* (New York, 1920), pp. 15–16.
4. There is no mention of Clemens in Trowbridge's autobiography, *My Own Story* (Boston, 1903).
5. 1825–1879.
6. William Dean Howells (1837–1920) was editor of the *Atlantic Monthly* 1872–1881. Trowbridge's story, "Pendlam," appeared in the first issue of the *Atlantic*. (See I, 70–85, November, 1857.) In all, sixty-nine of Trowbridge's stories, poems or articles were published in this magazine, seventeen of them during the period in which Howells was editor. Trowbridge's last *Atlantic* contribution, "An Early Contributor's Recollections," appeared in the issue for November, 1903.
7. For discussion of "The Dandy Frightening the Squatter," see F.J. Meine, *Tall Tales of the Southwest* (New York, 1930); Walter Blair, *Native American Humor* (New York, 1937); *American Literature* (November, 1931); Bernard DeVoto, *Mark Twain's America*, IV (Boston, 1932); and F.L. Pattee, *Mark Twain* (New York, 1933), introduction p. xix.
8. During the two-year period of this magazine's existence (March 29, 1851–March 23, 1852), Trowbridge, under the name of "Paul Creyton," contributed eleven sketches.
9. December 18, 1887.
10. Each guest was provided with an elaborate seating chart. For a copy of the one given Clemens, see A.B. Paine, *Mark Twain* (New York and London, 1912), III, opposite p. 1646. In the Trowbridge collection is an identical chart, according to which 58 people were provided for. Clemens' version of the incident, as well as a reprint of the speech itself, appears in *Mark Twain's Speeches* (New York and London, 1910), pp. 1–16. For other detailed accounts see Paine, *op. cit.*, II, 603–10, and for the speech itself, III, 1643, Appendix O; W.D. Howells, *My Mark Twain* (New York, 1910), pp. 58*ff.*; and DeVoto, *op. cit.*, pp. 196*ff.*
11. See *My Own Story*, pp 425*ff.*; also Samuel T. Pickard, *Life and Letters of John Greenleaf Whittier* (Boston and New York, 1899), II, 635–36.

12. Howells' comment in a letter to Charles Eliot Norton. See Mildred Howells, ed., *Life in Letters of William Dean Howells* (Garden City, New York, 1928), I, 243.

13. For the village-mindedness exemplified in this whole episode see DeVoto, *op. cit.*, pp. 220*ff.*

14. A few thought the speech excellent, one of these being Professor Child of Harvard, who read an account of the dinner in the next morning's paper. In later years Clemens himself came to look upon this as one of his best speeches. (See Mark Twain's Speeches, pp. 15–16.) The accounts of what followed after Clemens sat down are confused. Clemens, whose memory was notoriously faulty, differed in two of his versions. In one he wrote: "The programme for the occasion was probably not more than one-third finished, but it ended there. Nobody arose. The next man hadn't strength enough to get up." (*Mark Twain's Speeches*, p. 24.) On the other hand, Paine's biography (II, 605) reported him as saying that "Bishop, the novelist, did get up and began his speech but didn't get very far with it." Paine likewise reported Howells (II, 695) to the same effect. The Boston *Daily Advertiser* reported the dinner as if it had been a great success.

15. January 10, 1876.

16. Matthew Franklin Whittier (1812–1883) was the only brother of John Greenleaf, and five years his junior.

17. In the Trowbridge collection, at present in the possession of Mrs. Albert P. Madeira, granddaughter of Trowbridge.

18. Mrs. Alonzo Newton, the mother of Trowbridge's second wife.

19. Trowbridge's notebooks are full of references to this organization, of which he was a charter member. At the death of Thomas Wentworth Higginson, he was made honorary vice-president.

20. Mrs. Julia Ward Howe (1819–1910) has this to say of the occasion: ". . . I had worked hard all morning, but had managed to put together a scrap of rhyme in welcome of Mark Twain. A candle was lit for me to read by and afterwards M.T. jumped upon a chair and made fun, some good, some middling, for some three quarters of an hour. The effect of my one candle lighting up his curly hair was good and my rhyme was well received." (Laura E. Richards and Maud Howe Elliott, *Julia Ward Howe* [Boston and New York, 1916], II, 341.)

21. Item in Trowbridge notebook, dated October 25, 1905.

22. This anecdote was told to the writer by Nixon Waterman (1936), who was one of the group.

23. July 1, 1908.

24. Gilder had this to say: "Tuesday, the 20th at Portsmouth I read the little poem on The Singing River and another to Aldrich written

long ago and not published. The night before, Mrs. Aldrich had quite a large dinner party at the hotel and in the midst of it I asked her quietly if I could offer a 'silent toast.' She said, 'I wish you would,' knowing well what it would be—so we drank in silence to 'A bright and beautiful memory.'" (Rosamond Gilder, ed., *Letters of Richard Watson Gilder* [Boston and New York, 1916], p. 463.)

25. *Mark Twain in Eruption* (New York and London, 1940), pp. 295–99.

26. For a more concise account, see Paine, *op. cit.*, III, 1456.

27. Paine, *op. cit.*, III, 1456.

28. Item in Trowbridge's notebook, dated July 3, 1908.

Musings without Method

THE HILARITY OF LONDON—MARK TWAIN'S
MESSAGE OF MIRTH—THE LIMITATIONS
OF HUMOR—AN OBVIOUS INCONGRUITY—
THE EXAMPLE OF THE EIGHTEENTH
CENTURY—COTTON AND BRIDGES—'LIFE ON
THE MISSISSIPPI'—THE TALENT OF MARK
TWAIN—THE SIN OF EXAGGERATION—
PAGEANTS AND SPORTS.

For the last month London has suffered from a violent attack of hilarity. Painfully she has held her poor sides. So fiercely has she rocked with noisy laughter that her public monuments have been in danger of destruction. For Mark Twain has been in her midst, and has transmitted, through the voices of obsequious journalists, his messages of mirth. And Mark Twain is a humourist, a simple truth which nobody is permitted to forget. He is a humourist who cannot open his mouth without provoking the wonder of the world, and, thanks to the industry of energetic reporters, we have not lost one single pearl of his speech.

It is not Mark's fault,—Mark they call him, to prove their familiarity,—not the fault of the reporters, if a word spoken by the humourist has escaped us. All the world knows that the sublime heights of fun were climbed when Mark Twain referred happily to his own funeral. The compositors who set up this brilliant sally were so keenly conscious of their

Reprinted from *Blackwood's Magazine*, 182 (August 1907), 279–86.

privilege that they filled the master's incongruity with a bold series of misprints. Mark Twain designing his own funeral! Isn't it funny? Lives there a curmudgeon who will refrain from laughter when he hears of it? Still gayer was the phantasy which accused Mark Twain of stealing the Ascot Gold Cup. There's a pretty invention! Fleet Street accepted the joke as one man, and it will be surprising if the great man's luggage is not ransacked for the lost treasure by the Customs officers of this free and independent fatherland.

At last the humourist has left these shores. The echo of his last joke has died away, though the throats of his admirers are still husky with appreciative laughter. And so well did London play her part that if he rang his bell or asked for a lucifer match, the neighbourhood of Dover Street palpitated with excitement. Unhappily, upon this enthusiasm, as upon most others, time has and will have a chastening effect. Our exhausted capital is beginning to understand that it can have too much of a good joke, and that nothing stales so rapidly as the thing called "humour."

Humour as a solid quality and a lucrative trade is of modern invention. The ancients knew well that its effect was an effect of light and shade. They were humorous in flashes, and their humour was infinitely enhanced, because it was set against a background of gravity. To be funny at all hours and in all places is a vile a sin against taste as it would be to dissolve in floods of tears before strangers. The great men who dared to laugh in an earlier age than ours laughed in moderation and with a wise purpose. Aristophanes and Lucian, Chaucer and Rabelais, Shakespeare and Fielding, are the true humourists of the world. They did not jest and jibe out of season. They held up folly to ridicule, not to amuse the groundlings, but to reveal, in a sudden blaze of light, the eternal truths of wisdom and justice. Their humour is precious on account of its parsimony. They do not at every turn slap their reader on the back and assure him that there is nothing congruous in the visible world. Of the irreverence that turns whatever is beautiful or noble into a stupid jest they knew nothing. They kept their humour in its proper place; they used it for a wise purpose; they did not degrade it to catch an easy round of applause; and, fortunately for them, they are to-day refused the august title of humourist, which sits so appositely upon the shoulders of Mark Twain.

The essence of humour is that it should be unexpected. The modern humourist is never unexpected. He beats the drum from the moment at which he appears upon the stage. He does not cease to beat it until he quits the stage for the last time. His mouth is always awry, as though he fed upon sour apples, and he demands that his auditors, also should twist their lips. From morning till night he grins through a horse-collar and is surprised if all the world does not applaud his grimaces. To the rash fellow who confesses that he does not understand his fun, the professional humourist has a ready answer. He tells the wretch, with a shrug of pity, that he has no sense of humour, and has no right to criticise wholesome ribaldry. The boot, of course, is on the other leg. The professional humourist is the one person to whom the proper exercise of humour is forbidden, and he does but add insult to injury when he dares to criticise his victim's understanding.

Yet the professional humourist to-day inherits the earth. He is the most popular of God's creatures. He has his own "organs," in which he makes a desperate attempt to look at all things from a ridiculous point of view. He assures you, with a sentimental leer, that his fun is always amiable, as though amiability were a sufficient atonement for an imbecile lack of taste. He is prepared to tickle you with his jokes from early morn to nightfall, and he has been so grossly flattered that he believes there is a positive virtue in his antics. He is perfectly convinced that he is doing good, and he needs very little persuasion to believe that he is the only regenerator of mankind. Gradually, too, he is encroaching upon all the professions which are not legitimately his own. The pulpit knows him, and the senate. Worse still, he has invaded the Courts of Law, and sits grinning upon the bench at his own ineptitude, which appears to the obsequious barristers, who hope some day to wear his cap and bells, to sparkle with the brilliance of true Attic wit.

The secret of modern humour is revealed to all. Its basis is an obvious incongruity. Not the subtle παρὰ προσδοκίαν of the ancients, not a whimsical turn of phrase or twist of idea, which surprises us in the masters, but a coarse, crass confusion of past with present or of grave with gay. Its inventors, we regret to remind our readers, were Englishmen, aided and abetted by such Frenchmen as Motteux and D'Urfey, who were driven to these shores before or at the revocation of the Edict of Nantes, and whose native gaiety was not wholly extinguished by the persecutions endured by their fathers. Tom Brown the Facetious and the Inimitable Ned Ward were characteristic innovators. Inspired by joyousness and brandy, they laughed to scorn life and all its works. They were as cheerful a pair of ruffians as ever beat the pavement of a populous city since the infamous creatures of Petronius went splendidly upon the pad. They knew London as they knew their pockets, and they hunted the taverns with a zeal and an understanding worthy of their high purpose and higher spirits. They recalled the beggar-students of an earlier age, or the poets who, in Elizabeth's time, brought their plays to the Bankside. Ned Ward, inn-keeper though he was, had still a regard for letters, and Tom Brown was a real scholar. His style was flippant; his muse was ever down at heel, and wore a dressing-gown; his prose was alive with the slang of the gutter and the quip of the street corner. But when he took up his pen his mind went back to Lucian and to Horace; he kept always in the great tradition; and though he was determined to laugh at all things, he had too quick a sense of his art to be a humourist and nothing more.

Nevertheless, he sowed the seeds of the easy incongruity which has debauched the humour of to-day. He delighted in such mock-heroic exercises as an "Oration in praise of Drunkenness," and he taught the world to believe that nothing was beyond the reach of jocularity. One of the earliest of our comic reporters, he wore the cap and bells with a light indifference, and, Ned Ward aiding him, he understood that the journal and pamphlet were a useful substitute for the generosity of patrons. Had they lived under the Tudors or early Stuarts, Brown and Ward would have been jesters at court or in a country house. They would have worn the livery of king or duke, and repaid the munificence of their masters with a licensed effrontery. The liberal age of Anne threw them upon the people, and they forced their note to suit the foolish rufflers who bought their wares. Thus they showed the way, and their descendants in the world of humour have been only too ready to follow them.

Humour, in this baser sense, is a foolish travesty of life; and before Brown split the sides of Grub Street, Charles Cotton, fisherman and Cockney, had already converted travesty into a form of literature. If the poor humourists of to-day descend in one line from Tom Brown, in another they may trace their pedigree back to the admirable Cotton. Now Cotton, as became a gentleman of this education and pursuits, founded his humour upon the classics. He treated Virgil and Lucian precisely as the modern Yankee treats the older civilisation of Europe. He translated them into his own lingo and asked you to laugh with him at them. He delighted to trick out the heroes of antiquity in his own poor fustian, and as his knowledge of slang was as great as his daring, the result is often ludicrous. A passage or two in illustration will make the purpose of the old travesties as clear as daylight. Here is Dido's address of farewell to Æneas in Cotton's version:—

> But I'll waste on thee no more Breath,
> For whom the Wind, that fumes beneath,
> Is far too sweet: Avaunt, thou Slave!
> Thou lying coney-catching Knave,
> Be moving, do as thou hast told me!
> Nobody here intends to hold thee!
> Go: seek thy Farm, I hope 'twill be
> I' th' very bottom of the Sea:
> But shd'st thou 'scape, and not in Dike
>   lie
> Drown'd like a Puppy, as 'tis likely,

> Since in the Proverb old 'tis found,
> Who's born to hang, will ne'er be
>   drowned;
> Yet shd'st thou not be much the nigher
> I'll haunt thee like a going Fire,
> As soon as I can turn to a Ghost,
> Which will be in a week at most.

That is a fair specimen of Cotton's familiar style, and Cotton had many imitators. His contempt for grandeur, which is characteristic of the Cockney spirit, was emulated by many ingenious writers. The example which he set was followed for a century and more, and the best of his pupils handled the style with an even greater effrontery than his. Perhaps none of them, in ease of manner or bold anachronism, exceeded Bridges, whose burlesque translation of Homer is still ranked among "curiosities" in the catalogues. It is thus that in Bridges' version Agamemnon rates the angry Achilles:—

> The general gave him tit for tat,
> And answer'd, cocking first his hat,
> Go, and be hang'd, you blust'ring
>   whelp,
> Pray, who the murrain wants your
>   help?
> When you are gone, I know there are
> Col'nels sufficient for the war,
> Militia bucks that know no fears,
> Brave fishmongers and auctioneers;
> Besides, great Jove will fight for us,
> What need we then this mighty fuss?
> Thou lov'st to quarrel, fratch, and
>   jangle,
> To scold and swear, and fight and
>   wrangle.
> Great strength thou hast, and pray
>   what then?
> Art thou so stupid, canst not ken,
> The gods that ev'ry thing can see
> Give strength to bears as well as thee?

There in its origin and in its purpose is the whole of modern humour. The same flippant impertinence which distresses us in the works of popular Americans is already alive and alert. The same confusion of ancient and modern is already designed to evoke a hasty chuckle. We do not mean that the imitation is conscious; we do not suppose that Mark Twain or his predecessors ever heard the name of Charles Cotton; but when once the spirit of contempt for grave and reverend things was evoked, the worst enormities of contemporary humour were obvious and natural.

The end and aim of Mark Twain, then, are the end and aim of Cotton and Bridges. For him the art of Europe and the chivalry of King Arthur serve the purpose of Virgil and Homer. He travesties them with a kind of malignant joy. He brings whatever time has honoured down to the level of a Yankee drummer. In *The Innocents Abroad* he sets a slur of commonness upon beauty and splendour. With the vanity of a crude civilisation he finds every custom ridiculous that does not conform with the standard of the United States. The restraints of honour are food for his mirth. He holds his sides when he thinks of the old masters. They are not brought down to this our date. Nor does he understand that there are certain institutions, certain manifestations of genius, which should be sacred even for the jester. Newness is not the only virtue known to the world, and he who laughs at what is old, merely because it is old, proves a lack of intelligence which no whimsicality can excuse.

In other words, Mark Twain the humourist is a bull in the china-shop of ideas. He attempts to destroy what he could never build up, and assumes that his experiment is eminently meritorious. When, as in *A Yankee at the Court of King Arthur*, he gave full rein to his fancy, he achieved such a masterpiece of vulgarity as the world has never seen. His book gives you the same sort of impression which you might receive from a beautiful picture over which a poisonous slug had crawled. The hint of magnificence is there, pitilessly deformed and defaced. That Mark Twain is in perfect sympathy with his creature is perfectly evident. He frankly prefers Hartford, Conn., to Camelot. He believes that in all respects his native land is superior to the wisest and noblest society that the eye of Arthur saw or any other eye has seen. He is sure that refinement and "gentility" were unknown before his own time. The Knights of the Round Table, he declares, used words which would have made a Comanche blush. "Indelicacy is too mild a term to convey the idea." In our own nineteenth century, he informs us, "the earliest samples of the real lady and real gentleman discoverable in English history—or in European history, for that matter—may be said to have made their appearance." That is what it is to be a humourist. But even if we permit the humour we must still question the historical accuracy of the statement, and regret that Mark Twain ever thought it necessary to comment upon the ancients, against whom he cherishes a fierce antipathy.

His verbal humour, if less reckless than his history, is far more dismally deplorable. Here is his comment upon Merlin: "He is always blethering around in my way, everywhere I go; he makes me tired. He don't amount to shucks as a magician." Who can resist this amazing humour? And again, who, save a churl, would refuse the tribute of a laugh to the following exquisite criticism of the same wonder-worker? "Merlin's stock was flat," writes Mark Twain, "the King wanted to stop his wages: he even wanted to banish him; but I interfered. I said he would be useful to work the weather, and attend to small matters like that, and I would give him a lift now and then when his poor little parlour-magic soured on him." Isn't there a snigger in every word of it? And before this brilliancy must we not confess that humour, like delicacy and all the other virtues, made its first appearance in the nineteenth century and in America?

This monstrous incongruity demands two qualities for its indulgence: a perfect self-esteem, and an exaggerated common-sense. No one who is not confident that he engrosses the graces can affect to find pleasure in thus insulting the past. No one whose sense is not common in all respects can apply all the resources of a vulgar logic to the creations of fancy and emotion. That Mark Twain is fully equipped for his purpose is only too clear. His humour and his talk alike proclaim it. And it is the more pitiful, because he has a talent which stands in need of no folly for its embellishment. Had he never cut a joke, had he refrained always from grinning at grave and beautiful things, how brilliant a fame would have been his! When you are tired of his irreverence, when you have deplored his noisy jibes, when his funeral and his theft of the cup alike pall upon your spirit, take down his *Life on the Mississippi* and see what perfect sincerity and a fine sympathy can accomplish. Mark Twain writes of the noble river as one who knows its every change and chance. Yet he writes of it with an austere restraint and without any desire to humanise it out of its proper character. And there is humour, too, in his descriptions,—not the tortured humour of a later day, but humour sufficient to play, like light upon shade, in the grave places of his history. As he says himself, he loved the pilot's profession far better than any he has followed since, and his love and understanding shine in every page of his masterpiece. As the river kept no secrets from him, so his quick memory enabled him to recover the impressions of his youth. To cite his own expressive works, "The face of the water, in time, became a wonderful book—a book which was a dead language to the uneducated passenger, but which told its mind to me without reserve, delivering its most cherished secrets as clearly as if it uttered them with a voice. And it was not a book to be read once and thrown aside, for it had a new story to tell every day. . . . There was never so wonderful a book written by man." In this passage Mark Twain strikes the real note of his life and experience. With equal truth he tells us at what cost he acquired this deep knowledge of the river and its moods. "Now, when I had mastered the language of this water," says he, "and had come to know every trifling feature that bordered the great river as familiarly as I knew the letters of the alphabet, I had made a valuable acquisition. But I had lost something, too. I had lost something which could never be restored to me while I lived. All the grace, the beauty, the poetry had gone out of the majestic river. I still keep in mind a certain wonderful sunset which I witnessed when steamboating was new to me. . . . But, as I have said, a day came when I began to cease from noting the glories and the charms which the moon and the sun and the twilight wrought upon the river's face: another day came, when I ceased altogether to note them." Yet the very fact that Mark Twain recognised the change which had come over his vision is the best proof that he submitted willingly to the marvellous spell of the river. His mental process was the reverse of Wordsworth's. Wordsworth learned:

> To look on nature, not as in the
>   hour
> Of thoughtless youth; but hearing
>   oftentimes
> The still, sad music of humanity,
> Not harsh nor grating, though of ample
>   power
> to chasten and subdue.

Mark Twain, on the other hand, heard "the still, sad music of humanity" when he but half knew the river. A profounder knowledge silenced the music, and persuaded him to own, with sincerity, that he gazed upon the sunset scene without rapture, but with the understanding of an intimate.

The author of *Life on the Mississippi* was also the creator of Tom Sawyer and Huck Finn, two boys who will survive to cast shame upon all the humour of America. And it is for the sake of a genuine talent that we deplore Mark Twain's studied antics. It should not have been for him to light the thorns which crackle under the pot. It should not have been for him to encourage the gross stupidity of his fellows. The moderation of one who has known men and rivers should have been revealed to all the world. But Mark Twain, in submitting to the common demand, shares the general love of exaggeration. "Govern a great country as you would cook a small fish," said the Chinese philosopher; "that is, do not overdo it." The tendency of to-day is to overdo all things. Humour, which should be a relief, and nothing more, is now an end in itself. No experiment is made in any art or science but it must become a custom. Some years since an ingenious stage-manager invented what he was pleased to term a pageant. It was an attempt to reconstruct the life of an ancient town, to recover from the past the parti-coloured trappings and the forgotten background of history. Then every town, every village, must enjoy the pomp of the Middle Age. Peasants grow learned in costume and babble of "colour-schemes," whatever those may be. Even an ancient and honoured university has fallen so far beneath the level of its dignity as to connive at the creation of a vast circus and to provide a book of the words for a trifling performance. And the pageant, which might have served a useful end if handled with restraint and discretion, is plainly destined to be killed by ridicule.

And above all, the folly of exaggeration may be noted in our sports. If an English eight or an English eleven suffer defeat, it is proclaimed far and wide that England is in decay. The newspapers howl inappositely and ask the groaners to explain the ruin of their country. They forget that the sports upon which we pride ourselves are worth pursuing for their own sakes, and that it is only the professional who believes that victory alone justifies his exertion. A few weeks ago a Belgian crew carried off the Grand Challenge Cup from Henley. Its most dangerous opponent was the Leander Club, whose eight was composed of oarsmen from Oxford and Cambridge. The race was as good as conflicting courage and energy could make it, and the mere fact that the better crew won after a closely contested struggle has suggested to an idle press a mournful commentary, which is a clear negation of sportsmanship. In the first place, it is a regatta which is held at Henley, not an international meeting. The honour and enterprise of nations are not there put to a final test. If England and Belgium are to try conclusions, they must not meet in a sprint at Henley; they must fight it out, after due training, between Putney and Mortlake. And if the curse at Henley is ill fitted for an international battle, so also are the conditions of the meeting. The eight men, who represented not England but the Leander Club, had so little thought of their national responsibility that they rowed for their colleges or for themselves both before and after their race with the Belgians. They went to Henley not to defend their country against all comers but to get what enjoyment they could from the sport of rowing. But a simple understanding is not enough for this age. Exaggeration rules in humour. The amateur is blamed if he do not cultivate the vices of the specialist. The American critic assures us that the sole object of a game is to win, and our journals agree with the American critic. Some day there will be a reaction, and then it will be recognised that pleasure counts in life as much as success, and that solid blocks of humour are as blatant an outrage upon good sense as a daily pageant, or as games played with no other aim than by hook or by crook to snatch a victory.

Mark Twain and the
Old Time Subscription Book

George Ade

Mark Twain should be doubly blessed for saving the center table from utter dullness. Do you remember that center table of the seventies? The marble top showed glossy in the subdued light that filtered through the lace curtains, and it was clammy cold even on hot days. The heavy mahogany legs were chiseled into writhing curves from which depended stern geometrical designs or possibly bunches of grapes. The Bible had the place of honor and was flanked by subscription books. In those days the house never became cluttered with the ephemeral six best sellers. The new books came a year apart, and each was meant for the center table, and it had to be so thick and heavy and emblazoned with gold that it could keep company with the bulky and high-priced Bible.

Books were bought by the pound. Sometimes the agent was a ministerial person in black clothes and stove-pipe hat. Maiden ladies and widows, who supplemented their specious arguments with private tales of woe, moved from one small town to another feeding upon prominent citizens. Occasionally the prospectus was unfurled by an undergraduate of a freshwater college working for the money to carry him another year.

The book-agents varied, but the book was always the same,—many pages, numerous steel engravings, curly-cue

Reprinted from *Review of Reviews* 41 (June 1910), 703–704.

tail-pieces, platitudes, patriotism, poetry, sentimental mush. One of the most popular, still resting in many a dim sanctuary, was known as "Mother, Home, and Heaven." A ponderous collection of "Poetical Gems" did not involve the publishers in any royalty entanglements. Even the "Lives of the Presidents" and "Noble Deeds of the Great and Brave" gave every evidence of having been turned out as piece-work by needy persons temporarily lacking employment on newspapers. Let us not forget the "Manual of Deportment and Social Usages," from which the wife of any agriculturist could learn the meaning of R.S.V.P. and the form to be employed in acknowledging an invitation to a levee.

Nobody really wanted these books. They were purchased because the agents knew how to sell them, and they seemed large for the price, and besides, every well-furnished home had to keep something on the center table.

Subscription books were dry picking for boys. Also they were accessible only on the Sabbath after the weekly scouring. On week-days the boys favored an underground circulating library, named after Mr. Beadle, and the hay-mow was the chosen reading room. Let one glorious exception be made in the case of "Dr. Livingstone's Travels in Africa," a subscription book of forbidding size, but containing many pictures of darkies with rings in their noses.

Just when front-room literature seemed at its lowest ebb, so far as the American boy was concerned, along came Mark Twain. His books looked, at a distance, just like the other distended, diluted, and altogether tasteless volumes that had been used for several decades to balance the ends of the center table. The publisher knew his public, so he gave a pound of book for every fifty cents, and crowded in plenty of wood-cuts and stamped the outside with golden bouquets and put in a steel engraving of the author, with a tissue paper veil over it, and "sicked" his multitude of broken-down clergymen, maiden ladies, grass widows, and college students on to the great American public.

Mark Twain and the Old Time Subscription Book

Can you see the boy a Sunday morning prisoner, approach the new book with a dull sense of foreboding, expecting a dose of Tupper's "Proverbial Philosophy"? Can you see him a few minutes later when he finds himself linked arm-in-arm with Mulberry Sellers or Buck Fanshaw or the convulsing idiot who wanted to know if Christopher Columbus was sure-enough dead? No wonder he curled up on the hair-cloth sofa and hugged the thing to his bosom and lost all interest in Sunday-school. "Innocents Abroad" was the most enthralling book ever printed until "Roughing It" appeared. Then along came "The Gilded Age," "Life on the Mississippi," and "Tom Sawyer," one cap sheaf after another. While waiting for a new one we read the old ones all over again.

The new uniform edition with the polite little pages, high-art bindings, and all the boisterous wood-cuts carefully expurgated can never take the place of those lumbering subscription books. They were our early friends and helped us to get acquainted with the most amazing story-teller that ever captivated the country boys and small-town boys all over America.

While we are honoring Mark Twain as a great literary artist, a philosopher, and a teacher, let the boys of the seventies add their tribute. They knew him for his miracle of making the subscription book something to be read and not merely looked at. He converted the Front Room from a Mausoleum into a Temple of Mirth.

Mark Twain on the Lecture Platform

Will M. Clemens

The story of an unwilling orator, with extracts
and unpublished letters written
by the famous humorist

On Tuesday evening, September 29, 1866, Samuel Langhorne Clemens made his first appearance in public, at the Academy of Music in Pine Street, San Francisco. He had just returned from the Sandwich Islands, from where he had been writing letters on the islands and the islanders to the Sacramento *Union*. The appearance of Artemus Ward some months previous in San Francisco had aroused an ambition in Mark Twain, to "go and do likewise," not for the fame that might come to him, not from the money to be earned, but from a spirit of pure mischievousness. Twain was one of a coterie of Bohemians which included Bret Harte, Prentice Mulford, and Charles Warren Stoddard, and I can imagine how he chuckled to himself when he concluded to "learn a new trick and surprise the boys." He secured a hall and published a sort of Artemus Ward announcement that he would deliver a lecture about his trip to the Sandwich Islands.

Commenting upon the announcement, the San Francisco correspondent of a neighboring newspaper, wrote:

"We may expect either gay or grave remarks, for, by recently published letters, he very fully exhibited the

Reprinted from *Ainslee's Magazine* VI (August 1900), 25–32.

resources of the islands to the great satisfaction of our business community. His lecture at this time will have a peculiar interest, independent of his own rapidly augmenting popularity, from the fact that the queen (Emma) of said country is now in our midst. Everybody is going, and consequently a crowded audience will greet the maiden—I believe—lecture of the sage brusher. He is not at all an eloquent orator, and I fear, as he himself announces it, 'doors open at 7, the *trouble will* commence at 8 o'clock.'"

"The 'trouble' is over," wrote this same correspondent under date of October 3, 1866, "the inimitable 'Mark Twain' delivered himself last night of his first lecture on the Sandwich Islands, or anything else. Some time before the hour appointed to open his head the Academy of Music (on Pine street) was densely crowded with one of the most fashionable audiences it was ever my privilege to witness during my long residence in this city. The *élite* of the town were there, and so was the Governor of the state—occupying one of the boxes—whose rotund face was suffused with a halo of mirth during the whole entertainment. The audience promptly notified Mark by the usual sign—stamping—that the auspicious hour had arrived, and presently the lecturer came sidling and swinging out from the left of the stage. His very manner produced a generally vociferous laugh from the assemblage. He opened with an apology, by saying that he had partly succeeded in obtaining a band, but, at the last moment the party engaged backed out. He explained that he had hired a man to play the trombone, but he, on learning that he was the only person engaged, came at the last moment and informed him that he could not play. This placed Mark in a bad predicament, and wishing to know his reasons for deserting him at that critical moment, he replied 'that he wasn't going to make a fool of himself by sitting up there on the stage and blowing his horn all by himself.' After the applause subsided, he assumed a very grave countenance and commenced his remarks proper with the following well-known sentence: 'When, in the course of human events,' etc. He lectured fully an hour and a quarter, and his humorous sayings were interspersed with geographical, agricultural and statistical remarks, sometimes branching off and reaching beyond—soaring, in the very choicest language, up to the very pinnacle of descriptive power."

Thus we are told how Mark "tried it on the dog," and from all appearances the canine survived. Then came invitations from surrounding towns and from Nevada for Mark Twain to repeat his San Francisco success. Thereupon in January, 1867, he started forth upon a lecture tour through the smaller cities of California and Nevada. In those days almost any entertainment brought out a crowd, and when it was announced one day in Carson City that Mark was to deliver a lecture for the benefit of something or other at the Episcopal Church, it was generally understood that the house would be crowded.

"Well, the night arrived," writes a friend that was present. "Mark ascended the steps into the pulpit about 8 o'clock, there being a whole lot of the boys and young women, friends of his, as well as a good many old people in front. Mark made a very polite bow, and then unfolded a gigantic roll of brown paper. People thought at first it was a map, but it turned out to be his lecture written on great sheets of grocer's brown paper, with an ordinary grocer's marking brush. After his bow he turned his back around to the audience and craned his head up to the lamp, and thus read from the big sheets, as though it would be impossible for him to see any other way.

"The lecture was on 'The Future of Nevada,' and was the funniest thing I ever heard. He prophesied the great era of prosperity that was before us, and sought to encourage us residents of the sagebrush region by foretelling what appeared to be Golconda-like tales of impossible mineral discoveries. Right on the heels of it, however, came the remarkable discoveries at Virginia City, and then we thought he was not so far off in his humorous predictions."

In March, Mr. Clemens published his first book, "The Famous Jumping Frog of Calaveras," and soon after sailed for

New York by way of Panama. From New York he went to Washington, where he endeavored to earn his living by writing letters to the San Francisco *Alta*, and delivering a lecture or two. His lecture experience in Washington was brief but interesting, and he tells all about it in his inimitable way:

"Well, now, I'll have to tell you something about that lecture. It was a little the hardest and roughest experience I ever underwent in my whole career as a lecturer. Now, I had not been in Washington more than a day or two before a friend of mine came to my room at the hotel early one morning, wakened me out of a sound sleep, and nearly stunned me by asking if I was aware of the fact that I was to deliver a lecture at Lincoln Hall that evening. I told him no, and that he must be crazy to get out of bed at such an unseemly hour to ask such a foolish question. But he soon assured me that he was perfectly sane by showing the papers, which all announced that Mark Twain was to lecture that evening, and that his subject would be 'The Sandwich Islands.' To say that I was surprised would be drawing it mildly. I was mad, for I thought some one had put up a game on me.

"Well, on careful inquiry, I learned that an old theatrical friend of mine thought he would do me a favor. So he started out by getting drunk. While in this condition he made all the necessary arrangements for me to lecture, with the exception of the slight circumstance that he neglected to inform me of any of his intentions. He rented Lincoln Hall, billed the town, and sent the newspapers advertisements and notices about the coming lecture, and the worst of it was that he had done all his work thoroughly. After learning this I was in a dilemma. I had never prepared any lecture on the Sandwich Islands. What was I to do? I could not back out by telling the people that I was unprepared, and that my friend was intoxicated when he made these arrangements. No that was out of the question, because the public wouldn't believe it anyway. The billing of the town had been too well done for that. So there was only one thing left for me to do, and that was to lock myself in my room and write that lecture between the breakfast hour and half-past seven that evening. Well, I did it, and was on hand at the advertised hour, facing one of the biggest audiences I ever addressed.

"I did not use my manuscript, but in those days I always had my lecture in writing, and kept it on a reading stand at one end of the place where I stood on the platform. I was very good at memorizing, and rarely had any trouble in speaking without notes; but the very fact that I had my manuscript near at hand where I could readily turn to it without having to undergo the mortification of pulling it from my pocket, gave me courage and kept me from making awkward pauses. But the writing of that Sandwich Islands lecture in one day was the toughest job ever put on me."

The voyage to Europe, and the trip to Palestine came soon after this, and the subsequent publication of *Innocents Abroad*, in 1869, made Mr. Clemens famous on two continents. In the Autumn, James Redpath who was the manager of a Lyceum Bureau in Boston, encouraged Mark Twain to undertake a series of lectures or talks before church societies and lyceums in the New England states and the country round about New York. One of his first engagements was before a church society in Brooklyn, and the humorist was evidently disgusted at the spirit of the entertainment, for under date of December 4th, he wrote to Redpath:

> This is no regular course. It is an infernal mite society, a pure charity speculation.

His first lecture tour in the East was brief and disastrous to his nerves and temper. Meanwhile he had accepted an editorship on the Buffalo *Express* and had married. After his marriage he was in such demand as a platform attraction that he could not find time to reply to all the letters received, and was compelled on March 1st to have a circular printed:

Office Express Printing Co.,
Buffalo, March 1, 1870.

Dear Sir:

In answer, I am obliged to say that it will not be possible for me to accept your kind invitation. I shall not be able to lecture again during the present season.

Thanking you kindly for the compliment of your invitation, I am,

Yours Truly,
Sam'l L. Clemens.
(Mark Twain.)

But he relented at length, and during April and early in May was making lecture trips to towns in New York State, under the management of Redpath and Fall. On May 2d, he wrote to Redpath:

Buffalo, May 2, 1870

Dear Redpath:

I mislaid the letter inquiring about Cambridge, N.Y., till this moment. It got mixed with my loose papers.

They told me that the society I talked for was the leading and favorite. They half burned down the hall at 7 p.m. and yet at 8 had a full house, though a mighty wet and smoky one. It was a bad night, too.

Yours,
Mark.

Joel Benton, the author, tells a story of this period of Twain's platform career. Mark was to lecture in the village in which Benton managed the lyceum. He particularly requested the young chairman not to introduce him to the audience. It was a little whim of his, he explained. They mounted the rostrum together, and Twain gazed for a few long moments at the audience. But at last he arose, and taking a semi-circular sweep to the left, and then proceeding to the front, opened something like this. "Ladies and Gentlemen: I—have—lectured—many—years—and—in—many—towns,—large—and—small. I have traveled—north—south—east—and—west.

I—have—met—many—great—men; very—great—men. But—I—have—never—yet—in—all—my—travels—met—the—president—of—a—*country*—lyceum—who—could—introduce—me—to—an—audience—with—that—*distinguished*—consideration—which—my—merits deserve." After this deliverance, the house, which had stared at Benton for several minutes with vexed impatience, was convulsed at his expense.

Yet no sooner had Redpath printed circulars and arranged dates for Twain's appearance then the humorist balked. Under date of May 10th, he wrote a characteristic letter.

Elmira, N.Y., May 10, 1870

Friend Redpath:

I guess I am out of the field permanently. I am sending off those circulars to all lecture applicants now. If you want some more of them I can send them to you. ****The subscriber will have to be excused from the present season at least.

Remember me to Nasby, Billings and Fall. Luck to you!

Yours always and after,
Mark.

This last decision to cease lecturing was permanent for nearly a year, and the entreaties of Redpath and others proved of no avail. Redpath meanwhile had found a new platform star, John B. Gough, and concerning him, Mr. Clemens wrote in the following January, this letter to Redpath:

Buffalo, Jan. 22, 1871.

Friend Redpath:

Are you going to lecture Gough in California?? If so, take the advice of the only lecturer that ever *did* make lecture tours in California—and that advice is—lecture him three nights in succession and so advertise it. Then talk him two successive nights in Sacramento, one night or two in Virginia City, if you can get a church—they won't go to the nasty theatre. Then return and talk him three successive nights in San Francisco. There you are. If anybody says, "Go to San Jose, Petaluma, Grass Valley, Carson City or any other camp on the coast," tell them Artemus Ward and Mark Twain both lost money in each and every one of those places. But six nights in Platt's Hall, San Francisco, are the only ones in the ten I would give my old boots for—but they are worth close on to $8,000 gold, clean profit—more than that if you charge fifty cents extra for reserved seats (which ought to be done and you will have from 500 to 1,000 $1.50 seats that way.) I've had 1,400 reserved seats—sold them all in five hours and closed the box office at 3 p.m., at a dollar a ticket.

But maybe you ain't going to take Gough there after all. Well, put this letter where you can find it again when you do take somebody there. Nasby would have a big run there.

Yours ever,
Mark.

After persevering persuasion on the part of Redpath, Mark Twain was preparing to talk once more to delighted audiences during 1871. On obtaining a definite promise from the humorist, Redpath began booking him for an extended Eastern tour, while the lecturer settled down to his work of preparing the lectures. On June 27, 1871, he wrote from Elmira:

Dear Red:
Wrote another lecture—a third one—to-day. *It* is the one I am going to deliver. I think I shall call it "Reminiscences of Some Pleasant Characters Whom I Have Met," (or should the "whom" be left out?) It covers my whole acquaintance— kings, lunatics, idiots and all. Suppose you give the item a start in the Boston papers. If I write fifty lectures I shall only choose one and talk that one only.

Yours,
Mark

The same day, evidently in the evening, he wrote a second letter to Redpath:

Mark Twain on the Lecture Platform

Elmira, June 27, 1871.

Dear Redpath:
Don't be in any hurry about announcing the title of my lecture. Just say: "To be announced." Because I wrote a new lecture to-day, called simple[sic] "D.L.H." During July I'll decide which one I like best.

Yours,
Mark

In July, Mr. Redpath wrote to Mark, telling him that he had booked him for a lecture in a Brooklyn church, and incidentally mentioned that his partner, Mr. Fall, was suffering from the effects of a carbuncle. Twain's reply was characteristic:

Elmira, July 10, 1871.

Dear Redpath:
* * * I never made a success of a lecture delivered in a church yet. People are afraid to laugh in a church. They can't be made to do it in any possible way.
Success to Fall's carbuncle and many happy returns.

Yours,
Mark.

Four days later Redpath sent him news of further bookings, and to one engagement at least Mark demurred.

Elmira, July 14, 1871

Dear Redpath:
Don't lecture me at Jamestown, N.Y., unless Providence compels you. I suppose all lecturers hate that place.
Shall be in Hartford 3 or 4 weeks hence and then I shall run up and bum around with you a day or two if you ain't busy.

Yours,
Mark.

Mark Twain's uncertainty as to his lecture engagements, the final decision as to whether he wanted to lecture or not, and his unsettled condition of mind as to his future plans and movements were well illustrated in a very humorous letter written to Redpath, a month later. The letter reads:

> Hartford, Tuesday, Aug. 8, 1871.
>
> Dear Red:
>
> I am different from other men! My mind changes oftener. People who have no mind can easily be steadfast and firm, but when a man is loaded down to the guards with it, as I am, every sea of foreboding or inclination, maybe of indolence, shifts the cargo. See! Therefore, if you will notice, one week I am likely to give rigid instructions to confine me to New England; the next week, send me to Arizona; the next week withdraw my name; the next week give you full untrammelled swing; and the week following modify it. You must try to keep the run of my mind, Redpath, it is your business, being the agent, and it always was too many for me. It appears to me to be one of the finest pieces of mechanism I have ever met with. Now about the West, this week, I am willing that you shall retain all the Western engagements. But what I shall want *next* week is still with God.
>
> Let us not profane the mysteries with soiled hands and prying eyes of sin.
>
> Yours,
> Mark.
>
> P.S.—Shall be here two weeks, will run up there when Nasby comes.

In his next letter to Redpath he tells how to get sick just before an advertised appearance to lecture.

> Elmira, N.Y., Sept. 15, 1871.
>
> Dear Redpath:
>
> I wish you would get me released from the lecture at——
> ——. Otherwise I'll have no resource left but to get sick the day I am to lecture there. I can get sick easy enough, by the

simple process of saying the word—well never mind what word—I am not going to lecture there.

> Yours,
> Mark.

Among the earlier engagements of his lecture tour in 1871 was his appearance in Washington, upon which occasion he delivered for the first time a lecture on Artemus Ward. Writing to Redpath, he said:

> Washington, Tuesday, Oct. 28, 1871.
>
> Dear Red:
> I have come square out, thrown, "Reminiscences" overboard, and taken "Artemus Ward, Humorist," for my subject. Wrote it here on Friday and Saturday, and read it from MSS. last night to enormous house. It suits *me* and I'll never deliver the nasty, nauseous "Reminiscences" any more.
>
> Yours
> Mark.

The lecture on Artemus Ward evidently proved even less satisfactory to the lecturer than his much condemned reminiscences, for in December he telegraphed as follows:

> Buffalo Depot, Dec. 8, 1871.
>
> Redpath & Fall, Boston:
> Notify all hands that from this time I shall talk nothing but selections from my forthcoming book, *Roughing It*. Tried it last night. Suits me tiptop.
>
> Sam'l L. Clemens.

His reception in the Western and Central states pleased him so well that in a letter from Logansport, Indiana, he seemed thrilled with enthusiasm, and was apparently deeply in love with his platform life.

Logansport, Ind., Jan. 2, 1872.

Friend Redpath:
    Had a splendid time with a splendid audience in Indianapolis last night—a perfectly jammed house just as I have all the time out here and I like the new lecture but I hate the "Artemus Ward" talk and won't talk it any more. No man ever approved that choice of subject in my hearing, I think.

                Yours,
                Mark.

One never knows whether Mark is afoot or on horseback. In two weeks he had changed his mind again, and was begging for fewer engagements.

Jan. 17, 1872.

Dear Red:
    No, I can't lecture anywhere outside of New England in February except it be in Troy on the first. Wouldn't talk in Utica or Newburgh either for twice the money.
    Was glad Bellefontaine backed. Wish some more would. The fewer engagements I have from this time forth the better I shall be pleased.

                Yours,
                Mark.

Matters were going from bad to worse. Redpath was using his best endeavors to keep Twain on the platform, while the humorist was pulling like an army mule in the other direction. In February he telegraphed to Redpath from Hartford:

    How in the name of God does a man find his way from here to Amherst and when must he start? Give me full particulars and send a man with me. If I had another engagement I would rot before I would fill it.

                S. L. Clemens.

Summer came and Mark was glad—the lecture season was over. Then he sailed for England to arrange for the European publication of his works, and successfully secured Chatto & Windus as his English representatives, and the publishing house of Tauchnitz, at Leipzig, as his continental agent. Already he was widely known and quoted in England and was a welcome guest.

Mark tells a characteristic story, and at the same time comments upon the lecture business, in a letter written to Redpath in November.

> Langham Hotel, London, Nov. 3, 1872.
>
> Dear Redpath:
> * * * I was down for a speech at the Whitefriar's Club, and the chairman had done me the honor to make me his guest and appointed me a seat at his right, and as I know nearly all the Whitefriars, I expected to have a gorgeous time, but I got it into my head, that Friday was Thursday, so I stayed in the country stag-hunting a day too long and when I reached the club last night, nicely shaved and gotten up regardless of expense, I found that the dinner was the night before.
>
> I would like to stay here about fifteen or seventy-five years, a body does have such a good time. I am re-vamping, polishing, in other words fixing up my lecture on *Roughing It* and think I will deliver it in London a couple of times, about a month from now, just for fun.
>
> So Stanley gets $50,000 for 100 nights. That is as it should be. They charge $2 to hear Parepa sing two pieces (fifteen minutes all told) and if you charged a dollar to hear one of us fellows squeak it would become the fashion to hear us—and then the gates of hell could not prevail against us—we would always have a full house. When I yell again for less than $500 I'll be pretty hungry. But I haven't any intention of yelling at any price.
>
> Yours ever,
> Mark.

While in London he lectured not infrequently, and with striking success. The Rev. H. R. Haweis, the literary critic, who heard him, writes:

> I heard him once at the Hanover Square rooms. The audience was not large nor very enthusiastic. I believe he

would be an increasing success had he stayed longer. We had not time to get accustomed to his peculiar way, and there was nothing to take us by storm. He came on the platform and stood quite alone. A little table, with the traditional water-bottle and tumbler, was by his side. His appearance was not impressive, not very unlike the representation of him in the various pictures in his *Tramp Abroad*. He spoke more slowly than any other man I ever heard, and did not look at his audience quite enough. I do not think that he felt altogether at home with us, nor we with him. We never laughed loud or long. We sat throughout expectant and on the *qui vive*, very well interested and gently simmering with amusement. With the exception of one exquisite description of the Old Magdalen ivy-covered collegiate buildings at Oxford University, I do not think that there was one thing worth setting down in print. I got no information out of the lecture, and hardly a joke that would wear, or a story that would bear repeating. There was a deal about the dismal, lone silver-land, the story of the Mexican plug that bucked, and a duel which never came off and another duel in which no one was injured; and we sat patiently enough through it, fancying that by and by the introduction would be over, and the lecture would begin, when Twain suddenly made his bow, and went off! It was over. I looked at my watch, I was never more taken aback. I had been sitting there exactly an hour and twenty minutes! It seemed ten minutes at the outside. If you have ever tried to address a public meeting, you will know what this means. It means that Mark Twain is a consummate public speaker. If he ever chose to say anything, he would say it marvelously well; but in the art of saying nothing in an hour, he surpasses our most accomplished parliamentary speakers.

Upon his return to America and to Elmira, he found Mrs. Clemens ill, and consequently he telegraphed Redpath that he would not lecture again, and told his wife that there was not enough money in America to hire him to leave her for one day. He wrote Redpath that he might arrange a lecture tour later on, if Mrs. Clemens could accompany him. He appeared occasionally during the next few years in a few of the leading cities, but his decision to quit the platform was almost final.

Only once did he appear in public as a political speaker. As a conscientious Republican in his political preferences, Mr. Clemens took an active interest in the presidential campaign of 1880. While visiting in Elmira, New York, in the fall of that year, he made a short speech one Saturday night, introducing to a Republican meeting Gen. Hawley, of Connecticut. In the course of his remarks Mr. Clemens said:

"General Hawley is a member of my church at Hartford, and the author of 'Beautiful Snow.' Maybe he will deny that. But I am only here to give him a character from his last place. As a pure citizen, I respect him; as a personal friend of years, I have the warmest regard for him; as a neighbor, whose vegetable garden adjoins mine, why—why, I watch him. As the author of 'Beautiful Snow,' he has added a new pang to winter. He is a square, true man in honest politics, and I must say he occupies a mighty lonesome position. So broad, so bountiful is his character that he never turned a tramp empty-handed from his door, but always gave him a letter of introduction to me. Pure, honest incorruptible, that is Joe Hawley. Such a man in politics is like a bottle of perfumery in a glue factory—it may moderate the stench, but it doesn't destroy it. I haven't said any more of him than I would say of myself. Ladies and gentlemen, this is General Hawley."

In 1884, Mr. Clemens and George W. Cable made a tour of the country, giving readings from their own works, under the management of Major Pond. Cordial receptions and crowded houses greeted them everywhere. Strong inducements had been offered him to lecture abroad, even so far away as Australia. In 1884 he consented to lecture in America for a period not exceeding five months.

In December, Twain and Cable appeared in Cleveland. They arrived one afternoon and registered at the Forest City House. I called to pay my respects. Was Mr. Clemens in? Yes, but he had just eaten dinner, it then being 3 o'clock, and had gone to bed, not to be disturbed until 7 o'clock, excepting in case Mr. John Hay, the author of "Little Breeches," called. Mr. Clemens would see Mr. Hay, but no other human being could entice him from his bed. In the evening occurred the entertainment. Mr. Cable read passages from his novel, "Dr. Sevier." Mark Twain came upon the stage walking slowly, apparently in deep meditation. Those present saw a rather small man, with a big head, with bushy gray hair, heavy dark eyebrows, a receding chin, a long face, toothless gums visible between the lips, an iron-gray mustache, closely cut and stiff. The right hand involuntarily stroked the receding chin and a merry twinkle came into his eyes, as he advanced to the front of the stage and began to recite, in his peculiar, drawling and deliberate way, "King Sollerman," taken from advance sheets of *Huckleberry Finn*. When he had finished, he turned and boyishly ran off the stage, with a sort of dog trot. Then I remember that Mr. Cable came on, told us all about "Kate Riley" and "Ristofolo," and then, in imitation of Mark Twain, tried to run off the stage in the same playful manner. I remember also what a deplorable failure Mr. Cable made of the attempt, how his gentle trot reminded me of a duck going down hill, and how eventually he collided with one of the scenes, and lastly how the audience roared with laughter. Then Mark came forward again with his "Tragic Tale of the Fishwife," followed by Cable, who walked soberly now, like a Baptist deacon. Twain told us of "A Trying Situation," and finally concluded the entertainment with one of his inimitable ghost stories.

He is a good talker, and invariably prepares himself, though he skillfully hides his preparation by his method of delivery, which denotes that he is getting his ideas and phrases as he proceeds. He is an accomplished artist in his way. His peculiar mode of expression always seems contagious with an audience, and a laugh would follow the most sober remark. It is a singular fact that an audience will be in a laughing mood, when they first enter the lecture room; they are ready to burst out at anything and everything. In the town of Colchester, Connecticut, there was a good illustration of this, the Hon. Demshain Hornet having a most unpleasant experience at the expense of Mark Twain. Mr. Clemens was

Mark Twain on the Lecture Platform

advertised to lecture in the town of Colchester, but for some reason failed to arrive. In the emergency the lecture committee decided to employ Mr. Hornet to deliver his celebrated lecture on temperance, but so late in the day was this arrangement made that no bills announcing it could be circulated, and the audience assembled, expecting to hear Mark Twain. No one in the town knew Mr. Clemens, or had ever heard him lecture, and they entertained the idea that he was funny, and went to the lecture prepared to laugh. Even those upon the platform, excepting the chairman, did not know Mr. Hornet from Mark Twain, and so, when he was introduced, thought nothing of the name, as they knew "Mark Twain" was a pen-name, and supposed his real name was Hornet.

Mr. Hornet bowed politely, looked about him, and remarked: "Intemperance is the curse of the country." The audience burst into a merry laugh. He knew it could not be at his remark, and thought his clothes must be awry, and he asked the chairman, in a whisper, if he was all right, and received "yes" for an answer. Then he said: "Rum slays more than disease!" Another, but louder laugh followed. He could not understand it, but proceeded: "It breaks up happy homes!" Still louder mirth. "It is carrying young men down to death and hell!" Then came a perfect roar of applause. Mr. Hornet began to get excited. He thought they were poking fun at him, but went on: "We must crush the serpent!" A tremendous howl of laughter. The men on the platform, except the chairman, squirmed as they laughed. Then Hornet got mad. "What I say is Gospel truth," he cried. The audience fairly bellowed with mirth. Hornet turned to a man on the stage, and said: "Do you see anything very ridiculous in my remarks or behavior?" "Yes, ha, ha! It's intensely funny—ha, ha, ha! Go on!" replied the roaring man. "This is an insult," cried Hornet, wildly dancing about. More laughter, and cries of, "Go on, Twain!" Then the chairman began to see through a glass darkly, and arose and quelled the merriment, and explained the situation, and the men on the stage suddenly ceased laughing, and the folks in the audience looked sheepish, and they quit laughing, too, and then the excited Mr. Hornet, being thoroughly mad, told them he had never before got into a town so entirely populated with asses and idiots, and having said that, he left the hall in disgust, followed by the audience in deep gloom.

In Montreal, upon the occasion of Mark Twain's appearance in 1884, many Frenchmen were in the audience. This caused him to introduce into his lecture the following:

> Where so many of the guests are French, the propriety will be recognized of my making a portion of my speech in that beautiful language, in order that I may be partly understood. I speak French with timidity, and not flowingly, except when excited. When using that language, I have noticed that I have hardly ever been mistaken for a Frenchman, except, perhaps, by horses; never, I believe, by people. I had hoped that mere French construction, with English words, would answer; but this is not the case. I tried it at a gentleman's house in Quebec, and it would not work. The maid servant asked, "What would monsieur?" I said, "Monsieur So-and-So, is he with himself?" She did not understand. I said, "Is it that he is still not returned to his house of merchandise?" She did not understand that, either. I said, "He will desolate himself when he learns that his friend American was arrived, and he not with himself to shake him at the hand." She did not even understand that; I don't know why, but she did not, and she lost her temper, besides. Somebody in the rear called out, "Qui est donc la?" or words to that effect, She said, "C'est un fou," and shut the door on me. Perhaps she was right; but how did she ever find that out? For she had never seen me before till that moment. But as I have already intimated, I will close this oration with a few sentiments in the French language. I have not ornamented them. I have not burdened them with flowers of rhetoric, for, to my mind, that literature is best and most enduring which is characterized by a noble simplicity: *J'ai belle bouton d'or de mon oncle, mais je n'ai pas celui du charpentier. Si vous avez le fromage du brave menuisier, c'est bon; mais si vous ne l'avez pas, ne vous desolez pas, prenez le chapeau de drap noir de son beau frère malade. Tout a l'heure! Savoir faire! Qu'est ce que vous dites! Pâté de fois gras! Revanon à nos moutons! Pardon,*

Mark Twain on the Lecture Platform

messieurs, pardonnez moi; essayant à parler la belle langue d'Ollendorf strains me more than you can possibly imagine. But I mean well, and I've done the best I could.

Once when the late Richard Malcolm Johnston had been prevailed on a give a reading in Baltimore, Thomas Nelson Page volunteered to assist him. But a death in Mr. Page's family prevented him from appearing in the entertainment. Mark Twain heard of it. The people of Baltimore had long wanted to have Twain appear there, but he had steadfastly refused to resume his lectures. But he went on that occasion, for he appreciated the genius of Richard Malcolm Johnston, and, desiring to honor him, he left New York, at a great personal sacrifice, and appeared with him on that occasion. There was never such a crowded house in a Baltimore theatre. When the entertainment was over Col. Johnston, with his accustomed fairness and courtesy, tendered Twain the bulk of the receipts.

"No," said Mark, "not one cent shall I receive. It is such a great honor to know a man like you that I am the one who owes you the debt of gratitude."

"Well," said the colonel, "at least let me defray your expenses.""

"I have a through ticket," said Twain. "Good-by and God bless you!"

His last appearance in New York was during the winter of 1894, when he appeared at Madison Square Garden, with the late Bill Nye and James Whitcomb Riley. He had aged noticeably. The failure of his publishing firm in New York had told upon him in every way. His appearance on the platform at this time is best told in the words of a well-known journalist:

> And now comes dear old Mark. Those curly grayish locks, that drooping mustache, the half-closed eyes, the gentle expression of the mouth, almost melancholy, that historic dress suit, too, a relic of several decades ago. The waistcoat barely reached the trousers. Still there was a charming quaintness about him. His self-abnegatory way of speaking was more restful than the egotism of the other two.

I took my eyes off him but once, and then it was to look on the veteran historian, Parke Godwin, who was sitting a few seats in front. There was a resemblance between the two more striking than the difference in their ages. Both show the same disregard for the prevailing fashions in dress that frequently suggests genius. The paths of these two lives have been widely divergent; there is little in common between the author of Tom Sawyer and the historian of the French Revolution. But they are alike in that to either and to both one might apply the words of Homer:

> He was the friend of man,
> For he loved them all.

And now he begins his story. It is "The Jumping Frog." The sad expression begins to fade away, the half-closed eyes are opened wider and begin to twinkle; the point is reached and Twain has once more resumed the self-contemplative look and is again another Jacques.

His lecture tour of the world begun in 1895, under the management of Major Pond, was for a purpose—to earn money with which to pay the debts of his publishing firm—and all the world knows of his success in that grand endeavor.

Life Reviews *Huckleberry Finn*

Durant Da Ponte

The fact that *Huckleberry Finn* elicited only the scantest notice among the critics of its day is a commonplace of Mark Twain scholarship. The reasons for the neglect of Clemens's masterpiece are at best suppositional.[1] Whatever these reasons might be, the fact remains that the novel did not enjoy the critical attention which it might have been expected to call forth. Among the few reviews, one, which seems to have gone undetected by investigators of Clemens's contemporaneous reputation, appeared in the comic magazine *Life* on February 26, 1885 (V, 119), and is reproduced herewith entire.

Mark Twain's Blood-Curdling Humor

Mark Twain is a humorist or nothing. He is well aware of this fact himself, for he prefaces the "Adventures of Huckleberry Finn" with a brief notice, warning persons in search of a moral, motive or plot that they are liable to be prosecuted, banished or shot. This is a nice little artifice to scare off the critics—a kind of "trespassers on these grounds will be dealt with according to law."

However, as there is no penalty attached, we organized a search expedition for the humorous qualities of this book with the following hilarious results:

A very refined and delicate piece of narration by Huck Finn, describing his venerable and dilapidated "pap" as afflicted with delirium tremens, rolling over and over, "Kicking things every which way," and "saying there was

Reprinted from *American Literature* 31 (March 1959): 78–81.

devils ahold of him." This chapter is especially suited to amuse the children on long, rainy afternoons.

An elevating and laughable description of how Huck killed a pig, smeared its blood on an axe and mixed in a little of his own hair, and then ran off, setting up a job on the old man and the community, and leading them to believe him murdered. This little joke can be repeated by any smart boy for the amusement of his fond parents.

A graphic and romantic tale of a Southern family feud, which resulted in an elopement and from six to eight choice corpses.

A polite version of the "Giascutus" story, in which a nude man, striped with the colors of the rainbow, is exhibited as "The King's Camelopard; or, The Royal Nonesuch." This is a good chapter for lenten parlor entertainments and church festivals.

A side-splitting account of a funeral, enlivened by a "sick melodeum," a "long-legged undertaker," and a rat episode in the cellar.

The article is unsigned, but it appears as part of the weekly column entitled BOOKISHNESS, which was the special province of Robert Bridges, not to be confused with the British poet of the same name, who was literary critic for *Life* from 1883 to 1900, and who regularly signed his columns with the pen name "Droch." A note two weeks later in a column bearing Bridges's pseudonym refers to the Kemble illustrations "which enliven many a page of coarse and dreary fun."[2] Another comment a month later reads: "It is a pleasure to note that the Concord Library Committee agree with LIFE's estimate of Mark Twain's 'blood-curdling humor,' and have banished 'Huckleberry Finn' to limbo. If they will again take our advice, let them banish the School of Philosophy. Concord will then rank with other well-regulated Massachusetts towns."[3]

If these two brief comments bearing Bridges's pen name do not confirm beyond doubt his authorship of the *Huckleberry Finn* review, they at least indicate his whole-hearted agreement with the views of whoever wrote the critique in question. That Bridges, who is best remembered as being assistant editor of *Scribner's* magazine from its founding in

1887 until 1914 and editor from 1914 until 1930, failed to perceive the value of such an undeniable classic of American literature as *Huckleberry Finn* may seem odd indeed.[4] The fact is, however, that, regardless of his later development, Bridges's apprenticeship as a critic found him pretty firmly entrenched in the ranks of the romanticists. His BOOKISHNESS columns fairly bristle with attacks upon the new realistic school, the members of which he found "sadly limited."[5] His position as a spokesman in defense of the genteel tradition can best be summed up in his comments on the function of the critic: "If he is an honest critic, he will have some sincere convictions to express; if he is intelligent, he will be able to clearly present the central idea of the author to the reader, and perhaps reveal a purpose that would have remained concealed; and if he has any moral stamina, he can warn the ignorant but well-disposed against those books which can only count for evil."[6]

In addition, he believed that "A novel which faithfully though ideally reflects the life and country with which the author's deepest experiences are associated is the very best form of fiction...."[7] This last statement he made in a review of Charles Egbert Craddock's *The Prophet of the Great Smoky Mountains*. And here, I think, lies the answer to the riddle of Bridges's critical personality. Mark Twain did not idealize. Miss Murfree did, and in so doing perhaps even falsified. But as Huck himself tells us about the companion volume to the one of which he is hero: "That book was made by Mr. Mark Twain, and he told the truth, mainly." The truth, one might venture to suggest, was a commodity not especially congenial to readers of the time. And so it was that the comic magazine *Life* missed a good opportunity to assist in establishing the reputation of America's great humorist.

Notes

1. See Arthur L. Vogelback, "The Publication and Reception of *Huckleberry Finn* in America," *American Literature*, XI, 260–272 (Nov., 1939), in which the author reviews the pre-publication attention accorded the novel—the serialization of excerpts in the *Century*, Twain's reading of selections on a lecture tour with Cable, the lawsuit with the Boston publishing house of Estes and Lauriat over price cutting, and so forth—all of which no doubt tended to make *Huckleberry Finn* seem like "old stuff" when it appeared belatedly in February, 1885.

2. *Life* V (March 12, 1885): 146.

3. *Life* V (April 9, 1885): 202.

4. Frederick Lewis Allen has attested to the perspicacity of his mature judgment. "One likes to think," writes Allen, ". . . of Max Perkins. . . handing over to Bridges for serial publication. . . Hemingway's *A Farewell to Arms*, which aroused the disapproval of the Boston censors. . ." ("Fifty Years of Scribner's Magazine," *Scribner's* CI (Jan., 1937): 24.

5. *Life* X (Nov. 17, 1887): 274.

6. *Life* IX (Jan. 13, 1887): 20.

7. *Life* VI (Oct. 29, 1885): 243.

Huckleberry Finn:
The Book We Love to Hate

Leslie A. Fiedler

I like to think that it would have tickled Mark Twain that a defender of "sivilization" 1984-style rose at the first major symposium honoring the hundredth anniversary of the publication of *Huckleberry Finn* to demand—piously and solemnly—that it be banned from the school curriculum in State College, Pennsylvania. "Black kids," she contended of a book about a white boy willing to "go to hell" to insure the freedom of a runaway black slave, "can be humiliated by it, white kids who are sensitive feel somehow culpable and guilty, and others have their racial biases reinforced"; and she further urged that an English teacher who had assigned it to a ninth grade class, "be censured for manifestations of racial prejudice. . . ." But no one present, as far as I can gather from newspaper accounts of the occasion, had sense enough to laugh.

Instead, some of the other symposiasts seconded her plea, as unaware as she of the absurdity of advocating censorship in the name of "enlightened liberalism"; and apparently equally unaware that some decades earlier the book they advocated keeping out of the hands of the young lest it foster "racism" had been quite piously and solemnly condemned by unabashed white racists, including a now forgotten congressman called Joseph Shannon and the still infamous Senator Joseph McCarthy. The former, an unreconstructed

Reprinted from *Proteus* 1, no. 2 (Fall 1984): 1–8.

apologist for the Confederacy, had described Twain as "a foresaker of the interests of the South, a coward and deserter"; while the latter apparently considered him un-American, a source of aid and comfort for the Communist enemy.

To be sure, several of the academic participants in the centennial symposium rose valiantly to its defense; but they scarcely could have done otherwise, considering that they earned their living by teaching it. Besides, there was something almost as ridiculous as the attack which cued it in their humorless insistence on the moral integrity and classic status of a book to which its author had appended an ironic "Note" warning: "Persons attempting to find a motive in this narrative will be prosecuted; persons attempting to find a moral in it will be banished...." In any case, academic critics, as their latter day descendants did not trouble to remind their audience, have not always been so sure about the morality and greatness of *Huckleberry Finn*. As a matter of fact, when it first appeared it was reviewed favorably in only one "serious" literary periodical.

Part of the trouble seems to have been that it was not packaged and distributed like a "serious" book at all—but published by "subscription," which is to say, peddled like the sleaziest "commodity literature" of the time. Moreover, it seems to have disappointed the kind of genteel readers who had been encouraged by Twain's previous novel, *The Prince and the Pauper*, to believe he was shedding the bad habits he had acquired as a Western journalist, contemptuous of elegance and good taste, and learning at long last to produce books suitable for family reading in the civilized East. In *Huckleberry Finn*, however, he seemed to be reverting to inadvertent vulgarity and deliberate irreverence, farce and shameless burlesque. What is more, to make matters worse he had written his new book in colloquial backcountry American, with the deliberate misspellings and grammatical lapses on which newspaper humorists depended for easy laughs.

Small wonder then that most of the few notices he did get were more in the nature of rebukes than proper reviews.

Huckleberry Finn: *The Book We Love to Hate*

"Vulgar and coarse," the avowed enemies of the low comic called it, "trashy and vicious..no better than the dime novels. . . not elevating. . . more suited to the slums than to intelligent, respectable people. . . ." but even the polite humorists of the time found Twain offensive; a writer in *Life*, the leading comic magazine of the era, for instance, described *Huckleberry Finn* as "coarse and dreary fun"; and after detailing its many scenes of murder and mayhem, observed snidely that such fare was apparently being proffered as "especially suited to amuse children on long, rainy afternoons." But it was the humorless hardline which triumphed and persisted; so that as late as 1920, ten years after Twain's death, a certain Professor John T. Rice, is still insisting in the *Missouri Historical Review*, of that state's best-known writer, "he is often coarse, irreverent if not blasphemous. . . Mark Twain lacks the education absolutely necessary to be a great writer; he lacks the refinement which would render it impossible for him to create such coarse characters as Huckleberry Finn; furthermore, he is absolutely unconscious of all the canons of literary art. . . ."

By the time Rice had delivered himself of this blanket condemnation, however, a counter-effort to tout *Huckleberry Finn* as "the Great American Novel" had begun in earnest. Starting with the authorized and adulatory autobiography by Albert Bigelow Paine, it had even begun to penetrate the academy. But Twain's chief apologists up to the middle of our own century tended to be not objective critics, but cultural chauvinists bound and determined to find somewhere in our past a supreme American classic, or journalists with a strong populist bias, like Bernard DeVoto, bent on redeeming a homegrown novelist whom European-oriented academic critics had hitherto denigrated or ignored. When DeVoto's *Mark Twain's America* appeared in 1932, however, he was most directly responding to another freelance nonacademic, Van Wyck Brooks. In *The Ordeal of Mark Twain* (1920), Brooks had somewhat grudgingly granted that *Huckleberry Finn* attained a certain measure of greatness, but his chief emphasis was on the fact that it might have been even greater if Twain had not been himself the victim of the same genteel tradition which had found his novel vulgar and unrefined. During the Sexual Revolution of the 'twenties, that is to say— in one more typically ironic turn of the critical screw—Twain was blamed for expurgating his own work in response to the pressures of his timid family and friends—for failing, in short, to be vulgar and unrefined *enough*.

Moreover, just as he was found lacking by the "liberated" Freudian critics of the post-World War I era, he was adjudged inadequate by the two critical schools which dominated the American cultural scene during the Great Depression and immediately after World War II, the self-declared Marxists first and then the so-called "New Critics." To a hardline Stalinist like Granville Hicks, for instance, Twain seemed never to have fulfilled his promise of becoming "a great social novelist." Failing either to confront the social conflicts of his own time or "to regard the literary life as a serious enterprise," Twain— Hicks contends in *The Great Tradition*, published in 1933— ended bitter and frustrated. Ironically once more, despite their differences on almost every other score, the defenders of High Modernism, most of whom were politically reactionary, agreed. After all, their most admired literary ancestor, Henry James, had dismissed Twain as reading for the immature, and Newton Arvin echoed him in the 'fifties, writing that Twain's appeal was "chiefly to the very young. . . he is read not because he makes experience more intelligible, but because he cooperates with the desire to play hooky...."

It was Hawthorne and Melville whose fiction Arvin found infinitely more sympathetic, as did most of his more serious and sophisticated colleagues in the university and out; not merely teaching them assiduously, but producing numerous full-length studies of *The Scarlet Letter* and *Moby Dick*. They did not, however, perform a similar service for *Huckleberry Finn*. Indeed, Twain remains oddly invisible in the Age of Criticism which climaxed in the 'fifties. He is, for instance absent from F.O. Matthiessen's *The American Renaissance*, the critical study which established for that time a new canon of American literature, as he was also from an earlier work which much influenced it, D.H. Lawrence's *Studies in Classic American Literature.* Clearly, in the case of Matthiessen (who, unlike Lawrence, admired *Huckleberry Finn*) Twain was excluded for purely chronological reasons; but, in any case, neither Matthiessen himself nor anyone else hastened to fill the gap. To be sure, T. S. Eliot, who was not only the favorite poet of the first generation of New Critics, but a formidable critic as well, in 1950 declared himself convinced of the greatness of *Huckleberry Finn.* Eliot, though, was speaking nostalgically and sentimentally on the occasion of his temporary return from exile to the banks of the Mississippi, where he had been born; and he is, in any event, an erratic and untrustworthy judge of fiction. But Lionel Trilling, most literate and plausible of all American critics influenced by Karl Marx (and Sigmund Freud to boot) had gone on record to the same effect just a couple of years before. Consequently, despite the fact that both of their pieces are slight and occasional, they carried the day, making *Huckleberry Finn* as standard a part of the English curriculum as *Moby Dick* or the *Scarlet Letter* ; so that even the far later critics bent on making a negative case, have felt obligated to come to terms with so odd and formidable a united front.

This, however, is precisely what William Van O'Connor, a second-generation academic New Critic and hardline "Modernist" attempted to do in 1955, in a little essay much reprinted ever since, called "Why *Huckleberry Finn* is Not the Great American Novel." In it he argues that, in spite of Trilling and Eliot, "Twain, however gifted as a raconteur, however much genius he had as an improvisor, was not, even in *Huckleberry Finn,* a great novelist"; and he suggests as examples of writers who were: Jane Austen and Henry James. It is quite evident by the standards of Modernism that O'Connor finds Twain wanting—deficient in "serious wit," controlled form and precision of language. In light of this, then it is scarcely surprising that Cyril Connolly, drawing up in

1965 a list of the "one hundred key books" of the Modern Movement, excluded *Huckleberry Finn*, which he explained, "is over-praised, too involved and sentimental despite its prophetic use of American vernacular—a false dawn...."

For a long time, moreover, Twain fared as badly with his fellow-novelists as he had earlier on with the literary critics. His Continental contemporaries by and large ignored him, and even novelists who wrote in his own tongue, both American and English, though more likely to begin by granting that he possessed considerable talent, typically ended by denying his "greatness." The British, in fact, remained skeptical well into the twentieth century: Arnold Bennett, for instance, declaring that though some of Clemens' fictions were "episodically magnificent... as complete works of art they are of inferior quality;" and Frank Harris dismissing him even more summarily, with the observation, "I do not think *Huckleberry Finn* among the best boys' books. *Treasure Island* of Stevenson seems to me infinitely better." As late as 1941, V. S. Pritchett though urging an apparently reluctant English audience to read the book which he described somewhat condescendingly as, "granting the limits of a boy's mind in the hero and the author, a comic masterpiece," hastens to add that "It is not a book which grows spiritually, if we compare it to *Quixote*, *Dead Souls*, or even *Pickwick*; and it is lacking in that civilized quality which you are bound to lose when you throw over civilization—the quality of pity."

Considering the British inclination to identify their own culture with "civilization" itself, the response is understandable enough. But less understandably for a while at least, Twain was regarded just as suspiciously by eminent writers in his own country. Even William Dean Howells, his life-long advocate, as well as his editor and censor and close friend, though he rushed into print enthusiastically in behalf of *Innocents Abroad*, *The Prince and the Pauper*, and *A Connecticut Yankee in King Arthur's Court*, published no review of *Huckleberry Finn*. Good and sufficient reasons have been offered for this (he had no regular reviewing assignment at the moment; he was too deeply involved with editing the book *etc. etc.*); but his perhaps embarrassed silence is too much like that of most of his respectable contemporaries to be easily explained away. Certainly, he was aware of the resistance to Twain on the part of the eminent Brahmins of New England, whom he himself had wooed and won, though initially quite as much a suspect outsider as Twain, reporting a little ruefully that "I do not think Longfellow made much of him and Lowell made less."

Henry James, though more nearly of Twain's age and generation, regarded him, as we have already noted, with equal coolness; but this is scarcely surprising in light of the fact that the mass audience which spurned his work had made a rich man of his rival. What is surprising is that Walt Whitman, who one might have supposed would find Twain with his commitment to the vernacular and his populist politics profoundly sympathetic, thought him somehow not really on his side. "I think he misses fire," the Good Grey Poet told Horace Traubel of Twain, "he might have been something: he comes near to being something; but he never arrives." Similarly, the somewhat younger Theodore Dreiser, though he respected and admired Twain for his ideas, especially his religious skepticism and his hostility to American imperialism, found him inadequate as a maker of fictions; "never a novelist," was his final word on the subject, "He could not write a novel."

It seems clear, however, that Dreiser was deeply indebted to Twain in ways he could not confess even to himself. It was only with the emergence of Faulkner and Hemingway in the late 1920s that a generation of novelists appeared willing to acknowledge fully and generously what our literature in general and they in particular owe to Mark Twain. Fittingly enough, it is the judgment of the latter which has been quoted over and over ever since, till it has come to seem an article of faith. "All modern American literature comes from one book by Mark Twain called *Huckleberry Finn*." Hemingway wrote in *The Green Hills of Africa* in 1935, ". . . All American writing comes from that. There was nothing before. There has been nothing as good since."

The grandiloquent overstatement of the conclusion, dismissing as "nothing" all of Cooper and Poe, Hawthorne and Melville, is odd enough and is, therefore, generally ignored by those citing the passage in Twain's behalf. But even odder is the qualifying proviso, indicated by my three dots just before "all American writing," which most admirers of Twain and Hemingway tend to forget. "If you read it you must stop where the Nigger Jim is stolen from the boys. That is the real end. The rest is just cheating." In the first place (obviously Hemingway had not read the novel he so highly praised in a long time and had rewritten it in his memory), Jim is not stolen from "the boys" at all, only from Huck who is unaccompanied by Tom Sawyer at that climatic moment.

Moreover, as those of us who *have* read *Huckleberry Finn* recently are uncomfortably aware, the "rest" that is "just cheating"—the long passage full of cruel horseplay and tedious burlesque involving the mock stealing out of captivity of a black slave who Tom knows has long since been freed—constitutes nearly one third of the whole book. One must slog his way through it to reach what is perhaps the most famous pair of sentences in the book (the essential clue, as I hope finally to demonstrate, to why it has bugged so many self-righteous critics ever since): "But I reckon I got to light out for the Territory ahead of the rest, because Aunt Sally she's going to adopt me and sivilize me and I can't stand it. I been there before."

What Hemingway is saying, finally, is that all of American literature comes out of two thirds of a single book, the rest of which is an esthetic botch and moral failure; and almost all the critics who succeeded him have agreed. Ironically, however, Mark Twain himself did not. After completing the first sixteen or seventeen chapters, which is to say, the part of his novel which critics have found most authentic and moving, he temporarily abandoned the whole project for five or six years, vowing that he was well-nigh determined to "pigeon hole or burn the MS when it is done." But after he had completed the long anti-climax in which all that is potentially tragic in the work is dissolved into farce, he came to believe that he had produced a "rattling good" book after all, and declared that "*I* shall *like* it, whether anybody else does or not."

But that resolve was soon shaken by the treatment *Huckleberry Finn* received from the self-appointed guardians of public morality, to whom in some ways Twain attended more closely than he did to critics and fellow writers; since their opinions much influenced his wife and his daughters, whose approval was essential to his psychic well being. But Livy and Suzy turned out to be dubious about his new book, and eventually even he came like them to regard it as second best to more refined and pretentious works of his like *The Prince and the Pauper* and especially the almost unreadable *Joan of Arc*.

It was in the very heart of New England where he himself had settled that the voice of outraged moral protest against *Huckleberry Finn* was first raised; ironically enough in Concord, Massachusetts, the very cradle of American Liberty. It was there that an irate library committee banned Twain's book from their shelves as "rough, coarse, inelegant, dealing with experiences not elevating... the veriest trash." And a chorus of newspaper editorials—reaching eventually back into the West out of which Twain had emerged—repeated the charges: accusing him not only of a contempt for propriety and a willingness to pander to the gross tastes of the mass audience, but of fouling his own American nest, discrediting his country and culture in the eyes of the "civilized" world.

It was indeed this kind of attack on *Huckleberry Finn* which has persisted the longest. However critics may have changed their opinions and practicing writers altered their attitudes with the passage of time, the dogooders and righteous book-banners have continued to regard his masterpiece as subversive. As late as the time in which T. S. Eliot grew up, such a view prevailed in his genteel but cultured family (after all, his grandfather had brought enlightenment to the provinces by founding Washington University in Saint Louis). "I suspect," he wrote looking back from 1950, "that a fear on the part of my parents lest I should acquire a premature taste for tobacco, and perhaps other habits of the hero of the story, kept the book out of my way." It is interesting that Eliot discreetly specifies only smoking (not yet under fire from a new wave of puritan repression in his time) rather than lying and stealing and a contempt for school and church which constitute Huck's less venial faults. The truth is that, taken seriously, *Huckleberry Finn* is not merely "rough, coarse and inelegant" as charged, but also its anti-hero, convinced as he is that what parents, preachers and teachers advocate must be rejected at the behest of his own untutored heart, is a dubious sort of model for growing boys and girls.

It was therefore predictable from the start that scarcely a year would pass during the century since its publication that has not seen Twain's book forbidden somewhere in the United States. After all, the self-righteous we have always with us. What is surprising (though finally characteristic of an America, which like that novel is divided against itself) is that even as *Huckleberry Finn* has remained a banned book, it has also become a *required* one; and that this indeed, has seemed to exacerbate the resistance to it. Truly to understand the impact of Twain's most beloved and feared novel on our culture, then, we must be aware of both sides of our ambivalent response. But from a distance, what is most highly visible is the negative pole of that ambivalence—and the almost habitual scapegoating of poor Huck in which it periodically results.

It was, therefore, possible for a Soviet critic to claim in 1959, at the height of the Cold War, that the relationship of official America to "its greatest writer" is to "try to forget him," and when that fails, to forbid his books. In proof of this, that critic quoted from an English literary journal which a few months before had listed under the heading "Banned in America," *Lady Chatterley's Lover,* the novels of Henry

Miller—and *Huckleberry Finn*. The Russian spokesman, proud of the fact that up to that time eleven million copies of Twain's book had been distributed in his country, where everything not forbidden is required, did not mention that the two other authors were (and are still) under official ban there. Nor did he seem aware that, despite the occasional attempts to forbid it, *Huckleberry Finn* had sold even better in the United States. Instead, he alluded to the attacks on Twain by the long-dead Congressman Shannon and the recently discredited Senator McCarthy, citing as a clincher the fact that only two years earlier "The Board of Education of New York City crossed the book about Huck from the books permitted for reading in elementary and junior schools."

Clearly he was suggesting that Samuel Clemens had become *persona non grata* in the United States because of his satires of American capitalism and imperialism. But the final example scarcely supports this case; since the action of the New York School Board in 1957 was undertaken not at the instigation of the Chamber of Commerce or the Veterans of Foreign Wars, but the NAACP, an organization whose fight against the evils of American racism was then being supported by the American Communist Party. Moreover, in the quarter of a century since, most of the continuing efforts to ban *Huckleberry Finn* have been launched by enlightened liberals, though attacks from genteel conservatives have not utterly ceased.

Every year since 1971, for instance, the *School Library Journal* has given a mock award called the "Huck Finn Pin" to a new book adjudged by its editor to "ill serve the limited reading time of young people." It seems obvious to me that this gallant defender of "good taste" in literature for the young would in 1885 have awarded her booby prize to the book whose anti-hero she describes (explaining why she has thus used his name) as "illiterate and inclined to stay that way." But she feels obliged at least to justify and explain; while the book-banners on the Left have grown even bolder—and more shameless.

When word leaked out in 1957 that *Huckleberry Finn* had been "barred as a textbook" in New York City, school officials felt obliged to lie to the press; explaining that it had been dropped not because of political or ethical objections from anyone, but merely because "it was not really a textbook." The NAACP, however, gave away the game, insisting that they had in fact objected to its "racial slurs" and "belittling racial designations"—meaning its frequent use of the word "nigger." They could not bring themselves actually to say the six-letter word, which at that point was considered "dirtier" than any of the once taboo four-syllable Anglo-Saxon monosyllabics. By 1982, however, the self-righteous anti-racists were out of the closet, and willing, in a good cause, to call a spade a spade.

In that year, for instance, the Human Relations Committee of the Mark Twain (*sic*) Elementary School of Arlington, Virginia, recommending the removal of *Huckleberry Finn* from the curriculum, charged it with being "anti-American," a threat to the Fourteenth Amendment and the very notion that "all men are created equal" because of its "flagrant use of the word 'nigger'." Nor is there any point in denying that Twain is guilty as charged. That offensive epithet is, indeed, repeated over and over on the pages of his book like a *leitmotif* or an obsession; so that one can understand a black school boy in the midst of whites wincing as he reads.

But how could Twain have done otherwise in a book in which he boasted he had "painstakingly" recreated seven dialects spoken in the Mississippi Basin, in all of which, (including that spoken by blacks themselves) the sole name for Afro-Americans was indeed "nigger." The deeper truth told by America about *Huckleberry Finn*, whose last words are, after all, "*Yours Truly*," depends on its faithfulness to the language we Americans actually speak; especially terms like "nigger," which serve to remind us of not just our troubled history but of attitudes and values created by that history of which most of us have learned to be ashamed, yet from which none of us can feel wholly free. We should therefore prize Twain's dangerous and equivocal novel not in spite of its use of that wicked epithet, but for the way in which it manages to ironize it; enabling us finally—without denying our horror or our guilt—to laugh therapeutically at the "peculiar institution" of slavery.

One of my own favorite passages in the book is, indeed, the little interchange between Huck and Aunt Sally in Chapter XXXII, in which, after Huck lyingly tells her that the boat he had arrived on had blown a cylinder head, she asks, "Good gracious! anybody hurt?" "No'm, he answers; "Killed a nigger;" to which she responds, "Well, it's lucky; because sometimes people do get hurt." What initially makes this passage funny is that both of these essentially good people by thus dehumanizing the Negro diminish their own humanity; and what makes it even funnier is that Huck, obtuse of all obtuse narrators, a classically humorless "straight man," does not find it funny at all. But the real cream of the jest is that in our time self-righteous anti-racists still fail to get the joke, making it also a joke on them unto the third and fourth generation.

Ridiculous or not, however, one hundred years later they continue to suppress *Huckleberry Finn*—putting its defenders more and more on the defensive; so that some have even tried to appease the book-banners by expurgating the novel. It would appear, for instance, that in New York in 1957, the publishers of the textbook version then in use have already discreetly substituted "negro" for "nigger" throughout. As always, however, appeasement did not work, the adamant objectors protesting that that anachronistic and tasteless euphemism had not been properly capitalized. And there is no end in sight; since at this point even capital-N-Negro has become suspect to those who, however pale their actual hue, prefer to call themselves "blacks." In any case, the anti-racist objection to *Huckleberry Finn* is not finally to its language, but (once more in the words of the Human Relations Committee of the Mark Twain School) to "the demeaning way in which black people are portrayed in the book."

I must confess I find this second charge harder to grant, in light of the fact that the only black character portrayed fully in it is "Miss Watson's big nigger Jim," who is by all odds the most sympathetic of its characters. A loving parent and husband, a faithful friend, resourceful, courageous, self-sacrificing (he risks his life to save Tom's), he possesses a natural dignity and authority, which in one of the novel's most moving scenes compels Huck—whom Jim has just called "trash" for his heartlessness—to apologize abjectly. "It made me feel so mean," Huck writes. "I could almost kissed *his* foot to get him to take it back. It was fifteen minutes before I could work myself up to go and humble myself to a nigger—but I done it, and I warn't ever sorry for it afterwards, neither." It is an apology for all of white America, which its ironies (triggered once more by the key word "nigger") keep on the safe side of sentimentality. Moreover, Huck finds on the raft with Jim what he can find nowhere in the "sivilized" white world, a kind of love compatible with freedom. Together they establish a community of two, temporary and foredoomed perhaps, but providing for as long as it lasts a model for the reconciliation of blacks and whites in an America otherwise ethnically divided against itself.

But off the raft (and especially in the long farcical anti-climax which follows Chapter XXXI), the books, detractors protests,[sic] Jim is portrayed as ignorant, superstitious and gullible; thus perpetuating certain degrading "stereotypes about blacks" derived from the minstrel show, which—in the words of a Professor of Afro-American Studies who testified against *Huckleberry Finn* at the centennial symposium I began by describing—consists of "white men blacking up to entertain other whites at the expense of black people's humanity." Some thirty years earlier the same charges had been made by the eminent black American novelist, Ralph Ellison, who had explained to white readers that the Negro is "made uncomfortable" by Nigger Jim, because "Twain fitted Jim into the outlines of the minstrel tradition." Ellison, however, then went on to add—finally loving Twain's great book (and, he tells us, identifying with Huck, whatever his discomfort with Jim) that "it is from behind this stereotype mask that we see Jim's dignity and human capacity—and Twain's complexity—emerge."

What he suggests, and present enemies of the book fail to recognize, is that Twain not merely reflected but redeemed the "niggershow stereotype"—converting it to an archetype of great resonance and power: a mythic grid of perception, through which for a long time the whole world, black as well as white, perceived black Americans. The only two archetypal images of the Negro which can compete with Twain's Nigger Jim are Joel Chandler Harris' Uncle Remus and Harriett Beecher Stowe's Uncle Tom, both also created by white Americans and derived, directly or indirectly, from the minstrel show. Yet neither of the books in which they appear has ever been banned from libraries or classrooms at the behest of anti-racists. *Uncle Tom*, to be sure has been the target of Southern white racists, like *Huckleberry Finn*. Only the latter, however, has the unique distinction of having been censored not only by apologists for *both* sides in what eventuated in a bloody civil war—but also by those to whom culture and taste seemed more important than the "Negro Question," or indeed any social issue.

The persistent popularity of *Huckleberry Finn* has in fact always troubled members of any elite, esthetic, moral or political, whose members feel that they know better than the unredeemed masses what is good for them. I recall William Burroughs (improbable heir to Mark Twain as literary disturber of the peace) once observing that the world would be vastly improved if a weapon could be invented which would destroy "all those who think they are right," i.e., believe that the values in which they happen to believe are valid for everyone, everywhere and will for ever[sic] remain so. But *Huckleberry Finn,* it occurs to me, is precisely that weapon; killing no one, to be sure, but undermining all pretensions to final wisdom with ambiguity, irony, farce and burlesque: the universal solvent of laughter.

Without seeming to preach or teach it persuades us—at a level far below full consciousness—of the essential ridiculousness not only of our society's restrictive taboos against lying and stealing, "copping out" and "dropping out," but of its highest positive values as well: duty and hard work, heroism and honor. Moreover, in addition to mocking institutions despised by all right-thinking Americans by the end of the 19th century, royalty, aristocracy, slavery, the blood-feud and lynching, it satirizes others still dearly prized, like home, school and church, which is to say, bourgeois domesticity and Christian humanism. Certainly, the teachers and preachers and parents who defend them turn out in its pages always to be hilariously wrong. But it is worse even than this; since finally *The Adventures of Huckleberry Finn* undercuts, as Huck himself tells us (and we must—without ceasing to laugh—take him quite seriously) "civilization" itself: the reign of law and order and sweet reason, without which no community can survive, but for which the price we pay is, from the individual's point of view, in some sense too high.

To be sure, Twain himself did not live by Huck's antinomian, anarchic code but contented himself with dreaming of an orphan boy who did; and in his voice told the tale which—despite all censors—the world will not let die. Not that we who read and love it dare to "light out for the Territory" either; but turning its pages and evoking its images, we release vicariously all we have repressed in the daylight world of respectability and routine; thus therapeutically giving the devil of our unconscious his due.

Such therapeutic release of the repressed is what all literature which, like *Huckleberry Finn*, pleases many and pleases long, affords us; though not all writers are aware of this. Some indeed aspire to reinforce rather than to deliver us from the "restrictions" of civilization to justify God's ways (i.e., the reigning theology and morality of their time) to man. Mark Twain, however, was of the Devil's party and knew it. He therefore despised, as he did other preachers and teachers, those Apostles of the Art Religion who did not. About Poe and Jane Austen, for instance, he wrote, "I could read his prose on salary, but not Jane's. . . It seems a great pity they allowed her to die a natural death;" and of Henry James he once observed that he would "rather be condemned to Paul Bunyan's Heaven" than to be forced to finish *The Bostonians*.

Huckleberry Finn is a travesty of High Art quite as much as of conscience and duty and "sivilization"; and this Twain himself came finally to realize; writing in 1889, with a candor clearly bred by desperation, to Andrew Lang, one of the few critics he hoped might understand:

> Indeed I have been misjudged from the very first. I have never tried in even one single instance to help cultivate the cultivated classes. I was not equipped for it, either by native gifts or training. And I never had any ambition in that direction, but always hunted for bigger game—the masses. I have seldom deliberately tried to instruct them, but have tried to entertain them. . .to amuse them. . . .
>
> Yes, you see, I have always catered for the Belly and the Members but have been. . . criticized from the culture standard—to my sorrow and pain, because, honestly, I never cared what became of the cultured classes. They could go to the theater and the opera. They had no use for me and the melodeon.

That he did in fact win the "masses" he wooed, in *Huckleberry Finn* at least, is attested to by their having taken that book to their hearts long before official critics and moralists had managed to come to terms with it. But precisely because it has thus proved from the start available to the undereducated as well as the learned, the naive as well as the sophisticated, children as well as adults, the many as well as the few, the self-appointed guardians of culture and morality have continued to regard it with suspicion. Indeed, its scapegoating on ethical grounds has, as we have been noticing, never ceased, though those grounds have changed. But, in a sense, those who still insist that Twain's novel, written from as well as to "the Belly and the Members," rather than the

"Head," is dangerous and "vulgar" speak the truth. What falsifies *Huckleberry Finn* is the begrudged and belated praise of elitist critics, who have done their best recently to persuade us that Twain's untidy masterpiece, more improvised than structured, is "a great novel" in terms of the "culture standards" by which they also find *Pride and Prejudice* or *The Wings of the Dove* great.

The desperate plea with which Clemens ended his letter to Lang, that is to say, has never been truly or fully answered. "And now at last, " he wrote, "I arrive at my object and tender my petition, making supplication to this effect: that the critics adopt a rule recognizing the Belly and the Members, and formulate a standard whereby work done for them shall be judged. Help me, Mr. Lang. . . ." Lang did at least try but in the years since, and especially this side of the Atlantic, Twain's anguished appeal has been ignored, and the defense of popular art which underlies it dismissed as "self-serving" and insubstantial." His cry for help continues, however, to ring in my head, a reproach to me and the profession I practice. I have therefore taken advantage of the centennial celebration of the American book we most love to hate to begin at long last, tentatively—and with appropriate irony—to respond.

A Sound Heart and a Deformed Conscience

Henry Nash Smith

1

Mark Twain worked on *Adventures of Huckleberry Finn* at intervals over a period of seven years, from 1876 to 1883. During this time he wrote two considerable books (*A Tramp Abroad* and *The Prince and the Pauper*), expanded "Old Times on the Mississippi" into *Life on the Mississippi*, and gathered various shorter pieces into three other volumes. But this is all essentially minor work. The main line of his development lies in the long preoccupation with the Matter of Hannibal and the Matter of the River that is recorded in "Old Times" and *The Adventures of Tom Sawyer* and reaches a climax in his book about "Tom Sawyer's Comrade. Scene: The Mississippi Valley. Time: Forty to Fifty Years Ago."

In writing *Huckleberry Finn* Mark Twain found a way to organize into a larger structure the insights that earlier humorists had recorded in their brief anecdotes. This technical accomplishment was of course inseparable from the process of discovering new meanings in his material. His development as a writer was a dialectic interplay in which the reach of his imagination imposed a constant strain on his technical resources, and innovations of method in turn opened up new vistas before his imagination.

Reprinted from *Mark Twain: The Development of a Writer*. Cambridge: Harvard U.P., 1962; pp. 113–137.

The dialectic process is particularly striking in the gestation of *Huckleberry Finn.* The use of Huck as a narrative persona, with the consequent elimination of the author as an intruding presence in the story, resolved the difficulties about point of view and style that had been so conspicuous in the earlier books. But turning the story over to Huck brought into view previously unsuspected literary potentialities in the vernacular perspective, particularly the possibility of using vernacular speech for serious purposes and of transforming the vernacular narrator from a mere persona into a character with human depth. Mark Twain's response to the challenge made *Huckleberry Finn* the greatest of his books and one of the two or three acknowledged masterpieces of American literature. Yet this triumph created a new technical problem to which there was no solution; for what had begun as a comic story developed incipiently tragic implications contradicting the premises of comedy.

Huckleberry Finn thus contains three main elements. The most conspicuous is the story of Huck's and Jim's adventures in their flight toward freedom. Jim is running away from actual slavery, Huck from the cruelty of his father, from the well-intentioned "sivilizing" efforts of Miss Watson and the Widow Douglas, from respectability and routine in general. The second element in the novel is social satire of the towns along the river. The satire is often transcendently funny, especially in episodes involving the rascally Duke and King, but it can also deal in appalling violence, as in the Grangerford-Shepherdson feud or Colonel Sherburn's murder of the helpless Boggs. The third major element in the book is the developing characterization of Huck.

All three elements must have been present to Mark Twain's mind in some sense from the beginning, for much of the book's greatness lies in its basic coherence, the complex interrelation of its parts. Nevertheless, the intensive study devoted to it in recent years, particularly Walter Blair's establishment of the chronology of its composition, has demonstrated that Mark Twain's search for a structure capable of doing justice to his conceptions of theme and character passed through several stages. He did not see clearly where he was going when he began to write, and we can observe him in the act of making discoveries both in meaning and in method as he goes along.

The narrative tends to increase in depth as it moves from the adventure story of the early chapters into the social satire of the long middle section, and thence to the ultimate psychological penetration of Huck's character in the moral crisis of Chapter 31. Since the crisis is brought on by the shock of the definitive failure of Huck's effort to help Jim, it marks the real end of the quest for freedom. The perplexing final sequence on the Phelps plantation is best regarded as a maneuver by which Mark Twain beats his way back from incipient tragedy to the comic resolution called for by the original conception of the story.

2

Huck's and Jim's flight from St. Petersburg obviously translates into action the theme of vernacular protest. The fact that they have no means of fighting back against the forces that threaten them but can only run away is accounted for in part by the conventions of backwoods humor, in which the inferior social status of the vernacular character placed him in an ostensibly weak position. But it also reflects Mark Twain's awareness of his own lack of firm ground to stand on in challenging the established system of values.

Huck's and Jim's defenselessness foreshadows the outcome of their efforts to escape. They cannot finally succeed. To be sure, in a superficial sense they do succeed; at the end of the book Jim is technically free and Huck still has the power to light out for the Territory. But Jim's freedom has been brought about by such an implausible device that we do not believe in it. Who can imagine the scene in which Miss Watson decides to liberate him? What were her motives? Mark

Twain finesses the problem by placing this crucial event far offstage and telling us nothing about it beyond the bare fact he needs to resolve his plot. And the notion that a fourteen-year-old boy could make good his escape beyond the frontier is equally unconvincing. The writer himself did not take it seriously. In an unpublished sequel to *Huckleberry Finn* called "Huck Finn and Tom Sawyer among the Indians," which he began soon after he finished the novel, Aunt Sally takes the boys and Jim back to Hannibal and then to western Missouri for a visit "with some of her relations on a hemp farm out there." Here Tom revives the plan mentioned near the end of *Huckleberry Finn*: he "was dead set on having us run off, some night, and cut for the Injun country and go for adventures." Huck says, however, that he and Jim "kind of hung fire. Plenty to eat and nothing to do. We was very well satisfied." Only after an extended debate can Tom persuade them to set out with him. Their expedition falls into the stereotyped pattern of Wild West stories of travel out the Oregon Trail, makes a few gibes at Cooper's romanticized Indians, and breaks off.

The difficulty of imagining a successful outcome for Huck's and Jim's quest had troubled Mark Twain almost from the beginning of his work on the book. After writing the first section in 1876 he laid aside his manuscript near the end of Chapter 16. The narrative plan with which he had impulsively begun had run into difficulties. When Huck and Jim shove off from Jackson's Island on their section of a lumber raft (at the end of Chapter 11) they do so in haste, to escape the immediate danger of the slave hunters Huck has learned about from Mrs. Loftus. No longer-range plan is mentioned until the beginning of Chapter 15, when Huck says that at Cairo they intended to "sell the raft and get on a steamboat and go way up the Ohio amongst the free states, and then be out of trouble." But they drift past Cairo in the fog, and a substitute plan of making their way back up to the mouth of the Ohio in their canoe is frustrated when the canoe disappears while they are sleeping: "we talked about what we better do, and found there warn't no way but just to go along down with the raft till we got a chance to buy a canoe to go back in." Drifting downstream with the current, however, could not be reconciled with the plan to free Jim by transporting him up the Ohio; hence the temporary abandonment of the story.

3

When Mark Twain took up his manuscript again in 1879, after an interval of three years, he had decided upon a different plan for the narrative. Instead of concentrating on the story of Huck's and Jim's escape, he now launched into a satiric description of the society of the prewar South. Huck was essential to this purpose, for Mark Twain meant to view his subject ironically through Huck's eyes. But Jim was more or less superfluous. During Chapters 17 and 18, devoted to the Grangerford household and the feud, Jim has disappeared from the story. Mark Twain had apparently not yet found a way to combine social satire with the narrative scheme of Huck's and Jim's journey on the raft.

While he was writing his chapter about the feud, however, he thought of a plausible device to keep Huck and Jim floating southward while he continued his panoramic survey of the towns along the river. The device was the introduction of the Duke and the King. In Chapter 19 they come aboard the raft, take charge at once, and hold Huck and Jim in virtual captivity. In this fashion the narrative can preserve the overall form of a journey down the river while providing ample opportunity for satire when Huck accompanies the two rascals on their forays ashore. But only the outward form of the journey is retained. Its meaning has changed, for Huck's and Jim's quest for freedom has in effect come to an end. Jim is physically present but he assumes an entirely passive role and is hidden with the raft for considerable periods. Huck is also essentially passive; his function now is that of an observer. Mark Twain postpones acknowledging that the quest for freedom has failed, but the issue will have to be faced eventually.

The satire of the towns along the banks insists again and again that the dominant culture is decadent and perverted. Traditional values have gone to seed. The inhabitants can hardly be said to live a conscious life of their own: their actions, their thoughts, even their emotions are controlled by an outworn and debased Calvinism, and by a residue of the eighteenth-century cult of sensibility. With few exceptions they are mere bundles of tropisms, at the mercy of scoundrels like the Duke and the King who know how to exploit their prejudices and delusions.

The falseness of the prevalent values finds expression in an almost universal tendency of the townspeople to make spurious claims to status through self-dramatization. Mark Twain has been concerned with this topic from the beginning of the book. Chapter 1 deals with Tom Sawyer's plan to start a band of robbers which Huck will be allowed to join only if he will "go back to the widow and be respectable" and we also hear about Miss Watson's mercenary conception of prayer. In Chapter 2 Jim interprets Tom's prank of hanging his hat on the limb of a tree while he is asleep as evidence that he has been bewitched. He "was most ruined for a servant, because he got stuck up on account of having seen the devil and been rode by witches." Presently we witness the ritual by which Pap Finn is to be redeemed from drunkenness. When his benefactor gives him a lecture on temperance, it will be recalled,

> the old man cried, and said he'd been a fool, and fooled away his life; but now he was a-going to turn over a new leaf and be a man nobody wouldn't be ashamed of, and he hoped the judge would help him and not look down on him. The judge said he could hug him for them words; so *he* cried, and his wife she cried again; pap said he'd been a man that had always been misunderstood before, and the judge said he believed it. The old man said that what a man wanted that was down was sympathy, and the judge said it was so; so they cried again.

As comic relief for the feud that provides a way of life for the male Grangerfords Mark Twain dwells lovingly on Emmeline Grangerford's pretensions to culture—her paintings with the fetching titles and the ambitious "Ode to Stephen Dowling Bots, Dec'd.," its pathos hopelessly flawed by the crudities showing through like the chalk beneath the enameled surface of the artificial fruit in the parlor: "His spirit was gone for to sport aloft/In the realm of the good and great."

The Duke and the King personify the theme of fraudulent role-taking. These rogues are not even given names apart from the wildly improbable identities they assume in order to dominate Huck and Jim. The Duke's poses have a literary cast, perhaps because of the scraps of bombast he remembers from his experience as an actor. The illiterate King has "done considerable in the doctoring way," but when we see him at work it is mainly at preaching, "workin' camp-meetin's, and missionaryin' around." Pretended or misguided piety and other perversions of Christianity obviously head the list of counts in Mark Twain's indictment of the prewar South. And properly: for it is of course religion that stands at the center of the system of values in the society of this fictive world and by implication in all societies. His revulsion, expressed through Huck, reaches its highest pitch in the scene where the King delivers his masterpiece of "soul-butter and hogwash" for the benefit of the late Peter Wilks's fellow townsmen.

> By and by the king he gets up and comes forward a little, and works himself up and slobbers out a speech, all full of tears and flapdoodle, about its being a sore trial for him and his poor brother to lose the diseased, and to miss seeing diseased alive after the long journey of four thousand mile, but it's a trial that's sweetened and sanctified to us by this dear sympathy and these holy tears, and so he thanks them out of his heart and out of his brother's heart, because out of their mouths they can't, words being too weak and cold, and all that kind of rot and slush, till it was just sickening; and then he blubbers out a pious goody-goody Amen, and turns himself loose and goes to crying fit to bust.

4

Huck is revolted by the King's hypocrisy: "I never see anything so disgusting." He has had a similar reaction to the brutality of the feud: "It made me so sick I most fell out of the tree." In describing such scenes he speaks as moral man viewing an immoral society, an observer who is himself free of the vices and even the weaknesses he describes. Mark Twain's satiric method required that Huck be a mask for the writer, not a fully developed character. The method has great ironic force, and is in itself a technical landmark in the history of American fiction, but it prevents Mark Twain from doing full justice to Huck as a person in his own right, capable of mistakes in perception and judgment, troubled by doubts and conflicting impulses.

Even in the chapters written during the original burst of composition in 1876 the character of Huck is shown to have depths and complexities not relevant to the immediate context. Huck's and Jim's journey down the river begins simply as a flight from physical danger; and the first episodes of the voyage have little bearing on the novelistic possibilities in the strange comradeship between outcast boy and escaped slave. But in Chapter 15, when Huck plays a prank on Jim by persuading him that the separation in the fog was only a dream, Jim's dignified and moving rebuke suddenly opens up a new dimension in the relation. Huck's humble apology is striking evidence of growth in moral insight. It leads naturally to the next chapter in which Mark Twain causes Huck to face up for the first time to the fact that he is helping a slave to escape. It is as if the writer himself were discovering unsuspected meanings in what he had thought of as a story of picaresque adventure. The incipient contradiction between narrative plan and increasing depth in Huck's character must have been as disconcerting to Mark Twain as the difficulty of finding a way to account for Huck's and Jim's continuing southward past the mouth of the Ohio. It was doubtless the convergence of the two problems that led him to put aside the manuscript near the end of Chapter 16.

The introduction of the Duke and the King not only took care of the awkwardness in the plot but also allowed Mark Twain to postpone the exploration of Huck's moral dilemma. If Huck is not a free agent he is not responsible for what happens and is spared the agonies of choice. Throughout the long middle section, while he is primarily an observer, he is free of inner conflict because he is endowed by implication with Mark Twain's own unambiguous attitude toward the fraud and folly he witnesses.

In Chapter 31, however, Huck escaped from his captors and faces once again the responsibility for deciding on a course of action. His situation is much more desperate than it had been at the time of his first struggle with his conscience. The raft has borne Jim hundreds of miles downstream from the pathway of escape and the King has turned him over to Silas Phelps as a runaway slave. The quest for freedom has "all come to nothing, everything all busted up and ruined." Huck thinks of notifying Miss Watson where Jim is, since if he must be a slave he would be better off "at home where his family was." But then Huck realizes that Miss Watson would probably sell Jim down the river as a punishment for running away. Furthermore, Huck himself would be denounced by everyone for his part in the affair. In this fashion his mind comes back once again to the unparalleled wickedness of acting as accomplice in a slave's escape.

The account of Huck's mental struggle in the next two or three pages is the emotional climax of the story. It draws together the theme of flight from bondage and the social satire of the middle section, for Huck is trying to work himself clear of the perverted value system of St. Petersburg. Both adventure story and satire, however, are now subordinate to an exploration of Huck's psyche which is the ultimate achievement of the book. The issue is identical with that of the first moral crisis, but the later passage is much more intense and richer in implication. The differences appear clearly if the two crises are compared in detail.

In Chapter 16 Huck is startled into a realization of his predicament when he hears Jim, on the lookout for Cairo at the mouth of the Ohio, declare that "he'd be a free man the minute he seen it, but if he missed it he'd be a slave country again and no more show for freedom." Huck says: "I begun to get it through my head that he *was* most free—and who was to blame for it? Why, *me*. I couldn't get that out of my conscience, no how nor no way." He dramatizes his inner debate by quoting the words in which his conscience denounces him: "What had poor Miss Watson done to you that you could see her nigger go off right under your eyes and never say one single word? What did that poor old woman do to you that you could treat her so mean? Why, she tried to learn you your book, she tried to learn you your manners, she tried to be good to you every way she knowed how. *That's* what she done." The counterargument is provided by Jim, who seems to guess what is passing through Huck's mind and does what he can to invoke the force of friendship and gratitude: "Pooty soon I'll be a-shout'n' for joy, en I'll say, it's all on accounts o' Huck; I's a free man, en I couldn't ever ben free ef it hadn' ben for Huck; Huck done it. Jim won't ever forget you, Huck; you's de bes' fren' Jim's ever had; en you's de *only* fren' ole Jim's got now." Huck nevertheless sets out for the shore in the canoe "all in a sweat to tell on" Jim, but when he is intercepted by the two slave hunters in a skiff he suddenly contrives a cunning device to ward them off. We are given no details about how his inner conflict was resolved.

In the later crisis Huck provides a much more circumstantial account of what passes through his mind. He is now quite alone; the outcome of the debate is not affected by any stimulus from the outside. It is the memory of Jim's kindness and goodness rather than Jim's actual voice that impels Huck to defy his conscience: "I see Jim before me all the time: in the day and in the night-time, sometimes moonlight, sometimes storms, and we a-floating along, talking

A Sound Heart and a Deformed Conscience

and singing and laughing." The most striking feature of this later crisis is the fact that Huck's conscience, which formerly had employed only secular arguments, now deals heavily in religious cant:

> At last, when it hit me all of a sudden that here was the plain hand of Providence slapping me in the face and letting me know my wickedness was being watched all the time from up there in heaven, whilst I was stealing a poor old woman's nigger that hadn't ever done me no harm, and now was showing me there's One that's always on the lookout, and ain't a-going to allow no such miserable doings to go only just so fur and no further, I most dropped in my tracks I was so scared.

In the earlier debate the voice of Huck's conscience is quoted directly, but the bulk of the later exhortation is reported in indirect discourse. This apparently simple change in method has remarkable consequences. According to the conventions of first-person narrative, the narrator functions as a neutral medium in reporting dialogue. He remembers the speeches of other characters but they pass through his mind without affecting him. When Huck's conscience speaks within quotation marks it is in effect a character in the story, and he is not responsible for what it says. But when he paraphrases the admonitions of his conscience they are incorporated into his own discourse. Thus although Huck is obviously remembering the bits of theological jargon from sermons justifying slavery, they have become a part of his vocabulary.

The device of having Huck paraphrase rather than quote the voice of conscience may have been suggested to Mark Twain by a discovery he made in revising Huck's report of the King's address to the mourners in the Wilks parlor (Chapter 25). The manuscript version of the passage shows that the King's remarks were composed as a direct quotation, but in the published text they have been put, with a minimum of verbal change, into indirect discourse. The removal of the barrier of quotation marks brings Huck into much more intimate contact with the King's "rot and slush" despite the fact that the paraphrase quivers with disapproval. The voice of conscience speaks in the precise accents of the King but Huck is now completely uncritical. He does not question its moral authority; it is morality personified. The greater subtlety of the later passage illustrates the difference between the necessarily shallow characterization of Huck while he was being used merely as a narrative persona, and the profound insight which Mark Twain eventually brought to bear on his protagonist.

The recognition of complexity in Huck's character enabled Mark Twain to do full justice to the conflict between vernacular values and the dominant culture. By situating in a single consciousness both the perverted moral code of a society built on slavery and the vernacular commitment to freedom and spontaneity, he was able to represent the opposed perspectives as alternative modes of experience for the same character. In this way he gets rid of the confusions surrounding the pronoun "I" in the earlier books, where it sometimes designates the author speaking in his own person, sometimes an entirely distinct fictional character. Furthermore, the insight that enabled him to recognize the conflict between accepted values and vernacular protest as a struggle within a single mind does justice to its moral depth, whereas the device he had used earlier—in *The Innocents Abroad*, for example—of identifying the two perspectives with separate characters had flattened the issue out into melodrama. The satire of a decadent slave-holding society gains immensely in force when Mark Twain demonstrates that even the outcast Huck has been in part perverted by it. Huck's conscience is simply the attitudes he has taken over from his environment. What is still sound in him is an impulse from the deepest level of his personality that struggles against the overlay of prejudice and false valuation imposed on all members of the society in the name of religion, morality, law, and refinement.

Finally, it should be pointed out that the conflict in Huck between generous impulse and false belief is depicted by means of a contrast between colloquial and exalted styles. In moments of crisis his conscience addresses him in the language of the dominant culture, a tawdry and faded effort at a high style that is the rhetorical equivalent of the ornaments in the Grangerford parlor. Yet speaking in dialect does not in itself imply moral authority. By every external criterion the King is as much a vernacular character as Huck. The conflict in which Huck is involved is not that of a lower against an upper class or of an alienated fringe of outcasts against a cultivated elite. It is not the issue of frontier West versus genteel East, or of backwoods versus metropolis, but of fidelity to the uncoerced self versus the blurring of attitudes caused by social conformity, by the effort to achieve status or power through exhibiting the approved forms of sensibility.

The exploration of Huck's personality carried Mark Twain beyond satire and even beyond his statement of a vernacular protest against the dominant culture into essentially novelistic modes of writing. Some of the passages he composed when he got out beyond his polemic framework challenge comparison with the greatest achievements in the world's fiction.

The most obvious of Mark Twain's discoveries on the deeper levels of Huck's psyche is the boy's capacity for love. The quality of the emotion is defined in action by his decision to sacrifice himself for Jim, just as Jim attains an impressive dignity when he refuses to escape at the cost of deserting the wounded Tom. Projected into the natural setting, the love of the protagonists for each other becomes the unforgettable beauty of the river when they are allowed to be alone together. It is always summer, and the forces of nature cherish them. From the refuge of the cave on Jackson's Island the thunderstorm is an exhilarating spectacle; Huck's description of it is only less poetic than his description of the dawn which he and Jim witness as they sit half-submerged on the sandy bottom.

Yet if Mark Twain had allowed these passages to stand without qualification as a symbolic account of Huck's emotions he would have undercut the complexity of characterization implied in his recognition of Huck's inner conflict of loyalties. Instead, he uses the natural setting to render a wide range of feelings and motives. The fog that separates the boy from Jim for a time is an externalization of his impulse to deceive Jim by a Tom Sawyerish practical joke. Similarly Jim's snake bite, the only injury suffered by either of the companions from a natural source, is the result of another prank played by Huck before he has learned what friends owe one another.

Still darker aspects of Huck's inner life are projected into the natural setting in the form of ghosts, omens, portents of disaster—the body of superstition that is so conspicuous in Huck's and Jim's world. At the end of Chapter I Huck is sitting alone at night by his open window in the Widow Douglas' house:

> I felt so lonesome I most wished I was dead. The stars was shining, and the leaves rustled in the woods ever so mournful; and I heard an owl, away off who-whooing about somebody that was dead, and a whippowill and a dog crying about somebody that was going to die; and the wind was trying to whisper something to me, and I couldn't make out what it was, and so it made the cold shivers run over me. Then away out in the woods I heard that kind of a sound that a ghost makes when it wants to tell about something that's on its mind and can't make itself understood, and so can't rest easy in its grave, and has to go about that way every night grieving. I got so downhearted and scared I did wish I had some company.

The whimpering ghost with something incommunicable on its mind and Huck's cold shivers suggest a burden of guilt and anxiety that is perhaps the punishment he inflicts on himself for defying the mores of St. Petersburg. Whatever the source of these sinister images, they develop the characterization of Huck beyond the needs of the plot. The narrator whose stream of consciousness is recorded here is much more than the innocent protagonist of the pastoral idyl of the raft, more than an ignorant boy who resists being civilized. The vernacular persona is an essentially comic figure; the character we glimpse in Huck's meditation is potentially tragic. Mark Twain's discoveries in the buried strata of Huck's mind point in the same direction as does his intuitive recognition that Huck's and Jim's quest for freedom must end in failure.

A melancholy if not exactly tragic strain in Huck is revealed also by the fictitious autobiographies with which he so often gets himself out of tight places. Like the protocols of a thematic apperception test, they are improvisations on the basis of minimal clues. Huck's inventions are necessary to account for his anomalous situation as a fourteen-year-old boy alone on the river with a Negro man, but they are often carried beyond the demands of utility for sheer love of fable-making. Their luxuriant detail, and the fact that Huck's hearers are usually (although not always) taken in, lend a comic coloring to these inventions, which are authentically in the tradition of the tall tale. But their total effect is somber. When Huck plans his escape from Pap in Chapter 7, he does so by imagining his own death and planting clues which convince everyone in St. Petersburg, including Tom Sawyer, that he has been murdered. In the crisis of Chapter 16 his heightened emotion leads him to produce for the benefit of the slave hunters a harrowing tale to the effect that his father and mother and sister are suffering smallpox on a raft adrift in mid-river, and he is unable to tow the raft ashore. The slave hunters are so touched by the story that they give him forty dollars and careful instructions about how to seek help—farther downstream. Huck tells the Grangerfords "how pap and me and all the family was living on a little farm down at the bottom of Arkansaw, and my sister Mary Ann run off and got married and never was heard of no more, and Bill went to hunt them and he warn't heard of no more, and Tom and Mort died, and then there warn't nobody but just me and pap left, and he was just trimmed down to nothing, on account of his troubles; so when he died I took what there was left, because the farm didn't belong to us, and started up the river, deck passage, and fell overboard."

5

A number of characters besides Huck are presented in greater depth than is necessary either for purposes of satire or for telling the story of his and Jim's quest for freedom. Perhaps the most striking of these is Pap Finn. Like most of the book, Pap comes straight out of Mark Twain's boyhood memories. We have had a glimpse of him as the drunkard sleeping in the shade of a pile of skids on the levee in the opening scene of "Old Times on the Mississippi." His function in the plot, although definite, is limited. He helps to characterize Huck by making vivid the conditions of Huck's childhood. He has transmitted to his son a casual attitude toward chickens and watermelons, a fund of superstitions, a picaresque ability to look out for himself, and even the gift of language. Pap takes Huck away from the comfort and elegance of the Widow's house to the squalor of the deserted cabin across the river, and then by his sadistic beatings forces the boy to escape to Jackson's Island, where the main action of the flight with Jim begins. After the three chapters which Pap dominates (5–7) we do not see him again except as a corpse in the house floating down the river, but Huck refers to him several times later, invoking Pap's testimony to authenticate the aristocratic status of the Widow Douglas, and to support the family philosophy of "borrowing."

In the sociological scheme of the novel Pap provides a matchless specimen of the lowest stratum of whites who are fiercely jealous of their superiority to all Negroes. His monologue on the "govment" in Chapter 6, provoked by the spectacle of the well-dressed free Negro professor from Ohio, seizes in a few lines the essence of Southern race prejudice. Huck shrewdly calls attention to his father's economic code. When the flooded river brings down part of a log raft, he says: "Anybody but pap would'a' waited and seen the day through, so as to catch more stuff; but that warn't pap's style. Nine logs was enough for one time; he must shove right over to town and sell," mainly in order to buy whiskey.

A Sound Heart and a Deformed Conscience

But the documentary data supply only a minor part of the image of Pap in *Huckleberry Finn*. He provides some of the most mordant comedy in the book. The fashion in which he gives himself away in the monologue on "govment" is worthy of Jonson or Molière:

> It was 'lection day, and I was just about to go and vote myself if I warn't too drunk to get there; but when they told me there was a state in this country where they'd let that nigger vote, I drawed out. I says I'll never vote ag'in. Them's the very words I said; they all heard me; and the country may rot for all me—I'll never vote ag'in as long as I live. And to see the cool way of the nigger—why, he wouldn't 'a' give me the road if I hadn't shoved him out o' the way.

Even when the comedy verges on slapstick it retains its function as characterization. Pap is so completely absorbed in his diatribe that he barks his shins on the pork barrel:

> He hopped around the cabin considerable, first on one leg and then on the other, holding first one shin and then the other one, and at last he let out with his left foot all of a sudden and fetched the tub a rattling kick. But it warn't good judgment, because that was the boot that had a couple of his toes leaking out of the front end of it; so now he raised a howl that fairly made a body's hair raise, and down he went in the dirt, and rolled there, and held his toes; and the cussing he done then laid over anything he had ever done previous. He said so his own self afterwards. He had heard old Sowberry Hagan is his best days, and he said it laid over him, too; but I reckon that was sort of piling it on, maybe.

Pap's detached evaluation of his own accomplishment in swearing gives to his character an almost medieval flavor. In all his degradation he conceives of himself as enacting a role which is less a personal destiny than part of an integral natural-social reality—a reality so stable that he can contemplate it as if it were external to him. On election day he was drunk as a matter of course; it was an objective question, like an effort to predict the weather, whether he might be too drunk to get to the polls. When he settles down for a domestic evening in the cabin, he "took the jug, and said he had enough whiskey there for two drunks and one delirium tremens."

But when the delirium comes, it belies the coolness of his offhand calculation. Huck's description of the drunkard's agony is a nightmare of neurotic suffering that blots out the last vestige of comedy in Pap's image and relates itself in Huck's mind to the ominous sounds he had heard from his window in the Widow's house:

> [Pap] rolled over and over wonderful fast, kicking things every which way, and striking and grabbing at the air with his hands, and screaming and saying there was devils a-hold of him. . . Then he laid stiller, and didn't make a sound. I could hear the owls and the wolves away off in the woods, and it seemed terrible still. . . By and by he raised up part way and listened, with his head to one side. He say, very low:
>
> "Tramp—tramp—tramp; that's the dead; tramp-tramp-tramp; they're coming after me; but I won't go. Oh, they're here! don't touch me—don't! hands off—they're cold; let go. Oh, let a poor devil alone!"
>
> Then he went down on all fours and crawled off, begging them to let him alone, and he rolled himself up in his blanket and wallowed in under the old pine table, still a-begging; and then he went to crying. I could hear him through the blanket.

Pap's hallucinations externalize inner suffering in images of ghosts and portents. Presently he sees in Huck the Angel of Death and chases him around the cabin with a knife "saying he would kill me, and then I couldn't come for him no more." In fact, the mystery of Pap's anguished psyche has had a supernatural aura all along. He is in a sense a ghost the first time we see him, for his faceless corpse has been found floating in the river; and immediately before his dramatic appearance in Huck's room Jim's hair-ball oracle has announced, "Dey's two angels hoverin' roun' 'bout him. One uv' em is white en shiny, en t'other one is black. De white one gits him to go right a little while, den de black one sail in en bust it all up. A body can't tell yit which one gwyne to fetch him at de las'." Coming early in the story, at a time when Mark Twain had apparently not yet worked out the details of the plot, this sounds as if he had in mind the possibility of involving Pap more elaborately in the course of events. But aside from the relatively minor incidents that have been mentioned, what the angels might have led Pap to do is never revealed.

He does, however, have an important thematic function. He serves as a forceful reminder that to be a vernacular outcast does not necessarily bring one into contact with the benign forces of nature. Physical withdrawal from society may be plain loafing, without moral significance. Huck's life with Pap in the cabin foreshadows his life with Jim on the raft, but lacks the suggestion of harmony with the natural setting:

> It was kind of lazy and jolly, laying off comfortable all day, smoking and fishing, and no books nor study. Two months or more run along, and my clothes got to be all rags and dirt, and I didn't see how I'd ever got to like it so well at the widow's, where you had to wash, and eat on a plate, and comb up, and go to bed and get up regular, and be forever bothering over a book, and have old Miss Watson pecking at you all the time. I didn't want to go back no more... It was pretty good times up in the woods there, take it all around.

More explicitly, Pap's denunciation of Huck for the civilized habits the Widow and Miss Watson have imposed on him is a grotesque version of vernacular hostility toward the conventions of refined society:

> Starchy clothes—very. You think you're a good deal of a big-bug, *don't* you?... You're educated, too, they say—can read and write. You think you're better'n your father, now, don't you, because he can't?... you drop that school, you hear? I'll learn people to bring up a boy to put on airs over his own father and let on to be better'n what *he* is... First you know you'll get religion, too. I never see such a son.

This adds another nuance to the book by suggesting that civilized values have something to be said for them after all.

The extent to which Mark Twain's imagination was released in *Huckleberry Finn* to explore multiple perspectives upon the Matter of Hannibal and the Matter of the River can be realized if one compares Pap with the sociologically similar backwoodsmen observed from the steamboat in "Old Times." These "jeans-clad, chills-racked, yellow-faced miserables" are merely comic animals. Pap is even more degraded than they are, lazier, more miserable, but he is not an object of scorn. The fullness with which his degradation and his misery are presented confers on him not so much a human dignity—although it is also that—as the impersonal dignity of art.

In relation to the whole of *Huckleberry Finn*, Pap serves to solidify the image of Huck's and Jim's vernacular paradise by demonstrating that Mark Twain is aware of the darker possibilities confronting them when they escape from the shore to the river. The mass of superstitions with which Pap is so vividly connected (we recall the cross of nails in his boot heel to ward off the devil), standing in contrast to the intimations of blissful harmony with nature in the passages devoted to Huck and Jim alone on the raft, keeps that lyrical vision from seeming mere pathetic fallacy. And the appalling glimpse of Pap's inner life beneath the stereotype of the town drunkard makes him into what might be called a note of tragic relief in a predominantly comic story.

6

It has become a commonplace of criticism that the drastic shift in tone in the last section of *Huckleberry Finn*, from Chapter 31 to the end, poses a problem of interpretation. The drifting raft has reached Arkansas, and the King and the Duke have delivered Jim back into captivity. They make their exit early in the sequence, tarred and feathered as punishment for one more effort to work the "Royal Nonesuch" trick. Tom Sawyer reappears by an implausible coincidence and takes charge of the action, which thereafter centers about his

A Sound Heart and a Deformed Conscience

schemes to liberate Jim from confinement in a cabin on the plantation of Tom's Uncle Silas Phelps.

These events have for their prelude a vivid description of Huck's first approach to the Phelps place:

> When I got there it was all still and Sunday-like, and hot and sunshiny; the hands was gone to the fields; and there was them kind of faint dronings of bugs and flies in the air that makes it seem so lonesome and like everybody's dead and gone; and if a breeze fans along and quivers the leaves it makes you feel mournful, because you feel like it's spirits whispering—spirits that's been dead ever so many years—and you always think they're talking about *you*. As a general thing it makes a body wish *he* was dead, too, and done with it all.

And a few lines later:

> I went around and clumb over the back stile by the ash-hopper, and started for the kitchen. When I got a little ways I heard the dim hum of a spinning-wheel wailing along up and sinking along down again; and then I knowed for certain I wished I was dead—for that *is* the lonesomest sound in the whole world.

This passage has much in common with Huck's meditation before his open window in Chapter I. They are the two most vivid expressions of his belief in ghosts, and in both cases the ghosts are associated in his mind with a deep depression not fully accounted for by the context of the story.

It would be reasonable to suppose that the cause of Huck's depression is the failure of his long effort to help Jim toward freedom. The reader knows that even if Huck could manage to rescue Jim from the Phelpses, they face insuperable difficulties in trying to make their way back up the Mississippi to free territory. Yet oddly enough, Huck does not share this estimate of the situation. He is confident he can find a way out of the impasse: "I went right along, not fixing up any particular plan, but just trusting to Providence to put the right words in my mouth when the time come: for I'd noticed that Providence always did put the right words in my mouth if I left it alone." Somewhat later, Huck points out to Tom that they can easily get Jim out of the log cabin by stealing the key, and "shove off down the river on the raft with Jim, hiding daytimes and running nights, the way me and Jim used to do before. Wouldn't that plan work?" Tom agrees: "Why, cert'nly it would work, like rats a-fighting. But it's too blame' simple; there ain't nothing *to* it. What's the good of a plan that ain't no more trouble than that?"

The tone as much as the substance of the references to the problem of rescuing Jim makes it plain that Huck's view of his predicament cannot account for his depression as he approaches the Phelps plantation. The emotion is the author's rather than Huck's, and it is derived from sources outside the story. In order to determine what these were we must consult Mark Twain's autobiographical reminiscences. The Phelps place as he describes it in the novel has powerful associations for him because it is patterned on the farm of his Uncle John A. Quarles where he spent summers as a boy. "I can see the farm yet, with perfect clearness," he wrote in his *Autobiography*.

> I can see all its belongings, all its details; the family room of the house with a "trundle" bed in one corner and a spinning-wheel in another—a wheel whose rising and falling wail, heard from a distance, was the mournfulest of all sounds to me, and made me homesick and low spirited, and filled my atmosphere with the wandering spirits of the dead.

Additional associations with the Quarles farm are recorded in Mark Twain's "The Private History of a Campaign That Failed," written a few months after the publication of *Huckleberry Finn*. This bit of fictionalized autobiography describes his experiences as second lieutenant of the Marion Rangers, a rather informal volunteer militia unit organized in Hannibal in the early months of the Civil War. The Quarles farm is here assigned to a man named Mason:

A Sound Heart and a Deformed Conscience

> We stayed several days at Mason's; and after all these years the memory of the dullness, and stillness, and lifelessness of that slumberous farm-house still oppresses my spirit as with a sense of the presence of death and mourning. There was nothing to do, nothing to think about; there was no interest in life. The male part of the household were away in the fields all day, the women were busy and out of our sight; there was no sound but the plaintive wailing of a spinning-wheel, forever moaning out from some distant room—the most lonesome sound in nature, a sound steeped and sodden with homesickness and the emptiness of life.

The emotional overtones of the memories recorded in "The Private History" are made more explicit in a letter Mark Twain wrote in 1890:

> I was a *soldier* two weeks once in the beginning of the war, and was hunted like a rat the whole time. . . My splendid Kipling himself hasn't a more burnt-in, hard-baked and unforgettable familiarity with that death-on-the-pale-horse-with-hell-following-after which is a raw soldier's first fortnight in the field—and which, without any doubt, is the most tremendous fortnight and the vividest he is ever going to see.

But while there are references to fear of the enemy in "The Private History," they are mainly comic, and the dullness and lifelessness that afflict the neophyte soldiers at the Mason farm do not suggest the feeling of being hunted like a rat. More significant, perhaps is an incident Mark Twain places a few pages later in "The Private History." Albert B. Paine says it was invented; and it does have the air of fiction. But it reveals the emotional coloring of the author's recollections. He relates that he fired in the dark at a man approaching on horseback, who was killed. Although five other shots were fired at the same moment, and he did not at bottom believe his shot had struck its mark, still his "diseased imagination" convinced him he was guilty. "The thoughts shot through me that I was a murderer; that I had killed a man—a man who had never done

257

me any harm. That was the coldest sensation that ever went through my marrow."

Huck also experiences a strong and not easily explicable feeling of guilt a few pages after his arrival at the Phelpses'. When he sees the Duke and the King ridden out of the nearby town on a rail, surrounded by a howling mob, he says:

> It was a dreadful thing to see. Human beings *can* be awful cruel to one another... So we poked along back home, and I warn't feeling so brash as I was before, but kind of ornery, and humble, and to blame, somehow—though I hadn't done nothing. But that's always the way; it don't make no difference whether you do right or wrong, a person's conscience ain't got no sense, and just goes for him *anyway*. If I had a yaller dog that didn't know no more than a person's conscience does I would pison him.

The close linkage of the Phelps and Mason farms with Mark Twain's memory of the Quarles place strongly suggests that Huck's depression is caused by a sense of guilt whose sources were buried in the writer's childhood. It is well known that Mark Twain was tormented all his life by such feelings. A fable written in 1876, "The Facts Concerning the Recent Carnival of Crime in Connecticut," makes comedy of his sufferings; but they were serious and chronic. In his twenties, because of an imaginary error in administering an opiate, he had insisted he was to blame for the death of his brother from injuries received in the explosion of a steamboat. Later he accused himself of murdering his son Langdon when he neglected to keep him covered during a carriage ride in cold weather, and the child died of diphtheria.

But why was Mark Twain's latent feeling of guilt drawn up into consciousness at a specific moment in the writing of *Huckleberry Finn*? The most probable explanation is that at this point he was obliged to admit finally to himself that Huck's and Jim's journey down the river could not be imagined as leading to freedom for either of them. Because of the symbolic meaning the journey had taken on for him, the recognition was more than a perception of difficulty in contriving a plausible ending for the book. He had found a solution to the technical problem that satisfied him, if one is to judge from his evident zest in the complicated pranks of Tom Sawyer that occupy the last ten chapters. But in order to write these chapters he had to abandon the compelling image of the happiness of Huck and Jim on the raft and thus to acknowledge that the vernacular values embodied in his story were mere figments of the imagination, not capable of being reconciled with social reality. To be sure, he had been half-aware from the beginning that the quest of his protagonists was doomed. Huck had repeatedly appeared in the role of a Tiresias powerless to prevent the deceptions and brutalities he was compelled to witness. Yet Providence had always put the right words in his mouth when the time came, and by innocent guile he had extricated himself and Jim from danger after danger. Now the drifting had come to an end.

At an earlier impasse in the plot Mark Twain had shattered the raft under the paddle wheel of a steamboat. He now destroys it again, symbolically, by revealing that Huck's and Jim's journey, with all its anxieties, has been pointless. Tom Sawyer is bearer of the news that Jim has been freed in Miss Watson's will. Tom withholds the information, however, in order to trick Huck and Jim into the meaningless game of an Evasion that makes the word (borrowed from Dumas) into a devastating pun. Tom takes control and Huck becomes once again a subordinate carrying out orders. As if to signal the change of perspective and the shift in his own identification, Mark Twain gives Huck Tom's name through an improbable mistake on the part of Aunt Sally Phelps. We can hardly fail to perceive the weight of the author's feeling in Huck's statement on this occasion: "it was like being born again, I was so glad to find out who I was." Mark Twain has found out who he must be in order to end his book: he must be Tom.

In more abstract terms, he must withdraw from his imaginative participation in Huck's and Jim's quest for freedom. If the story was to be stripped of its tragic implications, Tom's perspective was the logical one to adopt because his intensely conventional sense of values made him impervious to the moral significance of the journey on the raft. Huck can hardly believe that Tom would collaborate in the crime of helping a run-away slave, and Huck is right. Tom merely devises charades involving a man who is already in a technical sense free. The consequences of the shift in point of view are strikingly evident in the treatment of Jim, who is subjected to farcical indignities. This is disturbing to the reader who has seen Jim take on moral and emotional stature, but it is necessary if everything is to be forced back into the framework of comedy. Mark Twain's portrayal of Huck and Jim as complex characters has carried him beyond the limits of his original plan: we must not forget that the literary ancestry of the book is to be found in backwoods humor. As Huck approaches the Phelps plantation the writer has on his hands a hybrid—a comic story in which the protagonists have acquired something like tragic depth.

In deciding to end the book with the description of Tom's unnecessary contrivances for rescuing Jim, Mark Twain was certain to produce an anticlimax. But he was a great comic writer, able to score local triumphs in the most unlikely circumstances. The last chapters have a number of brilliant touches—the slave who carries the witch pie to Jim, Aunt Sally's trouble in counting her spoons, Uncle Silas and the ratholes, the unforgettable Sister Hotchkiss. Even Tom's horseplay would be amusing if it were not spun out to such length and if we were not asked to accept it as the conclusion of *Huckleberry Finn*. Although Jim is reduced to the level of farce Tom is a comic figure in the classical sense of being a victim of delusion. He is not aware of being cruel to Jim because he does not perceive him as a human being. For Tom, Jim is the hero of a historical romance, a peer of the Man in the Iron Mask or the Count of Monte Cristo. Mark Twain is consciously imitating *Don Quixote*, and there are moments not unworthy of the model, as when Tom admits that "we got to dig him out with the picks, and *let on* it's case-knives."

But Tom has no tragic dimension whatever. There is not even any force of common sense in him to struggle against his perverted imagination as Huck's innate loyalty and generosity struggle against his deformed conscience. Although Mark Twain is indulgent toward Tom, he adds him to the list of characters who employ the soul-butter style of false pathos. The inscriptions Tom composes for Jim to "scrabble onto the wall" of the cabin might have been composed by the Duke:

1. Here a captive heart busted.
2. Here a poor prisoner, forsook by the world and friends, fretted his sorrowful life.
3. Here a lonely heart broke, and a worn spirit went to its rest, after thirty-seven years of solitary captivity.
4. Here, homeless and friendless, after thirty-seven years of bitter captivity, perished a noble stranger, natural son of Louis XIV.

While he was reading these noble sentiments aloud, Tom's voice trembled. . . and he most broke down.

7

Mark Twain's partial shift of identification from Huck to Tom in the final sequence was one response to his recognition that Huck's and Jim's quest for freedom was only a dream: he attempted to cover with a veil of parody and farce the harsh facts that condemned it to failure. The brief episode involving Colonel Sherburn embodies yet another response to his disillusionment. The extraordinary vividness of the scenes in which Sherburn figures—only a half-dozen pages all told—is emphasized by their air of being an intrusion into the story. Of course, in the episodic structure of *Huckleberry Finn* many characters appear for a moment and disappear. Even so, the Sherburn episode seems unusually isolated. None of the principal characters is involved in or affected by it: Jim, the Duke, and the King are offstage, and Huck is a spectator whom even the author hardly notices. We are told nothing about his reaction except that he did not want to stay around. He goes abruptly off to the circus and does not refer to Sherburn again.

Like Huck's depression as he nears the Phelps plantation, the Sherburn episode is linked with Mark Twain's own experience. The shooting of Boggs follows closely the murder of "Uncle Sam" Smarr by a merchant named Owsley in Hannibal in 1845, when Sam Clemens was nine years old. Although it is not clear that he actually witnessed it, he mentioned the incident at least four times at intervals during his later life, including one retelling as late as 1898, when he said he had often dreamed about it. Mark Twain prepares for the shooting in *Huckleberry Finn* by careful attention to the brutality of the loafers in front of the stores in Bricksville. "There couldn't anything wake them up all over, and make them happy all over, like a dog-fight—unless it might be putting turpentine on a stray dog and setting fire to him, or tying a tin pan to his tail and see him run himself to death." The prurient curiosity of the townspeople who shove and pull to catch a glimpse of Boggs as he lies dying in the drugstore with a heavy Bible on his chest, and their pleasure in the reenactment of the shooting by the man in the big white fur stovepipe hat, also help to make Bricksville an appropriate setting for Sherburn's crime.

The shooting is in Chapter 21, and the scene in which Sherburn scatters the mob by his contemptuous speech is in the following chapter. There is evidence that Mark Twain put aside the manuscript for a time near the end of Chapter 21. If there was such an interruption in his work on the novel, it might account for a marked change in tone. In Chapter 21 Sherburn is an unsympathetic character. His killing of Boggs is motivated solely by arrogance, and the introduction of Boggs's daughter is an invitation to the reader to consider Sherburn an inhuman monster. In Chapter 22, on the other hand, the Colonel appears in an oddly favorable light. The townspeople have now become a mob; there are several touches that suggest Mark Twain was recalling the descriptions of mobs in Carlyle's *French Revolution* and other works of history and fiction. He considered mobs to be subhuman aggregates generating psychological pressures that destroyed individual freedom of choice. In a passage written for *Life on the Mississippi* but omitted from the book Mark Twain makes scathing generalizations about the cowardice of mobs, especially in the South but also in other regions, that closely parallel Sherburn's speech.

In other words, however hostile may be the depiction of Sherburn in Chapter 21, in Chapter 22 we have yet another instance of Mark Twain's identifying himself, at least partially, with a character in the novel other than Huck. The image of Sherburn standing on the roof of the porch in front of his house with the shotgun that is the only weapon in sight has an emblematic quality. He is a solitary figure, not identified with the townspeople, and because they are violently hostile to him, an outcast. But he is not weaker than they, he is stronger. He stands above the mob, looking down on it. He is "a heap the best dressed man in that town," and he is more intelligent than his neighbors. The scornful courage with which he defies the mob redeems him from the taint of cowardice implied in his shooting of an unarmed man who was trying to escape. Many members of the mob he faces are presumably armed; the shotgun he holds is not the source of his power but merely a symbol of the personal force with which he dominates the community.

The Colonel's repeated references to one Buck Harkness, the leader of the mob, whom he acknowledges to be "half-a-man," suggest that the scene represents a contest between two potential leaders in Bricksville. Harkness is the strongest man with whom the townspeople can identify themselves. In his pride Sherburn chooses isolation, but he demonstrates that he is stronger than Harkness, for the mob, including Harkness, obeys his command to "*leave*—and take your half-a-man with you."

Sherburn belongs to the series of characters in Mark Twain's later work that have been called "transcendent figures." Other examples are Hank Morgan in *A Connecticut*

Yankee; Pudd'nhead Wilson; and Satan in *The Mysterious Stranger*. They exhibit certain common traits, more fully developed with the passage of time. They are isolated by their intellectual superiority to the community; they are contemptuous of mankind in general; and they have more than ordinary power. Satan, the culmination of the series, is omnipotent. Significantly, he is without a moral sense—that is, a conscience, a sense of guilt. He is not torn by the kind of inner struggle that Huck experiences. But he is also without Huck's sound heart. The price of power is the surrender of all human warmth.

Colonel Sherburn's cold-blooded murder of Boggs, his failure to experience remorse after that act, and his withering scorn of the townspeople are disquieting portents for the future. Mark Twain, like Huck, was sickened by the brutality he had witnessed in the society along the river. But he had an adult aggressiveness foreign to Huck's character. At a certain point he could no longer endure the anguish of being a passive observer. His imagination sought refuge in the image of an alternative persona who was protected against suffering by being devoid of pity or guilt, yet could denounce the human race for its cowardice and cruelty, and perhaps even take action against it. The appearance of Sherburn in *Huckleberry Finn* is ominous because a writer who shares his attitude toward human beings is in danger of abandoning imaginative insight for moralistic invective. The slogan of "the damned human race" that later became Mark Twain's proverb spelled the sacrifice of art to ideology. Colonel Sherburn would prove to be Mark Twain's dark angel. His part in the novel, and that of Tom Sawyer, are flaws in a work that otherwise approaches perfection as an embodiment of American experience in a radically new and appropriate literary mode.

A Connecticut Yankee Anticipated: Max Adeler's *Fortunate Island*

Edward F. Foster

According to Mark Twain the idea for *A Connecticut Yankee* came to him late in 1884. G. W. Cable, with whom he was on a lecture tour, gave him a copy of *Le Morte d'Arthur*, and Twain became so fascinated by Malory that he began shortly to plan a book dealing with the Middle Ages. By November, 1886, the first chapter was written; more work in 1887 and 1888 completed the tale, and it was published in 1889.[1]

Perhaps the most striking feature of the story was the imaginative power displayed in the theme—modern man in a medieval world—and readers have always been fascinated by this part of the work. Seven years before the appearance of *A Connecticut Yankee*, however, the humorist Max Adeler published a novelette, *The Fortunate Island*,[2] which contains an identical theme and numerous interesting parallels. This paper will present an analysis of the most important similarities between the two stories, for the connection has not been previously noted.

Adeler's story is shorter and employs a much simpler framework than *A Connecticut Yankee*. The hero is a sociologist, Professor E.L. Baffin, of Wingohocking University. Baffin and his daughter, Matilda, land on an uncharted, "floating" island following a shipwreck. This island, according to the natives, had broken away from England in King Arthur's time and drifted to a new location. Life on the island was frozen in the past: Knighthood flourishes; there are castles, jousts, love-sick maidens, and saintly hermits.

Professor Baffin and Matilda are taken to the castle of Sir Bors, a leading noble, where the Professor satisfies his curiosity about the new land, and amazes his hosts with demonstrations of modern inventions, his scientific gear luckily having been saved from the shipwreck. Enthralled by the possibilities before him, Baffin plans numerous projects and looks forward to a vast scheme of modernization. But before any of these technical plans can be put into practice, the Professor becomes involved in aiding a pair of lovers; he takes part in a joust, joins an expedition to rescue a kidnapped maiden, stars in a thrilling rescue, sustains the mandatory blow on the head—and wakes up aboard a rescuing vessel. He had been ill and delirious, the adventure on the Fortunate Island was a dream.

So much for the main plot details. A closer examination of certain features of Adeler's story will show that he anticipated Twain in numerous other ways. First the theme. Strictly speaking, Adeler's "frame" does not involve the temporal displacement and regression of an individual, but the net dramatic effect is the same as that of *A Connecticut Yankee*. A nineteenth-century American visits a medieval society, albeit through the medium of a dream device. The visitor plans to modernize the society, but he finds the same reverence for the past, the same unwillingness to accept change that Hank Morgan scoffed at so vigorously. Father Anselm, the hermit, tells Professor Baffin "we reverence the past. It is a matter of pride among us to preserve the habits, the manners, the ideas, the social state which our forefathers had when they were sundered from their nation."[3] The hermit also takes a gloomy view of any possibility of change or progress. "Sometimes. . . I have secret doubts whether our way is the best, whether in England and the rest of the world men may not have learned while we remained ignorant; but I cannot tell. And no one would be willing to change if we could know the truth."[4]

The respective heroes of the two stories are basically different types of men, but they react to their situation in much the same fashion. Professor Baffin, unlike Hank Morgan, is an intellectual, and when he discovers the nature of life on the island is most anxious to study it from a scientific viewpoint. Yet the Professor is at the same time a comic figure; he is neither the dreamy pedagogue nor the eccentric butterfly chaser of farce, but his nineteenth-century reactions to the discomforts of medieval housing and armor, and to the forwardness of medieval maidens lead to a number of humorous situations similar to those of Hank Morgan.

Both men share one important trait with equal force: the American zeal for progress, self-improvement, and getting ahead. When Sir Bleoberis laments his lack of fortune, the Professor remonstrates with him in proper Gilded-Age language: "Can't you go to work; go into business; start a factory, speculate in stocks, or something of that kind."[5] Another knight, Sir Agravaines, mentions that he has tried enchantment and philtres in an unsuccessful search for wealth. "Nonsense!" replies the Professor, "I don't operate with such trumpery as that. You agree to help me, and we'll give this island such a stirring up as will revolutionize it."[6]

Unlike Twain, Adeler does not venture on any criticism of medieval politics and religion. We are merely told that the ruler of the island, King Brandegore, is "wise and good." There is, moreover, no recognition of the major role played by the church in medieval society. The only religious figure in the story is the hermit, Father Anselm, who is treated sympathetically.

In the same manner, the foibles of medieval society and custom come in for only mild criticism. The nobility are pictured respectfully on the whole, though their illiteracy and disdain for work are underscored. Professor Baffin exhorts Sir Bleoberis to gain a fortune by hard work, only to receive the huffy reply, "persons of my degree never work."[7] Amorous customs of the time furnish materials for some comic situations. Both Sir Dinadan and Sir Agravaines are smitten with Matilda; each knight proposes to the lady on first meeting her, only to have his ears boxed for his audacity. Professor Baffin's rescue of Bragwaine, he finds to his discomforture, automatically makes him her fiancé. The lady is so persistent in her loving attention that the properly correct Baffin flees in confusion.

Adeler's strongest criticism of medieval customs is directed at the practice of duelling, an aspect of chivalry that Twain thoroughly detested. In one case, the joust between Sir Bleoberis and Baffin, the ludicrous aspects of the conflict are stressed. Later in the story, the tome grows more serious when Baffin is challenged by Sir Sagramor for refusing to marry Bragwaine, and Sir Bors volunteers to substitute for the American. "This," said the Professor, "is probably the most asinine proceeding upon record. Because I won't marry Sagramor's daughter, Sagramor is going to fight with a man who never saw his daughter."[8]

Perhaps the most striking parallel between *The Fortunate Island* and *A Connecticut Yankee* is the use of modern inventions to awe the natives and demonstrate the superiority of nineteenth-century American achievement. Professor Baffin employs an umbrella, a watch, a revolver, matches, cigars, and spectacles as magic objects from time to time. Following a performance by the court musician, a record of a song sung by Matilda is played on a phonograph, producing consternation in the audience. A telephone is passed off as an oracle on one occasion. Professor Baffin even makes some arrangements with Sir Bleoberis to build a short railroad line and a telegraph system, though he is as vague as Hank Morgan in explaining away the technical problems involved. While visiting King Brandegore, the Professor stages a series of electrical experiments which so impress the king that he orders the court magician executed as a fraud, an incident similar to the Yankee's vanquishing of Merlin. The climactic rescue of Ysolt is effected through a modern invention, a steam launch, just as the rescue of Hank Morgan and King Arthur is made by knights that speed to the scene on bicycles. Finally, Adeler also contrives a massacre, by no means as bloody as Twain's concluding holocaust, but gory enough to satisfy modest expectations. After the rescuers of Ysolt abandon their boat, the safety valve is tied down; the boiler explodes and kills Sir Dagonet and several of his followers as they are examining the craft.

These comparisons indicate numerous similarities of detail between *The Fortunate Island* and *A Connecticut Yankee*. Both writers move their respective heroes into another age and another time for the purpose of providing humorous and satiric contrasts between nineteenth-century America and medieval England. Adeler's work, it must be granted, is but the skeleton of a novel, because he fails to exploit his dramatic situation as does Twain, and he does not have Twain's compulsion for bitter satire. Given the unusual nature of the theme, however, the time span within which both works appeared, and the various parallels which have been noted, one must grant the existence of a remarkable literary coincidence.

There is no direct evidence in the published Twain material that Twain knew of Adeler's work, or was influenced by it. One cannot rule out absolutely the possibility of a connection, conscious or subconscious, however, because Twain read widely and was familiar with the other humorists of his time. Walter Blair, in dealing with the sources of *Huckleberry Finn* notes that Twain

> read much in several areas—in history, biography, philosophy, humor, and (though he believed he disliked it) fiction. His familiarity with contemporary literature helped him write a book which became a best seller. And in portraying more characters and incidents than students heretofore have noticed, consciously or unconsciously he echoed his wide-ranging reading.[9]

I have discovered only one published comment by Adeler on the similarities between *The Fortunate Island* and *A Connecticut Yankee*. Shortly before his death in 1915, Adeler published a collection of short stories which reprinted *The Fortunate Island.* On the first page of the story the following modest footnote appears: "It is necessary to say that this tale was first published in 1881 and antedates a story with a similar theme by a noted author."[10]

Notes

1. For detailed studies which offer differing conclusions concerning the origin of *A Connecticut Yankee,* see John Hoben, "Mark Twain's *A Connecticut Yankee:* A Genetic Study," *American Literature,* XVIII (1961), 195–214. See also Henry Nash Smith, *Mark Twain's Fable of Progress: Political and Economic Ideas in 'A Connecticut Yankee'* (New Brunswick, New Jersey, 1964).
2. *The Fortunate Island and Other Stories* (Boston, 1882). Max Adeler is the pseudonym of Charles Heber Clark (1847–1915). Clark was born in Berlin, Md., educated in Georgetown, D.C., and served as a Union soldier. He was a reporter and critic for various Philadelphia newspapers, and later became editor of the *Textile Record* and the *Manufacturer.* His most popular work was a series of humorous sketches of small-town life called *Out of the Hurly-Burly* (1874). He also published four novels and three books of short stories, none achieving the success of *Out of the Hurly-Burly.* See Stanley J. Kunitz and Howard Haycraft, *American Authors 1600–1900* (New York, 1938), p. 153. Other brief biographical sketches are in *Book Buyer* XXV (1902), 124–125; and J.F. Cooke, "Mysteries of Middle-C," *The Etude,* LXVI (1948), 4, 6, 10.
3. *Ibid.,* p. 25.
4. *Ibid.,* p. 26.
5. *Ibid.,* p. 40.
6. *Ibid.*
7. *Ibid.*
8. *Ibid.,* p. 98.
9. *Mark Twain & Huck Finn* (Berkeley, 1960), p. viii.
10. *By the Bend of the River* (Philadelphia, 1914), p. 98.

Yankee Slang

James M. Cox

A *Connecticut Yankee in King Arthur's Court* holds much the same position in Mark Twain's career that *Pierre* occupies in Melville's. Before both books stand single masterpieces; after them comes work of genuine merit, work of a higher order than they themselves represent, but work more quietly desperate, as if the creative force behind it had suffered a crippling blow. Moreover each book displays its author's ambitious effort to scale heights hitherto unattempted. Finally, the books share a similarity of substance, reaching resolutions involving self-destruction for the artist-hero. Melville's Pierre is a writer so caught in the involutions of love and creativity that suicide becomes a last refuge. Mark Twain's Hank Morgan, a brash superintendent of a Hartford Machine Shop transported into a sixth-century feudal world, assumes the role of a superman inventor in an effort to revolutionize the Arthurian world by accelerating the course of history. He does revolutionize it, only to destroy his technological marvels and defeat himself. Despite a certain audacity of conception, however, both works disintegrate into extravagant failures. Each involves an excess of energy, as if the energy invested had not been fully assimilated, leaving the author to force his way toward a destructive ending which would perforce break the identification between himself and the artist-hero.

Mark Twain:The Fate of Humor. Princeton: Princeton U. P., 1966, pp. 198–221.

Such a struggle is particularly evident in *A Connecticut Yankee*. The most revealing comment on the unfulfilled effort is Mark Twain's reply to Howells' praise of the novel: "Well, my book is written—let it go. But if it were only to write over again there wouldn't be so many things left out. They burn in me; & they keep multiplying & multiplying; but now they can't ever be said. And besides, they would require a library—& a pen warmed-up in hell."[1] This humorous exaggeration rests on two central assumptions: that the book is an incomplete expression of suppressed attitudes, and that the suppressions are self-generatively threatening the writer's personality. The entire passage points to the final incompleteness of *A Connecticut Yankee*, corroborating the incompleteness of the novel; or—to put it inversely—the novel realized the sense of incompleteness which the remark suggests. In this respect it is a new kind of failure for Mark Twain. He had failed before, and failed often, but usually in the midst of successes. For example, there is the failure of *The Innocents Abroad*—a failure of concentration and economy. And there is the failure of *Roughing It*, a failure to realize the true structure of the book. And even in *Huckleberry Finn*, there is, after everything one can say about the ending, a failure of proportion. But in all these instances the failure is directly related to and defined by a discovery in form.

In *A Connecticut Yankee*, however, the failure is as central and pervasive as it is in *The Prince and the Pauper*. Moreover, it is of greater magnitude for the simple reason that *A Connecticut Yankee* pretends to be more than *The Prince and the Pauper*. The earlier book had been addressed to a juvenile audience on the one hand and to a respectable audience on the other. It was a book which could be read aloud in the parlor to all the family. If it seemed tame, Mark Twain could rest in the solace of not having claimed it was profound, and also in the knowledge of having subtly conveyed the impression that the book had been written to please the respectable world in which he found himself. *A Connecticut Yankee* was a different thing. It was not peripheral but central; it was not respectable but genuinely irreverent; it offered itself not as an exercise but as an experiment. Like *Huckleberry Finn*, it did not come quickly but slowly, five years elapsing between the time of his first notebook entry in the late fall of 1884 and the date of publication in December, 1889. That first notebook entry—"Dream of being a knight errant in armor in the Middle Ages"—was supposedly inspired by Mark Twain's reading of Sir Thomas Malory to whose work he had been introduced by George W. Cable on their lecture tour in the fall of 1884.

Not until a year later, in December, 1885, did he actually begin to write; by March, 1886 he had written "A Word of Explanation" and the first three chapters. Then, much as he had done with *Huckleberry Finn*, he simply let the manuscript gather dust for a year and a half before returning to write sixteen chapters at Quarry Farm during the summer of 1887. This summer burst of writing carried him into Chapter 20, where Sandy and the Boss visit the Ogre's Castle. But when he returned to Hartford and the business world, his writing stopped. Not until he returned to Quarry Farm in July, 1888 did he begin the sustained assault which carried through disappointments and frustrating delays to the end of the manuscript in the spring of 1889.[2] This brief history of the composition points up the similarity between the emergence of *Huckleberry Finn* and *A Connecticut Yankee*. In each instance there was a beginning, a long delay, a return, another hesitation, and a final sustained push to, or near to, a conclusion.

But similarities have a way of pointing up essential differences, the difference in this instance being that the creative enterprise of *A Connecticut Yankee*, insofar as it parallels that of *Huckleberry Finn*, is on a slighter scale. The total time of its composition is shorter, the initial burst of writing is much less decisive, and the *literary* waste required to complete the book is almost minimal compared to the failures which marked the way toward the success of *Huckleberry Finn*. Yet—and here is the issue—*A Connecticut Yankee* sounds bigger than *Huckleberry Finn*. It makes more noise; it seems more aspiring; it is much more liberal; it exposes the evil as well as the folly of man and his institutions. It thus becomes the central book for those critics who want to see Mark Twain as a robust frontier spirit at war with tradition, and also for those who wish to measure literature in terms of political liberalism and social conscience. This is why Howells—whose awareness of Mark Twain was often so perceptive—singled out *A Connecticut Yankee* as his favorite book. It is why De Voto, though he thought the book a failure, followed Howells in thinking the *conception* extraordinarily bold. It is why, much more recently, Louis Budd, exposing Mark Twain's political conservatism, finds himself granting *A Connecticut Yankee* priority for its distinctly liberal views. Finally, it is why Henry Nash Smith considers the *Yankee* as the most difficult of Mark Twain's works to evaluate, yet the most necessary to understand.[3]

Yet for all the audacity the *Yankee* seems to have, it is actually a much tamer, safer performance. This fact is immediately evident in the Preface. Whereas the Preface to *Huckleberry Finn* was defiant and nihilistic, humorously warning the reader to look for something at the cost of his life, the *Yankee* Preface begins:

> The ungentle laws and customs touched upon in this tale are historical, and the episodes which are used to illustrate them are also historical. It is not pretended that these laws and customs existed in England in the sixth century; no, it is only pretended that inasmuch as they existed in the English and other civilizations of far later times, it is safe to consider that it is no libel upon the sixth century to suppose them to have been in practice in that day also. One is quite justified in inferring that whatever one of these laws or customs was lacking in that remote time, its place was competently filled by a worse one.[4]

Already there is the fatal appeal of *The Prince and the Pauper*: the appeal to history and at the same time the apology for fiction under the assurance of exposing eternal injustices. In a word, the Preface promises satire rather than humor, seriousness rather than mere laughter. Yet the language of *A Connecticut Yankee* was apparently vernacular, not genteel as it had been in *The Prince and the Pauper*. Promising a revolutionary revision of the past it invaded, it seemed a secure armor against the sentimentality of the earlier work. Yet *A Connecticut Yankee*, for all its hardheaded irreverence, succumbed to sentimentality.

The form of *A Connecticut Yankee* is what may be called an inverted Utopian fantasy. A graphic way to see the inversion is to compare it with Edward Bellamy's *Looking Backward*, which appeared in 1887 and was a best seller by the time the *Yankee* was ready for publication. Mark Twain himself was extremely fond of Bellamy's book, though he apparently did not read it until after the *Yankee* was completed.[5] In Bellamy's dream fantasy Julian West is precipitated into the future, where, faced with the material and ideological evolution evident in the year A.D. 2000, his own nineteenth century appears meager and startlingly inadequate. Through all his experience, West remains the observer, the listener, the interrogator who assimilates the persuasive criticism which the imaginary age affords. Bellamy's central achievement is to realize the terms of the Utopian fantasy, which is to say he conveys the notion of a dream of reason. Thus his hero finds himself being constantly persuaded that truths he had believed, values he had held, and causes he had supported are nothing more than outworn attitudes and trappings of a dead age. Being reasonable in the face of the disparity, he submits to the superior argument and assents to the promise of the strange new world.

Mark Twain, however, instead of sending his hero into an imaginary future territory outside history where the terms of criticism could operate freely to create the dream of reason, plunged him into history as if to invade and reform the past. The Yankee is not the innocent interlocutor but the chief actor of his chronicle. Just as his machine-shop lingo collides with the Malory-ese of the Age of Chivalry, his democratic ideology does battle with the aristocratic and religious dogmas of the king's realm. The superintendent of a Colt Arms machine shop, he emerges into the sixth-century Arthurian world and is able to see this feudal pastoral from the presumable advantage of democratic industrialism. Unable to resist the lure of potential power residing in his technological advantage, he finds himself "inventing" labor-saving devices, instigating reforms, and organizing the people in an effort to proclaim a republic in England. For a brief moment his regime prevails; but the Church, never quite defeated, plays upon the superstition of the populace, declares an interdict, and sends an army against the Yankee; he in turn blows up his technological world, along with the assaulting forces of Church and Chivalry. Surrounded and poisoned by the vast corpse he has made of the past, the Yankee is condemned to a thirteen-century sleep by Merlin, the old-time magician whom he initially ridiculed.

The energy generated by this incongruity between chivalric past and practical present made up—as near as one can tell—the central impulse for beginning the book. Mark Twain's letters and notebook entries say as much, and the early portions of the book itself, even after all revisions were made, are essentially built upon a burlesque contrast between two styles: Morgan's roughneck, irreverent abruptness sent against the exaggerated impersonation of Malory's circumlocutive archaism.[6] There are, particularly in the early chapters and from time to time throughout the book, amusing moments when Mark Twain is able to exploit the possibilities of the contrast to genuine advantage. His mounting the knights on bicycles, for example, or forcing them to wear placards advertising such items as Persimmons Soap or Peterson's Prophylactic Toothbrushes, have the genuine force of burlesque incongruity and exceed the expectations of the situation. And his utilizing the waste power of a genuflecting ascetic in order to operate a shirt factory has about it the old reckless irreverence which still has power to shock a safe gentility.

But as Morgan gains power in the Arthurian world, the democratic assumptions on which his identity rests assert themselves, causing the burlesque contrast to assume satiric form. Such a change produces a marked transformation of Hank Morgan's character. For insofar as the burlesque contrast is the dominant impulse, Hank Morgan is essentially the showman, his characterizing compulsion being his urge to gain attention. Wherever he appears, the Yankee must shine, and more than food or women or even life itself, he loves the effect. In a rare moment of insight, he observes that the crying defect of his character is his desire to perform picturesquely. His whole style—given to overstatement from the moment he appears until he finally collapses under Merlin's spell—is in large part a manifestation of his desire to show off. Even the sad-faced Mark Twain ruefully observes of the Yankee's dying call to arms, "He was getting up his last 'effect'; but he never finished it."

But as the satiric impulse comes to the fore, the surprise, bewilderment, and amusement with which Morgan had originally beheld the Arthurian world are displaced by the indignation he feels upon discovering the atrocities at the heart of chivalry. Whereas the burlesquing Morgan had been intent upon making fun of chivalry, the satiric Morgan becomes determined to make war upon it. Yet the satiric Morgan can never really be effective, because the narrow range of his burlesque style cannot tolerate enough analytic intelligence or wit to discharge his growing indignation. Instead, his outrage tends to reduce his democratic ideology to clamorous fulmination and noisy prejudice, so that he becomes an object of curiosity rather than an effective satiric agent. Constantly advertising his ideas, his mechanical aptitude, and his stagey jokes, he becomes a grotesque caricature of the nineteenth century he advocates. Prancing through every conceivable burlesque and flaunting himself before the stunned Arthurian world into which he bursts, he begins to be the real buffoon of the show he manages.

Mark Twain recognized the Yankee's limitations, going so far as to confide to his illustrator Dan Beard, ". . . this Yankee of mine. . . is a perfect ignoramus; he is boss of a machine shop; he can build a locomotive or a Colt's revolver, he can put up and run a telegraph line, but he's an ignoramus, nevertheless."[7] Aware of Morgan's career and Twain's own statements, certain critics have maintained that Mark Twain was directing his fire upon the nineteenth century as much as upon the sixth. Thus, Parrington insisted that Twain was "trimming his sails to the chill winds blowing from the outer spaces of a mechanistic cosmos,"[8] and Gladys Carmine Bellamy has more recently observed that the book is "a fictional working out of the idea that a too-quick civilization breeds disaster."[9]

Plausible though such arguments are in the light of the Yankee's ultimate failure, the logic of the narrative and the tone which sustains it move in precisely the opposite direction. For although the Yankee finally destroys himself, Mark Twain's major investment is in the Yankee's attitudes. After all, most of those attitudes were the same ones Mark Twain himself swore by at one time or another during his public life; and the usual response to the novel has been—and inevitably will continue to be—that he was lampooning monarchy, religion, and chivalry. There is abundant evidence that Mark Twain himself intended just such criticism. As early as 1866, he was attacking feudalism in the Sandwich Islands, and his belief in the superiority of democracy to monarchy goes back to the very beginning of his career; his hatred of an established church stretches equally far back—and further forward. Ten years after the Yankee's diatribes against organized religion, Mark Twain took special pleasure in mounting a sustained, logical attack upon Mary Baker Eddy, whose Christian Science he feared would become the official religion of the Republic. There is also clear evidence, as John B. Hoben long ago observed, that some of the Yankee's attitudes have their exact counterparts in Mark Twain's hostile responses to Matthew Arnold's strictures upon American culture.[10] Finally, Howard Baetzhold has shown that Mark Twain's picture of feudal England is at times almost a direct transcript of the elder George Kennan's lectures and writings on Russia, both of which Mark Twain particularly approved.[11]

What becomes evident is that during the composition of the *Yankee*, the hostility, anger, and indignation which were permanent aspects of his personality came into much fuller play. As he had done while writing *Huckleberry Finn*, he *gave himself up to these emotions.* To read his notebooks of either period is to come across long passages in which fury and brooding animus are often indulged, much as if the writer were cultivating those emotions in order to motivate himself to write.[12] But whereas in the vernacular of *Huckleberry Finn* he had discovered a vehicle to convert the indignation which stands behind both humor and satire into the ironic observation, apparent indifference, and mock innocence which constitute them, the vernacular of Hank Morgan lacked the inverted point of view which would convert the emotions of rage and hate into humor. Instead of being the instrument which transfers the indignation from writer to reader, as in the case of satire, or converts it to pleasure, as in the case of humor, Morgan—who is conceived as a rowdy agent of burlesque—comes to be invested with the indignation of his creator. He is therefore not fully dramatized and remains part of the author, who seems to struggle more and more desperately to free him into character. It is just this struggle which makes the ending seem like a fantasy in which the author is driving the mechanism of his hero faster and faster until it flies apart. Thus in the closing chapters of the book, what began as a burlesque dream assumes the character of a nightmare in which Morgan is electrocuting knights so rapidly and so thoroughly that the dead, being merely an alloy of brass and buttons, are impossible to identify. Trapped at the center of his destruction, the Yankee is condemned by Merlin to a thirteen-century sleep from which he awakens to find himself a stranger in his once-familiar nineteenth century. Unmoored from space, adrift in time, he lies down at last to death.

This relatively "sad" ending to what had begun as a burlesque contrast is what makes the book seem a turning point in Mark Twain's career, embodying as it does the shift from joy to despair, from dream to nightmare. The whole nature of the enterprise, in which Mark Twain finds himself killing the character who had given utterance to so many of his own criticisms and opinions, makes biographical speculation well-nigh inevitable. It is possible, for example, to show that Mark Twain's increasing involvement with the Paige Typesetter during the years the novel took shape had much to do with his growing desperation in the *Yankee*. For it was during these years, in the wake of his success with General Grant, that Mark Twain invested all his available capital in the typesetter. There is a sense in which the Yankee's demise is both a foreshadowing and a rehearsal of the fall which Mark Twain must have begun to see awaiting him. There is even a correspondence between the Yankee—whom Mark Twain indulges and almost glorifies, then brings to grief—and James Paige, the inventor of the typesetter who, like the Yankee, worked in the Colt Arms factory and was at first Mark Twain's hero, later his devil. The intricate relationship between book and typesetter is nowhere better revealed than in a letter Mark Twain wrote to his wife's brother-in-law, Theodore Crane, when, racing to finish the *Yankee*, he was also awaiting the advent of the mechanical miracle which Paige kept toying with.

> I am here in Twichell's house at work, with the noise of the children and an army of carpenters to help. Of course they don't help, but neither do they hinder. It's like a boiler-factory for racket. . . but I never am conscious of the racket at all, and I move my feet into position of relief without knowing when I do it. . . I was so tired last night that I thought I would lie abed and rest, today; but I couldn't resist. . . I want to finish the day the machine finishes, and a week ago the closest calculations for that indicated Oct. 22—but experience teaches me that their calculations will miss fire, as usual.[13]

Yankee Slang

The process of composition as Mark Twain describes it—a dumbly driven effort going on almost outside himself—is perfectly explained by his wish to finish the book on the day the machine was to be completed. He was saying, in effect, that he was a machine-driven writer; but more important, he revealed that the novel had come to be identified with the machine. There is, however, the hint of fatal doubt about Paige's invention. To accommodate his writing to its schedule was to be anchored to perpetual uncertainty. The machine was not perfected on October 22; nor was the novel completed on that date. Not until eight months later, after seasons of ecstatic hope punctuated by periods of depression or anxious alarm about the mechanical marvel, did Mark Twain succeed in completing his novel. As for the machine, it was never really completed. Paige, constantly taking it apart in an effort to perfect it to the last dimension of its complexity, was overtaken by the simpler Mergenthaler linotype. As for Mark Twain, he was left in bankruptcy.

That Mark Twain could bring the book to an end and break the identification discloses how much writing was his real business. It was the act he had ultimately to rely upon to recover from the financial involvements of his business ventures. Yet the recovery was as costly as it was desperate, for it required killing the Yankee. And the Yankee in the book is not simply a businessman or a mechanic in the Arthurian world, but an *inventor* as well; his power was indivisibly a part of Mark Twain's creative impulse. Killing the Yankee was symbolically a crippling of the inventive imagination, as if Mark Twain were driven to maim himself in an effort to survive. Understandably he considered this radical redefinition of himself to be the logical end of his writing life and went so far as to say jokingly to Howells that his career was over and he wished "to pass to the cemetery unclodded."[14] Of course, his career was not over. He wrote again and again, not simply because there were financial necessities which required it, but because writing was at last his life.

The priority of writing in Mark Twain's life brings us back to the matter of form in the *Yankee*. For it is finally the form—which is to say the style and character of Hank Morgan—that failed Mark Twain. Though a change in his outlook took place during the process of composition, and though this change is reflected in the book, it is difficult to say—as it was difficult to say about *Huckleberry Finn*—how much the art fed into the life and how much the life fed the art. Thus, while it can be said that Mark Twain's investment in his publishing hours and the Paige Typesetter "caused" him to run into writing difficulty, it is also possible to argue that Mark Twain's increasing tendency to invest in business rather than in art was a result, not a cause, of a lesion in his own creative faculties.

That there was such a lesion is evident in the slender frame he cast round the *Yankee*. In that frame—appropriately entitled "A Word of Explanation"—he employed the author-meets-narrator stratagem as a device for getting into the narrative and also for introducing his narrator. Following a guided tour through Warwick Castle, itself a representative of the storied past of the tourist's imagination, the author encounters a stranger "who wove such a spell about me that I seemed to move among the specters and shadows and dust and mold of a gray antiquity, holding speech with a relic of it!"[15] Here is the familiar impersonation of the cliches of travelogue nostalgia, and throughout the introduction Mark Twain continues to portray himself as the dreamy-eyed tourist bent on caressing images of the past. In this moment of sentimental retrospection—while the guide is attempting to explain the presence of a bullet hole in an ancient piece of armor—the stranger appears, like the fabulous genie come from a bottle, and into Mark Twain's ear alone proclaims himself the author of the bullet hole. The "electric surprise of the remark" momentarily shatters the tourist's dream, and by the time he recovers, the stranger has disappeared. That evening, however, sitting by the fire at the Warwick Arms, "steeped in a dream of the olden time," Mark Twain is again abruptly confronted by the stranger, who, knocking upon the door to interrupt the dream, takes final charge of the narrative.

The frame makes clear that Morgan, instead of being a companion character, is a projection, or, more accurately, an anti-mask of the tourist Mark Twain's stock nostalgia. In the same way that Morgan has put a bullet hole in the antique armor, he punctures the sentimental dream of the past. Moreover, he comes unbidden to menace the dreamer and his retrospective vision. Speaking with casual and confident authority, he proclaims himself the antithesis of sentimentality. "I am a Yankee of Yankees—and practical; yes, and nearly barren of sentiment, I suppose—or poetry, in other words." His entire narrative, appropriately preserved on a palimpsest, is the record of an attempt to overwrite as well as override the past.

The Yankee's role, as defined in the frame, is thus one of burlesquing "Mark Twain's" tourist version of the past. Taken together in the frame, Morgan and "Mark Twain" could be considered as the essential mechanism of Mark Twain's burlesque. There are the two attitudes—nostalgia and irreverence—in collision; both attitudes are at the heart of Mark Twain's creative impulse. For in order to make the irreverence work, Mark Twain had to impersonate reverence. Even as he specialized in burlesquing the piety of retrospection, he had to cultivate his longing for the past. Sentimental as that longing could be—he speaks in his *Autobiography* of "the pathetic past, the beautiful past, the dear and lamented past"—it nevertheless inspired, at the same time it drove him back upon, his memory.

Probably his chief protection against this intense longing for the past, which he indulged as necessarily as he had to indulge anger and indignation, was his capacity for burlesque. Burlesque was the means of both mocking and checking the nostalgic impulse. In *The Innocents Abroad* Mark Twain, by discovering a perspective along the borderland between pathos and ridicule, had developed a style which contained both attitudes in a new synthesis. Yet in the frame of *A*

Connecticut Yankee he reverted to the simple division of polite tourist and vulgar companion—a division he had used in his *Travels with Mr. Brown*, only to transcend it in *The Innocents Abroad*.[16] In giving over the narrative to Hank Morgan, Mark Twain attempted to transcend the essential division at the heart of the burlesque impulse; but in displacing "Mark Twain" with Morgan rather than Huck Finn, he had no way of producing the mock gravity so essential to his earlier humor. With Morgan as narrator, there was no possibility of impersonating pained seriousness or genteel piety. For Morgan is, as he proudly proclaims, a Yankee of Yankees and barren of sentiment. Instead of embodying the underside of language and experience in the manner of Huck Finn, Hank is the rowdy and irreverent genie of burlesque. Although both Hank and Huck are involved in reconstructing history, the mode of reconstruction is opposite at nearly every point. Huck is the apparently helpless figure drifting upon the current of the mighty Mississippi; Hank is both director and chief actor in his drama. Huck thinks all his heroism is wrong; Hank is sure that his revolution is right. But whereas Huck's successive evasions bring us to the awareness that a real revolution has taken place, Hank's revolutionary indignation involves him in an ever-enlarging fantasy.

All of which brings us to Hank Morgan's style, for Hank's style, like Huck's, will tell everything about the book. It is a loud and boisterous style, given to bluntness and dogmatic attitude. Unlike Huck's Southwestern vernacular, Morgan's Yankee lingo is essentially correct as far as its grammar is concerned. Though it runs toward a jaunty boastfulness and apparently reckless contempt for conventional attitudes, it does not play havoc with the proprieties of grammar. In the final analysis, Hank's vernacular is rather conventional language masquerading as burly, rough talk.

In Huck's vernacular, Mark Twain used the illusion of illiteracy to secure the impression of simplicity while at the same time retaining a complex syntactical structure. Set against the implications of conventional syntax, the illiteracies make possible a style capable of a vast range of expressive utterance. Take, for example, Huck's reflection upon Mary Jane Wilks's offer to pray for him:

> Pray for me! I reckon if she knowed me she'd take a job that was more nearer her size. But I bet she done it, just the same—she was just that kind. She had the grit to pray for Judus if she took the notion—there warn't no back-down to her, I judge. You may say what you want to, but in my opinion she had more sand in her than any girl I ever see; in my opinion she was just full of sand. It sounds like flattery, but it ain't no flattery. And when it comes to beauty—and goodness, too—she lays over them all.[17]

Here Huck's language defines perfectly the breach between his reality and her convention. Mary Jane can approve of him only sentimentally, only because she refuses to know the extent of his sin; and Huck can approve of her only in metaphors which are unwittingly abrasive. In a very real sense his praise of her "ain't no flattery." Yet neither Mary Jane's banality, Huck's self-depreciation, nor the implicit irony of his metaphors disturb the sentiment of his approval. Compare Huck's art of language to Hank's description of a girl he meets upon entering Camelot:

> Presently a fair slip of a girl, about ten years old, with a cataract of golden hair streaming down over her shoulders, came along. Around her head she wore a hoop of flame-red poppies. It was as sweet an outfit as ever I saw, what there was of it. She walked indolently along, with a mind at rest, its peace reflected in her innocent face. . . . But when she happened to notice me, *then* there was a change! Up went her hands, and she was turned to stone; her mouth dropped open, her eyes stared wide and timorously, she was a picture of astonished curiosity touched with fear. And there she stood gazing, in a sort of stupefied fascination, till we turned a corner of the wood and were lost to her view. That she should be startled at me instead of at the other man, was too many for me.[18]

This passage is as representative as it is revealing. The features which distinguish the passage as vernacular are clear—and few. First of all, there is a certain exaggeration of metaphor and figure, as illustrated by the "cataract of golden hair streaming down over her shoulders," and "hoop of flame-red poppies." This exaggeration is also present in other areas of the style. It is evident when the Yankee speaks of "astonished curiosity" and "stupefied fascination." The method here is to call into service an adjective which overlaps the meaning of the noun in an effort to intensify the description. This doubling effect, while it can produce a certain flamboyance of description, is more likely to result—as in the passage under scrutiny—in a redundancy and loss of nuance.

Aside from the exaggeration, the Yankee's style is pervaded with literary cliches. There is the "fair slip of a girl," the "golden hair," the "flame-red poppies," the "mind at rest." Then there are the elaborately stylized locutions—"Up went her hands," "her eyes stared wide and timorously," "she was a picture of astonished curiosity," and "there she stood gazing." These two tendencies—the one toward exaggeration and loud intensity, the other toward literary cliche—reach their logical end in the last sentence of the passage, where the sentence begins with the stilted noun clause as a subject and ends by veering into colloquialism. The entire passage illustrates the essential rhythm and feature of Morgan's language. Grounded in cliches and conventional syntax, its character emerges by means of exaggeration and calculated vulgarity. The exaggeration is achieved largely by relying on cliches which generalize images and impersonate Arthurian gentility; the slang is the means of dissociating from and exposing the overelaborate impersonation.

These revelations about Hank Morgan's style put us directly in touch with his action and his character, for Morgan's action bears the same relation to his style that Huck's action bore to his. Huck, it is worth remembering, was helplessly involved in doing the thing which his society disapproved—freeing a slave. It was an action which he himself disapproved but could avoid no more than he could avoid his grammatical blunders. Both morally and grammatically he "hadn't had no start." The humor in the book lay in involving Huck in a wrong action which his society might abhor yet the reader would heartily approve. Such a strategy required either setting the action in a primitive society and using space or geography as the point of reference; or setting the book in time and using history as the referent. The game lay in playing upon the reader's—and author's—instinctive belief in progress; and Mark Twain had played it admirably in *Huckleberry Finn*. Not only had he involved his protagonist in a revolution which his reader inexorably approved; the hero could not help himself. He simply found himself helplessly and ironically in revolution against a society which he kept thinking he should admire.

In *A Connecticut Yankee*, Mark Twain tried much the same strategy. His Yankee, finding himself in the Arthurian world, sets about revolting against the monarchy and the Catholic Church—institutions which were fairly safe game for a nineteenth-century Yankee. Certainly Mark Twain could count on a general audience approval of these aims almost as much as he could count on their disapproval of slavery. But the great difference between the Yankee and Huck is that the Yankee is a reformer whereas Huck is a helpless rebel. The Yankee acts upon principle and moral confidence; he is finally a Yankee, an abolitionist, an American, who never doubts that he is right. Huck, the fugitive and helpless outcast, acts out of a sense of being always wrong.

The Yankee's assurance that he is in the right contributes as much as anything else to alienating him from the reader. For a real problem arises the moment the Yankee begins to establish his republic. It is not that the reader disapproves of the Yankee's republicanism, but that he cannot approve the revolutionary zeal which goes along with it. As long as he is simply amused at the contrast between his own century and the quaint absurdities of the Arthurian world, the Yankee at least remains plausible; but when he begins to rail at the injustice of the past, his indignation becomes misplaced. The direction of the book discloses that the *intention* of the narrative can neither sustain nor account for the emotion of the central figure; for the emotion—the indignation—is a manifestation of the failure and inadequacy of the intention. The intention of the narrative is a burlesquing or *making fun* of the past. But what begins as making fun becomes making war. Insofar as the Yankee begins to make war upon the Arthurian kingdom he loses his sense of show and pleasure. His indignation is the index to his capacity, not for the destruction of the past, but for self-destruction.

Even more important, the Yankee's revolution is really as correct as his style. It *sounds* like revolution but is actually thoroughly safe and respectable gentility. Small wonder that Howells, who was himself at the threshold of a great "conversion" to political liberalism, should have congratulated his friend upon the bravery of the novel. And so, of course, did E. C. Stedman. Actually there is no courage about the novel. It marks a great turning back for Mark Twain—a turning back in technique and a betrayal of humor. Worst of all, Mark Twain seems to have been self-deceived since he apparently thought the Yankee was a rebel. Yet the reality of the situation is that there is scarcely anything rebellious about the Yankee. His language, as we have seen, is the index of his tameness. Although he sounds and thinks as if he were rebellious, he is quite clearly echoing the sentiments of a society fairly sunk in the complacent and institutionalized "liberalism" which had sponsored the Civil War in 1860–65.[19]

That is why the book, seen in a certain light, amounts to fighting the Civil War again. It is, after all, a tale of the Yankee doing battle with chivalry. Mark Twain himself had made it eminently plain in *Life on the Mississippi* that the South he could not abide was the South which had created itself in the image of Walter Scott and chivalry. Henry Nash Smith, in a fine discussion of Mark Twain's images of Hannibal, had shown decisively how the entire Arthurian kingdom is a thinly veiled picture of Southern regional culture which Mark Twain, as he grew older, came more and more to criticize. Smith points out that Arthur's Britain is "a projection of the benighted South," a "negative image of Hannibal, of Hannibal as Bricksville."[20]

Into this "backward" region the Yankee marches to free the people from religion, aristocracy, and slavery. It is here that he seeks to establish his republic. Insofar as the action of the book amounts to a fighting of the Civil War, Mark Twain assumes the role of the Yankee; he puts on—or better, indulges in—the Yankee conscience and commits aggression after aggression upon the South in himself. For Hank Morgan does, almost from the beginning, what Huck is finally driven helplessly to do—he commits himself to the Northern conscience. This commitment Mark Twain evidently believed was rebellious; actually it is nothing less—or more—than the *approved* action. Huck's rebellion lay not at all in his "All right, then, I'll *go* to hell," but in his rejection of conscience—of hell and heaven—altogether. Having committed himself to the "approved" rebellion, Hank Morgan sounds off louder and louder about it—and the more he commits himself to it, the less real rebellion there can be. This is Hank Morgan's and Mark Twain's self-deception—a self-deception which the style reveals. For Hank's supposed vernacular is not really vernacular at all but indulged colloquialism. It is, in a word, slang, which is to say that it is simply put-on vernacular. Mark Twain, in *A Connecticut Yankee*, succumbed to the lure of mere lingo, which so many writers since his time have done. He wanted to have a hero with an ideology *and* a vernacular. The vernacular was to ground the character in "reality" and give him a "realistic" and recognizable "social" quality. Such a hero really knows what ideas are and showily makes bright philosophical formulations in the rough and salty savor of colloquial speech. But what happens in *A Connecticut Yankee*, and in many another such attempt, is simply a faking and collapse in both directions. The ideas are so crudely simplified in Morgan's vernacular that they actually become pretentious evasions. And the vernacular is nothing but a *show*, an act. It is not necessary to the action, but simply decoration, a contrast. Nothing more than one of Hank Morgan's *effects*, it is in the last analysis an affectation.

To see this failure is to see the crucial difference between vernacular and slang. Slang is a patronizing indulgence of metaphor by someone consciously taking imaginative flights for purposes of mystification, in-group solidarity, or protective, secret communication. Vernacular, however, as we defined the term in *Huckleberry Finn*, is the "lower" or illiterate language whose very "incorrectness" at once indulgently implies a correct grammar and at the same time subverts the literary vision. The more a book is committed to a vernacular hero, the more it necessarily must produce a vision which displaces the genteel values it plays upon. *Huckleberry Finn* did carry such a vision—so much so that the vernacular and vision wait upon each other to produce a new reality of form and action. In the world of childhood which Huck's language reconstructed lay the central confrontations and discoveries which Mark Twain's humor could make. There lay the pleasure principle, which somehow gave the lie to the adult reality principle.

But in moving from Southwestern boy to Yankee adult, Mark Twain actually regressed. The Yankee is in many ways Tom Sawyer grown up—but Tom Sawyer grown up is, alas, somehow grown down. Mark Twain had refused to let Tom grow up on the grounds that he would "just be like all the other one-horse men in literature." And Morgan, if we look at him carefully, does do little but be like other one-horse men. That is why he comes to believe in himself, to take himself seriously. In *Tom Sawyer*, Mark Twain had kept Tom's speech contained within a frame—a frame half-indulgently patronizing, half-burlesque, which both indulges and exposes Tom's essential conformity with the imitation of adult ways. The indulgent narration of *Tom Sawyer* had greatly enriched Tom's reality by showing that it was somehow absurd yet pleasurably *real* in a lost nostalgic way.

When he dropped himself—the "Mark Twain" narrator—out of the action in *A Connecticut Yankee*, he could never compensate for the loss of perspective; instead, he was drawn inevitably to invest the fantasy Yankee with "serious" values. But the fate of the slang form inexorably produced a reduction in the intellectual content of Hank's "thought" and an attendant excess of emotion. The result is an increased amount of sound about ideas, yet a reduction of sense in expressing them.

The conclusion to be drawn from an examination of *A Connecticut Yankee* is that Mark Twain was deceived into believing that slang and vernacular were one and the same. But in vernacular humor, the *form* indulgently inverts conventional values, whereas in slang the *character* must attack them. The one inverts relationships and values; the other moves toward overt judgment and criticism. To realize the possibilities of slang form, Mark Twain would have had to reduce Hank Morgan's intelligence, thereby producing a burlesque, or increase his capacities of criticism and move toward satire. Yet he was able to do neither. It was as if the writer, having reached the top of his form in vernacular, was actually deceived by his masterpiece into believing that the sound of language was identical with its form. By failing to realize the necessities of his form, Mark Twain was never able to be fully responsible to the book he was making. Yet if he fatally confused vernacular and slang, he did no more than many of his successors have done. Believing that they are writing vernacular *Huckleberry Finns*, they produce instead slang *Connecticut Yankees*. Take Saul Bellow's *Henderson the Rain King* as a formidable example. Like the Yankee, Henderson speaks a salty colloquial idiom. Though much more intellectual than Morgan, Henderson nonetheless indulges language in a reckless, carefree way. Both the *Yankee* and *Henderson* try to be responsible by proposing themselves as fantasies, yet the consequences of slang indulgence take their revenge anyway. Whereas the burlesque Morgan turns serious and assaults the fantasy, the intellectual clown

Henderson requires excessive folds of fantasy to make his arrantly conventional sentiments seem boldly speculative. If in the process of becoming serious Morgan negates his own burlesque identity, Henderson in the act of sustaining his fantasy more and more depletes the reality of his speculations, making them seem mere tricks of thought. Both works, in trying to give serious content to the fantasy, succeed only in becoming more and more extravagantly fantastic—and tiresome.

Notes

1. *Mark Twain-Howells Letters*, II, 613.
2. For the best account of the writing of the book, see Howard G. Baetzhold, "The Course of Composition of *A Connecticut Yankee*: A Reinterpretation," *American Literature*, XXXIII (May, 1961), 195–214.
3. Howells, in *My Mark Twain* (p. 44), says, "I wish that all the work-folk. . . could know him their friend in life as he was in literature; as he was in such a glorious gospel of equality as the *Connecticut Yankee in King Arthur's Court*." In his essay "Mark Twain: An Inquiry," which appeared in the *North American Review* in February, 1901, and was included in *My Mark Twain* (pp. 165–85), he insisted that the book was Mark Twain's highest achievement in the way of "a greatly inspired and symmetrically developed romance" (*My Mark Twain*, p. 174). DeVoto, in *Mark Twain's America* (pp. 272–79) sees the bold satiric conception thwarted by the burlesque and frontier humor. Louis Budd (*Mark Twain: Social Philosopher* [Bloomington, Ind., 1962]) concludes his chapter on the *Yankee*: "When he snatched up the banners under which the middle-class was forcing the nobility to disgorge, he was eloquently sincere; his flaming calls to revolt against self-appointed masters are great statements of that right, and his genius at phrase-making left memorable appeals for self-respecting manliness and political equality" (p. 144). Smith has dealt extensively with the novel on two separate occasions: in *Mark Twain: The Development of a Writer* (pp. 138–70) and again in *Mark Twain's Fable of Progress* (New Brunswick, 1964). In the latter book, which is devoted exclusively to the *Yankee*, Smith feels that "at some point in the composition of this fable, he had passed the great divide in his career as a writer"

(p. 107), and that understanding an event so important is to understand the writer.

4. *Writings*, XVI, vii.

5. Budd, *Mark Twain: Social Philosopher*, p. 145.

6. Baetzhold, "Composition of *A Connecticut Yankee*," pp. 196–98.

7. Paine, *A Biography*, II, 887–88.

8. Vernon Louis Parrington, *Main Currents in American Thought*, 3 vols. in one (New York, 1930), III, 98.

9. Gladys Carmine Bellamy, *Mark Twain as a Literary Artist* (Norman, Olka., 1950), p. 314.

10. John B. Hoben, "Mark Twain's *A Connecticut Yankee*: A Genetic Study," *American Literature*, XVIII (November, 1946), 197–218.

11. Baetzhold, "Composition of *A Connecticut Yankee*," pp. 207–11.

12. Paine's edition of the notebooks omits most of Mark Twain's savage attacks, but in the years 1877–80 there are, in the unpublished notebooks, voluminous assaults on Whitelaw Reid and the French nation, to name but two targets. And during the composition of the *Yankee*, abuse is heaped on a variety of subjects.

13. *Letters*, II, 500.

14. *Mark Twain-Howells Letters*, II, 611.

15. *Writings*, XVI,I.

16. Franklin Rogers has an excellent discussion of the refined tourist and his vulgar companion (*Burlesque Patterns*, pp. 36–61). Rogers defines Mark Twain's problem of development as the difficulty of getting a narrative plank which would release the narrative from the stasis of the burlesque division. In the early travels with Mr. Brown, he merely inserted factual chapters between the burlesque chapters, but in *The Innocents Abroad* he assimilated the division into a single narrator who retained burlesque characteristics yet could narrate his travels.

17. *Writings*, XIII, 265.

18. *Writings*, XVI, 10–11.

19. Budd has an excellent account of Mark Twain's opinions in relation to the middle-class Liberalism of the period (*Mark Twain: Social Philosopher*, pp. 111–44).

20. Henry Nash Smith, "Mark Twain's Images of Hannibal: From St. Petersburg to Eseldorf," *University of Texas Studies in English*, XXXVII (1958), 15.

"I Kind of Love Small Game": Mark Twain's Library of Literary Hogwash

Alan Gribben

Mark Twain once observed that "if we read without understanding, there is no gain."[1] For him, reading with the benefit of understanding meant making judgments about what he read, and he did this almost by reflex, as the margins of books from his library testify. Indeed, Mark Twain's unliterary image may flourish so persistently partly because his unfavorable remarks about books and authors very nearly outweigh his praise. But he seldom commented on anyone's writing at length; Sydney Krause has pointed out that Mark Twain left behind not a single fully rounded book review—only desultory, scattered statements.[2]

From the miscellaneous opinions about literature that Mark Twain did set down, however, commentators have attempted to establish his critical standards. DeLancey Ferguson noted in 1943 that "pretentiousness, overwriting, inaccuracy of expression he detested. . . . His interest was always in the style, rather than the story."[3] Howard G. Baetzhold added that Mark Twain generally disliked absurdly romantic situations, excessive sentimentality, dearth of "interest," and lack of believable or likable characters.[4] Yet Mark Twain's marginalia from 1894 in his copy of Sarah Grand's *The Heavenly Twins*[5] show his willingness to over-

Reprinted from *American Literary Realism, 1870–1910* 9. no. 1 (Winter 1976): 65–76.

look objectionable plot conventions and bizarre characterizations provided that the prose style was succinct, the syntax clear, the diction appropriate.

Edgar M. Branch identified criteria applied by Mark Twain in his literary criticism between 1864 and 1866 which seem to hold for his later criticism as well: "clarity, exactitude, simplicity, honesty—all implied in his hatred for literary pretension or ambiguity."[6] Often this search for precision in style came down to a matter of diction. In 1905 Mark Twain explained that in written English prose "phrasing is everything, almost. Oh, yes, phrasing is a kind of photography: out of focus, a blurred picture; in focus, a sharp one."[7]

Generally it was easier for Mark Twain to identify and comment on examples of words used ineffectively, a practice that appealed more strongly to his instincts as a humorist. So adept did he consider himself at discovering specimens of atrocious writing, in fact, that eventually he compiled a special "Library of Literary Hogwash" for particularly delectable examples. Nearly all of these volumes of prose and verse were neglected in their own day and would have been forgotten today had not Clemens' attention fallen upon them. As Clemens confided to General Bryce on 13 October 1894 in another connection (concerning Bourget's *Outre-Mer*): "Paul's book is wretchedly small game, & not much short of idiotic; but I kind of love small game."[8] This preference for easy targets involved the type of perverse pleasure-seeking that Mark Twain had related of himself on 22 August 1878: when a young woman "cleaned out" the idlers in a hotel reading room with her "lacerating" piano rendition of "The Battle of Prague," Clemens alone remained to listen. "I staid," he explained in Notebook 15, "because the exquisitely bad is as satisfying to the soul as the exquisitely good—only the mediocre is unendurable."[9]

By at least 1870 Mark Twain had contrived a name for the literary small game he sought, and the term had associations with his journalism in Nevada and California. In a piece Mark Twain wrote for the June 1870 issue of *Galaxy*, he ridiculed as "the sickliest specimen of sham sentimentality that exists" a sketch entitled "A Touching Incident." In November 1870 he similarly derided the bathos of an obituary poem, scoffing: "There is something so innocent, so guileless, so complacent, so unearthly serene and self-satisfied about this peerless 'hogwash,' that the man must be made of stone who can read it without a dulcet ecstasy creeping along his backbone and quivering in his marrow." He added by way of explanation that "in California, that land of felicitous nomenclature, the literary name of this sort of stuff is '*hogwash*.'"[10] Accordingly, in 1876 he scrawled the words "This book belongs to S. L. Clemens's Library of Literary 'Hogwash'" across the flyleaf of his copy of Edward P. Hammond's *Sketches of Palestine*.[11] Clemens marked other volumes in his personal library with similar labels.

People who knew about Mark Twain's affection for bad writing were continually sending him fresh examples. To one such correspondent, John Horner of Belfast, Ireland, Mark Twain wrote on 12 January 1906: "Hogwash is a term which was invented by the night foreman of the newspaper whereunto I was attached 40 yrs ago, in the capacity of local reporter, to describe my literary efforts. Many years ago I began to collect Hog-Wash literature & I am glad of the chance to add to it the extraordinary book [Emanda Ros's *Irene Iddesleigh*] which you have sent to me."[12] In an Autobiographical Dictation of 16 December 1908 Mark Twain recorded that a letter from Howard P. Taylor (written on 1 December 1908) reminded him how Taylor, a Southerner on the staff of the Virginia City *Territorial Enterprise* (he was foreman of the composing room), coined the "word which I have often used in my books when I was talking about poor literary stuff that had a good opinion of itself—when I . . . wanted to compress my disparagement into a single word." Taylor used to wait while Clemens finished scribbling his day's output for the newspaper: "He never had any other name for my literature"—it was always "hog-wash" (MTP).

Not all of the inferior submissions Mark Twain received from admirers met his strict criteria as "hogwash." He dismissed the poems of Lewis Elmer Trescott of Glenwood, Long Island, for falling short in crucial areas. Clemens explained to a Mr. Lang on 21 August 1907 why Trescott was not a legitimate successor to Bloodgood H. Cutter, the "Poet Lariat" whose verse Mark Twain made celebrated in *Innocents Abroad*; Trescott's broadside poems lacked "incoherency," "idiocy," "windy emptiness," and "putrid & insistent bastard godliness" (MTP).

Mark Twain never actually made a list of selections for his "Library of Literary Hogwash," but the volumes he designated as belonging to it are easily enough identified from his inscriptions and marginalia.[13] A few other novels, sketches, and books of poetry can also be included on the basis of his comments about them, even though he did not specifically label them "hogwash." Had he ever set aside a special bookcase for this collection of literary horrors, its shelves probably would have contained:

Bishop, Levi. *The Poetical Works of Levi Bishop*. 3rd ed. Detroit: E.B. Smith, 1876/ 547 pp.
> *Inscription*: "This book belongs to / S.L. Clemens's / Library of Hogwash. / Hartford, 1876."
> *Marginalia*: Clemens underlined sentences in the biographical sketch of Bishop; at its conclusion he characterized Bishop as a useful citizen whose only failing was the delusion that his "jingling twaddle" qualified as poetry. Other marginal notes include the word "Rot" scrawled at the beginning of a poem entitled "The Oyster" (p. 490). Clemens also annotated Bishop's essay on the definition of poetry.

Location: The Newberry Library, Chicago, Illinois.

> *Copy examined*: I am grateful to Richard Colles Johnson, Bibliographer of the Newberry Library, for providing a photocopy of Clemens' notations for my use.

Caster, Andrew. *Pearl Island*. NY: Harper, 1903. 266 pp.
> *Marginalia*: Clemens penciled markings and sneering comments throughout the volume. On the front free endpaper he recorded his opinion that Caster's dialogues are "incomparably idiotic." Beside Caster's hint in the concluding paragraph (p. 267) concerning further adventures forthcoming in another volume, Clemens swore that the author should first be flayed and hanged.
> *Location*: Antenne-Dorrance Collection, Rice Lake, Wisconsin.[14]
> *Copy examined*: Clemens' copy.

Curtis, Elizabeth Alden. *One Hundred Quatrains from the Rubiyat of Omar Khyyam / A Rendering in English Verse*. Introd. by Richard Burton. Gouverneur, N.Y.: Brothers of the Book, 1899.
Clemens bristled at this attempt to supersede Edward FitzGerald's translation, writing incredulously from London to the Reverend Joseph H. Twichell of 1 January 1900 to say that Curtis had committed "sacrilege" upon "a noble poem" by endeavoring to recast it line by line. The result, he declared, was as though a Tammany Hall boss should demolish the Taj Mahal and then reconstruct it according to his own concept of what it ought to look like (MTP).

Curtis, Lillian E. *Forget-Me-Not / Poems*. Albany, N.Y.: Weed, Parsons, 1872. 112 pp.
> *Inscription*: Presented to Clemens by an admirer, Edwin F. Schirely, on 12 July 1889.

Marginalia: Clemens read the book thoroughly in search of humorous passages, commenting in pencil, correcting syntax and rhymes, and occasionally making outright gibes such as the one on page 56 (concerning "Letter to My Cousin, J.W.H., On His Birthday"): "Did he have to stand this every year?" On page 58, at the penultimate stanza of the same poem, Clemens urged Curtis to "hit him again next year" (copyright 1976, Mark Twain Company).
Location: Antenne-Dorrance Collection, Rice Lake, Wisconsin.
Copy examined: Clemens' copy.

Cutter, Bloodgood Haviland (1817–1906). *The Long-Island Farmer's Poems / Lines Written on the "Quaker City" Excursion to Palestine / And Other Poems*. NY: N. Tibbals, 1886. 499 pp.
Mark Twain preserved this poetaster's place in American letters by calling him the "Poet Lariat" and chuckling over his verse in *Innocents Abroad* (1869); thereafter Mark Twain took pleasure in encouraging Cutter's publication of his effusions. Notebooks 8 (1867) and 46 (1903) contain references to Cutter (MTP). Bradley, Beatty, and Long's edition of *Huckleberry Finn* reprints an example of Cutter's "lugubrious, sentimental, and semi-literate verse."[15]

Elmore, James Buchanan. *Love Among the Mistletoe / And Poems*. Alamo, Ind.: Published by the author, 1899. 164 pp.
Inscription: "Hogwash, but not atrocious enough to be first-rate," Clemens wrote in brown ink on the inner front cover, which he also signed and dated 1902 (copyright 1976, Mark Twain Company).

>   *Marginalia*: Ink markings on pages 48, 69, 70, 72, 213, 214.
>
>   *Location*: Antenne-Dorrance Collection, Rice Lake, Wisconsin.
>
>   *Copy examined*: Clemens' copy.

Gay, Mary Ann Harris. *Prose and Poetry / By a Georgia Lady*. Nashville, Tenn.: Privately printed, 1858. 199 pp.

Hamlin Hill, in "The Composition and the Structure of Tom Sawyer," *American Literature*, 32 (Jan. 1961), 379–392, identifies Gay's book as the one from which Mark Twain extracted two essays and a poem for graduation elocutions in Chapter 21 of *Tom Sawyer* (1876). In a footnote at the end of the chapter Mark Twain acknowledges that the declamations of Tom's female classmates "are taken without alteration from a volume entitled 'Prose and Poetry, by a Western [sic] Lady'—but they are exactly and precisely after the school-girl pattern, and hence are much happier than any mere imitations could be." Eight editions of Gay's book were issued between 1858 and 1873; the title varied. Sydney J. Krause—*Mark Twain as Critic*, pp. 114–117—found the style of Gay's volume to be "Miltonic ornamentation in a country version of the prose of sensibility."

Hammond, Edward Payson. *Sketches of Palestine / Descriptive of the Visit of the Rev. Edward Payson Hammond, M. A., to the Holy Land*. Introd. by the Reverend Robert Knox. Boston: Henry Hoyt, n.d. [Introd. is dated 8 Feb. 1868.] 180 pp.

>   *Inscription*: Clemens wrote in pencil on the recto of the front free endpaper: "This book belongs to S.L. Clemens's Library of Literary 'Hogwash.' Hartford 1876." The inside front cover is signed by Edward P. Judd.
>
>   *Marginalia*: Prolific annotations in pencil by Clemens, uniformly derisive. Choice passages have been

scissored from many pages, leaving the volume much mutilated. On page 148 Clemens referred to Hammond as a "putrid... humbug."
Location: Mark Twain Papers, Berkeley, California.
Copy examined: Clemens' copy.

Hammond wrote these "sketches" in the form of poems. On 27 October 1879 Clemens notified an unnamed correspondent that he had written a review of this "admirable singer" (Newberry Library, Chicago).

Joyce, John Alexander. *Edgar Allan Poe*. NY: F. Tennyson Neely, n.d. [cop. 1901]. 218 pp.
    Inscription: Katy Leary signed the inside front cover.
    Marginalia: Clemens made sarcastic notes in pencil throughout the entire volume, scoffing at Joyce's grammar as well as his conclusions. Clemens fixed his view of Joyce at the top of the first page of the text: "If he *had* an idea he couldn't word it. / The most remarkable animal that ever cavorted around a poet's grave" (copyright 1976, Mark Twain Company). Similarly belittling notes, brief ejaculations ("rot!" "bow-wow!"), and underlinings abound throughout the volume. Since Clemens compares Joyce's style to that of Mary Baker Eddy before her editors revised her writings (p. xii), he may have annotated this volume during or shortly after his intensive reading of Christian Science publications in 1902 and 1903.
    Location: Antenne-Dorrance Collection, Rice Lake, Wisconsin.
    Copy examined: Clemens' copy.

Kiefer, F.J. *The Legends of the Rhine from Basle to Rotterdam*. 2nd ed. Trans. by L.W. Garnham. Mayence: David Kapp, 1870. 313 pp.

Inscription: Original title page missing; Clemens has supplied a handwritten title page on the black recto for the frontispiece.
Marginalia: Clemens' annotations in pencil occur throughout. Inside the back cover is the sticker of a Leipzig bookseller.
Location: Mark Twain Papers, Berkeley, California.
Copy examined: Clemens' copy.

Kiefer's legends were the literary source for some of the stories Mark Twain told in *A Tramp Abroad* (1880). One legend, "The Converted Sceptic," Mark Twain reworked into the legend of Dilsberg Castle, giving a Rip Van Winkle theme to the narrative of a raft captain (chapter 19). But Garnham's cumbersome translation from the German tickled Mark Twain immensely. In chapter one of *A Tramp Abroad* he introduces Garnham's "toothsome" book to his readers, describing the translator's "quaint fashion of building English sentences on the German plan," and quoting a legend called "The Knave of Bergen" as an example. In chapter 16 he quotes Garnham's sorry attempt to translate the song titled "The Lorelei" into English: "I believe this poet is wholly unknown in America and England; I take peculiar pleasure in bringing him forward because I consider that I discovered him."

MacDonald, George. *Robert Falconer* (American edition published in 1870).

Though Clemens became friends with MacDonald and generally admired his writings, he found this novel extremely disappointing. To Mrs. Fairbanks, who had recommended the book, he complained on 2 September 1870 that he found nothing praiseworthy after the middle of the book; in fact he ended up "despising him [Robert] for a self-righteous humbug, devoured with egotism." Clemens culminated this (for him) unusually long literary disquisition by blasting "that tiresome Ericson & his dismal 'poetry'—hogwash, *I* call it." He felt that MacDonald should have omitted his moody gypsy and his thanatotic poetry.[16]

Miller, George Ernest. *Luxilla / A Romance.* [Mobile, Alabama], n.d. [cop. 1885]. 54 pp.

According to a note book Clemens kept during the summer of 1886, he had plans to "review 'Luxilla' that hogwash novel from the South" (Notebook 26, TS p. 9a, MTP).

Mills, S.M. *Palm Branches.* Sandusky, Oh.: Register Steam Press, 1878. 128 pp.

Marginalia: On the recto of the blank page opposite the copyright notice Clemens speculates that the writer must be about fifteen years old. He jotted derogatory remarks throughout the volume, first in black ink, then purple ink, and finally (in the latter half) in pencil. On page 65 he penciled his opinion that "puberty will do much for this authoress." Later, on page 120, he noted that when the character named Daisy remained the same "simple, beautiful maiden" despite Mr. Russell's lavishing every luxury upon her (including "pearls and precious gems that a princess might have coveted"), it was "a schoolgirl's idea of triumph" (copyright 1976, Mark Twain Company). There are numerous other sarcastic comments.

Location: Mark Twain Papers, Berkeley, California.
Copy examined: Clemens' copy.

Moore, Julia A. *The Sentimental Song Book.* Grand Rapids, Mich.: C.M. Loomis, 1877. 60 pp.

The "Queen & Empress of the Hogwash Guild" is how Clemens described this poetess to a correspondent in 1906.[17] It is generally agreed that the didactic doggerel of this farmer's wife inspired Emmeline Grangerford's lugubrious elegies in *Huckleberry Finn*.[18] In *Following the Equator* (1897) Mark Twain returned to *The Sentimental Song Book* ("Forgotten by the world in general, but not by me," he declared), and quoted from different poems in chapter 8 ("Frank Dutton"), 36 ("William Upson"), and 44 ("The Author's Early Life"). Moore, he wrote, had that ineffable and "subtle touch" necessary for genuine hogwash—"the touch that makes an intentionally humorous episode pathetic and an intentionally pathetic one funny" (ch. 36).

Ros, Emanda M'Kittrick. *Delina Delaney*. Belfast, Ireland: R. Aickin, n.d.

    Inscription: Signed by Clemens in ink and dated 1906.

    Marginalia: Notes and markings indicate Clemens' close reading of pages 51, 170, 178, 179.

    Location: Presently unknown; sold to a private buyer by Seven Gables Bookshop, New York City, in June 1970.

    Copy examined: I am indebted to Robert H. Hirst, an associate editor of the Mark Twain Papers in Berkeley, for the facts reported in this entry. Mr. Hirst inspected Clemens' copy in June 1970.

Emboldened by Clemens' delight with Ros's *Irene Iddesleigh* (see next entry), John Horner of Belfast, Ireland, mailed him a copy of her other work, *Delina Delaney*, on 21 April 1906 (ALS in MTP).

———. *Irene Iddesleigh*. Belfast, Ireland: W. & G. Baird, 1897. 189 pp.

    Marginalia: Numerous pencil and black ink annotations by Clemens up to page 55. John Horner of Belfast sent the volume to him on 15 December 1905; Horner's accompanying letter is pinned to the front free endpaper. In 1908 Clemens donated the volume to the Mark Twain Library

in Redding, Connecticut, and it still contains the bookstamps of that institution.
Location: Mark Twain Papers, Berkeley, California.
Copy examined: Clemens' copy.

In a letter to the book's sender on 12 January 1906, Clemens expressed his immense pleasure in the "enchanting" volume and speculated that Julia A. Moore's reign as undisputed Empress of the Hogwash Guild might finally be at an end (dictation copy of a TLS sent by Isabel V. Lyon, Clemens' secretary, MTP).

Royston, Samuel Watson. *The Enemy Conquered / Or, Love Triumphant*. New Haven, Conn.: T.H. Pease, 1845. 31 pp.
    Marginalia: Two copies once owned by Clemens are extant. One lacks the paper wrappers and contains numerous markings in brown ink; the other has pencil markings throughout. Clemens cut out sentences, paragraphs, and entire pages from both copies.
    Location: Mark Twain Papers, Berkeley, California.
    Copies examined: Clemens' copies.

Professor Francis Bacon of Yale purportedly lent a copy of this absurd novelette to George Washington Cable, and Cable then introduced Clemens to the tale of Indian fighter Major Elfonzo's courtship of Ambulinia Valeer, a Southern belle.[19] On 29 January 1884 Clemens requested Charles L. Webster to procure him a copy, instructing Webster to "pay two or three dollars if necessary."[20] But eventually it was Cable, who, in 1889, came through with copies of the book for which Clemens hungered; and on the blue envelope in which he kept them Clemens wrote, "Cable's precious pamphlet / Ambulinia, written by a jackass." Clemens made a note to remind himself to return "one of those old New Haven pamphlet novels" to Cable in 1889, and 1891 he again referred to "Cable's New Haven Idiot's Romance."[21] Eventually Clemens reprinted the entire novelette, with a satiric introduction, as "A Cure for the Blues" in *The £1,000,000 Bank-Note* (1893). Guy A. Cardwell has treated Mark Twain's obsession with this pathetic romance in an insightful article that accounts for his motives behind the writing of "A Cure" and his disappointing efforts to make Royston seem funny.[22]

Stedman, S. O. *Allen Bay / A Story.* Philadelphia: Lippincott, 1876. 152 pp.

On 23 November 1877 William Dean Howells asked Clemens, "Didn't you once read me some passages out of an idiot novel called Allen Bay?"[23] Clemens undoubtedly *had* singled out certain parts for Howells' amusement, but the copy of *Allen Bay* from which he had read was then no longer in existence; he had torn many pages from the volume in the course of writing a thirty-nine-page unpublished manuscript, "Burlesque Review of Allen Bay."[24] He used purple ink and Crystal Lake Mills ruled paper in writing the undated manuscript, a paper-and-ink combination that mainly occurred during 1876 and 1877. It is one of Mark Twain's fullest book reviews, inspired in this case by his abhorrence of Stedman's style. He claims to have reread the book seven times after a first reading and launches into a stylistic analysis of its mixed metaphors, marrings of tone, poor transitions, faulty diction, and other flaws. Gradually it dawns upon the reader that Mark Twain is producing a burlesque review, spoofing the vocabulary and cliches of book reviewers as well as the reprehensible tastes of the readers and writers of such sentimental trash. Moreover, in many instances Mark Twain's purple-ink revisions of the extracts he removed from the book distort the original wording and punctuation to heighten Stedman's already-woeful problems in syntax, diction, sense, and image. Mark Twain tore out pages 143–150 to demonstrate the fatuity of Stedman's highflown bathos and plundered other pages for shorter extracts. The narrative—about a misanthropic hermit who adopts a baby girl, Judith, only to watch her (as a teenager) die of grief over her boyfriend's drowning in a millpond—is undeniably atrocious, but Mark Twain's revisions emphasize its ludicrous qualities by compressing, italicizing, and isolating them.

Van Zandt, George Harrison. *Poems of George Harrison Van Zandt*. Philadelphia: Jay & Co., 1886. 256 pp.

In 1887, while Clemens was managing the business affairs of Charles L. Webster & Company, Van Zandt approached the publishing firm with a proposal to write a historical romance. In an undated letter to Charles L. Webster, Clemens recommended that Webster consult with Van Zandt about the project (ALS in Berg Collection, New York Public Library). At the top of a letter of 21 June 1887 from Van Zandt, however, Clemens advised Fred J. Hall, his representative at Charles L. Webster & Company, not to dispel Van Zandt's delusion that he could write another *Ben Hur*, but neither to encourage his proposals. "His volume of alleged 'poems,'" Clemens assured Hall, "is mere hogwash" (quoted from Philip C. Duschnes Catalog No. 49, item #125).

Warder, George Woodward. *The Cities of the Sun*. NY: G. W. Dillingham, 1901. 320 pp. [Paperback, wrappers missing, title-page defective.]
> *Marginalia*: Approximately two hundred words of marginal notations by Clemens; most comments and underlinings occur in chapter 12. Clemens connects Warder's philosophy with that of Mary Baker Eddy.
> *Location*: University of Rochester Library, Rochester, New York. (Purchased in 1940 from Goodspeed's bookshop in Boston.)
> *Copy examined*: A Xerox copy of the title page and a description of Clemens' marginalia were supplied to me by the University of Rochester Library. The fragile condition of this volume

does not permit the photocopying of its annotations.

A disparaging review—"About Cities in the Sun"—survives in the Mark Twain Papers at Berkeley (DV357) to display Mark Twain's amusement with the book. He planned to publish this piece, and even penciled notes to the editor in the margins of his manuscript, but it never appeared in print. Mainly he pokes fun at his fellow Missourian for taking literally St. John's vision of the New Jerusalem as located in the sun (Book of Revelation 21: 1–27), especially Warder's efforts to construct a precise picture of the heavenly city. Mark Twain's essay also derides Senator Chauncey M. Depew for endorsing "this turbulent philosopher."

Mark Twain entered the courtroom of critical opinion as though each of these twenty volumes were on trial and he were authorized to prosecute a vigorous case against the untalented author. In Mark Twain's marginalia and unpublished reviews he thus inverted the type of literary criticism practiced by his friend Howells; while Howells passed judgment on the upper crust of literature,[25] Clemens rummaged through the bottom shelves of the literary bookcase, finding and ridiculing the "exquisitely bad."

The satiric literary criticism Clemens yearned to write required a healthy dose of animosity, and he found it easy to work himself up to the proper pitch of indignation at the failings of these upstart writers. Why he carried so few of his abortive "reviews" into print is not clear: he may have sensed the unfairness of subjecting these pitiable publications to his mocking scorn; or his interest may have waned after an initial encounter with the book produced his marginalia or fragmentary manuscript and drained his hostility; or perhaps he sensed that he could not adequately educate the public to appreciate the sublimely poor in literature (as the relative failure of his "A Cure for the Blues"[26] seems to prove). But whatever the considerations that kept most of these sarcasms private, his travesty "reviews" of candidates for his "Library of Literary Hogwash" periodically whetted his critical implements in anticipation of the larger game he chose to carve up in print and in private correspondence—Harte, Austen, Eliot, Scott, Cooper, and Goldsmith.

Notes

1. Notebook 39 (dated 1896), TS, p. 15, Mark Twain Papers, University of California, Berkeley—hereafter cited as MTP. The Editor of that collection, Frederick Anderson, influenced the direction and content of this essay very considerably.

2. *Mark Twain as Critic* (Baltimore: Johns Hopkins Press, 1967), p. 1.

3. *Mark Twain / Man and Legend* (Indianapolis: Bobbs-Merrill, 1943), pp. 207–208.

4. *Mark Twain and John Bull / The British Connection* (Bloomington: Indiana U Press, 1970), p. 296.

5. The volume is now in the Henry W. and Albert A. Berg Collection, New York Public Library. Clemens' notations on its pages initially disparage the characters and dialogue, then reveal a grudging admiration for certain aspects of the novel, and finally become openly complimentary.

6. *The Literary Apprenticeship of Mark Twain* (Urbana: U of Illinois Press, 1950), p. 139.

7. "Three Thousand Years Among the Microbes," published in *Mark Twain's Which Was the Dream? And Other Symbolic Writings of the Later Years*, ed. John S. Tuckey (Berkeley and Los Angeles: U. of California Press, 1967), p. 460.

8. The Willard S. Morse Collection, Yale Collection of American Literature, Beinecke Library, Yale University.

9. TS p. 29, MTP. Mark Twain added a few variations in telling about this incident in chapter 32 of *A Tramp Abroad* (1880).

10. "Hogwash," *Galaxy* 9 (Jun 1870), 862, "Favors from Correspondents," *Galaxy*, 10 (Nov. 1870), 735.

11. The volume is in the Mark Twain Papers at Berkeley.

12. Quoted from a dictation copy kept by Isabel V. Lyon, Clemens' secretary (MTP).

13. The present writer has compiled an annotated catalog of Clemens' library books and marginalia in "The Library and Reading

of Samuel L. Clemens," unpublished doctoral dissertation, U of California, Berkeley, 1974. Henry Nash Smith directed this research.

14. Katy Leary, the Clemenses' maid and (later) housekeeper, selected and kept as mementos approximately ninety volumes from Clemens' personal library after he died in 1910. I have described the contents and the provenance of these books, now known as the Antenne-Dorrance Collection, in "The Dispersal of Samuel L. Clemens' Library Books," *Resources for American Literary Study*, 5 (Autumn 1975), 147–165. Robert and Katharine Antenne, co-owners of this collection along with James and Mary Dorrance, cooperated graciously with my research.

15. *Adventures of Huckleberry Finn / An Annotated Text, Backgrounds and Sources, Essays in Criticism*, ed. Sculley Bradley, Richmond Croom Beatty, and E. Hudson Long (NY: Norton, 1962), p. 252.

16. *Mark Twain to Mrs. Fairbanks*, ed. Dixon Wecter (San Marino, Calif.: Huntington Library, 1949), pp. 134–136.

17. Clemens to John Horner, 12 Jan 1906, dictation copy by Clemens' secretary, Isabel V. Lyon (MTP); quoted in Walter Blair's *Mark Twain & Huck Finn* (Berkeley and Los Angeles: U of California Press, 1960), p. 212.

18. See, for example, Walter Blair, *Mark Twain & Huck Finn*, pp. 209–213, 406 n. 13; *The Art of Huckleberry Finn / Text, Sources, Criticisms*, ed. Hamlin Hill and Walter Blair (San Francisco: Chandler, 1962), pp. 445–451; *Adventures of Huckleberry Finn*, ed. Bradley, Beatty, and Long. pp. 253–254; and *Huckleberry Finn / Text, Sources, and Criticisms*, ed. Kenneth S. Lynn (NY: Harcourt, Brace & World, 1961), pp. 156–160.

19. According to the preface in *A Cure for the Blues*, ed. Charles V. S. Borst (Rutland, Vt.: Charles E. Tuttle, 1964), pp. vii–viii, which seems mistaken in dating the incident as occurring in February 1884. Borst says that the Reverend Joseph H. Twichell subsequently obtained six copies of *The Enemy Conquered* in New Haven for Clemens' private amusement, but that Clemens somehow misplaced these and appealed to Cable for another copy in 1889. "I have searched everywhere and cannot find a vestige of that pamphlet," Clemens wrote to Cable. "I possess not a single book which I would not sooner have parted with."

20. *Mark Twain, Business Man*, ed. Samuel C. Webster (Boston: Little, Brown, 1946), p. 233.

21. Notebook 29, TS p. 6, MTP; Notebook 31, TS p. 17, MTP.

22. "Mark Twain's Failures in Comedy and The Enemy Conquered," *Georgia Review*, 13 (Winter 1959), 424–436.

23. *Mark Twain-Howells Letters*, ed. Henry Nash Smith and William M. Gibson (Cambridge: Harvard U Press, 1960), p. 209—hereafter cited as MTHL.

24. MS in MTP (Paine 59).

25. For the most part Clemens let Howells and other established critics take care of what he once—in 1887—called "high & fine literature" (MTHL, p. 587). Though he was grateful to Howells for introducing him to such arrivals of talent as William Allen White's *In Our Town* (MTHL, pp. 808, 814–815), Clemens' most fervent praise tended to be lavished on minor authors whom he had the pleasure of "discovering" himself: writers who published magazine short stories, out-of-the-way guidebooks, unnoticed novels, overlooked poems. Phoebe Brown's autobiography, for instance, never published and still in manuscript, kept him up far into the night with its quaint charm (MTHL, p. 381); and the issuance of E. W. Howe's *The Story of a Country Town* seemed to him an unheralded event that deserved congratulations (see C. E. Schorer, "Mark Twain's Criticism of *The Story of a Country Town*," *American Literature*, 27 [Mar 1955], 109–112).

26. The publication in 1893 of this mocking analysis of Samuel Watson Royston's forgotten *The Enemy Conquered* (1845) drew scarcely any public attention.

The American Claimant: Reclamation of a Farce

Clyde Grimm

Although Mark Twain's *The American Claimant* (1892) is a hastily and crudely fabricated novel, it is an interesting and significant work for at least two reasons. First, having been adapted by Twain from a farce drama written in collaboration with William Dean Howells, the novel provides an opportunity for study of Twain's imaginative conversion of pointless humor into meaningful satire. Second, because it reiterates with little ambiguity political and social themes which recur throughout Twain's work, the novel provides a clearer as well as more mature statement on cultural issues with which Twain had been concerned for years.

The play from which the novel grew has a curious history of its own, certain aspects of which warrant recapitulation.[1] Twain and Howells never intended more than to amuse themselves and, they hoped, a large audience by creating a ridiculously impractical schemer who would strut and fret his hour upon the stage in a series of ludicrous antics signifying nothing. Just as he had based his Colonel Sellers character in *The Gilded Age* (1873) on his eccentric cousin James Lampton, Twain proposed that they base the central figure of their play on his brother, Orion Clemens, whose fantastic schemes and inventions seemed rich material for a farce. Evidently, by the summer of 1878 Howells had become interested enough to start on such a play, referred to in their correspondence as both *The Steam Generator* and *Orme's Motor*, but he did not finish it. Twain continued enthusiastically to urge the project and in the spring of 1880 proposed as a model for the central character still another relative, a more distant cousin, Jesse Leathers, who was not only an inventor of laughable gadgets but also the current bearer of a longstanding family claim to the English peerage. By September 1881, as indicated in the following sketch sent to Howells, Twain's imagination had fused all three relatives into one character:

> Now I think the play for you to write would be one entitled "Col. Mulberry Sellers in Age" (75)—with that fool of a Lafayette Hawkins (aged 50) still sticking to him & believing in him & calling him "my lord" (S. Being American earl of Durham)—& has cherished his delusion until he & his chuckle-headed household believe he *is* the rightful earl & that he is being shamefully treated by the house of Lords. He is a "specialist" & a "scientist" in various ways; makes collections of pebbles & brickbats & discourses garrulously & ignorantly over them & projects original "theories" &c. Has a lot of impossible inventions, which cost somebody a good deal & then blow up & cripple disinterested parties, or poison them.

The Sellers character, originally bearing the peculiarities of only James Lampton, would thus acquire those of Orion Clemens and Jesse Leathers as well. Twain's enthusiasm seems to have blinded him to the potential danger of overloading one character with so many diverse idiosyncrasies: though the character might be original and extravagantly ridiculous, the play accommodating the number and variety of his antics might prove formless.

After having shown continued but ineffectual interest for several years, Howells proposed in April 1883 that they make definite plans to write the play in October and assured Twain that their idea had "the making of a good comedy in it without doubt." However, when in November and December of that year the two authors finally put the play together in short but

The American Claimant: *Reclamation of a Farce*

intense flurries of effort, they produced what Howells less than enthusiastically called "an extreme farce." The inferiority of "extreme farce" to "good comedy," though difficult to assess precisely, no doubt contributed to Howell's eventual loss of confidence in the play and his withdrawal from arrangements to stage it.

In August 1884, apparently discouraged and exasperated by faltering negotiations to produce the play, Twain declared to Charles Webster, his nephew and the manager of his publishing firm, "I'm going to elaborate it into a novel," thus revealing for the first time an intention it would take him seven years to make good.[2] At this same time, however, John T. Raymond, who had starred as Sellers in a successful stage version of *The Gilded Age* in 1876, promised to produce the play in September. Though Raymond agreed to accept it without alterations, he strongly urged excision of the claimant idea and one of Sellers' most incredible delusions, a scheme for reviving the dead called "materialization." He particularly objected to the latter because he felt it made Sellers appear a lunatic, and Raymond did not interpret the character's eccentricity that strongly. Howells at this time regarded both the claimant idea and materialization as "vital portions" of the play and opposed their excision. Twain, though granting that "Raymond's ideas are good," nevertheless rejected his advice because it would require too extensive rewriting. When Raymond peremptorily backed out of the arrangement, declining at the last minute to produce the play without revision, Twain once more heatedly vowed to "turn it into a novel."[3] There is no telling of course what shape a novel written at this time would have taken, but the unrestrained exuberance with which Twain seems to have exercised his imagination on the Sellers character and his reluctance to tone down the farce persuade one that the adaptation was fortunately postponed.

In May 1886 negotiations for production became as farcical as the play itself. Howells had reversed his judgment and now agreed with Raymond that the Sellers character seemed a lunatic and needed a good deal of modification; he believed too that the claimant idea was not sufficiently developed to be retained. And, finally, suggesting its lack of form, he lamented, "There is nothing in the play but the idea of Sellers' character, and a lot of comic situations." Though he had urged these views on Twain, he had neither absolutely refused to have the play staged nor effectively discouraged negotiations. Only after Twain had signed a contract with A.P. Burbank, who immediately leased Daniel Frohman's theater in New York, did Howells firmly decide against staging; the belated triumph of his misgivings cost each of them $500 (for the theater lease) and indefinitely committed the acting rights to Burbank. Twain persisted alone, however, and financed several performances in September 1887. Entitled *The American Claimant* or *Mulberry Sellers Ten Years Later*, with Burbank in the role of Sellers, the play was as poorly received as both Raymond and Howells had anticipated and was soon withdrawn, never to be staged again.[4]

Surprisingly, in spite of his earlier defection and the subsequent failure of the play on the stage, Howells made one final effort to reclaim it. In January 1890 he reported showing the play to James A. Herne, the prominent actor and playwright, and discussing with him a reconstruction of it. Confirming earlier opinions of the play's weaknesses, Herne recommended excision of the materialization idea, a general toning down of Sellers' eccentricity, and creation of a new plot. However, the proposal aroused neither author's enthusiasm, chiefly because of the financial complications caused by Burbank's possession of the acting rights, and their collaborative undertaking collapsed once and for all after more than a decade. Early in 1891 Twain made good his earlier vows to turn the play into a novel. Ironically, as A.B. Paine has noted, Augustin Daly, the famous producer, thought that the novel might be turned into a very good play, though nothing came of his proposal to do so.[5] Considering its history, especially each author's contribution and relative enthusiasm, it seems a final irony that the play, entitled

The American Claimant: Reclamation of a Farce

Colonel Sellers as a Scientist, now appears as one of *The Complete Plays of William Dean Howells*! [6]

Perusal of the play confirms Howells' objection that there is nothing to it but character and situation. The main "plot" focuses on Sellers the zany inventor, who amid impoverished surroundings displays a variety of fantastic gadgets from which he hopes to make a fortune; ironically, a modest, practical device in which he has shown little interest ultimately proves successful and redeems him. In one underplot Sellers lays claim to an English earldom but gratuitously renounces it in the end. A second underplot, the conventional romance, brings together with unusually little difficulty Sellers' daughter and the young English heir, who also gratuitously renounces his claim. The claimant idea contributes nothing essential to the action and as an addition to Sellers' eccentricity is superfluous. Another alleged weakness, the materialization idea, provides some incidental satire and also some farcical humor when Sellers twice expresses horror at the thought that a living girl is in love with what he supposes to be a "materialized" ghost. As for its contribution to Sellers' alleged lunacy, his belief in materialization does not appear any more incredible or insane than his confidence in a fire-making fire extinguisher, which none of the play's critics objected to and which Daniel Frohman even considered its only amusing element.[7] Neither materialization nor any of Sellers' other inventions or delusions seems inappropriate for "extreme farce," which after all seldom invites serious rational scrutiny. The play suffers most from the formal weaknesses sensed by Howells and Herne: its thinness of plot and the arbitrary employment of supporting elements.

When in May 1891 Howells inquired about the relation of the new novel to their collaborative work, Twain replied, "I found I couldn't use the play—I had departed too far from its lines when I came to look at it. I thought I might get a great deal of dialogue out of it, but I got only 15 loosely written pages—they saved me half a day's work. It was the cursing phonograph [another of Sellers' inventions]. There was abundance of good dialogue, but it couldn't be fitted into the new conditions of the story." Although he borrowed little verbatim, Twain nevertheless retained all of the basic elements of the farce. However in comparing the novel with the play, it is impossible to overemphasize the transforming effect of the "new conditions" Twain refers to. He had radically altered his view of the story material and its significance and had transformed it from meaningless farce into thoroughgoing political and social satire. In doing so, he showed remarkable ingenuity in adapting and integrating those elements which Howells and the others had most objected to. He revamped the claimant plot by expanding Sellers' role as a would-be English peer and also by adding for ironic contrast a fully developed complementary plot tracing the English heir's attempts to become an American democrat. Sellers' "lunacy" remains the same in terms of his devotion to fantastic projects but gains special significance in the new context. Even the materialization scheme becomes an effective vehicle for satire. Yet in spite of its ingenious thematic unity, the novel suffers from Twain's haste in putting it together in only "71 days."[8] For example, the new episodes devoted to the young Englishman's adventures, comprising roughly a third of the novel, are crudely inserted as a virtual block in the middle of the Sellers material. The satire in these episodes especially but in others as well is heavy-handed, as Twain's telling predominates over his showing.

Notwithstanding its shortcomings as art, however, *The American Claimant* is significant for the light it throws on Twain's political and social thought. Repeating themes and devices which appear in many of his earlier works, it invites comparisons which illuminate major cultural issues which preoccupied him for many years and indicates the direction in which, at the age of fifty-six, he sought or had found resolutions. Most apparent and interesting is Twain's recapitulation of the theme of disenchantment with democracy which he had employed just a few years earlier in

The American Claimant: Reclamation of a Farce

A Connecticut Yankee in King Arthur's Court (1889). The disillusioned figure in *The American Claimant* is not, however, like Hank Morgan, a native American raised on common-sense utilitarianism and democratic political principles; rather he is a young English nobleman, Viscount Berkeley, who has been raised as the heir to the Earldom of Rossmore. Twain assigns Berkeley the "candor, kindliness, honesty, sincerity, simplicity, [and] modesty" which suggest innate nobility of character antecedent to social status or political rank.[9] But like Prince Edward in *The Prince and the Pauper* (1882) and King Arthur in *A Connecticut Yankee*, two other characters of innate nobility, Berkeley is also naive and inexperienced, ignorant of many realities. He has been infected with the radical political theories of Lord Tanzy of Tollmache (whose Germanic name connotes insanity) and has determined to renounce his aristocratic station, emigrate to America and make his way by ability alone. The lesson taught by his subsequent adventures is two-fold: first, that in spite of its professed equalitarianism American democracy is a corrupt sham which perpetuates inequality and changes only its bases and the processes by which it is established; second, that the abstract principle of equality, no matter how sincerely adopted and earnestly pursued, will not produce the sentiment or feeling of equality, because it is contrary to human nature.

In America, though satisfied by the absence of the artificial titles peculiar to Europe, Berkeley is greatly disturbed by the misuse of two "titles" which he continues to believe valid as legitimate marks of genuine distinction: the titles "lady" and "gentleman." His landlady warns him that in America these titles are universally applied and that to deny them to anyone is a fighting matter. When the landlady's daughter asserts that "'everybody calls himself a lady or gentleman, and thinks he *is*, and don't care what anybody else thinks him, so long as he don't say it out loud,'" Berkeley's reaction is the obvious one: that calling oneself a lady or gentleman is not equivalent to being one. Another boarder, a Mr. Barrow, intrudes to explain the difference in usage between England and America:

> Over there, twenty thousand people in a million elect themselves gentlemen and ladies, and the nine hundred and eighty thousand *accept* that decree and swallow the affront which it puts upon them. Why, if they didn't accept it it wouldn't *be* an election; it would be a dead letter, and have no force at all. Over here the twenty thousand would-be exclusives come up to the polls and vote themselves to be ladies and gentlemen. But the thing doesn't stop there. The nine hundred and eighty thousand come and vote themselves to be ladies and gentlemen *too*, and that elects the whole nation. Since the whole million vote themselves ladies and gentlemen, there is no question about that election. It *does* make absolute equality, and there is no fiction about it; while over yonder the *inequality* (by decree of the infinitely feeble, and consent of the infinitely strong) is also absolute—as real and absolute as our equality. (p. 93)

The irony of this ostensible glorification of America over England is that in neither case does self-appointed gentility appear real and absolute or valid, and the irony strikes with greater impact against the *universality* of presumption and self-aggrandizement in America, a sham not differing in kind from that of England but differing colossally in extent or degree. Democratic leveling perverts the meaning of "equality" and by mocking the labels for superior intelligence, character, education and conduct tends to obliterate legitimate moral distinctions or gradations among human beings.

Berkeley finds, moreover, that the equalitarianism implied by this specious use of language is only nominal after all, for inequality and deference to rank or status are widespread in America. Immediately after arriving, he is disturbed by the deferential treatment he receives because of his English title. Adopting a pseudonym to avoid further such treatment, he tries to find a job. Though competent for government work, he fails to obtain even a modest clerkship. "Competency," Twain sneers, "was no recommendation; political backing, without competency, was worth six of it. He was glaringly English, and that was necessarily against him in the political center of a nation where both parties prayed for the Irish cause [home rule] on the housetop and blasphemed it in the cellar" (p. 85). The platitude that America is the land of unlimited opportunities is further belied by the selfish exclusivism of organized labor, which prevents Berkeley from finding employment elsewhere. He begins to realize that he is the victim of a discriminatory system just as real, just as impenetrable and, ironically, just as oppressive or tyrannous as any in Europe, "an aristocracy of the ins as opposed to the outs" (p. 108).

In the boarding-house where he resides, a microcosm of American society, Berkeley also observes travesties of rank and deference typical of democracy and records them in his diary:

> There is respect, there is deference here, but it doesn't fall to my share. It is lavished on two men. One of them is a portly man of middle age who is a retired plumber. Everybody is pleased to have that man's notice. He's full of pomp and circumstance and self-complacency and bad grammar, and at table he is Sir Oracle, and when he opens his mouth not any dog in the kennel barks. The other person is a policeman at the capitol-building. He represents the government. The deference paid to these men is not so very far short of that which is paid to an earl in England, though the method of it differs. Not so much courtliness, but the deference is all there. (p. 107)

A much more ominous example of popular deference occurs after Berkeley conquers the boarding-house bully in a fist-fight. The gang of boarders quickly transfer their fawning adulation from the bully to him, and though he had hoped for their comradeship, he senses that this sudden acceptance has been won on terms which prevent his feeling pride or satisfaction in it. He feels degraded by this deference because it seems nothing more than the instinctive acknowledgment by animals of the superior strength or brute force of another animal; as a consequence, he considers himself worse off than the prodigal son, who fed swine but "didn't have to chum with them" (p. 114).

Twain's frequent employment of zoological metaphors to describe the boarding-house and its residents (e.g., swine, barking dogs in a kennel, hive) suggests the brutishness of this microcosm of "free and open" democratic society. This image is confirmed by one incident in particular. Everyone applauds and abets the landlord's humiliation of one of the boarders, who is without work and therefore unable to pay his keep. In response to Berkeley's puzzlement at this cruel, inhumane behavior, the cynical Barrow exclaims, "'Don't you know that the wounded deer is always attacked and killed by its companions and friends?'" (p. 105). Whereas Berkeley had thought that "'equality ought to make men noble-minded'" (p.102), his experience suggests that on the contrary the "natural" society of a democracy depresses rather than elevates character and conduct by encouraging or condoning free exercise of the most bestial instincts. This dog-eat-dog, survival-of-the-fittest environment, dominated by the physically or economically strong, confirms the absolute travesty of calling everyone "lady" or "gentleman," for the moral superiority which these titles ought to denote is neither displayed, sought for, nor appreciated in this society of "common men."

Almost from the beginning of his tenure in America, Berkeley had been aware of a discrepancy between the principles he idealistically espoused and the sentiments he actually felt. "The equality of men was not yet a reality to him," Twain explains, "it was only a theory; the *mind* perceived, but the *man* failed to feel it" (p. 94). Ashamed of his continuing involuntary resistance and determined to overcome it, Berkeley struggled through the series of experiences summarized above, trying all the while to resolve not only the conflict he felt within himself but also the glaring contradiction he observed between the principles and the practice of Americans. At last, in the company of Barrow, he attends a meeting of a Mechanics' Debating Club and hears a tirade against "unearned titles, property, and privileges," which the speaker calls upon all the monarchs and nobles of the world to renounce. Though his entire experience in America has exposed the hypocrisy or delusion of such views and his own feelings continue to oppose them, he applauds the speech, dutifully struggling to persuade himself. Barrow, however, immediately and sharply condemns the mechanic's remarks as "'an idiotic damned speech'" (p. 122) which wholly ignores human nature and advocates what only a fool would do. Though opposed to the principle of inherited rank or privilege, he asserts that the speaker or any other man, including himself, would unhesitatingly accept an earldom if it were offered and that preaching renunciation is therefore hypocritical nonsense. This candid opinion from his American associate induces Berkeley to give up his unnatural struggle to become a "democrat" and to accept his heritage:

> He had been born an aristocrat, he had been a democrat for a time, he was now an aristocrat again. He marvelled to find that this final change was not merely intellectual, it had invaded his feeling; and he also marvelled to note that this feeling seemed a good deal less artificial than any he had entertained in his system for a long time. He could also have noted, if he had thought of it, that his bearing had stiffened, over night, that his chin had lifted itself a shade. (p. 128)

Berkeley thus resumes his inherited identity as an aristocrat much as Prince Edward and King Arthur do in earlier novels. It is important to note that in his case as in theirs the rank or title signifying superiority is accompanied by real distinction of character, breeding and conduct and therefore, unlike the titles and ranks adopted or conferred in America, has a legitimate moral basis.

This need not suggest that Twain sanctions the ordinary or traditional concept of hereditary aristocracy; in fact, through Barrow, he repudiates it. Yet he does dramatize a concept of natural aristocracy, in which innate nobility and superior breeding entitle one to social distinction. Not only do men naturally fail in the practice of equalitarianism, they also naturally fail to display an equal capacity for or inclination toward intelligent, moral behavior. Reminiscent of James

Fenimore Cooper's, Twain's chief criticism of democracy in America is not that men seek and society confers distinction but that the natural aristocrat is dispossessed and ignored in favor of ridiculous, corrupt and even brutal shams.

The remaining episodes of the novel, which are dominated by Colonel Sellers, develop these themes with variations peculiar to his special temperament and background. Though some pure farce remains, Twain did a remarkably thorough job of converting pointless elements from the play into meaningful and cohesive satire for the novel.

One of the most significant revisions concerns the claimant idea. As noted earlier, the idea derives from a family legend, which Twain first learned of from his mother, Jane Lampton Clemens, when he was a boy. The Lamptons believed themselves descendants of the Lambtons of England who had become Earls of Durham; Jesse Leathers, Twain's distant cousin, went so far as to proclaim himself the rightful earl, the victim of a mistaken succession several generations in the past.[10] Though Twain often made light of these claims to aristocratic lineage, the frequency of his allusions to them and his repeated employment of similar themes in his fiction suggest that he was compelled by the idea more than he preferred to admit. Further evidence of this is the curious modification which he made, over a decade, in Sellers' claimancy. In the sketch of Sellers which he sent to Howells in 1881, Twain clearly indicates that the claim is a delusion with no basis in fact and that Sellers is utterly foolish in believing himself the rightful earl. In the play itself, however, Sellers provides a vague but plausible explanation of his claim and he acknowledges that he is only third in line among the heirs to the title. Thus, in the play, neither the claim nor Sellers remains quite as absurd as in Twain's original conception. In the novel Sellers once again believes himself to be the rightful earl, having inherited his claim upon the death of his distant Arkansaw relative Simon Lathers, the former "earl." But of greatest significance is that Berkeley's father, the Earl of Rossmore, admits that a mistake in succession occurred years ago and, though he does not believe the courts would uphold it, confirms the moral right of the American claimant. What this radical change may suggest of Twain's attitude toward his own family's claims is conjectural, but its effect on the characterization of Sellers is quite plain. Sellers in the novel cannot be ridiculed for believing himself an heir or claimant to the peerage; Twain made him, in at least one sense a legitimate pretender. Thus, whatever else may remain laughable about Sellers, this particular element of his characterization invites serious consideration.

As a matter of fact, no matter how ridiculous many of his antics appear, Sellers is one of the most "sympathetic" adult characters Twain created. Mrs. Sellers describes her husband as "the same old scheming, generous, good-hearted, moonshiny, hopeful, no-account failure he always was" (p. 21). For all his absurd impracticalities, hair-brained schemes and romantic pretensions, Sellers is a moral aristocrat, whose innate nobility matches that of Berkeley. This is best illustrated by his impractical but humane patronage of two old Negroes who had been slaves of the family and who wandered back after the war "free" but decrepit and helpless. Though the Sellerses were themselves nearly destitute, his wife reports, the Colonel passionately rejected her plea for practicality:

> "Turn them out?—and they've come to me just as confidential and trusting as—as—why, Polly, I must have *bought* that confidence some time or other a long time ago, and given my note, so to speak—you don't get such things as a *gift*—and how am I going to go back on a debt like that? And you see, they're so poor, and old, and friendless..." (p. 23)

His innate humanity and his breeding as a southern gentleman (albeit an impecunious one) make him incapable of betraying a moral obligation, incurred in the prewar South, and of exploiting the cash nexus established by the North's victory as the prevailing basis of human relations.

Neither the crassness and cynicism of the age nor his personal disappointments alter his character, his temperament or his basic outlook. Yet he is not naive. On the contrary, he is well aware of unpleasant actualities and is capable of perfect candor. For example, he is momentarily incredulous when Hawkins denies seeking office or preferment: "Now look here, old friend, I know the human race; and I now that when a man comes to Washington, I don't care if it's from heaven, let alone Cherokee Strip, it's because he *wants* something" (p. 160). Sellers likewise candidly appraises his own failures as "an epitome of human ambition, and struggle, and the outcome: you aim for the palace and get drowned in the sewer" (p. 17). In spite of such insights, his prevailing mood, which only rarely lapses, is one of buoyant optimism, bright fancy, noble idealism and grandiose dreams. The key to this curious contradiction between his "realism" and his "romanticism" and to his unique personality is suggested by Mrs. Sellers:

> People who don't rightly know him may think he is commonplace, but to my mind he is one of the most unusual men I ever saw. As for suddenness and capacity in imagining things, his beat don't exist, I reckon. As like as not it wouldn't have occurred to anybody else to name this poor rat-trap Rossmore Towers, but it just come natural to him. Well, no doubt it's a blessed thing to have an imagination that can always make you satisfied, no matter how you are fixed. (p. 39)

Imagination is the key to Sellers' personality, as it is to the personalities of a number of other Twain characters. Like Tom Sawyer, for example, he "lets on" that his house with its impoverished furnishings is Rossmore Towers, a manor appropriate for the noble rank he "lets on" to possess. His illusions and pretensions, like these of Tom Canty in *The Prince and the Pauper* and Sandy Carteloise in *A Connecticut Yankee*, are attempts to sustain ideals and ennobling visions which transcend sordid and depressing realities. Sellers consciously chooses to indulge an image of himself and his surroundings commensurate with his own high moral ideals and aspirations. His awareness and acknowledgment of reality distinguish his imaginations from mere sentimental or naive delusions, and the repellent sordidness of that reality justifies his romanticism as a perceptual mode of adjustment which is not only satisfying but perhaps even necessary to his moral survival. Moreover, this adjustment may reflect Twain's estimate of the greatest felicity attainable in the democratic culture which emerged in America after the Civil War.

In any case, the new context demands a thoroughgoing reappraisal of Sellers' eccentricities as having a good deal more significance than they display in the farce. One peculiarity shared by both Sellers and his daughter is a culturally split personality. The Colonel's co-existent obsessions with Franklinian inventions and with dreams of an earldom suggest that he is a product of two different cultures. Likewise Sally Sellers, Twain explains, "was as practical and democratic as the Lady Gwendolen Sellers [her alter ego] was romantic and aristocratic" (p. 49). The Colonel himself defines this duality as "intensely and practically American by inhaled nationalism, and at the same time intensely and aristocratically European by inherited nobility of blood" (p. 50). The essence of this dichotomy, variants of which appear throughout Twain's work (e.g., Huck Finn and Tom Sawyer), may be reduced to the following terms: on the one hand, matter-of-fact "realism" (which usually insists upon the sordid and ugly), utilitarian practicality, and democratic political and social sentiments; on the other hand, romantic illusion and pretense, chivalric idealism and heroic aspiration, and an aristocratic sense of distinctions and gradations among men. With Sellers as with Berkeley the aristocratic identity is innate and "natural," whereas the democratic identity is "inhaled" and in a sense artificial.[11] Berkeley inhales the intoxicating abstractions of Tanzy, Sellers those of the culture in which he was raised. But the actualities of this culture conflict with their natural instincts and repel them. Most important, however, is that both Sellers and Berkeley display genuine nobility of character which distinguishes them from the common level of men who represent democratic culture and which vindicates their natural instincts, justifying both Berkeley's resumption of his aristocratic station and Sellers' aspiration to it.

The genuine or natural aristocrat must be distinguished from the sham, the legitimate from the presumptuous and false pretender. The distinction is crucial throughout Twain's work (e.g., the "King" and the "Duke" in *Huckleberry Finn*). In addition to the shams already noted in the Berkeley episodes, he satirizes in the Sellers episodes the vulgar pretensions of the *nouveaux riches* who dominate the school which Sally attends; Colonel Sellers' description recalls Twain's satiric portrayal of the Parvenus in *The Gilded Age* and his attack on the southern "she-college" in *Life on the Mississippi* (1883):

> Rowena-Ivanhoe College is the selectest and the most aristocratic seat of learning for young ladies in our country. Under no circumstances can a girl get in there unless she is either very rich and fashionable or can prove four generations of what may be called American nobility. Castellated college-buildings—towers and turrets and an imitation moat—and everything about the place named out of Sir Walter Scott's books and redolent of royalty and state and style; and all the richest girls keep phaetons, and coachmen in livery, and riding-horses, with English grooms in plug hats and tight-buttoned coats, and top-boots, and a whip-handle without any whip to it, to ride sixty-three feet behind them—(p. 37)

Sally Sellers, of course, is to be distinguished from these snobs; indeed she recognizes their corruptness and matches their disdain for her poverty with her own scorn for their moral bankruptcy.

Twain does not, however, limit his satire to the shams and pretensions of the Gilded Age alone; he enlarges the scope and significance of his criticism of American culture by broadening its historical perspective. He does so by once again transforming none-too-promising materials retained from the farce. The first of these is the "deadly chromos" which adorn the Sellers household:

> Some of these terrors were landscapes, some libelled the sea, some were ostensible portraits, all were crimes. All the portraits were recognizable as dead Americans of distinction, and yet, through labelling added by a daring hand, they were all doing duty here as "Earls of Rossmore." The newest one had left the works as Andrew Jackson, but was doing its best as "Simon Lathers Lord Rossmore, Present Earl." (p.12)

It is significant that the Lathers "pretender," a vulgar Arkansaw "blatherskite" who is killed by a falling log in the drunken chaos of a smoke house-raising on the frontier, is identified specifically with Andrew Jackson, the symbol of radical democracy and hero of the common man—but also, from a conservative point of view, the arch villain responsible for the corruption of government and the degradation of culture in America. By this symbolic identification Twain enlarges the significance of the Lathers story to national and historical proportions. The Lathers-Jackson alignment suggests the political revolution by which the common classes ascended to power during Jackson's pre-Civil War administration; the addition of Rossmore to this alignment suggests the continuing economic, social and moral revolution by which they aspire to respectability and further dominance of the culture. Once again, however, it is necessary to distinguish the legitimate pretender from the presumptuous sham. Though Berkeley's father confirms Lathers' moral right to the title, doubting only his legal claim, it would seem that in fact only his legal claim could have any validity, for the clamorous incongruity between his vulgarity and the nobility signified by the title precludes any genuine moral right. Yet Sellers' pretension not only retains the legal basis of Lathers' claim but also gains moral justification from his superior character. His dispossession of an English title, however, is less significant thematically than his dispossession of status in his native country, of which more will be said below.

Dixon Wecter has noted one of Andrew Jackson's vanities which may have been Twain's inspiration both for the chromo device discussed above and for another use of chromos in the Berkeley episodes of the novel; Wecter reports that "an artist named Earl was hired to live at the White House during the eight years of his Administration, and do nothing but paint one picture after another of the President."[12] Such a fact would have been widely publicized in Whig circles, both during and after Jackson's tenure in office, and Twain, whose family's affiliation with the Whig party is well documented, would almost certainly have known of it. The chromo of Jackson on Sellers' wall might well have been inspired by one of Earl's portraits and intended as a direct satiric allusion. The connection between his biographical item about Jackson and the other chromo episode may appear farfetched but, if not intended, is an astonishing coincidence. The only work that Berkeley can find in America is with two old hack artists, one a retired sea captain and the other a retired shoemaker, producing chromos which depict ordinary mechanics and other commoners in absurdly grandiose postures aping great historical figures like Napoleon. This portrait-making commissioned, as it were, by the common man is a travesty of the portrait-painting by great artists of the past under the commission of European royalty and nobility. Though it is a lucrative business, Berkeley's participation clearly indicates the triumph of desperation and necessity over pride and integrity, for he knows that he is no artist and that the chromos are vulgar parodies. His experience may epitomize the plight of the natural aristocrat in America: he is reduced to prostituting himself for the self-aggrandizement of his moral and intellectual inferiors. The vanity of the mechanics and the others who pose for mock-heroic portraits is like that of their hero Jackson, who commissioned endless and no doubt heroic images of himself. In producing these shams Berkeley is doing, in essence, exactly as Jackson's kept artist did, and though Berkeley has not yet succeeded to the title, he will one day be, again like Jackson's portrayer, an "Earl."

The American Claimant: *Reclamation of a Farce*

Twain further enlarges the historical perspective of the novel by adapting Sellers' materialization scheme. Although the incidental satire achieved by this device remains much the same in the novel as in the play (e.g., Sellers' intention to revive "the trained statesmen of all ages and all climes, and furnish this country with a Congress that knows enough to come in out of the rain. . ." [p. 29]), Sellers' mistaken identification of the young Englishman as a materialized ghost, while continuing to provide farcical humor, functions in the novel as satire also and contributes much to the development of primary themes. Twain expanded the function of this device by first of all complicating the confusion of identities. Early in the novel Berkeley escapes from a hotel fire dressed in the clothes of a notorious one-armed frontier bank robber, One-Armed Pete, who is burned to death in the fire. Dressed as a cowboy, Berkeley receives the deference of both ordinary citizens and government officials but mistakenly assumes that it is again due to his English rank. In fact, however, they defer to him not as a European noble but as a peculiarly American equivalent—the "noble" Westerner. The full significance of this misidentification evolves later when Colonel Sellers contrives a burlesque theory of evolution: "Every man is made up of hereditaries, long descended atoms and particles of his ancestors. This present materialization is incomplete. We have only brought it down to perhaps the beginning of this century" (p.164). By making Berkeley an ancestor of One-Armed Pete, Sellers' theory ironically suggests that an English lord is the proper historical antecedent of an American Frontier outlaw and, by extension, that European aristocracy is the origin and counterpart of the corrupt "peerage" that dominates America. Berkeley's obviously superior character and breeding, however, make ridiculous and untenable any such attempt to identify him with Pete. Even Sellers, who had planned to capture the bank robber and collect a reward, acknowledges the injustice of delivering Berkeley to the law to pay for the crimes of his alleged "posterity":

> In him there's atoms of priests, soldiers, crusaders, poets, and sweet and gracious women—all kinds and conditions of folk who trod this earth in old, old centuries, and vanished out of it ages ago, and now by act of ours they are summoned from their holy peace to answer for gutting a one-horse bank away out on the borders of Cherokee Strip, and it's just a howling outrage! (p. 165)

Properly identified—by his moral stature, not by his clothes—Berkeley absolves not only himself but also the centuries-old culture of which he is a product.

Though misapplied, Sellers' theory nevertheless invites us to view Berkeley and Pete in broad perspective and to relate them accurately. Because of his mistaken identification, Sellers distorts the relation between them by erroneously placing them in the same genealogical and cultural line of descent. But Berkeley is a contemporary of Pete, not an antecedent; neither is he blood-related to Pete through common ancestors as he is to Sellers. In fact Berkeley and Pete are related only as antitheses, and when they are viewed as representatives or symbols of their respective cultures this antithesis becomes of greatest significance. Like the contrast in *A Connecticut Yankee* between the original, sixth-century Knights of the Round Table and the "converted," nineteenth-century knights of the Yankee's stock exchange, this contrast in *The American Claimant* suggests that the development of democratic culture in America represents historical degeneration, not "progress" as Americans are accustomed to boast. One-Armed Pete, the frontier "knight" or literal "robber baron," symbolized democracy's inversion of the social order and of the moral values upon which it is based; Berkeley, on the other hand, represents the European institutions and culture from which America revolted. Though its distribution of rank may be imperfect, Europe nevertheless produced Berkeley, whose moral distinction matches his social rank and to that extent at least vindicates the culture which makes possible such a match.

The American Claimant: *Reclamation of a Farce*

In America, however, disparity between moral stature and social rank is the rule. One-Armed Pete, the moral bankrupt, enjoys the greatest prestige and power; Colonel Sellers, the natural aristocrat, Berkeley's true blood-relation and co-inheritor of high moral standards, is dispossessed and degraded. Pete epitomizes the travesty of America's democratic culture, Sellers its tragedy. For unlike Berkeley, who may repudiate this stultifying alien culture and return to his native land, Sellers cannot escape the "inhaled" influences of his native environment nor can he satisfactorily resolve the conflict between them and his natural instincts. His only recourse is imaginative withdrawal. Attempting to satisfy these instincts, he therefore expends his moral energies by indulging in romantic gestures and illusions which are usually ineffectual and often ridiculous. His compulsion to sustain romantic ideals and to strive for some measure of satisfaction on his own terms, as opposed to those prevailing in his environment, makes him an admirable and even heroic figure.

Sellers' absurdities, like those of Don Quixote, require that a distinction be made between spirit and manner; he is ridiculous not because of his romantic temperament, noble spirit and idealistic vision but because of the elaborate, archaic and incongruous manners and forms with which he identifies proper expression of these. In contrast to her father's ingrained and irremediable quixotism, Sally Sellers toward the end of the novel "reforms" by adopting a healthier, more mature view of aristocratic distinction, which of course complements Berkeley's reformed view of equalitarianism and democracy. She renounces the family's claimancy because of its "artificiality and pretense" but retains her respect for "real" aristocracy and nobility; moreover, she reassures Berkeley that his rank and title do not prejudice her against him because her feelings toward him are evoked by his intrinsic character, not by adventitious symbols. Thus, like Miles Hendon in *The Prince and the Pauper*, she values only essential moral distinction but repudiates or scorns its symbols only when they are false or incongruous.

Twain's deep personal involvement in the conflicts which dominate *The American Claimant* is suggested by an entry in his notebook, dated 1898, in which he makes the following confession:

> There are princes which I cast in the *Echte* (genuine) princely mold, and they make me regret—again—that I am not a prince myself. It is not a new regret but a very old one. I have never been properly and humbly satisfied with my condition. I am a democrat only on principle, not by instinct—nobody is *that*.[13]

In her report of her father's reaction to an invitation to visit German nobility, Twain's daughter Clara has provided confirmation of this profound inward conflict: ". . . we could tell that a battle was going on between a largely cultivated inclination toward democratic passions and a largely inborn inclination to worship distinction of position, which supposedly includes distinction of person."[14] Twain seems, therefore, to have revealed much of himself in his characterizations of Berkeley *and* Sellers, both of whom display this same dualism. Berkeley's conversions from aristocrat to democrat and back again no doubt parallel the alternation of Twain's own sentiments over a lifetime. Colonel Sellers' debt to his creator's personality is more complex. Though Twain had by 1881 already combined in Sellers the peculiarities of three people, he did not complete the characterization for the novel until in 1891 he added what appears to be something of himself. Beyond the dualism noted above, what he added was chiefly sympathy. Without altering the basic outlines of the Sellers character or adding substantially to the particulars of his behavior, Twain nevertheless radically changed the characterization by revising the contest in which Sellers appears and with it the tone of his presentation. It is as if Twain felt a new sympathy for James Lampton, his brother Orion, and Jesse Leathers because he recognized or acknowledged finally that he shared with them many of their "peculiarities," which he had ridiculed before but had since come to understand and appreciate. Judging by *The American Claimant*, what Twain had concluded was that for a person of the innate character and temperament of a Colonel Sellers the conditions of American life create a frustrating disparity between noble motives and opportunities for their fulfillment, which he can prevent from ending in despair only by indulging in absurd pretenses and illusions. From his revised and mature perspective—perhaps already that of despair—Twain could no longer treat these absurdities as farce but was compelled to display their tragi-comic aspect instead.

Notes

1. A useful introduction summarizing much of its history precedes the play, *Colonel Sellers as a Scientist*, in *The Complete Plays of William Dean Howells*, ed. Walter J. Meserve (New York, 1960), pp. 205–8. However, the richest source of information on the play is the two-volume *Mark Twain-Howells Letters*, eds. Henry Nash Smith and William M. Gibson (Cambridge, 1960), which in addition to the correspondence itself provides many detailed notes pertaining to the collaborative project. Except where otherwise indicated, all of the quotations and facts appearing in my summary have been drawn from this source; by this blanket acknowledgment I intend only to avoid a proliferation of footnotes, not to minimize my considerable indebtedness. I would hope that the many dates included in my text make relatively easy the locating of specific sources in the chronologically-arranged correspondence.

2. Samuel C. Webster, *Mark Twain, Business Man* (Boston, 1946), p. 273.

3. Webster, p. 277.

4. Meserve, p. 207.

5. *Mark Twain's Letters*, ed. A.B. Paine (New York, 1917), II, 563.

6. The published version of the play, appearing on pages 209–41, has been put together from a number of MSS, which Meserve identifies in his introduction (p. 208).

7. *Encore* (New York, 1937), p. 108.

8. *Mark Twain's Notebook*, ed. A.B. Paine (New York, 1935), p. 213.

9. Mark Twain, *The American Claimant and Other Stories and Sketches* (New York, 1896), p. 3. Page numbers of all subsequent citations from the novel appear in parentheses in the text and refer to this edition.

10. For a concise resumé of the Lampton and Leathers stories, see *Mark Twain-Howells Letters*, II, 869–71.

11. Although because of his nativism the pull of democracy appears to be stronger in Sellers than in Berkeley, his fantastic scheme for a republic of Siberia, the high point of his liberalism in the novel, is still essentially aristocratic: he envisions a Utopia populated entirely by the political exiles of Czarist Russia, a moral and intellectual elite which he considers "the very finest and choicest material on the globe for a republic" (p. 157)—perhaps, in Twain's view, the *only* constituency capable of creating and sustaining the ideal republic!

12. *The Saga of American Society* (New York, 1937), p. 93.

13. *Mark Twain's Notebook*, p. 357.

14. Clara Clemens, *My Father Mark Twain* (New York, 1931), p. 206.

Mark Twain—An Intimate Memory

Henry Watterson

Although Mark Twain and I called each other "cousin" and claimed to be blood-relatives, the connection between us was by marriage: a great uncle of his married a great aunt of mine; his mother was named after and reared by this great aunt; and the children of the marriage were, of course, his cousins and mine; and a large, varied and picturesque assortment they were. We were lifelong and very dear friends, however; passed much time together at home and abroad; and had many common ties and memories. The last time I saw him, a little less than two years ago, he came to lunch with me at the Manhattan Club, in New York, where he greatly amused my son, a buoyant, appreciative and promising young lawyer only a few weeks later snatched suddenly and tragically away, by his intimate reminiscences of Col. Sellers, of the "Earl of Durham," and of other fantastic members of our joint family.

Just after the successful production of his one play, "The Gilded Age," and the famous hit made by the late comedian, John T. Raymond, in its leading role, I received a letter from him in which he told me he had made in Col. Mulberry Sellers a close study of a certain mutual kinsman and thought he had drawn him to the life, "but for the love of Heaven," he said, "don't whisper it, for he would never understand, or forgive me, if he did not thrash me on sight."

Reprinted from *The American Magazine* 70 (July 1910): 372–5.

The True Col. Mulberry Sellers
Not a Comic Character

The pathos of the part, and not its comic aspects, had most impressed him. He designed and wrote it for Edwin Booth. From the first and always he was disgusted by the Raymond portrayal. Except for its amazing popularity and money-making quality, he would have withdrawn it from the stage as, in a fit of pique, Raymond himself did, while it was yet packing the theatres. The original Sellers had partly brought him up and been very good to him; a second and perfect Don Quixote in appearance and not unlike the knight of La Mancha in character. It would have been safe for nobody to laugh at him—nay, by the slightest intimation, look, or gesture, to treat him with inconsideration, or any proposal of his—however preposterous—with levity. He once came to see me upon a public occasion and during a function. I knew that I must introduce him, and with all possible dignity, to my colleagues; but he was very queer: tall and stately, wearing a black, swallow-tailed suit, shiny with age, a silk hat, bound with black crepe to conceal its rustiness, not to indicate a recent death; but his linen as spotless as new-fallen snow; and I had my doubts and fears. Happily, the company, quite dazed by the apparition, proved decorous to solemnity, and the dear old gentleman, pleased with himself and proud of his "distinguished young kinsman," went away highly gratified.

Not long after this, one of his daughters—lovely girls they were, too, and in charm altogether worthy of their Cousin Sam Clemens—was to be married, and he wrote me a lengthy summons: all-embracing, though stiff and formal; such as a baron of the Middle Ages might have indited to his noble relative, the Field Marshal, bidding him bring his good lady, and all his retinue to abide within the castle until the festivities were ended, though in this instance the Castle was a little suburban cottage not big enough to accommodate the immediate bridal party. I showed this bombastic but most hospitable and sincere invitation to Mr. Raymond, who chanced to be playing in Louisville when it reached me. He read it through with care and re-read it. "Do you know," said he, "it makes me want to cry. That is not the man I am trying to impersonate at all." Be sure it was not; for there was nothing funny about the spiritual being of Mark Twain's own Mulberry Sellers; he was as brave as a lion and as upright and stern as a covenanter.

When a very young man living in a woodland cabin down in the "Penny'rile" region of Kentucky, with a wife and two, or three, babies, he was so carried away by an unexpected windfall that he lingered over long in the village, dispensing a royal hospitality; in point of fact, he "got on a spree." Two or three days passed before he regained possession of himself. When at last he reached his home, he found his wife ill in bed and the children nearly starved for want of food. He said never a word, but walked out of the cabin, tied himself to a tree, and was literally horse-whipping himself to death when the cries of the frightened family called the neighbors and he was cut loose and brought to reason. He never touched an intoxicating drop from that day to the day of his death.

When Mark Twain had worked himself into a state of mind talking to one of us about "Old Jim," his eyes would flood with tears, and I cannot myself write about him without a choking sensation. Never such a hero lived in such a fool's paradise. Yet, as done by Raymond, never an impersonation on the American stage, or in any of our comic fictions, provoked louder and longer mirth. I do not know what Edwin Booth thought of Sellers, or indeed, whether he so much as read the part which had been intended for him. That Booth and Sellers were in Mark Twain's mind conjointly tells its own and quite a different story.

The "Earl of Durham" Touches Mark Twain for a Tenner

Another one of these mutual cousins was the "Earl of Durham." About the middle of the eighteenth century, before the War of the Revolution, there came to Virginia four brothers Lampton, younger scions of the House of Durham. From them the American Lamptons are sprung. Sam Clemens and I grew up on old wives' tales of estates and titles, which maybe it was a kindred sense of humor in both of us we treated with shocking irreverence.

It happened some forty years ago that there turned up, first upon the plains and afterward in New York and Washington, a straight descendant of the oldest of these Virginia Lamptons—he had somehow gotten hold of or had fabricated a full set of documents—who was what Theodore Roosevelt would call "a corker." He wore a sombrero, with a rattle-snake for a band, and a belt with a couple of six-shooters, and described himself and claimed to be the Earl of Durham. "He touched me for a tenner the first time I ever saw him," drawled Mark Twain, "and I coughed it up and have been coughing them up, whenever he's around, with punctuality and regularity." The "Earl" was indeed a terror especially when he had been drinking.

His belief in his peerage was as absolute as Col. Sellers' in his millions. All he wanted was money enough "to get across" and "state his case." During the Tichborne trial, Mark Twain and I were in London, and one day he said to me, "I have investigated this Durham business down at the herald's office. There's nothing to it. The Lamptons passed out of the Earldom of Durham a hundred years ago. There were never any estates. The title lapsed. The present earldom is a new creation not the same family at all. But, I tell you what, if you'll put up five hundred dollars, I'll put up five hundred more, we'll bring our chap over here and set him in as a claimant, and, my word for it, Kenealy's fat boy won't be a marker to him!"

He was so pleased with his conceit that later along he wrote a novel and called it "The Claimant." It is the only one of his books—though I never told him so—that I never could read. Many years after, I happened to see upon a hotel register in Rome these entries "The Earl of Durham," and in the same handwriting just below it, "Lady Anne Lambton" and "The Hon. Reginald Lambton." So the Lambtons—they spelled it with a b instead of a p—were yet in the peerage and earls of Durham. The next time I saw Mark Twain I tackled him on the deception. He did not defend himself—said something about its being necessary to perfect the joke. "Did you ever meet this present peer and possible usurper?" I asked. "No," he answered, "I never did, but if he had called on me, I would have seen him."

Next Door to the "Work'us"

His mind turned ever to the droll. Once in London I was living with my family at 103 Mount Street. Between 103 and 102 there was the parochial workhouse—quite a long and imposing building. One evening, upon coming in from an outing, I found a letter he had written on the sitting-room table and left with his card. He spoke of the shock he had received upon finding that next to 102—presumably 103—was the workhouse. He had loved me, but had always feared that I would end by disgracing the family—being hanged, or something—but the "work'us," that was beyond him; he had not thought it would come to that. And so on through pages of horse-play: his relief on ascertaining the truth and learning his mistake—his regret at not finding me at home—closing with a dinner invitation. Once at Geneva, in Switzerland, I received a long, overflowing letter, full of buoyant oddities, written from London. Two or three hours later came a telegram. "Burn letter. Blot it from your memory. Susie is dead."

How much of melancholy lay hidden behind the mask of the humorist it would be hard to determine. His griefs were tempered by a vein of philosophy. He was a medley of contradiction. Unconventional to the point of eccentricity, his sense of respectability was acute. Though lavish in the use of money, he had a full realization of its value and made close contracts for his work. Like Sellers, his mind soared when it sailed financial currents. He lacked sound business judgment in the larger things, while an excellent economist in lesser.

The book-publishing failure may be ascribed to lack of forecast along with an excess of optimism. So the failure of the type-setting machine. While that venture and its rival, the Mergenthaler invention, were in the experimental stage, Mr. Stillson Hutchins, who controlled the latter, made him an offer he should have accepted, and which, if it had been accepted, would indeed have ensured him "millions." They were old acquaintances and excellent friends. "Sam," said Hutchins, "let us merge these interests, you taking Europe and I this side." No, he would none of it; so, in the end, it cost him a pretty penny.

A Happy Marriage

His marriage was the most brilliant success of his life. He got the woman of all the world he most needed; a truly lovely and wise helpmeet; who kept him in bounds and headed him straight and right while she lived; the best of housewives and mothers, and the safest of counsellors and soundest of critics. She knew his worth; she understood his genius; and she clearly saw his oddities and his angles. Her death was a grievous disaster as well as a staggering blow. It was her sympathy and her love which enabled him to survive Susie's death. When the final tragedy came, it was too much for him— it broke his spirit—he could not react against it and sank beneath the load of accumulated sorrows and infirmities.

Mark Twain's place in literature, the bent of his genius and the merit of his writing, are made the subjects of varied commentation in England, in Germany and in his own country. Probably the works of no American author traveled farther, gave more pleasure, or were better known. It is not my purpose here to venture an estimate or take note of critical opinions; the rather to jot down a few intimate memories.

In the early seventies, he dropped into New York, where there was already gathered a congenial group to meet and greet him. This radiated from Franklin Square, where Joseph W. Harper—"Joe Brooklyn," we called him—reigned in place of his uncle, Fletcher Harper, the man of genius among the original four Harper Brothers, to the Lotus Club, then in Irving Place and Delmonico's, at the corner of Fifth Avenue and Fourteenth Street, with Southerland's in Liberty Street, for a downtown place of luncheon resort, not to forget Dorlon's, in Fulton Market. The Harper contingent, beside the Chief, embraced Tom Nast and Col. Seaver, whom John Russell Young named "Papa Pendennis," and described as "a man of letters among men of the world and a man of the world among men of letters," a very apt portrayal, albeit appropriated from Dr. Johnson, and Major Constable, a giant, who looked like a dragoon, and not a bookman, yet had known Sir Walter Scott and was sprung from the family of Edinburgh publishers. Bret Harte had newly arrived from California. Whitelaw Reid, though still subordinate to Greeley, was beginning to make himself felt in journalism. John Hay played high priest to the revels. Halstead and I used to make periodic pilgrimages to the delightful shrine.

Robustious Revels

Truth to say, it emulated rather the gods than the graces—though all of us had literary aspirations of one sort and another—especially late at night—and Sam Bowles would come over from Springfield to meet us. Often we had Joseph Jefferson, then in the heyday of his great career, with, once in a while, Edwin Booth, who could not quite trust himself to go our gait. The good fellows we caught from over sea were innumerable, from the elder Sothern and Sala and Yeats to Lord Dufferin and Lord Houghton. Times went very well those days, and, whilst some looked on askance—notably Curtis and, rather oddly, Stedman—and thought we were wasting time and convivializing more than was good for us, we were mostly young and hearty, ranging from thirty to five and forty years of age, with amazing capacities, both for work and play, and I cannot recall that any harm to any of us came of it. Although robustious, our frolics were harmless enough—ebullitions of gayety sometimes, perhaps unguarded—though each shade, or survivor, recurring to those Noctes Ambrosiae, might paraphrase to the other the words of Curran to Lord Avonmore:

> We passed them not in lust, or toys or wine, But in true poesy, wit and philosophy, Arts which I loved, for they, my friend, were thine.*

Mark Twain was the life of every company and of all occasions. I remember a practical joke of his suggestion played upon Halstead. A party of us were supping after the theatre at the old Brevoort House. A card was brought to me from a reporter of the *World*. I was about to deny myself, when Mark Twain said: "Give it to me, I'll fix it," and left the table.

Presently he came to the door and beckoned me to come to him. "I represented myself as your secretary and told this man," said he, "that you were not here, but that if Mr. Halstead would answer just as well, I would fetch him out. He is as innocent as a lamb and doesn't know either of you. I am going to introduce you as Halstead and we'll have some fun."

---

* I am writing from memory, without the opportunity to verify my quotation, which may not be strictly accurate.

"Fixing" a Reporter

No sooner said than done. The reporter proved to be a little bald-headed cherub newly arrived from the isle of dreams, and I lined out to him a column or more of very hot stuff, reversing Halstead in every expression of opinion. I declared him in favor of paying the national debt in greenbacks. Touching the sectional question which was then the burning issue of the time, I made the mock Halstead say: "The 'bloody shirt' is only a kind of Pickwickian battle-cry. It is convenient during political campaigns and on election day. Perhaps you do not know that I am myself of good old North Carolina stock. My father and grandfather came to Ohio from the old North State just before I was born. Naturally, I have no sectional prejudices, but I live in Cincinnati and am a Republican."

There was a good deal more of the same sort. How it passed through the *World* office I know not, but next day it appeared. On returning to table I had told the company what Mark Twain and I had done. They thought I was joking. It did seem inconceivable. Without a word to any of us, next day Halstead wrote a note to the *World* briefly repudiating the "interview," and the *World* printed his disclaimer with a line which said: "When Mr. Halstead talked with our reporter he had dined." It was too good to keep. John Hay wrote an amusing "story" for the *Tribune*, which set Halstead right and turned the laugh on me!

Now and then we did a little after-dinner speech-making all among ourselves—toward the wee sma' hours—perhaps to try our wings—certainly to try one another. Mark Twain made much the best speech. He had the gift to think clearly upon his feet. His oratory was a kind of easy dictation, and he was hard to follow, his words were so apt. Although he disliked audiences, they did not disconcert him. His method was slow, purposely halting, and the drawl, like Travers' stammer, assisted the humor.

Henry Watterson

Inherited His Drawl from His Mother

This drawl was not affected, as many supposed it. He inherited it from his mother; a bright and captivating woman, as were all the feminine Lamptons I have ever known. The men of that family were honest and courageous, but not successful on the material side. The women were immensely successful as wives and mothers. The family had the artistic temperament. Mark Twain's childhood, though passed upon the frontier, was enveloped by a certain semi-literary atmosphere. He got the hang of books in his cradle. There may not have been many of them, but they were select, incessantly read and talked about. His rude experiences on the river and in the mining camp accentuated the baby love of letters, and, when travel gave him the chance to proceed with his education, he made the most of it; a hard worker; a closer and a more intelligent student than he seemed, for, with John Hay, in the earlier time he liked to affect the rustic. Thus, after his years of foreign experience and residence, when he came to deal with other subjects than the pilot-house on the Mississippi and the "diggings" of Nevada, he applied a touch to his work which was unexpected and possessed the quality of the surprising.

I sometimes think we Americans are a little unjust to ourselves in our literary valuations. Irving, Bret Harte and Mark Twain followed the homely rescript that "the shoemaker should stick to his last." They wrote of things familiar and they wrote with both elegance and originality, and often with power; far and away in merit—even technical skill—the seniors of the chosen ones of larger fame, the "immortals" of France, and the worthies of England and Germany, whom we are wont to consider great in this world and in Valhalla cloisters to place upon pedestals.

Of the three, Mark Twain was the strongest and broadest, covering an ampler range of production, and striking a deeper note; as vivid as Harte, with none of Harte's insincerity; as conscientious and as true and simple as Irving, but with yet more potent hand and quicker and larger fancy, an American through and through in his genius, a cosmopolitan in his attainments and his art.

The Book Hunter

"Puddenhead Wilson," Mark Twain's latest story, is the work of a novelist, rather than of a "funny man." There is plenty of humour in it of the genuine Mark Twain brand, but it is as a carefully painted picture of life in a Mississippi town in the days of slavery that its chief merit lies. In point of construction it is much the best story that Mark Twain has written, and of men and women in the book at least four are undeniably creations, and not one of them is overdrawn or caricatured, as are some of the most popular of the author's lay figures. There is but one false note in the picture, and that is the introduction of the two alleged Italian noblemen. These two young men are as little like Italians as they are like Apaches. When challenged to fight a duel, one of them, having the choice of weapons, chooses revolvers instead of swords. This incident alone is sufficient to show how little Italian blood there is in Mark Twain's Italians. But this is a small blemish, and if Mark Twain, in his future novels, can maintain the proportion of only two lay figures to four living characters, he will do better than most novelists. The extracts from "Puddenhead Wilson's Almanac," which are prefixed to each chapter of the book, simply "pizon us for more," to use Huck Finn's forcible metaphor. Let us hope that a complete edition of that unrivalled almanac will be issued at no distant day.

Reprinted from *The Idler* 6 (August 1894): 222–3.

In Re "Pudd'nhead Wilson"

Martha McCulloch Williams

A better title, perhaps, would be "The Decline and Fall of Mark Twain;" for, looking at it solely as a piece of literature, there is no denying that his much-advertised serial is tremendously stupid. If it were nothing more, the reading, even the critical, world could afford to receive it in the charity of silence, remembering the merry heart it has had these twenty years past whenever it pleased Mr. Clemens to amuse it.

"Pudd'nhead Wilson" is more than stupid. So far as it has appeared—to the end of the second installment, that is—it is at once malicious and misleading. So much so, indeed, that involuntarily one recalls the gentleman who, it was said, "went to his memory for his wit, and his imagination for his facts."

It certainly seems to me that Mr. Clemens must have imagined all the local color of his tale. It has to do with Dawson's Landing, a small Missouri town on the Mississippi, populated largely with F. F. V.'s, all of whom are slaveholders, as are the rest of the inhabitants. Right here I wish to ask why it is that the Southern man who has an honest and decent pride in the fact that he comes of good stock fares so ill at the hands of certain literary gentlemen? Bret Harte gives us Colonel Starbottle as his type. Mr. Cable has won fame and fortune and the heart of the whole North by demonstrating to its entire satisfaction how heartlessly and continually all his

Reprinted from *Fetter's Southern Magazine* 4 (1894): 99–102.

well-born gentlemen overstep the color line. Last of all, Mark Twain has set himself the task of showing how impossible it is for a man to have a great-grandfather and, at the same time, any regard for the Decalogue.

Perhaps these gentlemen are bent on gleaning the full harvest of "Uncle Tom's Cabin." Perhaps, too, they are wise in so doing. In my seven years North, I have more than once been asked by people who regarded themselves as very well-informed "if there were still in the South any pure blacks at all, or any pure-blooded whites?" At first such questioning made me angry. Later, I have come to recognize it as the legitimate outcome of the deliverances of Mr. Cable and his school. Now that Mark Twain has come under their banner, the impression will doubtless become more than ever current. For he has—and has deserved—the widest public of any living American writer. And it is a melancholy fact that the sheep instinct of humanity is so strong as to make it follow *en masse* into any pasture of opinion where he may lead. A still more melancholy fact is the inability of many folk to judge a thing with eyes blinded by the glamour of a great reputation.

Otherwise, I think, some one would have risen ere this to protest against some of Mr. Clemens' gentle idiosyncrasies displayed in the first installment. For instance, the character of Pembroke Howard, introduced solely that the author might tell us that Howard, too, was an F.F.V., also that "he was popular with the people"—and that the story has no sort of concern with him. A while later he is permitted to die. At least, there is a line to that effect. What I want to know, and would like to ask Mr. Clemens, is how a man can be "popular with the people," since popular means of, by, or with the people. It does assuredly seem to me pretty queer usage for a man who was so lately toasted and feted by the Lotos Club, as the leading exponent of literary art.

That is by no means a solitary gem of its kind. Careful reading shows the like upon almost every page. It is not too much to say, in fact, that there is slovenly construction in every other paragraph. But the manner is a trifling burden compared with the matter of it. First to last, the writer seems to feel his burden of humor-with-malice-aforethought. He had chosen his place, his people. If the facts about them are not humorous, so much the worse for facts.

Witness the naming of the hero. He had come out of Western New York to practice law in the Missouri town. One day, hearing a dog bark, he indulges in the Joe-Millerism of wishing he owned half the dog so he might make an end of it. Thereupon the by-standers "fell away from him as something uncanny, and went into privacy to discuss him." One said:

"Pears to be a fool."

"Pears? said another "*Is*, I reckon. Said he wished he owned *half* the dog." "The idiot," said a third. "What did he reckon would become of the other half if he killed his half? Do you reckon he thought it would live?"

"In my opinion he ain't got any mind."

"No. 3 said: "Well, he's a lummox, anyway."

"That's what he is," said No. 4.

"He's a labrick; just a Simon pure labrick if ever there was one."

"Yes, sir, he's a damn fool, that's the way I put him up," said No. 5. "Anybody can think different that wants to, but those are my sentiments."

"I am with you gentlemen," said No. 6. "Perfect jackass—yes, and it ain't going too far to say he is a pudd'nhead. If he ain't a pudd'nhead, I ain't no judge, that all."

Mr. Wilson stood elected. The incident was told all over town and gravely discussed by everybody. Within a week he had lost his first name. Pudd'nhead took its place.

This is humor, as the great editors understand it. To one a little bit conversant with the folk who are supposed to be humorous, it seems, contrariwise, something cheap and thin. Throughout the Southwest, for at least seventy five years, "I'd like to own that dog—and kill my half" has been a cant saying so commonly current that it is laughed at only out of compliment to the user of it. The man who should now perpetrate it as original would perhaps be called something worse than "pudd'nhead," but very certainly nobody—not the most ignorant—would find in it a suggestion of uncanniness. For the thing is so common and proverbial that little children make use of it, or rather of its implication. More than one small lad has told me, rejoicing, "Ma has stopped her half of me from going to school." And one shrewd young person within my knowledge bought half of a coveted dolly, then insisted on a property-right to play with it all the time.

So, too, of Mr. Clemens' young man who went away East to college, and came back with "Eastern polish," whatever that may be—perhaps perfect fitting clothes and a habit of wearing gloves. His old friends overlooked the polish and the clothes but could not forgive the glove habit, so he was left solitary. This is some more, doubtless, of Mr. Clemens' very peculiar humor. He ought, however, to have stated the fact in a footnote. He might have been at the same pains about the reception to the Brothers Capollo. His account of the honors thrust upon them is doubtless a sly revenge upon the misguided Southern communities, which have stretched out admiring hands to Mr. Clemens when he would rather they did not.

So much for the accidentals of the tale. To deal adequately with the story itself, either in motif or atmosphere, would require more time and space than I, at present, command. It is built around the exchange of two children, born the same day, to one father. One is his wife's son; the other, his slave's. The wife dies; the slave mother, who has sixteen parts of white blood to one of black, has sole charge of both babies. After a while, her master (as is the custom of Virginia gentlemen in the hands of high literary persons), for some trifling fault, sells all the other house-servants, though as a mark of magnanimity he sells them at home instead of sending them down the river. The life-likeness of this part will be apparent to every ex-slave owner, especially to such as remember how far beyond rubies was in those days the price of a thoroughly excellent servant. Setting wholly aside the human affection that often subsisted between white and black, few men were so foolish as to inconvenience themselves by an entire change of *menage*, without the most imperative necessity for such a proceeding. All that is, however, beside the mark. This sale goes forward, and as a result, Roxy, the white slave, puts her son in his half-brother's place to save him from the possibility of such a fate.

She also puts her creator—Mark Twain—in rather a hard dilemma. To his mind the only man worth either saving or damning in all the South country is the black man. The exigencies of fiction, however, make it necessary that the slave baby, who normally would grow up a pin feathered angel, shall, as his own young master, grow up a pretty respectable devil. Similarly, the white child must be, by the change of position, endowed with all the virtues and graces of the subject race. Anybody can see that it is hard lines for the writer. One can fancy him apologizing beforehand to the little negro for the violence he is compelled to do his character. He makes the plunge and the double transformation boldly. It is more than a little amusing, though, to one who knows experimentally the autocracy of a "black mammy," to read how Roxy, after the exchange, was surprised to see how steadily and surely the awe which had kept her tongue reverent, her manner humble towards her young master, was transferring itself to her speech and manner toward the usurper. Roxy must have been a mighty exceptional character if she did not spank her charges with natural and noble impartiality, whether they were white or black.

She had christened her own child "Valet de Chambre—no surname. Slaves hadn't the privilege." That is some more news to us who owned them, and who keep lively memories of their pride in their surnames; and how tenaciously, after freedom came, they clung to the appellations whereunto they felt themselves born. In founding their families under the new conditions, it was often laughable to see the leaning to aristocracy. In more than one case within my own knowledge, negroes abandoned the names of the living masters, in favor of that of the master's grandfather from whom they were inherited and to whose family they leaned because of its greater distinction. Truly, if they had had no privilege of surnames, there must have been confusion worse confounded in the era '65.

Time and patience fail alike in bringing to book all such matters here set down. Suffice it to say that, first to last the whole recital is unveracious. If it is meant for caricature, the result is the same as would come from exaggerating the ears, nose, and coat-tails of a Bowery tough, and labelling the picture "Ward McAllister." So far as I know, all that the South, either "Old" or "New," has ever done to Mr. Clemens has been to buy his books, when it had precious little money to buy anything, and to set him upon a pedestal as the very prince of humorists. Wherefore, I quite fail to comprehend why it pleases him to villify us as he is doing in this book.

Let me add that I am no bigot in behalf of mine own people. Some have foibles, faults galore, even sins of deepest dye. There are knaves and fools among them—uncouth fellows not a few. So much I readily grant. I will go further and admit that there is that in the social constitution which, rightly handled, might give a humorist scope to add largely to the gaiety of nations. But take them by little and large, they are neither sordid nor stolid, nor lacking in the finer parts of humanity. All this Mr. Clemens makes them out to be. And because he is who he is, a large part of our common country will take his circus-posters for accurate photographs of life and people in the South. Solely for that reason, I make, here and now, my protest against this injustice. I can not comfort myself with the belief that he has sinned ignorantly against half his countrymen. His experience has been too wide, his intelligence is too keen, for that. He is, it seems to me, thus unveracious for revenue only. He has found out the sort of book that sells best. It is not that which speaks the truth as it is, but as the reader wishes to believe it to be. Beside, it is only against a background so lurid as the one he has manufactured that the action of his story could possibly take place. As an occasional dabbler in fiction, I recognize the strength of that necessity. But I can not hold that it is sufficient to justify the falsification of all historic conditions. A long time ago, I read a speech of Mr. Clemens in which he said, at the outset, that he had chosen something he knew nothing whatever about so as to be quite unhampered by facts. To judge from "Pudd'nhead Wilson," he has contracted a habit of being unhampered by facts,—a habit which seems to grow stronger with age.

"The Tales He Couldn't Tell": Mark Twain, Race and Culture at the Century's End: A Social Context for *Pudd'nhead Wilson*[1]

Shelley Fisher Fishkin

When Mark Twain began *Adventures of Huckleberry Finn* he thought he was writing another boys' book, a simple sequel to *Tom Sawyer*; but his story was soon hijacked by a black slave and a white boy on a quest for freedom. When Twain began the book that would end up as *Pudd'nhead Wilson* he thought he was writing a book about Angelo and Luigi, Italian Siamese twins with two heads, four arms and one torso; but *that* story was soon hijacked by a man who was one-thirty-second part black and a slave who had hoped to set him free. Two of the most powerful and most powerfully flawed books in American literary history were the result.

Where did these upstarts come from, the black man who "stole" his own freedom, and the man who looked white but whom society deemed black? And why did Twain let them crash their way into his plots and unleash, as he put it himself, "no end of confusion and annoyance"?[2]

Critics have focused on the composition history of both books to explain the roots of their markedly schizophrenic structures.[3] But understanding the order in which Twain put the pieces of his books together still doesn't explore the implications of the fact that both books were "taken over" by story lines that focused on black/white issues in the ante-

Reprinted from *Essays in Arts and Sciences* 19 (May 1990): 1–26.

bellum South. When Twain allowed his initial stories to be usurped by this new and troublesome theme, the result, in both books (as both Twain and the critics agree), was a certain amount of narrative chaos. That confusion, however, was not simply the result of a second story line bumping up against Twain's original plans. It was, I would argue, the subliminal subject of the second story line which helps account for the particularly thorny and unresolved contradictions and ironies that characterize the final versions of both books. That subliminal subject is American race relations, not in the time in which the books were set, but during the period in which they were written.

Sometimes a work of art can be a prism through which a historical moment becomes refracted into its constituent parts in stunning clarity and brilliant color. Elsewhere I have argued that *Adventures of Huckleberry Finn* performs this prismatic function for the period during which Twain wrote it, 1876 through the early 1880s.[4] Here I will examine the ways in which *Pudd'nhead Wilson* encodes and reflects the contradictions, tensions and ironies that characterized American race relations from the late 1880s through the turn of the century.

The social, legal, cultural and political history of American race relations immediately before, during and after Twain's publication of this book in 1894 is confusing and ironic. At the same time as black America produced writers, artists, composers, athletes, businessmen, and educators of the first rank, white America grew obsessed with asserting black inferiority, and with ensuring—legally and extralegally—the separation of the races. And as the project of ensuring the separation of the races was elaborated more and more meticulously in a byzantine code of laws, the possibility of actually delineating those sharp lines between black and white grew increasingly elusive: for despite white America's obsession with racial "purity," America was becoming an increasingly mulatto nation.

Against this backdrop, it is clearly folly to ascribe the difficulty of making sense of Twain's *Pudd'nhead Wilson* simply to botched artistry on Twain's part. Yes, the book is flawed, frustratingly so, sometimes veering in one direction, sometimes in another. But how, one might ask, could a book dealing with race and identity, written in this bizarre and contradiction-filled period, by a writer of Twain's sensitivity and moral awareness, be otherwise? An examination of the history of American race relations at the century's end can shed new light on the complexities of this puzzling novel; and, in turn, this deeply flawed book can illuminate the chapter of history that informs it in new and fruitful ways.

Part I of this essay will limn the history of American race relations in the period during and immediately preceding and following the book's publication. Part II will explore the ways in which the novel encodes and reflects that historical moment. Part III will compare Twain's treatment of these issues with that of several of his African-American contemporaries.

I

The late 1880s through the turn of the century was a period when white America made unprecedented moves to consolidate its power: it repeatedly stripped black Americans—legally and illegally—of hard-won rights, and took a myriad of steps—often violent ones—to make sure that the canvas on which black Americans could paint their lives was as constricted as possible.

Historians C. Vann Woodward, Rayford Logan, John Hope Franklin, George Frederickson, Joel Williamson, August Meier and others have laid out the details of the web of legal and illegal maneuvers through which white supremacy installed itself during this period, and have probed some of the reasons why such raw and open hostility was directed against blacks in both the South and the North, where liberals of every stripe beat a quick retreat from the race issue.[5] "All along the line," C. Vann Woodward notes, "signals were going up to indicate that the Negro was an approved object of aggression."

> These "permissions-to-hate" came from sources that had formerly denied such permission. They came from the federal courts in numerous opinions, from Northern liberals eager to conciliate the South, from Southern conservatives who had abandoned their race policy of moderation in their struggle against the Populists, from the Populists in their mood of disillusionment with their former Negro allies, and from a national temper suddenly expressed by imperialistic adventures and aggressions against colored peoples in distant lands.[6]

The hatred took many forms; two particularly common ones were the rise of "Jim Crow" laws and lynching. The 1890s saw the passage of the country's first segregation statutes, or "Jim Crow" laws. While these laws initially applied only to public transportation, eventually they would mandate the creation of separate water fountains, waiting rooms, parks, residences, textbooks, telephone booths, ticket windows, and bibles for witnesses in courtrooms.[7] As C. Vann Woodward observed, "the segregation code. . . lent the sanction of law to a racial ostracism that extended to churches and schools, to housing and jobs, to eating and drinking. Whether by law or by custom, that ostracism eventually extended to virtually all forms of public transportation, to sports and recreations, to hospitals, orphanages, prisons, and asylums, and, ultimately to funeral homes, morgues and cemeteries."[8]

The number of blacks killed by lynch mobs across the nation increased dramatically in the 1890s.[9] The lynchings were most often prompted by allegations of attempted rape of white women by black men, charges about which a writer like Ida B. Wells expressed acidic and eloquent skepticism.[10] Before 1889, as Joel Williamson has noted, lynching "was a Western and all-white phenomenon, often having to do with bands of cattle rustlers."[11] Starting in 1889, however, and continuing through the 1890s, "lynching became a special Southern occurrence in which black men were the special victims."[12]

> The recession of the late 1880s and the depression of the 1890s also produced profound psychological effects. Southern whites had been very much taken by sex and family roles prescribed in the Victorian era. Men saw themselves as the providers and protectors in their families. As the economic world constricted, men found themselves less and less able to provide for their women in the accustomed style, and there seemed to be no promise of an end to the decline. . . . It seems fully possible that the rage against the black beast rapist was a kind of psychic compensation. If white men could not provide for their women materially as they had done before, they could certainly protect them from a much more awful threat—the outrage of their purity, and hence their piety, by black men.[13]

Lynching, as George Frederickson had observed, "represented an ultimate sociological method of racial control and repression."[14] More than three times as many blacks were lynched in 1892 as had been lynched in any year during the previous decade. Throughout the 1890s an average of 110 blacks were lynched each year.[15] Despite these horrendous figures, efforts to pass anti-lynching legislation in Congress came to naught.

Even academic "scholars" of the day reflected the deterioration in race relations, producing books with titles such as *The Negro, A Menace to American Civilization*.[16] African-American novelist Charles W. Chesnutt said in 1903 that "the rights of Negroes are at a lower ebb than at any time during the thirty-five years of their freedom, and the race prejudice more intense and uncompromising."[17]

In the 1890s then, laws designed to separate white from black proliferated. And what could not be done within the law was accomplished extralegally by lynch mobs. The price one paid for the color of one's skin was higher than ever before; during the last two decades of the century it cost over twenty-five-hundred African-Americans their lives. At the same time, however, it was becoming more and more difficult to separate white from black on a practical level, for America was becoming an increasingly mulatto nation.

This increase was quite predictable, and could be explained, to a large extent, by simple arithmetic, the legacy of generations of miscegenation. That white slaveholders had fathered thousands of mulatto children who had now grown to adulthood and were producing light-skinned children of their own was a tacitly acknowledged, if distasteful, fact of life in the South; the migration patterns meant that light-skinned blacks were increasingly seen in the North, and that blacks who could pass for white were liable to appear anywhere, North or South, wreaking havoc on the bold lines of demarcation drawn by Southerners and Northerners alike to keep the races apart.

The United States, unlike many other racially mixed societies, classified anyone with a black or mulatto ancestor going back two, three or four generations as "black." Reasonable citizens had attempted to challenge this classification scheme for many years. In 1865, for example, P.T. Barnum gave a speech in the Connecticut legislature in support of the idea of striking the word "white" from the clause that defined voter qualifications in the state constitution: "The word 'white' in the Constitution cannot be strictly and literally construed," Barnum said,

> The opposition expresses great love for the white blood. Will they let a mulatto vote half the time, a quadroon three quarters, and an octoroon seven-eighths of the time? If not, why not? Will they enslave seven-eighths of a white man because one-eighth is not caucasian? Is this democracy? Shall not the majority seven control the minority one? . . ."[18]

Despite efforts like this to point up the ironies and absurdities that it engendered, the rigid "descent rule" classification scheme (mandating that "all descendants of mixed unions" get classed "with their black progenitors"[19]) remained largely intact throughout the nineteenth and much of the twentieth century. Scholars have had trouble coming up with a satisfying explanation for why this should have been so. In his book *White Supremacy: A Comparative Study in American and South African History*, George Frederickson has noted, for example, that "one of the major challenges for scholars of comparative race relations has been to explain the unique 'descent rule' that has been the principal basis of racial classification in the United States."[20]

The fiction of "racial purity"—the notion that it was, in fact, possible to divide society into "white" and "black"—remained the precious tenet which underlay the enormously cumbersome workings of the segregation laws. While white society tried to secure the dividing line between black and white through the courts and the law on the one hand, and through mob terror on the other, the population of Americans of mixed blood was increasing geometrically.

In addition to the rise of segregation laws and the increased mixing of the races, and despite the enormous obstacles in their paths, in the late 1880s and 1890s, African-Americans made impressive forays into literature, painting, music, journalism, economics, education, theater and sports. African Americans may have been forced to ride at the back of the bus and sleep on the "wrong" side of town, but that didn't stop them from writing stories for the *Atlantic Monthly*, building businesses, founding newspapers, winning boxing championships and horse-races, and publishing eloquent and accomplished books of fiction, non-fiction and poetry.

In 1886 Charles W. Chesnutt's story "The Goophered Grapevine" was published in the prestigious *Atlantic Monthly*. This was the first time a work of fiction by a black author reached a large white audience. In 1899 Houghton-Mifflin published two collections of Chesnutt's short stories, *The Conjure Woman* and *The Wife of His Youth, and Other Stories of the Color Line*, and in 1900 Chesnutt published his novel *The House Behind the Cedars*. Other literary achievements abounded as well: In 1892 Anna Julia Cooper published her eloquent book, *A Voice From The South* and in 1893 Paul

Laurence Dunbar published his first collection of poetry, *Oak and Ivy*, followed by *Majors and Minors* in 1895, which received a favorable, full-page review by William Dean Howells in *Harper's Weekly*. His *Lyrics of a Lowly Life* won national attention in 1896. With African-American literacy rising constantly, scores of African-American periodicals—newspapers, magazines, and literary and cultural journals—came into being. By 1898 there were one hundred thirty six weekly papers, three daily papers, eleven school papers, two quarterly reviews, and a monthly cultural journal.[21]

There were milestones in music, too: George W. Chadwick's Second Symphony was published in 1886, the first symphonic work using African-American folksongs; in 1892 Sisseretta Jones, an African-American singer, was invited to perform at the White House. African-Americans entered sports, as well: In 1890 George Dixon won the world bantamweight boxing championship, holding the title through 1892. In 1890 Pike Barns, an African-American jockey, won the Belmont and Alabama Stakes and Isaac Murphy, another African-American jockey, won the Kentucky Derby.[22]

In economics and business, there was progress: Thomy Lafon, a free black tycoon from New Orleans, worth half a million dollars at his death, had "contributed so much to the development of the city that in 1893 the State Legislature ordered a bust of him to be carved and set up in some public institution in New Orleans."[23] By 1891 in Virginia's sixteen major cities and towns, African-Americans owned over three million dollars worth of land, over a third of the total value of land owned. By 1900 nearly a quarter of America's African-American population owned their own homes. African-American entrepreneurs ran banks, drugstores, mining companies, and assorted other businesses. The African-American professional class had increased dramatically as well: in 1900 there were more than 21,000 teachers, more than fifteen thousand preachers, nearly two thousand doctors, three hundred journalists, and some seven hundred lawyers. There were over 2000 actors and showmen, 236 artists, sculptors and

"The Tales He Couldn't Tell"

art teachers, nearly 4000 musicians and music teachers, over 200 photographers, and some fifty architects, designers, draftsmen and inventors.[24]

There were milestones in education, too: In 1894 Harvard awarded a Ph.D. to an African-American student for the first time, a young man named W.E.B. Du Bois. His dissertation, *The Suppression of the African Slave Trade*, was soon published as a book. By 1900 more than 2000 African-Americans had college degrees.[25]

One would think that even the most die-hard "Redeemer" would be stumped to justify segregating some of the culture's finest artists, writers, musicians, businessmen, educators and athletes from the general populace on the grounds of their supposed inferiority—but racism has never been known for its rationality. Any individuals willing to open their eyes and look around them could see black Americans equalling and at times surpassing their white fellow citizens at the most complex and highly skilled endeavors. Clearly they could achieve whatever white America could achieve if they were given the opportunity. To an American aware of even a small portion of these diverse and impressive achievements, the ideology of inherent racial inferiority would have begun to ring increasingly hollow. It did for Mark Twain, whose skepticism about the supposed "superiority" of the white race would erode even further as he watched white nations brutally impose their brand of "civilization" on non-white peoples around the globe. Many of Twain's short, dark later works—"To the Person Sitting in the Darkness," for example—come out of this frame of mind.

II

What do these highly discordant elements add up to—the increased degradation and persecution of blacks coupled with increased achievement, progress and success of blacks? Or the rapidly increasing presence of blacks so light-skinned they didn't look black at all at a time when legislatures and courts tried to draw more sharply than ever the lines of demarcation between black and white? They add up to a confused and bitterly divided culture at war against itself, a society ready to sacrifice its ideals, its rational self-interest, and its prospects for a nonviolent future on a shaky altar of bigotry, hatred and racial pride.

Most of Twain's white contemporaries on the literary scene during the last two decades of the nineteenth century, both Northerners and Southerners, were content to ignore or sidestep these complicated issues when they addressed the subject of race and American culture in their fiction.[26] One looks in vain for any sense of tragedy or irony in the work of Joel Chandler Harris or Thomas Nelson Page, for example. Writers of the "plantation school" like Page offered a highly distorted view of what freedom meant to African-Americans. As Sterling Brown has noted: "Slavery was to be shown as not slavery at all, but a happy state best suited for an inferior, childish but lovable race. In this normal condition, the Negro was shown thriving. Then came his emancipation, which the better class of Negroes did not want, and which few could understand or profit by. Freedom meant anarchy. Only by restoring control (euphemism for tenant farming, sharecropping, black codes, enforced labor, segregation and all other ills of the new slavery) could equilibrium in the South, so important to the nation, be achieved."[27]

Theodore Gross has observed,

> the Southern authors' characterization of the Negro proved to be immensely popular. In the 1880s and 1890s such Northern writers as Frank Stockton, Harriet Spofford, and Constance Fenimore Woolson accepted the Southern version of Reconstruction; and the admirable freedman of Reconstruction was the devoted Negro who recalled his contented existence before the war and who voluntarily remained faithful to his past masters. The favorite formula of Reconstruction authors—Northern and Southern—was one in which the Negro alleviated his ex-master's poverty.[28]

In works by white authors written in the 1880s and 1890s that were set before the Civil War, Gross notes, most often "the noble Negro. . . refused to attempt freedom under any conditions."[29] The racism of these sentimental works from the 1880s and 1890s pales before the blistering racism of the novels Thomas Dixon would produce between 1902 and 1907.[30] However, in their dogged refusal to write about race and American culture *without* addressing any of the real anguished and contradictory tensions that marked the subject, these writers helped prepare the soil in which Dixon's foul-smelling, noxious plants would later bloom and flourish.

Mark Twain was tilling a different field.

Like many of the "plantation school" writers mentioned above, Twain sets his tale in ante-bellum days. But his ante-bellum tale is shot through with the acid irony, numbing pain and crippling despair that so many African-Americans must have found themselves struggling to overcome in the 1880s and 1890s in the face of lynchings, political intimidation, and social and cultural isolation and ostracism. In place of portraits of contented slaves who wouldn't for a moment attempt freedom, Twain gives us Roxanna, a woman who decides, by the book's third chapter, that death—for herself and her child—is preferable to slavery; it is while she plans her suicide/murder that the novel's plot is set in motion.[31] Twain's is clearly a different moral universe from that inhabited by Thomas Nelson Page. (History, as it happens, would eventually recognize the limitations of Page's world view and the strengths of Twain's. Page is now largely forgotten, while Twain has earned his niche—relatively secure if sometimes slippery—in the canon.)

Twain's Roxanna is one-sixteenth black, and her son is one thirty-second black. Still, as Twain tells us, by a "fiction of law and custom," both Roxanna and her son are black. Were Twain's numbers far-fetched? Perhaps not: as Susan Gillman has pointed out, "as late as 1970, . . . in Louisiana the legal fraction defining blackness was still one-thirty-second 'Negro blood'." "Most southern states," George Frederickson tells us, "were operating in accordance with what amounted to a 'one-drop rule'[32] meaning in effect that a person with any known degree of black ancestry was legally considered a Negro and subject to the full disabilities associated with segregation and disfranchisement."[33] This is precisely the nature of this "fiction of law and custom"—and its significance for society—that Twain's novel explores so pointedly. The everwinding spiral of absurdity that this "fiction" gets us into underlies the post-modern humor produced by Pudd'nhead Wilson himself.

David Wilson's downfall, when he first comes to town, as well as the source of his nickname and the ruin of his career, is a famous remark about a dog. (The story is not original with Twain—but in the context of the novel Twain gives it a new twist.[34]) Twain writes,

> He had just made the acquaintance of a group of citizens when an invisible dog began to yelp and snarl and howl and make himself very comprehensively disagreeable, whereupon young Wilson said, much as one who is thinking aloud:
> "I wish I owned half of that dog."
> "Why?" somebody asked.
> "Because I could kill my half."
> The group searched his face with curiosity, with anxiety even, but found no light there, no expression that they could read. They fell away from him as from something uncanny, and went into privacy to discuss him. One said:
> "'Pears to be a fool."
> "'Pears?' said another. "Is, I reckon you better say."
> "Said he wished he owned half of the dog, the idiot," said a third. "What did he reckon would become of the other half if he killed his half? Do you reckon he thought it would live?"
> "Why, he must have thought it, unless he is the downrightest fool in the world; because if he hadn't thought it, he would have wanted to own the whole dog, knowing that if he killed his half and the other half died, he would be responsible for that half just the same as if he had killed that half instead of his own. Don't it look that way to you, gents?"
> "Yes, it does. If he owned one half of the general dog it would be so; if he owned one end of the dog, and another person owned the other end, it would be so, just the same;

particularly in the first case, because if you kill one half of a general dog, there ain't any man that can tell whose half it was..."

No. 3 said, "well, he's a lummox anyway..."

"I'm with you, gentlemen," said No. 6. "Perfect jackass—yes, and it ain't going too far to say he is a pudd'nhead. If he ain't a pudd'nhead, I ain't no judge, that's all."[35]

"Irony" Twain observes, "was not for these people; their mental vision was not focused for it."[36]

We know from Twain's expressed views on the subject—as in "How to Tell a Story"—that David Wilson is a fine storyteller, too fine for his own good, perhaps. Master of the deadpan style that Twain had perfected, Wilson not only fails to crack a revealing smile during his initial performance, he also fails to let his audience know they've been "taken" for some twenty years hence! His comment is, of course, patently absurd. How can you kill half a dog? The halves are connected, kill a half and you've killed a whole. Any fool can see that. Or can he? Wilson's absurd comment that he would "kill his half" of the dog makes him a marked fool in his community. But aren't his fellow citizens engaged in just such a proposition? As they systematically degrade and destroy that "half" of the people in their land whose skin is the "wrong" color, don't they destroy their own community as well? If they don't within the confines of the book—for the book ends before the Civil War—we may be confident that this sleepy, comfortable, contented slaveholding town will be violently jarred quite shortly.

What if we think of the yelping, invisible "general dog" as the body politic or the country in 1894?[37] From the standpoint of law, custom and a range of other perspectives, the population of the United States in 1894, regardless of the actual numbers in each group, is divided into two parts: white and non-white. These two parts of the general populace together comprise the citizens of the United States of America, the equal citizens of the U.S. in fact, by virtue of the Fourteenth Amendment. Yet despite the fact that they make up an identifiable whole, the law, custom and popular parlance act as if the two parts are not only clearly identifiable, but easily separable: hence the ubiquitous Jim Crow laws designed to segregate black from white. Notwithstanding the fact that "Plessy v. Ferguson" in 1896 inscribed "separate but equal" as the law of the land, any American as clear-sighted as Mark Twain could see that there was nothing "equal" about the treatment black Americans received at the hands of the law and society.[38]

"We have ground the manhood out of them," Twain wrote on Christmas eve in 1885, referring to black people, "& the shame is ours, not theirs, & we should pay for it."[39] Throughout the 1880s and 1890s Twain embraced a variety of means to "pay for it." He paid with money (supporting black students in law school and college, or funding a black painter's apprenticeship in Paris); he paid with service (performing gratis in black churches whenever asked); he paid with his influence (writing publicity blurbs for the Fisk Jubilee Singers' international tour, interceding with President Garfield when Frederick Douglass was about to be dismissed from a Federal post); and he paid with his work—with "A True Story, Repeated Word for Word as I Heard It," with *Adventures of Huckleberry Finn,* and with *Pudd'nhead Wilson.* Twain himself, intensely conscious of the personal and national shame that was the legacy of Slavery, was prompted in the 1880's and 1890's to try, through the range of means cited here, to expand opportunities for black Americans. The majority of his fellow Americans, however, were engaged in a very different effort: as white supremacists garnered greater and greater influence in the North as well as the South, they tried to constrict the horizon of expectations of black Americans every way they could.

Despite the backing they had from the legislatures, the courts, and public opinion, however, the efforts of the white supremacists were doomed to fail. They could try to kill half a dog—but the other half—they themselves, would not escape unaffected.

"The Tales He Couldn't Tell"

Just as Slavery had dehumanized slaveholders as well as slaves in the ante-bellum era, post-war racism took its moral and psychological toll on whites as well as blacks. As Twain's contemporaries passed new Jim Crow laws, revoked rights, ostracized, reviled, insulted, abused and lynched in the 1890's, they thought they were simply killing "half a dog." The project was, of course, absurd: what they were really killing off were their own illegitimate children, the fruits of their own illegitimate power, a part of themselves, their fellow citizens, their country, their country's future.

The sickness of racism—designed to denigrate one group and elevate another—would send an entire nation, not half a nation—into painful, drawn-out convulsions. The violence and destruction of the race riots in the 1890's and at the turn of the century would be followed in the 1960's by the murder of civil rights workers, the blowing up of children in church, the assassination of Martin Luther King, Jr., and the uprisings that wracked so many cities; the legacy of the black underclass shaped by Jim Crow laws at the turn of the century is, unfortunately, all too with us as the end of our own century approaches.

Twain had an abiding affection for Pudd'nheads—and Sap-heads, which is what Huck Finn is called by Tom Sawyer when Huck fails to understand why the genies always do what "whoever rubs the lamp or ring" tells them to do. "Well," says Huck, "I think they are a pack of flatheads for not keeping the palace themselves."

> And what's more—If I was one of them I would see a man in Jericho before I would drop my business and come to him for the rubbing of an old tin lamp. "How you talk, Huck Finn. Why you'd have to come when he rubbed it, whether you wanted to or not." "What, and I as high as a tree and as big as a church? Alright, then: I *would* come; but I lay I'd make that man climb the highest tree there was in the country." "Shucks, it ain't no use to talk to you, Huck Finn. You don't seem to know anything, somehow—perfect sap-head."[40]

Not inculcated, as Tom Sawyer is, with genie lore from *Arabian Nights,* Huck sees no basis for the arbitrary authority the lamp-rubber exercises over a being many times his strength and size.

While Huck nay not make that leap of insight, clearly Twain does: in *Puddn'head Wilson*, so will Roxana. "What has my po' baby done, dat he couldn't have yo' luck," she moaned to her master's baby, as he sleeps not far from her own, "He hain't done noth'n. God was good to you; why warn't he good to him? Dey can't sell *you* down de river."[41] When she makes the fateful decision to switch her own baby with the baby of her master, Roxana is, in fact, to the best of her knowledge at the time, choosing to "keep the palace" herself.

"Sap-heads" and "pudd'nheads" have much in common. Both say things that are dumb or stupid in the eyes of those around them. Both of them seem to be blind to the "obvious." Both implicitly challenge the not-to-be-questioned premises of their peers. But both of them turn out to be more right than wrong: the notion of the genie keeping the palace for himself may be less absurd than Tom Sawyer thinks it is, and the question of killing half a dog holds more significance than the citizens of Dawson's Landing suspect. Twain uses both his famous "sap-head" and his famous "pudd'nhead" as vehicles to show society's assumptions—rather than the characters who question them—to be absurd.

As Twain explores various dimensions of the question of personal identity in *Pudd'nhead Wilson*, he gives heavy weight to the idea of training as the foremost shaper of character. "Training is everything," Pudd'nhead Wilson writes in his Calendar.[42] But is it? On the one hand, Twain traces numerous character traits to precisely the training one had as a child. "Tom got all the petting, Chambers got none. . . In consequence, . . . Tom was 'fractious,' as Roxy called it, and overbearing; Chambers was meek and docile."[43] "In babyhood," we learn, "Tom cuffed and banged and scratched Chambers unrebuked, and Chambers early learned that between meekly bearing it and resenting it, the advantage all lay with the former policy... Outside of the house the two boys were together all through their boyhood... Tom staked (Chambers) with marbles to play 'keeps' with, and then took all the winnings away from him... In the winter season Chambers was on hand, in Tom's worn-out clothes... to drag a sled up the hill for Tom, warmly clad, to ride down on; but he never got a ride himself... He was Tom's patient target when Tom wanted to do some snowballing, but the target couldn't fire back."[44]

Yet despite all his emphasis on "training" on numerous occasions in the book, at other times Twain seems to acquiesce to what seems, at bottom, a racist idea of heredity and environment. The fact that the one "natively vicious" character in the book is Tom, who is one thirty-second part black, has opened Twain, yet again, to the charge of being a racist: why is it that the child with black blood turns out completely immoral and selfish, lacking even the most basic compassion and decency, while his white counterpart is brave, kind, compassionate and generous?[45] Why make Tom such a villain? Why make the white child such a saint?

Critics have suggested several possible answers to this question. In "What Is Man?", as Judith Berzon notes, "Twain argues that man is controlled by the training which is brought to bear upon his inherited characteristics... While Twain's major emphasis is on the power of training, he makes it clear that temperament cannot be ignored. It is the 'disposition you were born with. You can't eradicate your disposition nor any rag of it—you can only put a pressure on it and keep it down and quiet'."[46] Thus Tom's "evil" and Chamber's "goodness." Another critic accounts for Tom's "utterly debased" behavior in terms of character and plot development: he has to be "made as diabolical as he is so that Roxy will be motivated to reveal his identity" and to overcome the force of her maternal affection.[47]

Twain's view on the nature vs. nurture argument in the book is, in fact, inconsistent and confused. But the central explanation for Tom's "native viciousness" may be that which appears in a passage included in Twain's working version of the novel, but deleted, for reasons unknown, before publication. In the Morgan manuscript of *Pudd'nhead Wilson*, Twain has Tom consider his motivation in refusing the duel. We are told that

> what was high came from either blood, & was the monopoly of neither color; but that which was base was the white blood in him debased by the brutalizing effects of a long-drawn heredity of slave-owning, with the habit of abuse which the possession of irresponsible power always created & perpetuates, by a law of human nature.[48]

In short, if heredity plays any role in creating the monster that is Tom, it is the white blood that has debased him, not the black. When a cadet who was one-sixteenth black was expelled from West Point in the 1880s for "conduct unbecoming an officer and a gentleman," William Dean Howells recalled Twain's caustic reactions to the proceedings: "The man was fifteen parts white, but 'Oh yes,' Clemens said with bitter irony, 'It was the one part black that undid him. It made him a 'nigger' and incapable of being a gentleman. It was to blame for the whole thing.'"[49] As the passage from the Morgan manuscript of *Pudd'nhead Wilson* suggests, if any blood were to blame for the cadet's ungentlemanly conduct, the white blood, and not the black, was the more likely suspect as far as Twain was concerned.

In *Pudd'nhead Wilson*, training teaches Chambers, a white child raised as a black slave, to be meek, docile, and self-effacing, to always expect less than equal treatment, to bear with equanimity being robbed, exploited, cuffed and pelted with snowballs by the boy he thinks is his master. Training teaches Tom, a black child raised as a white master, to be arrogant and overbearing, deceitful, cowardly, dishonest, and ready to rob, steal, cuff and pelt his way through life. The book doesn't make the argument that a black child raised as a white will be as good as a white: it argues that a black raised as a white will be as bad as a white. Whether one focused on heredity or on environment, then, the "master race", in Twain's view, contained ample seeds of its own undoing.

III

Twain's two great anti-racist works of fiction, *Adventures of Huckleberry Finn* and *Pudd'nhead Wilson* may be read as incisive commentaries on the time in which they were written, the 1870s, 1880s and 1890s. Why did Twain choose to set both books in the ante-bellum era? One reason, of course, was the special pull the time of his own youth had on his imagination. Another reason, however, may be the freedom this remote setting gave him to explore contemporary issues that may have been too threatening to explore directly. (When Twain did explore such issues directly—in "The United States of Lyncherdom," for example—he was likely to censor himself before publication. "I shouldn't have even half a dozen friends left, after it issued from the press," he wrote his editor only days after sending him the proposal for the book about lynchings.[50] Some topics were just too hot to handle.)

The choice Twain made when he set *Adventures of Huckleberry Finn* and *Pudd'nhead Wilson* in ante-bellum America was not unlike that made by the African-American writer Paul Laurence Dunbar in the virtuoso poem he wrote in 1896, "An Ante-Bellum Sermon." Just as Dunbar himself tells a story ostensibly set in slave times to offer truths about the 1890s, the preacher in the poem tells a story set in Biblical times to tell truths about the time in which he and his parishioners live, truths too dangerous to tell straight-out. The preacher's—and Dunbar's—strategy is highly effective, as these excerpts reveal:

> ... 'Now ole Pher'oh, down in Egypt,
>   Was de wuss man evah bo'n,
> An' he had de Hebrew chillun
>   Down dah wukin' in his c'n;
> Well de Lawd got tiahed o' his foolin'

> An' sez he: "I'll let him know—
> Look hyeah, Moses, go tell Pher'oh
> Fu'to let dem chillun go."
> ... But fu' feah some one mistakes me,
> I will pause right hyeah to say,
> Dat I'm still a-preachin' ancient,
> I ain't talkin' 'about today.
> ... So you see de Lawd's intention,
> Evah sence de worl' began,
> Was dat His almighty freedom
> Should belong to evah man,
> But I think it would be bettah
> Ef I'd pause agin to say,
> Dat I'm talkin' 'bout ouah freedom
> In a Bibleistic way....[51]

Here Dunbar, like the preacher in his poem, preached "ancient" to talk about "today." In other poems, however, such as "The Haunted Oak" and "We Wear the Mask," he wrote about contemporary problems—the physical and psychic toll taken by racism in the 1890s—in all their stark, unfiltered brutality.[52]

Twain, by way of contrast, never left off "preachin' ancient" in his published work of the 1880s and 1890s. Like the preacher in Dunbar's poem, he was always free to claim, "I ain't talkin' 'bout today." His decision to talk about freedom in an "ante-bellum way," may have insulated Twain from some of the more blatant hostility of his white contemporaries. It also may have prevented him from "connecting" intellectually, emotionally, and artistically, with black readers who might have responded to his work more intensely had he been willing to train his brilliant ironic vision on the contemporary scene. Despite his intense interest in the lives of black Americans, and despite the incisiveness with which he anatomized the dynamics of racism in his work, throughout his life he remained embedded, as an artist and as a man, in a world that was essentially white. If he read the African-American writers who were working through the same sorts of questions he was, often in the same literary forms that he himself was using, Twain unfortunately left us no record of the fact. Some interesting contrasts, however, emerge when one examines how two of Twain's African-American contemporaries, W.E.B. DuBois and Pauline Hopkins, handled some familiar themes.

The relationship Twain paints between Chambers and Tom brings to mind the story of a different pair of childhood playmates, one black and one white, who come of age in the years after Reconstruction in a story by W.E.B. Du Bois called "Of the Coming of John."[53] Each of the boys leaves home to go to school. The black boy, who had worked as a field-hand, finds the world of learning that opens up to him intoxicating: He

> wandered alone over the green campus peering through and beyond the world of men into a world of thought. . . . He caught terrible colds lying on his back in the meadows of nights, trying to think about the solar system; he had grave doubts as to the ethics of the Fall of Rome, and strongly suspected the Germans of being thieves and rascals, despite his textbooks; he pondered long over every new Greek word, and wondered why this meant that and why it couldn't mean something else, and how it must have felt to think all these things in Greek.[54]
>
> As he passed from preparatory school to college, he looked now for the first time sharply about him, and wondered he had seen so little before. He grew slowly to feel almost for the first time the Veil that lay between him and the white world; he first noticed now the oppression that had not seemed oppression before, differences that erstwhile seemed natural, restraints and slights that in his boyhood days had gone unnoticed or been greeted with a laugh. He felt angry now when men did not call him "Mister," he clenched his hands at the "Jim Crow" cars, and chafed at the color line that hemmed in him and his. . . Daily he found himself shrinking from the choked and narrow life of his native town. And yet he always planned to go back.[55]

His former playmate, a judge's son, goes to Princeton, where he learns the arrogance with which one must occupy one's rightful place in the ruling class. When he finds himself behind a black man on a ticket line for the opera, he entertains his date with the remark, "Be careful, you must not lynch the colored gentleman simply because he's in your way." He later "flushes to the roots of his hair" when the "Negro he had stumbled over in the hallway" turns out to be seated on the other side of his date in the reserved orchestra chairs. The music of the opera stirs the black man beyond anything he has known. "A deep longing swelled in all his heart," Du Bois writes, "to rise with that clear music out of the dirt and dust of that low life that held him prisoned and befouled... Who had called him to be the slave and butt of all? And if he had called, what right had he to call when a world like this lay open before men?" The usher soon interrupts his reverie to insist that he move to the colored seating area, much to the relief of the white man seated in his row, who didn't recognize his childhood friend.

Both young men return to their home town, each a conquering hero for his respective race. But the die is cast. The black man preaches education, sparks his people, opens a school, tries to open to others the world that was opened to him. His behavior threatens the white establishment. "This school is closed," the Judge announces to the stunned students that cram the rickety shanty where the black schoolmaster is teaching them to read. "You children can go home and get to work. The white people of Altamaha are not spending their money on black folks to have their heads crammed with impudence and lies. Clear out! I'll lock the door myself."[56]

The story races to a harrowing and tragic end: the promising young black scholar sees the Princeton n'er-do'well, the Judge's son, attempting to rape his sister. He strikes him mortally to stop the rape, and then drowns himself. The boldest visions and noblest dreams fall victim to one small battle in a large race war, devastating in its effects on white and black alike.

One wonders what Twain would have thought of this story, had he read it. Surely he would have been struck by its resonances with the story he himself had written: two childhood playmates, one black and one white, each destined for a very different fate. As he read Du Bois' lyrical and moving description of the black boy's growing intellectual excitement Twain might have wondered if these kinds of thoughts had ever passed through the mind of A.W. Jones, a black student whose education at Lincoln University Twain had funded. Twain would have found in Du Bois' description of the white boy's arrogance and ill manners support for his own increasingly cynical views about his race.

In Du Bois' story, which is set in the 1880s or 1890s, both of the childhood playmates are killed by the spiral of tragic events set off by ingrained patterns of racism. In *Pudd'nhead Wilson*, both of the childhood playmates emerge alive: damaged, no doubt, but very much alive. Du Bois' story is ultimately much darker than Twain's; tragedy, not irony, is the dominant mode.

Similar differences obtain, as well, between Twain's "A True Story, Repeated Word for Word as I Heard It," which appeared in *The Atlantic Monthly* in 1874, and Pauline Hopkins's story, "The Test of Manhood," which was published in *The Colored American* in 1902.[57] Like Twain in "A True Story," Pauline Hopkins in "The Test of Manhood" brings about the reunion of a black mother and son who have been separated for many years. In Twain's story the post-war reunion of mother and son is fortuitous and joyful: whatever pain there is in the story comes through in the mother's memories of the auction block, the terror of separation, the degradations of slavery. In Hopkins's story, however, the reunion is itself frought with searing pain and anguished decisions. The son had been "passing" as white, and acknowledging his mother means giving up his white fiancee, his job, his life, the person he has been so happy to "become." That is his "test of manhood"—and he passes. The "happy ending," for Pauline Hopkins, is thus bought with enormous psychic and emotional pain.

Shelley Fisher Fishkin

* * * *

As it encodes and reflects the history that shaped it, *Pudd'nhead Wilson* illuminates that history in fresh and memorable ways. The book engages our imagination both in spite of its flaws, and because of them. It challenges us to re-examine the moral underpinnings not only of Twain's society, but of our own. The book's greatest strengths—and its greatest weaknesses—stem from Twain's determination to grapple with the complex problem of American race relations. Nine years after *Pudd'nhead Wilson* appeared, Twain's insistence on the centrality and importance of this issue would be echoed by W.E.B. Du Bois.

In his preface to his magisterial 1903 book, *The Souls of Black Folk*, W.E.B. Du Bois wrote, "the problem of the Twentieth Century is the problem of the color line." On that point, Mark Twain most likely would have agreed. In his later years in such short works of nonfiction as "To the Person Sitting in the Darkness," and diatribes against racist imperialism in the Congo or the Philippines, Twain raged at the gall of a race that claimed to have a monopoly on civilization while exporting the most heinous brutality around the globe. In fragments of unfinished fiction, such as the novel "Which Was It?", Twain showed a prescient awareness of some of the forms that pent-up rage could take if the degradations of racism went unchecked.[58] Twain's disgust with his race was deep-going and well-founded, and his prognosis for America was not good. There was a long road to travel before any real change or progress could take place and Twain knew it wouldn't happen in his lifetime. "The shame," as Twain put it in 1885, "is ours."

Notes

1. An earlier version of this essay was presented as a lecture at the Mark Twain Memorial, Hartford, Ct. in 1989. I am greatly

indebted to Jeffrey Rubin-Dorsky and David E. E. Sloane for having taken the time to offer astute criticism and helpful editorial suggestions as I revised this material for publication.

2. When Tom Driscoll's story took over the story of the Siamese twins, Twain writes, he was left with "not one story, but two stories tangled together; and they obstructed and interrupted each other at every turn and created no end of confusion and annoyance." Mark Twain, *The Tragedy of 'Pudd'nhead Wilson' and the Comedy 'Those Extraordinary Twins'* (Hartford: American Publishing Company, 1894), p. 311.

3. In the hands of a talented critic like Hershel Parker, such an analysis is illuminating and compelling. See, for example, Hershel Parker, "*Pudd'nhead Wilson*: Jack-leg Author, Unreadable Text, and Sense-Making Critics," in *Flawed Texts and Verbal Icons: Literary Authority in American Fiction* (Evanston: Northwestern University Press), 1984, pp. 115–146. Other worthwhile studies of the composition history of either *Huckleberry Finn* or *Pudd'nhead Wilson* include: Walter Blair, "When Was Huckleberry Finn Written?", *American Literature*, 30 (March 1958): 1–25; Jeffrey Steinbrink, "Who Wrote *Huckleberry Finn*? Mark Twain's Control of the Early Manuscript" in *One Hundred Years of Huckleberry Finn*, ed. Robert Sattelmeyer and J. Donald Crowley (Columbia: University of Missouri Press, 1985), pp. 85–105; Victor Doyno, "*Adventures of Huckleberry Finn*: The Growth from Manuscript to Novel," in *One Hundred Years of Huckleberry Finn*, pp.106–116; Daniel Morley McKeithan, "The Morgan Manuscript of Mark Twain's *Pudd'nhead Wilson*,' *Essays and Studies on American Language and Literature*, No. 12 (Cambridge: Harvard University Press, 1961), pp. 1–64. Susan Gillman's fascinating essay "Racial Identity in *Pudd'nhead Wilson*" combines a discussion of the book's composition history with a sophisticated awareness of a number of the complex racial issues that intertwine with that history. See Susan Gillman, *Dark Twins: Imposture and Identity in Mark Twain's America* (Chicago: University of Chicago Press, 1989), pp. 53–95.

4. Shelley Fisher Fishkin, "'Smashed All to Flinders': *Huckleberry Finn* and the Breakdown of Reconstruction," in Fishkin, *The Stories He Couldn't Tell: Mark Twain and Race*, forthcoming, Oxford University Press. See also Shelley Fisher Fishkin, "Mark Twain and the Risks of Irony," in *Twain/Stowe Sourcebook: Curriculum Resource Materials for the Study of Mark Twain and Harriet Beecher Stowe*, ed. Elaine Cheesman and Earl French (Hartford: Mark Twain Memorial and Stowe-Day Foundation, 1989), pp. 49–52.

5. C. Vann Woodward, *The Strange Career of Jim Crow* (New York: Oxford University Press, 1955) and, also, *The Burden of Southern History* (New York: Vintage/Random House, 1960); Rayford W. Logan, *The Betrayal of the Negro: From Rutherford B. Hayes to Woodrow Wilson* (originally published as *The Negro in American Life and Thought: The Nadir, 1877–1901*) (London: Collier-Macmillan, 1965); John Hope Franklin, *From Slavery to Freedom: A History of Negro Americans*, third edition (New York: Alfred A. Knopf, 1967); George M. Frederickson, *The Black Image in the White Mind: The Debate on Afro-American Character and Destiny, 1817–1914* (New York: Harper & Row, 1971); Joel Williamson, *A Rage for Order: Black-White Relations in the American South Since Emancipation* (New York: Oxford University Press, 1986); August Meier, *Negro Thought in America 1880–1915: Racial Ideologies in the Age of Booker T. Washington* (Ann Arbor: University of Michigan Press, 1963).

6. Woodward, *The Strange Career of Jim Crow*, p. 64.

7. Woodward, *The Strange Career of Jim Crow*, pp. 82–83.

8. Woodward, *The Strange Career of Jim Crow*, p. 8.

9. Woodward, *The Strange Career of Jim Crow*, and Peter M. Bergman, *The Chronological History of the Negro in America* (New York: Harper & Row, 1969).

10. Ida B. Wells, *Crusade for Justice: The Autobiography of Ida B. Wells*, ed. Alfreda M. Duster (Chicago: University of Chicago Press, 1970), pp. 65–66. Ida B. Wells describes several stories like the following, which prompted her to write her famous 1892 editorial on lynchings: "I also had the sworn statement of a mother whose son had been lynched that he had left the place where he worked because of the advances made by the beautiful daughter of the house. The boy had fallen under her spell, and met her often until they were discovered and the cry of rape was raised. A handsome young mulatto, he too had been horribly lynched for 'rape.' It was with these and other stories in mind that last week in May 1892 that I wrote the following editorial: 'Eight Negroes lynched since last issue of the *Free Speech*. Three were charged with killing white men and five with raping white women. Nobody in this section believes the old threadbare lie that Negro men assault white women. If Southern white men are not careful they will over-reach themselves and a conclusion will be reached which will be very damaging to the moral reputation of their women.'" Wells' newspaper office was destroyed by some of the leading citizens of Memphis as a result of this column.

11. Williamson, *A Rage for Order*, p. 84.

12. Williamson, *A Rage for Order*, p. 84.

13. Williamson, *A Rage for Order*, p. 84.

14. Frederickson, *The Black Image in the White Mind*, p. 272.

15. These figures refer only to documented lynchings. Actual figures probably run substantially higher. Bergman, *The Chronological History of the Negro in America*, pp. 303–327.

16. Woodward, *The Strange Career of Jim Crow*, p. 78.

17. Woodward, *The Strange Career of Jim Crow*, pp. 80–81.

18. P.T. Barnum, in a speech before the Connecticut Legislature on May 26, 1865. Quoted in P.T. Barnum, *Struggles and Triumphs, or Forty Years' Record of P. T. Barnum, Written by Himself*, intro. by Roy F. Dribble (New York: Macmillan, 1930), pp. 459–460.

19. George M. Frederickson, *White Supremacy: A Comparative Study in American & South African History* (New York: Oxford University Press, 1981), p. 96; "For attempts by social scientists to explain the North American descent rule, see Marvin Harris, *Patterns of Race in the Americas* (New York, 1964), 56, 79–94; H. Hoetnik, *The Two Variants of Caribbean Race Relations: A Contribution to the Sociology of Segmented Societies* (London, 1967), 46–47; and passim; and idem, *Slavery and Race Relations in the Americas: An Inquiry into Their Nature and Nexus* (New York, 1973), 9–20 and passim," p. 305.

20. Frederickson, *White Supremacy*, p. 96.

21. Bergman, *The Chronological History of the Negro in America*, p. 323.

22. Bergman, *The Chronological History of the Negro in America*, pp. 298, 306.

23. Bergman, *The Chronological History of the Negro in America*, p. 311.

24. Bergman, *The Chronological History of the Negro in America*, pp. 306, 329.

25. Bergman, *The Chronological History of the Negro in America*, p. 329.

26. One exception to this pattern is the work of Albion W. Tourgee, who denounced ideas of white supremacy at political gatherings and in numerous novels, the most famous of which are *A Fool's Errand* (1879) and *Bricks Without Straw* (1880). Tourgee's work, however, tended to be dismissed as "purely propagandist" artistic failures. His books never achieved the widespread popularity of, say, the work of Joel Chandler Harris. (See Theodore Gross, "The Negro in the Literature of Reconstruction," p. 72 and also Brook Thomas, "Tragedies of Race, Training, Birth, and Communities of Competent Pudd'nheads." *American Literary History*, 1.4 (Winter 1989), pp. 754–785). Another exception is William Dean Howells' novel *An Imperative Duty* (1891), which addressed in subtle and sensitive ways contemporary dilemmas faced by the mulatto.

27. Sterling Brown, the American Race Problem as Reflected in American Literature," *Journal of Negro Education*, VIII (July, 1929), p. 282 (quoted in Theodore L. Gross, *op.cit.*, pp. 75–6).

28. Theodore L. Gross, "The Negro in the Literature of Reconstruction", in *Images of the Negro in American Literature*, ed. Seymour L. Gross and John Edward Hardy (Chicago: University of Chicago Press, 1966), p. 77 (reprinted from *Phylon*, 22 (1961), pp. 5–14).

29. Theodore L. Gross, "The Negro in the Literature of Reconstruction", p. 77. Gross notes that while a "condescending attitude toward the Negro is most obvious" in the fiction of Thomas Nelson Page and Thomas Dixon, it also "appears in the stories and novels of Joel Chandler Harris, Mary Murfree, Maurice Thompson, and innumerable minor writers" (p. 73).

30. Thomas Dixon, *The Leopard's Spots* (1902), *The Clansman* (1905), the *The Traitor* (1907). D.W. Griffith's 1915 film, "The Birth of a Nation" was loosely based on Dixon's novel, *The Clansman*. The film, and the three novels, chronicle and glorify the birth of the Ku Klux Klan.

31. Mark Twain, *Pudd'nhead Wilson* (New York: Bantam Books, 1959), pp. 13–18.

32. Susan Gillman, *Dark Twins*, p. 85. (For race classification in Louisiana, Gillman cites Virginia R. Dominguez, *White by Definition: Social Classification in Creole Louisiana* (New Brunswick, N.J., 1986).

33. George Frederickson, *White Supremacy: A Comparative Study in American and South African History* (New York, 1981), p. 130.

34. Twain may well have borrowed the story about H. Bailey, who, when cheated of the proceeds for exhibiting an elephant in which he owned half interest, announced "I am fully determined to shoot my half." P.T. Barnum, *The Life of P.T. Barnum, Written By Himself* (New York: Redfield, 1855) pp. 114–115. Twain kept Barnum's book on his bedside table. Another variant of the story appears in an article titled "Yankee Humor" in the *British Quarterly Review*, vol. 122, Jan.–April 1867, p. 221. In this story a minster asks blessings on "his half" of a negro slave. See David Sloane, *Mark Twain as a Literary Comedian* (Baton Rouge: Louisiana State University Press, 1979), pp. 178–179, ftnt. 12 p. 179. Sloane finds Don Marquis, in his short story "The Mulatto" published in 1916 dealing with the issue in the same terms, with seven drops of the hero's blood out of each eight being caucasian: "The eighth being African, classified him" (Sloane, 182).

35. Mark Twain, *Pudd'nhead Wilson*, pp. 23–4.

36. Mark Twain, *Pudd'nhead Wilson*, p. 28.

37. Evan Carton has explored the notion of the "general dog" as the "body politic" in an ante-bellum context. In his illuminating essay, "*Pudd'nhead Wilson* and the Fiction of Law and Custom" in *American Realism: New Essays*, ed. Eric J. Sundquist (Baltimore: Johns Hopkins University Press, 1982), pp. 82–94, he notes, "if. . . the 'general dog' implicates a body politic, half of whose members are owned by the other half, then it would follow that the possessors could not dispose of their own possessions without destroying themselves" (p. 84).

38. For an insightful and sensitive discussion of related issues see Eric Sundquist, "Mark Twain and Homer Plessy." *Representations*, 24 (Fall 1988): 102–27.

39. SLC to Francis Wayland, December 24, 1885 (in the private collection of Nancy and Richard Stiner). See Edwin McDowell, "From Twain, a Letter on Debt to the Blacks." *New York Times* (14 March 1985), pp. 1, 16.

40. Mark Twain, *Adventures of Huckleberry Finn*, ed., Leo Marx (Indianapolis: Bobbs-Merrill, 1967), p. 25.

41. Mark Twain, *Pudd'nhead Wilson*, p. 13.

42. Mark Twain, *Pudd'nhead Wilson*, p. 26.

43. Mark Twain, *Pudd'nhead Wilson*, p. 20.

44. Mark Twain, *Pudd'nhead Wilson*, p. 21.

45. Judith R. Berzon explores these questions in interesting ways in *Neither White Nor Black: The Mulatto Character in American Fiction* (New York: New York University Press, 1978). See pp. 40–48.

46. Judith Berzon, *Neither White Nor Black*, pp. 44–45.

47. Robert Rowlette, *Mark Twain's Pudd'nhead Wilson: The Development and Design* (Bowling Green, Ohio: Bowling Green University Popular Press, 1971), p. 97, quoted in Berzon, *Neither White Nor Black*, p. 45.

48. Mark Twain, *The Morgan Manuscript of Mark Twain's Pudd'nhead Wilson*, ed. Daniel Morley McKeithan (Cambridge, Mass., 1961), pp. 137–38 quoted in Judith R. Berzon, *Neither White Nor Black*, p. 46.

49. William Dean Howells quoted in James M. Cox, "*Pudd'nhead Wilson:* The End of Mark Twain's American Dream", in Seymour L. Gross and John Edward Hardy, ed., *Images of the Negro in American Literature* (Chicago: University of Chicago Press, 1966), p. 162.

50. Mark Twain, letter to Elisha Bliss, quoted in Everett Emerson, *The Authentic Mark Twain: A Literary Biography of Samuel L. Clemens* (Philadelphia: University of Pennsylvania Press, 1985), p. 238.

51. Paul Laurence Dunbar, "An Ante-Bellum Sermon," in Cleanth Brooks, R.W.B. Lewis and Robert Penn Warren, *American Literature: The Makers and the Making*, Vol. II, p. 1744.

52. Paul Laurence Dunbar, "We Wear the Mask" (1896) and "The Haunted Oak" (1903), in Brooks, Lewis and Warren, *American Literature*, pp. 1743–1744.

53. W.E.B. Du Bois, "Of The Coming of John," in *The Souls of Black Folk* (New York: New American Library, 1969), pp. 245–263.

54. W.E.B. Du Bois, *The Souls of Black Folk*, pp. 249–250.

55. W.E.B. Du Bois, *The Souls of Black Folk*, pp. 250–251.

56. W.E.B. Du Bois, *The Souls of Black Folk*, p. 261.

57. Mark Twain, "A True Story, Repeated Word for Word as I Heard It," *Atlantic Monthly* 34 (November 1874), pp. 591–594. Pauline Hopkins (Sarah A. Allen), "The Test of Manhood." *The Colored American*, 6 (December 1902), pp. 113–119.

58. See Shelley Fisher Fishkin, *The Stories He Couldn't Tell: Mark Twain and Race* (forthcoming, Oxford University Press).

The Later Career of Mark Twain:
The Comedian as a
Cultural Representative

Mark Twain: An Inquiry

William Dean Howells

Two recent events have concurred to offer criticism a fresh excuse, if not a fresh occasion, for examining the literary work of Mr. Samuel L. Clemens, better known to the human family by his pseudonym of Mark Twain. One of these events is the publication of his writings in a uniform edition, which it is to be hoped will remain indefinitely incomplete; the other is his return to his own country after an absence so long as to form a psychological perspective in which his characteristics make a new appeal.

The uniform edition of Mr. Clemens's writings is of that dignified presence which most of us have thought their due in moments of high pleasure with their quality, and high dudgeon with their keeping in the matchlessly ugly subscription volumes of the earlier issues. Yet now that we have them in this fine shape, fit every one, in its elect binding, paper, and print, to be set on the shelf of a gentleman's library, and not taken from it without some fear of personal demerit, I will own a furtive regret for the hideous blocks and bricks of which the visible temple of the humorist's fame was first builded. It was an advantage to meet the author in a guise reflecting the accidental and provisional moods of a unique talent finding itself out; and the pictures which originally illustrated the process were helps to the imagination such as the new uniform edition does not afford. In great part it could

Reprinted from Chapter XI from *My Mark Twain* (NY: Harper & Bros., 1910: 143–62), originally published in *North American Review* CLXXII (February 1901): 836–50.

not retain them, for reasons which the recollection of their uncouth vigor will suggest, but these reasons do not hold in all cases, and especially in the case of Mr. Dan Beard's extraordinarily sympathetic and interpretative pictures for *The Connecticut Yankee in King Arthur's Court.* The illustrations of the uniform edition, in fact, are its weak side, but it can be said that they do not detract from one's delight in the literature; no illustrations could do that; and, in compensation for their defeat, the reader has the singularly intelligent and agreeable essay of Mr. Brander Matthews on Mr. Clemens's work by way of introduction to the collection. For the rest one may acquit one's self of one's whole duty to the uniform edition by reminding the reader that in the rich variety of its inclusion are those renowning books *The Innocents Abroad* and *Roughing It;* the first constructive fiction on the larger scale, *Tom Sawyer* and *Huckleberry Finn;* the later books of travel, *A Tramp Abroad* and *Following the Equator;* the multiplicity of tales, sketches, burlesques, satires, and speeches, together with the spoil of Mr. Clemens's courageous forays in the region of literary criticism; and his later romances, *The Connecticut Yankee, The American Claimant,* and *Joan of Arc.* These complete an array of volumes which the most unconventional reviewer can hardly keep from calling goodly, and which is responsive to the spirit of the literature in a certain desultory and insuccessive arrangement.

So far as I know, Mr. Clemens is the first writer to use in extended writing the fashion we all use in thinking, and to set down the thing that comes into his mind without fear or favor of the thing that went before or the thing that may be about to follow. I, for instance, in putting this paper together, am anxious to observe some sort of logical order, to discipline such impressions and notions as I have of the subject into a coherent body which shall march columnwise to a conclusion obvious if not inevitable from the start. But Mr. Clemens, if he were writing it, would not be anxious to do any such thing. He would take whatever offered itself to his hand out of that mystical chaos, that divine ragbag, which we call the mind, and leave the reader to look after relevancies and sequences for himself. These there might be, but not of that hard-and-fast sort which I am eager to lay hold of, and the result would at least be satisfactory to the author, who would have shifted the whole responsibility to the reader, with whom it belongs, at least as much as with the author. In other words, Mr. Clemens uses in work on the larger scale the method of the elder essayists, and you know no more where you are going to bring up in *The Innocents Abroad* or *Following the Equator* than in an essay of Montaigne. The end you arrive at is the end of the book, and you reach it amused but edified, and sorry for nothing but to be there. You have noted the author's thoughts, but not his order of thinking; he has not attempted to trace the threads of association between the things that have followed one another; his reason, not his logic, has convinced you, or, rather, it has persuaded you, for you have not been brought under conviction. It is not certain that this method is of design with Mr. Clemens; that might spoil it; and possibly he will be as much surprised as any one to know that it is his method. It is imaginable that he pursues it from no wish but to have pleasure of his work, and not to fatigue either himself or his reader; and his method may be the secret of his vast popularity, but it cannot be the whole secret of it. Any one may compose a scrapbook, and offer it to the public with nothing of Mark Twain's good-fortune. Everything seems to depend upon the nature of the scraps, after all; his scraps might have been consecutively arranged, in a studied order, and still have immensely pleased; but there is no doubt that people like things that have at least the appearance of not having been drilled into line. Life itself has that sort of appearance as it goes on; it is an essay with moments of drama in it rather than a drama; it is a lesson, with the precepts appearing haphazard, and not precept upon precept; it is a school, but not always a school-room; it is a temple, but the priests are not always in their sacerdotal robes; sometimes they are eating the sacrifice behind the altar and pouring the libations for the god through the channels of their dusty old throats. An instinct of something chaotic, ironic, empiric in the order of experience seems to have been the inspiration of our humorist's art, and what finally remains with the reader, after all the joking and laughing, is not merely the feeling of having had a mighty good time, but the conviction that he has got the worth of his money. He has not gone through the six hundred pages of *The Innocents Abroad*, or *Following the Equator*, without having learned more of the world as the writer saw it than any but the rarest traveller is able to show for his travel; and possibly, with his average practical American public, which was his first tribunal, and must always be his court of final appeal, Mark Twain justified himself for being so delightful by being so instructive. If this bold notion is admissible, it seems the moment to say that no writer ever imparted information more inoffensively.

But his great charm is his absolute freedom in a region where most of us are fettered and shackled by immemorial convention. He saunters out into the trim world of letters, and lounges across its neatly kept paths, and walks about on the grass at will, in spite of all the signs that have been put up from the beginning of literature, warning people of dangers and penalties for the slightest trespass.

One of the characteristics I observe in him is his singleminded use of words, which he employs as Grant did to express the plain, straight meaning their common acceptance has given them with no regard to their structural significance or their philological implications. He writes English as if it were a primitive and not a derivative language, without Gothic or Latin or Greek behind it, or German and French beside it. The result is the English in which the most vital works of English literature are cast, rather than the English of Milton and Thackeray and Mr. Henry James. I do not say that the English of the authors last named is less than vital, but only that it is not the most vital. It is scholarly and conscious; it knows who its grandfather was; it has the refinement and subtlety of an old patriciate. You will not have with it the widest suggestion, the largest human feeling, or perhaps the loftiest reach of imagination, but you will have the keen joy that exquisite artistry in words can alone impart, and that you will not have in Mark Twain. What you will have in him is a style which is as personal, as biographical as the style of any one who has written, and expresses a civilization whose courage of the chances, the preferences, the duties, is not the measure of its essential modesty. It has a thing to say, and it says it in the word that may be the first or second or third choice, but will not be the instrument of the most fastidious ear, the most delicate and exacting sense, though it will be the word that surely and strongly conveys intention from the author's mind to the reader's. It is the Abraham Lincolnian word, not the Charles Sumnerian; it is American, Western.

Now that Mark Twain has become a fame so world-wide, we should be in some danger of forgetting, but for his help, how entirely American he is, and we have already forgotten, perhaps, how truly Western he is, though his work, from first to last, is always reminding us of the fact. But here I should like to distinguish. It is not alone in its generous humor, with more honest laughter in it than humor ever had in the world till now, that his work is so Western. Any one who has really known the West (and really to know it one must have lived it) is aware of the profoundly serious, the almost tragical strain which is the fundamental tone in the movement of such music as it has. Up to a certain point, in the presence of the mystery which we call life, it trusts and hopes and laughs; beyond that it doubts and fears, but it does not cry. It is more likely to laugh again, and in the work of Mark Twain there is little of the pathos which is supposed to be the ally of humor, little suffusion of apt tears from the smiling eyes. It is too sincere for that sort of play; and if after the doubting and the fearing it laughs again, it is with a suggestion of that resentment which youth feels when the disillusion from its trust and hope comes, and which is the grim second-mind of the West in the presence of the mystery. It is not so much the race-effect as the region-effect; it is not the Anglo-American finding expression, it is the Westerner, who is not more thoroughly the creature of circumstances, of conditions, but far more dramatically their creature than any prior man. He found himself placed in them and under them, so near to a world in which the natural and primitive was obsolete, that while he could not escape them, neither could he help challenging them. The inventions, the appliances, the improvements of the modern world invaded the hoary eld of his rivers and forests and prairies, and, while he was still a pioneer, a hunter, a trapper, he found himself confronted with the financier, the scholar, the gentleman. They seemed to him, with the world they represented, at first very droll, and he laughed. Then they set him thinking, and, as he never was afraid of anything, he thought over the whole field and demanded explanations of all his prepossessions—of equality, of humanity, of representative government, and revealed religion. When they had not their answers ready, without accepting the conventions of the modern world as solutions or in any manner final, he laughed again, not mockingly, but patiently, compassionately. Such, or somewhat like this, was the genesis and evolution of Mark Twain.

Missouri was Western, but it was also Southern, not only in the institution of slavery, to the custom and acceptance of which Mark Twain was born and bred without any applied doubt of its divinity, but in the peculiar social civilization of the older South from which his native State was settled. It would be reaching too far out to claim that American humor, of the now prevailing Western type, is of Southern origin, but without staying to attempt it I will say that I think the fact could be established; and I think one of the most notably southern traits of Mark Twain's humor is its power of seeing the fun of Southern seriousness, but this vision did not come to him till after his liberation from neighborhood in the vaster Far West. He was the first, if not the only, man of his section to betray a consciousness of the grotesque absurdities in the Southern inversion of the civilized ideals in behalf of slavery, which must have them upside down in order to walk over them safely. No American of Northern birth or breeding could have imagined the spiritual struggle of Huck Finn in deciding to help the negro Jim to his freedom, even though he should be forever despised as a negro thief in his native town, and perhaps eternally lost through the blackness of his sin. No Northerner could have come so close to the heart of a Kentucky feud, and revealed it so perfectly, with the whimsicality playing through its carnage, or could have so brought us into the presence of the sardonic comi-tragedy of the squalid little river town where the store-keeping magnate shoots down his drunken tormentor in the arms of the drunkard's daughter, and then cows with bitter mockery the mob that comes to lynch him. The strict religiosity compatible in the Southwest with savage precepts of conduct is something that could make itself known in its amusing contrast only to the native Southwesterner, and the revolt against it is as constant in Mark Twain as the enmity to New England orthodoxy is in Doctor Holmes. But he does not take it with such serious resentment as Doctor Holmes is apt to take his inherited Puritanism, and it may be therefore that he is able to do it more perfect justice, and impart it more absolutely. At any rate, there are no more vital passages in his fiction than those which embody character as it is affected for good as well as evil by the severity of the local Sunday-schooling and church-going.

I find myself, in spite of the discipline I intend for this paper, speaking first of the fiction, which by no means came first in Mark Twain's literary development. It is true that his beginnings were in short sketches, more or less inventive, and studies of life in which he let his imagination play freely; but it was not till he had written *Tom Sawyer* that he could be called a novelist. Even now I think he should rather be called a romancer, though such a book as *Huckleberry Finn* takes itself out of the order of romance and places itself with the great things in picaresque fiction. Still, it is more poetic than picaresque, and of a deeper psychology. The probable and credible soul that the author divines in the son of the town-drunkard is one which we might each own brother, and the art which portrays this nature at first hand in the person and language of the hero, without pose or affectation, is fine art. In the boy's history the author's fancy works realistically to an end as high as it has reached elsewhere, if not higher; and I who like *The Connecticut Yankee in King Arthur's Court* so much have half a mind to give my whole heart to *Huckleberry Finn*.

Both *Huckleberry Finn* and *Tom Sawyer* wander in episodes loosely related to the main story, but they are of a closer and more logical advance from the beginning to the end than the fiction which preceded them, and which I had almost forgotten to name before them. We owe to *The Gilded Age* a type in Colonel Mulberry Sellers which is as likely to endure as any fictitious character of our time. It embodies the sort of Americanism which survived through the Civil War, and characterized in its boundlessly credulous, fearlessly adventurous, unconsciously burlesque excess the period of political and economic expansion which followed the war. Colonel Sellers was, in some rough sort, the American of the day, which already seems so remote, and is best imaginable through him. Yet the story itself was of the fortuitous structure of what may be called the autobiographical books, such as *The Innocents Abroad* and *Roughing it*. Its desultory and accidental character was heightened by the co-operation of Mr. Clemens's fellow-humorist, Charles Dudley Warner, and such coherence as it had was weakened by the diverse qualities of their minds and their irreconcilable ideals in literature. These never combined to a sole effect or to any variety of effects that left the reader very clear what the story was all about; and yet from the cloudy solution was precipitated at least one character which, as I have said, seems of as lasting substance and lasting significance as any which the American imagination has evolved from the American environment.

If Colonel Sellers is Mr. Clemens's supreme invention, as it seems to me, I think that his *Connecticut Yankee* is his highest achievement in the way of a greatly imagined and symmetrically developed romance. Of all the fanciful schemes in fiction it pleases me most, and I give myself with absolute delight to its notion of a keen East Hartford Yankee finding himself, by a retroactionary spell, at the court of King Arthur of Britain, and becoming part of the sixth century with all the customs and ideas of the nineteenth in him and about him. The field for humanizing satire which this scheme opens is illimitable; but the ultimate achievement, the last poignant touch, the most exquisite triumph of the book, is the return of the Yankee to his own century, with his look across the gulf of the ages at the period of which he had been a part and his vision of the sixth-century woman he had loved holding their child in her arms.

It is a great fancy, transcending in aesthetic beauty the invention in *The Prince and the Pauper*, with all the delightful and affecting implications of that charming fable, and excelling the heartrending story in which Joan of Arc lives and prophesies and triumphs and suffers. She is, indeed, realized to the modern sense as few figures of the past have been realized in fiction; and is none the less of her time and of all time because her supposititious historian is so recurrently of ours. After Sellers, and Huck Finn, and Tom Sawyer, and the Connecticut Yankee, she is the author's finest creation; and if he had succeeded in portraying no other woman-nature, he would have approved himself its fit interpreter in her. I do not think he succeeds so often with the nature as with the boy-nature or the man-nature, apparently because it does not interest him so much. He will not trouble himself to make women talk like women at all times; oftentimes they talk too much like him, though the simple, homely sort express themselves after their kind; and Mark Twain does not always write men's dialogue so well as he might. He is apt to burlesque the lighter colloquiality, and it is only in the more serious and most tragical junctures that his people utter themselves with veracious simplicity and dignity. That great, burly fancy of his is always tempting him to the exaggeration which is the condition of so much of his personal humor, but which when it invades the drama spoils the illusion. The illusion renews itself in the great moments, but I wish it could be kept intact in the small, and I blame him that he does not rule his fancy better. His imagination is always dramatic in its conceptions, but not always in its expressions; the talk of his people is often inadequate caricature in the ordinary exigencies, and his art contents itself with makeshift in the minor action. Even in *Huck Finn*, so admirably proportioned and honestly studied, you find a piece of lawless extravagance hurled in, like the episode of the two strolling actors in the flatboat; their broad burlesque is redeemed by their final tragedy—a prodigiously real and moving passage—but the friend of the book cannot help wishing the burlesque was not there. One laughs, and then despises one's self for laughing, and this is not what Mark Twain often makes you do. There are things in him that shock, and more things that we think shocking, but this may not be so much because of their nature as because of our want of naturalness; they wound our conventions rather than our convictions. As most women are more the subjects of convention than men, his humor is not for most women; but I have a theory that, when women like it, they like it far beyond men. Its very excess must satisfy that demand of their insatiate nerves for something that there is enough of; but I offer this conjecture with instant readiness to withdraw it under correction. What I feel rather surer of is that there is something finally feminine in the inconsequence of his ratiocination, and his beautiful confidence that we shall be able to follow him to his conclusion in all those turnings and twistings and leaps and bounds by which his mind carries itself to any point but that he seems aiming at. Men, in fact, are born of women, and possibly Mark Twain owes his literary method to the colloquial style of some far ancestress who was more concerned in getting there, and amusing herself on the way, than in ordering her steps.

Possibly, also, it is to this ancestress that he owes the instinct of right and wrong which keeps him clear as to the conditions that formed him, and their injustice. Slavery in a small Missouri River town could not have been the dignified and patriarchal institution which Southerners of the older

South are fond of remembering or imagining. In the second generation from Virginia ancestry of this sort, Mark Twain was born to the common necessity of looking out for himself, and, while making himself practically of another order of things, he felt whatever was fine in the old and could regard whatever was ugly and absurd more tolerantly, more humorously than those who bequeathed him their enmity to it. Fortunately for him, and for us who were to enjoy his humor, he came to his intellectual consciousness in a world so large and free and safe that he could be fair to any wrong while seeing the right so unfailingly; and nothing is finer in him than his gentleness with the error which is simply passive and negative. He gets fun out of it, of course, but he deals almost tenderly with it, and hoards his violence for the superstitions and traditions which are arrogant and active. His pictures of that old river-town, Southwestern life, with its faded and tattered aristocratic ideals and its squalid democratic realities, are pathetic, while they are so unsparingly true and so inapologetically and unaffectedly faithful.

The West, when it began to put itself into literature, could do so without the sense, or the apparent sense, of any older or politer world outside of it; whereas the East was always looking fearfully over its shoulder at Europe, and anxious to account for itself as well as represent itself. No such anxiety as this entered Mark Twain's mind, and it is not claiming too much for the Western influence upon American literature to say that the final liberation of the East from this anxiety is due to the West, and to its ignorant courage or its indifference to its difference from the rest of the world. It would not claim to be superior, as the South did, but it could claim to be humanly equal, or, rather, it would make no claim at all, but would simply be, and what it was, show itself without holding itself responsible for not being something else.

The Western boy of forty or fifty years ago grew up so close to the primeval woods or fields that their inarticulate poetry became part of his being, and he was apt to deal simply and uncritically with literature when he turned to it, as he dealt with nature. He took what he wanted, and left what he did not like; he used it for the playground, not the workshop of his spirit. Something like this I find true of Mark Twain in peculiar and uncommon measure. I do not see any proof in his books that he wished at any time to produce literature, or that he wished to reproduce life. When filled up with an experience that deeply interested him, or when provoked by some injustice or absurdity that intensely moved him, he burst forth, and the outbreak might be altogether humorous, but it was more likely to be humorous with a groundswell of seriousness carrying it profoundly forward. In all there is something curiously, not very definably, elemental, which again seems to me Western. He behaves himself as if he were the first man who was ever up against the proposition in hand. He deals as newly, for instance, with the relations of Shelley to his wife, and with as personal and direct an indignation, as if they had never attracted critical attention before; and this is the mind or the mood which he brings to all literature. Life is another affair with him; it is not discovery, not a surprise; every one else knows how it is; but here is a new world, and he explores it with a ramping joy, and shouts for the reader to come on and see how, in spite of all the lies about it, it is the same old world of men and women, with really nothing in it but their passions and prejudices and hypocrisies. At heart he was always deeply and essentially romantic, and once must have expected life itself to be a fairy dream. When it did not turn out so he found it tremendously amusing still, and his expectation not the least amusing thing in it, but without rancor, without grudge or bitterness in his disillusion, so that his latest word is as sweet as his first. He is deeply and essentially romantic in his literary conceptions, but when it comes to working them out he is helplessly literal and real; he is the impassioned lover, the helpless slave of the concrete. For this reason, for his wish, his necessity, first to ascertain his facts, his logic is as irresistible as his laugh.

All life seems, when he began to find it out, to have the look of a vast joke, whether the joke was on him or on his fellow-beings, or if it may be expressed without irreverence, on their common creator. But it was never wholly a joke, and it was not long before his literature began to own its pathos. The sense of this is not very apparent in *The Innocents Abroad,* but in *Roughing It* we began to be distinctly aware of it, and in the successive books it is constantly imminent, not as a clutch at the heartstrings, but as a demand of common justice, common sense, the feeling of proportion. It is not sympathy with the under dog merely as under dog that moves Mark Twain; for the under dog is sometimes rightfully under. But the probability is that it is wrongfully under, and has a claim to your inquiry into the case which you cannot ignore without atrocity. Mark Twain never ignores it; I know nothing finer in him than his perception that in this curiously contrived mechanism men suffer for their sorrows rather oftener than they suffer for their sins; and when they suffer for their sorrows they have a right not only to our pity but to our help. He always gives his help, even when he seems to leave the pity to others, and it may be safely said that no writer has dealt with so many phases of life with more unfailing justice. There is no real telling how any one comes to be what he is; all speculation concerning the fact is more or less impudent or futile conjecture; but it is conceivable that Mark Twain took from his early environment the custom of clairvoyance in things in which most humorists are purblind, and that being always in the presence of the under dog, he came to feel for him as under with him. If the knowledge and vision of slavery did not tinge all life with potential tragedy, perhaps it was this which lighted in the future humorist the indignation at injustice which glows in his page. His indignation relieves itself as often as not in a laugh; injustice is the most ridiculous thing in the world, after all, and indignation with it feels its own absurdity.

It is supposable, if not more than supposable, that the ludicrous incongruity of a slaveholding democracy nurtured upon the Declaration of Independence, and the comical spectacle of white labor owning black labor, had something to do in quickening the sense of contrast which is the fountain of humor, or is said to be so. But not to drive too hard a conjecture which must remain conjecture, we may reasonably hope to find in the untrammelled, the almost unconditional life of the later and farther West, with its individualism limited by nothing but individualism, the outside causes of the first overflow of the spring. We are so fond of classification, which we think is somehow interpretation, that one cannot resist the temptation it holds out in the case of the most unclassifiable things; and I must yield so far as to note that the earliest form of Mark Twain's work is characteristic of the greater part of it. The method used in *The Innocents Abroad* and in *Roughing It* is the method used in *Life on the Mississippi*, in *A Tramp Abroad*, and in *Following the Equator*, which constitute in bulk a good half of all his writings, as they express his dominant aesthetics. If he had written the fictions alone, we should have had to recognize a rare inventive talent, a great imagination and dramatic force; but I think it must be allowed that the personal books named overshadow the fictions. They have the qualities that give character to the fictions, and they have advantages that the fictions have not and that no fiction can have. In them, under cover of his pseudonym, we come directly into the presence of the author, which is what the reader is always longing and seeking to do; but unless the novelist is a conscienceless and tasteless recreant to the terms of his art, he cannot admit the reader to his intimacy. The personal books of Mark Twain have not only the charm of the essay's inconsequent and desultory method, in which invention, fact, reflection, and philosophy wander after one another in any following that happens, but they are of an immediate and most informal hospitality which admits you at once to the author's confidence, and makes you frankly welcome not only to his thought but to his way of thinking. He takes no trouble in the matter, and he asks you to take none. All that he required is that you will have common sense, and be able to tell a joke when you see it. Otherwise the whole furnishing of his mental mansion is at your service, to make such use as you can of it, but he will not be always directing your course, or requiring you to enjoy yourself in this or that order.

In the case of the fictions, he conceives that his first affair is to tell a story, and a story when you are once launched upon it does not admit of deviation without some hurt to itself. In Mark Twain's novels, whether they are for boys or for men, the episodes are only those that illustrate the main narrative or relate to it, though he might have allowed himself somewhat larger latitude in the old-fashioned tradition which he has oftenest observed in them. When it comes to the critical writings, which again are personal, and which, whether they are criticisms of literature or of life, are always so striking, he is quite relentlessly logical and coherent. Here there is not lounging or sauntering, with entertaining or edifying digressions. The object is in view from the first, and the reasoning is straightforwardly to it throughout. This is as notable in the admirable paper on the Jews, or on the Austrian situation, as in that on Harriet Shelley, or that on Cooper's novels. The facts are first ascertained with a conscience uncommon in critical writing of any kind, and then they are handled with vigor and precision till the polemic is over. It does not so much matter whether you agree with the critic or not; what you have to own is that here is a man of strong convictions, clear ideas, and ardent sentiments, based mainly upon common sense of extraordinary depth and breadth.

In fact, what finally appeals to you in Mark Twain, and what may hereafter be his peril with his readers, is his common sense. It is well to eat humble pie when one comes to it at the table d'hôte of life, and I wish here to offer my brother literary men a piece of it that I never refuse myself. It is true that other men do not really expect much common sense of us, whether we are poets or novelists or humorists. They may enjoy our company, and they may like us or pity us, but they do not take us very seriously, and they would as soon we were fools as not if we will only divert or comfort or inspire them. Especially if we are humorists do they doubt our practical wisdom; they are apt at first sight to take our sense for a part of the joke, and the humorist who convinces them that he is a man of as much sense as any of them, and possibly more, is in the parlous case of having given them hostages for seriousness which he may not finally be able to redeem.

I should say in the haste to which every inquiry of this sort seems subject, that this was precisely the case with Mark Twain. The exceptional observer must have known from the beginning that he was a thinker of courageous originality and penetrating sagacity, even when he seemed to be joking; but in the process of time it has come to such a pass with him that the wayfaring man can hardly shirk knowledge of the fact. The fact is thrown into sudden and picturesque relief by his return to his country after the lapse of time long enough to have let a new generation grow up in knowledge of him. The projection of his reputation against a background of foreign appreciation, more or less luminous, such as no other American author has enjoyed, has little or nothing to do with his acceptance on the new terms. Those poor Germans, Austrians, Englishmen, and Frenchmen who have been, from time to time in the last ten years, trying to show their esteem for his humor as we could; we might well doubt if they could fathom all his wisdom, which begins and ends in his humor; and if ever they seemed to chance upon his full significance, we naturally felt a kind of grudge, when we could not call it their luck, and suspected him of being less significant in the given instances than they supposed. The danger which he now runs with us is neither heightened nor lessened by the spread of his fame, but is an effect from intrinsic causes. Possibly it might not have been so great if he had come back comparatively forgotten; it is certain only that in coming back more remembered than ever, he confronts a generation which began to know him not merely by his personal books and his fiction, but by those criticisms of life and literature which have more recently attested his interest in the graver and weightier things.

Graver and weightier, people call them, but whether they are really more important than the lighter things, I am by no means sure. What I am amused with, independently of the final truth, is the possibility that his newer audience will exact this serious mood of Mr. Clemens, whereas we of his older world only suffered it, and were of a high conceit with our liberality in allowing a humorist sometimes to be a philosopher. Some of us indeed, not to be invidiously specific as to whom, were always aware of potentialities in him, which he seemed to hold in check, or to trust doubtfully to his reader as if he thought they might be thought part of the joke. Looking back over his work now, the later reader would probably be able to point out to earlier readers the evidence of a constant growth in the direction of something like recognized authority in matters of public import, especially those that were subject to the action of the public conscience as well as the public interest, until now hardly any man writing upon such matters is heard so willingly by all sorts of men. All of us, for instance have read somewhat of the conditions in South Africa which have eventuated in the present effort of certain British politicians to destroy two free republics in the interest of certain British speculators; but I doubt if we have found the case anywhere so well stated as in the closing chapters of Mark Twain's *Following the Equator*. His estimate of the military character of the belligerents on either side is of the prophetic cast which can come only from the thorough assimilation of accomplished facts; and in those passages the student of the actual war can spell its anticipative history. It is by such handling of such questions, unpremeditated and almost casual as it seems, that Mark Twain has won his claim to be heard on any public matter, and achieved the odd sort of primacy which he now enjoys.

But it would be rather awful if the general recognition of his prophetic function should implicate the renunciation of the humor that has endeared him to mankind. It would be well for his younger following to beware of reversing the error of the elder, and taking everything in earnest, as these once took nothing in earnest from him. To reverse that error would not be always to find his true meaning, and perhaps we shall best arrive at this by shunning one another's mistakes. In the light of the more modern appreciation, we elders may be able to see some things seriously that we once thought pure drolling, and from our experience his younger admirers may learn to receive as drolling some things that they might otherwise accept as preaching. What we all should wish to do is to keep Mark Twain what he has always been: a comic force unique in the power of charming us out of our cares and troubles, united with as potent an ethic sense of the duties, public and private, which no man denies in himself without being false to other men. I think we may hope for the best he can do to help us deserve our self-respect, without forming Mark Twain societies to read philanthropic meanings into his jokes, or studying the Jumping Frog as the allegory of an imperializing republic. I trust the time may be far distant when the Meditation at the Tomb of Adam shall be memorized and declaimed by ingenuous youth as a mystical appeal for human solidarity.

The International Fame of Mark Twain

Archibald Henderson

> "Art transmitting the simplest feelings of common life, but such always as are accessible to all men in the whole world—the art of common life—the art of a people—universal art."—Tolstoy: "What is Art?"

It is a mark of the democratic independence of America that she has betrayed a singular indifference to the appraisal of her literature at the hands of foreign criticism. Upon her writers who have exhibited derivative genius—Irving, Hawthorne, Emerson, Longfellow—American criticism has lavished the most extravagant eulogiums. The three geniuses who have made permanent contributions to world literature, who have either embodied in the completest degree the spirit of American democracy or who have won the widest following of imitators and admirers in foreign countries, still await their final and just deserts at the hands of critical opinion in their own land. The genius of Edgar Allan Poe gave rise to schools of literature in France and on the continent of Europe; yet in America his name remained until now debarred from inclusion in a so-called Hall of Fame! Walt Whitman and Mark Twain, the two great interpreters and embodiments of America, represent the supreme contribution of democracy to universal literature. In so far as it is legitimate for any one to be denominated a "self-made man" in literature, these two men are justly entitled to that characterization. They owe nothing to European literature—their genius is transcendently

Reprinted from *North American Review* 192 (December 1910): 805–815.

original, native, democratic. The case of Mark Twain is a literary phenomenon which imposes upon criticism, peculiarly upon American criticism, the distinct obligation of tracing the steps in his unhalting climb to an eminence completely international in character. Mark Twain achieved that eminence by the sole power of brain and personality. In this sense his career is unprecedented and unparalleled in the history of American literature. Criticism must define those signal qualities, traits, characteristics—individual, literary, social, racial, national—which encompassed his world-wide fame. For if it be true that the judgment to foreign nations is virtually the judgment of posterity, then is Mark Twain already a classic.

Upon the continent of Europe, Mark Twain first received notable critical recognition in France at the hands of that brilliant woman, Mme. Blanc ("Th. Bentzon"), who devoted her energies in such great measure to the popularization of American literature in Europe. The essay on Mark Twain, in the series which she wrote, under the general title "The American Humorists," appeared in the "*Revue des Deux Mondes*" in 1872 (July 15th). In addition to a remarkably accurate translation of "The Jumping Frog" into faultless French, this essay contained a minute analysis of "The Innocents Abroad"' and at this time Mme. Blanc was contemplating a translation of "The Innocents Abroad" into French. There is no cause for surprise in the discovery that a scholarly Frenchwoman, reared on classic models and confined by rigid canons of art, should stand aghast at this boisterous, barbaric, irreverent jester from the Western wilds of America. When one reflects that Mark Twain began his career as one of the sage-brush writers and gave free play to his democratic disregard of the traditional and the classic as such, it is not to be wondered at that Mme. Blanc, while honoring him with elaborate interpretation in the most authoritative literary journal in the world, could not conceal an expression of amazement over his enthusiastic acceptance in English-speaking countries:

Mark Twain's "Jumping Frog" should be mentioned, in the first place, as one of his most popular little stories—almost a type of the rest. It is, nevertheless, rather difficult for us to understand, while reading the story, the "roars of laughter" that it excited in Australia and in India, in New York and in London; the numerous editions of it which appeared; the epithet of "inimitable"' that the critics of the English press have unanimously awarded to it. . . .

We may remark that a Persian of Montesquieu, a Huron of Voltaire, even a simple Peruvian woman of Madame de Graffigny, reasons much more wisely about European civilization than an American of San Francisco. The fact is that it is not sufficient to have wit or even natural taste in order to appreciate works of art.

It is the right of humorists to be extravagant; but still common sense although carefully hidden, ought *sometimes* to make itself apparent. . . . In Mark Twain the Protestant is enraged against the pagan worship of broken marble statues—the democrat denies that there was any poetic feeling in the Middle Ages. . . .

In the course of this voyage with Mark Twain ("The Innocents Abroad"), we at length discover, under his good-fellowship and apparent ingenuousness, faults which we should never have expected. He has in the highest degree that fault of appearing astonished at nothing—common, we may say, to all savages. He confesses himself that one of his great pleasures is to horrify the guides by his indifference and stupidity. He is, too, decidedly envious. . . . We could willingly pardon him his patriotic self-love, often wounded by the ignorance of Europeans, above all, in what concerns the New World, if only that national pride were without mixture of personal vanity. . . .

Taking the "Pleasure Trip on the Continent" altogether, does it merit the success it enjoys? In spite of the indulgence that we cannot but show to the judgments of a foreigner; while recollecting that those amongst us who have visited America have fallen, doubtless, under the influence of prejudices almost as dangerous as ignorance, into errors quite as bad—in spite of the wit with which certain pages sparkle—we must say that this voyage is very far below the less celebrated excursions of the same author in his own country.

It is only too patent that the humor of Mark Twain, the very qualities which won him his immense and sudden popularity, make no appeal to Mme. Blanc. She conscientiously and painstakingly upbraids him *au grand serieux* for those features of his work most thoroughly surcharged with *vis comica*. Three years later Mme. Blanc returns to the criticism of Mark Twain, in an essay in the *Revue des Deux Mondes* (March 15th, 1875), entitled "L'Age Dore en Amerique"—an exhaustive review and analysis of "The Gilded Age." The savage charm and genuine simplicity of Mark Twain are not devoid of attraction even to her sophisticated intelligence; and she is inclined to infer that jovial irony and animal spirits are qualities sufficient for the amusement of a young nation of people such as are the Americans, since they do not pique themselves upon being *blasés*. According to her judgment, Mark Twain and Charles Dudley Warner are lacking in the requisite mental grasp for the "stupendous tasks of interpreting the great tableau of the American scene." Nor does she regard their effort at collaboration as a success from the standpoint of art:

> From this association of two very dissimilar minds arises a work very difficult to read; at every moment we see the pen pass from one hand to the other and the romancer call the humorist to order, only too often call him in vain. . . Do not expect of Mark Twain either tact or delicacy, but count upon him for honest and outspoken shrewdness. . . .

The charm of Colonel Sellers wholly escapes her, for she cannot understand the truly loving appreciation with which this genial burlesque of the later American industrial brigand was greeted by the American people. The remarkable talents of Mark Twain as a reporter impress her most favorably; but she is repelled by "that mixture of good sense with mad folly—disorder," the wilful exaggeration of the characters, and the jests which are so elaborately constructed that "the very theme itself disappears under the mass of embroidery which overlays it." "The audacities of a Bret Harte, the temerities of a Mark

Twain still astonish us," she concludes; "but soon we shall become accustomed to an American language whose savory freshness is not to be disdained in lieu of still more delicate and refined qualities that time will doubtless bring."

In translating "The Jumping Frog" (giving Mark Twain the opportunity for re-translating it—"clawing it back"—into English which furnished amusement for thousands), in elaborately reviewing, with long citations, "The Innocents Abroad" and "The Gilded Age," Mme. Blanc rendered a genuine service to Mark Twain, introducing him to the literary world of France and Europe. In 1881 Emile Blémont still further enhanced the fame of Mark Twain in France by publishing in free French translation a number of his slighter sketches, under the title *"Esquisses Américaines de Mark Twain."* In 1884 and again in 1886 appeared editions of "Les Aventures de Tom Sawyer," translated by W. L. Hughes. In 1886 Eugéne Forgues published in the *"Revue des Deux Mondes"* (February 15th) an exhaustive review, with lengthy citations, of "Life on the Mississippi," under the title *"Les Caravanes d'un Humoriste."* His prefatory remarks in regard to Mark Twain's fame in France at this time may be accepted as authoritative. He called attention to the commendable efforts of French scholars to popularize these "transatlantic gayeties." But the result of all the efforts to import into France a new mode of comic entertainment was an almost complete check. There was one notable exception; for "The Adventures of Tom Sawyer" was really appreciated and praised as—an "exquisite idyll"! The peculiar twist of national character, the specialized conception of the *vis comica* revealed in Mark Twain's works, tended to confine them to a restricted *milieu*. To the French taste, Mark Twain's pleasantry appeared *macabre*, his wit brutal, his temperament dry to excess. By some, indeed, his exaggerations were regarded as "symptoms of mental alienation"; and the originality of his verve did not conceal from French eyes the "incoherence of his conceptions."

> "It has been said," remarks M. Forgues, "that an academician slumbers in the depths of every Frenchman; and this it was which militated against the success of Mark Twain in France. Humor, with us, has its laws and its restrictions. So the French public saw in Mark Twain a gross jester, incessantly beating upon a tom-tom to attract the attention of the crowd. They were tenacious in resisting all such blandishments... *As a humorist* Mark Twain has never been appreciated in France. The appreciation he has ultimately secured—an appreciation by no means inconsiderable, but in no sense comparable to that won in Anglo-Saxon and Germanic countries—was due to his shrewdness and penetration as an observer, and to his marvellous faculty for evoking scenes and situations by the clever use of the novel and the *imprévu*. There was, even to the French, a certain lively appeal in an intelligence absolutely free of convention, sophistication or reverence for traditionary views *qua* traditionary."

Although at first the salt of Mark Twain's humor seemed to be lacking in the Attic flavor, the leisurely exposition of the genially naive American in time won its way with the *blasé* Parisians. It is needless to cite those works of his which were subsequently translated into the French language. It has been recorded that tourists who could find no copy of the Bible in the street book-stalls of Paris were confronted on every hand with copies of "Roughing It"! When the English edition of Mark Twain's collected works appeared (Chatto and Windus: London), that authoritative French journal, the *Mercure de France* (December, 1899), paid him this distinguished tribute:

> His public is as varied as possible, because of the versatility and suppleness of his talent which addresses itself successively to all classes of readers. He has been called the greatest humorist in the world, and that is doubtless the truth; but he is also a charming and attractive storyteller, an alert romancer, a clever and penetrating observer, a philosopher without pretensions and, therefore, all the more profound, and finally a brilliant essayist.

The International Fame of Mark Twain

Perhaps the present writer may be pardoned for mentioning that when an essay of his on Mark Twain appeared in "Harper's Magazine," in 1909, M. Lux, reviewing it in *L'Indépendence Belge*, says:

> In Mark Twain's writings are to be distinguished, exalted and sublimated by his genius, the typically American qualities of youth and of gayety, of force and of faith. His countrymen love his philosophy, at once practical and high-minded. They are fond of his simple style, animated with verve and spice, thanks to which his work is accessible to all classes of readers. . . He describes his contemporaries with such an art of distinguishing their essential traits, that he manages to evoke, to *create* even, characters and types of eternal verity. The Americans profess for Mark Twain the same sort of vehement admiration that we have in France for Balzac.

In Italy, as in France, Mark Twain was regarded as a remarkable impressionist; and "The Innocents Abroad" had wide popularity in Rome. But with the peculiar *timbre* of Mark Twain's humor his Italian audience was not wholly sympathetic; they never felt themselves thoroughly *au courant* with the spirit of his humor.

> "Translation, however accurate and conscientious," as the Italian critic, Raffaele Simboli, has pointed out, "fails to render the special flavor of his work." And then in Italy, where humorous writing generally either rests on a political basis or depends on *risqué* phrases, Mark Twain's "Sketches" are not appreciated because the spirit which breathes in them is not always understood. The story of the "Jumping Frog," for instance, famous as it is in America and England, has made little impression in France and Italy.

It was rather among the Germanic peoples and those most closely allied to them racially and temperamentally, the Scandinavians, that Mark Twain found most complete and ready response in Europe. At first sight, it seems almost incredible that the writings of Mark Twain, with their occasional slang, their not infrequent colloquialisms, and their local peculiarities of dialect, should have borne translation into other languages, especially into so complex a language as the German. It must, however, be borne in mind that, despite these peculiar features of his writings, they are couched in a style of most marked directness, simplicity and native English purity.

> "He writes English," says Mr. Howells, "as if it were a primitive and not a derivative language, without Gothic or Latin or Greek behind it or German and French beside it. The result is the English in which the most vital works of English literature are cast..."

The ease with which Mark Twain's works were translated into foreign languages, especially the German and allied tongues, and the eager delight with which they were read and comprehended by all classes, high and low, constitute perhaps the most signal conceivable tribute not only to the humanity of his spirit, but to the genuine art of his natural and forthright style. "The Jumping Frog" one would imagine to be very recalcitrant to translation. But I was amazed to discover the naturalness and accuracy of both the French and German translations; not only was the spirit of the original preserved: the universality of the anecdote appeared in yet clearer light. Take a brief passage—that in which Smiley and the stranger touch their respective frogs in order to make them jump. First read M. Blémont's translation into French:

> "Maintenant, dit-il, êtes-vous prêt? Bon! Mettex votre bê à coté de Daniel, leurs pattes de devant bien alignées. Y êtes-vous? je donne le signal.
> "Et chacun d'eux pressa au même instant sa grenouille par derriére. La nouvelle grenouille sauta. Daniel voulut sauter aussi, Daniel fit un effort, haussa les épaules, tenez? comme ca, à la francais. Mais bah! Daniel ne pouvait plus bluger! La pauvre bête semblait plantée là aussi solidement qu'une enclume. On eût dit qu'elle était ancrée sur place. Smiley n'en fut pas médiocrement écoeuré. Mais il n'eut pas la moindre idée de ce qui s'était passé en son absence. Naturellement!"

The International Fame of Mark Twain

The translation is apt and clever, for M. Blémont has preserved the spirit—the *ton goguenard*—of the original—lacking in the translation of Mme. Blanc. Equally satisfactory, in catching the *tone* of the story, is the German translation of Herr Moritz Busch:

> "Na, wenn Sie jetst parat sind, so setzen Sie ihn neben Daniel'n hin, seine Vorderpfoten ganz in derselben Linie wie Daniel'n seine, und ich werde das Signal geben. Dann sagte er: 'Eins—zwei—drei—hopps!' und er und der Bursche gaben den Fröschen hinten einen Tipps, und der neue Frosch hüpfte fort. Aber Daniel that einen Säufzer und hob die Schultern—so—wie'n Franzose—aber's half nichts, er konnte sich nicht rippeln noch rappeln, er sass so fast wie ein Ambos, und er war nicht mehr im Stande, sich zu regen, als wenn er mit einem Anker festgekettet wäre. Smiley war sehr überrascht davon und sehr böse darüber, aber er hatte natürlich keine Ahnung, an was es lag."

One reason—by no means an insignificant reason—why Mark Twain is regarded in Germany almost as if he were a native German writer is that no other English or American author has had so many translators and editors. *Mark Twain's Ausgewählte Humoristische Schriften*, in twelve volumes (Lutz: Stuttgart), as the Viennese philologist, Dr. Leon Kellner, has pointed out, read "precisely like a German original"—a truly remarkable circumstance. And almost more remarkable still—Mark Twain's *Jugendschriften* have already, some years gone, passed into the fixed repertory of German school literature!

As early as 1872, Mark Twain had secured Tauchnitz, of Leipzig, for his Continental agent. German translations soon appeared of "The Jumping Frog and Other Stories" (1874, "The Gilded Age" (1874), "The Innocents Abroad" (1875), "The Adventures of Tom Sawyer" (1876). Numerous translations soon followed in Germany—published by Mann (Leipzig), Freytag (Leipzig), Lutz (Stuttgart), Reclam's *Universal-bibliothek*, etc. A few years later his sketches, many of them, were translated into virtually all printed languages, notably into Russian and modern Greek. His more extended works rapidly came to be translated into German, French, Italian, Dutch and the languages of Denmark and the Scandinavian peninsula.

The elements of the colossally grotesque, the wildly primitive, in the works of Mark Twain—the underlying note of melancholy, the strain of persistent idealism, not less than the bohemianism—awake a responsive chord in the Germanic consciousness. Mark Twain's stories of the Argonauts, the miners, and the desperadoes; his narratives of the wild freedom of the life on the Mississippi, the lawless and barbaric encounters—all appealed to the Germanic passion for the grotesque. To the Europeans, this wild genius of the Pacific Slope (strange misnomer!) seemed to function in a sort of unexplored fourth-dimension of humor—vast and novel—of which they had never dreamed. In his "*Psychopathik des Humors*," Schleich reserved for American humor, with Mark Twain as its leading exponent, a distinct and unique category which he denominated "*phantastish*," "*grossdimensional.*" In commenting upon the works of Mark Twain and his popularity in German Europe, Carl von Thaler unhesitatingly affirms that Mark Twain was entertained with absolutely unprecedented hospitality in Vienna—an honor hitherto paid to no German author! In Berlin the young Kaiser bestowed upon him the most distinguished marks of his esteem. He praised Mark Twain's work, notably "Life on the Mississippi," with the intensest enthusiasm; the passages in "A Tramp Abroad" dealing with German student life were also singled out for commendation. After hearing the Kaiser's eulogy on "Life on the Mississippi," Mark Twain was astounded and touched to receive a similar tribute, the same evening, from the *portier* of his lodging-hours.

> That a crowned head and a *portier*, the very top of an Empire and the very bottom of it, should pass the very same criticism and deliver the very same verdict upon a book of mine—and almost in the same hour and the same breath—

this, Mark Twain confessed, was the most extraordinary coincidence of his life.

By German critics Mark Twain was hailed as the leading exponent of American humor, not only in the United States, but, in Herr Ludwig Salomon's phrase, "everywhere that culture rules." "Robinson Crusoe" was held to exhibit a limited power of imagination in comparison with the ingenuity and resourcefulness of "Tom Sawyer." At times the German critics confessed their inability to discover the dividing-line between astounding actuality and humorously fantastic exaggeration. The description of the barbaric state of western America possessed an indescribable fascination for the Europeans. At times Mark Twain's bloody jests froze the laughter on their lips; and his "revolver humor" made their hair stand on end. "Such adventures," one bold critic observes, "are possible only in America—perhaps only in the fancy of an American!"

> "Mark Twain's greatest strength," says von Thaler, "lies in his little sketches, the literary snapshots. The shorter his work, the more striking it is. He draws directly from life. No other writer has learned to know so many different varieties of men and circumstances, so many strange examples of the *Genus Homo*, as he; no other has taken so strange a course of development."

The deeper elements of Mark Twain's humor did not escape the attention of the Germans, nor fail of appreciation at their hands. In his aphorisms, embodying at once genuine wit and experience of life, they discovered the universal human being; and it is chiefly for this reason that they found these aphorisms worthy of profound and lasting admiration. Franz Sintenis saw in Mark Twain a "living symptom of the youthful joy in existence"—a genius capable at will, "despite his boyish extravagance," of the virile formulation of fertile and suggestive ideas. On the occasion of Mark Twain's seventieth birthday, German Europe united in honoring the man and writer. Able critical reviews of his life and work were published in Germany and Austria—more in German Europe than in America! From these various essays—in such authoritative publications as the *Neue Freie Presse* (Vienna), *Tägliche Rundschau* (Leipzig), *Allgemeine Zeitung* (Munich), *Gymnasium* (Paderborn), and the *Illustrirte Zeitung* (Leipzig)—I select one short passage from the pen of the able critic, Dr. Leon Kellner, of Vienna:

> A bohemian fellow, who is full of mischief without the slightest trace of malice in it, an imaginative story-teller who is always ready to make himself and others ridiculous without coming anywhere near the truth, a fantastic and Johnny-look-in-air who nevertheless never loses the solid ground from under his feet, a vagabond and adventurer, who from crown to sole remains a gentleman and with the grand manner of a Walter Scott keeps his commercial honor unsoiled—that is the writer Mark Twain and the citizen Samuel Langhorne Clemens in one person.

He hails Mark Twain as "the king of humorists"—who understood how to transmute all earthly stuff, such as the negro Jim and the street Arab, Huckleberry Finn, into "the gold of pure literature." At the time of Mark Twain's death, when so many tributes were paid him all over the world, one of his German critics wrote, with genuine insight into the deeper significance of his work:

> Although Mark Twain's humor moves us to irresistible laughter, this is not the main feature in his works; like all true humorists, *ist der Witz mit dem Weltschmerz verbunden*, he is a witness to higher thoughts and higher emotions, and his purpose is to expose bad morals and evil circumstances in order to improve and ennoble mankind.

Mark Twain is loved in Germany, the critics pointed out, more than all other humorists, English or French, because his humor "turns fundamentally upon serious and earnest conceptions of life." It is a tremendously significant fact that the works of American literature most widely read today in

The International Fame of Mark Twain

Germany are the works of—striking conjunction!—Ralph Waldo Emerson and Mark Twain.

"The Jumping Frog" fired the laugh heard round the world; it initiated Mark Twain's international fame. "The Innocents Abroad" won the thoughtful attention of the English people. Since that day Mark Twain has been the adored author of England and the colonies; in lieu of a national author, the English chose Mark Twain for the national author of the English-speaking world. His popularity in England was as great as in America or Germany; all classes read his works with unfeigned delight; critics of the highest authority praised his works in the most glowing terms. The personal ovation to him in 1907, which I witnessed, was the greatest ovation ever given by the English public to a foreign visitor not a crowned head; and Oxford University honored him with her degree.

At that time the oldest of England's periodicals, *The Spectator*, paid Mark Twain this significant and comprehensive tribute:

> It is all, surely, the most admirable fun and light-heartedness. But fun, light-heartedness and an unrivalled sense of humor are by no means Mark Twain's only, not even, perhaps, his most commanding, characteristics. He has a peculiar power of presenting pathetic situations without "slush.". . . He is, above all, the fearless upholder of all that is clean, noble, straightforward, innocent and manly. . . He has his extravagances; some of his public, indeed, would insist on them. But if he is a jester, he jests with the mirth of the happiest of Puritans; he has read much of English knighthood, and translated the best of it into his living pages; and he has assuredly already won a high degree in letters in having added more than any writer since Dickens to the gayety of the Empire of the English language.

It is gratifying to citizens of all nationalities to recall and recapture the pleasure and delight Mark Twain's works have given the world for decades. It is peculiarly gratifying to Americans to rest confident in the belief that, in Mark Twain, America has contributed to the world an international and universal genius—sealed of the tribe of Moliére, a congener of

Defoe, of Fielding, of Le Sage—a man who will be remembered, as Mr. Howells has said, "with the great humorists of all time, with Cervantes, with Swift, or with any other worthy his company; none of them was his equal in humanity."

An Inspired Critic

Edith Wyatt

I

Among the journeys of one's dreams there is a certain experience familiar doubtless to many dream-travelers. I mean the great journey down the river. It is a green summer afternoon. The yellow water stretches away a half a mile on each side of your raft. The arrows of far silver ripples point to snags. Around you is the sight of low bluffs, cornbottoms, highland rolling prairie, up beyond the banks. You are a perfect pilot, in your dream-power; and as in other dream-countries you have always known this wonderful place, and yet it is all new and fresh to you.

It is not by the pages of *Tom Sawyer* alone, nor *Huck Finn* alone, that Mark Twain has piloted the world on that miraculous imaginary journey down the great valley, through the center of our national life; but by his whole philosophy, his tremendous propelling power as a social critic.

The Emperor of Germany once said that *Life on the Mississippi* was his favorite American book. The remark has always remained for me an instance of the German range and thoroughness in information. The Emperor could not I believe have chosen any other volume describing American life which would have expressed the virtues and vices of our nation as truly and as aptly as this work of genius.

It is only when one thinks over Mark Twain's writings in their entirety that one realizes how numerous his social

Reprinted from *North American Review* CCV (April 1917): 603-15.

criticisms were—criticisms favorable and unfavorable, and representing, taken together, one of the most far-sighted surveys of democracy that we possess.

It was as press-correspondent, from 1863-65, on the *Enterprise* in Carson City, and later in his letters to the *Enterprise* from San Francisco, that Mark Twain began that penetrating comment on the Government of the United States, and on her social injustice which he was to continue till the end of his life.

Mr. Albert Bigelow Paine tells us in his biography that

> Those who remember Mark Twain's *Enterprise* letters (they are no longer obtainable) declare them to have been the greatest series of daily philippics ever written. However this may be, it is certain they made a stir. Goodman (the editor of the *Enterprise*) permitted him to say exactly what he pleased upon any subject. San Francisco was fairly weltering in corruption, official and private. He assailed whatever came first to hand with all the fierceness of a flaming indignation long restrained.
>
> Quite naturally he attacked the police and with such ferocity and penetration that as soon as copies of the *Enterprise* came from Virginia (in Nevada) the City Hall (in San Francisco) began to boil and smoke and threaten trouble. Martin G. Burke, the chief-of-police, entered libel suit against the *Enterprise*, prodigiously advertising the paper, copies of which were snatched as soon as the stage brought them.

As a journalist he attacked at that period so many social abuses as to gain for himself the title of "The Moralist of the Main." On his return to Nevada to report the proceedings of the legislature at Carson City for the *Enterprise*, Mark Twain was the best-known figure at the capital. His power and courage as a writer, combined with Goodman's power and courage as an editor made him respected and feared in the State Government. Mr. Paine tells us that he could control more votes than any legislative member; and with two other journalists, Simmons and Claggett, could pass or defeat any bill offered.—"He was fearless, merciless and incorruptible."

An Inspired Critic

Mark Twain's contempt for the rabble of our State and national legislatures was lasting. In 1868 after he had gone East and become a Washington press-correspondent he was extremely dejected in the national capital, over the "pitiful intellects" governing the country. "This is a place to get a poor opinion of everybody in" he wrote of Congress. Thirty years later he put into the mouth of Pudd'nhead Wilson the remark that "It could probably be shown by facts and figures that there is no distinctly native American criminal class except Congress." And in 1907, in *Christian Science* he lists Congress and the American voter as among the moral failures of the Christian religion.

> If there are two tickets in the field in the city, one composed of honest men, and the other of notorious blatherskites and criminals he (the American voter) will not hesitate to lay his private Christian honor aside and vote for the blatherskites, if his "party honor" shall exact it. His Christianity is of no use to him and has no influence upon him when he is acting in a public capacity. He has sound and sturdy private morals, but he has no public ones. In the last great municipal election in New York, almost a complete one-half of the votes, representing about 3,500,000 Christians, were cast for a ticket that had hardly a man on it whose earned and proper place was outside of a jail. But that vote was present at church next Sunday the same as ever, and as unconscious of its perfidy as though nothing had happened.
>
> Our Congress consists of Christians. In their private life they are true to every obligation of honor; yet in every session they violate them all; and do it without shame.

One understands the fear and respect Mark Twain inspired as a commentator when one reads in the *Express*, the paper he owned in Buffalo soon after his marriage, the explicit manner of his statement. He was speaking of some farmers of Cohocton who had mobbed a couple whom they disapproved. "The men who did this deed are capable of doing any low, sneaking, cowardly villainy that could be invented in perdition." He appended a full list of their names.

It was with the same directness that he assailed Tammany in New York City in 1901 in his famous Waldorf-Astoria speech at the Acorn Club dinner—a paraphrase of Burke's Impeachment of Warren Hastings.

> I impeach Richard Croker of high crimes and misdemeanors.
> I impeach him in the name of the people whose trust he has betrayed.
> I impeach him in the name of all the people of America whose national character he has dishonored.
> I impeach him in the name and by virtue of those eternal laws of justice which he has violated.
> I impeach him in the name of human nature itself, which he has cruelly betrayed, injured and oppressed in both sexes, in every rank, situation and condition in life.

Our greatest humorist's critical examinations of various products of our social system, his defenses of the dumb, the oppressed, the human beings enduring injustice in our civilization, both in the United States and in almost every country in the globe, are innumerable. One may mention as prominent instances: *To the Person Sitting in Darkness*, *A Dog's Tale*, *A Horse's Tale*, *Cruel Treatment of a Boy* (a defense of Chinamen), the Croker Impeachment, the account of the Queensland-Kanaka Labor Traffic in *Following the Equator*, *The Stolen White Elephant* (a satire on the methods of American Detective Bureaus), *Leopold's Soliloquy* (a denunciation of King Leopold's Congo methods), *The Czar's Soliloquy* (a satire on the imperial divinity of the Emperor of Russia).

This was composed in the same year when a hideous massacre of Jews occurred in Moscow. At about the same time the author was asked for a Christmas sentiment for the New York press; and wrote: "It is my warm and all-embracing Christmas hope that all of us that deserve it may finally be gathered together in a heaven of light and peace, and the others permitted to retire into the clutches of Satan or the Emperor of Russia, according to preference if they have a preference."

Many people will recall with especial vividness Mark Twain's opinions on our annexation of the Philippines.

> We have bought some islands from a party who did not own them: with real smartness and a good counterfeit of disinterested friendliness, we coaxed a confiding, weak nation into a trap, and closed it upon them; we went back on an honored guest of the Stars and Stripes when we had no further use for him and chased him to the mountains; we are as indisputably in possession of a wide-spreading archipelago as if it were our property; we have pacified some thousands of islanders and buried them; destroyed their fields, burned their villages, and turned their widows and orphans out-of-doors; furnished heart-break by exile to some dozens of disagreeable patriots; subjugated the remaining millions by Benevolent Assimilation, which is the pious, new name of the market.

II

"There are many humorous things in the world," he says in *Following the Equator*, "among them the white man's notion that he is less savage than the other savages."

It will be seen that the United States of his chronicle is a land of savagery. Mr. Paine's just and absorbing biography seems to speak of Mark Twain's youthful experience of lawless violence, as somehow exceptional—or at least as the experience of a past, a pioneer condition in violence, a picturesque and bygone state. He points out that the author of *Life on the Mississippi* had seen in childhood a man shot down in the street, that his father Judge Clemens, as sheriff, had kept in his own house the body of a man killed in a local feud; and that he had known at close range in early boyhood of many barbarous horrors in the community of Hannibal. It is my own belief that one day in the municipal and criminal courts of Chicago would convince Mr. Paine that neither roughness nor ruffianism had abated in the Middle West since Mark Twain's boyhood.

The state of American society and government his stories and articles present is, broadly speaking, truthfully characteristic of the state of society and government we find now in Chicago—the most murderous and lawless civil community in the world. What is exceptional in our great humorist's view of our national life is not the ruffianism of the existence he describes for us on the Mississippi and elsewhere in the United States, but the fact that he writes the truth about it.

Indeed I think that it would be possible to show that if less rough, the United States of our own contemporary experience is far more ruffianly, far more violently bullied and more acquiescent in being bullied than the communities of Mark Twain's earlier novels and tales.

The United States is filled with what may be called an excessive moderation concerning the telling of truth—though the implication is not intended that Mr. Paine's candid consideration of his subject is shadowed by that fallacy in its truthfulness. She will not admit the presence of atrocity and horror in her own commonwealth. This admission would involve the inconvenient consequences of the necessity of her disapproval of these evils. Instead of acknowledging the plain, undeniable truth such as that which Mark Twain stated about our American mobs—that they are literally composed of persons who are low, sneaking, cowardly and villainous, she generally prefers to assume the timid and evasive air of what H.G. Wells calls our "vulgar refinement" and to dodge the truth by asserting that such a characterization is excessive.

Thus when Colonel Roosevelt called Judge Baldwin a liar for his conduct in the Hoxie decision (or was said to have called Judge Baldwin a liar), instead of looking to see whether an important member of the bench really had betrayed us by twisting the truth, and had behaved irresponsibly and unworthily, the American public focused its attention on the shock it had received from Colonel Roosevelt's "unmannerliness." But apparently no one was shocked by Judge Baldwin, whose decision to at least one lay-reader of its many pages seemed to assert that the American Government licensed railroads to murder their employees.

It is my own belief that if Judea had been peopled by Americans at the time of the Massacre of the Innocents, the main portion of the comment on the occurrence would have been devoted to the bad taste and persecutive sensationalism of referring to the incident as a massacre.

III

One reason doubtless why Mark Twain discriminated so clearly against our native atrocities was because he was in literal truth a great traveler. In his *weltanschauung* he shows you democracy not only absolutely as an experiment in the United States, along the river, in *Tom Sawyer* and *Huck Finn* and *Life on the Mississippi* and in *Roughing it*, but comparatively, and against the backgrounds of other countries, the pageantry of the nations of the globe.

"It does rather look," he says in *The American Claimant* "as if in a republic where all are free and equal property and position constitute rank." He fills you with indignation when he describes a white man cuffing a helpless Hindoo servant for nothing in particular, in a Bombay palace: and then he fills you with indignation again while he tells you how he has seen his own father cuff a little negro slave boy with the same offensive injustice, and in the midst of the same surrounding subservience to his detestable performance. And you wish that Mark Twain's penetration and fresh observation would show you all the kingdoms and customs of the earth, and all the United States' own social history against that background.

IV

Mark Twain considered democracy both geographically against the background of other lands, and historically against the background of other ages. His presentation of the subject historically has a brilliancy of sympathetic expression that seems to me unsurpassed. So that *The Prince and the Pauper* and *A Connecticut Yankee in King Arthur's Court* and *Joan of Arc* fire you with resentment, grief and amusement as quickly as their author's tales of today.

When he was a boy of fifteen, a compositor in a printer's office at Hannibal, as he walked to his work after dinner one afternoon, he noticed the loose page of a book blowing down the street. Picking is up, he read its fragmentary narrative. It was the account of a conversation of Joan of Arc in her prison at Rouen, with two brutal English soldiers who were taunting her. Mark Twain had never heard of Joan of Arc before. He had read no history. Thenceforth through the open door of the wind-blown page, flung to him by fate upon that warm afternoon in the little American town, he was to travel in the realms of gold for nearly sixty years—throughout the rest of his life-time. From that day he was a passionate reader of history.

"Was somebody asking to see the soul?" says Walt Whitman: and of course the reader of fiction is always asking to see the soul: and in *Personal Recollections of Joan of Arc* may look upon and know the soul of an inspired girl, of flaming genius, the soul of a great, a rich-hearted woman, as deeply as though she had been the profoundly loved and honored friend of a life-time. I think indeed she was a friend of Mark Twain's life-time: and that from the instant, when as a boy he read the words of her chronicled conversation he saw from afar the flash of the special force in her that made her what she was, and knew at once intensely and delicately the peculiar splendor of her nature. He said he had been forty years writing *Personal Recollections of Joan of Arc* and that he liked it better than any of his other books: and as you read the pity and terror of its tragedy you easily believe both these sayings. In many ways it is the most profound, the subtlest and the most searching of his novels.

In its superb story of the courage and truth of a woman's knowledge struggling forward under the puerile frivolities of the French rule of the king, and the evil trivialities, the mob stupidities and mob superstitions of the day you read a penetrating tale of patriotism for all time.

A Connecticut Yankee is filled too with patriotism—with the only kind of patriotism which will ever make a democracy successful, the sense of individual human responsibility for social justice. One of the most original works ever written, it is increasingly useful to us. For it presents a great democratic philosophy, a vast imaginative scheme of powerful rule whose humor and common-sense give it a pragmatic validity.

"My idea of our civilization," he wrote to a friend in 1900, "is that it is a shoddy, poor thing and full of cruelties, vanities, arrogancies, meannesses and hypocrisies."

Observing the truth of this saying as applied to our own country now, as well as to King Arthur's Court, American citizens are always turning to their great men to learn what to do if one intends to abide by our social agreement. On this absorbing question of what we are to do, few of our commentators of genius on democracy shed much light. Thoreau, of course, departed from the social agreement. He sheds a clear and blazing light nevertheless on the question of the honorable, individual conduct of free persons in a democracy; but unhappily, a strength almost divine, and beyond that of most mortal creatures, is required to climb the steep path the light indicates. Henry James, in another way from Thoreau, separated himself from our American social agreement; and sheds no light at all upon what we are to do in the general muddle—which he is indeed accredited with disparaging, but which in my own view, he simply ignored. Our greatest poet so beautiful to read, yet sheds no light at all, with his happy belief in "Good in all," etc. And even his outlined democracy, his fellow-roughs hanging about each other's necks, does not exactly represent a reality, and certainly not as democratic or livable a democracy as is presented by Huck's and the negro Jim's days on the raft.

Indeed it may be accepted as a proof of the magic of Mark Twain's genius of humor and the livable character of his democratic faith, that a nation periodically insane on the subject of the negro, and almost unable to recover from the shock of his having dined with a President, has selected as one of its most popular novels a work of fiction which presents the hero as dining, breakfasting, supping and sleeping for weeks with a negro on terms of complete social equality. In their different manners, William James, William Dean Howells and Mark Twain have all expressed great democratic philosophies, in whose light we can see a little distance into our own difficulties—philosophies that one can live by, and go along the road of one's existence by, at least at intervals, and according to one's worth.

To preserve and indeed to live in a sense of social responsibility and yet maintain a cheerful demeanor, this is a philosophy of the Connecticut Yankee which has never been expressed elsewhere, I think, in so convincing and thrilling a manner. On the tide of the author's humorous genius you are carried forward with an impetus which bears you on long after you have left the Connecticut Yankee and stopped laughing at Merlin.

Another carrying power of Mark Twain's philosophy, a force rather less obvious than his invincible humor, is its extraordinary sense of the beauty, the poetry and romance of personal relationship—not simply these qualities in relationships between opposite sexes, but throughout existence. His understanding of all human contacts has an exceptional keenness and delicacy. No persons in fiction are rougher than his characters; and yet no author has exhibited a quicker dislike of having anybody unfairly bullied or patronized. In a few pages of *Cashel Byron's Profession*, Alice Goff, the unfortunate, narrow-minded companion of the brilliant and generous Lydia Carew, who is presented by her creator as a person of exceptional gentleness and equity, is worse patronized and bullied by her mistress than anyone is unfairly bullied or patronized with the author's approval, in all the cursing and fighting and rowdiness of *Life on the Mississippi, The American Claimant, Tom Sawyer* and *Huck Finn* put together.

Mark Twain appreciated the injustices of civilization not only to the poverty-stricken, but to those of mediocre fortune. One of his most eloquent passages concerns the payment of a twenty years' debt of fifty dollars by a hard-working country clergyman. There are numberless instances of his sympathy not only with great wrongs, but with ordinary difficulties and struggles. Among these is the story of how one night at a club-meeting in New York, all the other members one by one slipped away, while he remained, listening patiently with respectful attention through to the end, while a young writer read aloud, a very, very long poem.

"How did you manage to sit through it?" someone asked afterwards.

"Well," he said quietly, "that young man thought he had a divine message to deliver, and I thought he was entitled to at least one auditor, so I stayed with him."

In the unusual social faith of that tale there speaks, I think the voice of the American spirit that may save us all at last.

Mark Twain was a penetrating and imaginative critic not only of the failures of democracy in the United States and in the countries of the globe and the ages of the past, but the failures of our prevailing theology.

His objections are sprinkled through all his books and his correspondence; and are crystallized in the sparkling speculative amusement of *Captain Stormfield's Visit to Heaven* and his posthumous story *The Mysterious Stranger* describing a sojourn of a nephew of Satan's upon earth. There is a power of imagination in these works of fiction on the subject of creation which is nothing less than titanic. Their fancies have a species of bulk, and one may almost say solidity, so that compared with them the gracile [sic] fancies of Poe seem made of air, and even Hawthorne's murky shadows appear to be cast by things ethereal. But the conception of Mark Twain's semi-theological tales of the cosmogony,

Captain Stormfield's race with the comet after his death, when the billions of natives of the comet run to one side, and make it careen—and the story of the dog who has a better heart than God, in *The Mysterious Stranger*, are composed of the same stuff of world-dreams as Thor with his hammer, and the Erl King, and Prometheus torn by the eagle.

Without wishing to speak with disrespect of a view of creation greatly solacing and inspiring to many, and to many noble persons, one may say that in general these fascinating works express one of the most interesting objections to the Judean religion that we know. This may be roughly summed up in the statement that what Mark Twain seems to say about both the old and the new Judean faith is simply that it is *too small*:

> When a man goes back to look at the house of his childhood [he says in a letter to Mr. Howells] it has *always shrunk*; there is no instance of such a house being as big as the picture memory and imagination call for. Shrunk how? Why, to its correct dimensions; the house hasn't altered; this is the first time it has been in focus. Well that's loss. To have house and Bible shrink so under the disillusioning corrected angle is loss—for a moment. But there are compensations. You tilt the tube skyward and bring planets and comets and corona flames a hundred and fifty thousand miles high into the field.

Before then he remarked one day to his friend the Reverend Joseph Twichell,

> Joe, I don't believe one word of your Bible was inspired by God any more than any other book. I believe it is entirely the work of man from beginning to end—Atonement and all. The problem of life and death and eternity and the true conception of God is a bigger thing than is contained in that book.

In declaring the doctrine of the Atonement an intrinsically mundane conception and in pointing out in numbers of other passages the pettishly self-referential and heartless manner of

An Inspired Critic

the God of the Bible, Mark Twain made a most valuable discrimination concerning the Christian theology. For him it is not simply as a physical but as a moral explanation of the universe that the Judean philosophy is too little.

It is this inherent objection to spiritual conceptions of a rather petty nature and his admiration of ideas of the universe which have greatness that make his tremendous monograph on Christian Science a suggestive and fascinating work.

If the author had never written any other book, this volume alone would have shown him to be a great social critic. Its candor, spontaneity and big, unique sense of human values place it with those creative criticisms and interpretative surveys of influential ideas which are among the world's most enlivening possessions—with *Thus Spake Zarathustra* and *Sartor Resartus* and Thoreau's *Civil Disobedience* and *The Shortest Way with Dissenters*.

At once a keenly analytic and a widely synthetic survey of the subject it has all the faculty of the close, detailed observation, and rapid, practical deduction of the river pilot. It is a masterpiece of clear consideration and powerful, natural expression from the author's candid praise of Mrs. Eddy's great contribution to human happiness, and her genius in execution to his exposition of her love of personal worship, and her taste for showy speech.

Not the least valuable and interesting part of the book, is its literary valuations. As a commentator on expression Mark Twain is always penetrating and imaginative. No more informing literary criticism is to be found than his reply to Matthew Arnold's strangely crass and ignorant remarks on General Grant's biography. His wit on the subject of the emptiness of Fenimore Cooper, his thorough-going praise of William Dean Howells' sustained power as a writer— everything he has to say concerning the art and craft of writing has conscientiousness, truth and independence.

One of Mark Twain's best attributes as a commentator on style, on men, on religious beliefs and on the ways of nations is his capacity for profound admiration. He has no poor provincial grudges against the souls and gifts of other peoples. He could praise well. He could admire greatly. He could admire with understanding. It is the obverse side of our American sin of judgment, and of condemnation in toto for a single obvious weakness or error that we are quite as likely to praise in toto for a single excellence. Public persons or foreign nations are entirely objectionable to us, or entirely commendable. Our regard is undiscriminating—a prejudice for or against its object. The reason why Mark Twain appreciated the greatnesses and the peculiar nobilities of the souls of nations was because he could also understand their smallnesses and their inferiorities. He could admire the beauties and contributive perceptions of our democracy because he could also know its stupidities and meannesses.

No one ever told the truth about us more relentlessly. No one ever laughed more uproariously, at our mussy, imbecile romanticism and our tenth-rate, ignorant feudal tastes and our mawkish imitative "refinement" or despised more completely our smug idealizing superstitions, or our sloppy subservient government, and our endless injustice.

But it is not alone because of Mark Twain's unique humorous genius, nor because he could admire well, nor because of his many-colored wide view of life as a citizen of America and a far-sighted traveler of lands and waters, of histories and of religions, that he has been so richly appreciated by his enormous and constant audiences of readers. He had besides a certain essentially masculine faculty, in which no author has equaled him in many hundreds of years—a faculty profoundly satisfactory to the human race, to everyone who has been wronged, to everyone who has done wrong. He could curse well.

Perhaps a person of another sex, and destitute of any talent in this respect may be able to exercise a more impartial discrimination among cursers than is possible for a masculine listener; and may be more readily struck by this ability in authors. In my own view, and within my own range of reading, Mark Twain is the best curser since Isaiah. To curse in a fine, forthright style and spirit seems to require at once more intensive and more extensive moral information—more knowledge of the states of Heaven and of Hell and of excellence and splendor and miserableness and meanness in mortal character than has ever been acknowledged. Mark Twain will long gratify his country as a magnificent, an immortal execrator.

He could curse the ways of the United States excellently, and could praise them excellently because he was ceaselessly interested in the success and failure of the fortunes of American democracy. He saw that tremendous undertaking I think as no other creature has seen it for us. He saw it at close range and in exact detail in his river-pilot days and as a journalist; he saw it geographically and historically against other ages and peoples and without class-consciousness; and he looked at the vast fallacies, and dangerous poverties of its prevailing religious belief, with a strangely independent, with a brave and humane vision.

> Praise is well. Compliment is well [he once said in recognition of the honor shown him by a great over-seas audience], but affection—that is the last and final and most precious reward that any man can win, whether by character or achievement, and I am very grateful to have that reward.

In the face of all our pettiness, it is, I think, something in our favor that our country was capable of instinctively giving that reward in overwhelming measure throughout his long life-time to a sincerely denunciatory and damaging critic of extraordinary genius. Down the ages somewhere I believe it will be set down to our eternal credit that one of our most popular recreations has always been the satisfaction of embarking with our magical and profane pilot and going down the river—going down the river with Mark Twain.

The Anecdotal Side of Mark Twain

Told in Stories and Anecdotes Contributed to the Journal by the Closest Friends of the Great Humorist, and Now Published for the First Time

The Funniest Man in America is Here Treated in the Fourth Article of the Series of The Ladies' Home Journal's New Form of Biography. Fully Equal in Interest is this Article to Those Published of Thomas A. Edison, in the April Issue; of Mrs. Cleveland, in June, and of President McKinley, in July.

Mark Twain's Dislike for Clothes

Mark Twain has an intense dislike for clothes, and if it were possible would remain in his pajamas day in and day out. And whenever he can do so he eats breakfast in them, receives his friends and works in them. His favorite mode of writing is to lie flat on the floor on his stomach in his pajamas, with a pipe in his mouth. When on lecture tours he never gets out of his sleeping clothes until it is time to go to hall or opera house. When the fit strikes him he likes to exercise, and then with his customary shamble will shuffle along for miles and exhaust his most athletic companion. But he feels far more at home in his pajamas than in a street suit or evening clothes, and in them he remains as great a part of the day as Mrs. Clemens will allow him.

Reprinted from *The Ladies' Home Journal* 15 (October 1898): 5–6.

He Could Shave in Church

Among the passengers who found excuses for addressing Mark one morning on board the steamer on which he was traveling on Lake Huron there was a young man who asked him if he had ever seen or used a shaving stone, at the same time handing him one. It was a small, fine-grained sandstone, the shape of a miniature grindstone and about the size of an ordinary watch, or perhaps a trifle larger. The young man explained to Mark that all one had to do was to rub the face with this stone and the rough beard would disappear, and that the shaver could, with the greatest ease, shave anywhere.

Mark looked at it doubtfully, rubbed it on his unshaven cheek and expressed great wonder at the result; then putting it in his vest pocket he remarked with a quiet, sort of reminiscent smile: "Well, the Madam (he generally spoke of Mrs. Clemens as 'the Madam') will have no cause to complain again of my never being ready for church because it takes me so long to shave. I will just put this in my vest pocket on Sunday. Then when I get in church I'll just pull the thing out and enjoy a quiet shave in my pew during the longer prayer."

His First Two Meetings With General Grant

When Mark was first introduced to General Grant the latter shook hands in a perfunctory manner and immediately relapsed into his customary attitude of reticence. There was an awkward pause; it grew longer and longer as the humorist tried to think of something bright to say. Finally, as if in sheer desperation, Twain looked up, with an assumed air of great timidity, and said, "Mr. President, I—I feel a little bit embarrassed. Do you?" The President could not help smiling, and Mark took advantage of the chance the incident presented to give place to others.

Ten years later, when statesman and humorist met again, General Grant, with a twinkle in his eye, said, before Twain

The Anecdotal Side of Mark Twain

The latest portrait of Mark Twain (photograph by Alfred Ellis, London).

The house at Hannibal, Missouri, in which Mark Twain was born.

had the chance to utter a word: "Mr. Clemens, I don't feel at all embarrassed. Do you?"

His Appeal To Baby Ruth Cleveland

Some years ago Mark Twain appeared at the Consulate of the United States at Frankfort, Germany, and found Captain Mason, the Consul-General, packing up his books and papers, and all of his personal belongings. "What's up?" he asked. "My time is up," returned Mason cheerfully. "We have a Democratic President, and as I am a Republican I have to get out and give my place to a good Democrat, soon to be appointed to this post." "That's a blessed shame!" said Mr. Clemens, and he started for the hotel, where he wrote this letter to Ruth Cleveland, then only about a year old:

> *My Dear Ruth*: I belong to the Mugwumps, and one of the most sacred rules of our order prevents us from asking favors of officials or recommending men to office, but there is no harm in writing a friendly letter to you and telling you that an infernal outrage is about to be committed by your father in turning out of office the best Consul I know (and I know a great many) just because he is a Republican, and a Democrat wants his place.

And then Mr. Clemens related what he knew of Captain Mason and his official record, and continued:

> I can't send any message to the President, but the next time you have a talk with him concerning such matters I wish you would tell him about Captain Mason and what I think of a Government that so treats its efficient officials.

Three or four weeks later Mr. Clemens received a little envelope postmarked Washington in which was a note, written in President Cleveland's own hand, that read:

Mark Twain talking to reporters in bed (photograph by Major James B. Pond)

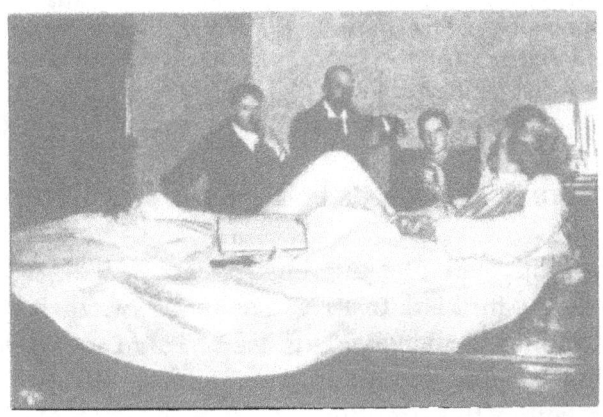

Mark Twain with his wife, and daughter, Miss Clara Clemens (photograph by Walter G. Chase)

Miss Ruth Cleveland begs to acknowledge the receipt of Mr. Twain's letter, and to say that she took the liberty of reading it to the President, who desires her to thank Mr. Twain for his information and to say to him that Captain Mason will not be disturbed in the Frankfort Consulate. The President also desires Miss Cleveland to say that if Mr. Twain knows of any other cases of this kind he will be greatly obliged if he will write him concerning them at his earliest convenience.

Compels His Manager To Keep His Contract

In order to keep a lecture engagement in the Northwest it was necessary for Mark to arrive one chilly morning in season to take the four o'clock overland train. There were five in the party, but no one grumbled. All reached the station five minutes before the time for the train, only to read on the bulletin, "Pacific Mail one hour and twenty minutes late." Mark began to grumble, saying that he had contracted to travel and give entertainments, and not to stand shivering around railroad stations. He kept this up for some time. Finally Mrs. Clemens asked him if he were not a little unreasonable. He was standing by the baggage wheelbarrow, and answered: "No, I am not. I insist on the Major's keeping his contract by keeping me traveling in this wheelbarrow." So Major Pond wheeled him up and down the platform just as the sun was coming up, when Miss Clara got the snap shot that is given above.

Mark Twain's Fondness for Cats

Mark Twain's American summer home for a number of years was at Quarry Farm, on the hill north of and overlooking Elmira, New York. Here he was invariably accompanied by a drove of cats—the cat being Mark's pet domestic animal. They followed him wherever he strolled about the place, and slept in a big chair beside the desk in his bower-study when he went there. He had for a long time four handsome cats—Beelzebub, Blatherskite, Apollinaris and Buffalo Bill—all under complete control. He would call them to "come up" on the chair, and they would all jump on the seat. He would tell them to "go to sleep," and instantly the group were all apparently fast asleep, remaining so until he called "Wide awake!" when in a twinkling up would go their ears and wide open would be their eyes.

His Way to Get Rid of Bores

Mark had an easy way, in the old days, of getting rid of bores. He delighted to smoke a pipe that he never cleaned and when any caller wearied him he would while seeming to be interested in what was said, puff like a locomotive, filling the room with such poisonous stuff as to make the unwelcome talker glad to go.

She Would Raise Melons: He Would Do the Rest

As everybody knows, the Secretary of Agriculture is authorized by Congress to distribute seeds among the farmers of the country for the ostensible purpose of introducing new vegetables and other crops from foreign countries. While he was Secretary of Agriculture the Hon. J. Sterling Morton received this communication:

Dear Sir: Your petitioner, Mark Twain, a poor farmer of Connecticut—indeed, the poorest one there in the opinion of envy—desires a few choice breeds of seed corn (maize), and in return will zealously support the Administration in all ways honorable and otherwise.

To speak by the card, I want these things to carry to Italy to an English lady. She is a neighbor of mine outside of Florence, and has a great garden and thinks she could raise corn for her table if she had the right ammunition. I myself feel a warm interest in this enterprise, both on patriotic grounds and because I have a key to that garden, which I got made from a wax impression. It is not very good soil, still I think she can raise enough for one table, and I am in a position to select the table.

If you are willing to aid and abet a countryman (and Gilder thinks you are), please find the signature and address of your petitioner below. Respectfully and truly yours,

"Mark Twain."

P.S. A handful of choice (Southern) watermelon seeds would pleasantly add to that lady's employment and give my table a corresponding lift.

Secretary Morton sent the seeds.

Once He Was Guilty of Punning

When Mr. and Mrs. Clemens were on their wedding tour he wrote to a Buffalo friend to secure board for them. This friend met them at the station on their return, and assured them that they would find their boarding-house satisfactory. On reaching there they were welcomed by the bride's parents, who asked them to accept the house as a wedding gift. Almost overcome by the surprise, Mark took his wife's hand, and stepping up to her parents simply said "Happy twain."

One of His Dry Queries

Several years ago Mr. Clemens met an Englishman traveling through this country with the unseeing eyes of the British tourist. The humorist told him, with much zest, one of his inimitable stories, which was received with a puzzled stare and no comment. Six months later Twain was in a London hotel when an Englishman rushed up to him and burst into a

As he often strolls out (photograph by Alfred Ellis, London)

roar of laughter as he grasped both Mark's hands, exclaiming, "I see the joke now!"

He proceeded to explain that the point of the story had suddenly struck him some time before, and when he heard of Mr. Clemens' presence in London he took the fastest train up to see him. The great joker looked at him gravely a moment and then queried, "You say you took the express? Why didn't you take the freight?"

An Example of His Devices To Get a Good Story

In Berlin when one pays his fare to the conductor of a street car he receives a ticket, which is soon afterward collected by an inspector, who boards the car at a fixed point. One day, just as a joke, Mark Twain paid his fare fifteen times on one trip, each time throwing the ticket out of the window or under his seat as soon as he had deposited the regular fare with the conductor. A few minutes later the inspector would get on the car and demand tickets all around. Of course Twain had none to show and had to buy another, apparently with reluctance. The performance amused the American, dumfounded the conductor, who had never met so reckless a passenger, and tickled the native passengers, who thought the foreigner well punished for his negligence. By this modest investment material was obtained for a capital story which netted Mark Twain just five hundred dollars.

Not So Bright As He Thought He Was

It was a busy morning in the Clemens household. Mrs. Clemens had had some etchings removed from their frames in order to clean them, and they were scattered about the floor of the library; upstairs Mark was digging away on some article

Mark Twain's four favorite cats: Beelzebub, Blatherskite, Appollinaris, and Buffalo Bill (photographs by permission of Major James B. Pond)

Mark insisted on traveling (photograph by Miss Clara Clemens)

that was absorbing all his attention; and just at this time an Englishman who had shown the family many courtesies and entertained them on his houseboat, rang the bell. Mrs. Clemens retreated to her chamber, and when the visitor's card was brought up told the maid to take it to Mr. Clemens and say that the gentleman was waiting and must be seen at once, as she herself was not prepared to meet him. Down came Mark, smothering the rage that was arising on account of the interruption. He had merely glanced at the card and had not recognized the name. Entering the library, and seeing the stranger bending over the array of etchings, he surmised that their caller was a dealer in pictures. "Well," he said rather brusquely, "I don't see that we need anything in your line," Then, glancing at the pictures, which he supposed had just been brought to the house, he added, "We already have this one, and this, and that one, too. At any rate, we don't need any more."

The Englishman was dumfounded. He politely offered an excuse for intruding, asked where Mr. Warner lived, and departed, while Mark returned to his writing. On the way past his wife's room he remarked triumphantly that he "got rid of that agent easily." Mrs. Clemens stared at him in horror, and then explained who the gentleman was. Mark instantly dashed across the back yard—a short cut to Warner's—with profuse apologies.

His Discovery in the New Testament

Mark Twain sat in his little library at Chelsea, London, one afternoon, when a friend who happened to be calling noticed an open Bible upon his table and inquired if he had taken to the study of the Holy Word.

"That's a good Book," Twain answered with his odd drawl. "That's about the most interesting Book I ever read. Joe Twitchell, a parson over in Connecticut recommended it to me, and I have been more interested in it than in any other book I have read for a long time. You better read it yourself. It beats any novel or history or work of science that I ever tackled. It is full of good stories and philosophy. It suggests lots of ideas, and there's news in it. I find things that I never heard of before. Did you ever know that the English people were mentioned in the Bible?"

"Why, yes, there is a theory that the lost tribes of Israel migrated over this way and settled the British Islands."

"Oh! I don't mean that. I discovered to-day that Christ spoke of the British people in the 'Sermon on the Mount.'" And, reaching over for the Book, he read:

"Blessed are the meek, for they shall inherit the earth."

Was Once a Perfumer

Probably few folk know that Mark Twain was once engaged in the perfumery business in Cleveland, Ohio, hanging out a sign: "Carl Faust, Late Perfumer to the King of Holland." He afterward told a friend that he bought all his supplies in New York, except his "pure bears' grease," which was a mixture of olive oil, wax and scent, made on the spot, and advertised by means of a bearskin hung now and then at the door. The venture was not a brilliant success, and Mark soon retired.

His Early Proclivity to Get into Trouble

One of the incidents of his boyhood in Hannibal, which does not figure in "Tom Sawyer," occurred while his sister Pamela was teaching music there. Frequently she used to entertain her pupils at her home. One night Mark was sent to bed early, while Miss Pamela and her young friends indulged in a candy-pull. At the proper moment the sweet mixture was set on the back porch to cool. Just about that time Mark was awakened by a cat fight. Here was a treat not to be missed. He crawled out of his window upon a trellis over the porch in order to get a good view, but missing his footing fell down into the pan of candy, making an alarming clatter. When the folks rushed out to see what had happened it appeared that Mark and the candy were inseparable.

Some of the Things He Likes

Mark Twain is a good billiard player and will drop almost any occupation for the sake of having a game. He likes to take long walks, and he also is fond of base-ball. Once, while at a ball game, he became so excited that he dropped his umbrella from the grandstand. Too lazy to go down under the seats for it at the time, he found, when looking for it at the end of the game, that it was missing. The next day he published this striking advertisement: "Five Dollars Reward for the umbrella, and several hundred for the body of the boy who stole it—dead or alive."

Saying a Good Word for General Hawley

Once in a while Mark has taken a hand in politics. On one occasion, being invited to speak in the interest of his fellow-townsman, Gen. Joseph Hawley, who was a candidate for reelection to the United States Senate, he said, in the course of a droll address: "General Hawley deserves your support, although he has about as much influence in purifying the Senate as a bunch of flowers would have in sweetening a glue factory. But he's all right; he never would turn any poor beggar away from his door empty-handed. He always gives them something—almost without exception a letter of introduction to me, urging me to help them."

Why Colonel Sellers Was Named "Mulberry"

One day while Mark and Charles Dudley Warner were walking together in Hartford they happened to begin a discussion of the modern novel, and one or the other suggested that it might be a good plan to burlesque it. Later, while journeying together to Boston, this suggestion took definite shape, and on their return the work was begun, one author writing a chapter, the other taking up the threads of the story the next day, and both critically examining the result each evening and asking the opinions of their wives as to the success of each stage of the undertaking. Finally they collected all the manuscript, of which there was too great a quantity, and jointly condensed it. It was owing to a suggestion by Mr. Warner that the chief character in the tale was called Colonel Eschol Sellers, and it is a fact that the man whose name was taken—a man supposed to be long dead—made a fiery demand for satisfaction, visiting Hartford for that purpose. In later editions of the story the name "Eschol" was changed to "Mulberry."

Afraid He would Run Out of "Smokes"

Mark Twain is an inveterate smoker and never lets a moment go by when possible without smoking his pipe or a cigar. When going on a long journey he has a mortal dread of running out of tobacco. When at Victoria, British Columbia, he was to sail next day for Honolulu. During a walk he espied a wholesale dealer in cheroots (small cigars) and bought three thousand of them, together with fifteen pounds of pipe tobacco. In the afternoon he went back to the store and bought three thousand more cheroots. That evening shortly after beginning his lecture he surprised his manager, who was in the audience, by beckoning him to come to the stage. The summons was obeyed with alacrity much to the curiosity of the audience. The manager mounted the platform, and when at the lecturer's side Mark Twain stopped in his talk, and turning to his manager said:

> Pond, I fear that cigar place may close before I get there. Go there now and get fifteen hundred more of those cheroots.

And turning to his audience Mark went on with his lecture as if nothing had happened. Next day he sailed with the seventy-five hundred cheroots and fifteen pounds of tobacco, perfectly happy and with his mind easy.

How He Made William II Laugh the Whole Evening

Hon. William Walter Phelps, who was the American Minister to Germany when Mark Twain first met William II, said that the incident was a striking one. "The Kaiser," said Mr. Phelps, "was then on speaking terms with but one American author, Fenimore Cooper. Now, Royal personages usually have a series of set speeches ready for emergencies. But William opened the conversation with a reference to "The Last of the Mohicans," or its author. A thoroughly well-drilled man of the world would have listened to His Majesty's remarks with the gravity becoming an apostle of wellbred boredom, and in that case the Kaiser would have done all the talking throughout the evening. Not so Mark Twain. He told His Majesty that he had come across a copy of "The Pathfinder" quite recently, and that it had struck him as the funniest thing out. And then he went on to speak of the moccasined person treading into the tracks of the moccasined enemy and thus hiding his own trail, and the master of woodcraft who had always a profusion of dry twigs ready on which somebody stepped, thereby alarming all the reds and whites for several hundred miles around. He led His Majesty "in the track of a cannon ball across the plain through a dense fog," and invited him to try and steer his yacht Hohenzollern in a gale for a particular spot on shore where he knew of an undertow that would hold her back against the gale and save her, as one of Cooper's skippers professed to have done. Then His Majesty forgot all about his fine set phrases and his desire to impress Mr. Clemens, and gave himself up to the enjoyment of American humor, its extravagance, its daring. Kaiser and humorist talked together the whole evening," concluded Mr. Phelps, "and the rest of the company received very little attention from either of them."

"3.—Mark Twain"

A.C. Ward

At one time it would have seemed an enormity equivalent to high treason to suggest that the real tragedy of Mark Twain's life might be found in the popular success of his literary gambols as a professional funny man. Now, however, it is not difficult to find those—Americans as well as Europeans—who agree that the necessities of farce, coupled with a defect of critical vision, turned some of Mark Twain's funny books into two-minded affairs, where verbal horse-play intermingles with savage satire aimed at a too-distant target. Almost certainly it would have been better for himself and for American literature if he had never discovered Europe. It is possible that his long-sighted preoccupation with the absurdities and injustices current in the Old World was in the first place determined by a well-founded conviction that America was so Europe-conscious as to put her own growth in danger of being seriously stunted; but when Mark Twain set the United States guffawing at trans-Atlantic queernesses he missed the chance of becoming his own country's most valuable satirist. There is no doubt in the minds of critics or of critical admirers that Mark Twain's work will be ruthlessly sifted by posterity, yet there is no common opinion as to what will be rejected. Since his death, a fuller portrait of the humorist's personality has revealed in him a considerable stratum of pessimism, which tended to grow in later years. This was so much at variance

Reprinted from *American Literature 1880–1930*, New York: The Dial Press, 1932, pp. 52–62.

with the common picture of him as a gay trifler (though a proper appreciation of his books could never have encouraged such a judgement) that his posthumous reputation seemed for a short time likely to rest upon such darker works as *The Mysterious Stranger* and *What Is Man?* But as the balance evens-out [sic] in a further reassessment of the various factors in his character, there will be less temptation to stress what seemed remarkable only because it had not been generally known.

In however brief an attempt to reconsider Mark Twain's contribution to the literature of his time, note must be taken of what he was qualified to do, and of how he reacted to certain contemporary influences. America from about the middle of the last century experienced the most extraordinary spate of professional funny men ever known in any country. The success of the dialect humorists depended chiefly upon the fact that their sayings and writings were a subtle if unconscious flattery of the great unlettered American public, which was tickled to death to find literary gentlemen speaking a language everybody could understand and cracking jokes comprehensible to the most unassuming intelligence. The popularity of Joe Miller, Artemus Ward and their like was not confined to the unliterary. Better-educated people found that type of humour quaint, refreshing and restful, though with this part of the audience its appeal was impermanent. Even poor jokes are always jokes to the four million, but to the four hundred a poor joke is only poor. Mark Twain grew up at a time when it was almost impossible for any ambitious popular writer to escape the spraying jet of farce, and he became at length saturated by it as a result of Artemus Ward's praise of his early journalistic writings. Though Mark Twain was then still under thirty, he had already accumulated the wide and varied experience of life which made him, at least potentially, America's most liberally informed and democratic writer. Born in the Middle West (Florida, Missouri) and owning a strain of Southern blood through his father's Virginian ancestry, Samuel Langhorne Clemens belonged to the new insurgent America which was travelling away from the puritan and intellectualist tradition. Beginning work after comparatively little schooling, the boy passed a few years in newspaper and printing offices, before he began those wanderings afield which eventually brought him to the most important of his adventures—the period (1857–61) spent on the Mississippi river-boats, upon which he became a licensed pilot and found, in a common cry of the leadsmen, his pen-name Mark Twain. With the outbreak of civil war, river-traffic was suspended and he returned, full of matter concerning men and places, to journalism, travelling, lecturing and ultimately to authorship in the full sense. Life and work on the Mississippi provided him with that swarming knowledge of humanity which populates his best books with diversified but mostly robust types. But if the pilot years taught him much, they failed to teach him some things by which he could have profited. He hated the merely anaemic virtues, and healthy readers can rejoice in his hatred; but in some respects he was disastrously insensitive, and this was in part responsible for his inability to recognize how many things he was incapable of so much as beginning to understand. As long as he could see the outsides of things he was inclined to believe that he saw and knew the whole. In an earlier generation one could have said solemnly that Mark Twain was "without reverence." The solemnity would not have injured the truth, for a man who lacks reverence (or the capacity for it) is automatically deficient in a sense of proportion and is so far unqualified to be a critic of life. Few humorists of Mark Twain's rank have had it in them to be, on occasion, so completely and finally boneheaded. To say that he was sometimes a bull in a china shop would be no more than a conventual whispered hint of the truth: at his worst he was a rhinoceros among porcelain. No doubt a rhinoceros would detect something a trifle inappropriate in such circumstances; apparently Mark Twain never did. He could barge and guffaw his way into any company without suspecting that he was the actual joke—and a bad one. If he had not been, at his best, a radiant dark angel, there would be no need to comment on his imbecilities, of which both *The Innocents Abroad* and *A Yankee at the Court of King Arthur* contain many. Nothing pleases half-baked democrats so much as demagogy, nor philistines so much as strident obtuseness. Mark Twain was in many respects a philistine, and though he was better than a half-baked democrat he did not disdain to truckle to such. It must have been with one eye steadily on this part of his audience that he wrote much of *The Innocents Abroad*, and in fairness to Mark Twain it should be remembered that he was writing the chapters (subsequently assembled to make a volume) as travel-letters for a Californian paper, and therefore for a community of average intelligences with no literary or artistic nonsense about them. In certain respects Mark Twain had something better than a *flair* for what the public wanted. Like Northcliffe in England later, he had only to consult his own taste in matters of art and politics with the assurance that popular taste would coincide. America was already horribly near becoming God's own country in Mark Twain's time; and, having only tenuous roots to its civilization, it suspected something shady at the roots of European civilization. The situation which had arisen in the American Middle and West was natural enough. The new self-consciously important nation, sickened by the Eastern States' slavish copying of European culture, was reacting with violence and, proceeding to damn or to guy what had hitherto been admired, was in danger of finding the European incubus on its shoulders in a new guise. If Mark Twain had said hail and farewell to Europe in one comprehensive Yankee cuss, no European would have begrudged him that measure of relief; but he spent several books wastefully and futilely nagging at the Old World, violently unearthing what had not been hidden, and proclaiming old abuses that a score of European writers had already laid bare. It has been remarked that *A Yankee at the Court of King Arthur* is "a sincere book, full of lifelong convictions earnestly held, a book charged with a rude iconoclastic humour, intended like the work of Cervantes to hasten the end of an obsolescent civilization." The comparison is inapposite both because the humour in *Don Quixote* is universal, whereas that in the *Yankee* is local; and because Cervantes thoroughly well understood what he tilted at, whereas there were many things in the "obsolescent civilization" of the Arthurian tradition that Mark Twain had neither the desire nor the insight to comprehend. He could not dispose of the Age of Chivalry by pointing out that it was also an age of barbarism, nor by suggesting analogies between medieval barbarism and that of the modern age. No intelligent European pretended that barbarity and a mystical apprehension of the universe were not co-existent in Arthurianism; but whereas Europe already knew about the barbarism, Mark Twain was incapable of responding to the mysticism. English people watching the Yankee's invasion of Arthurian territory feel very much as a cathedral custodian would if a boisterous holiday-maker vomited over an exquisite medieval carving. The visitor's companions might hail the disgusting exploit either as deliciously funny or as a magnificent proletarian gesture of contempt. Probably it was easier for Americans in the 'nineties than it is for English or Americans to-day to believe the book marvellously diverting and injurious to European obsolescence. America had still to learn the usefulness of a literary Munroe doctrine. What a perennially good travel-book *The Innocents Abroad* would be if the acute observations and the humor could be retained and the philistine spleen and facetiousness deleted! Yet uncontrolled by self-criticism and lacking taste or informed judgement, what a dull ass Mark Twain could be:

> We visited the Louvre... and looked at its miles of paintings by the old masters. Some of them were beautiful, but at the same time they carried such evidences about them of the cringing spirit of those great men that we found small pleasure in examining them. Their nauseous adulation of princely patrons was more prominent to me and chained my attention more surely than the charms of colour and expressions which are claimed to be in the pictures. Gratitude for kindness is well, but it seems to me that some

> of these artists carried it so far that it ceased to be gratitude, and became worship. If there is a plausible excuse for the worship of men, then by all means let us forgive Rubens and his brethren. (*Innocents Abroad*, ch. xiv.)

The fact that in *Innocents Abroad* Mark Twain could not let even the story of Abelard and Heloise go without making a long nose does at least enable us to calculate the extent of the changes and development his mind and heart underwent before he wrote such later works as (1896) *Personal Recollections of Joan of Arc* (an historical romance based upon a careful study of the evidence concerning her) and *Eve's Diary*. Although Joan was a lifelong heroine to him, Joan's oppressors would have been rich game for his peculiar humour twenty-five years before; and Adam and Eve would have offered many opportunities for facetious quirks. While *Eve's Diary* is a minor work, Mark Twain thought *Joan of Arc* his best book. Both are characterized by insight and a comprehensive sense of pity such as were lacking in the earlier books, which, however, demanded these qualities no less. The double strain in Mark Twain's nature caused his later capacity for pity and tenderness to be counterbalanced in other writings by a pessimism so deep as to approach despair. This is best illustrated in *The Man that Corrupted Hadleyburg* (written 1898), a long short story which recounts sardonically how nineteen "honest" citizens in the town of Hadleyburg were tricked into lying by the hope of securing a sack alleged to be full of gold. By the time that story came to be written Mark Twain had no disposition to turn his eyes upon European shortcomings. His vision of humanity as a whole had become gloomy, and in *Hadleyburg* he seems to be hinting that there are few "honest" men who cannot be bought. What had darkened his outlook? Probably no other answer need be attempted to that question than the suggestion that a tendency toward depression had always been latent in him, and found its outlet early on in the spleen already mentioned as trickling through his facetiousness in the *Innocents* and other books. Shortly after he returned from the first European tour Mark

"3—Mark Twain"

Twain married the woman upon whom he seems to be pronouncing an epitaph when he makes Adam say over Eve's grave, "Wheresoever she was, *there* was Eden." There are some who believe, despite those words, that Mark Twain chafed against the silken fetters of conventional respectability imposed upon their married life by Mrs. Clemens. Outwardly he wore the fetters with ease, but inwardly, it is clear, *something* chafed him desperately. If we do not yet know fully what it was, we can at least consider how far his two masterpieces—*Tom Sawyer* (1876) and *Huckleberry Finn* (1884)—may be used to suggest a portrait of Mark Twain himself, through their presentation of the conflict which leads nature to be at odds with custom and habit. Both Tom and Huckleberry are rebels—though (we might too readily assume) only normal boyish ones; but their rebellious instincts seem to be, in fact, more to Mark Twain than cubbish pranks. The boys are identified with their creator and he with them. Their original sin is the reflection of his mature outlook, of his impatience with conventional uses, of his firm and sweeping judgements. Tom goes unwillingly to church and Mark Twain takes the opportunity to say: "The choir always tittered and whispered all through service. There was once a church choir that was not ill-bred, but I have forgotten where it was, now. It was a great many years ago, and I can scarcely remember anything about it, but I think it was in some foreign country." (*Tom Sawyer*, ch. v.) When the public examination of the pupils attending Tom's school is held, Mark Twain comments upon the current educational system with evident contempt for its encouragement of "a nursed and petted melancholy," its insincerity and cultivation of emotional gush and stereotyped moral phraseology which infected the children's essays with an "inveterate and intolerable sermon that wagged its crippled tail at the end of each and every one of them."

> No matter what the subject might be, a brain-racking effort was made to squirm it into some aspect or other that the moral and religious mind could contemplate with edification. The glaring insincerity of these sermons was not

sufficient to compass banishment of the fashion from the schools, and it is not sufficient to-day; it will never be sufficient while the world stands, perhaps. (*Tom Sawyer*, ch. xxii.)

Over twenty years separated the writing of *Tom Sawyer* and *The Man that Corrupted Hadleyburg*, but the mood of the forty-year-old Mark Twain as displayed in the foregoing quotations is different only in degree, not in kind, from the mood of the old man whose work is bitter with disillusion. He hated the doctrine that Appearance is Everything, whether he detected it in the insincerities of the village school or in the hypocrisies of Hadleyburg; and if it is true that, in the service of domestic peace, he accommodated himself for years to a social virtue where "homely truth is unpalatable," the late outpouring of dammed-up distemper is explicable. That Mark Twain, with his actively sceptical and critical intelligence, should have filled the part of ideal husband was no doubt a triumph of domestic conquest, but its effect on Mark Twain's mind and spirit can be guessed. It is significant, too, that Tom Sawyer discovered "that to promise not to do a thing is the surest way in the world to make a body want to go and do that very thing." Did Mark Twain find, as Huck Finn found, that "whithersoever he turned, the bars and shackles of civilization shut him in and bound him hand and foot?" (*Tom Sawyer*, ch. xxiii.) From a stalactite in Injun Joe's cave, water fell slowly drop by drop every twenty minutes:

> That drop was falling when the Pyramids were new; when Troy fell; when the foundations of Rome were laid; when Christ was crucified; when the Conqueror created the British Empire; when Columbus sailed; when the massacre at Lexington was "news." It is falling now; it will still be falling when all these things shall have sunk down the afternoon of history and the twilight of tradition, and been swallowed up in the thick night of oblivion. Has everything a purpose and a mission? Did this drop fall patiently during five thousand

years to be ready for this flitting human insect's need, and had it another important object to accomplish ten thousand years to come? No matter. (*Tom Sawyer*, ch. xxxvi.)

The *farceur* of *Innocents Abroad*, who could vent his scepticism in splenetic references to Abelard and Heloise and other European "remains," was (by the time he came to *Tom Sawyer*) being driven inward to occasional broodings upon the follies and pretences of the human insect and upon his littleness as he faces the inescapable night of oblivion. From brooding he was to pass to disgust, perhaps to despair, and Mark Twain's pilgrimage was ended by the follower of Artemus Ward becoming not extravagantly unlike a disciple of Dean Swift. His duality could be illustrated further by reference to the rapid alternations between delicious comedy and violent tragedy in *Tom Sawyer* and *Huckleberry Finn*, but to dwell upon such points as these might be to forget the books while remembering only the evidence they offer in reference to The Case of Mark Twain. To this generation Mark Twain is interesting as a "case" because he had the misfortune to be considered in his lifetime as little more than a big-hearted and plain blunt funny man. Posthumous appreciation of his complexity and subtlety has caused some temporary overshadowing of his literary genius and his greatness as a humorist, as distinct from his quality as a verbal juggler and *farceur*. *Tom Sawyer* and *Huckleberry Finn* are among the few humorous masterpieces in world literature, altogether aside from what high merit they may also have as representations of the Eternal Boy—a creature particularly interesting to Mark Twain inasmuch as the Eternal Boy is also the Eternal Savage, the antithesis of civilized man. These two stories are honest and vigorous recreations of American life "in the raw" without trace of conscious starkness. *Huckleberry Finn* is an entirely successful continuation of the earlier book, no doubt for the very reason that it does not try to repeat a success but digresses from it into a more extensive sphere. The river adventures have the magnificent force of the realities Mark Twain knew from his Mississippi pilot days; and the two rogues—the Duke and the King—possess an almost Shakespearean amplitude with a more than Shakespearean repertory of ingenious dodges. Throughout both books hardly a sentence can be found in which humour and fun decline into facetiousness; and the tasteless insensitiveness of Mark Twain's farcical books has here become transformed into the sympathy and understanding necessary for true comedy. He was no longer living on the verbal dexterity and deliberate quaintness of approach which had served for the ramshackle structure of the *Innocents* and the *Yankee*.

No doubt it would be impossible to find three other writers with so many obvious differences as exist between Walt Whitman, Emily Dickinson and Mark Twain. Yet their fundamental qualities are not unlike, and might almost be said to be identical—for each had independent vision, and each dealt with experience in independence of the habitual attitude toward human affairs which passed for tradition and morality. Mark Twain was the most tragic figure among the three, for though each had endurances to cope with, he was the only one upon whom vital compromises were forced. By natural disposition, however (and in part in achievement also), he also confronted the universe without the chafing harness of civilization. In these three, at last, a new vision came to begin the making of a new literature for the New World.

Review of *Tom Sawyer Abroad*

It is more decent to parody Jules Verne than Sir Thomas Malory, and Mark Twain may therefore be deemed to have returned in his latest flight of humour to the limits of legitimate burlesque. We are introduced once more to Tom Sawyer, Huck Finn, and the invaluable nigger, Tim [sic]. These heroes obtain possession of a balloon, with a patent steering apparatus and a minimum pace of one hundred miles an hour. In this they cross the Atlantic, are driven by contrary winds to the middle of the Sahara, traverse Egypt, and finally come to anchor on "Mount Sinai, where the Ark was." On their way they fall in with oases, dust-storms, mirages, caravans, and other familiar marvels of African travel, and have a narrow escape from a somewhat improbable congregation of lions and tigers. The point of the jest appears to lie: firstly, in the shifts and expedients of the ingenious Tom Sawyer, who is certainly never at a loss for any emergency, and is able to point out to his companions the ruins of Joseph's granary, and the treasure hill of the Dervish and the Camel-driver in the *Arabian Nights*; and, secondly, in the attempt to express elementary scientific and geographical facts in terms of Yankee slang and Yankee logic. There are perpetual discussions, in which Tom Sawyer's fragments of book-learning are pitted against the ignorance and dialectic smartness of Huck Finn and the nigger, and, of course invariably get the worst of it. The chief fault of the book is that it does not strike one as particularly funny, which is perhaps a

Reprinted from *The Academy* XLVI, No. 1158 (14 July 1894): 27.

considerable defect in what is professedly a work of humour. It is a good thing, as someone once said, for a comic paper to have some jokes in it.

"Hadleyburg": Mark Twain's Dual Attack on Banal Theology and Banal Literature

Susan K. Harris

Recent criticism of Mark Twain's "The Man that Corrupted Hadleyburg" has primarily concerned itself with answering Gladys Bellamy's charge that the moralism of the story is philosophically inconsistent with its determinism. Pascal Covici, Jr., perhaps more interested in the psychological than the philosophical basis of free will, holds that "Hadleyburg" "has for its theme not the corrupting... but the awakening of the town to a sense of its innate depravity" and claims that the townsfolk welcome exposure and finally achieve a moral victory. In a more direct response to Bellamy, Clinton S. Burhams, Jr., feels that "Twain's determinism, . . . far from being inconsistent with his moralism, is the source of its real values. In his concern. . . with the relations between conscience and the heart, he views the moral values of conscience as determined by environment, by training; and one of his major aims is to show that such training. . . must be empirical, not merely prescriptive." Taking a slightly different tack, Henry B. Rule explicates the story in the light of R. W. B. Lewis's *The American Adam*, seeing Hadleyburg as "an ironic Eden . . . diseased by hypocrisy and money-lust" and claiming that "in Twain's treatment of the Eden myth, Satan plays the role of savior rather than corrupter," for the Stranger/Satan figure initiates the process whereby the Richardses and the town are morally reformed. Responding to Rule, Helen E.

Reprinted from *American Literary Realism, 1870–1910* XVI, No. 2 (Autumn 1983): 240–52.

Nebeker sees the original corrupter as the Calvinist God who, like the Stranger, punishes Adam and Eve by condemning their progeny to a "corrupt, moral life" of absolute depravity. Her reading of "Hadleyburg" sees the Richardses, despite their "moral bankruptcy," as "human, weak, but essentially guiltless" because they are the victims of God's vengeance. Finally, Mary E. Rucker's essay illustrates "the Richardses' freedom and their failure to attain a moral regeneration because of their not making the morally correct choices."[1]

With the exception of Covici and possibly of Rucker, the above commentators have assumed that Mary and Edward Richards, the central characters of "Hadleyburg," are intended to provide a focus for moral failings shared by the rest of the town, and that their fate is linked to the fate of the other citizens. Covici, however, notes that "Mary and Edward are overwhelmed by [the stranger's] hoax, but the rest of the town can laugh at themselves,"[2] and Rucker seems to imply that while the Richardses are damned by their failure to "act consciously and deliberately for primarily moral ends," the rest of the town is regenerated.[3] Following them, this essay will argue that, far from being representative of the town, Mary and Edward Richards are its most corrupt characters, and that their story differs both thematically and formally from the story of the town. Moreover, Mark Twain uses the elderly couple's tale not only to attack contemporary liberal notions of the power of free will but also to attack the way such ideas are embodied in current forms of short fiction.

"The Man that Corrupted Hadleyburg" actually contains two narratives, integral to each other but offering very different conclusions. The town's growth from pride in its untried virtue to humble willingness to learn how to resist temptation can be seen as an umbrella, or cover, tale for the far darker revelation of the Richardses' true nature. As William Macnaughton has pointed out, "The Man that Corrupted Hadleyburg" contains ideas from *What is Man?*, the heretical "gospel" Mark Twain was writing (but did not intend for publication in his lifetime) during the same period he was writing the short story. Because "Hadleyburg" *was* intended for publication, however, the author had to cater to popular expectations if he wanted to be read.[4] It is possible to see the apparent contradiction between moralism and determinism in the short story as evidence of Twain's ploy to make his ideas publishable: he hid his deterministic tale under a moralistic one that was both accessible and palatable to a readership accustomed to sentimental short stories which consistently implied not only that moral regeneration was possible, but that it was easy. Mark Twain uses Mary and Edward Richards to test his readers' ability to penetrate popular literary stereotypes, hoping that they will recognize that beneath the message of Christian hope implicit in the story of the town's reformation lies a message of Calvinist despair implicit in the story of the Richardses' ruin.

Because "The Man that Corrupted Hadleyburg" contains a pessimistic message disguised as an optimistic one, however, it can also be seen as an attack on the kind of short stories most often published in periodicals such as *Harper's*, *The Atlantic Monthly*, and *McClure's*, as well as in newspapers, a major market for American short fiction in the nineteenth century. Although it is a strikingly good story of its type and bears the unmistakable stamp of Twain's humor and style, the cover story, the story of Hadleyburg's reformation, nevertheless offers few surprises for readers of formulaic fiction: thematically inverting the plea from the Lord's Prayer to "lead us not into temptation" by juxtaposing to it Milton's strictures against a "blank virtue, not a pure," the cover tale formally resolves its tensions through the catharsis of the town meeting and overtly proclaims its moral through the town's revised motto. The narrative of Mary and Edward, on the other hand, dangles, neither thematically nor formally resolving its tensions. When the Richardses die they have neither recognized the magnitude of their own corruption nor exonerated the Reverend Burgess; little seems to have been learned by any of the characters concerned and there seems no "message" to the tale. Since the tensions are at best only partially resolved in the secondary tale, and since there is no neat moral to summarize the story's points, it seems inadequate and unfinished. Yet the structural raggedness of the Richardses' story is what makes it central to this work. Actively subverting the optimism projected by the cover story's design, the secondary story challenges us to re-examine our expectations of the difficulty of moral reform. It can be seen as a cautionary tale covertly seeking to awaken readers to the extent to which they have been duped by the sentimental optimism of the stories offered them in popular markets, the majority of whose careful plots, stereotyped characters, and neat resolutions convey the idea that human beings are essentially good-natured and will solve their problems once they recognize them. In fact, the subordinate story in "The Man that Corrupted Hadleyburg" can be seen as Mark Twain's rejection of the form and content of popular short stories, for in highlighting, by contrast, the facility with which moral problems are solved in formulaic fiction, it forces readers to realize that as not all stories can be resolved, so not all souls can be redeemed.

I

With the notable exception of Professor Rucker, the general tendency of readers of "Hadleyburg" has been to view Mary and Edward Richards as a rather benign elderly couple who, though sharing the moral failings of the town, are still relatively innocent and become the chief victims of the stranger's hoax only because they have been too defeated by the burdens of their lives to be able to redefine their moral universe and start a new life. They are, nevertheless, saved on their deathbeds and morally regenerated. Rucker, however, notes that "the couple's drives—fear and delirium—qualify the contention that the Richardses' death-bed confession signifies a moral regeneration."[5] Rucker's analysis of the Richardses should point us in a new—and fruitful—direction. For the

Richardses are not only driven by fear on their deathbeds, fear is one of the primary emotions of their lives. Rather than being less guilty than the rest of the town, Mary and Edward are like the boys of *The Chronicle of Young Satan* (also being composed during this period), who know that they are "not manly enough not brave enough to do a generous action when there [is] a chance that it could get [them] into trouble."[6] For instance, Mary, whose words always equate reputation and livelihood, assures Edward that he was right not to have valued his "manliness" before "public opinion" because "we couldn't afford it" (H, p. 236).

The narrator of "Hadleyburg" brings both Richardses into focus in a swift rhetorical descent from the general to the specific, a framework designed to trap the unwary reader into believing that this is a gentle old couple just like the ones he has met in stories like William Allen White's "The Home-Coming of Colonel Hucks."[7] Having introduced the town and explained its reputation for honesty, he appears to select one particular couple on whom to focus his drama, introducing them in stereotypical terms before ever naming them. The effect of their being introduced within a familiar context is to throw readers off the track instantly. For if we placidly accept the stereotype, we will never be able to see beyond it to the actual character delineated. Mary, for instance, is first heard rather than seen, "a woman's voice," which trustingly bids the stranger enter through the unlocked door. Next she is introduced as "the old lady who sat reading the *Missionary Herald* by the lamp," visual data designed to signal devoutness for readers of short stories in which simple, pious, and trusting old ladies were standard fare. In fact, the old lady is merely described in a series of cues—familiar signs directing readers to assume a particular set of characteristics—until she acts; only then does she attain a name, and only then does she begin to manifest anti-stereotypical behavior. Discovering that the man has left a sack full of gold, "Mrs. Richards" suddenly flies off to lock the door, draw the shades, and otherwise exhibit behavior ill-suited to one who believes herself surrounded by honest neighbors. Her change from passive trust to active mistrust suggests not only that she is not necessarily the gentle old soul "cued" so far, but that she expects others to respond to the money with a passion identical to her own.

Edward, too, is carefully introduced within a formulaic context before his particular character is revealed: arriving home late and tired, he moans that "it's dreadful to be poor, and to have to make these dismal journeys at my time of life," but at his wife's remonstrance ("Be comforted: we have our livelihood; we have our good name"[8]) he responds conventionally: "Yes, Mary, and that is everything. Don't mind my talk. . . Kiss me—there, it's all gone now, and I am not complaining any more" (H, p. 234). When he learns of the money, however, Edward's response is much like his wife's, though, being male, he lets her seem to bite the apple first. His proposal that they bury the sack and deny any knowledge of its existence is delivered "humorously," an emotive mask for desires he will not let himself express until she has made the first move. Yet although they are at pains to project an image of themselves which conforms to the mores of the town, both Richardses indicate their sense that they are actually spiritually alien to it. When they speculate on the identity of the good citizen whom the stranger has directed them to find, only Barclay Goodson, the local misanthrope, occurs to them as a possibility, for of all the town, he seems to have been the only citizen known to be capable of generosity. Not only do the Richardses identify him as untypically generous, they also identify him as untypically frank. Most importantly, they indicate that they share his view of Hadleyburg, thus identifying themselves as psychological outsiders rather than insiders. Although Goodson's response to Hadleyburg had been to attack it verbally, and the Richardses' has been to endorse it verbally, all three believe the town, for all its vaunted honesty, is also "narrow, self-righteous, and stingy" (H, p. 235).

Having cued readers to perceive the Richardses as decent folk, and then having hinted that their appearance may be deceptive, Twain proceeds to test his readers' ability to look behind the mask. Much of our reading of this story depends on whether we accept what the characters say or evaluate what they do. The Richardses' conscious verbal exchanges support the image they are seeking to project—for instance, they consistently counter their admissions of greed by piously acknowledging its sinfulness. Examination of their acts, however, especially their past acts, renders a very different idea of the couple's moral construction. In "The Man that Corrupted Hadleyburg" the Reverend Burgess, the town pariah, is the yardstick against which the Richardses' real moral standing is measured. For the first time, Edward confesses that he had been the instrument of Burgess's downfall years before: he had lacked the "manliness" to risk his own reputation to clear Burgess of a charge he alone knew was false. He is, then, guilty of a cowardice which, as readers of other works by Mark Twain well know, places him among the worst of the "human scum" Twain took delight in anathematizing. Moreover, Mary proves her affinities with her husband by justifying his act, despite delicately hesitating to indicate that she knows that what she is saying is "wrong." "As long as he [i.e., Burgess] doesn't know that you could have saved him, he—he—well, that makes it a great deal better," she concludes (H, p. 237).

Not only does Mark Twain undermine the stereotype the Richardses project by showing that by their acts they are consciously suspicious and cowardly, he also shows us that Edward is malicious on a subconscious level as well. If Richards's confession of cowardice does not convince us of his intrinsic corruption, his concept of a good deed should. It is significant that Mark Twain chose an incident concerning racial mixture to illustrate Richards's idea of the "favor" he might have done Goodson, because for Twain, white attitudes about blacks were always an index of moral development. When Richards convinces himself that he had been the man who had spread the word that Goodson's fiancee, "a very sweet and pretty girl," "carried a spoonful of negro blood in her veins" (H, p. 249), he shows himself a racist and a slanderer as well as a coward. The Mark Twain who had already denounced American concepts of racial "purity" in *Pudd'nhead Wilson* (1892) was not about to condone a character who saw a "spoonful" of Negro blood as defilement. For all their apparent humility and love for each other, the Richardses are—and apparently always have been—hypocritical, suspicious, cowardly, and racist.

They are, moreover, perfect exemplars of Mark Twain's concept of "the Moral Sense," the human Sense, as his spokesman defines it in *The Chronicle of Young Satan*, "whose function is to distinguish between right and wrong, with liberty to choose which of them he [i.e., man] will do... He is always choosing, and in nine cases out of ten he prefers the wrong" (CYS, p. 73). "The fact that man knows right from wrong proves his *intellectual* superiority to the other creatures," proclaims the Old Man in *What Is Man?* "but the fact that he can *do* wrong proves his *moral* inferiority to any creature that *cannot* " (WM?, p. 89).

As Professor Rucker points out, Mary and Edward constantly face crucial choices between right and wrong, and consistently choose the latter. Seemingly possessed of Free Will, they seem destined to make choices that will damn them. And Mark Twain clearly wants us to think of the Richardses' choices within the framework of Calvinist theology: both prate pulpit clichés which may well be intended to convey double meanings. "Ordered!" Mary cries when her husband reminds her that their age and poverty "must be for the best." "Oh, everything's *ordered,* when a person has to find some way out when he has been stupid" (H, p. 241). Just as their lives may be "ordered," so too may be their moral outlook. Suspecting that "this town's honesty is as rotten as mine is; as rotten as yours is" (H, p. 241), Mary repeatedly murmurs, as she faces temptation, "Lord, how we are made—how strangely we are made!" (H, p. 238). Made,

Twain may intend us to understand, to face temptation and to fall in full knowledge of the consequences. Furthermore, the couple's guilt is exacerbated by its secrecy: during the town meeting, even as Mary and Edward let pass the chance to confess and absolve themselves of one set of wrong choices, the townsfolk are unknowingly torturing them further by celebrating them as the only ones it "*does* like. . . ; *does* respect. . . ; more—it honors you and *loves* you—" (H, p. 263). Concealed guilt, as the Puritans well knew when they insisted that the secret places of a prospective member's soul be aired, is a sure sign of damnation, a "holding on" (in Huck Finn's words) to the worst sins of all.

Not only are the Richardses corrupt themselves, they project their spiritual worldview onto others. Like Young Goodman Brown, they see their own faults reflected in the faces of their neighbors. Burgess, grateful to Edward for having secretly warned him of the town's intent to tar and feather him during his original trouble, suppresses the Richardses' claim to the sack, and they are given the money as reward for their "honesty." But in the height of their "good fortune"—all stemming from Burgess's having lied to protect them—they suspect the minister of having learned of Edward's earlier silence and of having now turned against them, covertly exposing their claim to the money through the town. As Edward found it natural to pretend that he had spread the rumor about the racial taint of Goodson's fiancee, so now he finds it "natural and justifiable" (H, p. 277) that Burgess would "maliciously" betray him. Vicious and cowardly himself, Richards sees no barrier to suspecting others of a similar spiritual make.

Mary and Edward Richardses' acts, then, unlike their words, differ radically from those which readers of sentimental fiction had been led to expect, linking the secondary story of "Hadleyburg" closer to the naturalism of a Stephen Crane (compare, for instance, the difference between the Richardses' words and acts and the similar hypocrisy of Maggie's mother) or a Theodore Dreiser than to the more accessible—and far more prevalent—"realistic" short fiction of writers like Octave Thanet, Joseph Kirkland, or even Bret Harte. For although the general run of American short fiction published in the late nineteenth and early twentieth century often excelled at portraying American dialects or particularly American scenes, it also tended to suffer from its authors' discovery that particular formulas would get them published. Analysis of the Richardses is crucial to an understanding of Mark Twain's intention in "Hadleyburg" because without it his short story looks suspiciously like a rather sophisticated version of the optimistic—and usually sentimental—fiction with which it would have to compete for publication. While naturalistic stories were being published—Crane's "The Monster" (first published in August 1898), for instance, preceded "Hadleyburg" (December 1899) in *Harper's* by eighteen months—they were rare compared to the number of stories bearing far different underlying assumptions. In a domestic tale like Ella Higginson's "A Point of Knucklin' Down," for instance, the dramatic tensions are resolved because the young wife overcomes her pride and invites her mother-in-law back to live in her house.[9] In Rowland E. Robinson's "Out of Bondage," the protagonist, protecting an escaped slave only, at first, to win the favor of his abolitionist sweetheart, discovers the sacred pity the image of the black could inspire.[10] Similarly, stories by Ellen Olney Kirk, H.C. Bunner, Dorothy Lundt and others all involve a change of heart among their principal characters.

In 1923 Edward J. O'Brien, surveying the history of the American short story, complained that ever since Hawthorne "almost every American short story is the product of one or more of four heresies,—the heresy of types, the heresy of local color, the heresy of 'plot,' and the heresy of the surprise ending."[11] The cover story of "The Man that Corrupted Hadleyburg" reflects the prevailing tendency to overly control its plot as well as to stereotype its characters. Written by an author mindful of the perils of publication, it can be seen as a skillful piece of didactic, formulaic fiction, designed for a somewhat sophisticated audience familiar not only with the general run of writers—good and bad—of popular magazines but quite possibly also with current "theoretical" pieces concerning the aims of fiction, many of which contributed to the patterns to which O'Brien later objected. Readers of *Harper's* were of course familiar with William Dean Howells's rather moralistic essays in "The Editor's Study," but readers of the *Saturday Review* (London) and *Lippincott's Magazine* might also have read Brander Matthews's reflection on short fiction, first published in those periodicals in 1884 and 1885 respectively, then reprinted in *Pen and Ink: Essays on Subjects of More or Less Importance* in 1888, and, much later, published as *The Philosophy of the Short Story* in 1901.[12] More importantly, as the Columbia professor was Mark Twain's friend, literary correspondent, and, at times, literary antagonist (Twain had first attacked him in the *New Princeton Review* in 1888[13]) it is also probable that Twain had read the early versions of Matthews' *Philosophy*. Certainly he had Matthews on his mind during the period (May–October 1898[14]) of the composition of "Hadleyburg"; in early September 1898, Joe Twichell sent him an article by Matthews defending Goldsmith's *The Vicar of Wakefield* against Twain's attack on it in *Following The Equator*.[15]

The formal unity of the Hadleyburg tale satisfies many of the "laws" Matthews codified regarding the American short story (and which he observed himself in quaintly ethnocentric tales like "On the Steps of City Hall," where good old Judge Jerningham convinces headstrong young Van Dyne not to pollute his heritage by selling out to the political machine run by O'Donnell and McCann).[16] "Hadleyburg" has, as Matthews demanded, "The effect of 'totality,' as Poe called it, the unity of impression"—that is, a "sense of form."[17] It is "logical, adequate, harmonious," has "compression, originality, ingenuity" and "a touch of fantasy" as well.[18] It is, in fact, an extremely well-balanced story. When it opens, the town, falsely virtuous and unjustifiably proud of itself, is in a state of equilibrium. Action is precipitated when the equilibrium is disturbed (through the agency of an outsider who may be good or evil, the effect is the same); complications proliferate until the town is revealed to itself and recognizes its pretensions. The crisis is largely resolved through the cathartic effect of laughter; a new equilibrium is reached when it recognizes its errors, sheds its false pride, and vows to be wiser and better in the future. As the stranger whose machinations have brought it all about remarks to himself, the "dramatic unities" must be observed, and the story of Hadleyburg's reform is unified and therefore aesthetically satisfying as well as morally uplifting, meeting all the formal requirements its public—whether lay or professional consumers of fiction—could want.

In addition, the cover story of "The Man that Corrupted Hadleyburg" is thematically accessible, just complicated enough to flatter the intellectual ambitions of a moderately educated, upper-middle class who feel the occasional need to be reminded that they should examine their consciences, but who want assurance that if they try, they can do better. In fact, the specific audience Twain may have had in mind is signaled by the *Missionary Herald* Mary Richards is reading as the stranger enters her house. Established in 1805, the *Missionary Herald* was a congregational [sic] Church periodical that enjoyed immense popularity throughout the nineteenth century and well into the middle of the twentieth.[19] Largely consisting of journal reports from missionaries abroad, it provided stay-at-homes with vicarious thrills concerning the perils of the faith in alien climes. Certainly one reason for its inclusion in "Hadleyburg" was to provide a touch of local color; another was to provide ironic comment on Mrs. Richards's own lack of spiritual grace. As one of Twain's (always satiric) "practicing Christians," she feels more concern for the pagans abroad than for her own soul. But the name of the magazine also identifies Twain's target audience, people who read the *Missionary Herald* as well as literary journals— that is, literary (and usually wealthy) members of the Congregational Church. Part of the liberal Protestant Establishment, the *Missionary Herald*'s sponsors included not only congregations like Henry Ward Beecher's Plymouth Church (whose members Twain had satirized in *The Innocents Abroad* thirty years earlier) but also Hartford's Asylum Hill Congregational Church, where Twain's best friend, the Reverend Joseph Twichell, had occupied the pulpit since 1865.

The congregations from Brooklyn Heights and Asylum Hill fit the profile of the ideal readers for "Hadleyburg" exactly: grandchildren of Americans of a sterner faith, they were educated, affluent, and occasionally concerned about the effect of their money on their souls. In 1869 Twain had written Livy that he had "re-read Beecher's sermon on the love of riches being the root of evil,"[20] an indication that Beecher, at least in the early days of Twain's association with the wealthy Congregationalist crowd, was trying to instill some sense of moral conscience into his parishioners, but as Twain's portrayal of Beecher's "Pilgrims" in *Innocents* suggests, even then their consciences were of the verbal rather than the active breed. As the years passed, ministers like Beecher (in whom Twain lost faith after the minister's affair with Mrs. Tilton was exposed) and Twichell more often helped their congregations rationalize their money-lust than attacked them for it. Equally important, whatever attack they did mount was framed by the evolution of a liberal version of the doctrine of free will—or, from the opposite point of view, by the degeneration of the doctrine of predestination. Overseen by the spirit of reformers like Horace Bushnell, the Arminian strain of Congregationalist theology had come to the fore, emphasizing man's natural capacity for enlightened reform and de-emphasizing the concept of original sin.[21] Like the sentimental fiction which implied that all problems could be resolved by those willing to confront their difficulties and work hard to untangle them, the messages such ministers gave their people held that no sinner who truly wanted to change was incorrigible—a message so familiar that, in "Hadleyburg," when the Stranger claims it to have been Goodson's words to him, not one member of the community doubts that the misanthrope would have said it.

If the story of Hadleyburg's reform meets expectations of congregationalists of a later generation, however, the story of the Richardses' damnation meets the expectations of an earlier one. Offering no hope for moral redemption, its message of despair would be best grasped by the grandparents and great-grandparents of Twichell's or Beecher's flocks. For if the theme of the cover story implies that reform is possible, the theme of the subordinate story implies that it is not. In hiding his tale of Calvinist despair under a tale of latter-day Congregationalist hope, then, Mark Twain may have been aiming at the secret consciences of his affluent friends and neighbors, believing that despite the formulas taught them from the pulpit and the editor's chair they could still recognize a message that called them to a more profound examination of their spiritual state than they generally heard. Though adamantly not a professing Christian, Twain was nonetheless a man who agonized over moral questions, and by 1898, when he was writing "The Man that Corrupted Hadleyburg," *The Chronicle of Young Satan,* and *What Is Man?* he clearly felt that not enough careful consideration was being paid to the difference between the sin that was remediable, and the sin that was not.

II

One sign that the Richardses' story is not intended to provide easy answers to difficult moral problems is that it does not develop as neatly as Hadleyburg's. In fact, one of the reasons "The Man that Corrupted Hadleyburg" is so disturbing to read results from this formal dichotomy. If we insist on perceiving Mary and Edward within the scope and method of the cover story—that is, as the particular citizens whom Twain has chosen to illustrate the town's failings—we have real difficulty integrating the two conclusions, for the story of the town, on the whole, is resolved, while the story of the Richardses is not. Only if we perceive a different order

"Hadleyburg"

operating in the sub-tale will we understand how it functions to subvert the optimism of Hadleyburg's reform. For Mary and Edward, "caressing" each other on the couch, sharing their thoughts and supporting each others' ideas, seem to be paragons of faith and faithfulness. They even dupe the town. But, as we have seen, Mary and Edward are aliens to the town rather than integral parts of it, and although they know how to make the others think well of them, they—like Mark Twain—are preying on everyone's willingness to believe that because they *look* and *talk* like sweet old people, they actually are as good as they seem.

An important difference between the Richardses and the citizens of Hadleyburg is that while the latter are initially self-satisfied, the former are not. They seem, in fact, vastly discontented with their lot: their stringent "honesty" has been rewarded with grinding poverty. According to the Puritan work ethic, especially popular in the jargon of the Gilded Age, honesty and hard labor should bring some material success, some "sign" of God's grace to the elect. The Richardses, however, have received nothing but their "good name"—not enough to render contentment in their old age. Their poverty, their complaints, and their easy fall should be the first sign that they are neither of the Calvinist elect nor even of the community which, under a liberalized theology, could hope to be saved through self-examination and reform.

In addition, as we have already noted, the Richardses have a bad record, one for which they have never tried to make amends and which they do not try to amend until pushed by paranoia. Edward "confesses" on his deathbed only, one senses, because he will not be around to face the community's disappointment in him. Neither he nor Mary understands the depth of their own corruption, however; while they confess their claim for the sack in their delirium, and Edward confesses his cowardice regarding Burgess, neither ever recognizes that their hypocrisy is rooted in their apparently total lack of sympathy for anyone other than themselves and in their unquestioned assumption of the worst of the community's prejudices. Clearly, the major difference between the cover and the subordinate stories is that the first concerns remediable error, while the second concerns irremediable sin. The Richardses, unlike most of the town, are not mistaken but evil, and their tale cannot be resolved formally because evil, unlike error, simply will not disappear when it is unmasked.

There is, furthermore, a difference between the formal movements of the town's and the Richardses' tales: a movement of the protagonists in the former case, outwards, to increased objectivity, and in the latter, inward, to increased subjectivity. In the town's case, the truth-teller is Goodson. Dead before the events of the story begin but leaving a legacy of misanthropy and oddball generosity, he originally characterized the town as stingy and self-righteous. The stranger's function is to make the townsfolk concur with Goodson's assessment, to see themselves as others see them and to experience a collective change of heart. The town meeting, where the *Mikado* tune functions as a ritualistic chant, is the means through which the collectivity purges itself as the leading citizens are mocked by the less prominent citizens whom they had dominated. This does not mean that class antagonisms are expunged, nor all the citizens "saved" through the agency of the stranger and his sack; they only learn how to *earn* salvation, they are not suddenly all saved. Some, in fact, do not even learn the lesson. Clearly Harkness, for instance, who is willing to pay $40,000 for the sack so that he can defeat his political opponent, is not changed. Rather, the sum he pays—the sum originally supposed to be in it in gold—is Mark Twain's private symbol for dirty money: avoiding the obvious symbolism of $30.00, Twain consistently employs a variant of $40.00 whenever he wishes to indicate that sums being exchanged are morally tainted.[22] Thus $40,000 signals Harkness's recalcitrance. If he is one of the few who choose not to reform, however, the majority of the citizens do, and the town's revised motto signals its collective moral readiness.

The Richardses, however, go through no such process of reassessment. In contrast to the general movement of the town's consciousness outward, to greater objectivity about and evaluation of itself, the Richardses turn inward, towards an increasingly subjective vision of the way they are perceived by others. Always as alienated as Goodson, their response has always been crucially different: whereas he tried to make the town see itself, for its own good, the Richardses have tried to make it perceive them as they wish to be perceived. Since they have no power—or rewards—other than the satisfaction they derive from the image of themselves they have projected, the threat of discovery is tantamount to a threat of complete deprivation. Consequently, even when they are saved through Burgess's intervention, they live in terror of discovery, searching the community for clues that their suspicions are justified. While the town experiences a new community through shared shame (which greatly alleviates private guilt), the Richardses develop paranoia, assuming that the others are treating them as they would treat anyone in their situation: affecting love while feeling scorn, seeking to trick them into open confession. Instead of relieving their anxieties, the town meeting and its aftermath intensifies their isolation.

Finally, while the plot complications concerning the town are resolved, the plot complications concerning the Richardses are not. Rather, each apparent resolution generates a new complication. Although Edward clears Burgess of one accusation, he leaves him with another, this one of a most unchristian act of vengeance. Certainly the couple are not "saved" by these confessions. Nor is the evil they represent extirpated by their deaths. For even if the town is disillusioned about their honesty, it never knows that they have sinned against Burgess once again. Far from being resolved, the complications generated by the tangled plot of the secondary tale, like sin itself, live on.

"The Man that Corrupted Hadleyburg," then, combines Mark Twain's attack on the debased ideology of free will with an attack on the ideological optimism inherent in current forms of the short story. As he had satirized sermons, political speeches, courtroom speeches, recitation day speeches, initiation tales, European fables, romanticized landscape descriptions and guide books throughout his career in order to show his audience how such conventions falsified their perceptions of the world, so in "Hadleyburg" he undermines his stereotyped characters and tight, conventional plot in order to force his reader to look beyond the conventional message such formulas had taught them to expect. In doing so he unites his moral intentions with his concern for literary "truth": in a two-pronged attack on banal theology and banal literature, he challenges his readers to refuse easy solutions to moral problems at the same time that they refuse easy resolutions to formal ones.

Notes

1. Gladys C. Bellamy, *Mark Twain as a Literary Artist* (Norman: Univ. of Oklahoma Press, 1950), pp. 308–309; Pascal Covici, Jr., *Mark Twain's Humor: The Image of a World* (Dallas: Southern Methodist University Press, 1962): Clinton S. Burhans, Jr., "The Sober Affirmation of Mark Twain's Hadleyburg," *American Literature*, 34 (Nov. 1962), 375–384; Henry B. Rule, "The Role of Satan in 'The Man that Corrupted Hadleyburg'," *Studies in Short Fiction*, 6 (Fall 1969), 619–626; Helen E. Nebeker, "The Great Corrupter or Satan Rehabilitated," *Studies in Short Fiction*, 8 (Fall 1971), 635–637; Mary E. Rucker, "Moralism and Determinism in 'The Man That Corrupted Hadleyburg,'" *Studies in Short Fiction*, 14 (Winter 1977), 49–54.

2. Covici, p. 203.

3. Rucker, p. 53. Rucker is not explicit on this point. However, her last line claims that "If we are to see a relation between action and the Miltonic moral embodied in the revised motto. . . we must not center attention on the individualized characters, rather, we must accept on faith what the narrator tells us about the town's achieved willingness to face temptations in an effort to attain a viable morality."

4. William R. Macnaughton, *Mark Twain's Last Years as a Writer* (Columbia: Univ. of Missouri Press, 1979), p. 100.

5. Rucker, p. 53.

6. Mark Twain, *The Chronicle of Young Satan*, in William M. Gibson, ed., *Mark Twain: The Mysterious Stranger* (Berkeley: Univ of California Press, 1970), p. 82. Hereafter abbreviated CYS and documented internally, as will be all primary works in this essay. H refers to the edition of "The Man that Corrupted Hadleyburg" in Justin Kaplan, ed., *Great Short Works of Mark Twain* (New York: Harper and Row, 1967); WM? to *What Is Man?* (New York: Harper and Brothers, 1917).

7. *McClure's*, 8 (Feb. 1897), 326–443.

8. Mary's response may be seen as a further revelation of her real values; again she equates reputation with money. Wouldn't the "real" stereotyped old woman value "good health" before "livelihood"?

9. *McClure's*, 6 (Dec. 1895), 71–75.

10. *The Atlantic Monthly*, 80 (Aug. 1897), 200–216.

11. Edward J. O'Brien, *The Advance of the American Short Story* (New York: Dodd, Mead and Co., 1923), p. 6.

12. For the publication history of Matthews's ideas see the Prefatory Note to his *Philosophy of the Short Story* (London: Longmans, Green, and Co., 1912), pp. 7–8.

13. Alan Gribben, *Mark Twain's Library: A Reconstruction* (Boston: G.K. Hall and Co., 1980), I, 458–460. Professor Gribben's work has made Mark Twain research far more coherent and accessible; it is an invaluable aid to Mark Twain scholarship.

14. See Macnaughton, pp. 100–103.

15. Albert Bigelow Paine, ed., *Mark Twain's Letters* (New York: Harper and Brothers, 1917), II, 666–667. In the same letter Twain remarks that he is receiving copies of *Harper's Century*, and *McClure's* magazines in Kaltenleutgeben.

16. *Harper's New Monthly Magazine*, 98 (Mar. 1899), 525–530.

17. Matthews, p. 17.

18. Ibid., p. 23.

19. *The Missionary Herald At Home and Abroad* ceased publication with volume 147, in 1951.

20. This letter is quoted in Gribben, (I, 55), and is available at the Mark Twain Papers. Dixon Wecter does not include it in *The Love Letters of Mark Twain* (New York: Harper and Brothers, 1949) but does include a subsequent letter (1/19/69) which makes it clear not only that Livy was sending her fiancee copies of Beecher's *Plymouth Pulpit: A Weekly Publication of Sermons Preached by Henry Ward Beecher in Plymouth Church, Brooklyn*, but that he was reading them. Clearly Twain's association of Congregationalists and wealth was laid during the sixties, when he first came into contact with Beecher's congregation, with Thomas K. Beecher (Henry Ward's half-

brother), pastor of Livy's church in Elmira; with young Joseph Twichell, and with the whole Brooklyn/Hartford "connection."

21. For a brief review of the evolution of Congregationalist theology in America, see Sydney E. Ahlstrom, *A Religious History of the American People* (New Haven: Yale Univ. Press, 1971), esp. Ch. 46, "The Golden Age of Liberal Theology." A biography of Twichell is Leah A. Strong's *Joseph Hopkins Twichell: Mark Twain's Friend and Pastor* (Athens: Univ. of Georgia Press, 1966). Recent works on Beecher are William G. McLoughlin, *The Meaning of Henry Ward Beecher* (1970), and Clifford E. Clark, Jr., *Henry Ward Beecher: Spokesman for a Middle-Class America* (Urbana: Univ. of Illinois Press, 1978).

22. This motif is consistent throughout Mark Twain's works, and has been noted by various critics. Most familiar should be the sums associated with moral inadequacies in *Adventures of Huckleberry Finn*. For instance, the slave hunters give Huck $40 instead of helping his allegedly sick family; the King trades Jim for $40; Tom gives Jim $40 for having been such a "good" prisoner.

Is The Philippine Policy of the Administration Just?

"No"
By Mark Twain

In the North American Review *for February, Mark Twain publishes an article "To the Person Sitting in Darkness," which we are permitted to reprint in part as follows:*

Extending the Blessings of Civilization to our Brother who Sits in Darkness has been a good trade and has paid well, on the whole.

There is more money in it, more territory, more sovereignty and other kinds of emolument, than there is in any other game that is played. But Christendom has been playing it badly of late years, and must certainly suffer by it, in my opinion. She has been so eager to get every stake that appeared on the green cloth, that the People who Sit in Darkness have noticed it. They have become suspicious of the Blessings of Civilization. More—they have begun to examine them. This is not well. The Blessings of Civilization are all right, and a good commercial property; there could not be a better, in a dim light. In the right kind of a light, and at a proper distance, with the goods a little out of focus, they furnish this desirable exhibit to the Gentlemen who Sit in Darkness:

LOVE,	LAW AND ORDER,
JUSTICE,	LIBERTY,

Reprinted from *Harper's Weekly* 45 (9 February 1901): 154–5.

GENTLENESS,	EQUALITY,
CHRISTIANITY,	HONORABLE DEALING,
PROTECTION TO THE WEAK,	MERCY,
TEMPERANCE,	EDUCATION,

—and so on.

There. Is it good? Sir, it is pie. It will bring into camp any idiot that sits in darkness anywhere. But not if we adulterate it. It is proper to be emphatic upon that point. This brand is strictly for Export—apparently. *Apparently.* Privately and confidentially, it is nothing of the kind. Privately and confidentially, it is merely an outside cover, gay and pretty and attractive, displaying the special patterns of our Civilization which we reserve for Home Consumption, while *inside* the bale is the Actual Thing that the Customer Sitting in Darkness buys with his blood and tears and land and liberty.

We all know that the Business is being ruined. The reason is not far to seek. It is because our Mr. McKinley, and Mr. Chamberlain, and the Kaiser, and the Czar and the French have been exporting the Actual Thing *with the outside cover left off.*

It is a distress to look on and note the mismoves, they are so strange and so awkward. Mr. Chamberlain manufactures a war out of materials so inadequate and so fanciful that they make the boxes grieve and the gallery laugh. Next, to our heavy damage, the Kaiser went to playing the game without first mastering it. He lost a couple of missionaries in a riot at Shantung, and in his account he made an over-charge for them. And by-and-by comes America, and our Master of the Game plays it badly—plays it as Mr. Chamberlain was playing it in South Africa. It was a mistake to do that; also it was one which was quite unlooked for in a Master who was playing it so well in Cuba. In Cuba he was playing the usual and regular *American* game, and it was winning, for there is no way to beat it. The Master, contemplating Cuba, said: "Here is an oppressed and friendless little nation which is willing to fight to be free; we go partners, and put up the strength of seventy million sympathizers and the resources of the United States:

play!" Nothing but Europe combined could call that hand: and Europe cannot combine on anything. There, in Cuba, he was following our great traditions in a way which made us very proud of him, and proud of the deep dissatisfaction which his play was provoking in Continental Europe. Moved by a high inspiration, he threw out those stirring works which proclaimed that forcible annexation would be "criminal aggression"; and in that utterance fired another "shot heard round the world." The memory of that fine saying will be outlived by the remembrance of no act of his but one—that he forgot it within the twelvemonth, and its honorable gospel along with it.

****

For, presently, came the Philippine temptation. It was strong; it was too strong, and he made that bad mistake: he played the European game, the Chamberlain game. It was a pity; it was a great pity, that error; that one grievous error, that irrevocable error. For it was the very place and time to play the American game again. The game was in our hands. If it had been played according to the American rules, Dewey would have sailed away from Manila as soon as he had destroyed the Spanish fleet—after putting up a sign on shore guaranteeing foreign property and life against damage by the Filipinos, and warning the Powers that interference with the emancipated patriots would be regarded as an act unfriendly to the United States.

The more we examine the mistake, the more clearly we perceive that it is going to be bad for the Business. The Person Sitting in Darkness is almost sure to say: "There is something curious about this—curious and unaccountable. There must be two Americas: one that sets the captive free, and one that takes a once-captive's new freedom away from him, and picks a quarrel with him with nothing to found it on; then kills him to get his land."

The truth is, the Person Sitting in Darkness *is* saying things like that; and for the sake of the Business we must persuade him to look at the Philippine matter in another and healthier way. We must arrange his opinions for him. I believe it can be done; for Mr. Chamberlain has arranged England's opinion of the South-African matter, and done it most cleverly and successfully. He presented the facts—some of the facts—and showed those confiding people what the facts meant. He did it statistically, which is a good way. He used the formula: "Twice 2 are 14, and 2 from 9 leaves 35." Figures are effective; figures will convince the elect.

Now, my plan is a still bolder one than Mr. Chamberlain's, though apparently a copy of it. Let us be franker than Mr. Chamberlain; let us audaciously present the whole of the facts, shirking none, then explain them according to Mr. Chamberlain's formula. This daring truthfulness will astonish and dazzle the Person Sitting in Darkness, and he will take the Explanation down before his mental vision has had time to get back into focus. Let us say to him:

"Our case is simple. On the 1st of May Dewey destroyed the Spanish fleet. This left the Archipelago in the hands of its proper and rightful owners, the Filipino nation. Their army numbered 30,000 men, and they were competent to whip out or starve out the little Spanish garrison; then the people could set up a government of their own devising. Our traditions required that Dewey should now set up his warning sign, and go away. But the Master of the Game happened to think of another plan—the European plan. He acted upon it. This was, to send out an army—ostensibly to help the native patriots put the finishing-touch upon their long and plucky struggle for independence, but really to take their land away from them and keep it. That is, in the interest of Progress and Civilization. The plan developed, stage by stage, and quite satisfactorily. We entered into a military alliance with the trusting Filipinos, and they hemmed in Manila on the land side, and by their valuable help the place, with its garrison of 8000 or 10,000 Spaniards, was captured—a thing which we

Is the Philippine Policy of the Administration Just?

could not have accomplished unaided at that time. We got their help by—by ingenuity. We knew they were fighting for their independence, and that they had been at it for two years. We knew they supposed that we also were fighting in their worthy cause—just as we had helped the Cubans fight for Cuban independence—and we allowed them to go on thinking so *until Manila was ours and we could get along without them.* Then we showed our hand.

"We kept the positions which we had beguiled them of; and by-and-by we moved a force forward and overlapped patriot ground—a clever thought, for we needed trouble, and this would produce it. A Filipino soldier, crossing the ground, where no one had a right to forbid him, was shot by our sentry. The badgered patriots resented this with arms, without waiting to know whether Aguinaldo, who was absent, would approve or not. Aguinaldo did not approve; but that availed nothing. What we wanted, in the interest of Progress and Civilization, was the Archipelago, unencumbered by patriots struggling for independence; and War was what we needed. We clinched our opportunity. It is Mr. Chamberlain's case over again—at least in its motive and intention; and we played the game as adroitly as he played it himself.

"We and the patriots having captured Manila, Spain's ownership of the Archipelago and her sovereignty over it were at an end—obliterated—annihilated—not a rag or shred of either remaining behind. It was then that we conceived the divinely humorous idea of *buying* both of these spectres from Spain! In buying those ghosts for twenty millions, we also contracted to take care of the friars and their accumulations. I think we also agreed to propagate leprosy and small-pox, but as to this there is doubt. But it is not important; persons afflicted with the friars do not mind other diseases.

"With our Treaty ratified, Manila subdued, and our Ghosts secured, we had no further use for Aguinaldo and the owners of the Archipelago. We forced a war, and we have been hunting America's guest and ally through the woods and swamps ever since."

Having now laid all the historical facts before the Person Sitting in Darkness, we should bring him to and explain them to him. We should say to him:

"They look doubtful, but in reality they are not. There have been lies; yes, but they were told in a good cause. We have been treacherous; but that was only in order that real good might come out of apparent evil. True, we have crushed a deceived and confiding people; we have turned against the weak and the friendless who trusted us; we have stamped out a just and intelligent and well-ordered republic; we have stabbed an ally in the back and slapped the face of a guest; we have bought a Shadow from an enemy that hadn't it to sell; we have robbed a trusting friend of his land and his liberty; we have invited our clean young men to shoulder a discredited musket and do bandit's work under a flag which bandits have been accustomed to fear, not to follow; we have debauched America's honor and blackened her face before the world; but each detail was for the best. We know this. The Head of every State and Sovereignty in Christendom and ninety per cent of every legislative body in Christendom, including our Congress and our fifty State Legislatures, are members not only of the church, but also of the Blessings-of-Civilization Trust. This world-girdling accumulation of trained morals, high principles, and justice, cannot do an unright thing, an unfair thing, an ungenerous thing, an unclean thing. It knows what it is about. Give yourself no uneasiness; it is all right."

Now, then, that will convince the Person. You will see. It will restore the Business. Also, it will elect the Master of the Game to the vacant place in the Trinity of our national gods; and there on their high thrones the Three will sit, age after age, in the people's sight, each bearing the Emblem of his service: Washington, the Sword of the Liberator; Lincoln, the Slave's Broken Chains; the Master, the Chains Repaired. It will give the Business a splendid new start. You will see.

****

Is the Philippine Policy of the Administration Just?

Everything is prosperous now; everything is just as we should wish it. We have got the Archipelago, and we shall never give it up. Also, we have every reason to hope that we shall have an opportunity before very long to slip out of our Congressional contract with Cuba and give her something better in the place of it. It is a rich country, and many of us are already beginning to see that the contract was a sentimental mistake. But now—right now—is the best time to do some profitable rehabilitating work—work that will set us up and make us comfortable, and discourage gossip. We cannot conceal from ourselves that, privately, we are a little troubled about our uniform. It is one of our prides; it is acquainted with honor; it is familiar with great deeds and noble; we love it, we revere it; and so this errand it is on makes us uneasy. And our flag—another pride of ours, our chiefest! We have worshipped it so; and when we have seen it in far lands—glimpsing it unexpectedly in that strange sky, waving its welcome and benediction to us—we have caught our breath, and uncovered our heads, and couldn't speak for a moment, for the thought of what it was to us and the great ideals it stood for. Indeed, we *must* do something about these things; we must not have the flag out there, and the uniform. They are not needed there; we can manage in some other way. England manages, as regards the uniform, and so can we. We have to send soldiers—we can't get out of that—but we can disguise them. It is the way England does in South Africa. Even Mr. Chamberlain himself takes pride in England's honorable uniform, and makes the army down there wear an ugly and odious and appropriate disguise, of yellow stuff such as quarantine flags are made of, and which are hoisted to warn the healthy away from unclean disease and repulsive death. This cloth is called khaki. We could adopt it. It is light, comfortable, grotesque, and deceives the enemy, for he cannot conceive of a soldier being concealed in it.

And as for a flag for the Philippine Province, it is easily managed. We can have a special one—our States do it: we can have just our usual flag, with the white stripes painted black and the stars replaced by the skull and cross-bones.

And we do not need that Civil Commission out there. Having no powers, it has to invent them, and that kind of work cannot be effectively done by just anybody; an expert is required. Mr. Croker can be spared. We do not want the United States represented there, but only the Game.

By help of these suggested amendments, Progress and Civilization in that country can have a boom, and it will take in the Persons who are Sitting in Darkness, and we can resume Business at the old stand.

"Yes"
By John Kendrick Bangs

When, a few days ago, I took up my copy of the *North American Review* for February, it was with a great deal of pleasure that I observed, in perusing the table of contents, that Mark Twain had provided for the delectation of its readers an article entitled "To the Person Sitting in Darkness." Here, assuredly, was a treat in store, for I felt that Mr. Clemens, more than any other living writer, was entitled, because of his intrinsic sanity, to speak to those in need of light, no matter by what precise species of darkness they might be enveloped. I sat down to read and to rejoice.

I had not read far before I began to rub my eyes in astonishment, and the more I read the more did my amazement increase and my rejoicement diminish. It was incredible, and yet there it was, and the marvel grew upon me, although I was quite unable to decide at which I marvelled the more, the hardihood of the humorist in writing his article, or the temerity of the editor of the *North American Review* in printing it. But there it stood before me in plain black and white, a sort of after-dinner speech in a *Review*, in which missionary effort in heathen lands is openly and drastically discredited because of the somewhat too strenuous behavior of certain muscular Christians in the Far East; in which the extension of the blessings of civilization by the strong nations of the earth is likened to that particular kind of business in which selfishness is predominant, and in the operations of which the weak and worthy are crushed into lifelessness by the strong and vicious; and in which, for merely performing the required functions of his office, the President of the United States is held up to public contempt and classed with the land-grabbing statesmen of the Old World. I could scarce believe my eyes. I looked again at the title and the authorship.

"Surely this is not by Mark Twain," I muttered. "Perhaps Senator Pettigrew has taken to writing; or may it not be that the editor of the *Review* has got his authors mixed, and a manuscript by some member of the Atkinson Society for the Prevention of National Growth, marked for rejection, has got by mistake into the Mark Twain envelope!"

Alas! neither was the case. The article, investigation showed, was authentic, and for the first time in my life, or his, I seemed to find the great American somewhat astray in his Americanism; the great satirist wielding the bludgeon instead of the rapier; the great purveyor of sunshine to his fellow-men joining the ranks of the prophets of evil, spreading the gospel of discontent, and being governed by his disgusts rather than by his admirations.

****

As to the methods employed by the missionaries of China, I propose neither to attack nor to defend them. I prefer to take the Rev. Mr. Ament, to whom Mr. Clemens refers, exacting enormous fines from the Boxers either as an unduly muscular Christian acting with a zeal not wholly to his discredit, or as a man who in the face of a great provocation has exceeded the bounds of propriety, if indeed the newspaper stories upon which Mr. Clemens bases his attack are ever confirmed. A man may be a minister of the gospel and still remain a man of force and conviction. To be a Christian does not require that one shall be pusillanimous, and I see no more reason why a missionary should be required to sit meekly down and suffer himself and his followers to be robbed, his family to be outraged, and murder and arson committed in his own neighborhood, than that any other self-respecting man should be expected to emulate the action of the dove when the circumstances call for a tiger. To inspire respect for the Christian religion in the field to which this has been carried, the official representatives of that institution must be as strenuous in the maintenance of the principles of justice as are the representatives of the law in law-abiding communities, who are no more popular with the criminal classes than are missionaries with the Boxers. Whether the missionaries have a right to carry the gospel, as they know it, into other lands is a question which may not be discussed here. Many worthy people think that missionary work, like charity, should begin at home. Others think it should be carried far afield. It is enough to say that it is only in those lands into which the principles of Christianity have been carried by noble bands of self-sacrificing men and women that we find that enlightenment which stands for progress, for law, for order, and for a decent respect for the rights of the individual. I, for one, would rather see one acre of the pest-ridden East Side of the city of New York redeemed from vice than to have every follower of the teachings of Confucius won over to the Church; but when the Church undertakes to win over the followers of Confucius, with the consent and approbation of its greatest minds, I should regret to see its efforts fail because its missionaries were unable to inspire respect for its teachings, either for the lack of physical courage, or for yielding to a policy of non-resistance based upon pusillanimous sentimentality.

Nor do I care much when Mark Twain likens the Extension of the Blessings of Civilization to our Brother in Darkness to a business; if it has become so, so much the better

Is the Philippine Policy of the Administration Just?

for our Brother in Darkness. Organized effort in its results is far more beneficial than the well-meaning but ill-considered independent effort of the idealist. Mr. Clemens and I would have no country to be ashamed of or to be proud of respectively to-day if, in the extension of the blessings of civilization to this land, the foundations upon which our national being rests had not been laid by men who, in addition to their ideals, were gifted with practical heads and a good, hard common-sense, which goes with what men term business. That people are coming to recognize the value of organized effort is shown by the comparatively new methods of the charitably inclined. Organized charity of to-day is doing a thousandfold more and better work than could ever have been accomplished under old methods, in which there was no co-ordination of forces and under which the kindly generosity of the philanthropist was rendered of no avail in the accomplishment of permanent good. Unless we attack charity as being unmoral, then, for having become a business, we are not justified in assaulting the "Blessings-of-Civilization Trust," as Mr. Clemens calls it, for going at its work in a businesslike manner. And for the reason that one unworthy follower cannot destroy the good name of the Charity Organization Society, may we also assure ourselves that one selfish act here or one high-handed arbitrary act of aggression there is powerless to cast a blot upon the escutcheon of the nations which have undertaken to spread the principles of civilization in immediately unresponsive localities.

****

It is when Mr. Clemens flings at the President of the United States that I am inclined to find the most fault with him, because, in my judgement, his arrows are tainted with the poison of injustice. One does not like to hear him suggest a modification of the American flag for use in the Philippine Islands so that its stripes shall be black and red and its stars shall be superseded by a skull and cross-bones, because there is absolutely nothing in the Philippine situation as it exists today that warrants the humorist in making such a suggestion. Law is law, and it can never be superseded by mere sentimentality. The facts are so simple that it is a wonder they are at all in controversy. Our authority in the Philippine Islands is so clearly defined and our title to it so absolutely indisputable that the veriest child should be able to grasp the fact. The question that arises is as to whether or not we shall maintain that authority in the face of an armed rebellion against it. There is no other question immediately involved in the situation. It is all very well for pamphleteers, whose chief mission in life seems to be to tear down that which others are striving to build up, to try to befog the issue with all sorts of sentimental reflections upon a noble people fighting for their liberty, upon the purity of the motives of the great leader of this rebellion—a man who sold himself to the enemy, deserted his people, robbed his fellow-conspirators, and did not even keep faith with those who bought him. It invariably happens in the face of a conflict between a strong nation and a weak, the sentimentalist, right or wrong, takes the side of the weak. We had a great deal of this kind of thing at the beginning of the Transvaal trouble; indeed Mr. Clemens ladles out a lot of it to us in this latest effort of his. Mr. Kruger was the Washington of the Transvaal to these people, just as Aguinaldo is the Washington of the Pacific. Very soon some one will rise up and call Prince Tuan the Washington of China. And as time goes on we shall find the earth girdled with Washingtons, some more worthy than others, perhaps, but every man jack of them trying to stand in the way of the inexorable march of civilization, and with the inevitable result that they will be crushed to earth never to rise again. It is a wonder that Captain Herlihy has not been set down by these sentimentalists as the "Washington of the Red Light District."

I have yet to meet the man, woman, or child who is glad that we have the Philippine Islands to deal with. I think it is quite probable that ninety-nine out of every one hundred thinking men wish that Dewey might have sailed away from

Is the Philippine Policy of the Administration Just?

Manila after having destroyed the fleet of Spain. I deem it likely that all who are not idle dreamers know that Dewey could not honorably have done so, leaving a community entitled to the protection of law of some kind to inevitable chaos. To accuse the Administration, which could not possibly have foreseen the complications that Dewey's victory entailed, of playing the game of the land-grabber, is, to my mind, a lamentable perversion of the facts. Publicly to endorse the act of a scheming adventurer in armed rebellion against the forces of the United States in other days would have been called treason, and those who ventured along similar lines during the dreadful years of 1860 to 1865 were known by the significant title of Copperhead. I should not, for one instant, think of calling Mr. Clemens either a traitor or a Copperhead, for he is neither, but I do think that upon his return last autumn after a prolonged absence from his native land, during which time he may reasonably have been expected to get out of touch with things American, he should have been inoculated against what I might call the contagion of the Atkinsonian bacillus, lately discovered in Boston, the effects of which are to promote irresponsible speech, to impair the political vision, and to stunt one's patriotic development. We have had so much destructive nonsense from the Anti-Imperialist League and so little really constructive criticism of the Philippine policy of the Administration that it is positively disheartening to find one from whom we have a right to expect so much as we expect from Mark Twain, joining the ranks of the merely captious—for Mr. Clemens indulges not at all in argument. A Philippine Philippic I should rather call this latest screed of his. I, for one, should much have preferred to hear Mark Twain's clarion voice uttering the following words at this intellectual feast of the *North American Review*: "Gentlemen,—You have asked me to speak upon the Philippine question. There is no Philippine question. When we find the situation in the Philippine Islands such that an American soldier may wear his honorable uniform without peril to his life, when we find the properly acquired authority of this great and well-meaning republic of ours respected in these islands of the far Pacific, where we find our beloved flag, the purest emblem of liberty afloat, honored in the Philippines as we honor it, then there may be a Philippine question. Until then there shall be no such thing. We do not want the Philippine Islands. We never have wanted them, but the inevitable trend of the circumstances of war, beyond our power to control, forced them upon us, and we must deal with them. I am confident that when it is possible for this nation to consider what shall be their status among the communities of the world, we shall find that the pure common-sense of the American people, the love of justice among us, our innate sympathy with the desire of all people in the world to be free, to enjoy the largest measure of self-government and liberty, have resulted in a solution of this now most difficult problem which shall prove to be of the greatest good to the greatest number of the Filipinos. Upon a great many points, which I shall not enumerate, I regret to find myself at variance with the authorities at Washington, but I must admit that the gentleman to whom we have entrusted the administration of our affairs knows more about the situation than I do. In any event, as an American citizen, I place my trust in the President. Personally, caring little for William McKinley, I care much about my President, and him I shall speak well of publicly, even though in private I may write him a letter or two which he may not care to read over a second time. Gentlemen, I give you the President of the United States, the political incarnation of ourselves, the embodiment of the power, of the conscience, of this nation. In all matters outside of our borders we and he must be one. His enemies are ours. Those who defy him, defy us, and in the face of shotten cannon, directed against the authority which he wields, let us not be found skulking at the rear, baiting our general at every move, and by our captious criticism in the face of danger distracting his mind from problems which God knows are in themselves hard enough to solve. Advice? yes, constructive—not destructive. Warnings? yes—the more the better, but whispered, and in a friendly, helpful spirit. Support? when lack of it comforts his enemies—always. Gentlemen, the President—standing."

This, it seems to me, is what Mark Twain would have said as an Innocent Abroad.

As an Oracle at home he pleases me only in the evidence which we may derive from his paper in the *North American Review* that he is, after all, merely human, and not the demigod some of us had begun to think him. There is positive comfort in the thought that even Mark Twain is not infallible.

Reconstructing the "Imagination-Mill": The Mystery of Mark Twain's Late Works

Susanne Weil

When the University of California Press began to publish Mark Twain's suppressed late works, readers expected undiscovered Hucks and Yankees—and found mysterious strangers. These posthumous publications seem so different from Twain's best-known writing (and from one another) that a reader might be forgiven for thinking they must have been written by a different person—perhaps by several different persons. Read as a group, the later manuscripts leave the impression that during the 1890s, Twain's familiar, wryly humorous narrative voice was radically transformed: to mix a metaphor, it is as if that voice had been projected through a prism and refracted into a broad spectrum of literary tones, even genres. Moralism, sentimentality, polemic, homely philosophy, fable, and science fantasy are all represented among his late works. Some see the extreme range and varied quality of these manuscripts as evidence that Twain's voice did not simply refract but splintered and broke; certainly the old white light of humor had disappeared. Few, if any, of the late manuscripts resemble the work of a certain wickedly funny steamboat pilot-turned-writer who became the authentic voice of the American West.

But why should they? During his life, Twain deliberately suppressed the manuscripts now emerging from the Mark Twain Papers—suppressed them despite the 1898 contract which invited him to submit whatever he wrote to Harper's and Brothers under their exclusive agreement (Hill, xxii).

Twain's refusal to publish these manuscripts should serve as a flashing neon "buyer beware" sign to new readers; instead, even critics have approached the late works hoping to sate their appetites for unread vintage Twain. They have often been disappointed, and their unrealistic expectations have obscured the different, but genuine, value of much that Twain wrote in his later years. It has become commonplace to say that Twain's late writing is inferior, an embarrassment, and to explain that writing away by citing his biography. The critics' refrain sounds something like this: poor Mark Twain was so undone by personal disasters like the death of his most talented, best-loved daughter in 1896 that he lost his sense of humor and became artistically paralyzed. Led by Hamlin Hill, who in *Mark Twain: God's Fool* (1973) branded the entire body of late writing a "literary junkyard," (273) even editors of some new volumes have denigrated them in the act of writing their introductions.

Before consigning the later Twain to this literary lunatic asylum, let us review the high points in his last fifteen years of writing. Manuscripts he opted to publish include "Fenimore Cooper's Literary Offenses" (1895); "The Man That Corrupted Hadleyburg" (1898), "To the Person Sitting in Darkness" and "To My Missionary Critics" (1901); "Eve's Diary" (1904); "The War Prayer" (1904); "The $30,000 Bequest" (1905); and the final version of "An Extract From Captain Stormfield's Visit to Heaven" (1907). Those which he withheld from publication include *The Mysterious Stranger Manuscripts* (begun in 1897 and culminating in 1905 with the finished novel *#44, The Mysterious Stranger*); the unfinished but fascinating "3,000 Years Among the Microbes" (written in 1905); *Letters from the Earth* (written during the period from 1906–1909); and the massive *Autobiography* (composed between—roughly—1904 and 1909: Twain declared these finished in December of 1909 with "The Death of Jean" [Twain 403fn]).

Even by themselves, these often-anthologized texts would represent a strong showing for any author. Add to them some of the other late writing whose value even late-Twain partisans debate (such as *What Is Man?*, the *Fables of Man* sketches, and the sentimental tales from *The Personal Recollections of Joan of Arc* on down); add the now-published "fragments"—the clusters of related, unfinished fictional pieces representing repeated attacks on ideas Twain could not get out of his head concerning the "damned human race"; and, finally, add the thousands of pages catalogued but not yet published by the Mark Twain Papers: all these comprise a body of work which, however wide its range of quality, proves that Twain's last fifteen years were hardly a creative wasteland.

It is not my intention to argue that Twain's late works are "as great as" or "greater than" his "mature" work: *The Adventures of Huckleberry Finn*, *Life on the Mississippi*, and the other classics of Twain's major period staked out authentic American diction and experience as the new frontier of our literature, and his late works will not have such an impact. Instead, I propose to re-evaluate Twain's late work on its own ground, leaving behind disappointed nostalgic yearnings for more *Hucks* and *Toms* to ask *why* the late works are so different. Those last fifteen years represent a major literary mystery, one which most critics have treated more like a disease in need of a cure than a question in need of an answer.

What happened? Why did Twain stop writing humorous, realistic fiction? Even recent critics who see the value of his later writing, such as John Tuckey, Sholom Kahn, and William Macnaughton, focus on rehabilitating the reputations of selected manuscripts, not on analyzing the shift in Twain's style or clarifying the relationship between the disastrous events of the 1890s and the change in Twain's view of himself as man and writer. Critics who do try to examine Twain's late years as a distinct epoch in his literary life, notably Hamlin Hill and Justin Kaplan, focus on Twain's biography rather than analyze the late works themselves in any detail: in fact, they dismiss the later manuscripts without even excerpting passages for close readings. I shall argue that through this omission—made possible by the assumption that the less one of Twain's manuscripts is like Huck, the less it is worth reading—they have lost an opportunity to look inside Twain's mind.

The unwillingness of the critical community to analyze the change in Twain's writing seems even more mysterious when we consider that Twain's shift occurred just as American realism, whose frontier Twain had helped to open, was coming into its own. No one has, as yet, offered a comprehensive, plausible analysis of why Twain's writing changed just at the moment when the American public (segments of it, at least) was beginning to sample the wares of Dreiser, Norris, Crane, et al.—just at the moment when that public was presumably ready to swallow what Twain was so sure it could not: his own social criticism unmediated by humor. What is at stake in asking why Twain's style changed is, in effect, an explanation of his refusal to join the literary movement he had helped bring to life.

If we take on the role of literary detectives, trying first to track down the time and the circumstances in which Twain's narrative style changed, we may be able to deduce the reasons why it changed. Using this approach, the crucial question becomes not which was Twain's last "great book," but which book represents Twain's last *characteristic*, completed work of fiction. I would argue that this must be *Pudd'nhead Wilson*, written in 1893 and published both serially and in book form in 1894.* *Pudd'nhead Wilson* is a tale set on the banks of the Mississippi, told with the bite of ironic humor, couched in Midwestern dialect, and expressive of the themes with which Twain was so often concerned: both the evils of slavery and

---

* One could make a case for "Fenimore Cooper's Literary Offenses" or "An Extract from Captain Stormfield's Visit to Heaven" as characteristic Twain. However, these brief works seem more like flickers within his later period, and I am concerned here with the question of why Twain did not choose to write longer works of fiction in his characteristic voice.

the conflict between conscience, social conditioning, and instinct in the decisions of individuals. Few would assert that anything Twain wrote after Pudd'nhead contains its mixture of the elements that made Twain's "mature" writing unique.

1894 was not only the year in which Twain published his last characteristic, completed work of fiction: it was the year in which his luck ran out. In the wake of the national economic panic of 1893, Twain's publishing business, Charles L. Webster and Company, like many other companies, swirled into the vortex of debt (Leary, 10–26). Twain, like other would-be captains of industry, had become accustomed to using credit in lieu of working capital, and the result was bankruptcy when the Mount Morris Bank called in Webster & Company's massive outstanding loans on April 18, 1894 (Leary, 23). 1894 also marked the failure of Twain's brainchild, the Paige typesetter, in a critical test before prospective investors (25). With that catastrophe, Twain's finances were ruined. He had invested the equivalent of modern millions in the machine, as well as an immeasurable amount of hope: not only had he intended the machine to free him of the need to write for profit, but after his bankruptcy, he had expected that its sales would make him solvent again (Kaplan, 280–81).

Finally, 1894 marked the start of Twain's financial and personal relationship with Henry Huttleston Rogers, the powerful Vice President of Standard Oil. Rogers, who became Twain's closest friend, assumed power of attorney over Twain's assets and rescued him from his financial morass by negotiating both his bankruptcy settlement and his Harpers' contract. The Twain/Rogers correspondence makes Rogers' deep respect for Twain clear; the man was ruthless in business, but he was loyal and fair to those he liked, and he liked Twain. However, their correspondence documents how, in transaction after transaction, Rogers quietly persuaded Twain to relinquish control over yet another area of his life. Although there is no evidence that Rogers ever took advantage of Twain's trust or rubbed his nose in his own poor business sense, Twain's regard for Rogers often took the form of debilitating personal comparisons: Rogers came to epitomize for him the kind of steady responsibility which he himself had never been able to maintain, and the insight was lacerating (Kaplan, 322–25; 359–60). When "the mill refused to go"—Twain's metaphor for the times when he could not write—he would go to Rogers' office and, with morbid fascination, watch his friend's "master brain and master hands" tirelessly working (Leary, 10–26).

Rogers fulfilled another of Twain's needs: reading what he wrote. Both Livy, Twain's wife, and William Dean Howells, his longtime friend and literary comrade, shrank from the corrosive bitterness of *What Is Man?* and similar works; but Rogers was willing to read them and ready to accept the views they voiced (10–26). As Twain began to bifurcate his world into realms of "sentiment" and "business," Rogers was the only close friend who would inhabit with him the regions he had come to feel were truly "real." It was precisely because Rogers was the ultimate man of business that his remark that Twain's fortune and fame had "cost no one a pang or a penny" meant so much to him. Twain might have examined the source of this comfort more closely: after all, it seems that none of Standard Oil's shenanigans—wide-reaching and brutal as Twain's never were—cost Rogers a pang, either. But in the mid-1890s, Twain desperately needed to hear those words from someone who could never be accused of sentimentality.

If we accept the proposition that *Pudd'nhead Wilson* was Twain's last characteristic work, it seems logical to conjecture that something about the bankruptcy which closely followed its publication "changed" Twain: changed him well before his daughter Susy's death and more fundamentally than the diversion of time and energy into the bankruptcy negotiations would suggest. An examination of his correspondence and notebooks from the period supports this idea (as we shall see). As Bernard DeVoto has argued, Twain's identity not simply as a success but as the real-life hero of a Horatio Alger-style romance was rocked to its basis and with it, temporarily, his power as an artist (DeVoto; Smith, 140–158).

It seems reasonable to suggest that if Twain had not been fundamentally changed by his bankruptcy, he would have been able (or would have wished) to return to his old style once his financial problems were resolved. However, it is undeniable that what came next cemented the change in him and confirmed the view of life he adopted after becoming a bankrupt. To pay off his debts, Twain realized that he would have to undertake a world lecture tour at the age of 60, depressed and in poor health. Even worse, he would have to grind out books according to the bankers' timetable. The books he would have to write would not, legally, even belong to him, but to Livy. Since Livy's inheritance had been liberally "borrowed" by Charles L. Webster & Co., Rogers was able to make her Twain's preferred creditor; thus, a large portion of the debt became "owed" to Livy and written off (Leary, 24); this also meant that until such time as all debts were completely settled, the copyrights to his books, not only present, but future—his creativity itself, in a sense—belonged to Livy. During the negotiations, he wrote to her about the mental shift this required:

> ... It was confoundedly difficult for me to be always saying "Mrs. Clemens's books," "Mrs. Clemens's copyrights," "Mrs. Clemens's type-setter stock," and so on; but it was necessary to do this, and I got the hang of it presently. I was even able to say with gravity, "My wife has two unfinished books, but I am not able to say when they will be completed or where she will elect to publish them, when they are done." [5/4/1894] (Wecter, *LLMT*, 302)

The above letter in its entirety suggests that Twain enjoyed this role-playing, but legally, it was not a game. Twain had been determined from the moment of their engagement that he would never live on Livy's income (Kaplan, 94–102), but Rogers' arrangement made Twain financially dependent upon her. Although Livy did not want to be Twain's preferred creditor, and the record of their correspondence suggests that she did not exploit her role, it is difficult to imagine any writer feeling very good about resigning the rights to his own creativity.

In January of 1895, while planning out his lecture tour and writing *Joan of Arc*, Twain outlined the first of a series of autobiographical fantasies: tales of a phenomenally successful man who became a bankrupt and saw his life change so quickly and catastrophically that he could not be sure which, if either, was real and which was a dream—former success or current ruin. Even if the parallels between these manuscripts and Twain's life were less clear, their autobiographical nature would be evident from his notebooks, in which he set down "keys" to which characters represented which people in his life (Tuckey, 9, 151). The connection in Twain's mind between the "dream" motif and his financial disasters was so strong that he mentioned the story idea to Rogers in the same letter with which he responded to Rogers' news that the typesetter had failed (Leary, 115–16). He would never finish a single one of these "dream" tales. If unfinished, they could not be published; if not published, they could not become anyone else's property. Refusing to publish these and other highly personal, experimental manuscripts may have become Twain's way of keeping control over them, a possibility I have explored elsewhere (Weil).

The evolution of the "dream" manuscripts through a series of major changes in plot while retaining essentially the same set of autobiographical characters provides us, as DeVoto argued, with something like a road map of Twain's changing view of himself as a man and artist beginning in 1894, the year of catastrophe (140–41). DeVoto urged future critics to take that road map and explore its uncharted territory, but no one has, as yet, gone beyond his general observation that Twain became obsessed with the problem of guilt and responsibility (from the personal to the cosmic scale) to show precisely how that obsession changed Twain's characteristic voice.

In *Mr. Clemens and Mark Twain*, Justin Kaplan has convincingly shown how Twain forged that voice while writing of *The Innocents Abroad*, the watershed book that marked him as not merely a funny Western fellow but a nationally popular humorist (Kaplan, 70–72). Twain believed that he had been "forced by fate" to adopt humor "as a medium of truth" (Hill, 17), but he had adopted more than humor. Through elaborate self-fashioning, he had shaped himself to assume an ingenious comic stance, a bad-boy pose: what Leslie Fiedler, writing not of Twain as an artist but of Tom and Huck, calls "the good bad boy" (Fiedler; Smith, 130–39). The good bad boy could play pranks, swear and use slang, skip church, break rules and commit venial sins: but because he was charming, funny, and "had his heart in the right place," he would always be forgiven, even beloved.

Twain made his good-bad-boy pose a popular phenomenon. Before Mark Twain, most American literary characters, even rugged frontier scouts like Cooper's Natty Bumppo, tended to speak and act in ways that would not be out of place in the most proper parlor. Twain found his pose an attractive way to "package" his Western material for the Eastern literary establishment, as Kaplan has argued (70–72). It freed him to use then-nontraditional material—bawdy jokes, slang, and irreverence both social and religious—because the pose could be understood and rationalized by a "mature" American audience of that time: boys were allowed to tread on borderlines, as long as they did not "go too far." As Louis Budd points out in *Our Mark Twain: The Making of His Public Personality*, Twain's pose was liberating to Americans working to fit themselves into the proprieties of the increasingly corporate, post-Civil War world of business that Twain named "the Gilded Age": in his writing, he "intimated that the secret of coping was play, the spirit that burst through the workaday routine or reduced it to feckless confusion" (71). In short, Twain's audience could live vicariously through his printed escapades without outraging propriety; he could expose the "shadow" of the American middle class to light in ways acceptable to that class as a literary audience.

Twain found his bad-boy pose an invaluable asset. For example, he used it to get the license he wanted from his friends and, later, from Livy, in their role as his "literary censors." In writing, the pose intrigued and entertained them; socially, it became the Trojan Horse in which Twain was able to insinuate his remarkably unreconstructed social presence into their milieu. As we shall see, he did this less as an exercise in conscious manipulation than as a matter of habit: the role he played to tease Mary Fairbanks, one of his early literary mentors (Wecter, *MTMF*, 1–120), and played more earnestly to win well-bred Livy Langdon as his wife, became a convenience. It worked, and since it worked so well, he fell into it with ever-increasing ease.

When we examine Twain's correspondence, we can see that Twain came to use the pose in his business ventures as well, but fatally (Weil, chapters 2 and 3, *passim*). He ran his publishing company into bankruptcy with his whirlwind financial maneuvers, hopping from one scam to the next like a grown-up Tom Sawyer. When his schemes failed to pan out (their usual fate), he blamed Charley Webster and then Frederick J. Hall, his hapless business managers, even though the record of their contracts and business correspondence shows that Twain held a controlling interest in the company and that he routinely ordered his managers to "drop everything" at a moment's notice in order to attend to his financial whims and "inspirations" (Hill, *MTP* 290–99). When Twain became a bankrupt, however, he finally had to face a situation not susceptible to his persuasive charm: for once, the good-bad-boy pose could not create license. His anger and consternation at his publishers for "failing" him and at his bankers for wanting their money back turned into vehement, morbid self-blame. By the summer of 1894, he had begun to imagine life as a hellish dream: his correspondence swelled with references to this theme, and he began to consider writing something about it. Once the typesetter, too, failed him, he outlined the first of the dream manuscripts (Tuckey, 31; Leary, 115–16).

Through the metamorphoses of the fragmentary dream manuscripts, we can trace the disintegration of Twain's narrative pose. The wry narrator vanished; in the first manuscript, *Which Was the Dream?* (1897–98), there were no "good bad boys" (or men), only figures fixed at the extremes of good and evil. These figures were essentially autobiographical: as noted above, Twain's notebooks from this period list his fictional characters and the real people whom he meant them to represent; even where lists are lacking, analogies are impossible to ignore. For example, as Twain had blamed his business managers for the bankruptcy, "Tom X" blames "Jeff Sedgewick," their fictional counterpart, for his own ruin in *Which Was the Dream?* When Twain shifted from *Which Was the Dream?* to *Indiantown* (1899) and finally to *Which Was It?* (1899–1902), he made a crucial psychological shift as well: he moved his terrible sense of guilt from the purely evil Sedgewick character and invested it in a character representing himself, but with more realistically mixed motives (George Harrison in *Which Was It?*, a respectable man who discovers that he will do anything to avoid the stigma of debt). I would argue that Twain's decision to cut Sedgewick as he moved on to *Indiantown* and *Which Was It?* reflected his realization that his own Tom Sawyer-like escapades were responsible for his bankruptcy. Twain's treatment of the well-intentioned "plots" contrived by young "Tom," Harrison's son in *Which Was It?*, to surprise his father with the funds he needs, as well as Harrison's realization that those "plots" have led him into a situation in which he commits murder, lend strong support to this contention.

I have found no single letter or notebook entry that expresses any conscious realization by Twain that living his pose effectively bankrupted him, but comparisons of the plot and characters of the fragments with Twain's view of his bankruptcy (as expressed in his correspondence) make this conclusion difficult to escape. In his business ventures, he had behaved as though his actions could have no consequences: behavior typical of "good bad boys," but hard to condone in a man sixty years of age. Once illuminated by the bankruptcy, the pose became untenable. Twain rejected both the bad-boy figure and the bad-boy pose—the slyly humorous characters and narrative voice that had gotten away with so much—because, consciously or not, they had become indelibly associated with his misfortunes (Weil).

Through the process of writing the dream manuscripts, Twain not only abandoned his characteristic narrative pose but he transformed his use of his classic Midwestern setting as well. In rejecting the Eastern milieu of *Which Was the Dream?* in favor of the Midwestern locale of *Which Was It?* Twain dispensed with the setting, "family" characters, and trappings of social class that represented the life which he had built for himself as an adult: as "Mark Twain," the successful man of letters and businessman at home in the Eastern establishment. It is as if that created world and self could not coexist in Twain's mind with the cravenness that he attributed to himself not only in his letters and notebooks, but in the character representing himself in *Which Was It?* In that final fragment of the dream series, Twain placed this guilt-ridden figure in a Midwestern town closely resembling Hannibal—and infected the aspirations of every other person in that town with cravenness and guilt as well. Twain had diffused his crushing sense of self-blame throughout a world whose nature could not be "blamed" on him since he neither made nor chose it but merely found himself in it as a child and young man.

Twain's location of guilt and blame in the land of his origins poisoned the "matter of Hannibal" like a corpse in a well: everything he drew from it after the bankruptcy ("Hadleyburg," for example) tasted of the death of his faith in himself and others. To use his own metaphor for his creativity, the old "tanks" were not going to "fill up" again. He replaced them with the bitter figures and voice of *Which Was It?* He also chose other extremes: he knew that good still existed and allowed himself to embrace it blindly in the sentimental tales like *Joan of Arc*. But in his best late work, he succeeded in fusing both black and white visions in morality plays and essays written from the God's eye view of white-hot satire. This technique enabled him to handle human weakness in a more detached, analytical fashion than he did in his autobiographical writings. In his satires, he succeeded in making the question of evil less excruciatingly personal and thus more amenable to literary effort.

Twain's first self-justifying, finally self-condemnatory view of his bankruptcy, then, led him to abandon his unique, carefully forged narrative persona and voice as well as his characteristic treatment of his richest source material and locale in an attempt to contain his sense of guilt. Because this solution required a new pose and voice, Twain suddenly began to experiment with many new modes of expression. I have traced in detail the parallel disintegration of Twain's finances and his literary persona—his "imagination-mill"—as well as his work to reconstruct the "mill" in the dream manuscripts; drawing again upon (but substantially qualifying) Bernard DeVoto, I have attempted to show that Twain turned his transformed idea of himself as an artist into, in essence, the theme unifying the *Mysterious Stranger Manuscripts* (Weil). In those manuscripts, Twain set up the "stranger" characters as authorial analogues, what Henry Nash Smith has called "transcendent," powerful figures who appear mysteriously in provincial towns to play havoc with the moral assumptions of the people they find there (Smith, 135–37). Like many of Twain's later satires, the *Stranger* manuscripts are dominated not by boys (good or bad), but by these transcendent figures capable of commanding everyone around them with the sheer power of their words: Colonel Sherburn in *Huck* and Hank Morgan in *A Connecticut Yankee in King Arthur's Court* are the evolutionary forerunners of these later characters. They are isolated by their intellectual superiority to their communities, have power almost or actually supernatural, are contemptuous of mankind as a species, and are not torn by the inner conflict of "conscience and moral sense" (122–23). Because they can resist the "blurring of attitudes caused by social conformity" (118), they can be effective critics of human nature. Having lost his will to write as a "good bad boy," Twain needed to find another type of character who could perform the service which Smith, writing of Huck Finn, so aptly identifies: to "speak as moral man viewing an immoral society, an observer who is himself free of the vices and even the weaknesses he describes" (118).

The "transcendent figures" whom Smith defines served this purpose for Twain, but Smith finds in them the source of what he considers Twain's late diminution of artistic power. Writing of "The Chronicle of Young Satan," the first of the *Stranger* manuscripts, Smith alludes to the famous sequence in which the stranger figure, Young Satan, creates and then destroys a miniature village full of tiny people as

> the symbolic gesture of a writer who can no longer find any meaning in man or society. Twain's only refuge is to identify himself with a supernatural spectator for whom mankind is but a race of vermin, hardly worth even contempt. And this marks the end of his career as a writer, for there was nothing more to say. (188)

But Twain had plenty more to say in the two manuscripts with which he followed "Chronicle." In both, Twain endows #44, the new stranger figure, with the power of Young Satan, but he strikingly limits 44's willingness to abuse that power as he attempts to enlighten the people he encounters. Twain also limits 44's effectiveness in opening men's eyes to the truths he bears. Even in the scene in "Chronicle" which Smith defines as an expression of the contempt which he feels destroyed Twain's creative power, Twain emphasizes the narrator's horror and grief at Young Satan's wanton destruction—and the ease with which Satan (the creating character and authorial analogue) can manipulate people (the literary audience). When Twain shifts the function of his authorial analogues to make them less destructive, more compassionate, and more limited in their impact upon others, it seems that he is not identifying himself with contemptuous power in the simple way Smith suggests; rather, he is exploring the question of a writer's capacity to enlighten his audience.

Twain's answer to this question is the key to his decision to withhold so much of his late writing from publication in his lifetime. This analysis may, finally, reveal Twain's conception of himself as an artist: how it originally enabled him to write his best-known work, and how its metamorphosis transformed his later writing. My argument, like DeVoto's, will necessarily be speculative, but I believe that the vast evidence of Twain's manuscripts, notebooks, journals and correspondence will make it persuasive.

Before making that argument, I feel obligated to explain more fully my rather harsh view of Twain's critics. In fact, the work that Hill, Macnaughton, and Kaplan have done in their efforts to make sense of the later Twain is a provocative starting point for a detailed exploration of "what happened" to the writer in the 1890s.

Although Hamlin Hill's account of Twain's last decade in *Mark Twain: God's Fool* is detailed and painstaking biography, it becomes more descriptive than analytical when Hill discusses Twain's literary sea-change. In fact, by beginning his analysis in 1900, he avoids even touching upon Twain's transitional years. Hill writes that Twain's humor could not express the rage and indignation which became his emotional constants during the personal tragedies of 1900 onward, a time dotted with the deaths of people Twain loved. He argues that such rage and indignation must inevitably overwhelm humor and irony unless channeled with greater care than Twain could muster at that time in his life; but he also argues that Twain was actually struggling to toss off the "comic pose" that employed humor and irony and replace it with a new, "authentic" voice, primarily through writing nonfiction (to Hill, the *Autobiography* was Twain's one great late achievement [xxiii]). I agree that Twain was trying to change that pose, but what Hill argues is self-contradictory: if Twain was not even trying to use humor and irony, how could they be "overwhelmed" by rage and indignation? Hill is right to observe that Twain was trying to find a new "pose," but when he sees it he criticizes it primarily for failing to be ironic humor, Twain's old vein. In his earlier work, Twain tended to rein in his rage and indignation through the strategic use of subjective narrators like Huck, or *Connecticut Yankee*'s Hank Morgan, or the "greenhorns" of *Roughing It* and his other Western writing: this strategy for expressing "the antagonisms within him"—this use of limited or unreliable narrators to "get away with" social criticism—is not the strategy Twain used in later works like *Hadleyburg* or *Letters from the Earth*, which deliberately employ omniscient narrators. These later works are Swiftian satires, which not only can "accommodate" rage and indignation, but burn them as fuel.

A presumption that the later Twain was utterly out of control prejudices a reading of his works: it misses the possibility that in turning to acrid satire (or moral fable, or syrupy sentimentality) Twain could have made deliberate artistic choices. They may in some cases have been bad choices, but they should still be analyzed as choices—choices which may have unconscious undercurrents, even compulsions, without yet signalling the onset of senile dementia. I would argue that often they were not bad choices, and that even when they were, they opened windows onto Twain's creative processes at work.

Let us compare Hill's treatment of Twain's work in finishing *#44, the Mysterious Stranger*, with the evidence of the notebooks and manuscripts. *#44* was the final manuscript in a series of fragments concerning the incursion of a stranger with mysterious powers into a provincial village and his effect upon the people, especially the boys, who live there. Twain worked on earlier versions intermittently, beginning in 1897, before concocting the combination of narrative elements that he could bring to closure in *#44*. These manuscripts appear in holograph form in the Mark Twain Papers, and their dating has been thoroughly documented by both John Tuckey and William M. Gibson. In this excerpt from *Mark Twain: God's*

Reconstructing the "Imagination-Mill"

Fool, Hill analyzes the work Twain did on *#44* in 1905 through Twain's correspondence:

> On June 29th, [Twain] switched from *3000 Years Among the Microbes* to the final version of *The Mysterious Stranger*. He reported to Clara, "I have spent the day reading the book I wrote in Florence. I destroyed 125 pages and expect to go over it again tomorrow and destroy 25 more. . . ." Mark Twain continued working on the "wonderful 44 story" in July and gave the manuscript of *#44, the Mysterious Stranger* to Miss Lyon to read. . . . He told Rogers, with irresistible interest in his own productivity: "my output grows smaller daily. It has dwindled from high-water mark—32 pages a fortnight ago, one day—to 12 day before yesterday, 10 yesterday, and 8 to-day." (111)

Taking his cue from Twain's own frustration, Hill focuses on the bumpy progress of composition. Twain's "output" was dwindling—at 70, he could not "produce" at the rate he could, for example, at 50, when he finished *Huck*. Nevertheless, his notebooks clearly show that Twain did compose 155 pages in the month Hill discusses and actually finished the book (Gibson 10–11). When Hill next mentions *#44*, he calls it "a jumble of confused motives and ideas, in those parts written in 1905 as well as the segments composed earlier. The 'mysterious stranger' creates 'Duplicates' to run a printing shop, performs burlesque miracles, and in general vitiates the possibilities for effective social satire or philosophical writing with his pranks" (113). Hill's analysis of *#44* never becomes more specific than this, perhaps because his sense of the emotional context in which Twain wrote becomes his judgment of the quality of the writing itself, which he does not quote. Thus, Hill came to see Twain's late works as a "junkyard of unfinished manuscripts and ill-conceived literary ideas (which) was the most enduring testimony of the failure of Mark Twain to retain creative control over his world" (273).

Hill tends to refer to the three separate "Stranger" manuscripts collectively as *The Mysterious Stranger*, the title which Paine and Duneka used for their 1916 edition of "The

Chronicle" with the final chapter of *No. 44* improbably appended as the conclusion; this is a conjunction of materials which Twain never intended. "The Chronicle" was, as the evolutionists might say, a dead end in development: Twain never returned to it except to append its opening chapter to *No. 44*. Though related, it was very different. Its "mysterious stranger," Philip Traum, is a young, unfallen cousin of Satan out to study mankind, whereas 44 is revealed as neither an angel nor a devil but a dream emanating from the mind of August, the human narrator. 44's purpose is not to study mankind but to enlighten August concerning August's true nature, that of the world, and of God. The other major difference is that *No. 44* is a finished work: at least, Twain himself wrote in his working notes that he had finished it. To label it a "fragment" begs the question of what a literary fragment is. Whatever else may be said of *No. 44*, its narrative structure is tightly knit around the premise, revealed only in the final chapter, that 44 is one of the narrator's own recurring dreams made material, an emanation of the unconscious mind attempting to enlighten its conscious counterpart concerning its own true nature. The only instances in which August is other than shocked at 44's world-view are times when he uses it to justify his own manipulation of others (disposing of his Duplicate in order to win Marget, duping her as to his identity, etc.). These are not inconsistencies but part of a coherently conceived design which I shall elaborate below. "The Chronicle," ultimately, is a string of episodes, some surpassing *No. 44* in vividness—and necessarily, since August's straight-man tone is essential to Twain's later conception. Twain was a master in the use of the "unreliable narrator" as a satiric technique, but he always unmasks him as a fool at the close of his tale (as in his early tall tales, such as "The Notorious Jumping Frog" and "Jim Blaine and His Grandfather's Old Ram").

In his introduction to the *Mysterious Stranger Manuscripts*, William Gibson criticizes these texts for reasons which arise partly from his perspective on the significance which the stranger figure held for Twain. He writes,

> Satan, alias "No. 44," is the primary character in all three manuscripts and the most complex in his acts, in his satirical bent, the "fatal music of his voice," his Socratic way of speaking, his origins... In Mark Twain's theology, he is the truth-speaker momentarily banished from heaven, the preacher Koholeth, the new Prometheus who is "courteous to whores and niggers."... It is Satan the rebel, nonetheless, who figures most often in Twain's writings and who exhibits the richest development. (Gibson 14–15)

These remarks would work better if applied to the unfinished "Letters to Satan" and to *Letters from the Earth* than to the *Mysterious Stranger Manuscripts*. If it was Satan the rebel who most interested Twain, why is the stranger figure of all three manuscripts unfallen? Gibson says that "The Chronicle" was born out of Mark Twain's note of "Satan's boyhood—going around with other boys and surprising them with devilish miracles," and it is true that most of the "Chronicle's" action deals with this theme. The only discrepancy is that Young Satan is not Satan. Rather, he is his unfallen nephew and, far from having been cast out, has come to Earth on his own accord to study mankind. Only "Schoolhouse Hill," of the three fragments, genuinely centers on the figure of the young Satan (already at that point in Twain's progression called "44"). In that brief, unfinished tale, 44 is the son of Satan, again unfallen, and he takes up a vocation which is precisely the opposite of his father's: to rehabilitate mankind, which has been "diseased" by the fruit of the knowledge of good and evil.

Gibson assumes that Twain abandoned "Schoolhouse Hill" because

> ... certain inherent contradictions within the character of 44 and his projected actions proved too great for Twain to resolve. Apparently he wanted to make his stranger both a boy and an angel, both a companion to Tom and Huck and a Prometheus-figure who was to enlighten the citizens of St. Petersburg concerning the damnable Moral Sense. (9)

The idea of a boy or adolescent angel is not inherently contradictory, nor is the notion that such a boy angel might, almost by definition, be Promethean in intention and effect. It seems more plausible that Twain ultimately abandoned "Schoolhouse Hill" because the figure of the mysterious stranger was ultimately more interesting to him as a foil to man than as the center of his own drama. Twain wrote "Schoolhouse Hill" in a departure from work on "The Chronicle"; after abandoning both, his next attempt to sound the stranger motif was *No. 44*, in which, again, the main figure is the naive *human* narrator, drawn to the charismatic stranger and his mysteries.

By the time Twain came to write *No. 44*, however, his emphasis had shifted. The stranger is no longer related to any figure in the Christian cosmology: he is a dream. Where previously he was utterly separate from mankind, alternately amused by and contemptuous of it ("The Chronicle") or compassionate toward it ("Schoolhouse Hill"), here, as an emanation of August's unconscious mind, he is a part of it. He tells August in the famous final chapter,

> "Nothing exists; all is a dream. God,—man,—the world,—the sun, the moon, the wilderness of stars: a dream, all a dream, they have no existence. *Nothing exists save empty space—and you!*"
> "I!"
> "And you are not you—you have no body, no bones, you are but a *thought*. I myself have no existence, I am but a dream—your dream, creature of your imagination. In a moment you will have realized this, then you will banish me from your visions and I shall dissolve into the nothingness out of which you made me . . . But I your poor servant have revealed you to yourself and set you free. Dream other dreams, and better! . . ." (404)

Like Twain himself, 44 may mock the human race for its pretensions, but he is always involved with it: the embittered tone of his mockery betrays his inescapable attachment. "On the whole," he says, "I am more sorry for the race than ashamed of it": but why should he feel ashamed of it unless he is somehow responsible for it, part of it? 44 appears whenever August is unhappy to cheer him and is hurt whenever August gets angry at him for his "blasphemies."

But Young Satan is never so solicitous of his human companions; he maintains a tone of lofty indifference throughout their Satanic dialogues. He sums up his attitude toward the human race in a speech whose tone recalls neither of the other two strangers, but Colonel Sherburn denouncing the mob which comes to lynch him for cold-blooded murder in *Huck Finn*:

> . . . Men have nothing in common with me—there is no point of contact. They have foolish little feelings, and foolish little vanities and impertinences and ambitions, their foolish little life is but a laugh, a sigh, and an extinction . . . I will show you what I mean. Here is a red spider, not so big as a pin's head; can you imagine an elephant being interested in him; caring whether he is happy or isn't; or whether he is wealthy or poor; or whether his sweetheart returns his love or not . . . Those things can never be important to the elephant, they are nothing to him, he cannot shrink his sympathies to the microscopic size of them. Man is to me as the red spider is to the elephant. The elephant has nothing against the spider, he cannot get down to that remote level— I have nothing against man . . . The elephant would not take the trouble to do the spider an ill turn; if he took the notion he might do him a good turn, if it came in his way and cost him nothing. I have done men good service, but no ill turns. (114)

It is disingenuous for the elephant to display such elaborate indifference to the red spider; it cannot be unconscious of the spider's existence and sensations if it can dilate upon them at such length nor can Young Satan. This pose of chilling severance is a convenience to him, and it is not the attitude of either 44.

These three "mysterious strangers" are not the identical beings Gibson describes, ciphers to be shuffled into whatever plot drifted across Twain's ephemeral field of attention. We may begin to sense why Twain made them different through analyzing their relationships with the boys whom they choose for companions. Early in "The Chronicle," Young Satan tells the boys that

> Man's mind clumsily and tediously and laboriously patches little trivialities together, and gets a result—such as it is. My mind *creates*! Do you get the force of that? Creates anything it desires—and in a moment. Creates without materials; creates fluids, solids, colors—anything, everything—out of the airy nothing which is called Thought. A man imagines a silk thread, imagines a machine to make it, imagines a picture, then by weeks of labor embroiders it on a canvas with the thread. I *think* the whole thing, and in a moment it is before you—created. (114)

Young Satan, creating characters and orchestrating events like a wildly imaginative author run rampant in his own text, seems at times like an authorial analogue. In the passage above, however, Twain makes him directly confront the difference between laborious physical creation and imaginative creation. An author cannot, of course, create a real silk thread with his thoughts, but he can create a representation of one; and in fact, Twain seems to play out the relationship between an author and his audience in these exchanges between Young Satan and the boys. If Young Satan is in some sense an authorial analogue, however, he represents a rather brutal author. What he creates, he feels free to destroy whenever it suits him: he concocts a miniature Creation scene to amuse the boys, only to squash between his fingers two workmen whose tiny brawl distracts him from conversation. When

> the small noise of the weeping and praying [over the dead workmen] began to annoy him, then he reached out and took the heavy board seat out of our swing and brought it down and mashed all those people into the earth just as if they had been flies, and went on talking just the same. (50)

Writers can wipe out multitudes of characters and "keep on talking," although in literature of any value such symbolic destruction will be to some purpose. To Young Satan, it is just a reflex. The boys are horrified, but Twain tells us that Young Satan "was bent on putting us at ease, and he had the right *art*" (italics mine). Before two pages have elapsed, he inspires them with "the fatal music of his voice" to dance upon the grave he has just created: "he was bent on making us feel as he did, and of course his magic accomplished his desire. It was no trouble to him, he did whatever he pleased with us."

In his San Francisco days, Twain learned the art of stand-up comedy from Artemus Ward, one of the best-known Western humorists of that day. Justin Kaplan, among others, has argued that as Twain developed his own brand of lecture-platform humor, the demands of its practice led him to see his audience as a pack of dumb, vile, pathetic sheep: the more successfully he manipulated them, the less he respected them (Kaplan, 226–27). As Kaplan says, Twain tended to think of his own humor as "something violent and painful that he did to someone else." (227) I would suggest that Twain invested in Young Satan his own contempt of his audience: the flip side of his courtship, in fact his need, of it. Young Satan's games seem to play out on a symbolic level the power Twain felt he himself could wield.

Despite the power and success of his own imagination, throughout his life Twain displayed uneasiness with the power of the imagination to wish evil on others, even though, and perhaps partially because, he could himself be so vindictive to anyone who he felt had crossed him. In *The Innocents Abroad*, Twain mused that the sea-travelers praying for a storm to pass them by were, by extension, wishing the storm on someone else; in 1905, in "The War Prayer," he drove home the point that those who pray for their country's victory in war are wishing pain and annihilation upon another country, populated by people like themselves. Twain's rigidly Presbyterian upbringing enforced upon him a sense that man is fully responsible for everything he does; although he struggled against the idea that with free will goes the guilt of human action, it was a belief too deeply ingrained to discard. After his bankruptcy and the cycle of disasters that followed it, Twain felt terrible guilt at what he called "robb[ing] my family to feed my speculations." (Leary, 351) Responsibility, a theme that runs throughout his writing, became a preoccupation after his bankruptcy, and we may see it further illustrated in *No. 44*.

When Twain turned from "The Chronicle" to *No. 44*, he chose to make the stranger figure, the authorial analogue, nonviolent. The absence of Satan's destructiveness in 44's brand of "creativity" is striking. 44 creates things, people, and considerable mischief, but destroys nothing—only himself, in two mock self-immolations. August, however, says the word that destroys his Duplicate. Further, 44 is always careful not to hurt the feelings of those around him; but August is capable of callous manipulation (again, the means by which he ensures that his Duplicate has no success with Marget) and cowardice (he never tries to help 44 when 44 is being attacked by the print-shop workers). But we must remember that August and 44 are linked: August is the conventional, prosaic-minded, waking self, and 44 is the power of his dreams, we might even say of his imagination, able to create with thought. Together, they seem to represent a polarization of the impulses which warred within Twain during his final years, with 44 representing the wild, fantastic imagination and sense of moral outrage which seeps through all of his fiction—in short, the creativity which made Twain a writer—and August representing the side of him that feared the righteous rage of public morality and desperately wanted to keep his public self from "going too far."

Early in *No. 44*, 44 absolves August of guilt for his lack of courage of his convictions, saying, "You did not make yourself. How then are you to blame?" August, it seems, is permitted his moral weakness and intellectual dullness because he is merely human, and so by definition stupid, limited, and unconscious.

But 44, having insight and creative power, is not to be permitted such weakness. I would suggest that in the progression from "The Chronicle" to *No. 44*, Twain curtailed the destructive impulses of the "authorial" figure of the mysterious stranger with whom he most strongly identified: it is as if he felt there could be no excuses for him. Thus, rather than to destroy or even to create, 44's primary mission becomes one of revelation. 44 shows August his own true nature: "But I your poor servant have revealed you to yourself and set you free. . . ." 44 is a black-comedy rendition of Dante's Virgil, treating exclusively the province of the first third of Dante's epic: he acts as a guide to the underworld of the human unconscious.

After Livy's death, Twain wrote a letter to his close friend, the Reverend Joe Twichell, of which the "nothing exists; all is a dream" close of *No. 44* is virtually a paraphrase. Quoting this letter, Gibson writes that the "almost unrelievedly dark tenor of [Twain's] letter" is only "half lightened in the 'Conclusion' [to *No. 44*] by blessed and hopeful feelings." (33) It is strange that Gibson finds anything "lightened," even by half, in such a conclusion: to end a novel with the narrator's realization that the world as we know it is only an illusion—a realization which the narrator experiences as a great relief—is surely a condemnation of that world. In justifying his view that No. 44 represents a cheerier perspective on Twain's part than does the letter to Twichell, Gibson writes, "Clemens valued the creative life above all other lives; it is a vulgar error to suppose that he did not." (33)

Certainly Twain did value "the creative life," but that does not mean that he never suffered ambivalence over its results, actual or potential. If the parallels which I have drawn between both Young Satan and 44 with Twain as an artist are plausible, we can see through Twain's use of Young Satan as an authorial surrogate his ambivalence about the moral nature of authorship: that he scrapped "The Chronicle" and went on to let 44 create, but, pointedly, not destroy, suggests that the analogy between himself and his mysterious stranger had grown too close for comfort. If the episode of the miniaturized Creation in "The Chronicle" seems more like a comment on the nature of God than of writing, I would suggest that on some level, Twain was analogizing the two: both create, and since both can, Twain felt, profit from that creation, they should bear responsibility for that creation.

In this creation sequence, Young Satan plunges the little people he has made into hellfire; Theodor, along with the other boys, feels their pain.

> [Young Satan] made us see all these things, and it was as if we were on the spot and looking at them with our own eyes. And we *felt* them, too, but there was no sign that they were anything to him, beyond being mere entertainments. Those visions of hell, those poor babes and women and girls and lads and men shrieking and supplicating in anguish—why, we could hardly bear it, but he was as bland about it as if it had been so many imitation rats in an artificial fire. (50)

The scene is eerily similar to Books XI and XII of *Paradise Lost*, in which the archangel Michael conveys to Adam the vision of the future life of the human race which God has decreed that he should see. It is ostensibly a vision of hope (at least, this was Milton's view), and yet Adam must witness Cain killing Abel, among other tragic spectacles. Having seen such a vision, how will Adam be able to take any joy in his sons when they are born? The scene is punishment masquerading as helpful information; insisting on its kind intent, as the Father does through Michael, amounts to sadism.

Twain knew *Paradise Lost* well; the similarity between the two scenes may have been intentional. After all, Twain saw the Christian God as a cosmic stand-up comic (McMichael, et al. 331–2), with Christians as the stupid, self-righteous butts of an absurd joke. In both "The Chronicle" and *Paradise Lost* XI and XII, the characters within the story suffer through the "fatal music" of the speaker's voice and the vision it gives them. Telescope the relation of speaker to listener outward to the level of author and reader, and that relation is duplicated: the reader, granted, participates in the author's effort with a consenting imagination, but the more felicitous the writer's art, the more vivid the painful impression upon the reader will be. What makes the passage above seem to serve as evidence of Twain's ambivalence about the "creative life" is that it emphasizes the boys' continuing pain and horror at the acts of their idol, Young Satan, not any ennobling (or even justifiable) purpose for those acts. Young Satan creates a race of tiny people and puts them in hell *because he can*, and Theodor says that this "made us miserable, for we loved him, and had thought him so noble and beautiful and gracious, and had honestly *believed* he was an angel; and to have him do this cruel thing—ah, it lowered him so, and we had such pride in him." (49) It "lowers" him in their eyes, but, as we have seen, they remain in thrall to him. 44 has the excuse of bearing a genuinely moral message: the visions of hell which he evokes are part of his program to lead August to an enlightened perspective on human nature, from which August may be able to "dream other dreams" (since human nature itself, at the close of *No. 44*, is a dream) "and better!" But August cannot dream a better dream: he can only relive the story he knows, grim as it is. Twain seems to suggest that the human mind is a sadomasochistic organ. Through this irony, Twain betrays his final ambivalence about the power of imaginative writing: the question of whether or not it can make any impact upon real human actions.

If we read 44 as representative of the power of the creative mind, and August, as I suggested above, as representative of the prosaic, conventional, conscious aspect which such a mind may wear, then the following description by 44—recapitulating Young Satan's view of the imagination in Twain's new context—of the radically different modes of thought possible to each one becomes especially suggestive:

> . . . But, August, I don't mean *your* kind of thought, I mean my kind, and the kind that the gods exercise. . . . A man *originates* nothing in his head, he merely observes exterior things, and *combines* them in his head—puts several observed things together, and draws a conclusion. His mind

> is merely a machine, that is all—an *automatic* one, and he has no control over it; it cannot conceive of a *new* thing, an original thing, it can only gather material from outside and combine it into new forms and patterns. But it always has to have the materials from the outside, for it can't make them itself. That is to say, a man's mind cannot *create*—a god's can, and my race can. That is the difference. *We* need no contributed materials, we create them—out of thought. (332–33)

In keeping with roles which 44 and August seem to play in Twain's figurative drama, we may speculate that Twain imagines the creative imagination as godlike, conjuring matter and events out of thought with sweeping effects. Its prosaic side is capable only of mechanical construction from pre-existing materials: this is the merely human aspect which seems to embody Twain's disgust with himself and is represented by August—appropriately, a printer's apprentice. Herr Stein, taking 44's side and promoting him to "printer's devil," elevates publishing to the level of an "art . . . the noblest and most puissant of all arts, and destined in the ages to come to promote the others and preserve them." (251)

But 44's duties turn out to be the most trivial, mechanical, and tiresome in the shop, requiring vast reserves of physical energy. "What a devil to work he was!" says August, watching his labors. The active, though nasty laborers of the printshop are called "diligent and devilish spirits." "Devilish," in *No. 44*, comes to be synonymous with "energetic"; 44's title of "printer's devil" is the only hint of the original derivation of the mysterious stranger figures. Twain said of Milton's Satan that "the grandest thing in *Paradise Lost* . . . [is] [t]he Arch-Fiend's terrible energy." (Gibson 16) In *No. 44*, Twain stressed the tremendous effort involved in the printing process; he knew it well, having been apprenticed to a printer at the age of twelve (Wecter, *SCH*).

Again, 44 seems to stand in for Twain: just as in Twain's own life the creative effort of writing supplanted the physical drudgery of the printer's trade, 44 supplants grinding physical labor with the ease of his own imaginative creation. When the workmen go on strike, 44 first makes invisible sprites and, later, the Duplicates to carry out the printing process. The entire episode mocks the tremendous human effort which the mechanical production of an author's imaginative work required. The result is that the creative mind of the stranger (writer) is elevated at the expense of the pathetic, mechanical efforts of men (publishers, whose conventional attitudes and rapacious business practices Twain loathed but knew necessary to the fame he craved).

Looking back from the conclusion of *No. 44* to 44's distinction between his and August's brands of thought, it seems that in making both inhabit the same being, Twain dramatized his own sense of imaginative limitation. The idea that human beings create nothing and are capable only of mechanical construction was a conviction that Twain may have held throughout his life, but it was surely reinforced by his reading of Hume: his copy of *The Origin of Ideas* has been catalogued by Alan Gribben as part of Twain's vast, heavily annotated library. Compare the following passage from Hume with 44's exposition of the distinction between "his kind of thought" and August's:

> ... But though our thought seems to possess this unbounded liberty, we shall find, upon a nearer examination, that it is really confined within very narrow limits, and that all this creative power of the mind amounts to no more than the faculty of compounding, transposing, augmenting, or diminishing the materials afforded us by the senses and experience. When we think of a golden mountain, we only join two consistent ideas, gold and mountain, with which we were formerly acquainted. A virtuous horse we can conceive; because, from our own feeling, we can conceive virtue; and . . . a horse . . . is an animal familiar to us. In short, all the materials of thinking are derived either from our outward or inward sentiment: the mixture and composition of these belongs alone to the mind and will. Or, to express myself in philosophical language, all ideas and more feeble perceptions are copies of our impressions or more lively ones. (Hume)

The parallels are close: 44 tells August that the human mind is incapable of creating "a new thing, an original thing; it can only gather materials from the outside and combine it into new forms and patterns." Hume summarizes the problem pithily: "the most lively thought is still inferior to the dullest sensation." Could Twain have read this without wondering whether the most lively writing would not, in terms of effect on the thoughts of his human readers, be inferior to the dullest physical experience?

Given Twain's fluctuations between guilt at his actions and doubt over their effects, we may have in his view of imagination a partial answer to the question of why he published so little of the material he wrote in the last decade of his life. If he had held such a view, it could have worked in several ways. In one mood, he might focus on the inability of his prosaic audience to comprehend or even to bear the message of his growing pessimism about the "damned human race"; in another, he might doubt that his own artistic powers were sufficient to make that audience feel the force of what he wanted to say.

Certainly Twain could have felt ambivalence about his own artistic powers without Hume's encouragement, but the similarity between 44's and Hume's exposition of the same problem makes it reasonable to suggest that in Hume's philosophy, Twain found a framework in which to express his ambivalence about his own creative capacities. In venting his frustration with August's limited understanding, 44 blurts out, "one cannot pour the starred and shoreless expanses of the universe into a jug!" The title page of *No. 44* bears the legend, "An Ancient Tale found in a Jug, and freely Translated from the Jug."

In the year before his death, Twain reveled in the discovery of a new literary form: expressing his more vitriolic views in letters he never meant to send. These were letters to his closest friends, who were well acquainted with his heterodox notions. Gibson writes, "He told Howells, 'when you are on fire with theology, you'll write it to [Reverend]

Twichell because'—in imagination—'it would make him writhe and squirm and break the furniture.'" (Gibson 31) Gibson sees a "literary impulse" outweighing Twain's "private sorrow" in concocting this strategy; as Hill aptly says in *God's Fool*, Twain felt he had been "forced by fate to adopt fiction as a medium of truth," and "in his final years, he gained confidence in his autobiographical voice to express unpleasant truths." (17)

Twain may have gained some confidence but not enough to allow that autobiographical voice to be heard. If these letters had been written in the spirit of attempting to make, for example, his friend the minister understand how he felt about theology, why not send them, unless he felt that he could not make his beliefs either acceptable or comprehensible even to the people closest to him? Imagining one's friends being driven to "break the furniture" because of something you wrote to them sounds like a hostile wish or an uneasy premonition.

Since Twain's contract with Harper's obligated them to publish—literally—whatever he submitted to them, we must see Twain's failure to publish so much of his late writing as a refusal to publish. There could be no stronger testament to the sense of alienation under which Twain labored in his last years nor to the vacillations of his attitude toward his own artistic power than this refusal to make public so much of what he wrote. He knew that he could make an impact on the minds he chose to influence, but the nature and degree of that impact he could not predict. He was well aware that the sort of fiction he wanted to write, and did write, could cost him his reading public, just as sending the "imaginary" letters might have destroyed his closest relationships; he was willing to risk neither. As Ferguson has written,

> [Twain] withheld his most vitriolic comments, as he continued to withhold "The War Prayer" and his many criticisms of the God of the Old Testament. Yet it was probably not Livy's dead hand which checked him. His estimate of what would shock the public was formed before

he ever knew Livy; like his philosophy, it had its roots in the Presbyterian Sunday School of Hannibal. He never in his life wrote anything more scathing than the "Defense of General Funston," and the controversy with the missionaries; he published them, and the heavens did not fall. But it flattered him to believe that he was full of thoughts so devastating that the world could not take them. (302)

Ferguson is correct that Twain found perverse comfort in believing that the world was not ready for his work. And yet, it is striking to note that Twain was willing to publish some of his political late writing, such as "Funston" and "To the Person Sitting in Darkness," but not works treating the subject of religion in any substantive way. He knew from Hannibal, surely, that such material as *Letters from the Earth* would truly be more than that audience could "take" and that its publication could hurt the royalties from his collected works. As he wrote to Rogers during the negotiation of his Harper's contract,

> Whenever a Uniform and a Deluxe can be marketed, *that's* the time to do it; a delay of a year can be fatal, for a literary reputation is a most frail thing—any trifling accident can kill it, and its market along with it. (Leary, 348)

Any audience that could be so fickle would not, one would think, be much worth courting. And yet Twain had courted it from the 1860s onward, and, I would suggest, once his collected works began to issue, he chose to stop courting it at book length. Platform lectures, essays, and the occasional short story were sufficient to keep his memory green in the public mind, and, considering the way he spoke of his audience, calling them "sheep" and likening himself to a "trained seal barking for fish," it is not surprising that Twain felt that it could not absorb his criticisms without the teasing tenor of the good-bad-boy voice. Further, he came to see that audience more and more from a God's-eye-view. In a suggestive jotting in a notebook of 1896, Twain dilated upon the sort of God he would construct. Above all, this deity would not "trade on salvation":

> ... He would not be a merchant, a trader... He would not sell, or offer to sell, temporary benefits or the joys of eternity, for the product called worship. I would have him as dignified as the better sort of men in this regard. (*MTN*, 300–301)

Twain loved worship: it exhilarated him. But perhaps, in the omniscient mood of his later works, using technically limited narrative voices that nonetheless read minds (George Harrison's tactic for telling "truth" in *Which Was It?*), creating authorial analogues who resemble deities, moods like the above as well as fears for his profits helped keep his most challenging later works out of the public eye.

At the close of *No. 44*, the fate of 44, the authorial analogue—whether he, and imagination with him, disappear altogether, or find a way to merge with August, the straight man—is left ambiguous, as the question of whether imagination could be reconciled with the demands of public life remained ambiguous for Twain until his death. If there is no way to prove that anything exists outside the mind, we are left helpless, stuck inside the joke played upon us. Twain could shake off that suspension by writing books deflecting that helplessness onto his audience, but in *No. 44*, where both satiric author and audience are symbolically contained within one mind, there is no escape, only irritation as the mind perpetually retells its own story.

Twain's last years were plagued by just such an irreducible irritation over the questions of creativity and its power, guilt, and atheism. His refusal to publish his most powerful late work was not a failure of artistic power, but a failure of will. His lack of faith—in himself as well as in God— was the agitated sort that the playwright-hero of Beckett's *Endgame* expresses when his prayer for more characters goes unheard ("The bastard! He doesn't exist!"); and in fact, Beckett's "I can't go on—I'll go on" could serve as an epigraph to the fascinating fragments and finished works that grew out of his last fifteen years. His achievement in *No. 44* was in finding and finishing a narrative structure that could play out the questions that plagued him, even if he could not solve them.

Mark Twain came to believe that effective exercise of such power was only possible to those gigantic figures who, like Young Satan, have no compassion for the suffering of those whom their actions affect; that those who, like 44, undertake a consciously Promethean role, are doomed to suffering and failure. Only when these latter figures cloak their intent in humor does Twain concede any possibility that their Promethean mission might succeed: for, to steal the words of Young Satan, "against the assault of laughter nothing can stand." Believing this, Twain withheld the bulk of his most seriously intended later work from publication during his lifetime. In so doing, he flung down the gauntlet for later generations: if it's not a joke, can we take it?

Works Cited

Budd, Louis J. *Our Mark Twain: The Making of His Public Personality.* Philadelphia: U. of Pennsylvania P., 1983.

Clemens, Samuel Langhorne: see Twain, Mark.

DeVoto, Bernard. "The Symbols of Despair," rpt. in *Mark Twain: A Collection of Critical Essays.* Ed. Henry Nash Smith. Englewood Cliffs: Prentice-Hall, 1963. 119–29.

Ferguson, Delancey. *Mark Twain: Man and Legend.* New York: Bobbs-Merrill Co., Inc., 1943.

Fiedler, Leslie A. "As Free As Any Cretur . . ." rpt. in *Mark Twain: A Collection of Critical Essays.* Ed. Henry Nash Smith. Englewood Cliffs: Prentice-Hall, 1963. 130–39.

Gibson, William. Introduction to Mark Twain's *The Mysterious Stranger Manuscripts.* Berkeley: U. of California P., 1968. 1–34.

Gribben, Alan. *Mark Twain's Library: A Reconstruction.* Boston: G. K. Hall & Co., 1980. Volume I.

Hill, Hamlin. *Mark Twain: God's Fool.* New York: Harper and Row, 1973.

Hill, Hamlin, ed. *Mark Twain's Letters to His Publishers, 1867–1894*. Berkeley: U. of California P., 1967.

Hume, David. *An Enquiry Into Human Understanding*. Ed. Steven M. Cahn. *Classics of Western Philosophy*. Indianapolis: Hackett Publishing Co., 1977.

Kahn, Sholom J. *Mark Twain's Mysterious Stranger: A Study of the Manuscript Text*. Columbia: U. of Missouri P., 1979.

Kaplan, Justin. *Mr. Clemens and Mark Twain*. New York: Simon and Schuster, 1966.

Leary, Louis, ed. *Mark Twain's Correspondence with Henry Huttleston Rogers, 1893–1910*. Berkeley: U. of California P., 1969.

Macnaughton, William R. *Mark Twain's Last Years as a Writer*. Columbia: U. of Missouri P., 1979.

McMichael, George, Crews, Frederick, Levenson, J.C., Marx, Leo, and Smith, David E., eds. *Anthology of American Literature*. New York: Macmillan Publishing Co., 1980.

Smith, Henry Nash. *Mark Twain: The Development of a Writer*. New York: Atheneum, 1962 (rpt. 1972).

Tuckey, John S. *Mark Twain and Little Satan: The Writing of the Mysterious Stranger*. West Lafayette, Indiana: Purdue University Studies, 1963.

Twain, Mark. *The Autobiography of Mark Twain*. Ed. Charles Neider. New York: Harper and Row, 1959.

—— *The Devil's Race-Track: Mark Twain's 'Great Dark' Writings*. Ed. John S. Tuckey. Berkeley: U. of California P., 1966.

—— *Mark Twain's Notebook*. Ed. Albert Bigelow Paine. New York: Harper and Brothers, 1935.

—— *Mark Twain's Which Was the Dream? and Other Symbolic Writings of the Later Years*. Ed. John S. Tuckey. Berkeley: U. of California P., 1966.

—— *The Mysterious Stranger Manuscripts*. Ed. William M. Gibson. Berkeley: U. of California P., 1969.

Wecter, Dixon. *Sam Clemens of Hannibal*. Boston: Houghton Mifflin Co., 1952.

—— ed. *The Love Letters of Mark Twain*. New York: Harper and Brothers, 1949.

—— ed. *Mark Twain to Mrs. Fairbanks*. Los Angeles: Plantin Press, 1949.

Weil, Susanne. "Reconstructing the 'Imagination-Mill': Mark Twain's Literary Response to Bankruptcy." Diss. University of California, Berkeley, 1991.

Coming Back to Humor: The Comic Voice in Mark Twain's Autobiography

Michael J. Kiskis

Literary and biographical studies of the years between 1890 and 1910 focus on Mark Twain's dual tragedies—his bankruptcy in 1894 and Susy's death in 1896—as defining events: the shock, we are told, moved Twain away from humor toward a darker vision of the world, and that darker vision became the controlling theme of, as well as the impetus for, his increased output of social criticism and his preoccupations with a dream self. His life and writings succumbed to that darkness. It choked his creative process and led to his seeming inabilty to complete any lengthy fiction. He lost his counterbalance to life's pain and put aside humor, the primary ingredient in his successful storytelling. We are left with an image of a deeply troubled misanthrope who sank into bitterness and rage as he outlived his immediate family and became increasingly uncomfortable with and suspicious of his staff. We are left with a picture devoid of humor, the end of storytelling. We are left wondering what happened to Mark Twain's sense of humor.[1]

While it was certainly toned down and mixed with heavy doses of depression and anger and guilt, Mark Twain's humor remained a renewable resource.[2] It was too much a part of his public and private self to slip away unnoticed. He was much too sensitive to the call of humor and much too reliant on it as a personal and literary muse to forsake it entirely. The nature of his humor changed, however, as he worked through the range of emotions connected both with the death of his favorite daughter and with the personal sense of loss that played so heavily upon him as he witnessed the deaths of family and friends. During his final years (1906–1910), humor became less a tool for social criticism and more a hook to use to knit together the variety of his interests and memories. But Twain needed a vehicle that would allow him to revisit his muse so that he could find the raw materials he needed to build his stories. Autobiography reawakened and refocused Mark Twain's humor.[3]

This refocusing was no easy task since many of Mark Twain's writings during 1890–1910 were rooted in the difficulties of business and family tragedy. In 1890 Twain faced the growing threat from the mismanagement of the Charles Webster Company and the false optimism in the Paige typesetter. His mother, Jane Lampton Clemens, died during that year. His family faced severe financial problems. His bankruptcy in 1894 gave rise to the world lecture tour of 1895–96, which eased his debt but ended with the greater loss of Susy to spinal meningitis in 1896. His older brother Orion died in 1897. His youngest daughter Jean's condition as an epileptic became clearer during these years. Throughout this period, Twain sought solace and peace by plunging into his work; however, while that work is often dark in tone, the pattern of darkness and disappointment was not new to the 1890s. Mark Twain's adult life was haunted by rapid mood swings. If we are looking for instances of Twain's darkening vision, we are hard pressed to find images more disturbing than the violence of "A Bloody Massacre near Carson" (1863) and the tragedy of *Huckleberry Finn* (1885) or the destruction of the sand belt in *A Connecticut Yankee in King Arthur's Court* (1889). If we are looking for examples of frantic composition, we need look only to his work on *Innocents Abroad* (1869) and *Roughing It* (1872). Twain approached the precipice of darkness throughout his career as a writer. He constantly mixed the contraries of violence and depression with humor, and that mixture must be kept in mind as we examine his final decades.

Perhaps the most problematic of Twain's shifts during these years is his move away from fiction. That movement, however, did not put a stop to his writing. A quick review of Mark Twain's publication record starting as early as 1894 with *Pudd'nhead Wilson* and *Tom Sawyer Abroad* suggests that his creative drive had begun to slow or, at least, had been redirected. While he continued to publish, the nature of his work changed from the extended narratives that assured his reputation as a novelist to the essay, with only occasional forays into extended tales. After *Personal Recollections of Joan of Arc* and *Tom Sawyer, Detective* (1896), Twain completed *Following the Equator* (1897). From that point on, he devoted more attention to the essay, especially the political essay.[4] His new-found position as commentator and sage, as reformer and activist, pushed him to write more directly to the public, and the essay was best suited for direct and timely commentary. That in itself leads to an impression that he became increasingly haunted by social and political issues and less interested in humor or storytelling. We should, however, think of his explicitly designed and overtly stated social criticism as a stage of his evolution as a public figure.[5] As he tuned his satiric voice, his essays became increasingly biting and increasingly effective. And—though he would eventually stumble and then ease out of the picture—he became a leading voice in America for the Anti-imperialist movement.[6]

Though Twain completed several extended pieces after 1897—*What Is Man?* (1898; 1906), *Christian Science* (1907), *Captain Stormfield's Visit to Heaven* (1907), and *Is Shakespeare Dead?* (1909)—his work might be discussed from two perspectives: his public offerings as an essayist and satirist; his private experiments in fiction and storytelling. That split was indeed quite clear during the work that Twain completed between 1900 and 1905. Among his public offerings were the scathing essays "To The Person Sitting in Darkness," "To My Missionary Critics" (1901), "Defense of General Funston" (1902), "Tsar's Soliloquy" (1904), and "King Leopold's Soliloquy" (1905). His satires made ample use of the incongruous and burlesque as he developed his images of the imperialist powers. Their humor was severe in its tone and volume. His private writing, on the other hand, produced a variety of fragmented tales: among them "The Secret History or Eddypus, the World-Empire" (1901–02) and "The Stupendous Procession" (1901), each of which offers a blend of fiction and political essay. Other unfinished pieces are "No. 44, The Mysterious Stranger," (1902; incorporating materials from "The Chronicle of Young Satan," on which Twain worked between 1897 and 1900), "Three Thousand Years Among the Microbes" (1905), and "The Refuge of the Derelicts" (1905). While the private pieces reflect Twain's growing restiveness and interest in ontological questions, they also contain their share of humorous insights and burlesque images.

This all leads us back to Twain's work on the autobiography. With the advent of 1906 Mark Twain began to integrate the public and private as he prepared to work on his autobiography. That integration was possible because Twain used autobiography to reinvigorate himself by resurrecting humor and storytelling. We must keep in mind that humor and irony were Mark Twain's primary tools. He kept them sharp and he used them (even though he did not always publish the results). There is much to be said about the vitality of Mark Twain's humor and his use of humor as a palliative and as a recuperative tonic.

Humor was one way Twain dealt with the distractions that became especially acute with the onset of the financial storm in 1894. That blast contributed to his seeming inability to gather up the steam necessary to navigate an extended fiction. But Twain's composing process was always rather fickle: he worked until his interest fagged and then he pigeonholed the manuscript. From 1870 through 1906, manuscripts earmarked as autobiography were constantly pigeonholed. Eventually, this jackrabbit composing style worked to Twain's advantage. He went right along piling up tales and anecdotes with little concern for the overarching structure or intent. That removed the demand for consistency and logic and made it possible for a variety of tales—some tall, some poignant—to be told.

As Twain relocated himself in autobiography, he became increasingly interested in the process of the story. He was excited by the series of autobiographical dictations (at least through 1906 and 1907) because of the emphasis on talk. Twain claimed that talk was at the heart of true autobiography and the reason for his enjoyment. When he returned to dictating in 1904, he wrote William Dean Howells:

> You will never know how much enjoyment you have lost until you get to dictating your autobiography; then you will realize, with a pang, that you might have been doing it all your life if you had only had the luck to think of it. And you will be astonished (& charmed) to see how like talk it is, & how real it sounds, & how well & compactly & sequentially it constructs itself, & what a dewy & breezy & woodsy freshness it has, & what a darling worshipful absence of the signs of starch, & flatiron, & labor & fuss & other artificialities! . . . There are little slips here & there, little inexactednesses, & many desertions of a thought before the end of it has been reached, but these are not blemishes, they are merits, their removal would take away the naturalness of the flow & banish the very thing—the nameless something—which differentiates real narrative from artificial narrative & makes the one so vastly better than the other—the subtle something which makes good talk so much better than the best imitation of it that can be done with a pen (MT to WDH 1/16/04; SMTHL, 370–371).

In effect, Mark Twain found himself facing his own beginnings as a storyteller: talk was the primary currency of his youth as he sat and listened to tales around slave kitchens, of his piloting days as he sat in the wheelhouses, of his adulthood as he and Jim Gillis told and retold the story of the jumping frog and as he stood night after night on the lecture platform. Talk was the basis for much of Twain's fiction: he wove lively dialogues for any number of his characters from Simon Wheeler to Demoiselle Alisande la Carteloise, from Huck Finn to No. 44. And the potential for humor—or at least for the basic incongruities that sire that humor—is best found in his talk.

In effect, Twain's return to the autobiography in 1906 rekindled his sense of direction and revived his interest in presenting one final story to the public. But while the idea of beginning the work appealed to Twain, the dominance of the spoken word in the autobiographical dictations was not enough to keep Twain on track. He again fell prey to distractions and devoted a good deal of time to supplementing the story of his life with contemporary newspaper reports, fragments of work that he had long since pigeonholed, and long submerged but still potent affronts. The dictations became an attic, or at least a storage trunk, into which he poured memories and commentary and sentiment and vitriol.

This combination changed as Twain's conception of the project shifted—what started out as a series of interviews that Albert Bigelow Paine would use as the foundation for his biography of Twain soon developed into an intentional attempt to pile up materials for an autobiography (perhaps as a way to block Paine's work[7]). The explanation that Twain used to rationalize his private freedom from publication—"I am not interested in getting done with anything. I am only interested in talking along and wandering around as much as I want to, regardless of results to the future reader" (MTA I, 327)—would eventually succumb to the possibility of profit. While Paine's projected biography sparked Twain's interest, their work together remained private. George Harvey assured the continuation of Twain's public storytelling when he purchased and serialized chapters from Twain's autobiography.

The project changed substantially when Twain was approached by Harvey. Until that point, Twain had been using the dictations themselves as a distraction. They kept him busy. His intention was to simply present his story to his small and approving audience (at first made up of only Paine and Josephine Hobbey, a stenographer). With the arrival of Harvey, however, and with the resulting contract with the *North*

American Review, Twain adjusted his sights once more on the wider public audience. The demands of serialization, of presenting consecutive and self-contained pieces forced Twain to impose more control on his meandering commentary so that the tale would develop in a form more suitable for publication. This brought him back to the careful pruning that had always been a part of his composing process and to his tried and true formula for effective storytelling: "To string incongruities and absurdities together in a wandering and sometimes purposeless way, and seem innocently unaware that they are absurdities, is the basis of the American art... Another feature is the slurring of the point. A third is the dropping of a studied remark apparently without knowing it, *as if one were thinking aloud.* The fourth and last is the pause" (Essays, 158; my emphasis). Talk is basic. This talk brought Mark Twain back to humor and its variety of tools and voices. It helped him warm to the prospect of jumping back into public storytelling.

The material that Twain finally presented to his public as "Chapters from my Autobiography" during 1906 and 1907 is markedly different from the raw material that he had been accumulating in the dictations.[8] It is different in the range of topics that are covered within its twenty-five chapters, and it is different in the structure that is imposed on the materials. It is also a very different text because it is a tapestry—it weaves together his written and dictated passages. Mark Twain knew his readers, and that combination of material helped him reach his audience. He knew what would sell. And he made a conscious attempt to give the audience a self-portrait that would not vary too far from the image they already had of him—he would solidify his image as a man of letters by offering a text rich in self-effacing tales and bouts of sentiment.

Twain's success with the autobiography can be seen best if we consider the text a full and complete tale, one that has a beginning, a middle, and an end. Of course, narrative has a way of falling into that rough structure, especially autobiography because it usually grows out of the basic chronology of the life. But Twain does not rely on the cradle to grave chronology to control the tale. It is controlled by the frame that he builds: the body of the narrative exists squarely within that frame. If we unite the twenty five chapters to form a single text, the autobiography joins "The Jumping Frog," "A True Story," and *A Connecticut Yankee in King Arthur's Court* in its use of the framing device to enter and exit the tale. It is also related to several fragments of Twain's later years: "The Great Dark," "Which Was It?," "The Secret History of Eddypus" and "Three Hundred Years Among the Microbes" use the frame. With the autobiography, however, Twain returned to humor as the basic material for his frame. In this way the autobiography is more closely related to Simon Wheeler's tale than to Hank Morgan's or to Henry Edwards'.

The connection to Wheeler reverberates in the voice that dominates the frame. Throughout his career Twain made ample and successful use of one of the staples of southwestern humor—the deadpan voice: "The humorous story may be spun out to great length, and may wander around as much as it pleases, and arrive nowhere in particular... [it] is told gravely; the teller does his best to conceal the fact that he even dimly suspects that there is anything funny about it" (Essays, 155–156).[9] It is Wheeler's and it is Huck's. It is Sandy's. As the autobiography continues, it will be Susy's.[10] At the opening, it is Mark Twain's:

> Howells was here yesterday afternoon, and I told him the whole scheme of this autobiography and its apparently systemless system—only apparently systemless, for it is not really that. It is a deliberate system, and the law of the system is that I shall talk about the matter which for the moment interests me, and cast it aside and talk about something else the moment its interest is exhausted. It is a system which follows no charted course and is not going to follow any such course. It is a system which is a complete and purposed jumble—a course which begins nowhere, follows no specified route, and can never reach an end while I am alive, for the reason that, if I should talk to a stenographer two hours a day for a hundred years, I should

still never be able to set down a tenth part of the things which have interested me in my lifetime. I told Howells that this autobiography of mine would live a couple of thousand years, without any effort, and would then make a fresh start and live the rest of the time.

He said he believed it, and asked me if I meant to make a library of it.

I said that this was my design; but that, if I should live long enough, the set of volumes could not be contained merely in a city, it would require a State, and that there would not be any multi-billionaire alive, perhaps, at any time during its existence who would be able to buy a full set, except on the installment plan.

Howells applauded, and was full of praises and endorsement, which was wise in him and judicious. If he had manifested a different spirit, I would have thrown him out of the window. I like criticism, but it must be my way (MTOA, 3–4).

There are several points bubbling along beneath the surface of this introduction. Along with the steady and very serious voice, we also get an explanation of Twain's process, a pitch for a continual series of volumes (we might think of these as a variation on encyclopedia yearbooks), an endorsement by a major literary figure, and then a final threat which underlines the serious nature of the text ahead. And none of this is presented as remarkable or unusual. It is all very plain and clear and stable. In a compact preface, Twain has put his readers on notice that his tale will alternate between the comic and the serious. His potential attack on Howells and warning to readers sets a decidedly humorous tone (the warning functions in much the same way as does the comic disclaimer that opens *Huckleberry Finn*), and as we move into the main portion of the tale, a serious and strong personal interest supports the comedy.

The tale gets under way with a nod toward the expected family history and another backhand swipe at the reader:

Back of the Virginia Clemenses is a dim procession of ancestors stretching back to Noah's time. According to

> traditions, some of them were pirates and slavers in Elizabeth's time. But this is no discredit to them, for so were Drake and Hawkins and the others. It was a respectable trade then and monarchs were partners in it. In my time I have had desires to be a pirate myself. The reader—if he will look deep down in his secret heart, will find—but never mind what he will find there; I am not writing his Autobiography, but mine (MTOA, 4).

In a movement reminiscent of *Mark Twain's (Burlesque) Autobiography and First Romance* (1871), Twain pushes his ancestry back to Noah in a bid to claim deep and impressive roots.[11] It smacks of the tall tale, and of the raftman's boast. The connection to privateers ties him to the disreputable—regardless of the official stamp of approval—and reminds us of Tom Sawyer's conventional pirate band on the one hand and of Huck and Jim's rebellion on another. By calling attention to these professions, Twain draws the reader closer. He sets the stage for his own tale with hints of shady dealing and outlaw behavior. He keeps those dealings firmly for himself as he abruptly ends the ancestral line that would allow his readers that same connection. In all, then, Twain invites his readers to gather around, sit by the fire, and listen to his tale. His is the unmistakable voice of the seasoned storyteller.

The storyteller dominates the remaining chapters. While Twain's method of butting present and past together to explore the effect is prominent throughout the twenty-five chapters, it is possible to identify five general patterns of associations that unite the text: comments on Twain's early writing (chapter 2), tales of the Clemens family (chapters 1, 3, 4, and 5), famous acquaintances (chapters 6 and 7), Twain's experience in Hannibal and Nevada (chapters 8 through 14), the Clemenses in Hartford and Elmira, a loosely tied series of comments on Twain's writing, his literary acquaintances, recent experiences, and a replay of the Whittier Birthday speech (chapters 16 through 25). This is not as clean as it appears from this breakdown, since Twain weaves in and out of memories and associations as he continues his tale; however, the thematic links do help begin to refute the charge of literary chaos that has been leveled against the autobiography.

The essential link, however, is Mark Twain's voice. He constantly modulates his voice to fit the explicit tales and anecdotes, but these separate pieces are stitched together much like a quilt. The essential voice—the controlling consciousness and perspective—remains consistent throughout the text: it resonates with an appreciation for the incongruities that have made up a life and cherishes the contrasts when past events are filtered through the irony that is possible only with distance. The point is that Twain uses the autobiography to reconnect with the creative formula that was at the heart of his regional, national, and international success. He mixes the tall tale with the familiar anecdote; he undercuts his tales of public acclaim with sharp blasts powered by events and details of his inept behavior in the midst of his family life. And while there are moments of supreme pathos and seemingly genuine sentiment, there are many more that focus on the comic adventures that combine to describe Twain's western and family life. All of these are interpreted by Twain as he looks back through the haze of time.

Twain's comic voice that reverberates within these sketches and anecdotes and tales is a derivative of the tenderfoot pose that he used so well in *Roughing It*.[12] This seems a very deliberate choice. Twain's version of his life offers very little of the commentary on contemporary politics that plays so prominent a role in Albert Bigelow Paine's and Bernard DeVoto's collections of dictations. Throughout the autobiography, Twain presents himself as perpetually hampered by his slow wits, his lack of social skills, his inabilty to live up to expectations. He is the quick-tempered novice editor in the west who is ultimately betrayed both by his own lack of judgement and his friends' and colleagues' joy in the preliminaries to a duel. He is the muddled husband: he places his social reputation at risk because of his decidedly low style, he fails to understand the basic workings of household items, he has temper tantrums. He is also the doting and misunderstood father: he spins yarns for his children, he keeps careful record of the children's reactions to the life around them, he wonders at the observations that Susy offers as part of her biography of him.[13]

As Twain looks into his past, his images are tempered by his at times overwhelming sense of loss. This leads him to use the autobiography as an extended eulogy for family and friends on the one hand and for an idyllic and elegiac childhood on another. Each of these movements, however, is touched by Twain's puckishness. Two well-known pieces of the autobiography help to establish this trend: Twain's shirt-throwing tantrum and his look back at the Quarrels farm.

In chapter five, Twain recalls his temper and his vain attempts to hide it and the resulting language from Livy. While dressing he was piqued at finding buttons missing from his shirts. That pique devolved into venom as he put on three shirts and just as quickly dispatched each offender out of the window. Throughout, Twain's language expanded "both in loudness and vigor of expression" until he reached for the third shirt: "I was too angry—too insane—to examine the third shirt, but put it furiously on. Again the button was absent, and that shirt followed its comrades out the window. Then I straightened up, gathered my reserves, and let myself go like a cavalry charge. In the midst of that great assault, my eye fell upon the gaping door, and I was paralyzed" (MTOA, 46–47). Livy had, of course, heard the final assault. Twain continues:

> I tried to hope that Mrs. Clemens was asleep, but I knew better. I could not escape by the window. It was narrow, and suited only to shirts. At last I made up my mind to boldly loaf through the bedroom with the air of a person who had not been doing anything. I made half the journey successfully. . . . I had to stop in the middle of the room. I hadn't the strength to go on. I believed that I was under accusing eyes—that even the carved angels were inspecting me with an unfriendly gaze. You know how it is when you are convinced that somebody behind you is looking steadily

at you. You have to turn your face—you can't help it. I turned mine. . . .

Against the white pillows I saw the black head—I saw that young and beautiful face; and I saw the gracious eyes with a something in them which I had never seen there before. They were snapping and flashing with indignation. I felt myself crumbling; I felt myself shrinking away to nothing under that accusing gaze. I stood silent under that desolating fire for as much as a minute, I should say—it seemed a very, very long time. Then my wife's lips parted and from them issued—*my latest bathroom remark*. The language perfect, but the expression velvety, unpractical, apprenticelike, ignorant, inexperienced, comically inadequate, absurdly weak and unsuited to the great language. In my lifetime I had never heard anything so out of tune, so inharmonious, so incongruous, so ill-suited to each other as were those mighty words set to that feeble music. I tried to keep from laughing, for I was a guilty person in deep need of charity and mercy. I tried to keep from bursting, and I succeeded—until she gravely said, "There, now you know how it sounds."

Then I exploded; the air was full with my fragments, and you could hear them whiz. I said, "Oh Livy, if it sounds like that I will never do it again."

Then she had to laugh herself. Both of us broke into convulsions, and went on laughing until we were physically exhausted and spiritually reconciled (MTOA, 46–48).

This long passage shows off Twain's storytelling (it can easily stand on its own as a complete tale). The contrast between Twain and Livy is, of course, at the heart of the passage. There would be no tale if that contrast were not so clear and so pronounced: he is volcanic and well acquainted with the rigors of "bathroom" remarks; she is, to say the least, inexperienced with and unappreciative of the genre. That conflict between western ruffian and eastern innocent recurs throughout the autobiography whenever Twain places himself within Livy's hearing or reach. Here it supplies the context for the humor, since the linchpin for the tale is the repeated curses.[14]

Beyond that, however, we have a scene reconstructed to offer readers a memorable image—of Livy. As a eulogist, Twain worked to present the various members of his family in an almost saintly light (like Livy, Orion survives as fundamentally innocent and honest). Here he introduces Livy not only as inexperienced with the nuances of cursing (something that is especially important to our image of her as perpetually innocent) but as unusually naive when it comes to the very sound and intention of the language. Twain drives this point home forcefully by describing Livy with an extended series of adjectives: her face is "young and beautiful"; her eyes "gracious." Her flash of anger dissipates because her version of the curse is "velvety," "unpractical," "apprenticelike," "ignorant," "inexperienced," "comically inadequate," "absurdly weak." The irony, of course, is that adjectives that normally indict—especially if they are used to describe the tenderfoot—are put together here to applaud and to praise. This twist is especially important for Twain since he is working to offer a memorial to Livy. He does that not only by placing his own increasingly disreputable self in opposition to Livy's goodness but also by turning the tenderfoot—once despised and ridiculed—into a hero. Surely part of this construction has its foundation in Twain's own perception of Livy as well as in his Victorian sensibilities. The vigor of his protection of Livy is, however, even more notable because of the combination of humor and eulogy and the conflict between civilizing (constructive in its opening new vistas to the individual) and "sivilizing" (destructive in its intention to beat naturalness and freedom out of the individual) efforts.

While Twain spent considerable time and effort composing memorials to family and friends, he also moved beyond that to offer a deeply felt tribute to youth and childhood. His tales of Nevada and Hannibal hum with good humor and well-aimed irony. He presents stories of frontier reporting, aborted duels, and a variety of games. Most importantly, however, Twain returned to Hannibal and the

Coming Back to Humor

Mississippi with a clear eye and a yearning for an idyllic past. His yarns of the frozen Mississippi, measles, Jim Wolf's trials with cats and wasps, and the visiting mesmerizer all bring him (and his readers) back to an Edenic childhood.

To capture the idyll Twain worked back through his earlier manuscripts and resurrected a portion of the "Early Days" fragment that he had composed during 1897. The piece holds a prominent place in the structure of the autobiography: as the thirteenth of the twenty-five chapters it falls in the middle of the narrative. While that placement may actually have been somewhat fortuitous (Twain eventually came to a point where he was composing material for the serial, and that may inhibit a finding of definite intention), the content and the circumstance of composition certainly place this piece at the heart of Twain's attempt at autobiography.

Twain's move back to his childhood was one way for him to deal with the pain of Susy Clemens' death in 1896. He often retreated to autobiography during times of emotional and creative stress, and the years after Susy's unexpected death were among the most troubled of his life. His sense of loss and his sense of guilt pushed him to find solace not only in some general plan of work but in a specific and deliberate return to his boyhood. This was one way that he could transcend his pain and reconnect with his western beginnings. That return to his beginnings also reignited the basic humor that was part and parcel of those early experiences.

Twain's description of his uncle's farm is especially notable. And two sections of that description call for closer attention. The first introduces the farm itself:

> In "Huck Finn" and in "Tom Sawyer Detective" I moved [the farm] down to Arkansas. It was all of six hundred miles, but it was no trouble, it was not a very large farm: five hundred acres, perhaps, but I could have done it if it had been twice as large. And as for the morality of it, I cared nothing for that: I would move a State if the exigencies of literature required it.
>
> It was a heavenly place for a boy, that farm of my uncle John's. The house was a double log one, with a spacious

> floor (roofed in) connecting it with the kitchen. In the breezy floor, and the sumptuous meals—well it makes me cry to think of them. Fried chicken, roast pig, wild and tame turkeys, ducks and geese; venison just killed; squirrels, rabbits, pheasants, partridges, prairie-chickens; biscuits, hot batter cakes, hot buckwheat cakes, hot "wheat bread," hot rolls, hot corn pone; fresh corn boiled on the ear, succotash, butter-beans, string-beans, tomatoes, pease, Irish potatoes, sweet-potatoes; butter milk, sweet milk, "clabber"; watermelons, muskmelons, cantaloups—all fresh from the garden—apple pie, peach pie, pumpkin pie, apple dumplings, peach cobbler—I can't remember the rest (MTOA, 113).

Twain's comments about moving the farm set a tone for his description and, in fact, alert readers that some of what follows may in fact have been "moved"—created—by the "exigences of literature." Twain winks at his readers. He lets them know that they should be skeptical of his claim to truth telling. Anyone who would move a complete farm with so little concern would have even fewer scruples when it came to describing its fine points.

The humor is this passage is understated: it does not call attention to itself but rather builds slowly during the recitation of Twain's overloaded menu. The relentless collection of food pushes the image of home cooking and hospitality to its limit: the reader is overcome by the simple accumulation of detail. And Twain undermines his own list as be pushes back from the imagined table and gives up trying to offer a complete description: "I can't remember the rest." The passage works, too, because Twain weds it to his introductory comments tied to the Clemens family's Tennessee Land: he precedes the description of the banquet with a brief recounting of the Tennessee Land's history and an accounting of the profits he made from writing about that land; he ties the experience to the Sellers-like optimism that fed the family's dreams: "It is good to begin life poor; it is good to begin life rich—these are wholesome; but to begin it prospectively rich! The man who has not experienced it cannot imagine the curse of it" (MTOA, 111).

Twain's reference to Sellers—"Whenever things grew dark [the Tennessee Land] rose and put out its hopeful Sellers hand and cheered us up" (MTOA, 111)—establishes an important counterweight for the tales and images to come. In effect, it undercuts his position by linking the episodes with daydreams and fantasy. The combination of a Sellers boast and dream enhances Twain's characterization of the importance of his birth in Florida, Missouri: "The village contained a hundred people and I increased the population by one per cent. It is more than the best man in history ever did for any other town. It may not be modest for me to refer to this, but it is true. There is no record of a person doing as much—not even Shakespeare. But I did it for Florida, and it shows that I could have done it for any place—even London, I suppose" (MTOA, 112). It is a pretentious boast, but one made within a context ripe for hubris and inflated self images.[15]

A bit farther into the chapter, Twain comes back to his strategy of making lists. This time, however, he focuses on a series of images connected to the farm experience:

> As I have said, I spent some part of every year at the farm until I was twelve or thirteen years old. The life which I led there with my cousins was full of charm, and so is the memory of it yet. I can call back the solemn twilight and the mystery of the deep woods, the earthy smells, the faint odor of the wild flowers. . . I can call it all back and make it as real as it ever was, and as blessed. I can call back the prairie, and its loneliness and peace. . . . I can see the woods in their autumn dress. . . I can see the blue clusters of wild grapes hanging amongst the foliage of the saplings, and I remember the taste of them and the smell. I know how the wild blackberries looked, and how they tasted. . . I know the taste of maple sap, and when to gather it, and how to arrange the troughs and the delivery tubes, and how to boil down the juice, and how to hook the sugar after it is made; also how much better hooked sugar tastes than any that is honestly come by, let bigots say what they will. I know how a prize watermellon looks when it is sunning its fat rotundity

among pumpkin-vines and "siblins"; I know how to tell when it is ripe without "plugging" it; I know how inviting it looks when it lies on the table in the sheltered great floor-space between house and kitchen, and the children gathered for the sacrifice and their mouths watering; I know the crackling sound it makes when the carving-knife enters its end, and I can see the split fly along in front of the blade as the knife cleaves its way to the other end. . . I know how a boy looks behind a yard-long slice of that melon, and I know how he feels; for I have been there. . . . and I can hear Uncle Dan'l telling the immortal tales which Uncle Remus Harris was to gather in his books and charm the world with, by and by; and I can feel again the creepy joy which quivered through me when the time for the ghost story of the "Golden Arm" was reached—and the sense of regret, too, which came over me, for it was always the last story of the evening, and there was nothing between it and the unwelcome bed. . . .

I remember the pigeon seasons, when the birds would come in millions, and cover the trees, and by their weight break down the branches. They were clubbed to death with sticks; guns were not necessary, and were not used. I remember the squirrel hunts, and the prairie-chicken hunts, and the wild-turkey hunts, and all that; and how we turned out mornings, while it was still dark, to go on these expeditions, and how chilly and dismal it was, and how often I regretted that I was well enough to go. A toot on a tin horn brought twice as many dogs as were needed, and in their happiness they raced and scampered about, and knocked small people down, and made no end of unnecessary noise. At the word, they vanished away toward the woods, and we drifted silently after them in the melancholy gloom. But presently the gray dawn stole over the world, the birds piped up, then the sun rose and poured light and comfort all around, everything was fresh and dewy and fragrant, and life was a boon again. After three hours of tramping we arrived back wholesomely tired, overladen with game, very hungry, and just in time for breakfast (MTOA, 120–123).

The passage offers an image of calm and enjoyment. Twain evokes the idyll using the homely images of small children living in a prelapsarian Eden.

The domestic sphere is the focal point for the rather gentle humor that permeates this section of the autobiography. The chapter is unified by the references either to the variety of foods or to methods of gathering those foods, whether by "hooking" it or by hunting it. The idyll is given a burst of energy by memories seasoned with humor. For example, Twain turns away from his collection of sensuous images to swipe at bigots who fail to realize the improved taste of "hooked" maple sap. This move from recollection and description to a moral judgement interrupts the rhythm of the passage and calls attention to the conflict between ethical and sensual rewards—the child revels in the sensual, and so does Twain. We are also told of the watermelon that sacrificed itself for the wonder and joy of a small boy, of the creepy joy of ghost stories, and of the opening moments of the hunt when excited dogs knocked down excited—but "small"—people. There is a nod to the tall tale in the description of the multitude of birds that fell from the trees when branches broke from their weight. And all these are supplement to the variety of other comic touches: Jane Clemens' and Patsy Quarrels' aversion to bats (of his mother Twain writes, "It was remarkable the way she couldn't learn to like private bats" [MTOA, 117]), "General" Gaines' rescue from the local cave, the variety of broken bones from hickory bark swings and medical treatments, and Twain's recollection of his mother's own brand of humor:

> I was always told that I was a sickly and precarious and tiresome and uncertain child, and lived mainly on allopathic medicines during the first seven years of my life. I asked my mother about this, in her old age—she was in her 88th year—and said:
> "I suppose that during all that time you were uneasy about me?"
> "Yes, the whole time."
> "Afraid that I wouldn't live?"
> After a reflective pause—ostensibly to think out the facts—
> "No—afraid you would" (MTOA, 119).

The incongruity of the mother's reply, the direct challenge to conventional expectations, and the finish with the snapper (Jane Clemens' adept handling of the pause is a highlight) all challenge readers. In "How to Tell a Story" Twain described the humorous story as one that "bubbles gently along" (Essays, 156). His tale of the Quarrels farm presents us with the full complement of humorous devices, the most important of which is the consistency and strength of the teller's personality—his voice.

Throughout the remaining chapters, Twain continues to juxtapose his past experiences with his present position. He makes good use of his meetings with the famous (especially his experience in Germany as a dinner guest of Emperor William II [MTOA, chapter 14]); he spins yarns about George Washington Cable, Livy's "editing," games of chance, his Oxford degree. He is repeatedly caught between humor and pathos as he offers selections from Susy Clemens' biography of him and comments on her observations. But Twain most often chooses to come back to humor to control the narrative movement.

Twain approaches the end of the autobiography with a decidedly humorous emphasis. Chapter twenty-four is a mix of humor and sentiment as he recounts a series of acquaintances who have died, offers more of Susy's biography, and presents himself as representative of the race. But he also tells the tale of Jim Wolf and the wasps and recounts riotous matches of billiards and bowling. In the final chapter he comes solidly back to humor as he resurrects the text of the Whittier Birthday speech—"I have read it twice, and unless I am an idiot, it hasn't a single defect in it from the first word to the last. It is just as good as it can be" (MTOA, 237)—and recounts his days as a reporter in Washington. The autobiography ends with one of the more effective uses of comic undercutting to be found in Twain's writings. It closes the frame that was set up in the brief preface that brought Howells into the picture.

Twain sets up the punch line by introducing us to the tale of his first meeting with General Nelson A. Miles in Washington. The meeting revolves around Twain's selling Miles a dog for three dollars (MTOA, 238–242). Of course, the dog was not Twain's. The tale revolves around what happened when the animal's rightful owner eventually showed up. The final exchange between Miles and Twain is a masterful bit of comic dialogue. First, Twain:

"I am sorry, but I have to take the dog again."
. . . "Take him again? Why he is my dog; you sold him to me, and at your own price."
"Yes," I said, "it is true—but I have to have him, because the man wants him again."
"What man?"
"The man that owns him; he wasn't my dog."
. . . "Do you mean to tell me that you were selling another man's dog—and knew it?"
"Yes, I knew it wasn't my dog."
"Then why did you sell him?"
. . . "Well, that is a curious question to ask. I sold him because you wanted him. You offered to buy the dog; you can't deny that. I was not anxious to sell him—I had not even thought of selling him, but it seemed to me that if it could be any accommodation to you—"
He broke me off in the middle, and said,
"Accommodation to me? It is the most extraordinary spirit of accommodation I have ever heard of—the idea of your selling a dog that didn't belong to you—"
I broke him off there, and said, "There is no relevancy about this kind of argument; you said yourself that the dog was probably worth a hundred dollars, I only asked you three; was there anything unfair about that? You offered to pay more, you know you did. I only asked you three; you can't deny it."
"Oh, what in the world has that to do with it? The crux of the matter is that you didn't own the dog—can't you see that? You seem to think that there is no impropriety in selling property that isn't yours provided you sell it cheap. Now, then—"
I said, "Please don't argue about it any more. You can't get around the fact that the price was perfectly fair, perfectly

reasonable—considering that I didn't own the dog—and so arguing it is only a waste of words. I have to have him back again because the man wants him; don't you see that I haven't any choice in the matter? Put yourself in my place. Suppose you had sold a dog that didn't belong to you; suppose you—"

"Oh," he said, "don't muddle my brains any more with your idiotic reasonings! Take him along and give me a rest."

So, I paid back the three dollars and led the dog downstairs and passed him over to his owner, and collected three for my trouble.

I went away then with a good conscience, because I had acted honorably; I never could have used the three that I sold the dog for, because it was not rightly my own, but the three I got for restoring him to his rightful owner was righteously and properly mine, because I earned it. That man might never have gotten that dog back at all, if it hadn't been for me. My principles have remained to this day what they were then. I was always honest; I know I can never be otherwise. It is as I said in the beginning—I was never able to persuade myself to use money which I had acquired in questionable ways.

Now, then, that is the tale. Some of it is true (MTOA, 240-242).

There are three sections to this tale: the introduction of Miles and the opening of the Washington tale in which the dog first appears, the bickering to reclaim the dog for its owner, and Twain's reflection on the moral of the tale and on his own basic honesty. Of those three pieces, the bickering carries the most humor because of the conflict between the contrasting moral views held by Twain and Miles. That conflict—a replay of the battle between the western rough and the eastern establishment—is traced through six turns in the argument, turns that are controlled by Twain as he weaves his tale: his announcement that he did not own the dog, his point that Miles had asked to buy the dog, his statement that he sought only to accommodate the request, his asking only three dollars for the dog, his argument that the price was fair, and his asking Miles to imagine himself selling the dog. The sequence is vital to the success of the tale. Each turn sparks a stronger and more heated response from Miles and leads to the last twist—the proposed exchanging of roles. Twain's responses also become more complex and more innocent until he is finally able to use his deadpan delivery to exasperate Miles. The deadpan voice becomes stronger as Twain pronounces, "That man might never have gotten that dog back at all, if it hadn't been for me. . . . I was always honest; I know I can never be otherwise" (MTOA, 242). Honesty, of course, is the central question. Of the dog story. And of the autobiography as a whole.

The tag line illuminates the notion of honesty. It is a disclaimer not only for the modified tall tale of the general and the dog but for the the entire autobiography. It brings the autobiography full circle by suggesting the potential hoax. The introduction established the boundaries of the hoax by laying out the extremes of the autobiography's length and depth and Twain's love of criticism that is bent his way. Readers were invited to see the joke within the historical references that lampooned the conventional autobiography's reliance on family and ancestors. The final line brings us back to Twain's storytelling roots and undermines the whole tale. It performs double duty: it ends a minor tale and simultaneously brings the full autobiography to a close. The frame is complete: the tale began with Twain's deadpan voice and it ends with Twain's deadpan voice. And we are left with a vague feeling of having been conned by a comic master.

While Twain's creative output decreased during the final years of his life, he nevertheless remained true to the humor that influenced him and that he helped shape. Resurrecting the image of Mark Twain as a master storyteller—and master con man—is important to a balanced treatment of his final decades. We can begin to add shading to Twain's portrait by taking the whole of his creative output during his final decades into consideration. It is especially important to include the completed autobiography in that package. That work offers clues of just how inextricably Twain's creative self was bound to a tradition energized by strains of southwestern and northeastern humor and by a potent mix of the oral storytelling that he experienced in slave kitchens, mining camps, saloons, and boarding houses. Mark Twain's autobiography can focus an exploration of the ways in which he remained tuned to that tradition and faithful to humor even as he turned away from publishing his fiction. It can help us relocate and reaffirm Mark Twain's humor.

Notes

1. It is virtually impossible to write about Mark Twain's life without moving into the realm of literary biography. His life was so intimately tied to his literary work that the line between literary critic and biographer is often blurred. That has meant a landslide of works focusing on Mark Twain's development as a writer and on the relationship between his professional and personal life. Some of the more important studies include Clara Clemens Gabrilowitsch's *My Father Mark Twain*, William Dean Howells' *My Mark Twain*, Van Wyck Brooks' *The Ordeal of Mark Twain*, Bernard DeVoto's *Mark Twain's America* and *Mark Twain at Work*, Henry Nash Smith's *Mark Twain: The Development of a Writer*, DeLancy Ferguson's *Mark Twain: Man and Legend*, Dixon Wecter's *Sam Clemens of Hannibal*, Justin Kaplan's *Mr. Clemens and Mark Twain*, Everett Emerson's *The Authentic Mark Twain: A Literary Biography of Samuel L. Clemens*, William R. Macnaughton's *Mark Twain's Last Years as a Writer*, Hamlin Hill's *Mark Twain: God's Fool*, Louis Budd's *Our Mark Twain: The Making of His Public Personality*, Guy Cardwell's *The Man Who Was Mark Twain: Images and Ideologies*, John Lauber's *The Making of Mark Twain* and *The Inventions of Mark Twain: A Biography*, and John C. Gerbers' *Mark Twain*. Albert Bigelow Paine's *Mark Twain: A Biography* remains the central text for much of Twain's life, even though subsequent biographers have managed to deepen and broaden the image that Paine offers.

2. See James M. Cox, *Mark Twain: The Fate of Humor*.

3. Mark Twain's autobiography has been presented in a variety of forms by a variety of editors. To compare these editions, see Albert Bigelow Paine's *Mark Twain's Autobiography*, Bernard DeVoto's *Mark Twain in Eruption: Hitherto Unpublished Pages About Men and Events*, Charles Neider's *The Autobiography of Mark Twain*, and Michael J. Kiskis' *Mark Twain's Own Autobiography: The Chapters from the North American Review*.

4. See Philip S. Foner, *Mark Twain: Social Critic* and Louis J. Budd, *Mark Twain: Social Philosopher.*

5. That evolution should be neither unusual nor unappealing. It mirrors the movement that Benjamin Franklin charted as he composed his autobiographical manuscripts: the completed sections follow Franklin as he evolves a social, a community consciousness. Twain's career—while certainly not as overtly political—follows a similar course as he takes to the issues of imperialism during the final years of the nineteenth and early days of the twentieth centuries.

6. The scandal connected to Maxim Gorky's visit to America in 1906 (Gorky's "wife" was actually his mistress, Maria Andreyeva) led Twain and Howells to resign as sponsors of a major fund raising banquet. The proceeds were to aid the Russian revolt against the Czar.

7. See G. Thomas Couser, "Autobiography as Anti-biography: The Case of Twain vs. Paine."

8. "Chapters from My Autobiography," *North American Review* 183 (1906), 184, 185, 186 (1907): various issues.

9. See Franklin R. Rogers, *Mark Twain's Burlesque Patterns*, Kenneth S. Lynn, *Mark Twain and Southwestern Humor*, and David E. E. Sloane, *Mark Twain as a Literary Comedian*. Sloane's *The Literary Humor of the Urban Northeast, 1830–1890* is also helpful.

10. This opens up a series of questions related to Twain's use of the biography of him that Susy wrote during her thirteenth year. His strategy of offering bits and pieces of her writing may, in fact, foster the deadpan delivery since he juxtaposes her basic narrative with his much more energetic responses.

11. The *(Burlesque) Autobiography* is actually a list of felons presented as ancestors: an inmate of Newgate prison, a highwayman, a series of cowards, a forger, an idler and a thief, a pirate, a missionary, and a renegade. There is also a supplementary list naming more ancestors: Guy Fawkes, Sixteen-String Jack, Jack Sheppard, Baron Munchausen, Captain Kydd, George Francis Train, Tom Pepper, Nebuchadnezzar, and Baalam's Ass. The inclusion of Munchausen undercuts the list because of the Baron's reputation as the premier teller of tall tales.

12. See John C. Gerber, "Mark Twain's Use of the Comic Pose."

13. See Charles Neider's edition *Papa: An Intimate Biography of Mark Twain.*

14. The battle between East and West is basic to southwestern humor. Twain, of course, had used that conflict since 1852 in "The Dandy Frightening the Squatter."

15. The passage is reminiscent of Twain's description of his birth in the *(Burlesque) Autobiography*: "I was born without teeth—and there Richard III had the advantage of me; but I was born without a humpback, likewise, and there I had the advantage of him. My parents were neither very poor nor conspicuously honest" (24–25).

Works Cited

By Mark Twain

Adventures of Huckleberry Finn. ed. Walter Blair and Victor Fischer. Berkeley: University of California Press, 1988.
The Adventures of Tom Sawyer, Tom Sawyer Abroad, Tom Sawyer, Detective. ed. John C. Gerber, Paul Baender, and Terry Firkins. Berkeley: University of California Press, 1980.
The Autobiography of Mark Twain. ed. Charles Neider. New York: Harper & Row, 1959.
Captain Stormfield's Visit to Heaven. New York: Harper and Brothers, 1907.
"Chapters from My Autobiography," *North American Review* 183 (1906), 184, 185, 189 (1907): various issues.
Christian Science. New York: Harper and Brothers, 1907.
The Complete Essays of Mark Twain. ed. Charles Neider. Garden City: Doubleday & Company, Inc., 1963.
A Connecticut Yankee in King Arthur's Court. ed. Bernard L. Stein. Berkeley: University of California Press, 1979.
Early Tales and Sketches, vol. 1 (1851–1864). ed. Edgar M. Branch and Robert H. Hirst. Berkeley: University of California Press, 1979.
Early Tales and Sketches, vol. 2 (1864–1865). ed. Edgar M. Branch and Robert H. Hirst. Berkeley: University of California Press, 1981.
Following the Equator. The Writings of Mark Twain: Definitive Edition 20 and 21. New York: Gabriel Wells, 1923.
The Gilded Age: A Tale of Today. The Writings of Mark Twain: Definitive Edition 5 and 6. New York: Gabriel Wells, 1922.
The Innocents Abroad or the New Pilgrim's Progress. The Writings of Mark Twain: Definitive Edition 1 and 2. New York: Gabriel Wells, 1922.
Mark Twain in Eruption: Hitherto Unpublished Pages About Men and Events. ed. Bernard DeVoto. New York: Harper and Brothers, 1940.

Mark Twain's Autobiography. 2 vols. ed. Albert Bigelow Paine. New York: Harper and Brothers, 1924.
Mark Twain's (Burlesque) Autobiography. Norwood: Norwood Editions, 1975.
Mark Twain's Fables of Man. ed. John S. Tuckey. Berkeley: University of California Press, 1972.
Mark Twain's 'Mysterious Stranger' Manuscripts. ed. William M. Gibson. Berkeley: University of California Press, 1969.
Mark Twain's Own Autobiography: The Chapters from the North American Review. ed. Michael J. Kiskis. Madison: University of Wisconsin Press, 1990.
Mark Twain's 'Which was the Dream?' and Other Symbolic Writings of the Later Years. ed. John S. Tuckey. Berkeley: University of California Press, 1979.
Personal Recollections of Joan of Arc. New York: Harper & Brothers Publishers, 1896.
Pudd'nhead Wilson. The Writings of Mark Twain: Definitive Edition 16. New York: Gabriel Wells, 1923.
Roughing It. ed. Franklin R. Rogers. Berkeley: University of California Press, 1972.
Selected Mark Twain—Howells Letters, 1872–1910. ed. Frederick Anderson, William M. Gibson, and Henry Nash Smith. Cambridge: Harvard University Press, 1967.
Selected Shorter Writings of Mark Twain. ed. Walter Blair. Boston: Houghton-Mifflin Company, 1962.
'What Is Man?' and Other Essays. The Writings of Mark Twain: Definitive Edition 26. New York: Gabriel Wells, 1923.
'What Is Man?' and Other Philosophical Writings. ed. Paul Baender. Berkeley: University of California Press, 1973.

Secondary Works

Brooks, Van Wyck. *The Ordeal of Mark Twain.* New York: E. P. Dutton & Company, 1920.
Budd, Louis J. *Mark Twain: Social Philosopher.* Bloomington: Indiana University Press, 1962.
———. *Our Mark Twain: The Making of His Public Personality.* Philadelphia: University of Pennsylvania Press, 1983.
Cardwell, Guy. *The Man Who Was Mark Twain: Images and Ideologies.* New Haven: Yale University Press, 1991.
Clemens, Olivia Susan. *Papa: An Intimate Biography of Mark Twain.* ed. Charles Neider. Garden City: Doubleday & Company, Inc., 1985.

Couser, G. Thomas. "Autobiography as Anti-Biography: The Case of Twain vs. Paine." *Auto/Biography Studies* 3, no. 3 (Fall 1987): 13–20.

Cox, James M. *Mark Twain: The Fate of Humor*. Princeton: Princeton University Press, 1966.

DeVoto, Bernard. *Mark Twain's America*. Boston: Little, Brown, and Company, 1932.

———. *Mark Twain at Work*. Cambridge: Harvard University Press, 1942.

Emerson, Everett. *The Authentic Mark Twain: A Literary Biography of Samuel L. Clemens*. Philadelphia: University of Pennsylvania Press, 1984.

Ferguson, DeLancey. *Mark Twain: Man and Legend*. New York: The Bobbs-Merrill Company, 1943.

Foner, Philip S. *Mark Twain: Social Critic*. New York: International Publishers, 1958.

Gabrilowitsch, Clara Clemens. *My Father Mark Twain*. New York: Harper & Brothers Publishers, 1931.

Gerber, John C. *Mark Twain*. Boston. G. K. Hall & Co., 1988.

———. "Mark Twain's Use of the Comic Pose." *PMLA* LXXXVII (June 1962): 297–304.

Hill, Hamlin. *Mark Twain: God's Fool*. New York: Harper & Row, Publishers, 1973.

Howells, William Dean. *My Mark Twain: Reminiscences and Criticisms*. New York: Harper Brothers Publishers, 1910.

Kaplan, Justin. *Mr. Clemens and Mark Twain*. New York: Simon and Schuster, 1966.

Lauber, John. *The Inventions of Mark Twain: A Biography*. New York: Hill and Wang, 1990.

———. *The Making of Mark Twain*. New York: American Heritage Press, 1985.

Lynn, Kenneth S. *Mark Twain and Southwestern Humor*. Boston: Little, Brown, 1959.

Macnaughton, William R. *Mark Twain's Last Years as a Writer*. Columbia: University of Missouri Press, 1979.

Paine, Albert Bigelow. *Mark Twain: A Biography*. 1912; rpt. with author's note to the 1935 edition and introduction to the 1923 edition by William Lyon Phelps. New York: Chelsea House, 1980.

Rogers, Franklin R. *Mark Twain's Burlesque Patterns*. Dallas: Southern Methodist University Press, 1960.

Sloane, David E. E. *The Literary Humor of the Urban Northeast, 1830–1890*. Baton Rouge: Louisiana State University Press, 1983.

———. *Mark Twain as Literary Comedian*. Baton Rouge: Louisiana State University Press, 1979.

Smith, Henry Nash. *Mark Twain: The Development of a Writer*. Cambridge: Harvard University Press, 1962.

Wecter, Dixon. *Sam Clemens of Hannibal*. Boston: Houghton Mifflin Company, 1952.

"The Mysterious Stranger": Absence of the Female in Mark Twain Biography

Laura E. Skandera-Trombley

"Absence of the Female" refers to two related issues: the absence of female Mark Twain biographers and the absence of women within Twain biography. By identifying the first and exploring the polemics of the second, a paradigm will be introduced where the women in Clemens' life are granted their importance and where the field of Twain biography may be made more accessible to interested women.

With the sheer mass of criticism that has been published concerning Mark Twain, it appears that writing about Samuel Langhorne Clemens has become a *rite de passage* for any serious scholar of American literature. Such luminaries as Van Wyck Brooks, Bernard DeVoto, Leslie Fiedler, Everett Emerson, and Hamlin Hill have all commented on Clemens; Justin Kaplan's *Mr. Clemens and Mark Twain* was awarded the Pulitzer prize. Although there is a spread of sixty years among these biographical scholars, they share two common denominators: their gender and their critical positions. The field of Twain studies has always been and continues to be one of the most heavily male-dominated areas of American scholarship; and to date only two paths of accepted biographical discourse have emerged, those of Brooks' division of self, and, in opposition, that of DeVoto's integration of the self.

With the Brooks-DeVoto battle lines drawn, so were the divergent paths that all subsequent Twain biographers would follow. In what has become a compulsory initiation ritual, biographers must choose on which side of the Brooks-DeVoto net to play. The Brooks side maintains that Clemens had a divided self and that this division became so pronounced that his capacity for fiction writing was irreparably damaged. On the DeVoto side, critics undertook to prove that Clemens' later fiction was intact—and so was his personality. This writer found both sides of the court flawed and at the same time was struck by the dearth of discussions concerning the impact female familial members and colleagues had upon Clemens. The tacit admission that Clemens was surrounded by women has been made from Brooks to Hill, but why always seen in that way—surrounded—as though no productive interaction took place?

Writing in reaction to Albert Bigelow Paine's and William Dean Howells' sympathetic biographies of Clemens, Brooks charged that there were inconsistencies in the version of Clemens portrayed by Paine and Howells and claimed that instead of perceiving Clemens as a rustic, charming storyteller, a more accurate interpretation of Clemens was as embittered, artistic failure. To examine the question of Clemens' personality, Brooks used what has been identified as one of the earliest psychoanalytic interpretations of an author (Fraiberg). Brooks asserted that there was a split in Clemens' personality and viewed the women in his life as firmly entrenched within the realm of a hostile Other. Not much has changed since Brooks first denounced then discarded Clemens' female intimates; subsequent biographers' interpretations of the role they played run the negative gamut: women were the psychological ruin of Clemens; women were the monetary ruin of Clemens; women had no effect upon Clemens; Clemens managed to survive the effect women had upon him.

A significant defect of past scholarship has been the tendency to view the women in Clemens' personal life as an indistinguishable whole. An Olivia Clemens could be substituted for a Mary Fairbanks, a Mary Ann Cord for a Katy

Leary, Susan Crane for Mary Rogers, with the three daughters interchangeable. No individual differentiation was made and simplistic conclusions were reached: women had either a debilitating effect or were nullities. What these studies all had in accord was that women were forever on the periphery, and if in particular instances they moved to the fore it would have been far better for Clemens had they not.

Cynthia Fuchs Epstein, in *Deceptive Distinctions: Sex, Gender and the Social Order*, addresses the impetus for the existence of dichotomous categorization: "It is no surprise that dichotomous models as an ideological weapon survive challenge because it is easier to propose a dichotomy than to explicate the complexities that make it invalid" (15). Clearly such a dichotomous structure currently exists in Twain scholarship. Twain biographers have identified a dichotomy in his relationships with women; but what they have failed to find is the explanation for this dichotomy—or to consider the possibility that this dichotomy may not exist outside their own constructions. With the virtual exclusion of women from studies exploring Clemens' fiction-making process (aside from the occasional articles referring to the editing by Mary Fairbanks and Olivia Clemens), these two schools and their critical offshoots have engendered and promoted this kind of dichotomous model. Why?

To date, there are no critical studies on Olivia Langdon Clemens and her first biography, by Resa Willis, is scheduled for publication in the spring of 1992. There are no published articles about Clemens' relationship with his sister-in-law Susan Crane and none discussing the Clemens family's connection with Dr. Rachael Gleason. There has been nothing published on the relationships Clemens had with suffragettes Isabella Beecher Hooker and Anna Dickinson.[1] Aside from scattered mention in biographies and select articles focused on the individual, Clemens' relationship with his contemporary female writers has been left untreated. This researcher has discovered that Clemens maintained an extremely active correspondence with over one hundred women writers from five different countries. Along with other writers of fiction, Clemens corresponded with feminists, social reformers, and women educators.

The result of this lack of scholarship on women is a distorted view of Clemens as man and as writer. A particularly odd by-product of this kind of exclusionary biography is that critics were left with the problem of Clemens' sexuality. Women were considered extraneous but Clemens' sexuality certainly was not. For the past thirty years quite an industry has been built by biographers about Clemens' supposed ambivalence toward sexual relations climaxing with Hill accusing Clemens of pedophilia. Only within the past two years, with the publication of the first volume of letters, have critics begun to reinterpret Clemens as an adult man involved with adult women.

What biographers have not recognized is that throughout his life Clemens intentionally surrounded himself with women. Clemens desired women to help define his boundaries, both personal and literary; he was a man both voluntarily controlled and influenced by women. Women shaped Clemens' life, edited his books, provided models for his fictional characters, and their correspondence and literary works heavily influenced his fiction. This absence of women is not restricted just to Twain scholarship; male writers have been historically portrayed as "immune" or "beyond" the influence of women. This gendercentric scholarship results in the male writer being interpreted as operating within an asocial context. Closeted away from the tainting influence of those "damned scribblers," male writers supposedly relied upon their one true source of inspiration—themselves. Clemens has been variously described by biographers as a King Lear, an American Adam, a fallen angel. These labels have removed Clemens, the man, into the realm of Mark Twain, the fiction. This fallacy is evident throughout Twain scholarship. The critical quorum's opinion concerning his fiction-writing ability was that outside sources and influences were unnecessary (and in fact considered potentially ruinous) as long as Clemens relied solely upon himself for inspiration. Alan Gribben's massive work, *Mark Twain's Library: A Reconstruction*, challenged the long-held misconception of Clemens as unread man. What must now be recognized is that not only was Clemens highly aware of what was being written by his female colleagues and that he utilized their work as impetus for his own fiction, but that the women in his family circle allowed Clemens access to a feminine consciousness that enabled him to create a unique brand of literature.

Departing from the Brooksian based critical position of dual selves, I contend that Clemens was indeed an integrated personality; yet, the dichotomous type of biography that has been employed has failed to recognize the major wellspring of Clemens' inspiration. Due to this exclusionary methodology, in examining Clemens' final years critics such as DeVoto and Hill have been hard-pressed to account for the waning of his fiction-writing ability and the rise of his pronounced cynicism. To examine this problem and to give a more credible reading of Clemens' final years, I have developed a paradigm consisting of the component "feminine consciousness." This feminine consciousness, provided in part by the women both in and outside Clemens' family circle, allowed Clemens entree into the female community during the latter half of the nineteenth-century.

Sydney Janet Kaplan, in her text *Feminine Consciousness in the Modern British Novel*, begins her discussion of "feminine consciousness" with a given, that "novelists have most definitely attempted to depict the consciousnesses of men and women and to show that each has a different quality" (3). According to Kaplan, feminine consciousness should be viewed as a "literary device," a method of characterization of females in fiction" (3). Kaplan is quick to qualify that the term "feminine consciousness" does not necessarily entail the "full range of any given woman's consciousness in a novel," instead just the "aspects . . . which are involved with her definition of self as a specifically feminine being" (3). Kaplan's discussion of fiction is restricted to works authored by women; I think one can open the discussion to include particular male authors such as Clemens. Clemens too was interested in depicting the variegated consciousnesses of males and females, characters such as Pudd'nhead Wilson and Roxana come immediately to mind, yet he was also interested in going beyond gendered portrayals of consciousness; in such characters as Huckleberry Finn, Judith Loftus, and Joan of Arc, Clemens questioned, satirized, and ultimately discarded the very attitudes and behaviors comprising socialized gender roles.

The valuable insights Clemens gained from his access to the feminine point-of-view were reinforced by his writing techniques and surfaced in his classic realist novels. Clemens' female half has been previously overlooked by biographers; without his feminine consciousness his ability to create extended works of fiction was eventually lost. And this is what ultimately happened. Women in effect functioned collectively as Clemens' personal and creative touchstone. Rather than envisioning Clemens as continually turning away from a harmful Other, it would be more accurate to view him as embracing and allying himself with the female. Shortly before their marriage Clemens joyfully proclaimed to Olivia: "'I' mean both of us, & 'both of us' means I of course—for are not we Twain one flesh?" (Wecter, *Mark*, 73).[2] Clemens viewed himself and his art as inseparable from Olivia. When Clemens was composing, he would retreat into his study during the day and return to his family at sundown. After the evening meal, the family would gather and he would present the day's output. Clemens did the bulk of his writing at his sister-in-law's home, Quarry Farm, in Elmira, New York, and there his audience consisted of his three daughters, his wife Olivia, his wife's adopted older sister, Susan Crane, and Mary Ann Cord, a former slave, who worked as a cook for Susan Crane. To this female audience, then, Clemens would read his work. The varied opinions Clemens received constituted his literary wellspring. Alan Gribben stresses the necessity of audience for Clemens' writing:

> Nothing else known about Clemens' reading habits seems as significant as his preference for oral readings before other people, a practice that surely helped develop the flexible narrative voice he strove to reproduce in his fiction. He read his daily output of prose to his family and friends. . . . ("Unsatisfactory," 55–56)

Yet this reading before a female audience resulted in more than perfecting Clemens' narrative voice. The women became, in a sense, the text's co-constructors. Clemens received the insights and opinions of individuals who were as estranged from patriarchal Victorian society as was the Southerner Clemens from literary Brahmin New England, and as was the young Huckleberry Finn from the slave-holding society of St. Petersburg, Missouri.

In Olivia Louise Langdon Clemens, Clemens had a writing partner who came from a family well known for sailing against the tide of repressive nineteenth-century mores. When Presbyterian church elders refused to sign an anti-slavery pledge, the Langdons broke away and founded a Congregationalist church that would. Rejecting allopathic medicine's heroic practices, such as bloodletting, leechings, and cauterization, the Langdons embraced the tenets of hydropathic medicine (one of the irregular schools of nineteenth-century medicine) with its emphasis on therapeutic treatments. The Langdon's (and later the Clemens') family physician was Dr. Rachael Gleason. Gleason is listed in *Medical Women of America* as the fourth woman to receive her medical degree in America; just two years earlier, in 1849, Elizabeth Blackwell was granted the first such degree. The Langdons advocated women's education and were major supporters of Elmira Female College, founded in 1855. Elmira College was the first to grant degrees to women which were equal to those of men, and both Langdon daughters studied there. At an early age, Olivia became close to such radical suffragettes as Isabella Hooker and Anna Dickinson. In fact, Dickinson proved so influential in Olivia's development that at one point Olivia agonized whether she, too, should join the public ranks of the women's movement. In a letter to Mary Fairbanks, co-written by Olivia and Clemens shortly after their marriage, Olivia defiantly proclaimed: "I am woman's rights" (Wecter, *Love*, 127).

Before their marriage, as early as their first meeting in Elmira, Olivia knew that Clemens intended to propose. From that point on, Olivia composed the movements of Clemens' suit. It was Olivia who rejected Clemens' first proposal but left the relationship intact; Olivia who insisted he write to her as a brother would a sister; Olivia who engaged in subterfuge by having Clemens address his letters to her brother; Olivia who installed Hattie Lewis as a romantic decoy so she could deliberate Clemens' overtures without public pressure; Olivia who had Clemens prove his sincerity about his intentions by writing scores of letters. It was a carefully thought-out wooing and Olivia neatly concluded it in her methodical way when she wrote on the envelope of his final letter before they married: "184th—Last letter of a 17 months' correspondence" (Wecter, *Love*, 139).

Nor did her control end at the altar. When the Clemenses decided to build a home in Hartford, it was Olivia who drew the initial sketch and was in charge of planning the construction of the house and, like her mother and older sister before her, she was the sole title holder of the land. This was the woman who married Samuel Clemens: a far cry from Hamlin Hill's characterization of her as "a delicate figurine, the Victorian ideal of a 'lady'" (xxiv). Nor does her behavior support Joyce Warren's condemnation of Clemens, that he intended "to keep [Olivia] in a state of childlike innocence—or ignorance. . . . She is Twain's ideal woman: gentle and sweet, but ignorant as a child" (167).

Following the example set by her mother, Olivia was a voracious reader who organized reading and study groups throughout her life. Judging from the contents of personal letters to friends and her Commonplace Book, Olivia was well-versed in classic and modern American and British literature. Olivia was widely read in contemporary American women's fiction and she must have been cognizant of the themes and images considered, by Susan Gubar and Sandra Gilbert, to constitute a nineteenth-century female literary tradition. Gilbert and Gubar contend that "images of enclosure and escape," are representational of Victorian women's novels (xi). These elements of entrapment, enclosure, and escape, that Gilbert and Gubar identify as evident within Victorian women's novels, also compose the primary themes and images of *Adventures of Huckleberry Finn*. I do not view this as coincidence.

Elaine Showalter urges the necessity of viewing women's writing within a historical context and regards women's literature as a kind of subculture with its own specific images and themes. Showalter emphasizes that she is uncomfortable with past attempts to develop what she terms a "female sensibility" that constitutes itself in a form specific to women's writing because of its ahistorical stance. For Showalter, this kind of interpretation runs perilously near to echoing what she calls "familiar stereotypes. . ." (12). Showalter argues that such a concept as female imagination must

> not be handled as a romantic or Freudian abstraction. It is the product of a delicate network of influences operating in time. . . including the operations of the marketplace. . . . (12)

I agree with Showalter regarding the limitations of creating a kind of female imaginary list; such an action would be dangerously inhibiting. According to Showalter the female literary tradition evidences itself not in an innate sexual attitude but in the relation women maintained with society during a particular time-span; the nature of the images Gilbert and Gubar identify reflect the sociological construct Showalter promotes. This experience of being part of, yet not a part of, patriarchal, white Victorian society was particularly valid for individuals, such as the Langdon women, who attempted to go beyond the purely domestic sphere. Clemens was granted valuable access to the feminine consciousness through Olivia's experience of estrangement from society because of her family's views concerning religion, health, and women's education, and through her awareness of what was being written by contemporary women writers.

Olivia's part in co-creating Clemens' texts was in functioning not so much as editor, although that is the role to which she has been traditionally relegated, as it was to provide an educated audience familiar with transforming and reforming social standards. Olivia was concerned with the scope and treatment of the fictive subject, not with censoring the end product. With Olivia as guide, Clemens could not overindulge in the burlesque; to elicit her approval he had to provide finesse behind the fireworks. Clemens described how necessary Olivia was in the generation of the novels in a letter to Archibald Henderson:

> I learned from her that the only right thing was to get in my serious meaning always, to treat my audience fairly, to let them really feel the underlying moral that gave body and essence to my jest. (Henderson, 183)

The connection between the expectations of the first two-thirds of Clemens' audience and *Adventures of Huckleberry Finn*, overall, is apparent. The burlesque is left intact for the amusement of the children, as in Jim's soothsaying prowess with the ox hairball, and Olivia's "serious meaning" takes precedence with this one sentence by Huck: "All right, then, I'll go to hell." In keeping with Olivia's advice to Clemens, Leland Krauth observes that the climax of the book represents "both [Huck's] greatest moment of pathos and one of the most humorous moments. . ." (382). The reason this combination can exist is that "of course we know that no one of such fine and tender feeling can be damned" (383).

Mary Ann Cord had a crucial role in the shaping of Clemens' fiction. Born a slave in Virginia, Cord claimed she had been sold twice and had all of her children taken from her before she escaped to the North (Jerome, 8). Ida Langdon, in an address she delivered at the Elmira College Convocation in

"The Mysterious Stranger"

1960, remembered Cord as a "dogmatic Methodist" (Jerome, 62). Cord was very likely a member of the African Methodist Episcopal Zion Church, the first African American church founded in Elmira in 1841 (Sorin, 15). Cord's denomination is shared by Roxana in *Pudd'nhead Wilson*; in *Pudd'nhead Wilson* Clemens attributes Roxana's recent conversion to Methodism as saving her from being sold down the river by her master.

While summering at Quarry Farm Clemens composed a short story written partly in black dialect, which Sherwood Cummings first noted that he later utilized as the genesis for the main plot and theme for the first section of *Adventures of Huckleberry Finn*. This short story provided Clemens an entree into the November 1874 issue of the *Atlantic*. The piece was entitled, "A True Story Repeated Word for Word as I heard It," and related the travails of "Rachel" Cord. After reading the piece, William Dean Howells was commendatory: "I think it extremely good and touching with the best and reallest [sic] kind of black talk in it" (*Twain-Howells*, 24). The cross-over between "A True Story" and *Adventures of Huckleberry Finn* is readily apparent: in "A True Story," "Rachel" scolds a young man (who unbeknownst to her is her long-lost son) and says, "I wa'nt bawn in de mash to be fool' by trash!" (*Unabridged*, 408); in *Adventures of Huckleberry Finn* Jim utters a similar line when he rebukes Huckleberry for playing a cruel trick on him: "Dat truck dah is trash; en trash is what people is dat puts dirt on de head er dey fren's en makes 'em ashamed" (72). "A True Story Repeated Word for Word as I Heard It" is of particular importance not only because it marked the beginning of Clemens' contributions to the *Atlantic* but also because this oral history of an African American woman's road to freedom might also have served as an impetus for the composition of Clemens' greatest work.

At Quarry Farm, the wide variety in temperament, education, experience, culture, race, and age, ranging from Jean (the Clemens' youngest daughter) to Mary Ann Cord, meant that for Clemens to maintain his disparate audiences' attention he had to produce fiction that was multigenerational, multicultural, multiracial, and, most significantly, themes with which these women could identify. Viewed within the context of Clemens' female audience/feminine consciousness, the absence of overt masculine themes from *Adventures of Huckleberry Finn* should not come as entirely unexpected. Leland Krauth isolates the various episodes that traditionally comprise Southwestern humor and remarks that *Huckleberry Finn* is striking for what it is not: "[*Adventures of Huckleberry Finn*] ignores, first of all, those subjects, like courtings, frolics, dances, weddings, and honeymoons, that naturally involve adult sexuality. And secondly, it omits entirely or else skims over those activities, like hunting, fighting, gambling, gaming, horse racing, heavy drinking, and military maneuvering, that are the traditional pastimes of manly backwoods living. (Whenever such activities do appear briefly they are targets of ridicule.) In short, Twain purges from the Southwestern tradition its exuberant celebration of rough-and-tumble masculinity" (374).

What Clemens does with the character of Huck, Krauth continues, is also unprecedented within the genre of Southwestern humor; Clemens departs from the archetype of the Man of Feeling to make Huck "a comic Man of Feeling. Huck never feels good about his goodness; his altruistic emotions—with the possible exception of his aid to Mary Jane—never give him egoistic satisfaction" (381). Krauth asserts that this is one of the reasons *Adventures of Huckleberry Finn* is still so intriguing today, because the portrayal of the "Man of Feeling" still challenges conventional stereotypes of manhood. Krauth also points out, quite rightly, that while Huck is a lost boy afraid in a man's world, he is never frightened by the world of women. Clearly both Huck's and Clemens' Angst was reduced when they were with females. Krauth ends his article with this intriguing statement: "[Huck's] kind of manliness seems to elude our language for it, even today" (384). Clemens could create this sense of manliness combined with delicate sensitivity because his female collaborators, with their essential feedback into his writing process, enabled him to synthesize their feminine consciousness with his own. During his trip down the river, Huck metamorphoses into the student he was never allowed to become in St. Petersburg, and he learns about natural humanity from Jim and about the falsity of gender roles from Judith Loftus. The result of these lessons is that a radically changed conception of the traditional Southwestern character came to life in Clemens' novel.

This product by Clemens and the feminine consciousness was also clearly subject to what Showalter terms the "operations of the marketplace." Upon completion of *Tom Sawyer* and *Adventures of Huckleberry Finn* Clemens was undecided as to whether they should be considered children's or adult books. Clemens wrote to William Dean Howells to declare that he had written *Tom Sawyer* for adults: "It is not a boy's book, at all. It will only be read by adults" (*Twain-Howells*, 91). Howells replied: "I think you ought to treat it explicitly as a boy's story" (110). Clemens wrote back to Howells agreeing, "Mrs. Clemens decides with you that the book should issue as a book for boys, pure and simple—and so do I" (112). What probably proved instrumental in changing Clemens' mind was Howells' insistence that "the book consumer[s] par excellence in Victorian America" were young women (Wecter, *Sam*, 172). Howells was correct; by 1872 nearly three-quarters of all published books in America were authored by women (Coultrap, 2). Clemens ultimately took Howells' advice to heart for he finally wrote him that "the book is now professedly & confessedly a boy's & girl's book" (*Twain-Howells*, 122).[3]

The critic must not underestimate Clemens' awareness of what was successful within the literary marketplace. Clemens' knowledge about the female-authored fiction then being published came about in a few different ways: one, the novels both he and the women in the family read; two, the manuscripts submitted to him for publication within his own publishing firm; and, three, the voluminous correspondence he maintained with women writers. Clemens made it his business to know what women wanted. Clemens supported women authors by corresponding and exchanging ideas with them and by providing a commercial outlet for their work, which he did by having his company publish their writings.

What sounded the deathknell to Clemens' fiction, was the demise of Olivia on June 5, 1904. With her death, the linchpin of his connection to the feminine consciousness was gone. After 1904, Clemens produced mainly polemical writing; he attempted to write extended works of fiction a multitude of times, but the manuscripts were left incomplete. Clemens became a man bereft of his favorite audience and of the secure home life in which this feminine circle surrounded him. Without his female circle, Samuel Clemens the writer disappeared; what remained was merely the public persona. For the rest of his life, Clemens was condemned to try to recreate his source of feminine consciousness, but what he managed to construct with Isabel Lyon and the angel fish was only a poor imitation; the happiest days and most productive times of his life were over, and on a deeper level—not always consciously—Clemens knew it. Clemens became tragically morose, and his bitterness arose from his keen awareness that all of his efforts to bring back the earlier days were futile.

Samuel Langhorne Clemens' greatest achievement in writing was the novel *Adventures of Huckleberry Finn*. In Huckleberry Finn, Clemens created an androgynous character. Throughout the novel, Huckleberry (as does Jim) adopts and abandons various male and female disguises as well as rejects the world of the purely male or female. In addition, Huck enters and flees various representations of so-called "civilization" that he and Jim encounter periodically during their flight down the Mississippi. This rejection of sexual segregation is reinforced by Clemens' creating Huckleberry as a prepubescent youth, a time in his development when Huckleberry is non-sexual. At the end of the novel, Huckleberry ultimately chooses to "light out for the Territory," but what he is embarking on is a search for an integrated world where he can be freed from the confines of gender to pursue a higher realm of truth and justice. Leland Krauth states that Huckleberry Finn's kind of manliness "seems to elude our language for it, even today" (384). Huckleberry possesses the dual traits of manliness and femininity.

Contrary to Leslie Fiedler's famous argument that the novel is homo-erotic and portrays "a conventionally abhorrent doctrine of ideal love" (147), what *Adventures of Huckleberry Finn* actually concerns itself with is introducing a new kind of quest archetype, one that concentrates upon two figures both disenfranchised from the predominating white, patriarchal society. Fiedler begins his argument by automatically assuming *Adventures of Huckleberry Finn* is "precisely, [a] boy['s] book"—thus dismissing without a backward glance the female audience for whom Clemens originally wrote the novel. What Fiedler fails to perceive is that Clemens cleverly bypasses what he terms an archetypal "homo-erotic crush," thus excluding the female, by making both Huck and Jim non-sexual. Both are considered "boys": Huck by age, as prepubescent, and Jim by race, as a slave he has been symbolically castrated; equally important, by virtue of their cross-dressing, both Huck and Jim are at times identified with the female.

At the beginning of the story, both are at the mercy of their surrounding culture and are rendered powerless. Huckleberry, son of "pap" the town drunk, has been marginalized by the society of St. Petersburg. Huckleberry does not attend church, live in a conventional dwelling, or attend school until he is adopted by the Widow Douglas—and this societal rejection ultimately saves him as it is far easier for him to abandon this culture than someone who grew up within it, for instance Tom Sawyer. Jim's caste is even lower than Huckleberry's, at least that is what "pap" would like to believe, because of his slave status. Jim is objectified by Southern culture, as he is well aware, yet even before the two take raft to river Jim resists the predominating ethos: "I owns myself, en I's wuth eight hund'd dollars" (*Adventures*, 42).

As they sail down river, the world around the seemingly helpless duo becomes increasingly violent. On the river, the raft provides respite and shelter from the shore madness, yet that refuge is violated with the arrival of the Duke and the Dauphin. While on shore, the only relative safety that can be found is when females are present as with Judith Loftus and the Wilks girls. As the novel progresses, the power balance changes as both Huck and Jim repeatedly manage to outwit and escape the prevailing white, patriarchal society of the South. While Huck is perceived as an ignorant youth by the adults around him, he struggles with such issues as truth and freedom—these being beyond the grasp of his elders. Jim comes to symbolize both faith and love. To attain the goal of their quest, both Huck and Jim remain in their androgynous states, and they eventually succeed in transcending their gender-specific, racially segregated, societal confines. Huck and Jim are freed to pursue a higher quest for a kindly humanity which is more universally "feminine" in nature than the violence of the masculine format Clemens studiously avoided.

James Cox questions whether *Adventures of Huckleberry Finn* should be considered a quest novel. Cox maintains that interpreting the text as a quest is to do so in error: "A quest is a positive journey, implying an effort, a struggle to reach a goal. But Huck is escaping. His journey is primarily a negation, a flight *from* tyranny, not a flight toward freedom" ("Uncomfortable," 350). Cox's point is well taken. Clemens is not crafting a traditional quest tale here; there is, however, something Huck is seeking, a sense of selfhood that has been repeatedly denied to him, first by "pap," Huck has no sense of belonging to family, and second by the town of St. Petersburg, Huck constantly remains on the periphery. Huck finds these signifiers of acceptance, family, and community, on the raft with Jim. The only element missing is that Huck must discover who and what *he* is. Throughout the novel Huck desperately seeks an identity, and by the end of the story, he has found one—that of writer.

Instead of interpreting Clemens' literary efforts, as Brooks and his subsequent critical followers do, as the result of a fragmentation of self, Clemens' genius ultimately resided in the joining of different consciousnesses to forge an androgynous whole. Within *Adventures of Huckleberry Finn*, the elements of both the traditional masculine quest novel and the sentimentalized female novel are apparent. Joseph A. Boone, in his essay "Male Independence and the American Quest Genre: Hidden Sexual Politics in the All-Male Worlds of Melville, Twain and London," recognized that "in rejecting the shore world's negative models of masculine aggression and feminine piety alike," Huck becomes a cultural misfit, like Clemens, like the Langdon women, like Mary Ann Cord. Boone identifies Huckleberry's journey as his personal response to a bifurcated sexual ethos that blocks individual wholeness or self-expression. Huckleberry, instead of attempting to gain re-entry into society, Boone concludes, "embraces an independent truth of self, rooted in an ethos of compassionate love that runs counter to all social hierarchies" (200). For it is Huckleberry's loving relationship with Jim, above all else, that becomes the measure of Huck's status as a cultural misfit and of his unretraceable deviation from a traditional standard of manhood. (199–200)

Clemens created his own genre—the androgynous quest novel, and he continued his androgynous experiments in *The Personal Recollections of Joan of Arc*.[4] Clemens' circle of female advisors underlined this self-knowledge on his part that if he was going to write fiction integrating both male and female experience and produce fiction that would appeal to both genders, he needed to have access to the feminine consciousness. To write a fully integrated novel, he required a feminine point-of-view with which he could integrate his masculine perception. When Clemens wrote to Frederick Duneka at *Harper's Magazine*, on September 15, 1902, "My wife being ill, I have been—in literary matters—helpless all these weeks. I have no editor—no censor," he was identifying a very real, and frightening situation—the loss of his most important source of female consciousness (MTP). Clemens, like Huck, had found his sense of self in his identity of writer and with the loss of his female circle, this identity, this selfhood, was threatened.

Clemens indeed, as DeVoto suggested, accepted "tuition" when he came East and he also possessed, as Edward Wagenknecht proclaimed, too much "vitality" to be averted from what he deemed important; but what Clemens realized himself and what critics have failed to perceive is that this "tuition" and "vitality" of which they speak were in effect Clemens' signaling of his openness to the world of the female.

Clemens realized early on that his fictional powers were enhanced—more than enhanced, empowered—by his interactions with women. As is evident from the time of Ann E. Taylor to the era of the "Angel Fish," Clemens relied upon his female audience for their creative inspiration. To create his greatest works of fiction, Clemens abandoned the realm of the purely male and investigated, and ultimately incorporated, the world of the female. Clemens' genius lay in his ability to synthesize these disparate forms of consciousness provided in part by his familial circle, and ultimately this ability enabled him to create his unique and masterful androgynous vision. The absence of female Twain biographers and the critical cold shoulder that the women in Twain's life have received is more than mere coincidence; it is time that both omissions be corrected so that the full multi-sexual universality of Clemens' vision may be more clearly understood.

Notes

1. For the first time, at the 1990 MLA Conference, a panel was formed to examine the issue of women in Mark Twain biography. The panel participants and paper titles are: Laura Skandera, panel organizer, "'I am Woman's Rights': Olivia Langdon Clemens and Her Feminist Circle"; Sherwood Cummings, "The Commanding Presence of Rachel Cord"; John Stahl, "Samuel Clemens and 'Mother' Fairbanks"; Michael Kiskis, "'A man's house burns down':

Father/Daughter Collaboration in Mark Twain's Autobiography." A paper on the relationship between Clemens and Susan Crane was delivered by Gretchen Sharlow, "The Cranes of Quarry Farm," September 1988, at the Center for Mark Twain Studies.

2. A line strikingly similar to the one in Clemens' letter is found in Mary Abigail Dodge's novel, *A New Atmosphere* (1865): "Neither is the man superior to the woman, nor the woman to the man, but they twain are one flesh" (284). In Alan Gribben's *Mark Twain's Library: A Reconstruction*, two works by Dodge are listed, *Skirmishes and Sketches* and *Stumbling Blocks*, as belonging to Clemens' library but not *A New Atmosphere*; however, it is likely that Clemens was aware of Dodge's *Atmosphere*.

3. Four letters in question are dated July 3, 1875; November 21, 1875; November 23, 1875; January 18, 1876.

4. Clemens often referred to androgyny in other works such as "Hellfire Hotchkiss." "Hellfire Hotchkiss [the girl] is the only genuwyne male man in this town and Thug Carpenter's [the boy] the only genuwyne female girl, if you leave out sex and just consider the business facts." Clemens was not the only nineteenth-century author to explore the novelistic possibilities of androgyny. William Dean Howells, in *The Rise of Silas Lapham*, introduced the character of Penelope, a young woman who functions as Silas' surrogate son, and who, by the end of the novel, is banished to Mexico in hopes she will find a society more accepting of her than Brahmin New England. Sarah Orne Jewett, a friend of Clemens', also introduced an androgynous narrator in *The Country of the Pointed Firs*. Jewett's narrator functions as an androgynous bridge between the opposing factions of male and female in the village of Dunnet's Landing. Clemens predated Virginia Woolf's experiments with androgyny in her novel *Orlando* by some four decades.

Works Cited

Boone, Joseph A. "Male Independence and the American Quest Genre: Hidden Sexual Politics in the All-Male Worlds of Melville, Twain and London." *Gender Studies*. Ed. Judith Spector. Bowling Green: Bowling Green State U. Popular Press, 1986.

Brooks, Van Wyck. *The Ordeal of Mark Twain*. New York: Dutton, 1933.

Coultrap-McQuin, Susan. *Doing Literary Business: American Women Writers in the Nineteenth Century*. Chapel Hill: U. North Carolina P., 1990.

Cox, James M. "The Uncomfortable Ending of *Huckleberry Finn*." *The Adventures of Huckleberry Finn*. Ed. Sculley Bradley. New York: W. W. Norton, 1977.

DeVoto, Bernard. *Mark Twain at Work*. Cambridge: Harvard U. P., 1942.

Epstein, Cynthia Fuchs. *Deceptive Distinctions: Sex, Gender and the Social Order*. New Haven: Yale U. P., 1989.

Fiedler, Leslie. *The Collected Essays of Leslie Fiedler*. Vol 1. New York: Stein & Day, 1971.

Fraiberg, Louis. "Van Wyck Brooks versus Mark Twain versus Samuel Clemens." *Psychoanalysis and American Literary Criticism*. Detroit: Wayne State U. P., 1960.

Gilbert, Sandra, and Susan Gubar. *The Madwoman in the Attic*. New Haven: Yale U. P., 1979.

Gribben, Alan. "'It Is Unsatisfactory to Read to One's Self': Mark Twain's Informal Readings." *Quarterly Journal of Speech* 62 (1976): 49–56.

———. *Mark Twain's Library: A Reconstruction*. 2 Vols. Boston: G. K. Hall, 1980.

Henderson, Archibald. *Mark Twain*. Philadelphia: Folcroft Press, Inc. 1969 [1912].

Hill, Hamlin. *Mark Twain: God's Fool*. New York: Harper, 1973.

Jerome, Robert D., and Herbert A. Wisbey, Jr., eds. *Mark Twain in Elmira*. Elmira: Mark Twain Society, 1977.

Kaplan, Justin. *Mr. Clemens and Mark Twain*. New York: Simon and Schuster, 1966.

Kaplan, Sydney Janet. *Feminine Consciousness in the Modern British Novel*. Chicago: U. of Illinois P., 1975.

Krauth, Leland. "Mark Twain: The Victorian of Southwestern Humor." *American Literature* 54 (October 1982): 368–84.

The Mark Twain Papers (MTP). University of California, Berkeley.

Showalter, Elaine. *A Literature of Their Own*. Princeton, N.J.: Princeton U. P., 1977.

Sorin, Gretchen Sullivan. "The Black Community in Elmira." *A Heritage Uncovered: The Black Experience in Upstate New York: 1800–1925*. Ed. Cara Sutherland. Chemung County Historical Society, 1988.

Twain, Mark. *Adventures of Huckleberry Finn*. Ed. Sculley Bradley. New York: W. W. Norton, 1977.

———. *Mark Twain—Howells Letters*. Eds. Henry Nash Smith and William M. Gibson. Cambridge: Harvard U. P., 1960.

———. *The Unabridged Mark Twain.* Ed. Lawrence Teacher. Philadelphia: Running Press, 1976.

Wagenknecht, Edward. *Mark Twain: The Man and His Work.* 3rd ed. Norman: U. Oklahoma P., 1971.

Warren, Joyce W. "Old Ladies and Little Girls." *The American Narcissus: Individualism and Women in Nineteenth-Century American Fiction.* New Jersey: Rutgers U. P., 1984.

Wecter, Dixon, ed. *The Love Letters of Mark Twain.* New York: Harper, 1949.

———. *Mark Twain to Mrs. Fairbanks.* San Marino: Huntington Library, 1949.

———. *Sam Clemens of Hannibal.* Boston: Houghton Mifflin, 1952.

SELECTED BIBLIOGRAPHY

Items listed in the anthologies are usually not listed separately in the following bibliography, which is largely oriented toward materials from 1980 forward. Other listings may be found in numerous bibliographies in works cited here and in other Twain criticism.

Anthologies of Criticism

A number of collections of articles and sections of books have already appeared concerning Mark Twain. Several of the most prominent, useful, and readily accessible are listed here with their contents.

Mark Twain, the Critical Heritage. Frederick Anderson, editor. New York: Barnes & Noble, 1971. Contains

The Innocents Abroad or The New Pilgrim's Progress (1869)
    Unsigned review, *Nation*, 1869
    Unsigned review, *Packard's Monthly*, 1869
    Unsigned review, Buffalo *Express*, 1869
    William Dean Howells, review, *Atlantic*, 1869
    "Tom Folio," review, Boston *Daily Evening Transcript*, 1869
    Bret Harte, review, *Overland Monthly*, 1870
    Unsigned review, *Athenaeum*, 1870
    Unsigned review, *Saturday Review*, 1870
    William Ward, "American Humorists." Macon (Mississippi) *Beacon*, 1870

Roughing It, or The Innocents at Home (1872)
    Unsigned review, Manchester *Guardian*, 1872

Selected Bibliography

William Dean Howells, review, *Atlantic*, 1872
Unsigned review, *Overland Monthly*, 1872

Sketches, New and Old (1875)
William Dean Howells, review, *Atlantic*, 1875
Matthew Freke Turner, "Artemus Ward and the Humourists of America," *New Quarterly Magazine*, 1876

The Adventures of Tom Sawyer (1876)
William Dean Howells, review, *Atlantic*, 1876
Moncure D. Conway, review, London *Examiner*, 1876
Unsigned review, *Athenaeum*, 1876
Unsigned review, London *Times*, 1876
Unsigned review, New York *Times*, 1877

A Tramp Abroad (1880)
William Ernest Henley, review, *Athenaeum*, 1880
Unsigned review, *Saturday Review*, 1880
William Dean Howells, review, *Atlantic*, 1880
H.H. Boyesen, review, *Atlantic*, 1881
E. Purcell, review, *Academy*, 1881
Unsigned review, *Athenaeum*, 1881
Unsigned review, *Century Magazine*, 1882
John Nichol on Mark Twain (1882)
William Dean Howells, "Mark Twain," *Century Magazine*, 1882
Thomas Sergeant Perry, "An American on American Humour," *St. James's Gazette*, 1883

Life on the Mississippi (1883)
Lafcadio Hearn, review, New Orleans *Times-Democrat*, 1883
Unsigned review, *Athenaeum*, 1883
Robert Brown, review, *Academy*, 1883
Unsigned review, *Graphic*, 1883

The Adventures of Huckleberry Finn (1884–5)
Unsigned review, *Athenaeum*, 1884
Brander Matthews, review, *Saturday Review*, 1885

Robert Bridges, review, *Life*, 1885
Unsigned article, "Modern Comic Literature," *Saturday Review*, 1885
Thomas Sergeant Perry, review, *Century Magazine*, 1885
Andrew Lang, "The Art of Mark Twain," *Illustrated London News*, 1891
Sir Walter Besant, "My Favourite Novelist and His Best Book," *Munsey's Magazine*, 1898
Andrew Lang, "Jubilee Ode to Mark Twain," *Longman's Magazine*, 1886

A Connecticut Yankee in King Arthur's Court (1889)
Sylvester Baxter, review, Boston Sunday *Herald*, 1889
William Dean Howells, review, *Harper's Magazine*, 1890
Desmond O'Brien, review, *Truth*, 1890
Unsigned review, *Speaker*, 1890
Unsigned review, London *Daily Telegraph*, 1890
Unsigned review, *Scots Observer*, 1890
William T. Stead: review, *Review of Reviews* (London), 1890
Unsigned review, *Athenaeum*, 1890
Unsigned review, Boston *Literary World*, 1890
Unsigned review, *Plumas National*, 1890
H. C. Vedder: article, New York *Examiner*, 1893

The Tragedy of Pudd'nhead Wilson (1894)
William Livingston Alden: review, *Idler*, 1894
Unsigned review, *Athenaeum*, 1895
Unsigned review, *Critic*, 1895

Personal Recollections of Joan of Arc (1896)
William Peterfield Trent, review, *Bookman* (New York), 1896
Brander Matthews, "Mark Twain—His Work," *Book Buyer*, 1897
Unsigned article, "Mark Twain, Benefactor," *Academy*, 1897
David Masters, "Mark Twain's Place in Literature," *Chautauquan*, 1897

D.C. Murray, article, *Canadian Magazine*, 1897

Following the Equator, or More Tramps Abroad (1897)
Unsigned review, *Academy*, 1897
Unsigned review, *Speaker*, 1897
Unsigned review, *Saturday Review*, 1898
Unsigned review, *Critic*, 1898
Hiram M. Stanley, review, *Dial*, 1898
Theodore De Laguna, "Mark Twain as a Prospective Classic," *Overland Monthly*, 1898
Anne E. Keeling, "American Humour: Mark Twain," *London Quarterly Review*, 1899
Henry Harland, "Mark Twain," London *Daily Chronicle*, 1899
Harry Thurston Peck, "As to Mark Twain," *Bookman* (New York), 1901
R. E. Phillips, "Mark Twain: More than Humorist," *Book Buyer*, 1901
T. M. Parrott, "Mark Twain: Made in America," *Booklover's Magazine*, 1904
Harry Thurston Peck, "Mark Twain at Ebb Tide," *Bookman* (New York), 1904
Hammond Lamont, "Mark Twain at Seventy," *Nation*, 1905
Unsigned article, "Mark Twain," *Spectator*, 1907
William Lyon Phelps, "Mark Twain," *North American Review*, 1907
Charles Whibley, column, *Blackwood's Magazine*, 1907
H. L. Mencken, review, *Smart Set*, 1909
Unsigned notice, *Saturday Review*, 1910
Frank Jewett Mather, "Two Frontiersmen," *Nation*, 1910
Unsigned notice, *Dial*, 1910
Arnold Bennett, comment, *Bookman* (London), 1910
Sydney Brooks, "England and Mark Twain," *North American Review*, 1910
Harry Thurston Peck, article, *Bookman* (New York), 1910
William Lyon Phelps, "Mark Twain, Artist," *Review of Reviews* (New York), 1910

Selected Bibliography

Simeon Strunsky, article, *Nation*, 1910

Archibald Henderson, "The International Fame of Mark Twain," *North American Review*, 1910

John Macy on Mark Twain, 1913

H.L. Mencken, "The Burden of Humor," *Smart Set*, 1913

Critical Essays on Mark Twain, 1867–1910. Edited by Louis J. Budd. Boston: G. K. Hall, 1982. Includes

[Charles Henry Webb], "Advertisement"

[Edward H. House], "Mark Twain as a Lecturer"

Anonymous, [Review of *The Innocents Abroad*]

Henry Wheeler Shaw, "The Josh Billings Papers/Sum Biographical—Mark Twain"

[William A. Croffut], "Mark Twain Last Night"

Anonymous, [Review of a Lecture on the Sandwich Islands]

George T. Ferris, "Mark Twain"

William Dean Howells, [Review of *Mark Twain's Sketches, New and Old*]

[Robert Underwood Johnson], "A New Boy Book by Mark Twain"

Edmund H. Yates, "Mark Twain at Hartford"

Anonymous, "Not Quite an Editor/The Story about Mark Twain's Connection with the Hartford *Courant*"

Anonymous, "Mark Twain Home Again"

Anonymous, [Review of *The Stolen White Elephant*]

W. D. Howells, "Mark Twain"

John Henton Carter, "A Day with Mark Twain"

C., "Mark Twain"

Anonymous, "Mark Twain as Lecturer/How He Feels When He Gets on the Stage before an Audience"

[Frank George Carpenter], "Such Is Mark Twain"

Anonymous, "Talk with Twain. . . His Comments on Authors, Magazines and General Literature"

Edgar C. Beall, "Mark Twain's Head Analyzed"

Charles H. Clark, "Mark Twain at 'Nook Farm' (Hartford) and Elmira"

Selected Bibliography

Oliver Wendell Holmes, "To Mark Twain (*On His Fiftieth Birthday*)"
Anonymous, "An Interview with the Famous Humorist/He Chats of Past and Present/His Life as a Reporter"
Andrew Lang, "The Art of Mark Twain"
Henry C. Vedder, "Mark Twain"
Frank R. Stockton, "Mark Twain and His Recent Works"
[Lute Pease], "The Famous Story-Teller Discusses Characters/Says That No Author Creates, but Merely Copies"
[Samuel E. Moffett], "Mark Twain to Pay All/On His Way Around the World Now to Raise the Money"
Anonymous, "Mark Twain in Sydney/A Further Interview"
R. C. B., "Mark Twain on the Platform"
William Peterfield Trent, "Mark Twain as an Historical Novelist"
Brander Matthews, "Mark Twain—His Work"
Anonymous, "Mark Twain Smiling through His Tears, but in Sore Straits"
Carlyle Smythe, "The Real 'Mark Twain'"
Anonymous, "Mark Twain in London/He Talks of His Visit and His Doomsday Book"
Henry Harland, "Mark Twain"
Anonymous, "Mark Twain to Spend Winter Here/Author Returns an Anti-Imperialist"
James L. Ford, "An American Humorist"
James B. Pond, [Paying Off His Debts]
Anonymous, "A Little Man and a Great Subject"
[Rollo Ogden], "Mark Twain on McKinley"
R. E. Phillips, "Mark Twain: More Than Humorist"
Anonymous, "Mrs. Astor Injures Mark Twain's Feelings"
Anonymous, "Degree for Mark Twain"
Anonymous, "Mark Twain's Farewell?"
Henry Van Dyke, "A Toast to Mark Twain!"
Anonymous, "Happy Pessimist Is Mark Twain"
William Dean Howells, "Sonnet to Mark Twain"

Selected Bibliography

   [Hammond Lamont], "Mark Twain at Seventy"
   Anonymous, "Mark Twain's Clothes"
   Anonymous, "Mark Twain"
   William Lyon Phelps, "Mark Twain"
   Hamilton W. Mabie, "Mark Twain the Humorist"
   Archibald Henderson, "Mark Twain"
   Anonymous, "Twain Pokes Fun at Union Station and Pities City"
   Henry M. Alden, "Mark Twain: Personal Impressions"
   Clarence H. Gaines, "Mark Twain *the* Humorist"
   Anonymous, "Mark Twain"
   Anonymous, "Chief of American Men of Letters"
   Anonymous, "Mark Twain: An American Pioneer in Man's Oldest Art, Whose Death Is Mourned by the World at Large"
   Anonymous, "Mark Twain"
   Anonymous, "The Death of Mark Twain"
   [Simeon Strunsky], "Serious Humorists"
   George Ade, "Mark Twain as Our Emissary"

Critical Essays on Mark Twain, 1910–1980. Edited by Louis J. Budd. Boston: G. K. Hall, 1983. Contains
   Archibald Henderson, "The International Fame of Mark Twain"
   Anonymous, "Mark Twain's Portrait"
   [Stuart P. Sherman], "A Literary American"
   [William Dean Howells], [Review of A. B. Paine's *Biography*]
   H. L. Mencken, "The Man Within"
   Alvin Johnson, "The Tragedy of Mark Twain"
   Brander Matthews, "Mark Twain and the Art of Writing"
   Carl Van Doren, "Mark Twain and Bernard Shaw"
   Fred Lewis Pattee, "On the Rating of Mark Twain"
   Newton Arvin, "Mark Twain: 1835–1935"
   Mark Van Doren, "A Century of Mark Twain"
   Owen Wister, "In Homage to Mark Twain"
   Robert Herrick, "Mark Twain and the American Tradition"

Selected Bibliography

Robert T. Oliver, "Mark Twain's Views on Education"
Robert M. Gay, "The Two Mark Twains"
Herman Wouk, "America's Voice is Mark Twain's"
Kenneth Rexroth, "Humor in a Tough Age"
Leslie Hanscom, "Twain: A Yearning for Yesterday"
John C. Gerber, "Mark Twain's Use of the Comic Pose"
Glauco Cambon, "Mark Twain and Charlie Chaplin as Heroes of Popular Culture"
Edward Field, "Mark Twain and Sholem Aleichem"
C. Merton Babcock, "Mark Twain, Mencken and 'The Higher Goofyism'"
Richard Schickel, "Hal Holbrook Tonight!"
Maurice F. Brown, "Mark Twain as Proteus: Ironic Form and Fictive Integrity"
Stanley Brodwin, "The Theology of Mark Twain: Banished Adam and the Bible"
Janet Holmgren McKay, "'Tears and Flapdoodle': Point of View and Style in *Adventures of Huckleberry Finn*"
Arthur G. Pettit, "Mark Twain and His Times: A Bicentennial Appreciation"
Anonymous, "Mark Twain and the Pope"
Judith Fetterley, "Mark Twain and the Anxiety of Entertainment"
Leland Krauth, "Mark Twain Fights Sam Clemens' Duel"

Mark Twain: A Sumptuous Variety. Edited by Robert Giddings. London: Vision Press, 1985. Contains
Philip Melling, "Sport on the River and the Science of Play"
John S. Whitley, "Kids' Stuff: Mark Twain's Boys"
William Kaufman, "The Comedic Stance: Sam Clemens, His Masquerade"
Robert Goldman, "Mark Twain as Playwright"
A. Robert Lee, "*Huckleberry Finn*, 'Sivilization', and the Civilization of the Heart"
Lyall Powers, "Mark Twain and the Future of Picaresque"

Selected Bibliography

Peter Messent, "Towards the Absurd: Mark Twain's *A Connecticut Yankee, Pudd'nhead Wilson* and *The Great Dark*"

Robert Giddings, "Mark Twain and King Leopold of the Belgians"

Eric Mottram, "A Raft Against Washington: Mark Twain's Criticism of America"

Huck Finn Among the Critics, A Centennial Selection, 1884–1894. Edited by M. Thomas Inge. Washington, D. C.: United States Information Agency, 1984.

    M. Thomas Inge, "Introduction"
    Arthur G. Pettit, "Mark Twain and His Times"
    Hamlin Hill and Walter Blair, "The Composition of *Huckleberry Finn*"

Reviews by
    William Ernest Henley,
    Brander Matthews,
    Thomas Sergeant Perry

Andrew Lang, "The Art of Mark Twain"

Sir Walter Besant, "My Favorite Novelist and His Best Book"

William Dean Howells, "Mark Twain: An Inquiry"

H. L. Mencken, "The Burden of Humor"

V. S. Pritchett, "America's First Truly Indigenous Masterpiece"

Lionel Trilling, "The Greatness of *Huckleberry Finn*"

Leslie Fiedler, "Come Back To The Raft Ag'in, Huck Honey"

T. S. Eliot, "Mark Twain's Masterpiece"

Leo Marx, "Mr. Eliot, Mr. Trilling and *Huckleberry Finn*"

W. H. Auden, "Huck and Oliver"

Joseph Wood Krutch, "Bad Novels and Great Books"

James M. Cox, "Remarks on the Sad Initiation of Huckleberry Finn"

Lauriat Lane, Jr., "Why *Huckleberry Finn* Is a Great World Novel"

Richard P. Adams, "The Structure of *Huckleberry Finn* "
Glauco Cambon, "Mark Twain and Charlie Chaplin as Heroes of Popular Culture"
Janet Holmgren McKay, "Tears and Flapdoodle": Point of View and Style in *Adventures of Huckleberry Finn* "
Bruce Michelson, "Huck and the Games of the World"
Hamlin Hill, "*Huckleberry Finn's* Humor Today"
Beverly R. David, "The Pictorial *Huck Finn*: Mark Twain and His Illustrator, E. W. Kemble"
Perry Frank, "*Adventures of Huckleberry Finn* on Film"
M. Thomas Inge, "A Mark Twain Chronology"
Thomas A. Tenney, "An Annotated Checklist of Criticism on *Adventures of Huckleberry Finn*, 1884–1983"

Critical Approaches to Mark Twain's Short Stories. Edited by Elizabeth McMahan. Port Washington, NY: Kennikat Press, 1981.

How Mark Twain Writes
    S. L. Clemens, "Report to the Buffalo Female Academy"
    S. L. Clemens, "How to Tell a Story"
    George Feinstein, "Mark Twain's Idea of Story Structure"

"The Celebrated Jumping Frog of Calaveras County"
    A. B. Paine, "The Jumping Frog"
    Gladys Bellemy, "The Art of 'The Jumping Frog'"
    Kenneth Lynn, "Upset Expectations in 'The Jumping Frog'"
    Henry Nash Smith, "The Mysterious Charm of Simon Wheeler"
    Sydney J. Krause, "The Art and Satire of Twain's 'Jumping Frog' Story"
    James M. Cox, "The Structure of 'The Jumping Frog'"

Selected Bibliography

"A True Story"
- Philip Foner, "A True Story"
- Gerald J. Fenger, "Telling it Like it Was"
- William H. Gibson, "The Artistry of 'A True Story'"

"The Facts Concerning the Recent Carnival of Crime in Connecticut"
- Maxwell Geismar, "A Curious Parable"
- William M. Gibson, "Mark Twain's 'Carnival of Crime'"

"The £1,000,000 Bank-Note"
- Philip Foner, "A Satire on the System"
- Maxwell Geismar, "Twain on the 'Get-Rich-Quick' Mania"
- Ricki Morgan, "Mark Twain's Money Imagery in 'The £1,000,000 Bank-Note' and 'The $30,000 Bequest'"

"The Man That Corrupted Hadleyburg"
- Gladys Bellemy, "Moralism Vs. Determinism in 'Hadleyburg'"
- Clinton S. Burhans, Jr., "The Sober Affirmation of Mark Twain's 'Hadleyburg'"
- Henry Nash Smith, "Twain's Mathematical Demonstration of Human Greed"
- Henry B. Rule, "The Role of Satan in 'The Man That Corrupted Hadleyburg'"
- Maxwell Geismar, "Twain's Ironic Parable on the Hypocrisy of Human Virtue"
- Stanley Brodwin, "Mark Twain's Mask of Satan in 'Hadleyburg'"

"The $30,000 Bequest"
- Maxwell Geismar, "Twain's Parody of Small Souls on the Make"
- Gerald J. Finger, "The Complete Irony of 'The $30,000 Bequest'"

"Captain Stormfield's Visit to Heaven"
- S. L. Clemens, "The Literary Evolution of Captain Ned Wakefield"

Selected Bibliography

    Gladys Bellemy, "The Narrative Perfection of 'Captain Stormfield's Visit to Heaven'"
    Louis Budd, "Twain's Satire on Racism"
    James M. Cox, "Captain Stormfield as Pure Burlesque Figure"
    William M. Gibson, "The Imaginative Achievement of 'Captain Stormfield's Visit to Heaven'"

"The Mysterious Stranger"
    John S. Tuckey, "'The Mysterious Stranger': Mark Twain's Texts and the Paine-Duneka Edition"
    John R. May, "The Gospel According to Philip Traum: Structural Unity in 'The Mysterious Stranger'"
    Raymond Verasco, "Divine Foolishness: A Critical Evaluation of 'The Mysterious Stranger'"

Edited with an Introduction by Barry A. Marks. Boston: D. C. Heath & Co., 1959. "Problems in American Civilization" Series.

Selections from
    Van Wyck Brooks, *The Ordeal of Mark Twain*
    Walter Blair, *Mark Twain and Native American Humor*
    Bernard De Voto, *Mark Twain at Work*

Essays
    Lionel Trilling, "The Greatness of *Huckleberry Finn* "
    Leo Marx, "Mr. Eliot, Mr. Trilling, and *Huckleberry Finn*"
    James M. Cox, "Remarks on the Sad Initiation of Huckleberry Finn"
    Frank Baldanza, "The Structure of *Huckleberry Finn*"
    Richard P. Adams, "The Unity and Coherence of *Huckleberry Finn*"
    Lauriat Lane, Jr., "Why *Huckleberry Finn* Is a Great World Novel"
    William Van O'Connor, "Why *Huckleberry Finn* Is Not the Great American Novel"

Selected Bibliography

Mark Twain: A Collection of Critical Essays. Edited By Henry Nash Smith. Englewood Cliffs, NJ: Prentice-Hall, 1963.
    Henry Nash Smith, "Introduction"
    Van Wyck Brooks, "Mark Twain's Humor"
    Maurice Le Breton, "Mark Twain: An Appreciation"
    Kenneth Lynn, "*Roughing It*"
    Leo Marx, "The Pilot and the Passenger"
    Walter Blair, "*Tom Sawyer*"
    Henry Nash Smith, "A Sound Heart and a Deformed Conscience"
    Daniel G. Hoffman "From Black Magic—and White—In *Huckleberry Finn*"
    W. H. Auden, "Huck and Oliver"
    James M. Cox, "*A Connecticut Yankee*: The Machinery of Self-Preservation"
    Leslie Fiedler, "As Free as Any Cretur"
    Bernard De Voto, "The Symbols of Despair"
    Tony Tanner, "The Lost America—The Despair of Henry Adams and Mark Twain"

One Hundred Years of Huckleberry Finn. Edited by Robert Sattelmeyer and J. Donald Crowley. Columbia: University of Missouri Press, 1985. All the essays deal with *Huckleberry Finn* and are new with this text.

The Critical Response to Mark Twain's Huckleberry Finn. Edited by Laurie Champion. Westport: Greenwood Press, 1991. Includes some standard essays and an ABC "Nightline" dialogue "Huckleberry Finn: Literature or Racist Trash?" of limited interest.

Articles and Books

Alden, W. L. "The Book Hunter." *Idler*, VII (May 1895): 565–76. Comments on *Personal Recollections of Joan of Arc* in the April *Harper's Magazine* as "by the Sieur Uquel Berri-Finn, and that they were originally translated into English by M. Marc Touêne. Nothing that the Sieur Uquel Berri-Finn has written is more characteristic of that charming author than are the opening chapters of this new romance," as quoted in Tenney.

Andrews, Kenneth R. *Nook Farm: Mark Twain's Hartford Circle.* Cambridge, MA: Harvard University Press, 1950; rpt. Hamden, CT: Archon Books, 1967.

Arnold, St. George, Jr. "The Twain Bestiary: Mark Twain's Critters and the Tradition of Animal Portraiture in Humor of the Old Southwest." *Southern Folklore Quarterly*, 41 (1977): 195–211.

Bacheller, Irving. "Mr. Paine's Biography of Mark Twain." *Literary Digest*, XLV (16 November 1912): 909. Tenney notes this to be less a review of Paine's biography than Bacheller's tribute to Twain: "He found the East still in the bondage of Puritanism. Lincoln freed the negro. Mark Twain freed the white man."

Ballorain, Rolande. "Mark Twain's Capers: A Chameleon in King Carnival's Court." In *American Novelists Revisited*, Fritz Fleischmann, ed. Boston: G. K. Hall, 1982. Pp. 143–70. Contends that Twain is a European writer in his sense of the "carnivalesque."

Barchilon, Jose, and Joel S. Kovel. "*Huckleberry Finn:* A Psychoanalytic Study." *Journal of the American Psychoanalytic Association*, XIV (October 1966): 775–814. A psychoanalysis of Huck Finn as a legitimate patient, excluding Twain's biography.

Bassett, John E. "*Life on the Mississippi:* Being Shifty in a New Country." *Western American Literature*, 21 (1986): 39–45. Disguise and performance as central elements in the canon and especially in *Life on the Mississippi*.

———. "*Roughing It:* Authority through Comic Performance." *Nineteenth-Century Literature*, 43 (1988): 220–34. Language is used to control audience by withholding information and creating contradictions.

Bentzon, Th. "Les Humoristes Américains, I: Mark Twain." *Revue de Deux Mondes,* 204 (15 July 1872): 313–35.

Selected Bibliography

An early and thoughtful examination of Twain's humor before the establishment of his reputation as a novelist, in French.

Berkove, Lawrence I. "The Reality of the Dream: Structural and Thematic Unity in *A Connecticut Yankee.*" *Mark Twain Journal*, 22, I (1984): 8–14. The novel is tightly structured around the endless repetitions of human error, as reflected by the unreliable narrator.

Blair, Walter, and Hamlin Hill. *America's Humor from Poor Richard to Doonesbury.* London: Oxford, 1978. A comprehensive study of the historical field and Twain's humor in six brief but illuminating chapters on his role as actor and storyteller within his own canon.

Blair, Walter. *Native American Humor.* San Francisco: Chandler, 1960 [1937]. The basic study of the field of American humor leading to Twain, with valuable critical and bibliographical information.

Branch, Edgar M. "'The Babes in the Wood': Artemus Ward's 'Double Health' to Mark Twain." *PMLA*, 93 (1978): 955–2. A reconstruction of the comic lecture by Ward which Twain probably heard and may have taken as inspiration for his story-telling and lecturing mode.

———. "Mark Twain: Newspaper Reading and the Writer's Creativity." *Nineteenth-Century Fiction*, 37 (1983): 576–603. Twain's extensive use of newspaper material documented and analyzed.

———. "A New Clemens Footprint: Soleather Steps Forward." *American Literature*, 54 (1982): 497–510. Finds an 1859 sketch by Twain indicating his drive to comedy even while piloting.

Brodwin, Stanley. "The Humor of the Absurd: Mark Twain's Adamic Diaries." *Criticism*, XIV (Winter 1972): 49–64. Twain's diaries of Adam, Eve and Satan highlight the grotesque irony of innocence pitted against determinism.

———. "Wandering Between Two Gods: Theological Realism in Mark Twain's *A Connecticut Yankee.*" *Studies in the Literary Imagination*, 16, II (1983): 57–82. Calvinism,

Deism, and Darwinism mixed within historical experience to create the dream-ending perspective on human life.

Budd, Louis J. "Mark Twain and the Magazine World." *University of Mississippi Studies in English*, No. 2 (1982): 35–42. Shows Twain treating the magazine audience as appreciating a higher class of writing than the more generalized public he addressed.

———. *Our Mark Twain: The Making of His Public Personality*. Philadelphia: University of Pennsylvania Press, 1983. An analysis of the making of the staged persona Mark Twain as author/entertainer/entrepreneur.

———. "Who Wants to Go to Hell? An Unsigned Sketch by Mark Twain?" *Studies in American Humor*, No. 1 (1982): 6–16. Identifies a sketch by Twain subsequently verified by a set of proofs in the Mark Twain Papers.

Cheesman, Elaine, and Earl French, eds. *Twain-Stowe Sourcebook*. Hartford: Mark Twain Memorial and Stowe-Day Foundation, 1988. A teaching sourcebook including numerous lesson plans and abstracts of presentations by Louis Budd on "Humor and Ethics," Shelley Fisher Fishkin on "Mark Twain and the Risks of Irony," Hamlin Hill on "Humor and Pessimism," and David E. E. Sloane on "Mark Twain as an Urban Northeast Humorist" and "Mark Twain's Heroes: Huck and Hank," among other topics.

Cox, James M. "Humor and America: The Southwestern Bear Hunt, Mrs. Stowe and Mark Twain." *Sewanee Revue*, 83 (1975): 573–601. *Huck Finn* is a historical lie combining elements of Southwestern humor and northern consciousness into a portrait of a civilization that is a cruel joke even on readers who seek to conscientiously perfect it.

———. "*Life on the Mississippi* Revisited." In *The Mythologizing of Mark Twain*, Sara deS. Davis and Philip D. Biedler, eds. University, Alabama: University of Alabama Press, 1984. Pp. 95–115. Identifies unity in the novel in tension between Clemens the man and Twain the comic persona.

———. "Toward Vernacular Humor." *Virginia Quarterly Review*, 46 (1970): 311–30. Surveys Twain, Ring Lardner, and J. D. Salinger.

Cunliffe, Marcus. "Mark Twain and His 'English' Novels." *Times Literary Supplement*, 25 December 1981: 1503–04. Suggests *The Prince and the Pauper* was an attempt to capture the audience of the English historical novel and finds a Bulwer-Lytton analog to *Connecticut Yankee*.

Durden, Fred. "The Aesthetics of Bitterness in *Following the Equator*." *American Literary Realism, 1870–1910*, 16 (Autumn 1981): 277–85. Language, context, and landscape merge into Twain's most bitterly ironic travel narrative, completing the technique found in earlier works.

Eby, Cecil D. "Dandy Versus Squatter: An Earlier Round." *Southern Literary Journal*, 20, I (1987): 33–36. Finds Joseph Doddridge's "Dialogue of the Backwoodsman and the Dandy" as an 1821 analog.

Emerson, Everett. "A Send-Off for Joe Goodman: Mark Twain's "The Carson Fossil-Footprints." *Resources for American Literary Study*, 10 (1980): 71–78. Identifies a sketch written for Goodman in 1884 which is in the comic style of his Virginia City local newspaper writings.

Farrell, James T. "Mark Twain's *Huckleberry Finn* and *Tom Sawyer*." In *The League of Frightened Philistines*. New York: Vanguard Press, 1945. Pp. 25–30. Twain as democrat and cynic made Tom and Huck symbols of human possibilities in a spoiled world of chattel slavery.

Fischer, John Irwin. "How to Tell a Story: Mark Twain's Gloves and the Moral Example of Mr. Laurence Sterne." *Mark Twain Journal*, 21, III (1982): 17–21. Influence of Sterne's *Sentimental Journey* on Twain's glove-buying episode and the novel generally.

———. "Mark Twain, Mount Tabor, and the Triumph of Art." *Southern Review*, 14 (1978): 692–705. Close analysis of a chapter in *Innocents* suggests the conflict between art and philosophy in Twain's writing.

Selected Bibliography

Fischer, Victor. "Huck Finn Reviewed: The Reception of *Huckleberry Finn* in the United States, 1885–1897." *American Literary Realism, 1870–1910*, 16, No. 1 (Spring 1983): 1–57. A complete introduction to the critical vulnerabilities of a humorist and the attempt to define American humor in the newspapers and periodicals of the 1885–1895 period, reprinting many perceptive and revelatory reviews of *Huck Finn* and of Twain.

Fisher, Marvin. "'Do Not Bring Your Dog': Mark Twain on the Manners of Mourning." In *Continuities and Ideas in American Literature*. Lanham, MD: University Press of America, 1986. Pp. 106–25. "The Tomb of Adam" sequence in *Innocents Abroad* exemplifies Twain's attack on false gentility as carried out through the funeral in *Huck Finn*.

Galligan, Edward L. "True Comedians and False: *Don Quixote* and *Huckleberry Finn*." *Sewanee Review*, 86, I (1977): 66–83. Huck and Jim show up Tom Sawyer's humor as cruel and false even better than Twain wished.

Ganzel, Dewey. *Mark Twain Abroad*. Chicago: University of Chicago Press, 1968. Excellent background on the conscious creation of a persona and philosophy in *Innocents Abroad*.

Gibson, William M. *Theodore Roosevelt among the Humorists: W. D. Howells, Mark Twain, and Mr. Dooley*. Knoxville: University of Tennessee Press, 1980. Insights by contemporary humorists on the politician's achievements.

Goudie, Andrea. "'What Fools These Mortals Be!' A Puckish Interpretation of Mark Twain's Narrative Stance." *Kansas Quarterly*, 5, IV (1973): 19–31. Relates Twain's humorousness to Puck's role in Shakespeare's play.

Grenander, M. E. "'Five Blushes, Ten Shudders and a Vomit': Mark Twain on Ambrose Bierce's *Nuggets and Dust*." *American Literary Realism, 1870–1910*, 17 (1984): 170–79. Studies relations between Twain and Bierce.

Gribben, Alan *Mark Twain's Library: A Reconstruction*. Boston: G. K. Hall, 1980. A massive and informative listing of volumes related to Twain with annotations on his reading of and response to them.

———. "Mark Twain Reads Longstreet's *Georgia Scenes*" in *Gyascutus: Studies in Antebellum Southern Humorous and Sporting Writing*, James. L. W. West, III, ed. Atlantic Highlands, NJ: Humanities Press, 1978. Pp. 103–11. Reading of the southwestern humorist by Twain.

Harris, Susan K. "Mark Twain's Bad Women." *Studies in American Fiction*, 13 (1985): 157–68. Treats Laura in *The Gilded Age* and Roxy in *Pudd'nhead Wilson* as showing that Twain adhered to the Victorian concept of woman's role.

Hawkins, Hunt. "Mark Twain's Involvement with the Congo Reform Movement: 'A Fury of Generous Indignation'." *New England Quarterly*, 51 (1978): 147–75. An extensive study of "King Leopold's Soliloquy."

Karnath, David. "Mark Twain's Implicit Theory of The Comic." *Mosaic*, 9 (1976): 207–18. Contends that reversing the reality of the fiction underlies Twain's sense of the comic.

Ketterer, David. "'Professor Baffin's Adventures' by Max Adeler: The Inspiration for *A Connecticut Yankee in King Arthur's Court?*" *Mark Twain Journal*, 24, I (Spring, 1986): 24–34. A valuable expansion of the work by Foster on these items reprinted in this volume.

Khouri, Nadia. "From Eden to the Dark Ages: Images of History in Mark Twain." *Canadian Review of American Studies*, 11 (1980): 151–74. Twain's methodology for handling the discontinuity between the American dream and its reality in his major works.

Kolb, Harold H. Jr. "Mark Twain, Huck Finn, and Jacob Blivens: Gilt-Edged, Tree-Calf Morality in *The Adventures of Huckleberry Finn*." *Virginia Quarterly Review*, 55 (1977): 653–69.

———. "Mere Humor and Moral Humor: The Example of Mark Twain." *American Literary Realism, 1870–1910*, 19 (1986): 52–64. A consideration of the nineteenth-century belief that humor was a low calling, shared by Twain himself, as opposed to the moral purpose which developed increasingly strongly in Twain after 1874.

Krauth, Leland. "Mark Twain: The Victorian of Southwestern Humor." *American Literature*, 54 (1982): 368–84. Twain avoided sensuality, as evident in his reworking of southwestern materials, and makes Huck genteel.

Lee, Mary K. "The Overt, Unreliable, Naive Narrator in the Tall Tale and *Huckleberry Finn*." *Mark Twain Journal*, 21, III (1983): 39.

Lenz, William. *Fast Talk & Flush Times: The Confidence Man as a Literary Convention*. Columbia, Missouri: University of Missouri Press, 1985. Sellers, Dilworthy, and the society of *Huck Finn* treated in relation to the southwestern tradition of fraud.

Lloyd, James B. "The Nature of Twain's Attack on Sentimentality in *The Adventures of Huckleberry Finn*." *University of Mississippi Studies in English*, 13 (1972): 59–63. How Twain balances head and heart through tears in *Huck Finn*.

Masters, Edgar Lee. *Mark Twain, A Portrait*. New York: Charles Scribner's Sons, 1938. Rpt. New York: Biblo & Tannen, 1966. Without historical insight or philosophical genius, Twain was a clown elevated above other comedians only by his pages about boys and the Mississippi.

Matheson, Terence J. "The Devil and Philip Traum: Twain's Satiric Purposes in *The Mysterious Stranger*." *Markham Review*, 12 (1982): 5–11. Theodor is an unreliable respondent to Young Satan's logic and the authorial voice is more ironic than has been presumed by critics.

Matthews, Brander. "The Penalty of Humor." In *Aspects of Fiction, and Other Ventures in Criticism*. New York: Charles Scribner's Sons, 1896. Pp. 43–56. Largely devoted to a historical survey of humorous writers concluding with a page or two on Twain.

Maxwell, D. E. S. "Twain as Satirist." In *American Fiction: The Intellectual Background*. New York: Columbia University Press, 1965; London: Routledge and Kegan Paul, 1965. Pp. 192–235; 292. Eighteenth-century satire related to Twain.

Selected Bibliography

Mencken, H. L. "The Burden of Humor." *Smart Set*, XXXVIII (February, 1913): 151–54. Rpt. in Anderson (1971), 327–31. *Huck Finn, Life on the Mississippi, Connecticut Yankee*, and *Captain Stormfield's Visit to Heaven* "are alone worth more, as works of art and as criticisms of life, than the whole out-put of Cooper, Irving, Holmes, Mitchell, Stedman, Whittier and Bryant." Also Rpt. in *A Mencken Chrestomathy, Edited and Annotated by the Author* (New York: Alfred A. Knopf, 1967), p. 485.

Michelson, Bruce. "Ever Such a Good Time: The Structure of Mark Twain's *Roughing It*." *Dutch Quarterly Review of Anglo-American Letters*, 17 (1987): 182–99. The work moves from fun and playfulness to disillusion to thirty chapters of less enjoyable reality.

Morris, Wright. "The Lunatic, the Lover, and the Poet." *Kenyon Review*, XXVII (Autumn 1965): 727–37; rpt. in *Twainian*, XXVI (January–February, 1967). Pudd'nhead Wilson charts Twain's personal crisis.

Nolle-Fischer, Karen. "Selling Mark Twain's *Connecticut Yankee* in America: Marketing and Illustrations." *Revue Francaise d'Etudes Americaines*, 8 (1983): 265–81. Illustrations help interpret two impulses in the novel, one toward popularity and the other toward populism.

O'Connor, Mrs. T. P. "Sir Walter Scott and the Civil War." In *My Beloved South*. New York and London: G. P. Putnam's Sons, 1913. Treats *Life on the Mississippi* as unjust to the South.

Parker, Hershel. "Pudd'nhead Wilson: Jack-leg Author, Unreadable Text, and Sense-Making Critics." *Flawed Texts and Verbal Icons: Literary Authority in American Fiction*. Evanston: Northwestern University Press, 1984. Pp. 115–45. Sees attempts to find continuity in this novel at variance with the evidence.

Pullen, John J. *Comic Relief: The Life and Laughter of Artemus Ward, 1834–1867*. Hamden: Archon, 1983. An interpretive study of one of Twain's most important predecessors as a literary comedian.

Selected Bibliography

Quirk, Thomas. "'Learning a Nigger to Argue': Quitting *Huckleberry Finn*." *American Literary Realism, 1870–1910*, 20 (Fall 1987): 18–33. Adding the King Sollermun chapter to *Huck Finn* at the end of composition shows Twain's despair over the imperfectibility of his characters, muffled because he had decided not to conclude with Jim being lynched as a final nihilistic statement.

Regan, Robert. "The Reprobate Elect in *The Innocents Abroad*." *American Literature*, 54 (1982): 240–57. Twain's attack on the genteel pilgrims through a management of facts, intensified from the letters to the book.

Robinson, Forrest G. "'Seeing the Elephant'," Some Perspectives on Mark Twain's *Roughing It*." *American Studies*, 21, II (1980): 43–64. A somber view finding paradoxical moral ambiguity in western experiences such as the Slade episode and the coyote description. The mining frontier was an unpleasant practical joke replayed over and over on the innocent self.

Rosen, Robert C. "Mark Twain's 'Jim Blaine and His Grandfather's Ram'." *College Literature*, 11 (1984): 191–94. The story is a logical and artistic expression of the skeptical state of mind.

Rourke, Constance. *American Humor: A Study of the National Character*. Garden City: Doubleday, 1953 [1931]. A broad history of American humor emphasizing its relation to folk-tales and myths among other elements of backwoods humor.

Rowe, Joyce A. "Mark Twain's Great Evasion: *Adventures of Huckleberry Finn*." *Equivocal Endings of Classic American Novels: The Scarlet Letter, Adventures of Huckleberry Finn, The Ambassadors, The Great Gatsby*. London: Cambridge University Press, 1988. Pps. 46–74. The Phelps Farm episode shows the impossibility of the raft ideal being realized.

Rowlette, Robert. "Mark Ward on Artemus Twain: Twain's Literary Debt to Ward." *American Literary Realism, 1870–1910*, 6 (Winter 1973): 13–25. Substantial attention to *Roughing It* to illustrate Twain's borrowings from Ward.

Sax, Richard A. "Living in the Realm of Possibility: Beriah Sellers in *The Gilded Age*." *Mark Twain Journal*, 21, IV (1983): 38–41. Treats Sellers as a positive rather than negative figure.

Schmitz, Neil. "On American Humor." *Partisan Review*, 47 (1980): 559–77. Only touching lightly on *Huck* while surveying American literature, this article contends that Huck's language is a metaphor undercutting formal speech and metaphoric social transactions.

Seelye, John. "The Craft of Laughter: Abominable Showmanship and *Huckleberry Finn*." *Thalia*, 4, I (1981): 19–25. Practical jokes in *Huck Finn*.

Sewell, David R. *Mark Twain's Languages, Discourse, Dialogue, and Linguistic Variety.* Berkeley: University of California Press, 1987. Language, grammar, syntax, and diction are identified as central to Twain's concept of social corruption and truth and thus to the plots and meanings of his stories as well as his methods as a writer.

Sloane, David E. E. *Adventures of Huckleberry Finn: American Comic Vision.* Boston: Twayne, 1988. Analysis of the novel in relation to historical sources and reader-response criticism.

———. "A Connecticut Yankee and Industrial America: Mark Twain's Lesson." *Essays in Arts and Sciences*, 10 (1982): 197–205. Patriotic pride in industrialism, as shown in other American writers and Twain's Yankee, potentially leads to catastrophe.

———. *The Literary Humor of the Urban Northeast, 1830–1890.* Baton Rouge: Louisiana State University Press, 1982. Establishes a continuum of northeastern urban and literary humor which places Twain's short writings and burlesques in that tradition.

———. *Mark Twain as a Literary Comedian.* Baton Rouge: Louisiana State University Press, 1979. Identifies the ethical outcomes of Twain's relation to literary comedy as defined through a close study of Twain's predecessor Artemus Ward.

———. "Mark Twain's Comedy: The 1870's." *Studies in American Humor*, 2, III (January 1876): 146–56. By warping real events into comic fantasy, Twain's semifictional travel works raised him above contemporary literary comedians of the decade such as Nasby, Kerr, and Adeler.

Smith, Henry Nash. *Mark Twain's Fable of Progress: Political and Economic Ideas in a Connecticut Yankee.* New Brunswick: Rutgers University Press, 1964. A careful analysis of the novel as a political and economic fable.

Smith, Lawrence R. "Mark Twain's 'Jumping Frog': Toward an American Heroic Ideal." *Mark Twain Journal*, 20, I (1979): 15–18. Sees Twain's opposition to artificial ideals.

Sousa, Raymond J. "'Be It What It Will, I'll Go To It Laughing': Mark Twain's Humorous Sense of Life." *Thalia*, 2, I–II (1979): 17–24. Applies late Freud to *Roughing It*.

Stahl, John Daniel. "Mark Twain and Female Power." *Studies in American Fiction*, 16 (1988): 51–63. Explicates "A Memorable Midnight Experience" and *1601* in terms of women's role in society.

Steinbrink, Jeffrey. "How Mark Twain Survived Sam Clemens' Reformation." *American Literature*, 55 (1983): 299–315. Sees Twain as stabilizing as a humorist while courting Livy Langdon.

Strong, Leah A. *Joseph Hopkins Twichell: Mark Twain's Friend and Pastor.* Athens: University of Georgia Press, 1966. Twichell was "Harris" in *A Tramp Abroad*, first recipient of *1601*, and influential on Twain's philosophy particularly as expressed through Hank Morgan in *A Connecticut Yankee*.

Sumida, Steven H. "Reevaluating Mark Twain's Novel of Hawaii." *American Literature*, 61 (1989): 586–609. Explores a "lost" Twain novel on Hawaii from 1884 and suggests its views on natives and missionaries.

Tanner, Tony. "Mark Twain." In *The Reign of Wonder: Naivety and Reality in American Literature.* Cambridge: Cambridge University Press, 1965. Pp. 97–183. Discusses the implications of the vernacular from a critical but not a historical or linguistic viewpoint.

Tenney, Thomas A. "Black Writers on *Adventures of Huckleberry Finn*: One Hundred Years Later." *Mark Twain*

Journal: Special Issue, 22, II (1984). Subsequently reprinted as a book by Duke University Press, this symposium offers a wide splay of perspectives on Twain's novel in relation to Afro-Americans.

———. *Mark Twain: A Reference Guide*. Boston: G. K. Hall, 1977. An invaluable compendium of annotated abstracts of Mark Twain criticism from 1858 to 1975, subsequently updated in *American Literary Realism, 1870–1910* and the *Mark Twain Journal*.

Thoreson, Trygve. "'Virtuous According to Their Lights': Women in Mark Twain's Early Work." *Mark Twain Journal*, 21, IV (1983): 52–6. Finds evidence of kind treatment of women of dubious virtue in 1860's sketches versus humor directed at the genteel.

Tulip, James. "Huck Finn—The Picaresque Saint." *Balcony/The Sydney Review*, No. 2 (Winter, 1965): 13–18. Twain and Huck are fused in their continual escaping from the past in picaresque moments; the novel is at its best when Twain's voice supersedes Huck's.

Vallin, Marlene Boyd. "Mark Twain, Platform Artist: A Nineteenth-Century Preview of Twentieth-Century Performance Theory." *Text and Performance Quarterly*, 9 (1989): 322–33. Indicates how Twain diverged from common platform styles in his era, anticipating in his relation to the audience twentieth-century modes.

Wade, Clyde. "Twain's Psychic Farce." *Papers of the Arkansas Philological Association*, 13 (1987): 59–66. On the power of irrational humor in "The Jumping Frog," "Grandfather's Old Ram," and "Jim Baker's Blue-Jay Yarn."

Westendorp, Tjebbe A. "'He Backed Me into a Corner and Blockaded Me with a Chair': Strategies of Mark Twain's Literary Campaigns." *Dutch Quarterly Review of Anglo-American Letters*, 16 (1986): 22–36. How Twain uses narrative modes.

Wetzel-Sahm, Brigit. "Deadpan Emotionalized: American Humor in a German Translation of Mark Twain's 'Journalism in Tennessee'." *Svensak Akademiens Handlinger*, 5 (1988): 3–

Selected Bibliography

16. Shows how a German translator changed the story for a German readership.

Wilson, James D. *A Reader's Guide to the Short Stories of Mark Twain.* Boston: G. K. Hall, 1987. A useful guide to plots and characters along with summaries of Twain's shorter works.

———. "In Quest of Redemptive Vision: Mark Twain's *Joan of Arc.*" *Tennessee Studies in Literature*, 20 (1978): 181–98. Sees the book as a religious-historical allegory which is hopeful rather than pessimistic.

"Yankee Humor." *Quarterly Review*, CXXII (January, April 1867): 212–37. One of the earliest and most accurate attempts to analyze American literary humor from the British perspective and thus useful background on Twain as a literary comedian.

Zall, P. M. *Mark Twain Laughing: Humorous Anecdotes by and about Samuel L. Clemens.* Knoxville: University of Tennessee Press, 1985. A usefully condensed collection of brief comic statements, stories, and jokes by Twain, most of which are available elsewhere.

INDEX

Abbott, Jacob, *Little Rollo* books, 137*ff.*, 151(n4)
Academy, The (London), xxii, 467–8
Adams, Charles Francis, Jr., 88
Adams, Henry, 51
   The Education, 45, 47
Ade, George, xv, xx, xxi–xxii, 189–92
Adeler, Max (Charles H. Clark), xxi, 139
   The Fortunate Island, 265–70
Aguinaldo, 493, 500
Albert, Prince, 100
Aldrich, T.B., 140, 170–73
Alger, Horatio, and novels by, 137–38*ff*, 144, 510
Allgemeine Zeitung (Munich), 420
Alta California, 14, 40, 109, 123–24, 196
Ament, John C., xix
Ament, Rev. Mr., 497
American humor, xiv, xviii, xxii–xxiii, 19, 34, 59–60, 127–128, 158–164, 183–84*ff.*, 396–97, 409–22
Americanism, 73, 80, 121–24, 158–60, 274, 330–32, 346–47, 395, 402, 409–10, 428–29, 436, 458–60, 467–68, 499–500
American Literary Scholarship: An Annual, xxv

AME Zion Church, 581
"Angel Fish, The," 588
Angel's Camp, 4
Animals, 6–29
Arabian Nights, 467
Aristophanes, 178
Arnold, Matthew, 278, 435
Arvin, Newton, 220
The Athenaeum (London), 135–36
Atkinson Society, 497
Atlantic Monthly, xi, 102, 156, 161, 166–67, 381, 471, 581
Auerbach, Eric, 43
Austen, Jane, 221, 233–34, 310
Austrian situation, 405
Authority, authoritarian, xvi, 586, *passim*.

Baender, Paul, 24
Baetzhold, Howard, 279, 295
Bailey, James M., 140
Baldwin, J. G., *Flush Times*, 90
Baldwin, Judge, 428
Bangs, John Kendrick, xv, xix, 496–503
Barns, Pike, 366
Barnum, P.T., xix, xxii, 111–115, 118, 122–23, 364, 386(n34)
Beadle's dime novels, 190
Beard, Dan, 278, 392
Beckett, *Endgame*, 537
Beecher, H.W., 139–40, 481–82

Index

Bellemy, Edward, *Looking Backward*, 275
Bellemy, Gladys, 6, 469
Bellow, Saul, *Henderson the Rain King*, 291
Ben Hur, 308
Bennett, Arnold, 222
Benton, Joel, 198*ff.*
Bentson (Blanc), Mme. Th., xvii, 410–13, 417
Berzon, Judith, 375
The Bible, 450–51
Bierstadt, A., 121
Billings, Josh, 110, 116, 127, 158
Bishop, Levi, *The Poetical Works of . . .*, 298–99
The Black Avenger, 139
The Black Crook, 122
Blackwell, Elizabeth, 577
Blackwood's Magazine, xvii, xxii–xxiii, 177–88
Blair, Walter, xiv, xvi, xx, xxv, 137–54, 236
Blémont, Emile, 413, 416–17
Bliss, Elisha, 31–32
Boatright, Mody C., 51
Boone, Joseph A., 587
Booth, Edwin, 338–39, 343
The Boston *Carpet-Bag*, xi
Botkin, B.A., xiv
Bourget, Paul, *Outre-Mer*, 296
Bowles, Sam, 343
Boxer Rebellion, xix, 497
Boy, bad, 513–16, 536, *see also* Boy books and individual titles
Boy books, *see* Children's books
Branch, Edgar M., xvi, xviii, xx, 3–29, 110, 296
Bridges, Robert, xxi, 213–16
Bridges [Thomas] and burlesque classics, 182
British humor, 32–34, 39–40, 177*ff.*
Literature, 578
Brooks, Van Wyck, xxv, 219, 571–72, 575, 587
Brown, Phoebe, Autobiography, 312(n23)
Brown, Sterling, 368
Brown, Tom, 180–81
Browne, Charles F. (Artemus Ward), xi, xx, xxii–xxiii, 7, 14, 16–18, 22, 109–110, 113*ff.*, 121–125, 135, 158, 163, 203, 458, 527
Browne, J. Ross, 37
Bryce, Gen., 296
Budd, Louis, xx, xxi, 85–108, 117, 274, 513
Buffalo, NY, 85*ff.*
    Buffalo *Express*, 86*ff.*, 425
Bunner, H.C., 478
Bunyan, Paul, 233
Burbank, A.P., 316
Burhams, Clinton, Jr., 469
Burlesque, 32–49, 110*ff.*, 124, 141, 277, 279–80, 307, 400, 580, *passim*.
Burroughs, William, 231
Burton, *A Pilgrimage to Al-Medinah and Meccah*, 37
Busch, Moritz, 417

Cable, G.W., 207, 265, 306, 351–52, 560
Californian, 4
Calvinism, 138
Captain Cuttle, in Brougham's *Domby and Son*, 18
Cardwell, Guy A., 307
Cargill, Oscar, 47
Carlyle, Thomas, *French Revolution*, 262
    Sartor Resartus, 435
Cashel Byron's Profession, 432
Caster, Andrew, *Pearl Island*, 299

Index

Cervantes, *Don Quixote*, 33, 35, 222, 260, 338, 422, 460–61
Chadwick, George W., 366
Chamberlain, Mr., 490*ff.*
Champion, Anthony, 32
"Charity Organization Society," xix
Chatto & Windus, 205, 414
Chaucer, 178
Chesnutt, Charles W., 363, 365
"Chicago," xxiii, 428
    Chicago *Times*, 105
Child, Francis J., and Whittier Dinner speech, 175(n14)
Children's books, 136, 137–154
China, xix
Christianity, xiv, xvi, 96, 425, 434–35, 471–85, 489–503, 527–38, *see also* Religion
Christian Science, 278, 435
Circus, 122–123
Civil War, Post-Civil War, 45, 120, 156–57, 288, 501
Claggett, 424
Clemens, Clara, 334, 443–44
Clemens, Jane Lampton, xi, 346, 542, 559–60
Clemens, Jean, xii, 542, 581
Clemens, John Marshall, xi, 64, 156, 427, 429
Clemens, Langdon, xi
Clemens, Olivia Langdon, xi–xii, xiv, 85, 206, 225, 342, 439–48, 463, 510–11, 529, 535–36, 542, 552–54, 560, 571–91, 584
Clemens, Orion, xi, 11, 17, 19, 21, 313*ff.*, 334, 542, 554
Clemens, Pamela, 451–52
Clemens, Samuel Langhorne, *passim*, 155–58, 436, 439–55, 541–69, 571–91
    Cats, 449
    Characters of, *see* individual books
    Cigars, 453–54
    Literary opinions, 295–312
    Person, Personality, *passim*, xx, 18–22, 157, 337–47, 404, 450, 514–17*ff.*, 533–35, 551–52, 574*ff.*, 584–88
    Pessimism, 457*ff.*, 513–38
    Works of
        "About Cities in the Sun," 309
        "A Cure for the Blues," 309, 311(n19)
        "Adventures in Hayti," 87
        Adventures of Huckleberry Finn, xii, xiii, xviii, xx, xxi, xxv, 54, 60–64, 67, 90, 104, 109, 186, 208, 213–16, 217–34, 235–64, 273, 282–85, 290–91, 305, 327–28, 349, 359–60, 372–74, 377, 392, 396–400, 420, 423, 429, 431, 433, 463, 465–66, 507, 517–18, 525, 542, 545, 548–50, 555, 576, 580–87
        Adventures of Tom Sawyer, xii, xvi, xx, 104, 135–154, 155, 161, 186, 191, 235, 290, 301, 327, 359, 392, 397–99, 413, 417, 418, 423, 429, 433, 463–65, 507, 514–15, 583
        Huck, 144, 150
        Structure, 145–47
        Tom as bad boy, 141–44, 148
        American Claimant, xii, xvii, xxiii, 313–36, 340–41, 392, 429, 433

Index

"An Appeal on...
 Suffrage... to Boys,"
 98
"Barnum's First Speech
 in Congress," 118–123,
 128
"Bishop Southgate's
 Matinee," 122
"Bloody Massacre," 118,
 542
"Burlesque Review of
 Allen Bay," 307
"Cannibalism in the
 Cars," 115–116, 118–
 120
"Captain Stormfield's
 Visit to Heaven," 433,
 506, 543
"The Celebrated Jumping
 Frog of Calaveras
 County," xi, xviii, xx,
 3–29, 119, 195, 212,
 408, 410–13, 416–17,
 421, 548
    Andrew Jackson, 10,
     19–21, 23, *passim*.
    Dan'l Webster, 13–14,
     23, 28(n19), *passim*.
    Digression, 16
Christian Science, 425,
 543
"The Chronicle of Young
 Satan," 473, 482, 528–
 30, 544
A Connecticut Yankee,
 xii, xxi–xxii, xxiii, 71–
 73, 81, 90, 101, 183–84,
 222, 263–64, 265–70,
 271–94, 319, 326, 332,
 392, 398–99, 430–32,
 460–61, 517, 520, 542,
 545, 548
"Cruel Treatment of a
 Boy," 426

"A Curious Dream," 87
"The Curious Republic of
 Gondour," 102–03
"The Czar's Soliloquy,"
 426
"The Dandy Frightening
 the Squatter," xi, 74
"The Death of Jean," 506
"Defense of Gen.
 Funston," 536, 543
"A Dog's Tale," 426
"Earthquake Almanac,"
 11
Eve's Diary, 462, 506
Fables of Man, 507
"The Facts Concerning
 the Late Carnival of
 Crime in Connecticut,"
 xxiv, 161, 258
"Fenimore Cooper's
 Literary Offenses," 506,
 508
Following the Equator,
 xii, 305, 392–94, 404,
 406, 426–27, 479, 543
The Gilded Age, xi, xxiv,
 89–91, 93–99, 101–02,
 113, 116–118, 155, 162,
 191, 313, 328, 398,
 412–13, 417
"The Great Beef
 Contract," 99
"The Great Dark," 548
"Hellfire Hotchkiss,"
 589(n4)
A Horse's Tale, 426
"How Are the Mighty
 Fallen!," 111–112
"How to Tell a Story,"
 16–18, 371, 560
"Huck Finn and Tom
 Sawyer Among the
 Indians," 238
Indiantown, 515

Index

Innocents Abroad, xi, xx, 31, 38, 40, 42, 75–79, 88–89, 120–128, 158, 183, 191, 197, 222, 272, 283–84, 392–94, 398, 403–04, 408, 410, 417, 421, 460–62, 465, 481, 513, 527, 542
"Inspired Humor," 86
"Is Shakespeare Dead?," 543
Joan of Arc, xii, xvii, xx, xxiii, 225, 392, 399, 430–31, 462, 507, 512, 517, 543, 576, 587
"King Leopold's Soliloquy," 426, 543
Letters from the Earth, 506, 520, 523, 536
Life on the Mississippi (Old Times on the Mississippi), xii, xvii, xxii, xxiii, 46, 156, 185–86, 191, 235, 250, 254, 288, 328, 404, 413, 418, 423, 427, 429, 433, 507
"The Man that Corrupted Hadleyburg," xvi, xx, 462, 464, 469–88, 506, 516, 520
Mark Twain's Autobiography, xx, xxiv, 171, 256, 506, 519–20, 541–69
Mark Twain's Burlesque Autobiography, 88, 550, 565(n11), 566(n15)
Mark Twain's Travels with Mr. Brown, 42, 115
"Memoranda," 87–88
"The £1,000,000 Bank-Note," 307
"The Monopoly Speaks," 86
The Mysterious Stranger and "#44," xx, 264, 433–34, 458, 506, 517–38, 544–45
"Open Letter to Commodore Vanderbilt," 85, 88
"The Petrified Man," 118
"Petticoat Government," 117–18
The Prince and the Pauper, xii, 158, 161–62, 218, 222, 225, 234, 272, 274–75, 326, 333, 399, 430
"The Private History of a Campaign that Failed," 256–58
Pudd'nhead Wilson, xii, xix, 264, 349, 351–57, 359–88, 425, 476, 508, 510, 543, 576, 581
"Punch, Brothers, Punch," 105
"The Refuge of the Derelicts," 544
Roughing It, xi, xviii, 31–49, 68–70, 88–90, 118, 157, 191, 205, 392, 398, 403–04, 414, 429, 520, 542, 551
Slade, 44–45
"Running for Governor," 87
"Schoolhouse Hill," 523–24
"The Secret History of Eddypus, . . .," 544, 548
"The Secret of Dr. Livingston's . . . Exile," 92

623

Index

Sketches, New and Old, 104
"A Small Piece of Spite," 15
The Stolen White Elephant, 426
"The Story of the Bad Little Boy," 141
"The Story of the Good Little Boy," 141
"The Stupendous Procession," 544
"The Temperance Crusade and Woman's Rights," 99
"The $30,000 Bequest," 70–71, 506
"3,000 Years Among the Microbes," 506, 544, 548
Tom Sawyer Abroad, xxii, 467–68, 543
Tom Sawyer, Detective, 543, 555
"To My Missionary Critics," 506, 543
"To the Person Sitting in Darkness," xii, xv, xix, 367, 426, 489–503, 506, 536, 543
"Tragic Tale of the Fishwife," 208
A Tramp Abroad, xi, 158, 206, 235, 303, 392, 404, 418
Travels with Mr. Brown, 284
"A True Story," xi, 372, 381, 548, 580–81
"A Trying Situation," 208
"Tsar's Soliloquy," 543
"An Unbiased Criticism," 5

"The United States of Lyncherdom," 377
"A Voice for Setchell," 18
"The War Prayer," 506, 527, 535–36
What Is Man?, xii, xv, 375, 458, 482, 507, 510, 543
"Which Was It?," 515–16, 537, 548
"Which Was the Dream?," 515–16
Whittier Dinner Speech, 167–69, 175n
see also Lecturing
Clemens, Susy, xii, 225, 510, 541–42, 548, 552, 555, 560
Clemens, Will, xvii, 152(n19), 193–212
Cleveland, Mrs., 439
President, 442–44
Ruth, 442–44
Clubs, English, 178, 205, 352, American, 433
Coleman, Rufus, xvi, 165–176
Combe, William, *The Tour of Dr. Syntax*, 32–35, 39–40, 42
Comedy, humor, xiii, xvi–xviii, xxi, xxv, 17–19, 24, 56–57, 60–61, 127–128, 135, 159–64, 178–88, 233, 260, 353, 400–06, 457, 465, 467–68, 541–69, *passim.*
Communism, 218, 220, 226–27
Confederacy, 218
Connolly, Cyril, 221–22
Conservatism, xxi, 85–108, 274
Constable, Major, 343
Cooper, Anna Julia, 365–66
Cooper, J.F., 224, 310, 324, 405, 435, 454

Index

Natty Bumppo, 45, 513
Indians, 89
Cord, Mary Ann, 572, 576, 580–81, 587
Cotton, Charles, 181–83
Courant (Hartford), 91, 93*ff.*, 100
Courier, Hannibal (MO), 156
Covici, Pascal, xx, 51–84, 469–70
Cox, James M., xxi, 271–94, 586
Crabbe, George, 32
Crane, Steven, 477–78, 508
Crane, Susan, 573, 576
Crane, Theodore, 280
Croker, Richard, 426, 496
"Crow, Jim," see "Jim Crow" Laws
Cuba, 490*ff.*
Culture, xvii
Cumberland, George, 32
Curtis, G.W., 344
Curtis, Lillian E., *Forget-Me-Not*, 299–300
Curzon, *Monasteries of the Levant*, 37
Cutter, Bloodgood, 298, 300
Czar, The, 490

Daily Advertiser (Boston), 167
Daly, Augustin, 316
Da Ponte, Durant, xx
Darwin, Charles, 160
Dead Souls, 222
DeFoe, Daniel, 422
 Moll Flanders, 124
 Robinson Crusoe, 419
De Forest, John W., *Honest John Vane*, 98
Democratic ideals, xix, xxi, xxiii, 89–90, 97–98, 100–105, 277*ff.*, 287, 320–23, 402*ff.*, 429–32, 437, *see also* Equality
De Quille, Dan, 89

Derby, George H. (John Phoenix), xi, 163
DeVoto, B., 51, 60, 126, 172, 219, 274, 510–12, 517, 551, 571–72, 575, 588
Dewey, Admiral, 491–92, 501
Dickens, Charles, 34
 Hard Times, 127, 131(n20), 163
 Pickwick Papers, 222
 Sam Weller, 35
Dickinson, Anna, 573, 577
Dickinson, Emily, 466
Dixon, George, 366
Dixon, Thomas, 369
Dr. Livingstone's Travels in Africa, 190
Dodge, Mary A., *A New Atmosphere*, 589(n2)
Dreiser, Theodore, 223, 477, 508
 Sister Carrie, xxii
Du Bois, W.E.B., 367, 379–82
Dufferin, Lord, 344
Dumas, A., 260*ff.*
Dunbar, Paul Laurence, 366, 377–78
Duneka, F., 522, 587
Durham, Earl of, *see* Lampton, James; Leathers, Jesse

East, Yankee, Brahmin, 44, 52, 99, 181, 183*ff.*, 223, 225, 271*ff.*, 401, 460, 467, 577
Eddy, Mary Baker, 278, 302, 308, 435
Edison, Thomas A., 439
Eliot, George, 310
Eliot, T.S., 221, 225–26
Ellison, Ralph, 230
Elmira Female College, 577
Elmore, James B., *Love Among the Mistletoe*, 300–01
Emerson, Everett, 571

Index

Emerson, R.W., 167–68, 409, 421
England, 99–100, 160, 222, 319–20*ff.*, 341–42, 407, 421, 451
English humor, 32–39*ff.*, 56–59, 446–48, *see also* British humor
Epstein, C.F., *Deceptive Distinctions: Sex, Gender and the Social Order*, 573
Equality, 46–47, 56, *passim*.
Europe, xiv, xvii, 35–37, 75–77, 123–27, 342, 406, 409–22, 460, 490*ff.*
Evening Post (New York), 93
Exaggeration, 73, 419, *passim*.
Express, (Buffalo), 86*ff.*

Fairbanks, Mrs. Mary, 303, 514, 572–73, 578
Farrell, James T., xxiii
Faulkner, William, 223
"Faust, Carl," Twain pseudonym, 451
Fawcett, Edgar, xxi
Ferguson, DeL., 535
Fiedler, Leslie, xx, xxi, 217–34, 571, 585
Fielding, Henry, 178, 422
  Joseph Andrews, 33, 56, 137
Finlay, Frank D. (*Northern Whig*, Belfast), 100
Fishkin, Shelley Fisher, xix, 359–88
Fisk, Jim, 88
FitzGerald, Edward, 299
Florida, Missouri, xi, 155, 557
Folk humor, 74, *passim*.
Foster, Edward P., xxi, 265–70
France, *see* Europe
Franklin, Benjamin, 74, 327, 565(n5)
Franklin, John Hope, 361

Frederickson, George, 361*ff.*
French language, *see* Language, French
Freud, Sigmund, 221
Freytag (Leipzig), 417
Frohman, Daniel, 316
Fun, 34

Gaines, "General," 559
Galaxy Magazine, xxi, 87, 89, 296
Ganzel, Dewey, 121
Garnham, L.W., 302–03
Gay, Mary A.H., *Prose and Poetry*, 301
Genteel, xxiii, 219, 240, 277, 463
German, 416–18*ff.*, 423, 448, *see also* Europe
Gibson, William, xxiv, 521–25*ff.*, 534–35
Gilbert, Sandra, 579
Gillis, Jim, 5, 7, 545
Gillman, Susan, 369
Gilpin, William, 32
Gleason, Rachael, 573, 577
Godkin, E.L., 97
Godwin, Parke, 212
Goldoni, 159
Goldsmith, 310
  The Vicar of Wakefield, 479
Goodman, Joseph T., 4, 11, 424
Gough, John B., 199*ff.*
Gould, Jay, 88
de Graffigny, Madame, 411
Grand, Sarah, *The Heavenly Twins*, 295
Grant, U.S., 100, 102, 159, 170, 394, 435, 440–442
Greeley, Horace, 92, 343
Gribben, Alan, xvi, xxiv, 295–312, 533, 575–76
Grimm, Clyde, xvii, xxiii, 313–36
Gross, Theodore, 368*ff.*

Index

Gubar, Susan, 579
Gymnasium (Paderborn), 420

Hale, E.E., 166
Hall, Fred J., 308, 514
Halstead, Murat, 343–45
Hammond, Edward P., *Sketches of Palestine*, 297, 301–02
Hannibal, Missouri, xi, 105, 155, 235, 262, 289, 430, 441, 451, 516, 536, 550, 554
Harper, Joseph W., 343
Harper's Uniform Edition of Twain's Works and contract with, 192, 391–92*ff.*, 505–06, 535
Harper's Weekly and *Monthly*, xv, xix, 366, 415, 471, 479, 489–503, 587
Harris, Frank, 222
Harris, G.W., 53*ff.*, 62
Harris, Joel Chandler, 231, 368, 558
Harris, Susan, xvi, xx, 469–88
Harte, Bret, 7, 89, 157, 193, 310, 343, 346, 351, 412, 478
Hartford, Connecticut, *see* Nook Farm
Harvard, 367
Harvey, George, 546
Haweis, H.R., 205
Hawley, Gen., 207, 452
and "Beautiful Snow," 207
Hawthorne, N., 51, 62, 220, 224, 409, 433, 478
"Young Goodman Brown," 477
Hay, John, 207, 343, 345–46
Heart, 66, 235*ff.*
Hemingway, Ernest, 223–24
Henderson, Archibald, xvii, 409–422, 580
Herald, (New York), 81

Herlihy, Capt., 500
Hero, 46
Hicks, Granville, 220
Higginson, Ella, 478
Higginson, T.W., 166, 171
Hill, Hamlin, xxiv, 301, 506–39, 519–24, 535*ff.*, 571–72, 575, 578
Hobbey, Josephine, 546
Hoben, John B., 278
Holmes, O.W., 168, 397
Hooker, Isabella Beecher, 573, 577
Hooper, J.J., 53*ff.*
Hopkins, Pauline, 379, 381
Horner, John, 297, 305
Hornet, Demshain, 208–10
Houghton, Lord, 344
Howe, E.W., *The Story of a Country Town*, 312(n19)
Howe, Julia Ward, 169–70, 175(n20)
Howells, William Dean, xv, xxiv, 102, 104, 149, 155–64, 166*ff.*, 171, 173, 222, 272, 274, 288, 307, 309, 313*ff.*, 324, 366, 376, 385(n26), 391–408, 416, 432, 434–35, 479, 510, 534–35, 545, 548–49, 560, 572, 581, 583, 589(n4)
Huck Finn Pin, 227
Hughes, W.L., 413
Hume, D., *The Origin of Ideas*, 533
Hutchings, J.M., "Dr. Dotitdown," 35
Hutchins, Mr. Stillson, 342

Idealism, xiv
Illustrirte Zeitung (Leipzig), 420
L'Independence Belge, 415
Indians, 89

Index

Iowa-California Edition of Twain's works, xviii, 505*ff.*
Irving, Washington, 346, 409
Italy, *see* Europe, *Pudd'nhead Wilson*

Jackson, Andrew, 10*ff.*, 330
James, Henry, 51, 66, 73, 81, 221, 223, 233–34, 394, 431
   The American (Newman), 34, 78–80
   Portrait of a Lady (Isabel Archer), 47–48
James, William, 432
Jefferson, Joseph, 343
Jewett, S.O., *The Country of the Pointed Firs*, 589(n4)
Jews, 405, 426
"Jim Crow" Laws, 362*ff.*, 372
Joe Miller, 353, 458
Johnson, Andrew, 115
Johnson, Dr., 343
Johnston, Richard Malcolm, 211
Jones, A.W., 381
Jonson, Ben, 251
Joyce, John Alexander, *Edgar Allan Poe*, 302
Judy, 34

Kahn, Sholom, 507
Kaiser William II, 454–55, 490, 560
Kaplan, Justin, 507, 513, 519, 527, 571
Kaplan, Sydney Janet, *Feminine Consciousness . . .*, 575–76
Keifer, F.J., *The Legends of the Rhine*, 302–03
Kellner, Dr. Leon, 417, 420
Kenealy's fat boy, 340
Kennan, George, 279

Keokuk *Gate City*, 12, 42
Kerr, Orpheus C. (R.H. Newell), 120
Kirk, Ellen Olney, 478
Kirkland, Joseph, 478
Kiskis, Michael, xv, xx, xxiv, 541–569
Know-Nothings, xvi
Krause, Sydney, 295, 301
Krauth, Leland, 580, 582, 585
Kruger, Mr., 500

Ladies' Home Journal, The, xv, xix, 439–55
Lady Chatterley's Lover, 226
Lafon, Thomy, 366
Lampton, James, 313*ff.*, 334, 340–41
Lang, Andrew, 233
Langdon, Ida, 580
Langdon, Jervis, and family, 31, 85–86, 577, 579, 587, *see also* Clemens, Olivia
Langdon, Crane, Susan
Language, 67–70, 90, 115, 136, 162, 275*ff.*, 284*ff.*, 394–95, 416, 436–37, 458, 467, 552–53, 581
   French, 210–11, 413
Lawrence, D.H., 221
Leary, Kate, 302, 572–73
Leathers, Jesse, 314*ff.*, 324, 329, 334–35
Lecturing, xii, xvii, 157, 166, 175(n20), 193–212, 345, 453–54, 545
Le Sage, 422
Lewis, C.B. (M. Quad), 140–41
Lewis, Hattie, 578
Lewis, R.W.B., 469
Lewis, Sinclair, 73, 77–81
Life, xxi, 213–16, 219
Lincoln, A., 59, 159, 395, 494
Lincoln University, 381

628

Lippincott, *Haps and Mishaps . . . in Europe*, 37
Literary comedy, 109*ff.*
Little Eva, 137–138
Logan, Rayford, 361
London, Jack, 587
Longfellow, 165, 167–68, 223, 409
Longstreet, A.B., 53, 112
Lovingood, Sut, 54–55*ff.*, 74, 139, *see also* G.W. Harris
Lowell, J.R., 159, 223
Lucian, 178, 181
Lundt, Dorothy, 478
Lutz (Stuttgart), 417
Lux, M., 415
Lynching, 363*ff.*, 377
Lynn, Kenneth, xx, 51–52

Mabie, H.W., 171
MacDonald, George, *Robert Falconer*, 303–04
Macnaughton, William, 470–71, 507, 519
Malory, Sir Thomas, *Le Morte d'Arthur*, 265, 275–76, 467
Manhattan Club, 337
Mann (Leipzig), 417
Manners, 56
Mark Twain, *see* Clemens, Samuel L.
Mark Twain Journal, xxv
Mark Twain's Ausgewählte Humoristische Schriften, 417
Marx, Karl, 220–21
Mason, Capt., 442
Masses, 90, 103, 105*ff.*, 233, 262, 352, 458, 536
Masters, Edgar Lee, xxiii, 147
Mattheissen, F.O., 220–21
Matthews, Brander, xxiii, 392, 479

Maude, Thomas, 32
McAllister, Ward, 356
McCarthy, Sen. Joseph, 217, 227
McClure's, 471
McKinley, Pres., 439, 490*ff.*, 502
Meier, August, 361
Meine, Franklin, 51
Melville, H., 51, 62, 66, 220, 224, 271, 587
Mencken, H.L., xxiii, 80
Mercure de France, 414
Mergenthaler Linotype, 281, 342
Mikado, 484
Miles, Gen. Nelson A., story, 561–63
Miller, George E., *Luxilla*, 304
Miller, Henry, 227
Miller, Joe, *see* Joe Miller
Mills, S.M., *Palm Branches*, 304
Milton, John, 301, 394, 471
Paradise Lost, 530, 532
Missionary Herald, 480*ff.*
Mississippi River, xi, 53, 185–86, 235, 349, 459, 554–55
Missouri Democrat, 109, 116
Molière, 251, 422
Monroe Doctrine, 461
Monroe, Lewis, 166
Montesquieu, 411
Moore, Julia A., *The Sentimental Song Book*, 304–06
Morality, justice, *passim.*, 161, 355, 377, 391–408, 423–37
Morton, J. Sterling, 445–46
Mukherjee, Arun, *The Gospel of Wealth in the American Novel*, xxii
Mulford, Prentice, 157, 193
Murfree, M.N. (C.E. Craddock), 215
Murphy, Isaac, 366

NAACP, 228
Narrator, 41–46, 109–131, 279*ff.*, 293(n16), 545–52*ff.*, 562–63
Nasby, Petroleum V. (David R. Locke), 37, 120, 158
Nast, Thomas, 99, 343
Nebeker, Helen, 470
Negro, 58, 75, 111–12, 114–15, 217–34, 250, 352*ff.*, 359–88, 432, 467, 581, *see also* Race
New York School Board, 227–28
Noah, Mordecai, 166
Nook Farm, Hartford, CT, xi, xv, 105, 550, 578
Norris, Frank, 508
North, 289, 361, 396–97, *see also* East
North American Review, xii, 489, 496–97, 501, 546–47
Northcliffe, 460
Northeast humor, xiv, 564, *passim.*
Norton, C.E., 168
Nye, Bill, 211
Nye, Emma, 31
Nye, Sen. James W., 93

O'Brien, Edward J., 478–79
O'Connor, William Van, 221
"On the Steps of City Hall," 479
Optimism, pessimism, xv, 338–40, 556
Our Young Folks, 140, 165
Oxford University and degree, xii, 421, 560

Page, Thomas Nelson, 211, 368–69
Paige (James) Typesetter, xii, 280–81, 342, 509, 514, 542

Paine, Albert B., 219, 257, 424, 427, 522, 546, 551, 572
Pamela, 137
Parepa, 205
Parody, 87, *see also* Satire, Burlesque
Parrington, V.L., 45
Partington, Ike, 139
Persona, *see* Narrator
Pessimism, 462*ff.*, 514*ff.*, 541*ff.*, *see also* Optimism
Pettigrew, Sen., 497
Phelps, William Walter, 454–55
Philippine War, xix, 427, 489–503
Poe, E. A., 51, 233, 302, 409, 433, 479, *Tales*, 35, 224
Point of view, 41
Politics, political corruption, 91, 95–98, 100, 111–113, 118–120, 207, 287, 318–19, 331, 371–72, 424–25, 442, 543
Pomeroy, Sen. Samuel C., 93
Pond, Major, 207, 212, 444
Popularity, xvii, xx, xxi–xxii, 135, 391–438, *passim*, 536, *passim.*
Pritchett, V.S., 222
Punch, 34, 36
Punch and Judy, 34

Quaker City, 40, 125, *passim.*
Quarles, John A., farm, 256–58, 552, 555–56, 559
Quarry Farm, Elmira, NY, 444–45, 550, 576, 581

Rabelais, 178
Race, 352, 354–57, 359–88
Raymond, Mr. John, 315*ff.*, 337–39, *see also* Sellers, Col.
Read, Opie, *Mark Twain and I*, 130–31(n19)

Index

Realism, 43–44, 53–55, 60, 67, 121, 145, 356–57, 508, *passim*.
Reclam's *Universal-bibliothek*, 417.
Redpath, James, 197*ff*.
Regionalism, xxiv, 54–55, 91, 163, 395–97, 459, 513, *see also* Southwestern humor, West, Northeast humor, East
Reid, Whitelaw, 92–93, 343
Religion, 17, 21–22, 58, 105, 110, 126–127, 148, 232, 241, 267, 278, 433, 464, 517–38, 580, *see also* Christianity
Republican party, 92
Revue des Deux Mondes, 410–13
Rice, Prof. John T., 219
Richard III, 11, 21
Riley, James W., 17, 211
Robinson, E.A., 33
Robinson, Rowland E., 478
Rogers, Franklin, xvi, xviii, 31–49
Rogers, H.H., 509–11
Rogers, Mary, 573
Roosevelt, Theodore, 165, 340, 428
Ros, Imanda, *Irene Iddesleigh*, *Delina Delaney*, 297, 305–06
Royston, Samuel W., *The Enemy Conquered*, 306–07, 312(n19)
Rucker, Mary E., 470, 472*ff*.
Rule, Henry B., 469

Sacramento Union, 32, 39
St. Nicholas, 165
Sala, G. A., 344
Salomon, Ludwig, 419

Sandwich Islands (Hawaii), 24, 32, 92–93, 193–94, 196–97, 278
San Francisco, 527, in "Jumping Frog," 3–29
  Call, 4, 8–10, 157
  Dramatic Chronicle, 4, 11, 19–20
  White's Museum, 11
Satan, 426, 433, 469, 518–38, 532
Satire, 56*ff*., 87, 232, 236*ff*., 247, 277*ff*., 426, 486, 543–44, *passim*.
Schleich, *Psychopathik des Humors*, 418
Scott, Walter, 288, 310, 328, 343, 420
Scribner's magazine, 214
Seaver, Col., 343
Sellers, Col., xvii, xxiv, 162, 313–36, 337–41, 398–99, 412, 453, 556–57
Setchell, Dan, 17–18
Shakespeare, 159, 178, 557
Shannon, Joseph, 217, 227
Shelley, P.B. and Harriet, 402, 405
Shillaber, B.P., 152(n11), 166
Showalter, Elaine, 579
Simmons, 424
Sintenis, Franz, 419
Skandera-Trombley, Laura, xiv, xxiv–xxv
Slaves, slave-holding, 156, 242*ff*., 354–55, 359–88, 396–97, 400–01, 403–04, 429, 494, 545
Sloane, David E.E., xvi, xxv, 109–131
Smarr, Sam/Owsley shooting, 261–64
Smiley, Jim, 3, 15, 24, *passim*.

631

Smith, Henry Nash, xx, xxi, 42, 235–264, 274, 288–89
Society, 43–44, 52–54, 240*ff.*, 253, 266, 433
South, 241, 288–89, 351–57, 361*ff.*, 396–97, 401, 577
South Africa, 407, 490
Southern, the elder, 344
Southwestern humor, xiv, xx, 51–83, 353, 548, 564, 583, *passim.*
Spectator, The (London), 421
Speculation, invention, enterprise, 96, 279–287, 313–35, 398, *passim.*
Spofford, Harriet, 368
Springfield *Republican*, 86
Stanley, 205
Stedman, E.C., 288, 344
Stedman, S.O, *Allen Bay*, 307–08
Stendhal, 43
Sterne, Laurence, 34
Stockton, Frank, 368
Stoddard, C.W., 157, 193
Stowe, H.B., *Uncle Tom's Cabin*, 231, 352
    Sunny Memories of Foreign Lands, 37
Strong, Leah, xiv
Structure of works, 31–50, 137–54, 235*ff.*, 247, 392–94, 404, 472*ff.*, 479, 544–47
Subscription books, 189–92, 391
Suggs, Simon, 55*ff.*, 67–68, 72, 81, 139, *see also* J.J. Hooper
Sumner, Charles, 395
Swift, Jonathan, xiv, 59, 422, 435

Tägliche Rundschau (Leipzig), 420

Tammany, 426, *see also* Tweed
Tarkington, Booth, 153(n23), 166
Tauchnitz, 205, 417
Taylor, Ann E., 588
Taylor, Bayard, *Views A-Foot*, 37
Taylor, Howard, 297
Tenney, Thomas, *Mark Twain: A Reference Guide*, xxv
Thackeray, William, 34, 163, 394
Thaler, Carl von, 418
Thanet, Octave, 478
Thompson, William T., *Major Jones*, 53, 55, 64–66, 74
Thomson, Mortimer, *Doesticks, What He Says*, 121
Thoreau, H.D., 431, 435
Thus Spake Zarathustra, 435
Tichborne Claimant, *see* Lampton, James; Leathers, Jesse
Ticknor, C., 171–72
Toledo *Blade*, 86
Tourgee, Albion W., 385(n26)
Traubel, Horace, *see* Whitman, Walt
Travers' stammer, 345
Treasure Island, 222
Trescott, Lewis E., 298
Tribune (New York), 92–93
Trilling, Lionel, xviii, 46, 221
Trowbridge, John T., xvi, 151(n3), 165–176
Tuan, Prince, 500
Tuckey, John, 507, 520
Tupper's Proverbial Philosophy, 191
Twain, Mark, *see* Clemens, Samuel L.
Tweed, Boss, and Tammany Hall, 94, 102–03, 299

Index

Twichell, Joseph, xiv, xvi, 280, 299, 434, 450–51, 479, 481–82, 529, 535
Tyler, Royall, *The Contrast*, 75

Union (Sacramento), 193

Vanderbilt, Comm., 103, *see also* "Open Letter to ..."
Van Zandt, G.H., *Poems of ...*, 308
Vernacular values and speech, 246–48, 253, 279, 290–91
Verne, Jules, 467
Victoria, Queen, 112
Virginia City (Nevada) *Territorial Enterprise*, xi, 4, 89, 157, 297, 424
Vocabulary, 7
Voltaire, xiv, 411
Vote, 99*ff.*
Vulgarity, xxiii, 99*ff.*, 121, 184–85, 218–19, 225*ff.*, 233–34, 513

Wagenknecht, E., 588
Warburton, *The Crescent and the Cross*, 37
Ward, A.C., xvii, 457–66
Ward, Artemus, *see* C.F. Browne
Ward, Ned, 180–81
Warder, G.W., *The Cities of the Sun*, 308–09
Warner, C.D., 94*ff.*, 398, 412, 450
Warren, Joyce, 578
Washington, G., 494, 500
Watterson, Henry, xvi, xvii, xxiv, xxv, 337–48
Webb, C.H., 4, 157
Webster, Charles L., and Company, 306, 308, 315, 509, 511, 514, 542

Wecter, Dixon, 330
Weil, Susanne, xv, xx, xxiv, 505–39
Wells, H.B., 428
Wells, Ida B., 362, 384(n10)
Welsch, Roger, xiv
West, western, 44, 46, 52, 225, 274, 331, 395, 401–02, 418–19
West Point, 376
Wheeler, Simon/Ben Coon, 4–7, 14, 17, 22–24, 119, 545, 548
White, W.A., *In Our Town*, 312(n19)
Whitman, Walt, 45, 166, 223, 409, 431, 466
Whittier Dinner, 167–69, 550
Whittier, J.G., 167–70
Whittier, Matthew, 168
Williams, Martha McCulloch, xix, 351–57
Williamson, Joel, 361*ff.*
Willis, Resa, 573
Women, Woman's Suffrage, xxv, 95, 98–99, 102, 111, 116–117, 400, 430–31, 571–91
Woodward, C. Vann, 361*ff.*
Woolson, Constance Fenimore, 368
Wordsworth, William, 32
World (New York), 344–45
Wyatt, Edith, xvii, xx, xxiii, 423–37

Yale, xii, 75
   Prof. Francis Bacon of, 306
Yankee, 283, *see also* East
Yeats, 344
Young, John Russell, 343
Youth's Companion, 165

For Product Safety Concerns and Information please contact our EU
representative GPSR@taylorandfrancis.com
Taylor & Francis Verlag GmbH, Kaufingerstraße 24, 80331 München, Germany

www.ingramcontent.com/pod-product-compliance
Lightning Source LLC
Chambersburg PA
CBHW070904300426
44113CB00008B/933